Praise for Ramachandra Guha

The Unquiet Woods

'Dr Guha's book is a pathfinding work on the Chipko movement and its people. It assumes all the more importance in view of the developmental crossroads on which the nation stands.'
—*The Economic Times*

'The book is lucidly written and highly readable.'
—*The Eastern Anthropologist*

'This is not merely a chronological narration, but the work of an accomplished social scientist, who articulates his conclusions with scholarly care.'
— *Sunday*

'Fascinating reading. Guha is to be commended for his effort which constitutes a significant illustration of the insights which the trained historian and sociologist can offer in the examination of a contemporary social movement.'
— *Indian Express Magazine*

'...a stimulating and useful book.'
— *Economic and Political Weekly*

'This is an excellent book, a job done thoroughly and painstakingly. There are no unnecessary flourishes of theory and trivialities of facts if found, seem to be relevant. ... his book reflects an intensity rarely found in books on sociology.'
— *Book Review*

'Guha's book with the startling title is a welcome addition to the subaltern studies on peasant movements. [It] is a well documented, serious study of a subject that is likely to engage the attention of social scientists and planners for a long time to come.'

— *The Book Review*

'It is a significant contribution to the literature in this area, based on painstaking scholarship and rich insights into the nature of peasant society and its aspirations.'

— *Sunday Herald*

Environmentalism: A Global History

'...a volume of eminently readable narrative. ...[it] conveys its message in a highly palatable form. The author's interest, and the clarity he gives to...events, is endlessly refreshing.'

— *Biblio*

'This is the first truly global history of environmental thought and activism. Superbly crafted, it deserves to be read by all concerned with the well-being of the environment on our lonely planet kept in mind.'

— *The Hindu*

'[Guha's] style is trademark—free flowing and peppered with biographical details of the people he is writing about.'

— *Business Line*

'Guha needs to be congratulated on this meticulously researched book. [It] is...like an introduction to the global history of environmentalism.'

— *The Book Review*

'Guha has written a compelling and highly readable history of the environment.'

— *Contributions to Indian Sociology*

Savaging the Civilized

'A wrenching and grand biography in the classical mould, that sounds the gong for the coming of age of the modern Indian biography. In the largeness of the theme, in the writer's tireless efforts to get into the mind

PRAISE FOR RAMACHANDRA GUHA

and soul of his subject...in the ease with which he straddles disciplines to grasp a prolific, difficult persona, in the finesse of language and execution, this book is beyond all other Indian attempts at life-sketching.'

— Binoo John, *Outlook*

'Almost forgotten now in Britain, Elwin deserves this excellent biography by Ramachandra Guha, an enthusiast writing about an enthusiast, an anthropologist and ecological historian who shares and understands his subject's principal concerns. Biographer and subject are well matched, even in the quality of their prose...[Elwin] understood, loved and defended the people he studied, and thoroughly merits this rehabilitation.'

— David Gilmour, *The Spectator*

'In documenting the fascinating life of a man turned native, [Ramachandra Guha] has compromised neither scholastic rigour nor idiomatic English. He has told the story of an Englishman abroad with style, understanding, a lot of sympathy and devotion to detail. Guha has put biography on the publishing map of India. He has not only rescued Elwin from the dead weight of anthropological morbidity, he has reestablished good, liberal scholarship...*Savaging the Civilized* is a landmark.'

— Swapan Dasgupta, *India Today*

'*Savaging the Civilized* is well researched, well-written and makes fascinating reading.... An excellent biography.'

— Khushwant Singh, *The Hindustan Times*

'*Savaging the Civilized* is a major achievement. Guha has understood Elwin well—his triumphs, truancies and tribulations—and shows genuine respect for the Englishman whom he never met. This scholarly yet lively book will, one hopes, revive interest in Elwin's life and vision and serve as an inspiration and resource for scholars, policy-makers and all thinking people concerned with tribal issues, issues of development and social and spiritual issues in general.'

— Sunil Janah, *The Times Higher Educational Supplement*

The Ramachandra Guha Omnibus

OUP India's Omnibus collection offers readers a comprehensive coverage of works of enduring value, woven together by a new introduction, attractively packaged for easy reference and reading.

The Ramachandra Guha Omnibus

The Unquiet Woods
Ecological Change and Peasant
Resistance in the Himalaya

Environmentalism
A Global History

Savaging the Civilized
Verrier Elwin, His Tribals, and India

UNIVERSITY PRESS

YMCA Library Building, Jai Singh Road, New Delhi 110 001

Oxford University Press is a department of the University of Oxford.
It furthers the University's objective of excellence in research, scholarship, and education
by publishing worldwide in

Oxford   New York

Auckland   Cape Town   Dar es Salaam   Hong Kong   Karachi   Kuala Lumpur
Madrid   Melbourne   Mexico City   Nairobi   New Delhi   Shanghai   Taipei   Toronto

With offices in

Argentina   Austria   Brazil   Chile   Czech Republic   France   Greece   Guatemala
Hungary   Italy   Japan   Poland   Portugal   Singapore   South Korea   Switzerland
Thailand   Turkey   Ukraine   Vietnam

Oxford is a registered trademark of Oxford University Press
in the UK and in certain other countries

Published in India
by Oxford University Press, New Delhi

© Oxford University Press 2005

The moral rights of the author have been asserted
Database right Oxford University Press (maker)

The Unquiet Woods
© Oxford University Press 1989
First Indian edition 1989, New expanded edition 1999
Environmentalism: A Global History
© Ramachandra Guha 2000
Savaging the Civilized
© Ramachandra Guha 1999
First published 2005
Fourth impression 2009

All rights reserved. No part of this publication may be reproduced,
or transmitted in any form or by any means, electronic or mechanical,
including photocopying, recording or by any information storage and
retrieval system, without permission in writing from Oxford University Press.
Enquiries concerning reproduction outside the scope of the above should be
sent to the Rights Department, Oxford University Press, at the address above

You must not circulate this book in any other binding or cover
and you must impose this same condition on any acquirer

ISBN-13: 978-0-19-566811-7
ISBN-10: 0-19-566811-1

Printed in India by Pauls Press, New Delhi 110 020
Published by Oxford University Press
YMCA Library Building, Jai Singh Road, New Delhi 110 001

Contents

Introduction   xiii

The Unquiet Woods
Ecological Change and Peasant Resistance in the Himalaya

Preface to the New, Expanded Edition
Preface to the First Edition
Acknowledgements
Glossary
Abbreviations
Map of Uttarakhand

1. A SOCIOLOGY OF DOMINATION AND RESISTANCE
2. THE MOUNTAINS AND THEIR PEOPLE
3. SCIENTIFIC FORESTRY AND SOCIAL CHANGE
4. REBELLION AS CUSTOM
5. REBELLION AS CONFRONTATION
6. THE MARCH OF COMMERCIAL FORESTRY
7. CHIPKO: SOCIAL HISTORY OF AN 'ENVIRONMENTAL' MOVEMENT
8. PEASANTS AND 'HISTORY'

   Epilogue
   Appendix
   Bibliography
   Index

Environmentalism
A Global History

Series Editor's Preface

Author's Preface

PART I: ENVIRONMENTALISM'S FIRST WAVE

1. GOING GREEN
2. BACK TO THE LAND!
3. THE IDEOLOGY OF SCIENTIFIC CONSERVATION
4. THE GROWTH OF THE WILDERNESS IDEA

   Afterword: SOME WHO DON'T FIT

PART II: ENVIRONMENTALISM'S SECOND WAVE

   Prologue: THE AGE OF ECOLOGICAL INNOCENCE

5. THE ECOLOGY OF AFFLUENCE
6. THE SOUTHERN CHALLENGE
7. SOCIALISM AND ENVIRONMENTALISM
8. ONE WORLD OR TWO?

   Bibliographic Essay

   Index

Savaging the Civilized
Verrier Elwin, His Tribals, and India

Prologue

1. EVANGELICAL GHETTO
2. OXFORD REBELLION
3. BETWEEN CHRIST AND THE CONGRESS
4. BREAKING RANKS

5. AN ASHRAM OF ONE'S OWN

6. DEFENDING THE ABORIGINAL

7. GOING GOND

8. ANTHROPOLOGIST AT LARGE

9. STAYING ON

10. AN ENGLISHMAN IN INDIA

11. A SAHIB (SOMETIMES) IN THE SECRETARIAT

12. NEHRU'S MISSIONARY

13. AN ENGLISHMAN FOR INDIA

14. OUTSIDER WITHIN: THE WORLDS OF VERRIER ELWIN

Epilogue

Appendices

Acknowledgements

Notes

Index

Introduction

PLURAL HISTORIES

> From my assiduous reading I learned two lessons: first, the historian should avoid burrowing into his own hole and should keep a close eye on what goes on in related disciplines; and second, that doing research with all the requisite rigor need not mean that, when it comes time to divulge one's results, one must adopt a frigid style. The scholar performs his function better if he knows how to please his readers, if he has the ability to capture and hold their attention with the amenities of his style.
>
> —*Georges Duby*

Becoming a Historian

This Omnibus brings together three works of history, written by a man who never formally studied the subject. I became a historian through a series of chance encounters. The first took place in the summer of 1978, in an adivasi village of the Koraput district in Orissa. I was then a student of the Delhi School of Economics, and had come to Koraput to study the impact of industrialization in a tribal belt. In these remote mountain ranges, Hindustan Aeronautics Limited (HAL) had built a factory to manufacture MIG airplanes. (One reason for the choice of location, apparently, was that it was safely away from the range of enemy aircraft.) For six weeks I worked in the HAL unit, analysing the productivity records of individual workers. I finally proved, at the 1% level of statistical significance, that tribal workers were as efficient as non-tribals. When the last number had been crunched, my local host, a kindly man called Patro, took me in his jeep to see some Gadaba villages. At one of these I met a veterinary doctor named Das, who asked whether I had heard of an anthropologist called Verrier Elwin who, he said, had once roamed these hills and forests.

By this time I already knew that I was spectacularly ill-suited to the study of economics. Thus, on my return to Delhi, I searched for the works of Verrier Elwin. My college library had a copy of Elwin's diary of his life among the Gonds of Central India, *Leaves from the Jungle*. Next I read his autobiography, *The Tribal World of Verrier Elwin*. Both works communicated learning with elegance and wit. Here was stuff about society made human in prose; not, as in economics, camouflaged in tables and equations and matrices.

Dr Das of Koraput sent me to Elwin, and Elwin in turn inspired me to seek a change of discipline. In July 1980 I began a doctorate in Sociology at the Indian Institute of Management, Calcutta. Six months into my studies, I attended a lecture by a visiting scholar, Jayanta Bandopadhyaya. After the talk (which, as I recall, was on the use and abuse of science) I had tea with the speaker. He asked me what topic I would take up for my dissertation. I said that I was torn between studying caste in a village or workers in a factory. Where are you from, asked Dr Bandopadhyaya. Dehradun, I replied. Then why don't you do a study of the Chipko movement, he said.

It was an inspired suggestion, for the Chipko movement was then less than a decade old. It was the stuff of newspaper stories, but not yet the staple of academic research. At this time there was scant interest in environmental issues in the Indian academy. Among sociologists the topics of the day were caste, class, kinship and religion; among historians, agrarian structure and the evolution of Indian nationalism. Had I not met Dr Bandopadhyaya I might have written the three hundredth thesis on caste, or perhaps the fiftieth thesis on workers. But meeting him got me interested in the as yet underexplored field of environmental studies.

In the summer of 1981, I travelled up the Alakananda valley to the town of Gopeshwar, where lived the pioneer of the Chipko movement, Chandi Prasad Bhatt. After talking to Bhatt I moved on to Mandal, the hamlet where, back in March 1973, the first Chipko protest had taken place. One of the people I interviewed here was Alam Singh Rawat, who had been village headman at the time of that protest. I had come to the hills determined to locate Chipko in the modern environmental debate. Alam Singh, however, insisted it formed part of a long history of social protest within Garhwal. When the colonial state had attempted to take over the forests, he claimed, his ancestors surrounded the Commissioner of Kumaun Division and branded his face with a cattle iron.

It was an intriguing story, which set me off in search of the evidence to back it. Two historian friends, Sumit Guha and Hari Sen, took me to the National Archives of India, where they taught me how to search for and order old records. In a faded file of the Foreign and Political Department I discovered Alam Singh's story to be true, in essence if not in fine detail. (The incident took place in the valley of the Bhageerathi rather than the Alakananda; and the target of the peasants' rage was a Conservators of Forests, not a Divisional Commissioner.) It was my first experience of archival research, and I much enjoyed it. I discovered, in fact, that I preferred it to field-research. Dead documents spoke to me in a way that living people could not.

As it happened, my work on Chipko and its antecedents coincided with a nation-wide controversy about forest policy. This was sparked by the draft forest act of 1982, which aimed at replacing a piece of legislation that was more than a century old. 23% of India' is legally under the control of the Forest Department. Every single Indian, be he peasant, tribal, artisan, pastoralist, or city-dweller, is dependent on forests and forest produce. When I got drawn into the debate over the forest act, I found that the subject had been comprehensively neglected by historians of India. The state and national archives had the records of the colonial forest department; these were incredibly detailed and extensive, and a window into social, political and legal history. However, since in a scholarly sense forests were 'off the map', these records lay more-or-less untouched. This surprised but certainly did not dismay me. For there is nothing as thrilling as stumbling upon an undiscovered archive, touching, feeling and reading documents not seen by one's peers. Georges Duby describes it well:

> I was alone. I had finally managed to have a carton brought to the table. I opened it. What was this box going to turn up? I withdrew a first packet of documents. I untied it and slipped my hand between sheets of parchment. Taking one of them, I unfolded it, and already I felt a peculiar pleasure: these old skins are often exquisite to touch. Along with the palpable delight goes the sense of entering a secret preserve. When the sheets are opened

out and flattened, they seem to fill the silence of the archives with the fragrance of long-vanished lives. One can almost feel the presence of the man who, eight hundred years earlier, took up his goose quill, dipped it in ink, and began to form his letters at an unhurried pace, as if engraving an inscription for eternity—and the text is there, before one's eyes, as fresh as the day when it was written.

The documents I was reading were a hundred rather than eight hundred years old. That scarcely dimmed the excitement. To the contrary, it was heightened by the knowledge that there was something transgressive in what I was doing. For Indian sociologists were not meant to do archival research; nor were they supposed to seriously study the past. (By the same token, Indian historians are discouraged from doing fieldwork, or for venturing beyond the year of Indian independence, 1947.) With my work on forests began a life-long addiction, so that there is still nothing that gives me a greater thrill than reading old letters and documents. Every few months, preferably every few weeks, I have to soil my hands in them.

Dr Das and Dr Elwin brought me to *sociology*; Dr Jayanta Bandopadhyaya to *ecology*; and the unlettered Alam Singh Rawat to *history*. Two of the three books reprinted here lie at the intersection of those three disciplines. However, while *The Unquiet Woods* is confined to one part of India, *Environmentalism* takes in the world. In some ways the books complement one another: the first a regional study mindful of similar conflicts at other times and other places; the second a global overview that pays attention to numerous, locally articulated, ideas and movements.

Through the nineteen-eighties, as I worked on environmental issues, the figure of Verrier Elwin was never far from my mind. For Elwin was a precocious critic of colonial forest policy, who wrote with sensitivity and engagement about the adivasi's relations with the natural world. In the early nineties, I began work on a project which I had at first entitled: 'The Tribal Question in Modern India'. Gradually, however, one man took over the project, the process captured in these shifts in title: 'Verrier Elwin and the Tribal Question in Modern India'; then 'Verrier Elwin: An Intellectual Biography'. The final product, sent to the world as *Savaging the Civilized: Verrier Elwin, His Tribals, and India*, is (I hope) both a personal biography and an intellectual one, as much a portrait of the time as of the individual.

My research in environmental history left me with an abiding skepticism of what academic journals and academic icons deemed important or significant. When I began work on Elwin, I had once more to overcome the tyranny of fashion. Scholars in general, and Indian scholars in particular, are deeply suspicious of the genre of biography. I felt this prejudice with some force, for whenever a colleague heard I was writing a book on Elwin he would be gently—and not always gently—dismissive. It did not do to spend several hundred pages on an individual, especially if his skin was white, and even more so if he was born an Englishman. (In the postcolonial academy, there is nothing as unfashionable as a dead, white, British male.) On the other hand, friends outside the academy, be they journalists, artists, or housewives, were invariably excited by my project. 'A biography of Verrier Elwin? What a wonderful idea!', is what they would say. These laymen disregarded the colour of Elwin's skin and recalled only that he had led an extraordinarily interesting life.

Working on Elwin also furthered my interest in the craft of historical narrative. My previous work had foregrounded history's relation to the social sciences. Now, writing a biography, I was compelled to see history as a branch of literature. I had to venture into areas taboo to the sociologically oriented historian: such as an individual's moods and motives, and his emotional and sexual relationships.

The Tyranny of the Discipline

I like to think of these three books as 'plural histories'. They each move back and forth between the individual and society, between culture and politics, between the past and the present, between humans and nature, and between India and the world. If there is a credo that unites them, it is this: Thou Shall Not be Bound by the Tyranny of thy Discipline.

There are some very good reasons why university departments are structured around disciplinary lines, and why it is so hard to start centres or programmes of inter-disciplinary research. For every scientific discipline has its own history, logic, and socialization process. There is no gainsaying the achievements of individual disciplines, and yet, these walls between departments can come to constitute a form of tyranny. Very early in his career, a scholar is made to declare his disciplinary affiliation. This loyalty oath is total, in that one has not just to state a primary affiliation, but also a sole one. I have heard inter-disciplinary research defined as 'that which you do after you get tenure'. At any rate, it is almost impossible for a young PhD scholar to say that he is a sociologist as well as a historian; he has to squarely say that he is either one or the other.

Even for older and established scholars, to proclaim a multiple allegiance is only to invite the condescension of one's peers. When I was a student at Delhi University, there was a Professor who described himself as both a sociologist and an economist. What was said about him (behind his back) was this: 'When Professor K is with sociologists, he talks about economics; when he is with the economists, he talks sociology; and when he is with both, he talks about the weather'. There is an older version of this sneer, associated with none other than Karl Marx. His great rival Pierre Joseph Proudhon once wrote a book called *The Philosophy of Poverty*. Marx titled his rejoinder *The Poverty of Philosophy* where he remarked (I quote from memory): 'In Germany, where they understand no history, Monsieur Proudhon calls himself a historian; in France, where they know no philosophy, he passes off as a philosopher.'

And there were disciplinarians much before Marx. Thus, when I recounted his jibe to Professor Robert Goldman of the University of California at Berkeley, that distinguished Sanskritist quoted an ancient verse which ran like this:

> *yatra shastrinah tatra vaidika, yatra vaidikas tatra shastri*
> *yatra cobhayam tatra nobhayam, yatra nobhayam tatra cobhayam*

> (Where there are shastrins, there he is a vaidika; where there are vaidikas, there he is a shastrin;
> Where there are both, there he is neither; where there is neither there he is both.)

As we can see, scholarly specialization, and turf battles over disciplinary terrain, have been with us from time immemorial.

Closely allied to the tyranny of the discipline is a *fetishization of method*. Each discipline in the humanities has its own privileged method of research. The historian goes to the archives where he seeks out primary unpublished material: letters, government records, legal documents, manuscripts, diaries. The anthropologist goes to a village or factory where he spends twelve months or more. The sociologist designs and administers a series of questionnaires. And the applied economist runs a series of regressions. Each of these methods is meant to be mutually exclusive, each the preserve of a specific discipline. Thus the historian is not supposed to do extensive fieldwork. The sociologist is not expected to dig deep into the archives. The anthropologist is not meant to run regressions, and the economist is prohibited from conducting qualitative interviews.

A third barrier to the progress of inter-disciplinary research is what I call the *partitions of time*. In the Indian university, a single date, 15th August 1947, decisively demarcates history from the other disciplines. The boundary is scrupulously observed on both sides; thus historians are mandated not to stray into the period after Independence, whereas sociologists and anthropologists stay clear of the period of colonial rule.

A fourth barrier is what one might term the *partitions of knowledge*. I refer here to the wall erected between what in India are termed the Arts and the Sciences. This partition is erected very early and runs right through one's student years. In high school, one is made to choose between Arts and Science; and there is no going back on the choice.

If nothing else, the works in this Omnibus represent a challenge to the tyranny of the discipline, the fetishization of method, the partitions of time and the partitions of knowledge. They are the works of a historian originally trained in sociology and social anthropology. They are chiefly based on primary archival research, yet also draw upon material from personal interviews. These works all begin before 1947 but come right down to the present. And, wherever necessary or desirable, they use insights and inputs from ecological science.

It seems to be the case that disciplinary boundaries are more rigidly observed in India than in other parts of the world. Here, it is a struggle to break free of academic shackles, as it is to break out from social shackles in general—to escape from being stereotyped according to one's caste or religion or gender. I was myself fortunate in coming under the influence of three Indians who were noticeably heterodox. One was my teacher, Anjan Ghosh, a man with an unusually wide range of intellectual interests. A Marxist by political conviction, Anjan suppressed his faith in the classroom, teaching me the works of Durkheim and Weber with as much engagement and understanding as he did the works of Marx. A second influence was the sociologist Shiv Visvanathan, who introduced me to the literature on the environmental debate, and taught me to see science as inseparable from its cultural mileu. A third mentor was the ecologist Madhav Gadgil, a scientist with both an unusual penchant for fieldwork and a deep understanding of Indian history. These teachers and friends taught me never to privilege a specific discipline, research method, or ideology.

Such were the direct, tangible influences; but in retrospect there were probably also other, less perceptible ones. For it was in the eighties that historians of India came to display, almost for the first time, an interest in sociology and social anthropology. Coming from the other side (the side of sociology), I followed the work of these disciplinary traitors with keen interest. Some of them—notably David Hardiman, Sanjay Subrahmanyam, and Shahid Amin—were also personal friends. Although they worked on topics and periods very different from mine, I took heart from what I saw as a shared disinclination to adhere to boundaries drawn by academic tradition and training.

And then there was the example of Verrier Elwin himself. Here was a man who could only be described as a serial transgressor. Here was an individual who became a traitor to his race, his class, his religion, and his nationality. Here was a scholar who, in disciplinary terms, was shockingly promiscuous, who blurred and challenged academic genres decades before it became respectable to do so. Elwin wrote and published poetry, novels, works of theology, anthropological monographs, folklore collections, official reports, polemical pamphlets, and art criticism. His last work was an autobiography that is generally regarded as the finest of all his books.

Elwin not merely breached the boundaries between disciplines; he challenged the wall that divides the academy from the wider world. His best books are solidly researched, and yet very readable. He was an anthropologist who was also a writer. From Elwin, and from the British historian E. P. Thompson—another of my early and enduring heroes—I learnt that scholarly rigour and elegant prose need not necessarily be at odds.

My final bow must be to the country I was born into and which Elwin made his own. For a historian of India must count himself exceptionally lucky—more so a historian who cherishes variety and experimentation. There may be richer countries, more powerful countries, but none that are remotely as interesting. In both cultural and ecological terms, there is no society as complex, or as diverse, as ours. In modern India there is a plenitude of exciting research topics that await their historians. May these be open-minded and undogmatic, impervious to fashion, and sensitive to style.*

RAMACHANDRA GUHA

---

* I am grateful to Rukun Advani and Sujata Keshavan for commenting on an earlier draft of this introduction.

THE UNQUIET WOODS

Ecological Change and Peasant
Resistance in the Himalaya

New, Expanded Edition

RAMACHANDRA GUHA

For
Amma, Appa and Suja

Contents

Preface to the New, Expanded Edition	vi
Preface to the First Edition	vii
Acknowledgements	xiii
Glossary	xv
Abbreviations	xvii
Map of Uttarakhand	xviii

1 A SOCIOLOGY OF DOMINATION AND RESISTANCE — 1
TWO APPROACHES TO THE STUDY OF LOWER-CLASS PROTEST — 1
THE LANDSCAPE OF RESISTANCE — 5

2 THE MOUNTAINS AND THEIR PEOPLE — 9
Political history — 10
SOCIAL STRUCTURE — 11
Caste — 11
Agrarian relations — 14
Community traditions — 21
Role of women — 21
State and society — 22
The 'begar' system — 25
THE CULTURAL ECOLOGY OF THE HIMALAYANS — 27
Forests and social institutions in the indigenous system — 28

3 SCIENTIFIC FORESTRY AND SOCIAL CHANGE — 35
THE FORESTS OF UTTARAKHAND — 35
THE GROWTH AND DEVELOPMENT OF STATE FORESTRY IN UTTARAKHAND — 37
State forestry in Tehri Garhwal — 39
Forestry in Kumaun division — 43
SCIENTIFIC FORESTRY AND SOCIAL CONTROL — 48
Alienation of humans from nature — 55
THE AGENDA OF SCIENTIFIC FORESTRY — 59

CONTENTS

4 REBELLION AS CUSTOM — 62
RAJA AND PRAJA IN TEHRI — 62
  The king as 'Bolanda' Badrinath — 63
  The motif of the wicked official — 65
  The dhandak — 67
EARLY RESISTANCE TO FOREST MANAGEMENT — 69
THE DHANDAK AT RAWAIN, 1930 — 72
THE KISAN ANDOLAN, 1944–8 — 79
  Peasants and parties — 87
ELEMENTARY ASPECTS OF CUSTOMARY REBELLION — 89
  Paternalism from above and from below — 96

5 REBELLION AS CONFRONTATION — 99
EARLY RESISTANCE TO FORCED LABOUR — 100
EARLY RESISTANCE TO FOREST MANAGEMENT — 104
THE UTAR AND FOREST MOVEMENTS OF 1921 — 110
  The Forest Movement of 1921 — 114
SOCIAL PROTEST: 1921–42 — 120
FROM CUSTOM TO CONFRONTATION — 125
NATIONALISM AND THE VANGUARD PARTY — 131

6 THE MARCH OF COMMERCIAL FORESTRY — 138
ECOLOGICAL CHANGE AND THE MONEY-ORDER ECONOMY — 143
FRAGMENTS OF A PRISTINE CONSCIOUSNESS: 'COMMUNITY' MANAGEMENT — 148

7 CHIPKO: SOCIAL HISTORY OF AN 'ENVIRONMENTAL' MOVEMENT — 152
CHIPKO: ITS ORIGINS AND DEVELOPMENT — 153
  The background — 153
  The 1970 flood — 155
  Mandal — 157
  Reni — 158
  The government steps in — 159
  Chipko spreads to Tehri — 161
  Chipko in Kumaun — 162

Chipko returns to Chamoli 163
THE BADYARGARH ANDOLAN 165
The andolan 166
Chipko and popular consciousness 168
Chipko in a history of protest 170
CUSTOM AND CONFRONTATION IN CHIPKO 172
CHIPKO AS AN ENVIRONMENTAL MOVEMENT 177
The widening of Chipko 178
Three environmental philosophies 179

8 PEASANTS AND 'HISTORY' 185
THE UNQUIET WOODS: FOREST CONFLICTS IN
TWO CONTINENTS 185
AGAINST EUROCENTRICISM 191

Epilogue 197
Appendix 211
Bibliography 223
Index 240

Preface to the New, Expanded Edition

For this new edition of *The Unquiet Woods* I have added two freshly written sections. An epilogue brings the story of Himalayan social protest up-to-date. It reflects on the Chipko movement's continuing influence in the wider world, even as within the hills it has been completely supplanted by a popular upsurge calling for a separate state. An appendix charts the progress of environmental history in India. It explores the social factors that have made this a real 'growth area' for historical research, marks the major debates and arguments, and suggests possible areas of future work. With the incorporation of this new material I have also revised the bibliography and index.

Preface to the First Edition

Since the early seventies a wave of social movements has swept Uttarakhand, the region embracing the eight hill districts of the state of Uttar Pradesh.[1] By far the best known of these movements is the peasant initiative against commercial forestry, the Chipko movement. Chipko has been followed in rapid succession by movements directed at the siting of large dams, the environmental consequences of mining, and the sale and consumption of illicit liquor in Uttarakhand. At the time of writing the region is once again astir, in the grip of a renewed call for a separate hill state.

These movements have helped Uttarakhand emerge from a position of relative obscurity to one which more accurately reflects its ecological and cultural importance to the life of the subcontinent. Himalayan deforestation is by now widely recognized as India's most pressing environmental problem. It has attracted wide attention, as has the chain of events which has come in its wake: the eroding basis of subsistence agriculture, large-scale outward migration, and the creation of a 'money-order' economy in the villages of Uttarakhand. Meanwhile, Chipko has almost universally been hailed as a significant step forward in the fight to save Himalayan ecology and society from total collapse. While this attention is certainly welcome, what it tends to obscure is that Chipko, like the processes of ecological and social fragmentation which it attempts to reverse, is itself only part of a much longer history of resistance and protest. As this work shows, Chipko is the last in a long series of peasant movements against commercial forestry which date from the earliest days of state intervention, i.e. the closing decades of the nineteenth century.

This study was originally conceived as a sociology of Chipko. Despite the token genuflection to the movement in national and

[1] These eight districts are Pauri, Chamoli, Tehri, Uttarkashi, and Dehradun (which collectively constitute 'Garhwal'); and Almora, Pithoragarh and Nainital (which constitute 'Kumaun').

international debates on ecologically sound development alternatives, and its widespread coverage in the media, there was a surprising lack of sociologically informed analyses of the movement. Perhaps the media attention itself contributed to this lacuna: by assimilating the movement to the modern discourses of feminism, environmentalism, and the revival of Gandhism, it glossed over the local roots of Chipko, its embeddedness in the specific historical and cultural experiences of the Uttarakhand peasantry. Meanwhile, with the emergence of several wings within the movement, such accounts as did exist were seriously vitiated by the a priori partisan stance they took in favour of one or other wing of Chipko.[2] In the circumstances, a non-partisan analysis of the movement, which would in addition restore Chipko to its original home, seemed long overdue. A sociological perspective significantly reveals that the most celebrated 'environmental' movement in the Third World is viewed by its participants as being above all a *peasant* movement in defence of traditional rights in the forest, and only secondarily, if at all, an 'environmental' or 'feminist' movement. At the same time, a historical approach contributes to a decentring of Chipko, by showing it to be part of a much longer tradition of peasant movements in the Himalaya. Consequently, this study has turned into a more general history of ecological decline and peasant resistance in this region, whose main focus is on recovering the history of forest-based resistance within which Chipko is a small though undoubtedly distinguished part. In this sense my study is both more and less than the history and sociology of the Chipko movement.[3]

As it happens, this shift towards a more historically rooted analysis coincided with the timely arrival of the Subaltern Studies project. That series, as well as the individual monographs on peasant movements by some of its contributors, notably David Hardiman, Gyan Pandey, and Ranajit Guha, has greatly enriched our understanding of the origins and

[2] See, in this connection, the exchange between Jayanta Bandopadhyay/Vandana Shiva and myself in *Seminar*, New Delhi, issues of February, June, August and November 1987.

[3] The definitive history of the Chipko Andolan is currently being written by Dr. Shekhar Pathak of Kumaun University, a person uniquely qualified for the task; for he is perhaps the leading historian of modern Uttarakhand and an activist in Chipko from its inception in 1973.

modalities of tribal/peasant movements in the nineteenth and twentieth centuries.[4] One reason the Subalternists have written better history is because they have cast a wider net: apart from a more critical use of conventional sources (records of the Home Department and of the All India Congress Committee), they have made more extensive use of materials in Indian languages, utilized neglected series of official documents (e.g. forest, medical and judicial records), conducted fieldwork, and on the whole shown a greater sensitivity to local variations in class and culture. At the same time, their studies have substantially drawn upon the work of sociologists and anthropologists in combating the excessively empiricist orientation of Indian history.

While placing my work in the context of the debates which the Subaltern Studies project has given rise to, I find myself both an insider and an outsider to what more than one Subalternist has referred to as their 'collective odysssey'. While sharing their concern for a more interpretive understanding of lower-class resistance, my own intellectual background diverges in at least two ways.

First, I have tried to bring an ecological dimension to the study of agrarian history and peasant resistance. The relationship between colonialism and ecological decline is one neglected by historians of modern India, who have been rather more aware of the social and political consequences of British rule. However, in Uttarakhand by far the most important consequence of colonial rule was the system of commercial forestry it introduced. Yet the conflict between state forestry and the peasantry, while perhaps at its most intense in Uttarakhand, was played out (with variations) in other forest regions of the subcontinent as well. Its origins were as much ideological as economic: for peasant use and state use were embedded in very different understandings of the social role of the forests. I argue, therefore, that ecological history cannot merely be the history

See Ranajit Guha (ed.), *Subaltern Studies: Writings on South Asian History and Society*, volumes I to IV (1982–85); David Hardiman, *Peasant Nationalists of Gujarat* (1981); Hardiman, *The Coming of the Devi* (1987); Gyanendra Pandey, *The Ascendancy of the Congress in Uttar Pradesh* (1978); Ranajit Guha, *Elementary Aspects of Peasant Insurgency in Colonial India* (1983), all published by Oxford University Press, New Delhi.

of changes in the landscape; it must link environmental changes with changing, and competing, human perceptions of the 'uses' of nature.

Second, I am not a historian but a sociologist trying write history. This is a work of historical sociology, in which I am, as compared to most historians, more consciously theoretical and comparative in my approach. Here I am on slippery ground, for historians have in general a sharp scepticism of the pretensions of sociologists. E. P. Thompson, for example, rarely misses an opportunity to side-swipe at the sociologist's penchant for arid abstraction. Twenty years ago John Womack prefaced his great study of the peasantry in the Mexican Revolution with these words, in which he made clear his relative evaluation of the two disciplines:

[T]his is a work not in historical sociology but in social history. It is not an analysis but a story because the truth of the revolution in Morelos is in the feeling of it, which I could not convey through defining its factors but only through telling of it. The analysis that I thought pertinent I have tried to weave into the narrative, so that it would issue at the moment right for understanding it.[5]

Around the same time, but probably unknown to Womack, an Indonesian historian was completing his own opus on peasant movements against the Dutch in Java, a magisterial study which deserves to be much better known in ex-colonial countries like India. Sartono Kartodirdjo could not have disagreed more with Womack for, he wrote, 'the one subject matter which certainly does exhibit the actual or potential interdependence of history and sociology is the social movement.'[6] While appreciating Womack's reservations—and which sociologist will deny that historians write with so much more feeling?—I am, like Sartono, more hopeful of a potential union, provided sociologists stop waiting for historians to provide them 'data' from which to generalize, and learn the tools of historical research themselves. It seems to have escaped most historically-minded sociologists that generalizations are far more convincing when based on more, not less, primary

[5] John Womack, *Zapata and the Mexican Revolution* (New York, 1969), p. x.
[6] Sartono Kartodirdjo, *The Peasants' Revolt in Banten in 1888* (The Hague, 1966), p. 12.

data. As things stand, 'primary' data usually passes through several hands, and several interpretations, before it reaches the generalizing sociologist. It is well to remember that those two masters of historical sociology, Marx and Weber, were often wildly off the mark in their assessments of Indian society not only because of their strong prejudices about non-European cultures in general, but also because they relied exclusively on other peoples' already loaded interpretations of an alien culture. At the same time, by rejecting the historian's obsession with the accumulation of certified facts, Marx and Weber did provide an array of sociological concepts that have scarcely outlived their usefulness—concepts that have found their way into the work of even the most atheoretical historian.[7] As far as the study of peasant resistance is concerned, the work of James Scott, Teodor Shanin and Barrington Moore Jr—to name only three sociologists—and of Ranajit Guha, Sartono Kartodirdjo and E. P. Thompson—to mention but three historians—is ample proof of the potential interdependence, one denied by historians even as they practise it, of sociology and history.

[7] A comparative work spanning several continents and several centuries may of course have to rely exclusively on secondary sources; yet it is the sociologist (like Marx and Weber) with some experience of doing primary research who is more likely to carry off a large-scale work of synthesis.

Acknowledgements

Having accumulated an unusually large number of debts for a work of this kind, I can do no better than start in chronological order.

C. S. Venkatachar, possessed of a scholarly detachment quite remarkable in a former civil servant of the raj, first evoked an interest in the study of Indian society. My first teachers in sociology, Anjan Ghosh and Kamini Adhikari, encouraged me to take up what was for sociologists uncharted territory, even as they insisted I locate my empirical findings in wider theoretical debates. Two scholars with an unrivalled knowledge of Uttarakhand, Shekhar Pathak and Thakur Shoorbeer Singh Panwar, were always forthcoming with advice and encouragement. Anil Agarwal, Acharya Gopeshwar Narain Kothiyal, Paripurnanand Painuli, Thakur Sarop Singh and Smt. Lalita Devi Vaishnav gave me ready access to valuable source material in their possession. I am greatly indebted to the many scholars who commented on the manuscript in whole or in part: Kamini Adhikari, Anjan Ghosh, David Hardiman, Louise Fortmann, Rukun Advani, Michael Adas, James Scott, John Richards, Dharma Kumar, K. Sivaramakrishnan and an anonymous reader for the University of California Press. I owe a special debt to Jim Scott for introducing me to a wide range of comparative work on peasant protest in Europe and Asia.

I am grateful to the staff of the following institutions for their help in locating documents for this study: Forest Research Institute Library, Dehradun; National Archives of India, New Delhi; National Library, Calcutta; Uttar Pradesh State Archives, Lucknow; Regional Archives, Dehradun and Nainital; and Nehru Memorial Museum and Library, New Delhi. Two of my previous employers, the Centre for Studies in Social Sciences, Calcutta, and the Centre for Ecological Sciences, Indian Institute of Science, Bangalore, provided a congenial atmosphere for the completion of this work.

Among the many other individuals who provided help of various kinds, I must especially mention the following: Sunderlal Bahuguna, Jayanta Bandopadhyay, Chandi Prasad Bhatt, Bill Burch, Partha Chatterjee, Robi Chatterji, J. C. Das. Bernard d'Mello, Madhav Gadgil, Jean Claude Galey, Vinay Gidwani, Sumit Guha, Ashis Nandy, Gyan Pandey, K. S. Pundir, Ajay Rawat, Satish Saberwal, Atul Saklani, Hari Sen, and Shiv Visvanathan.

My parents and my wife followed the course of this work with interest and a growing exasperation. Their support at all times has been critical.

Finally, I should note that earlier versions of chapters 3 and 5 respectively were published in the *Economic and Political Weekly*, special number, 1985, and in Ranajit Guha (ed.), *Subaltern Studies IV* (New Delhi: Oxford University Press, 1985).

Glossary

andolan   popular movement
bandh   general strike (see *hartal*)
banj   oak
bardaish   supply of provisions
begar, utar, coolie utar   forced labour
chaukidar   watchman
chir   long-leaved pine
darbar, dirbar, durbar   royal court
deodar   cedar
dewan, diwan   chief minister
gaddi   throne
ghar   house
gherao   to surround
hartal   general strike (see *bandh*)
hookah   pipe
kand   firing
kisan   peasant
kisan andolan   peasant movement
jati   caste
jath   country fair
jatha   group
lakh   one hundred thousand
malikhana   rent
padayatra   walking tour
padhan, pradhan   headman
pahari, paharee   hillman
panchayat   village council
pargana   county
patti   a group of villages
patwari   revenue official in charge of a **patti**
praja   citizens, subjects
praja mandal   citizens' forum
quintal   one hundred kilograms

raja king
rawal head priest
sabha association
sarvodaya (here) belonging to the Gandhian movement

Abbreviations

F & P	Foreign and Political Department
F.D.	Forest Department
For. Div.	Forest Division
GAD	General Administration Department
GRH	*Garhwali*
IF	*Indian Forester*
ISR	*Indian States Reformer*
NAI	National Archives of India
NMML	Nehru Memorial Museum and Library
RAD	Regional Archives, Dehradun
RAN	Regional Archives, Nainital
UPSA	Uttar Pradesh State Archives, Lucknow
WP	Working Plan
YV	*Yugvani*

TIBET
TIBET
TEHRI
GARHWAL
STATE
R. Bhagirathi
SIMLA
HILL STATES
(Himachal Pradesh)
Uttarkashi
Badrinath
R. Alakananda
NEPAL
Tehri
Gopeshwar
Dehradun
Srinagar
Rudraprayag
Narendra
nagar
Pauri
BRITISH GARHWAL
DISTT
ALMORA
DISTT
Hardwar
Lansdowne
Bageshwar
Ranikhet
KUMAUN
DIVISION
Almora
Pithoragarh
UTTARAKHAND
1815 - 1949
Nainital
Bhawali
NEPAL
NAINITAL
DISTT
Haldwani
ROHILKHAND
Scale : 1 : 1 000 000

CHAPTER 1

A Sociology of Domination and Resistance

> [The] peasantry is a class neglected by the throng of writers in quest of new subjects. This neglect, it may be, is simple prudence in days when the working class have fallen heir to the courtiers and flatterers of kings, when the criminal is the hero of romance, the herdsman is sentimentally interesting, and we behold something like an apotheosis of the proletariat. Sects have arisen among us, every pen among them swells the chorus of 'Workers arise!' even as once the Third Estate was bidden to 'Arise'! It is pretty plain that no Herostratus among them has had the courage to go forth into remote country districts to study the phenomena of a permanent conspiracy of those whom we call 'the weak' against those who imagine themselves to be the 'strong'—of the Peasantry against the Rich.
>
> —Balzac

TWO APPROACHES TO THE STUDY OF LOWER-CLASS PROTEST

The historical and sociological study of lower-class protest is a relatively recent phenomenon. As a separate field it emerged only after World War II. Among a host of factors, the growing influence of academic Marxism in Europe and the rise of anti-colonial movements in Asia and Africa were particularly important in initiating a reappraisal of the two fundamental projects of modernity: the rise of capitalism in Europe, and its transplantation, in the form of colonialism, in non-European territories. Challenging the view that these processes of social change were by and large harmonious, historians were able to document the deep-rooted and endemic opposition to the economic and political changes initiated by capitalism and colonialism. As part of a larger movement from 'consensus' to 'conflict' approaches in sociology, and from 'top down' to 'bottom up' in history, these works have firmly placed the study of lower-class resistance on the scholarly agenda.

It would serve little purpose here to review the voluminous literature on peasant and working class movements that has accumulated in the past decades.[1] While the field's importance has been widely commented upon, what is less apparent is the emergence of two distinct approaches in the literature. As I believe this divergence to be of methodological and theoretical significance for future work in the field, I have attempted, in what follows, to characterize these two trends.

The first approach, which I call the Structural–Organizational (S–O) paradigm, is concerned with analysing large-scale historical processes—e.g. capitalism, imperialism, and the rise of the nation-state—what Charles Tilly, one of its most influential practitioners, has called the 'master processes' of social change.[2] It investigates the impact of these changes on different social classes, identifying those classes likely to be adversely affected, and among these the classes likely to revolt against their superiors. It is keenly interested in the role of political parties (whether regional, nationalist or communist) in organizing the disaffected, in the role of the state as a mechanism of repression, and finally in the historical outcome of movements of social protest.

The second approach, termed here the Political–Cultural (P–C) paradigm, accepts the importance of large-scale economic change. It argues, however, that if economics is the only important determinant of collective action, many peasants and labourers living at the margins of subsistence would be rebelling all the time. Crucial to a fuller understanding of resistance

[1] Even the major studies are too numerous to be listed here. A partial listing of works in English could include: Barrington Moore, *Social Origins of Dictatorship and Democracy* (Harmondsworth, 1966); Eric Wolf, *Peasant Wars of the Twentieth Century* (New York, 1969); Rodney Hilton, *Bond Men Made Free* (London, 1973); Eric Hobsbawm, *Primitive Rebels* (Manchester, 1959); George Rudé, *The Crowd in History* (New York, 1964); Hobsbawm and Rudé, *Captain Swing* (Harmondsworth, 1969); E. P. Thompson, *The Making of the English Working Class* (Harmondsworth, 1963); Sartono Kartodirdjo, *The Peasant Revolt in Banten in 1888* (The Hague, 1966); J. C. Scott, *The Moral Economy of the Peasant* (New Haven, 1976); Ranajit Guha, *Elementary Aspects of Peasant Insurgency in Colonial India* (New Delhi, 1983).

[2] Charles Tilly, *Big Structures, Large Processes, Huge Comparisons* (New York, 1985).

are systems of political legitimacy and the interplay between ideologies of domination and subordination. Looking more closely at local class relations and their cultural idiom, the P–C paradigm asks—how is legitimacy claimed by the superordinate classes, how is it granted, and when does it break down? While accepting that economic deprivation is often a necessary condition for resistance, it suggests that protest will take place only when there is a perceived erosion, whether partial or total, of patterns of legitimate authority. Lastly, this approach has a more sophisticated view of the role of political organizations, arguing that the rank and file, far from uncritically accepting the ideology of the leadership, often reshape and rework it to suit their own purposes.[3]

Flowing from these theoretical differences are certain methodological preferences. The S–O paradigm is prone to view protest as instrumental, oriented towards specific economic and political goals. Here, success is the gauge by which the significance of protest is measured. By contrast, the P–C paradigm is more likely to emphasize the expressive dimensions of social protest—its cultural and religious idioms. The significance of lower-class resistance, it argues, consists not merely in what the rebels accomplish or fail to accomplish, but also in the language in which social actors express their discontent with the prevailing arrangements. Second, implicit in the S–O paradigm is a unilinear progression from 'spontaneous' to 'organized' forms of protest, with individual action at one end of the scale and organized party activity at the other. The P–C approach, on the other hand, distinguishes between different mechanisms of protest, relating specific actions to specific systems of domination. While accepting that certain forms of protest are likely to predominate in particular societies and historical periods, it does not accept the historical inevitability of a progression from unorganized to organized forms. For most rebels have available a wide range of protest mechanisms, with the use of one tactic (e.g. organized revolt) not precluding the use of another, ostensibly more 'primitive', tactic (e.g. arson) at a later date.[4]

[3] Cf. J. C. Scott, 'From Protest to Profanation: Agrarian Revolt and the Little Tradition', *Theory and Society*, vol. 4, 1977.

[4] See, in this connection, Michael Adas, 'From Footdragging to Flight: The

In sum, the practitioners of the S–O approach look for underlying regularities, draw large generalizations, and adhere to strict notions of causality in analysing social protest: they are closer to the 'science' end of the social-science spectrum. The P–C approach, on the other hand, stresses differences in the language and mechanisms of protest, relating these differences to particular cultural contexts: thus it is closer to the 'interpretive' end of the spectrum. The S–O paradigm stands at the confluence of structural Marxism and organizational sociology, a meeting captured in Charles Tilly's organizing trinity of concepts, 'interest, organization, and opportunity'.[5] Among the major works in this genre are those by Eric Wolf and Charles Tilly, and Barrington Moore's classic on dictatorship and democracy.[6] The P–C paradigm consists of a more eclectic brew, drawing selectively on Marxism, Weber, and the interpretive turn in social science. Perhaps its most influential Western exponent is James Scott, while in India the pathbreaking studies of the Subaltern Studies school come within its ambit.[7] The division also mirrors the schism emerging in the sociology of social movements, with the P–C paradigm standing close to the Collective Behaviour school, the S–O paradigm to Resource Mobilization theory.[8]

Evasive History of Peasant Avoidance Protest in South and South-east Asia', *Journal of Peasant Studies*, vol. 13, no. 2, 1986.

[5] Charles Tilly, *From Mobilization to Revolution* (Reading, Mass., 1978); idem, *The Contentious French* (Cambridge, Mass., 1986). See also George Rudé's review of the latter work in *Times Literary Supplement*, 4 April 1986.

[6] Wolf, *Peasant Wars*; Tilly, *The Contentious French*; Barrington Moore, *Social Origins*.

[7] J. C. Scott, *Weapons of the Weak: Everyday Forms of Peasant Resistance* (New Haven, 1986); Ranajit Guha, *Subaltern Studies: Writings on South Asian History and Society*, volumes I to IV (New Delhi, 1982–5). Cf. also Richard Cobb, *The Police and the People: French Popular Protest, 1769–1820* (Oxford, 1970).

It is difficult to place the pioneering works of Hobsbawm and Rudé in either category. While their interest in the culture of resistance draws them close to the P–C approach, their 'progressive' view of history and faith in the Leninist party as the perfect embodiment of the aspirations of the oppressed classes are more typical of the S–O school. The other distinguished British Marxist historian of lower-class protest, E. P. Thompson, can be more easily placed in the P–C camp.

[8] J. Craig Jenkins, 'Resource Mobilization Theory and the Study of Social Movements', *Annual Review of Sociology*, no. 9, 1983; J. R. Gusfield, 'Social Move-

THE LANDSCAPE OF RESISTANCE

While the orientation of this work places it within the P–C paradigm, both the approaches described above have their distinctive strengths and weaknesses. While the S–O framework may be particularly suited to studying Tilly's master processes of social change, case studies of the cultural idiom of resistance would draw largely upon the organizing concepts of the P–C school. Here, two caveats are in order. First, a close attention to the language of domination and subordination in any one society does not preclude either the use of theoretical concepts drawn from the social sciences or the formulation of generalizations based on the careful comparative analysis of protest in different conjunctures.[9] Second, one must be wary of the pitfalls of an exclusively 'interpretive' approach—namely the downplaying of the material basis of human society so characteristic of anthropological attempts to analyse a culture from within and on its own terms.[10]

In this work the material structure of Uttarakhand society serves as the 'landscape of resistance'.[11] Following Marx's postulate that social being conditions social consciousness, I argue that the social relations and forces of production set certain limits to the forms a culture (and within it, resistance) may take. However, a truly materialist approach would begin not with the economic landscape but with the natural setting in which the economy is embedded. For if production relations sharply define the boundaries of political structures and cultural-symbolic systems, they in turn are limited by the eco-

---

ments and Social Change: Perspectives of Linearity and Fluidity', in Louis Kriesberg (ed.), *Research in Social Movements, Conflict and Change*, vol. 4 (Greenwich, Conn., 1981).

[9] This is exemplified by a culturally sensitive work pitched at an extremely high level of generality, Barrington Moore's *Injustice*. Interestingly, while his earlier work (*Social Origins*)—a vastly influential study in the S–O genre—is quite deaf to the cultural idiom of protest, *Injustice* is a major contribution to a culturally rooted political sociology.

[10] This neglect of structure is quite apparent in the later works of the cult figure of interpretive anthropology, Clifford Geertz. See especially his *The Interpretation of Cultures* (New York, 1973), and *Local Knowledge* (New York, 1980).

[11] I owe this term to James Scott, *Weapons of the Weak*. My usage is somewhat different from Scott's.

logical characteristics—the flora, fauna, topography, and climate—of the society in which they are placed.

It is not my intention to substitute, for explanations based exclusively on economic and social factors, an equally uncritical ecological determinism.[12] Yet I would emphasize that in a region so markedly influenced by its ecological setting as the Indian Himalaya, a study of processes of social change would be seriously flawed unless set in the context of simultaneous processes of environmental change. Thus the 'ecological landscape of resistance', outlined in the following two chapters, will incorporate the linkages between forests and agriculture, the management of forests in the indigenous system, the specific forms of state intervention and the changes it induced, and of course the agrarian relations of production normally regarded as the material base. Once this landscape has been set in place, we can turn to the study's major concern: the· nature and form of social protest movements asserting traditional claims over the forest. In this manner the book spans the gap between two distinct scholarly traditions: the sociology of lower-class protest and the ecologically oriented study of history.

The fusion of these hitherto parallel discourses will hopefully help move the study of popular opposition to colonial rule in India beyond the current preoccupation with the role of the Congress party. Until the recent advent of the Subaltern Studies school, historical research on Indian nationalism was located firmly in the S–O genre: in focusing on the part played by the Congress party in organizing the peasantry, it had little time for what one critic has called the 'internal face' of Indian nationalism.[13] Consequently, we have as yet a very primitive understanding of the social composition, culture and ideology of many of the tribal and peasant movements in twentieth-century India. A second area of neglect germane to this work is the study of the often considerable impact of colonial forest/environmental policies on agrarian economy and peasant protest. For, by looking only at social conflicts around land and within the workplace, historians have for the most part been

[12] The best-known example of which is, of course, Marvin Harris, *Cows, Pigs, Wars, and Witches: The Riddles of Culture* (New York, 1974).

[13] Gyanendra Pandey, *The Ascendancy of the Congress in Uttar Pradesh* (New Delhi, 1978), p. 215.

curiously unaware of the equally bitter conflicts concerned with the control and utilization of forests, water and other natural resources.[14] Much work on social movements has, moreover, been marked by provincialism; very rarely are Indian developments located or analysed in a wider comparative framework.

In trying to overcome these limitations this book has three major aims. Its primary focus is on the links between structures of domination and the idioms of social protest. Here Uttarakhand is a fascinating case study, for between 1815 and 1949 it was divided into two distinct socio-political systems—the princely state of Tehri Garhwal and the colonial territory of Kumaun. While the region was quite homogeneous in terms of economy and culture, during this period the structure of the state, and especially the style of rule, differed substantially in the two domains. The ruler of Tehri Garhwal, representative of a dynasty that stretched back 1200 years and that was perhaps the oldest in north India, could also call upon his symbolic status as the head of the Badrinath temple—one of the holiest in Hinduism—in pursuance of his claims of legitimate authority. Of much more recent origin, the colonial government of Kumaun was also separated from its subjects by a gulf of race and language. Consequently, the structure of authority was quite different in the two contexts, one approximating Weber's 'traditional' authority, the other 'bureaucratic' authority.[15] At the same time, the peasantry in both territories was subject to virtually identical processes of ecological change. An elaboration of these similarities and differences will help us appreciate the interplay between structures of domination and styles of protest. We shall also see how these distinct sociopolitical systems and histories of protest influence the trajectory

[14] Cf. Ramachandra Guha and Madhav Gadgil, 'State Forestry and Social Conflict in British India', *Past and Present*, no. 123, May 1989.

[15] Max Weber, *Economy and Society*, translated by Guenther Roth and Claus Wittich (Berkeley, 1968). Weber is not concerned with the colonial situation, in which bureaucratic authority does not have the positive features he sometimes associates it with. Colonial bureaucratic structures have no popular sanction; they are legitimized only by the superior force of alien rulers. The two elements in Weber's treatment relevant here are the impersonal character of authority in bureaucracies (as opposed to the personalized systems of traditional authority), and his conception of bureaucracy as the most efficient way of exercising authority over human beings.

of a contemporary social movement, the Chipko Andolan.

The second major focus is on the links between competing systems of forest use and management, ecological decline, and agrarian protest. There are voluminous histories of Indian forestry written by forest officials.[16] Set in a region whose forests were among the most intensively worked in the subcontinent, this book traces a different path, directing attention away from the perceptions of the forest department towards the perceptions of the villagers of Uttarakhand affected by its policies.[17] In contrast to other regions, where peasant subsistence was not so closely interwoven with the forests, in Uttarakhand the ecological dimension is crucial to a fuller understanding of the social idiom of popular protest.

Finally, while the book's core consists of a comparative analysis of social protest in Tehri Garhwal and Kumaun divisions, it also attempts three additional kinds of comparison. First, I use the Tehri Garhwal case to develop a theory of customary rebellions in traditional monarchies which takes issue with Max Gluckman's germinal treatment of the subject.[18] Second, I use the Kumaun case to make a larger critique of party-centred histories of nationalism, arguing that the connections between the peasantry and 'organized' politics are more complex and more surprising than has hitherto been supposed. Third, in the concluding chapter I compare movements in twentieth-century Uttarakhand with movements in defence of forest rights in early-capitalist Europe. The persistence of forest conflicts in the one case, and their diminution and eventual disappearance in the other, is, I suggest, indicative of the ecological limits to full-blown industrialization on the Western model in ex-colonial countries. The union of history and ecology is therefore not merely a methodological imperative; it is also an invaluable guide to the understanding of contemporary social concerns.

[16] Especially E. P. Stebbing, *The Forests of India*, three volumes (London, 1922-7).
[17] For a more detailed study, at an all-India level, see Madhav Gadgil and Ramachandra Guha, *This Fissured Land: Humans and Nature in the Indian Subcontinent*, forthcoming (Oxford University Press, New Delhi).
[18] Max Gluckman, *Order and Rebellion in Tribal Africa* (London, 1963).

CHAPTER 2

The Mountains and Their People

> We entered an enchanted garden, where the produce of Europe and Asia—indeed of every quarter of the world—was blended together. Apples, pears and pomegranates, plantains, figs and mulberry trees, grew in the greatest quantity, and with the most luxuriant hue. Blackberries and raspberries, hung temptingly from the brows of the broken crags, while our path was strewed with strawberries. In every direction, were blooming heather—violets and jasmine, with innumerable 'rose trees in full bearing' ... I have beheld nearly all the celebrated scenery of Europe, which poets and painters have immortalized, and of which all the tourists in the world are enamoured; but I have seen it surpassed in these ... unknown regions [of the Himalaya.]
>
> — Thomas Skinner, *Excursions in India, Including a Walk over the Himalaya to the Source of the Jumna and the Ganges* (1832)

Through most of recorded history the Indo-Gangetic plain, a vast unbroken territory extending westwards to the Arabian Sea and eastwards to the Bay of Bengal, has been the political 'core' of India, the epicentre of the great kingdoms that have risen and fallen with the centuries. Rising sharply from this plain the Himalaya, source of the holy rivers of Hinduism, has loomed large in the spiritual and religious life of the subcontinent. The transition from this plain to the Himalaya is achieved via the Siwaliks, a line of hills fifteen to fifty kilometres in breadth and from a few hundred to a few thousand feet in elevation, that run along the southern edge of the Himalaya. Separating these outer hills from the fertile plain is a band of swamp and forest called the Terai. Inhabited only by a few hunting and gathering communities, and highly malarial, the Terai formed an effective barrier to the penetration of large armies from the plains.

The Himalayan region proper, lying a few kilometres north

of the Siwaliks, rises quickly to an average elevation of 7000 feet. The inner hills extend a hundred kilometres to the north, culminating in the great snowy peaks that surpass in elevation all other parts of the world. The hills are criss-crossed by river valleys, resembling gigantic ravines carved out of hillsides. At the bottom of each valley flows the river with narrow strips of cultivable land adjoining it. Alongside the river are steeply sloping hills, rising up to 9000 feet. It is this ecological region, lying between the snowy peaks and the outer hills, that is the focus of this study.

Political history

Garhwal and Kumaun refer to the two kingdoms that ruled Uttarakhand through much of the medieval period. At one stage both territories were under the sway of one dynasty, the Katyuris. The Katyuris ruled for several centuries, first from Joshimath in the Alakananda valley and later from the Katyur valley in present-day Almora district.[1]

Following the decline of the centralized political authority of the Katyuris, which cannot be dated with certainty, the area broke up into many small principalities. The independent chiefdoms of Garhwal were first subjugated by Ajaypal Panwar in the thirteenth century, while the unification of Kumaun took place under Som Chand around AD 960.[2] 'Kshatriyas' from Malwa (Gujarat) and Rajputana respectively, the Panwars and the Chands soon consolidated their rule. In this they were helped by the isolated nature of their territories, bounded on the north by the Greater Himalaya and separated from the Indo-Gangetic plain in the south by the Siwalik hills. Thus they neither came under the sway of the Mughals nor were they subject to invasion from the north. They were seriously threatened only after the unification of Nepal in 1768 under the Gurkha chief Prithvinarayan Sah. After repeated attempts the Gurkhas conquered Kumaun in 1790 and Garhwal in 1804.

The Gurkhas introduced certain changes in the agrarian

[1] See L. D. Joshi, *The Khasa Family Law* (London, 1929), pp. 28–9.
[2] These dates are currently the subject of controversy amongst historians of Uttarakhand. They were first put forward by E. T. Atkinson in his massive work, *The Himalayan Districts of the North-western Provinces of India*, 3 volumes, (Allahabad, 1882–6).

structure—built around strong village communities, with most members enjoying a vested interest in land—via the system of military assignments. Their rule was, however, short-lived. When the Anglo-Gurkha wars culminated in the treaty of 1815, the East India Company had annexed both Kumaun and Garhwal. Retaining Kumaun and eastern Garhwal (now known together as Kumaun division), the British restored the western portion—known as Tehri Garhwal after the new capital—to the son of the last Garhwali ruler.

The boundaries of the treaty of 1815 were fixed with a view to controlling the route to Tibet and the passes used for trade. It was the prospect of commercial intercourse with Tibet, and not considerations of revenue, that induced Lord Hastings to embark on the hill campaign. While Kumaun bordered Nepal in the east, both northern Almora and British Garhwal had important trade routes to Tibet.[3] Its location, strategic from the viewpoints of both defensive security and trade, played an important part in the evolution of British land policy in Kumaun.[4]

The boundaries of Kumaun division coincided with well defined physical features. The river Kali separated it from Nepal in the east; the Himalaya separated it from Tibet in the north; in the west it was divided from the state of Tehri Garhwal by the Alakananda and Mandakini rivers; in the south the outer hills demarcated it from the adjoining division of Rohilkhand. Tehri Garhwal, likewise bounded in the south and north by the Siwalik hills and Tibet respectively, was separated from Dehradun district by the Tons and Yamuna rivers in the west.

SOCIAL STRUCTURE

Caste[5]

The social structures of Kumaun and Garhwal share marked similarities. The largest ethnic stratum is made up of the Khasa

[3] British Garhwal refers to the portion of Garhwal now constituted as a British district. Along with Nainital and Almora it formed 'Kumaun division'.
[4] John Pemble, *The Invasion of Nepal* (London, 1971), chapter III, 'The Matter of Himalayan Trade'. Cf. also B. P. Saksena (ed.), *Historical Papers Relating to Kumaun, 1809–1842* (Allahabad, 1956).
[5] This section draws on the following works: R. D. Sanwal, 'Social Stratifica-

or Khasiya which comprise the traditional peasantry, while the next largest stratum consists of the Doms serving the cultivating body as artisans and farm servants. Numerically the smallest but ritually the highest are the Thuljat—Brahmins and Rajputs claiming to be descendants of later immigrants from the plains.[6]

Most writers adhere to a 'conquest' theory whereby the Doms are viewed as the original inhabitants who were conquered and enslaved by the Khasas. While the Khasas were a widespread race in prehistoric Asia, the origins of the hill Khasas is obscure. They have, however, adhered to a Vedantic form of Hinduism at least since the eighth century.[7] The Khasas in turn were subjugated by later immigrants from the plains who came to hold both political power and ritual status.

This three-tiered structure—Thuljat/Khasa/Dom—emerged, then, out of what were originally distinctions between ruler and ruled. The structure can be conceptualized as a series of binary distinctions, of which the two basic oppositions were (*i*) Bith (clean) *vs.* Dom (unclean); (*ii*) within Bith, Thuljat (immigrant) *vs.* Khasa (indigenous). While both Thuljat and Khasa had Brahmin and Kshatriya segments, Thuljat as a whole ranked higher than Khasa; for example, a Thuljat Kshatriya was considered superior to a Khasa Brahmin. These distinctions can be pictorially represented, as in the following chart:

---

tion in the Hill Region of Uttar Pradesh', in Indian Institute of Advanced Study, *Urgent Research in Social Anthropology* (Simla, 1969); *idem, Social Stratification in Rural Kumaun* (Delhi, 1976); G. D. Berreman, *Hindus of the Himalayas* (Berkeley, 1973); Pannalal, *Hindu Customary Law in Kumaun* (1921; rpt. Allahabad, 1942); A. C. Turner, 'Caste in the Kumaun Division and Tehri Garhwal State', *Census of India*, 1931, vol. 18, pt 1; E. H. H. Eyde, 'The Depressed Classes of the Kumaun Hills', *Census of India*, 1921, vol. 16, pt 1, appendix C.

[6] An analysis of the 1931 census data from UP showed Kumaun and Garhwal as being 'a highly distinctive caste region that also has a high degree of homogeneity'. While the index of dissimilarity for Almora and Garhwal, 0.08, was 'considerably lower than the value for any pair of contiguous plains districts', the index reached its highest value, 0.81, across the mountain/plain boundary between Garhwal and Bijnor districts. See D. E. Sopher, 'Rohilkhand and Oudh: An Exploration of Social Gradients across a Political Barrier', in R. G. Fox (ed.), *Realm and Region in Traditional India* (Delhi, 1977), p. 289.

[7] That is, following the advent of Adi Sankaracharya in the hills. Prior to this Buddhism exercised a vigorous influence that can still be discerned in the iconography of hill temples.

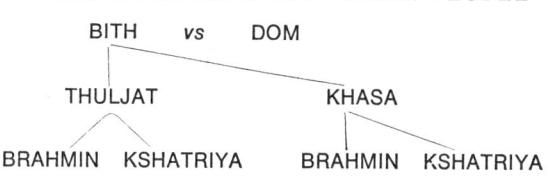

```
             BITH   vs   DOM
              |_____|
              |          |
           THULJAT      KHASA
           /    \       /    \
      BRAHMIN KSHATRIYA BRAHMIN KSHATRIYA
```

SOURCE: After R. D. Sanwal, *Social Stratification in Rural Kumaun* (Delhi, 1976).

The geographical isolation of the hill tracts fostered an ambiguous relation with the so-called 'Great Tradition' of Hinduism. On the one hand, contact with plains Hinduism was maintained through the pilgrims who came annually to visit the famous temples in the hills. As a result, one finds little evidence of an 'almost universal antipathy' which hillmen are believed to feel towards the inhabitants of the plains.[8] On the other hand, caste restrictions and other rules of orthodox Hinduism were singularly lax. Brahmins customarily used the plough and ate meat, while there was a great deal of informal interaction between high and low castes, especially on festive occasions. And as the opening out of the economy under British rule facilitated status mobility, over time the Khasa merged with the Thuljat.

With reference to the untouchable Doms, ritual rules of purity and pollution were not defined as exclusively as in the plains.[9] While each village had two water sources, one for the Bith, the other for the Dom, the Dom could smoke from the same pipe as the Khas–Rajput (the dominant peasant caste) and touch without polluting food not cooked or mixed with water (e.g. fruit and grain). Mostly artisans and tenants, the

[8] David Arnold, 'Rebellious Hillmen: The Gudem Rampa Risings, 1839–1924', in Ranajit Guha (ed.), *Subaltern Studies I* (Delhi, 1982), p. 13.

[9] According to the 1921 census the population of Doms was as follows:

District	Total population	Population of depressed classes
Nainital	276,875	32,970
Almora	530,338	108,659
British Garhwal	485,186	77,334
Tehri Garhwal	318,414	54,325

Doms formed an integral part of the village community. This was especially true of the Bajgis and Aujis, the drummers who played a leading part in all religious and social ceremonies. In conflicts between *lohars* (ironsmiths) of adjoining villages, each was backed by his *padhan* (headman) and *panchayat* (council). On occasions when the artisan was fined, the people of his village collectively paid up on his behalf. Commercialization of the economy, by giving artisans outside employment as masons, carpenters, etc., also helped mitigate the iniquities of the system.

Agrarian relations

Social anthropologists studying ritual hierarchy in Garhwal and Kumaun have stressed the similarities between hill society and the rest of India, seeing the former as a variant of the pan-Indian trend.[10] While this may be true in so far as caste is concerned, there are significant differences in terms of control over land and in political structure. The (attenuated) presence of caste notwithstanding, hill society exhibits an absence of sharp class divisions. Viewed along with the presence of strong communal traditions, this makes Uttarakhand a fascinating exception which one is unable to fit into existing conceptualizations of social hierarchy in India. This distinctive agrarian structure, described below, is germane to the specific forms taken by the movements of social protest that are the subject of this study.[11]

The Central Himalaya are composed of two distinct ecological zones: the monsoon-affected middle and low altitude areas, and the high valleys of the north, inhabited by the Bhotiya herdsmen who had until 1962 carried out the centuries-old trade with Tibet.[12] Along the river valleys cultivation was carried out, limited only by the steepness of land and more frequently by the difficulty of irrigation. Two and sometimes

[10] The standard works are those by Berreman and Sanwal.

[11] Cf. chapters 4 and 5, where the democratic nature of the village community and its communal traditions are seen to play an important role in shaping the idiom of protest.

[12] The Bhotiyas, who are peripheral to this study, have been described in R. P. Srivastava, 'Tribe/Caste Mobility in India and the Case of Kumaun Bhotias', in C. von Fürer Haimendorf (ed.), *Caste and Kin in Nepal, India and Ceylon* (Bombay, 1966).

three harvests were possible throughout the last century, wheat, rice, and millets being the chief cereals grown. The system of tillage and methods of crop rotation bore the mark of the hillfolk's natural environment. With production oriented towards subsistence needs, which were comfortably met, there remained a surplus of grain for export to Tibet and southwards to the plains. Usually having six months' stock of grain in hand, and with their diet supplemented by fish, fruit, vegetable, and animal flesh, the hill cultivators were described by Henry Ramsay, commissioner from 1856 to 1884, as 'probably better off than any peasantry in India'.[13]

Through the nineteenth century European travellers and officials were frequently given to lyrical descriptions of peasant life in the Himalaya, comparing it favourably not merely to social conditions in the adjoining Indo-Gangetic plain but also to the everyday existence of British and Irish villagers. One official, returning from a trip to Tibet, compared the 'homely sight' of the 'pretty hamlets nestling in [the] fertile valleys' of Almora district with the 'barren wilderness' and 'treeless landscape' characteristic of life on the other side of the Himalaya.[14] That grain production easily exceeded subsistence was testified to by various mountaineering expeditions, who welcomed climbing in Upper Garhwal because the surplus produce of the interior villages made it 'very easy to live off the country'.[15] Perhaps the most evocative picture was drawn by the military adventurer Thomas Skinner, whose description of a scene in the Yamuna valley begins this chapter. Skinner marvelled at the 'remarkably clean' and 'well cultivated' villages whose 'terraces are bound by hedges, and neatly kept as they would be in England'. Apologizing for talking too much of 'green fields', he explains that he has only tried to 'convey as truly as I can, a

[13] H. G. Walton, *Almora: A Gazetteer* (Allahabad, 1911), pp. 57–9; S. D. Pant, *The Social Economy of the Himalayans* (London, 1935), p. 137; 'Correspondence Relating to the Scarcity in Kumaun and Garhwal in 1890', in *British Parliamentary Papers*, vol. 59 (1890–2).

[14] C. A. Sherring, *Western Tibet and the Indian Borderland* (1916; rpt. New Delhi, 1974), pp. 366–7.

[15] Eric Shipton, 'More Explorations round Nanda Devi', *The Geographical Journal*, vol. 90, no. 2, August 1937, p. 104; F. S. Smythe, 'Explorations in Garhwal around Kamet', *The Geographical Journal*, vol. 79, no. 1, January 1932, p. 3.

picture of the most delightful scenery, and most lovely spots on the face of the earth'. Coming across a shepherd boy playing his pipe, he comments that 'the notes were sweet and simple, and in such a situation, among such scenes, could not fail to bring to the mind an Arcadian picture.' Clearly, Skinner's evocation of mountain landscape is the more effusive for his having spent many years in the plains of India. At the same time, it is noteworthy that his Himalayan Arcadia is not an uninhabited wilderness but a composite picture of fields, houses, woods, fruit trees, birds, and streams.[16]

The hill land-tenure system inherited by the British differed no less strikingly from that in the plains. The first commissioner, G. W. Traill, observed that at least three-fourths of the villages were *hissedari*—i.e. wholly cultivated by the actual proprietors of the land, from whom the revenue demand was perforce restricted to their respective shares of the village assessment. The remaining villages were divided into (*i*) those in which the right of property was recognized in earlier recipients of land grants (many dating only from the period of Gurkha rule), while the hereditary right of cultivation remained with the original occupants (called *khaikar*); (*ii*) a handful of villages owned by a single individual. Here too, individual tenants (called *khurnee*) were able to wrest easy terms owing to the favourable land–man ratio.[17] As even the most important landowners depended not on any legal right but on the actual influence they exercised over village communities, there was not one estate which could be termed 'pure zamindari'. Government revenue and certain customary fees were collected by the *elected* village padhan, who reported in turn to a higher revenue official called the *patwari* (in charge of a *patti* or group of villages) who was entrusted with police duties and the responsibility of collecting statutory labour for public works.[18] While over time much of the class of khurnee merged with that

[16] Thomas Skinner, *Excursions in India, Including a Walk over the Himalaya Mountain to the Sources of the Jumna and the Ganges*, two volumes (London, 1832), I, pp. 223, 242, 246–7, 260, 268, etc.

[17] G. W. Traill, 'Statistical Sketch of Kumaun', in *Asiatic Researches*, vol. 16 (1828; rpt. Delhi, 1980).

[18] J. H. Batten, 'Report on the Settlement of the District of Garhwal' (1842); idem, 'Final Report on the Settlement of Kumaun', both in Batten (ed.), *Official Reports on the Province of Kumaun* (1851; rpt. Calcutta, 1878). The extent of land

of khaikar, the latter differed from the hissedar only in that he could not transfer land and had to pay a fixed sum as *malikhana* to the proprietor. This sum represented the conversion into a cash payment of various cesses and perquisites earlier levied. But, by the end of the century, fully nine-tenths of all hillmen were estimated to be hissedars, cultivating proprietors with full ownership rights.[19]

Some evidence from census returns is given in Table 2.1. Not strictly comparable with the other mountainous districts, Nainital comprised a few hill pattis and a large area of the Terai which had begun to be settled by the end of the nineteenth century.[20] Within the hill districts proper, one observes that around 60 per cent of the agrarian population were owner-cultivators. Having already noted the position of *khaikhari* tenures, we can conclude that around 80 per cent of the total population farmed largely with the help of family labour. The extraordinarily low proportion of agricultural labour confirms

cultivated and share of gross produce retained by different classes of cultivators as estimated by Batten were:

Class	Per cent share of gross produce	Per cent of land cultivated
Cultivating proprietors (hissedar)	80	60
Original occupants reduced to occupancy tenants (khaikhar)	70–5	20
Tenants settled by proprietor (khurnee)	66	20
Non-resident tenants	NA	

Under the earlier rulers 'the agricultural assessment originally fixed was extremely light, and its rate and amount would appear to have been very rarely revised.' Traill, quoted in E. K. Pauw, *Report on the Tenth Settlement of the Garhwal District* (Allahabad, 1896), p. 53.

[19] B. H. Baden-Powell, *The Land Systems of British India* (1892; rpt. Delhi, 1974), vol. II, pp. 308–15; V. A. Stowell, *A Manual of the Land Tenures of the Kumaun Division* (1907; rpt. Allahabad, 1937). The latter statement, attributed to Pauw, is obviously an overestimate, but significant in so far as it reflects a strongly perceived contrast with the land systems of the plains.

[20] See B. K. Joshi, 'Underdevelopment of Hill Areas of UP', GIDS, Lucknow, mimeo, 1983, for the distinction between hill and terai.

TABLE 2.1

Occupational Classification of Agricultural Households in Kumaun, 1911–1921 (Workers and Dependants)

Category	Nainital 1911	Nainital 1921	Almora 1911	Almora 1921	British Garhwal 1911	British Garhwal 1921
Those whose income is						
I. Primarily from rent:						
(a) landlords	3,023		681		102	
(b) occupancy tenants	5,025		21		2	
(c) ordinary tenants	15,199		22		17	
Total class I	23,247 (9.89)	722 (0.35)	724 (0.15)	530 (0.11)	121 (0.03)	155 (0.03)
II. From cultivation of their holdings						
(a) landlords	48,887 (20.80)		287,952 (59.31)		292,649 (66.60)	
(b) occupancy tenants	22,449 (9.55)		107,519 (22.15)		104,793 (23.85)	
(c) ordinary tenants	118,411 (50.38)		88,337 (17.16)		34,799 (7.92)	
Total class II	189,747 (80.73)	184,276 (89.15)	478,808 (98.62)	486,776 (98.04)	432,241 (98.37)	448,649 (99.11)

III. Farm servants and field labourers	14,212 (6.05)	15,261 (7.38)	1,771 (0.36)	2,411 (0.49)	3,917 (0.89)	1,744 (0.39)
IV. Goatherds, shepherds and herdsmen	4,886 (2.07)	3,741 (1.81)	3,151 (0.65)	6,035 (1.21)	1,507 (0.34)	642 (0.14)
V. Others (including forestry)	2,956 (1.26)	2,698 (1.31)	1,053 (0.22)	763 (0.15)	1,609 (0.37)	642 (0.14)
VI. Agriculture and pasture (total)	235,428	206,698	485,507	496,515	439,395	451,832
VII. Total population	323,519	276,875	525,104	530,338	480,167	485,186
VIII. VI as % of VII	72.65	74.65	92.46	93.62	91.51	93.30

NOTE: (i) A simpler classification was adopted in 1921 owing to the non-co-operation movement.
(ii) Figures in parentheses denote percentage of agricultural population (VI).
SOURCE: *Census of India*, 1911 and 1921.

the picture of an egalitarian peasant community, a picture used more often as an analytical construct than believed to exist in reality.[21] The land system of Tehri Garhwal differed only in that theoretically all land vested in the sovereign. While landlords could not alienate their holdings, land was hereditary and could be gifted to religious endowments or leased out to tenants. Except for the *muafi* (revenue-free holding) of Saklana, there were few large landowners. As in Kumaun division, the agrarian system was dominated by peasants cultivating their holdings with the help of family labour. This is corroborated by the census figures.

TABLE 2.2

Land Holdings in Tehri Garhwal[1]

	1911	1921
Total population	300,819	318,414
Occupancy tenants	251,722	300,365[2]
Ordinary tenants	22,503	—
Rentiers	747	133
Farm servants and field labourers	1,799	922

[1] All figures for workers and dependants
[2] Includes ordinary tenants

SOURCE: As in Table 2.1.

Thus, over 80 per cent of the population corresponded to the category of hissedar in Kumaun division, except that they enjoyed hereditary rights of usufruct and not of ownership. Land revenue, paid directly to the king, was collected by patwaris who, along with the padhans, got a fixed share of the revenue as well as certain customary fees from the villagers. The kinsmen of the raja were, however, exempt from revenue. An indication of the dominance of small peasant production is given by the land revenue figures of 1910. Of the Rs 115,000 collected as revenue, 96,100 (or about 84 per cent) was col-

---

[21] Cf. D. Thorner, 'Peasant Economy as a Category in Economic History', in T. Shanin (ed.), *Peasants and Peasant Societies* (Harmondsworth, 1972).

lected as *khalsa*, i.e. revenue paid directly by the cultivator, and 18,900 as paid by *jagirs*, muafi and *gunth* (temples).[22]

Community traditions

The absence of sharp inequalities in land ownership within the body of cultivating proprietors—who formed the bulk of the population—was the basis for the sense of solidarity within the village community. Exhibiting a strong sense of clanship, peasants often derived their caste name from the village they inhabited. The institutional expression of this solidarity was the village panchayat. With every adult member of the 'clean' castes having a voice, the hill panchayat differed markedly from the caste panchayat of the plains. While not accorded formal rights, the Doms could also invoke the authority of the panchayat to settle their affairs.

Covering a wide range of activities, the panchayat dealt not only with social and religious matters but with judicial questions as well. Well after the establishment of colonial law in Kumaun, panchayats frequently continued to deal internally with matters technically under the jurisdiction of civil and criminal courts. In Tehri Garhwal, although the state had taken over some of its duties, the panchayats continued to be very powerful. While there was virtually no crime, Tehri peasants rarely ventured to the monarch's court, preferring to settle disputes amongst themselves.[23]

Role of women

A peculiar characteristic of hill agriculture—prevalent from Kashmir in the west to Arunachal in the east—is the important role assigned to women. In the difficult terrain no single economic activity can sustain the household. Typically, there is a 'basket' of economic pursuits—cultivation, cattle rearing, outside employment, perhaps some trade—that requires the equal participation of women. Thus,

the women of the house are also equal partners in the struggle to achieve economic security. Their labour is in no way less valued than

---

[22] Based on H. K. Raturi, *Garhwal Varnan* (Bombay, 1910); *idem*, *Garhwal ka Itihas* (1928; rpt. Tehri, 1980); and conversations with Acharya G. N. Kothiyal.

[23] Joshi, *Khasa Family Law*, pp. 34, 194–9; Turner, 'Caste System', pp. 559–60; E. A. Blunt, *The Caste System of Northern India* (1931; rpt. Delhi, 1969), p. 145; Skinner, *Excursions in India*, vol. II, pp. 16–17.

that of the male members. They work equally with men in the fields, help them in looking after domestic animals and, of course, take physical care of husband and children. Except ploughing, a wife does virtually everything to help her husband in cultivation, which [elsewhere] are the men's task.[24]

Here the disproportionate role played by women in cultivation is ascribed to the imperatives of economic security in an inhospitable environment. Other writers, notably S. D. Pant in his pioneering work on Kumaun,[25] have tended to see in this unnatural division of labour incipient signs of sexual oppression. It may be pointed out that apart from her contribution to the tasks of cultivation, the woman of the household is exclusively responsible for household chores (cooking, cleaning, etc.), the rearing of children, and the collection of fuel, fodder and water. Foreign travellers were invariably struck by the importance of women in economic life, in stark contrast to male-dominated European agriculture.[26] These chores often involved 16 to 18 hours of hard work, and the husband was prone to chastise and even beat his wife when the tasks were not performed to his satisfaction. Reformers hoped that the spread of education, if it took women into its fold, would go a long way towards mitigating these evils.[27] Others commented more sharply on the disproportionate share of farm and family labour borne by women, and visualized a rebellion that 'has been lacking so far, but discontent is daily increasing and a change may occur any time.'[28]

State and society

Its isolated position and, later, its status as a recruiting ground for army personnel were reflected in the administrative policies

[24] Ramesh Chandra, 'Sex Role Arrangements to Achieve Economic Security in Northwest Himalayas', in C. von Fürer Haimendorf (ed.), *Asian Highland Societies in Anthropological Perspective* (New Delhi, 1981), p. 209.
[25] Pant, *Social Economy*.
[26] 'Mountaineer', *A Summer Ramble in the Himalayas* (London, 1860), p. 207; James Kennedy, *Life and Work in Benares and Kumaun 1839–1877* (London, 1884), p. 239.
[27] See *Garhwali* (Dehradun), 5 May 1928, 22 September 1928, etc.
[28] See Pant, *Social Economy*, p. 192. While this revolt may have been delayed, the participation of women in contemporary social movements (cf. chapter 7) bears witness to this prophetic statement.

followed in Kumaun division. While the 'peculiar circumstances of Kalee [i.e. Eastern] Kumaun and its position on the borders of the Nepal territory render a moderate [revenue] demand especially expedient', in Garhwal too the settlement officer was advised 'to form the settlement on the same principles of moderate demand . . .'[29] That these instructions were faithfully adhered to is borne out by Table 2.3.

TABLE 2.3

Land Revenue in Kumaun and British Garhwal, 1848

	Kumaun			British Garhwal			Average for province		
	Rs	a.	p.	Rs	a.	p.	Rs	a.	p.
Rate/acre/ total area	NA			NA			0	14	1
Rate/acre/ total Malguzaree	0	7	3	0	12	14	1	3	8
Rate/acre/ total cultivation	0	12	9	1	1	2	1	12	1

SOURCE: R. A. Shakespear, *Memoir on the Statistics of the North Western Provinces of the Bengal Presidency* (Calcutta, 1848).

Army recruitment had started by the mid nineteenth century, with both Kumauni and Garhwali soldiers being drafted into Gurkha units. The Garhwali Regiment, with headquarters at Lansdowne in the outer hills, was formed in 1890, becoming the 39th Garhwal Rifles in 1901. Essentially peasant farmers who returned to cultivate their holdings upon retirement, hill soldiers enjoyed an enviable record for their bravery.[30] In these circumstances, British land-revenue assessment was extraordinarily light—around Rs 3 per family—and

[29] R. Alexander, asst secretary to the comm., 3rd Div., Sudder Board, Camp Futtegurh, 7 February 1837, in Saksena (ed.), *Historical Papers*, pp. 233-4.

[30] A. L. Mumm, *Five Months in the Himalayas* (London, 1909), pp. 13-15; J. C. G. Lewer, *The Sowar and the Jawan* (Ilfracombe, Devon, 1981), pp. 46-50; P. Mason, *A Matter of Honour* (London, 1975), pp. 384-92. Garhwalis won three out of the five Victoria Crosses awarded to Indians during World War I, and were to win

its revision barely kept up with the increase in population. A rapid expansion of cultivated area was watched over by a highly personalized administration exemplified in the person of Henry Ramsay,[31] whom fellow Englishmen hailed as the uncrowned king of Kumaun.[32]

At one stage the hills had afforded distinct possibilities of tea cultivation. In 1862-3 over 35,000 pounds of tea was produced in Dehradun and Kumaun, and an estimate of waste land fitted for tea cultivation revealed that it was feasible to match the entire export trade of China from this region alone. As the climate, elevation and variety of vegetative types all suited Europeans, some officials strongly recommended large-scale colonization by white settlers. Holding out the 'certain prospect of comfort', colonization would be a 'perfect god-send to the starving peasantry of Ireland and of the Scotch Highlands'.[33] The refusal of the hill peasant to shed his subsistence orientation, and the opposition anticipated at the introduction of white settlers, led to these plans being shelved.[34] In fact, in the odd year when the monsoon failed, grain was imported by the authorities and sold at remunerative prices—a measure, it was stressed, necessitated not by the poverty of the population (who could well afford to buy grain) but by the inaccessibility of many villages and the lack of markets in an economy characterized by an absence of traders in food grains. Such measures may help explain the absence of any revenue-based agitations in either the nineteenth or the twentieth century.[35]

---

undying fame when they refused to fire at a crowd of Khudai Khitmatgars at Peshawar in 1930. For the latter episode, see Shekhar Pathak, *Peshawar Kand ki Yad* (Almora, 1982).

[31] Pant, *Social Economy*, p. 88; H. Ramsay, comm., KD, to secy, Sudder Board of Revenue, NWP & O, no. 147, 14 July 1856, in file no. 2, pre-Mutiny records, Regional Archives, Dehradun.

[32] See Jim Corbett, *My India* (Bombay, 1952), chapter IV, 'Pre-Red-Tape Days'.

[33] B. H. Hodgson, 'On the Colonialization of the Himalaya by Europeans' (1856), in his *Essays on the Languages, Literature and Religion of Nepal and Tibet* (1874; rpt. Varanasi, 1971), pt II, pp. 83-9.

[34] 'Reports on Tea Plantations', in *Selections from the Records of Government of the North Western Provinces*, vol. v (Allahabad, 1869); Walton, *British Garhwal*, pp. 37-9.

[35] Census of India, 1891, vol. 16, pt 1, NWP & O (general report); A. S. Rawat, 'Administration of Land Revenue in British Garhwal (1856-1900)', in

If anything, state interference in the everyday world of peasant agriculture was even less in Tehri Garhwal. Not only was land revenue pitched lower than in the adjoining British territory, at marginally above Rs 2 per family in the early decades of this century,[36] but cultivators were also allowed to bring uncultivated land under the plough between two settlements without incurring any liability to enhanced assessment. And as income from forests came to constitute a major proportion of the king's revenue (chapter 3), there was little incentive to induce peasants to change their subsistence mode towards a market-oriented agriculture. The opening out of Tehri Garhwal was a slow process, hastened only after the world wars and the recruitment of Tehri peasants into the British Indian army. It was only in the last decade of the Tehri raj that the advent of a more revenue-oriented administration and radical revisions of the land settlement led to transformations in peasant society (chapter 5), whose scale far exceeded the gradual social changes of the preceding century and a half.

The 'begar' system

If land policy in British Kumaun did not quite exhibit the revenue orientation of colonial governance in other parts of India, Tehri Garhwal too resembled the archetypal 'feudal' princely state more in the breach. Indeed, the only major intrusion by the state in the life of the peasant before its takeover of the forests was the system of forced labour. Known by various names during the colonial period (*coolie utar, bardaish, begar, godam*), it has been the subject of a fine recent study.[37] The British operated the system, a legacy of the petty hill chiefs who preceded them, from Darjeeling to Simla, on grounds of administrative convenience in tracts whose physical situation made both commercial transport and boarding houses economically unattractive. As embodied in their settle-

Quarterly Review of Historical Studies (Calcutta), vol. 21, nos. 2 and 3, pp. 36-40 (1981-2).

[36] For details see the various annual reports of Tehri Garhwal deposited at the National Archives.

[37] Shekhar Pathak, 'Uttarakhand mein Coolie Begar Pratha: 1815-1949', unpublished Ph.D. thesis, Department of History, Kumaun University, 1980; this has now been published as a book by Radhakrishnan Publishers, Delhi.

ment agreements,[38] landholders were required to provide, for all government officials on tour and for white travellers (e.g. shikaris and mountaineers), several distinct sets of services. The most common of these involved carrying loads and building *chappars* (temporary rest huts), and the supply of provisions (bardaish) such as milk, food, grass, wood and cooking vessels. The actual operations, governed by custom, were far more complex than those sanctioned by custom. Although only hissedars and khaikars were technically liable to be called upon to provide coolie-bardaish, *sirtans* (tenants at will) were also held liable 'as a matter of custom and convenience'. Other forms of statutory labour included the collection of material and levelling of sites for building, roads and other public works, transporting the luggage of regiments moving from Lansdowne, and the carrying of iron and wood for the building of bridges in the interior. Old men and widows were exempt from these burdens at the discretion of the DC (district collector); otherwise remissions were rarely granted. According to the settlement villagers were to be reimbursed for these services, but in actual fact they were often rendered free.[39] While convinced of the 'inequity of the practice' as early as 1850, the government concluded after an enquiry that there existed no available substitute.[40]

In Tehri the different kinds of unpaid labour which could be requisitioned by the state, in addition to bardaish (provisions), were as follows: *gaon begar*, where villagers had to carry the luggage of subordinate officials; *manzil begar*, where villagers had to supply labour for the convenience of higher officials travelling on duty, for guests of the state, or for the carriage of

[38] As Taradutt Gairola argued, the Allahabad high court had passed judgments that the practice was in fact illegal. See his speech in the UP Legislative Council, 16 December 1918, in file no. 21 of 1918–19, dept xv, Regional Archives, Nainital.

[39] Note by D. A. Barker on '*quli-bardaish*', 13 April 1915, in GAD file 398/1913, UPSA ('Begar System in the Kumaun Division'); Shekhar Pathak, 'Kumaun mein Begar Anmulan Andolan', paper presented at seminar on peasant movements in UP, at Jawaharlal Nehru University, on 19 and 20 October 1982, pp. 1–2.

[40] NWP, Board of Revenue Proceedings, vol. 491, cons. 97, pro. 289, 'Forced Labour in Kumaun and Garhwal', India Office Library, London (notes collected by Shri Dharampal).

building materials which could not be transported by mules; *benth*, where labour was supplied for the construction of important buildings or for state occasions (e.g. royal marriages). While the extent of the household's contribution was proportional to the land revenue it paid, remissions were usually granted to village headmen, old men, widows and the handful of jagirdars and muafidars.[41]

THE CULTURAL ECOLOGY OF THE HIMALAYANS

With land revenue fixed at a comparatively low level, in both Tehri Garhwal and Kumaun divisions the begar system constituted the one major intervention by the state in the day-to-day life of the village. The absence of a class of 'feudal' intermediaries further reinforces the image of an independent peasantry firmly in command of its resources. As compared to the sharply stratified villages of the Indo-Gangetic plain, Uttarakhand came much closer to realizing the peasant political ideal of 'a popular monarchy, a state without nobles, perhaps without churchmen, in which the peasantry and their kings are the only social forces'.[42]

It has been suggested that this relative autonomy came about only through a long drawn out process of struggle between the peasantry and the overlord.[43] The absence of sharp class cleavages *within* village society, however, clearly owes its origins to the ecological characteristics of mountain society. Whereas the possibilities of 'extensive' agriculture were limited by the extent of culturable land and the paucity of irrigation, 'intensive' agriculture for the market was severely hampered by the fragility of the soils and poor communications. There

[41] 'Note on the Employment of Unpaid Labour in the Tehri Garhwal State' (prepared by Tehri durbar), enclosed with no. 1885, XVI-63, 17 January 1914, from P. Wyndham, comm., KD, to CSG, UP, in GAD file 398/1913.

[42] Rodney Hilton, *The English Peasantry in the Later Middle Ages* (Oxford, 1975), p. 15, quoted in Rosamund Faith, 'The Great Rumour of 1377 and Peasant Ideology', in T. H. Ashton and R. H. Hilton (eds), *The English Rising of 1381* (Cambridge, 1984), p. 63.

[43] Cf. Joshi, *Khasa Family Law*. For a theoretical exposition of the conflict between 'feudal' and 'communal' modes of power, see Partha Chatterji, 'More on Modes of Power and the Peasantry', in Ranajit Guha (ed.), *Subaltern Studies II* (Delhi, 1982).

have always existed major ecological constraints to the generation of surplus and consequently to the emergence of social classes in hill societies. In Uttarakhand, as in the Alps, Andes, and other comparable ecosystems, agrarian society has had a more or less uniform class structure, composed almost wholly of small peasant proprietors, and with a marginal incidence of big landlords and agricultural labourers. This distinctive class structure meshed nicely with the other ecologically determined hallmark of mountain society, the close integration of agriculture with forests and pasture.

Forests and social institutions in the indigenous system

The best class of cultivation in these mountains was to be found in villages between three and five thousand feet above sea level, having access on the one hand to good forest and grazing ground, and on the other to riparian fields in the depths of the valley. Village sites were usually chosen halfway up the spur, below oak forests and the perennial springs associated with them, and above the cultivated fields along the river bed. In such a situation all crops could be 'raised to perfection', a healthy elevated site was available for houses, and herds of cattle could be comfortably maintained. Until 1910 most villages came close to this ideal.[44]

With animal husbandry being as important to their economy as grain cultivation, the hillfolk and their cattle migrated annually to the grass-rich areas of the forest. Temporary cattle sheds (*kharaks*) were constructed and the cultivation of small patches carried out. In localities where sheep and goats were reared, they were taken to the alpine pastures above the tree line where they stayed till the first autumn snows.

In the permanent hamlets oak forests provided both fodder and fertilizer. Green and dry leaves, which served the cattle as litter, were mixed with grass and the excreta of the animals and fermented to give manure to the fields. In winter manure was moulded from dry leaves and subjected to rot. Thus the forest augmented the nutritive value of the fields, directly through its foliage and indirectly through the excreta of the cattle fed with

[44] Walton, *Almora*, pp. 47–8; idem, *British Garhwal: A Gazetteer* (Allahabad, 1911), p. 167.

fodder leaves and forest grass. Broad-leaved trees also provided the villagers with fuel and agricultural implements.[45]

In the lower hills the extensive *chir* forests served for pasture. Every year the dry grass and pine needle litter in the chir forest was burnt to make room for a fresh crop of luxuriant grass. Simultaneously, the needle litter, whose slippery surface endangered the otherwise sure-footed hill cattle, was destroyed. Very resistant to fire, chir was used for building houses and as torch-wood. In certain parts where pasture was scarce, trees were grown and preserved for fodder.[46]

In such multifarious ways the extensive forests were central to the successful practice of agriculture and animal husbandry. In addition, they were the prime source of medicinal herbs, and in times of dearth, of food as well. Indeed, the hillman was 'especially blessed by the presence in almost every jungle of fruit, vegetables or roots to help him over a period of moderate scarcity'.[47]

This dependence of the hill peasant on forest resources was institutionalized through a variety of social and cultural mechanisms. Through religion, folklore and tradition the village communities had drawn a protective ring around the forests. Across the region covered by this study there existed a highly sophisticated system of conservancy that took various forms. Often, hilltops were dedicated to local deities and the trees around the spot regarded with great respect. Many wooded areas were not of spontaneous growth and bore marks of the hillfolk's instinct for the plantation and preservation of the forest; indeed 'the spacious wooded areas extending over the mountain ranges and hill sides [bore] testimony to the care bestowed upon them by the successive generations of the Kumaunies.'[48] With villages usually sited halfway up the spur,

[45] This paragraph is drawn from Franz Heske, 'Problem der Walderhaltung in Himalaya' (Problems of Forest Conservation in the Himalaya; hereafter referred to as 'Problem'), *Tharandter Forstlichien Jahrbuch*, vol. 82, no. 8, 1931. I am grateful to Professor S. R. D. Guha for translating from the German. See also Patiram, *Garhwal: Ancient and Modern* (Simla, 1916), pp. 53-4; E. C. Mobbs, 'Life in a Himalayan Valley', in four parts, *Indian Forester*, vol. 60, nos. 10, 11 and 12; and vol. 61, no. 1 (1934-5).
[46] Heske, 'Problem', pp. 555, 564-5; Pauw, *Garhwal*, pp. 23, 47.
[47] Walton, *Almora*, p. 59.
[48] G. B. Pant, *The Forest Problem in Kumaun* (Allahabad, 1922), pp. 30-1.

sacred groves had an obvious functional role in stabilizing water flows and preventing landslides. Particularly in eastern Kumaun and around temples, *deodar* plantations had become naturalized, some way east of the trees' natural habitat. Temple groves of deodar varied in extent from a few trees to woods of several hundred acres.[49] This magnificent tree, one surveyor remarked, is 'frequently planted by the Hindus in all parts of the mountains, and attains a gigantic size'.[50] As late as 1953 it was reported that the finest stands of deodar were found near temples, venerated and protected from injury.[51] Commenting on the numerous sacred places in deodar forests, an official observed that 'such spots are frequently prominent places where a good view is obtained, or a beautiful glade in the forest, or where there is some unusual natural phenomena, as a large rock split with a tree growing between the two halves.' Sacred spots were normally marked with cloth or coins.[52] Nor was tree worship restricted to the deodar; a Swiss geologist expedition found, in a village in the Upper Dhauli valley in Garhwal, a sacred birch tree remarkable in its size: with a spread of eighty feet and a double trunk ten feet in diameter.[53] In such sacred groves, the 'traditional form of forest preservation', and one found all over India, no villager would injure the vegetation in any way.[54] In fact, the planting of a grove was regarded as 'as a work of great religious merit'.[55] In parts of Tehri, even today, leaves are offered to a goddess known as Patna Devi (goddess of leaves), this being only one of several

[49] S. B. Bhatia, *WP for the East Almora Forest Division, UP, 1924–25 to 1933–34* (Allahabad, 1926), pp. 13, 32. (WP stands for 'Working Plan'. I use the abbreviation even within monograph titles.)
[50] R. Strachey, 'On the Physical Geography of the Provinces of Kumaun and Garhwal in the Himalaya', *Journal of the Royal Geographical Society*, vol. 21, 1851, p. 76.
[51] N. L. Bor, *Manual of Indian Forest Botany* (Delhi, 1953), p. 18.
[52] E. C. Mobbs, 'Life in a Himalayan Valley', pt IV, *Indian Forester* (IF), vol. 61 (1935), pp. 1–8.
[53] A. Heim and A. Gansser, *The Throne of the Gods: An Account of the First Swiss Expedition to the Himalayas*, translated by Eden and Cedar Paul (London, 1939), p. 116.
[54] D. Brandis, *Indian Forestry* (Woking, 1897), p. 12.
[55] S. M. Edwardes, 'Tree Worship in India', *Empire Forestry*, vol. 1, no. 1 (March 1922), pp. 78–80.

examples of the association of plants with gods.[56] Cases were not unknown of open land being left uncultivated that were dedicated to fairies of the forests, who were believed to come there at night to play.[57] In the Tons valley, tubers and roots—the peasantry's food during times of scarcity—are used only during culturally specified times to inhibit overexploitation.[58]

While sacred groves testified to the role played by traditional religious beliefs in the preservation of nature, in other instances it was informal management practices that regulated the utilization of forest produce by the community. A civilian newly posted to the hills in the 1920s was struck by the way communal action continued to survive in the considerable areas serving as village grazing ground, and by fuel and fodder reserves walled in and well looked after. Despite official apathy the old customary restrictions on the use of the forests operated 'over large areas'; while no formal management existed, practical protection was secured by customary limitations on users. In many patches of oak forest there were rules that prohibited the lopping off of leaves in the hot weather, while the grass cut by each family was strictly regulated. The penalty for the infringement of these rules included boycott and/or the exclusion from the forest of the offender.[59] Traditionally, many villages had fuel reserves even on *gaon sanjait* (common land) measured by government, which the villagers cut over in regular rotation by common consent. With the planting of timber trees a fairly common phenomenon, the jungles preserved within their boundaries were zealously guarded by villages nearby. Thus, Tehri officials observed that peasants strongly asserted their claim to species like *bhimal*, a valuable fodder tree usually found near habitations.[60] In British Garhwal, Chaundkot *pargana* was singled out for its oak forests within village boundaries, called *bani* or *banjanis*, where branches of trees were cut only at specified times, and then with the permission of the entire village

---

[56] R. K. Gupta, *The Living Himalayas: Volume 1: Aspects of Environment and Resource Ecology of Garhwal* (Delhi, 1983), p. 295.
[57] Mobbs, 'Himalayan Valley', pp. 10–11.
[58] Sunderlal Bahuguna, personal communication.
[59] Note by J. K. Pearson, December 1926, in FD file 83/1909, UPSA.
[60] H. K. Raturi, *Garhwal Varnan* (Bombay, 1910), p. 36.

community.[61] In remote areas, untouched by commercial exploitation of forests, one can still come across well maintained banjanis containing oak trees of a quality rarely observed elsewhere.[62]

Undoubtedly, this situation was facilitated by the near-total control exercised by villages over their forest habitat. As 'the waste and forest lands never attracted the attention of former [i.e. pre-British] governments',[63] the peasant communities enjoyed the untrammelled use of their produce. While the native kings did subject the produce of the forests, such as medicinal herbs, to a small cess as and when they were exported, the products of the forests consumed by the people themselves were not taken into account.[64] In such circumstances, where they exercised full control over their forest habitat, co-operation of a high order was exhibited by adjoining villages. Every village in the hills had fixed boundaries, existing from the time of the pre-Gurkha rulers, and recognized by G. W. Traill in the Kumaun settlement of 1823 (the so-called *san assi* boundaries). Within these limits the inhabitants of each village exercised various proprietary and other rights of grazing and fuel, secured by long usage and custom.[65] Quite remarkably, this co-operation existed even across political boundaries; thus, the adjoining villages in Tehri and Bashar state amicably grazed their flocks and fetched wood from common forest and pasture land without any kind of dispute.[66]

Although the above account consists largely of fragments reconstituted from official discourse, it is apparent that the role of forests in hill life was highlighted by the existence of social and cultural institutions which enabled the peasantry to re-

[61] Note by V. A. Stowell, D. C. Garhwal, n.d., probably 1907; note of August 1910 by Dharmanand Joshi, the late deputy collector, Garhwal, both in FD file 83/1909.
[62] Observations in villages of Pithoragarh district, October 1983.
[63] E. K. Pauw, *Report*, p. 53.
[64] See E. T. Atkinson, *The Himalayan Districts of the North Western Provinces*, vol. 1 (Allahabad, 1884).
[65] T. D. Gairola, *Selected Revenue Decisions of Kumaun* (Allahabad, 1936), p. 209.
[66] Joint Report, 26 October 1910, of Mr Darling, political assistant commissioner, Simla, and Dharmanand Joshi, retired deputy collector on special duty, in file no. 210/1910, political department, UPSA.

produce its existence—this notwithstanding the later construction of an ideology which viewed the usurpation of state monopoly over forests as a logical corollary of the lack of 'scientific' management practices among the original inhabitants of forest areas.[67] The 'intimate and reverential attitude toward the land', which Robert Redfield regards as being a core value of peasant society, seems to have incorporated, in Uttarakhand, a reverential attitude towards the forest as well.[68] In other parts of India where forests are closely interwoven with material life, we observe very similar patterns of cultural restraints on resource utilization. Thus, in tribal India even today, 'it is striking to see how in many of the myths and legends the deep sense of identity with the forest is emphasized.'[69] In such forest areas not only did the forests have a tremendous influence in moulding religious and spiritual life,[70] the inhabitants also exhibited a deep love of vegetation, often acting 'entirely from a sense of responsibility towards future generations' by planting species whose span of maturity exceeded a human lifetime.[71]

As this description of traditional conservation systems suggests, these hardy peasant communities had been primed for collective action. The absence of serious economic differences greatly facilitated social solidarity, as did the ties of kinship and caste shared by villagers. In its democratic characteristics and reliance on natural resources Uttarakhand is representative of mountain societies in general, in which ecological constraints to the intensification and expansion of agriculture have historically resulted in an emphasis on the close regulation of the common property resources so crucial for the subsistence of individual households. Tailored 'to the characteristics of the community's own environment and population', the detailed rules for the management and utilization of forests and pasture

[67] See Ramachandra Guha, 'Forestry in British and Post-British India: A Historical Analysis', in two parts, *Economic and Political Weekly*, 29 October and 5–12 November 1983.

[68] Robert Redfield, *Peasant Society and Culture* (Chicago, 1961), pp. 19, 63–4.

[69] *Report of the Scheduled Areas and Scheduled Tribes Commission, Volume I, 1960–61* (Delhi, 1967), p. 125.

[70] See M. K. Raha, 'Forest in Tribal Life', *Bulletin of the Cultural Research Institute*, vol. 2, no. 1, 1963.

[71] C. von Fürer Haimendorf, *Himalayan Barbary* (London, 1955), pp. 62–3.

account in large measure for the stability and persistence of many mountain communities.[72] Lucien Febvre's description of Andorran highlanders applies quite beautifully to Uttarakhand —namely that there was an 'effective solidarity among them and a special development of certain rules in their scheme of government, especially those which relate to common property and grazing rights'.[73] As Uttarakhand was virtually unaffected by external political forces in the millennia before the Gurkha invasion, these systems of resource use had become an integral, seemingly permanent part of the social fabric. They were superseded by another system of forest management, propelled by powerful economic and political forces, which rested on a radically different set of priorities. The socio-ecological characteristics of this new system, and its impact on traditional patterns of resource use, are spelt out in the next chapter.

[72] See Robert Netting, *Balancing on an Alp* (Cambridge, 1981), chapter III, 'Strategies of Alpine Land Use'.
[73] Lucien Febvre, *A Geographical Introduction to History* (1925: rpt. London, 1925), translated by E. G. Mountford and J. H. Paxton, p. 176 f.

CHAPTER 3

Scientific Forestry and Social Change

Then began a life of guerilla warfare for [head forester] Michaud, his three foresters, and Groison. Unweariedly they tramped through the woods, lay out in them of nights, and set themselves to acquire that intimate knowledge which is the forest-keeper's science, and economizes his time. They watched the outlets, grew familiar with the localities of the timber, trained their ears to detect the meaning of every crash of boughs, of every different forest sound. Then they studied all the faces of the neighbourhood, the different families of the various villages were all passed in review, the habits and characters of the different individuals were noted, together with the ways in which they worked for a living. And all this was a harder task than you may imagine. The peasants who lived on the Aigues, seeing how carefully these measures had been concerted, opposed a dumb resistance, a feint of acquiescence which baffled this intelligent police supervision.

— Balzac, *The Peasantry*

THE FORESTS OF UTTARAKHAND

Early travellers were impressed by the extent and density of the Himalayan forests. In 1793 a visitor to the court of the king of undivided Garhwal proclaimed that 'the forests of oak, fir, and boorans [rhododendron] are here more extensive and the trees of greater magnitude, than any I have ever seen.'[1] An early commissioner of Kumaun, investigating sources of fuel for a proposed iron mine, was bold enough 'to declare that the forests of Kumaun and Garhwal are boundless and, to all appearances, inexhaustible'.[2] Almost a century later two Swiss

[1] T. Hardwicke, 'Narrative of a Journey to Srinagar', *Asiatic Researches*, vol. 6 (1809; rpt. Delhi, 1979), p. 327.

[2] J. H. Batten, comm., KD, to W. Muir, secy to govt, NWP, 6 August 1855, in 'Papers regarding the Forests and Iron Mines in Kumaun', in *Selections from the Records of the Government of India (Home Department)*, supplement no. VIII (Calcutta, 1855), pp. 6-7.

geologists were likewise 'surprised at the vast extension of the wooded ranges in the lower Himalaya'.[3] The varied conditions of topography and altitude in Uttarakhand had given rise to a wide variety of forest types. While a detailed description would be out of place here, a brief statement of the forest types is given in Table 3.1.[4]

TABLE 3.1

Distribution of Vegetation by Altitude in the Central Himalaya

Altitude (in feet)	Characteristic vegetation
13,000	Vegetation entirely ceases
12,000	Birch and blue pine
11,000	Fir, spruce, yew, cypress and bush
10,000	Rhododendron and chestnut limit; grassy slopes begin
9,000	Higher level oaks (*tilonj* and *kharsu*) chiefly occur
8,000	*Banj* oak limit
7,000	Blue and chir pine limit; banj oak and rhododendron in abundance
6,000	Deodar begins; banj and rhododendron begin to give way to pine
5,000	Chir pine in abundance
4,000	*Sal* limit; *haldu* and *tun*

SOURCE: Adapted from S. D. Pant, *Social Economy of the Himalayans* (London, 1935).

The major division is between the conifers and the broadleaved species. Within this division the most important and common species, especially in the altitudes inhabited by human populations, are the banj or *ban* oak (*Quercus incana*) and the chir or *chil* pine (*Pinus roxburghii*). In general, the species distribution reflects the process of *ecological succession* whereby stable forest cover is established on any terrain. This succession can generally be divided into three stages:[5] (*i*) the initial stage,

[3] A Heim and A. Gansser, *Central Himalaya* (1939; rpt. Delhi, 1975), p. 229.
[4] This is dealt with exhaustively in the working plans for each forest division.
[5] Based on R. S. Troup, *Silviculture of Indian Trees* (Oxford, 1921), Introduction and *passim*.

in which certain species of trees, usually with small or light seeds, take possession of newly exposed ground; (*ii*) the transitional stages, in which changes take place on ground already clothed with some vegetative cover; (*iii*) the climax stage, which represents the farthest advance towards a hygrophilous (i.e. adapted to plentiful water supply) type of vegetation which the locality is capable of supporting. While it could be said that in the Himalaya the oaks and other broad-leaved species represent stage (*iii*) and the conifers stage (*ii*), in the days before forest management mixed forests were the norm. In general, the more favourable the locality is for vegetation the greater the number of species struggling for existence in it.

Two points are noteworthy. While the oaks (and other broad-leaved species) are more valuable for hill agriculture, on both ecological and economic grounds the conifers have had, since the inception of 'scientific' management, a variety of commercial uses. Second, while 'progressive' succession—from stage (*i*) to (*iii*)—occurs in nature, 'retrogressive' succession— from stage (*iii*) to (*ii*) to (*i*)—can be caused by the hand of man, either accidentally or deliberately. Foresters are cautioned that in many cases 'the natural trend of this succession may be diametrically opposed to what is desirable from an economic point of view.'[6] This disjunction between the natural trend of ecological succession—whereby oak is the climactic stage— and the imperatives of commercial forestry—which favoured the extension of conifers—has had a major influence on the development of scientific forestry in Uttarakhand.

THE GROWTH AND DEVELOPMENT OF STATE FORESTRY IN UTTARAKHAND

The landmark in the history of Indian forestry is undoubtedly the building of the railway network. The large-scale destruction of accessible forests in the early years of railway expansion led to the hasty creation of a forest department, set up with the help of German experts in 1864. The first task before the new department was to identify the sources of supply of strong and durable timbers—such as sal, teak and deodar—which could be used as railway sleepers. With sal and teak being very heavily

[6] Ibid., pp. iv–v.

worked out,[7] search parties were sent to explore the deodar forests of the Sutlej and Yamuna valleys.[8] Intensive felling in these forests forced the government to rely on the import of wood from Europe. But with emphasis placed on substituting indigenous sleepers for imported ones, particularly in the inland districts of northern India, the department considered the utilization of the Himalayan pines if they responded adequately to antiseptic treatment.[9]

Successful forest administration required checking the deforestation of past decades,[10] and for this the assertion of state monopoly right was considered essential. A prolonged debate within the colonial bureaucracy on whether to treat the customary use of forests as based on 'right' or on 'privilege' was settled by the selective use of precedent and the principle that 'the right of conquest is the strongest of all rights—it is a right against which there is no appeal.'[11] An initial attempt at asserting state monopoly through the forest act of 1865 having been found wanting, a comprehensive all-India act was drafted thirteen years later. This act of 1878 provided for the constitution of 'reserved' or closed forests, divested of existing rights of user to enable sustained timber production. The act also provided for an elaborate procedure of forest settlement to deal with all claims of user, which, if upheld, could be transferred to a second class of forest designated as 'protected'.[12] While the

[7] Thus, by 1869, the sal forests of the outer hills were all 'felled in even to desolation'. See G. F. Pearson, 'Sub Himalayan Forests of Kumaun and Garhwal', in *Selections from the Records of the Government of the North Western Provinces*, 2nd series, vol. 2 (Allahabad, 1869), p. 132 (hereafter *Selections*).

[8] See G. P. Paul, *Felling Timber in the Himalayas* (Lahore, 1871).

[9] D. Brandis, 'Memorandum on the Supply of Railway Sleepers of the Himalayan Pines Impregnated in India', IF, vol. 4 (1879), pp. 365–85.

[10] A vivid account of the official measures that induced this deforestation can be found in E. P. Stebbing, *The Forests of India*, 3 volumes (London, 1922–7), 1, pp. 36–62, 288–9, 505–9, 523–30, etc. By 'successful' forest administration I mean successful from the viewpoint of strategic imperial needs.

[11] C. F. Amery, 'On Forest Rights in India', in D. Brandis and A. Smythies (eds), *Report of the Proceedings of the Forest Conference held at Simla, October 1875* (Calcutta, 1876), p. 27.

[12] For the 1878 act which, apart from minor modifications continues to be in operation, the basic documents are: B. H. Baden-Powell, 'On the Defects of the Existing Forest Law (Act VII of 1865) and Proposals for a New Forest Act', in B. H. Baden-Powell and J. S. Gamble (eds), *Report of the Proceedings of the Forest*

burden of proof to establish 'legally established rights' was on the people, the state could grant both 'non-established rights' and 'terminable concessions' at its discretion.[13]

State forestry in Tehri Garhwal

The commercial exploitation of the forests of Tehri Garhwal predates similar operations in the British territory. The Yamuna valley, particularly, harboured the finest stands of deodar found anywhere, with the tree's resilient wood being in great demand for railway sleepers. In fact, around 1850 an intrepid Englishman named Wilson had leased the state's forests for a paltry sum of Rs 400 per annum and pioneered the water transport of timber. On the expiry of Wilson's lease in 1865 the government of the North Western Provinces, well aware that 'the importance of adding as much as possible to the limited area of forest now capable of yielding large timber is very great',[14] successfully negotiated a twenty-year lease of all forests in the state for Rs 10,000 per annum. Clearly, strategic imperial needs, and not disinterested motives of forest preservation, led the British to enter into this contract.[15] In April 1885 the lease was renegotiated whereby the chir forests of the Tons valley reverted to state control, the deodar forests remaining with the Imperial Forest Department. Although the lease was renewed for a further twenty-year period in 1905, from 1902 'as an act of grace' the raja was paid 80 per cent of net profits in lieu of an annual rental.[16]

The leased forests were divested of existing rights of user enjoyed by the surrounding population and worked for the extraction of railway sleepers. Preliminary surveys, which

---

Conference, 1873–74 (Calcutta, 1874), pp. 3–30; D. Brandis, *Memorandum on the Forest Legislation Proposed for British India (Other than the Presidencies of Madras and Bombay)* (Simla, 1875).

[13] 'Instructions for Forest Settlement Officers in the NWP & O', no. 682/XIV, 328–63, dated 29 May 1897, in file no. 279, dept IV A, list no. 2, post-Mutiny records, RAD.

[14] Col. R. Strachey, secy, GOI, to secy to govt, NWP, in the PWD, 29 March 1864, foreign dept, revenue B prog., May 1864, no. 10, NAI.

[15] P. D. Raturi, *WP for the Jamuna For. Div., Tehri Garhwal State 1932–33 to 1952–53* (Tehri, 1932), p. 49.

[16] J. C. Tulloch, *WP for the Leased Deodar Forests in Tehri Garhwal* (Allahabad, 1907), pp. 1–5.

identified the nature of timber growth in the different forest zones, established beyond doubt that the property acquired at a nominal lease would 'yield a fine yearly revenue, besides supplying the wants of both government and the railways for timber'.[17] The forests were then brought under working plans that regulated the yearly extraction and prescribed appropriate silvicultural practices to enable adequate reproduction of species like chir and deodar. Forming 'perhaps the largest and most compact deodar forest in the world', the Yamuna woods exported 6,500,000 deodar sleepers in the period 1869–85.[18] At the time when the rate of forest destruction imperilled further railway expansion, the forests of Tehri Garhwal proved a strategically valuable resource for British colonialism.

Meanwhile the raja had constituted a skeletal forest staff in 1885 and, twelve years later, Pandit Keshavanand Mamgain, a native Garhwali, was deputed from the forest department of the North Western Provinces. Keshavanand, who began the work of demarcating the forests, was succeeded as conservator of forests by Sadanand Gairola in 1905. In 1907 Rama Dutt Raturi took over the post and demarcated the forests and waste land into three classes: (*i*) the first class or reserved forests; (*ii*) the second class, intended for the exercise of forest concessions; and (*iii*) a class for the constitution of village forests.

While the third class remained largely inoperative, over time the distinction between the first two classes was abolished. As the 'legal' property right in the forest was claimed by the sovereign, the peasantry was only allowed to exercise certain 'concessions' notified by the durbar. Regulations fixed the amount of building timber allotted to households, while free grazing was allowed in the second and third class forests within a five-mile radius of each village. Villagers could also collect dry fallen wood and cut grass in specified areas. In return the peasants were to help in extinguishing forest fires as and when

[17] G. F. Pearson, 'Forests in the Bhageerathi Valley', in *Selections*, vol. 2, p. 121. Also *idem*, 'Report on the Bhageerathi Valley Forests', in *Selections*, vol. 3 (Allahabad, 1870), pp. 106–16.

[18] N. Hearle, *WP for the Tehri Garhwal Leased Forest, Jaunsar For. Div.* (Allahabad, 1888), pp. 1–16.

SCIENTIFIC FORESTRY AND SOCIAL CHANGE 41

these occurred. In addition, a tax of half a *seer* of ghee was levied on every buffalo possessed by a state subject.[19]

TABLE 3.2

Durbar Revenue from Leased Forests, 1909–1924

Average for period	Raja's share of surplus (in lakhs)
1909–10 to 1911–12	0.96
1912–13 to 1914–15	1.52
1915–16 to 1917–18	1.72
1918–19 to 1920–21	2.03
1921–22 to 1923–24	1.45

SOURCE: Computed from E. C. Mobbs, *WP for the Tons For. Div., T.G. State, 1925–46* (Allahabad, 1926).

As Table 3.2 indicates, British management demonstrated the commercial value of the Tehri forests, and in common with other native chiefs the raja became 'generally very much alive' to the value of his forest property.[20] On the leased forests reverting totally to state control in 1925, the durbar invited Dr Franz Heske, a renowned German expert, to survey the forests and advise on their systematic working. Based on Heske's recommendations, forest settlement operations were embarked upon during 1929–31, and officers sent to the Forest Research Institute to undergo training.[21] Several new forest divisions were constituted, and gradually the entire forests of the state came to be managed under working plans.[22] Under state management the revenue orientation became more marked

[19] M. N. Bahuguna, *WP for the Tehri For. Div., Tehri Garhwal State, 1939–40 to 1969–70* (Tehri, 1941); Tehri durbar circular no. 21 of 1930, reproduced in V. P. S. Verma, *WP for the Tehri For. Div., Garhwal Circle, UP, 1973–74 to 1982–83* (Nainital, 1973), appendix, pp. 580–4.
[20] E. A. Smythies, *India's Forest Wealth* (London, 1925), p. 27.
[21] *Garhwali* (hereafter GRH), 20 October 1928; file no. 730–1/26, F. and P. dept, NAI.
[22] Four new divisions were constituted: Tehri, Uttarakashi, Yamuna and Tons.

(Table 3.3). While exact figures are unobtainable, the extraction of timber was considerable, especially during World War II. In the first three years of the war, over 1.4 million cubic feet—double the average extraction in normal years—of timber was exported for use on the front. Over 20,000 trees were

TABLE 3.3

Revenue and Surplus of Tons Forest Division, Tehri Durbar, 1925–1945

(in lakhs)

Year	Gross revenue	Net revenue (surplus)
1925–26	3.01	2.41
1926–27	4.20	3.55
1927–28	2.81	2.43
1928–29	2.49	1.79
1929–30	2.31	1.89
1930–31*	1.31	0.53
1931–32*	1.82	0.53
1932–33*	1.01	0.50
1933–34*	1.77	0.80
1934–35	1.99	1.31
1935–36*	1.24	1.09
1936–37	0.92	0.73
1937–38	1.10	0.50
1938–39	1.64	1.41
1939–40	4.16	3.94
1940–41	3.12	2.87
1941–42	2.30	2.08
1942–43	6.04	5.83
1943–44	4.02	3.80
1944–45	3.49	3.39

* Does not include revenue from departmental timber operations.

SOURCE: K. P. Pant, *WP for the Tons For. Div. (leased forests), T.G. State, 1945-6 to 1964-5* (Dehradun, 1948).

exported annually from the Tons valley alone.[23] Over time, forests came to constitute the largest single item of revenue for the durbar, a far cry from the days when the king had leased out a seemingly valueless property for a pittance. In 1935–6, for example, forests accounted for 7.3 lakhs out of a total of 17.94 lakhs that accrued to the exchequer on all heads.[24] As the state took greater interest in the commercial management of its woodland, village access to the forests was correspondingly reduced.

Forestry in Kumaun division

The systematic management of the Kumaun hill forests commenced with the constitution of small blocks of reserved forests to furnish a permanent supply of fuel and timber to the administrative centres of Nainital and Almora and the cantonment town of Ranikhet.[25] A survey was commissioned to report on the detailed composition of the hill forests, particularly those within 'reasonable distance' of land and water, and select sites for roads and saw mills.[26] This was followed in 1893 by the declaration of all unmeasured land in Kumaun division as 'district protected forest' (DPF)—what was thought 'of primary importance was to assert the proprietary right of Government in these forests' and lay down certain limits to the hitherto unregulated access of rightholders.[27] Official interest in these forests, dominated by the long-leaved or chir pine, quickened further with two important scientific developments being reported by Indian forest officials. The tapping of chir pine for oleo-resin had been started on an experimental basis in the 1890s. By 1912 methods of distillation had been evolved which would enable the products to compete with the American and French varieties that had hitherto ruled the market. At the same time, fifty years of experimentation on a process to pro-

[23] See P. D. Raturi, 'War Effort of Tehri Garhwal State Forest Department (1939–42)', IF, vol. 68 (1942), pp. 631–4.

[24] See *Annual Administrative Report of the Tehri Garhwal State, 1936–37* (Tehri, 1937).

[25] D. Brandis, *Suggestions Regarding Forest Administration in the Northwestern Provinces and Oudh* (Calcutta, 1882).

[26] T. W. Webber, *The Forests of Upper India* (London, 1902), pp. 38–43.

[27] Note by J. S. Campbell, Kumaun division, 6 July 1910, in FD file no. 83/1909, UPSA.

long the life of certain Indian woods for use as railway sleepers through chemical treatment finally bore fruit. Of the timbers successfully treated the chir and blue pines were both found suitable and available in substantial quantities, and could be marketed at a sufficiently low price.[28]

Four distinct phases, representing the progressive diminution of villagers' rights in the forests of Kumaun, can be distinguished:[29]

(*i*) Between 1815 and 1878 the state concentrated on the submontane sal forests of the foothills, while the forests of Kumaun proper were left untouched. However, the forests around Nainital were demarcated in the 1850s and those around Ranikhet and Almora in 1873 and 1875, respectively.

(*ii*) Between 1878 and 1893 these forests were notified as reserved under the 1878 act, while grants of forest made to iron companies and several other tracts in Almora and Garhwal districts were declared reserved or protected forests.

(*iii*) On 17 October 1893 all waste land not forming part of the measured area of villages or of the forests earlier reserved was declared to be DPF under the act, although the necessary enquiry (vide section 28) had not been made. Thus, DPF comprised, apart from tree-covered lands, snow-clad peaks, ridges and cliffs, river beds, lakes, buildings, temple lands, camping and pasture grounds, and roads and shops.[30] A skeletal forest

---

[28] Puran Singh, 'Note on the Distillation and Composition of Turpentine Oil from the Chir Resin and the Clarification of Indian Resin', *Indian Forest Records* (IFR), vol. IV, pt I (Calcutta, 1912); R. S. Pearson, 'Note on the Antiseptic Treatment of Timber in India, with Special Reference to Railway Sleepers', IFR, vol. II, pt I (Calcutta, 1912). Also *idem*, 'A Further Note on the Antiseptic Treatment of Timber, with Results Obtaining from Past Experiments', IFR, vol. VI, pt IX (Calcutta, 1918). These two sets of findings finally led to the constitution of the Kumaun circle on 2 October 1912, and forest settlements being undertaken in the three districts.

The two chief products of oleo-resin, turpentine and rosin, had a wide variety of industrial uses. While resin was used in the manufacture of shellac, soap, paper, oil cloth, linoleum, sealing wax, printing inks, electric installations, and gramophone records, turpentine was the chief thinner and solvent used in the manufacture of paint and varnish, the basis of synthetic camphor, and an ingredient of bootpolish and liniments. See Smythies, *India's Forest Wealth*, p. 80.

[29] Following Pant, *Forest Problem*, pp. 6-26.

[30] As I have noted, this proclamation was made with a view to asserting proprietary right in these lands.

SCIENTIFIC FORESTRY AND SOCIAL CHANGE 45

staff was constituted and on 24 October 1894 eight types of tree—including deodar, chir and sal—were reserved. Rules were framed for regulating the lopping of trees for fuel and fodder and claims for timber, while trade by villagers in any form of forest product was prohibited. On 5 April 1903 the Kumaun DPF were divided into two classes: closed civil forests, which the state considered necessary for reproduction or protection; and open civil forests, where villagers could exercise their rights subject to the rules prescribed in 1894.

(iv) All these cumulative incursions culminated in 1911 with the decision to carve extensive reserves out of the DPF. Forest settlements carried out in the three districts between 1911 and 1917 resulted in the constitution of almost 3000 square miles of reserved forest in Kumaun division. Elaborate rules were framed for the exercise of rights, specifying the number of cattle to be grazed and amount of timber and fuelwood allotted to each rightholder. Villagers had to indent in advance for timber for construction of houses and for agricultural implements, which would be supplied by the divisional forest officer (DFO) from a notified list of species. The annual practice of burning the forest floor for a fresh crop of grass was banned within one mile of reserved forests. As this excluded few habitations in these heavily forested hills, the prohibition virtually made the practice illegal.[31]

Within a few years of commercial working the Kumaun forests had become a paying proposition. When one full fifteen-year cycle (1896-1911) had revealed that resin tapping did not permanently harm trees, attempts were made to 'develop the resin industry as completely and rapidly as possible'.[32] Between 1910 and 1920 the number of resin channels tapped rose from 260,000 to 2,135,000,[33] a rate of increase matched by the production of rosin and turpentine (Table 3.4). When the construction of a new factory at Bareilly was completed in 1920—

[31] Details of these rules can be found in A. E. Osmaston, *WP for the North Garhwal For. Div., 1921-22 to 1930-31* (Allahabad, 1921), appendix.
[32] E. A. Smythies, 'The Resin Industry in Kumaun', *Forest Bulletin No. 26* (Calcutta, 1914), p. 3. Cf. also R. G. Marriot, *The Resin Industry in Kumaun, Compiled in the Kumaun Circle*, bulletin no. 9, United Provinces forest department (Allahabad, 1936).
[33] Stebbing, III, p 660. The work was done by small contractors (practically all from outside Kumaun), under the supervision of the forest department.

TABLE 3.4

Imports into and Production in India of Rosin and Turpentine, 1907–1923

Year April to March	Rosin Imports	Rosin Indian production	Rosin Total (cwts)	Turpentine Imports	Turpentine Indian production	Turpentine Total (gallons)
1907–8	76,200	4,845	81,045	225,560	16,086	241,646
1910–11	41,600	6,625	48,225	197,720	17,051	214,771
1913–14	45,769	20,100	65,869	193,937	58,803	252,740
1916–17	18,760	43,500	62,260	80,000	125,663	205,663
1919–20	13,855	46,700	60,555	113,638	148,680	262,318
1921–22	10,602	57,200	67,802	70,369	163,151	233,520
1922–23*	18,037	82,000	100,037	90,364	279,100	369,464

* Calendar year 1922.

NOTE: Until 1920 two factories accounted for total production—Bhowali (UP) accounted for roughly 60 per cent and Jalloo (Punjab) for the rest.

SOURCE: E. A. Smythies, *India's Forest Wealth* (London, 1925).

with a rated capacity of 64,000 cwts of rosin and 240,000 gallons of turpentine, a capacity that could be easily expanded fourfold —production was outstripping Indian demand. This put under active consideration proposals for the export of resin and turpentine to the United Kingdom and the Far East.[34] Indeed, the only impediment to increased production was the lack of adequate means of communication. The extensive pine forests in the interior had to remain untapped, with extraction restricted to areas well served by mule tracks and sufficiently close to railroads.[35]

The war provided a fillip, as well, to the production of chir sleepers. The cessation of antiseptic imports proved a 'blessing in disguise' when the Munitions Board requisitioned untreated sleepers.[36] In 1914 three large antiseptic treatment centres were established at Tanakpur, Hardwar and Kathgodam respectively, where the Sarda, Ganga and Gaula rivers debouched onto the plains.[37] Almost four lakh sleepers were supplied during 1916–18, and the Kumaun circle began to show a financial surplus for the first time, with all stocks being cleared. The government saw-mill was unable to deal with all the indents it received. Nevertheless, over 5000 chir trees were felled and sawn annually. For the forest department its activities during the war were adequate justification for the recent and controversial forest settlement in the hills.[38]

[34] Imperial Institute, Indian Trade Enquiry, *Report on Lac, Turpentine and Resin* (London, 1922), esp. pp. 29–51. India was the only source of oleo-resin within the British dominions.

[35] The available technology of transportation crucially affected the working of these forests. Coniferous timber could be floated out to railheads by water. The oaks, though durable, were too heavy and consequently did not merit commercial exploitation. All attempts to float resin in cans having remained unsuccessful, the pine forests of Almora and Nainital, at a lesser distance from the plains, were tapped earlier than those in Garhwal. While proposals for building a railway line through the Alakananda valley up to Karanprayag were mooted at various times, in the latter forests resin-tapping on a large scale had to await the construction of motor roads after 1947. See R. N. Brahmawar, *WP for the Garhwal For. Div.*, *1930–31 to 1939–40* (Allahabad, 1932), p. 138 and *passim*.

[36] Stebbing, III, pp. 658–9.

[37] J. E. C. Turner, 'Antiseptic Treatment of Chir Pine Sleepers in the Kumaun Circle, UP', IF, vol. 40 (1914), pp. 427–9.

[38] *Annual Progress Report of Forest Administration in the United Provinces for the Forest Year 1916–17* (hereafter APFD) (Allahabad, 1918), pp. 20, 38, 45; APFD,

After the forest movement of 1921 (see chapter 5) the Kumaun Forest Grievances Committee (KFGC), in a bid to allay the discontent with forest regulations, constituted the so-called class I forests. These forests were handed over to the district administration and the remaining forests—called class II reserves—continued to be vested directly with the forest department, the principle of demarcation being that all forests not considered of commercial importance were to be excluded from the class II reserves. Thus a large proportion of the class I forests consisted of high-level fir, spruce and oak forests.[39]

Although the recommendations of the KFGC withdrew the forest department's jurisdiction over large areas, the class II reserves continued to be worked, on a sustained basis, for both timber and resin. Operations were considerably stepped up during World War II, when 'fellings and sawings were pushed into the remotest forests of the Himalayas . . .' In 1940–1 alone, 440,000 sleepers were supplied to the railways, mostly of chir pine.[40] The recorded figures show an increase (at an all-India level) over pre-war outturn of about 65 per cent. In the hills, working-plan prescriptions were considerably upset by war requirements, the excess fellings being estimated at as much as six annual yields.[41] As at the time of the expansion of the railway network, the Kumaun forests proved to be an important resource for British colonialism during the two world wars.

SCIENTIFIC FORESTRY AND SOCIAL CONTROL

Aiming at a radical reorientation of existing patterns of resource utilization, commercial forestry was to initiate a major transformation in agrarian relations. In the years following the introduction of forest management, protest at the onerous regulations was a recurrent feature in Uttarakhand. Apart from

---

1917–18, pp. 22–3. I have estimated the number of trees felled from figures (pertaining to recorded fellings only) given in different working plans.
[39] See C. M. Johri, *WP for the Garhwal For. Div., Kumaun Circle, UP, 1940–41 to 1954–55* (Allahabad, 1940), esp. the attached map.
[40] H. G. Champion and F. C. Osmaston, *E. P. Stebbing's Forests of India*, vol. IV (Oxford, 1962), chapter IX.
[41] Ministry of Agriculture, *India's Forests and the War* (Delhi, 1948), pp. 107–11.

social movements (cf. chapters 4 and 5) which occurred at regular intervals, the contravention of forest laws represented the most tangible evidence of such protest. While the trajectory of social protest is described more fully in later chapters, it suffices to say here that breaches of the forest law led to the evolution of management strategies of considerable sophistication which could ensure the sustained output of commercially valued timber species.

The mechanisms of protest—the contravention of rules concerning the lopping of trees and grazing, and the burning of the forest floor for a fresh crop of grass—were in effect an assertion of traditional rights whose exercise was now circumscribed by the imperatives of scientific forestry. By its very nature commercial forestry—which divides the forests into blocks which are completely closed after the trees are felled—disrupts existing patterns of resource utilization. In order to enable regeneration to take place in the logged areas, closure to humans and cattle is essential. Likewise, in the areas under reproduction fire is to be avoided as hazardous to young saplings. Thus the continuance of customary patterns of forest use represented a major threat to commercial timber operations. This was especially true of the firing of the forest, in contravention of the forest act, which sometimes resulted in a total annihilation of recent regeneration.

Faced with recurrent and widespread protest, forest officials in Uttarakhand had to develop and perfect a set of silvicultural strategies which could simultaneously exercise control over the customary use of the forest and enable the reproduction of favoured species of trees. In the circumstances, an earlier emphasis on ensuring regeneration and enforcing control over large areas of forest came under close scrutiny. A change of focus, from extensive to intensive methods of forest management, was advocated as the only solution. Drawing on the lessons gleaned from a tour of European forests, an eminent silviculturist observed:

> everything points to the concentration rather than to diffusion of work as the ground-work of successful forest management in India. Concentration implies more efficient and economical work on natural and artificial regeneration with subsequent tending operations, more economical and thorough exploitation under a definite system of roads

or other export works, the possibility of using fire in effecting regeneration, the conduct of special fire protective measures in definite areas where protection is most urgently required, a more economical use of the staff and better supervision over it, a more workable arrangement as regarded to closure to grazing, and, what is of great importance in the mixed forests of India, special facilities for regulating the proportion of valuable species to what is economically and silviculturally desirable.[42]

In Uttarakhand three elements in the customary use of the forest—grazing, lopping and the burning of the forest floor—constituted the most serious threat to rationalized timber production. However, the changeover from extensive to intensive operations enabled silviculturists to successfully manipulate these practices to subserve the ends of commercial forestry. Thus grazing, far from being an unmitigated evil (as forestry textbooks would have it), in many areas actually helped the reproduction of favoured species like chir and deodar by keeping down the thick undergrowth of grass and brushwood. As one report observed, the concentration of regeneration operations helped divert grazing from areas closed for reproduction and towards the rest of the forest where 'far from being a curse the grazing would in many cases be a blessing in tending to keep down inflammable undergrowth'. However, even where grazing was found beneficial on silvicultural grounds, it would introduce an element of 'insecurity' in forest operations, particularly as 'all forest rights tend to get more onerous'. Officers were therefore cautioned that while allowing grazing under favourable silvicultural conditions, it must be strictly regulated: villagers were to be told unambiguously that grazing was being allowed as a favour and could not be claimed as a matter of right.[43]

Lopping, likewise, was skilfully used to promote one of the primary aims of forest management: increasing the proportion of the commercially valuable species (chiefly conifers) in the forest crop. Working plans prescribed detailed operations,

[42] R. S. Troup, *A Note on Some European Silvicultural Systems with Suggestions for Improvements in Indian Forest Management* (Calcutta, 1916), pp. 3-4.
[43] Ibid., p. 4; W. F. d'Arcy, 'Grazing Rights in Forests', IF, vol. 9 (1883), pp. 359-61; H. G. Champion, 'The Influence of the Hand of Man on the Distribution of Forest Types in the Kumaun Himalayas', IF, vol. 49 (1923), pp. 131-2.

covering thousands of hectares, that included the felling and girdling of broad-leaved species in order to 'help' the conifers 'in their struggle' with other species. In addition, villagers were allowed unrestricted access to oak and other broad-leaved species, it being later reported with satisfaction that this selective lopping and girdling was likely to transform mixed forests into pure stands of chir pine.[44]

Perhaps the most important management innovation, however, was designed to combat the centuries-old custom of burning the chir forests for pasture. The needles of chir falling on to the forest floor both suppressed the grass and rendered the hillside dangerous for cattle. Thus, in late April or early May, villagers resorted to the time-honoured remedy of fire to obtain a fresh crop of grass, and, 'when no restrictions exist burning [was] resorted to everywhere at this season.'[45] Although mature chir trees are remarkably resistant to fire, continuous reproduction in areas of commercial logging operations rendered the young growth particularly vulnerable to fire. Fire protection was at once 'the most important as well as the most difficult question concerned with the management of our [forest department's] chir forests', more particularly as villagers were 'very averse to this measure'.[46] Not accustomed to any interference with their customary practices, it was evident that for the peasants universal fire protection would 'always be a source of complaint'.[47] The resolution of this problem assumed a growing importance with the growth of the resin industry and the perfection of antiseptic treatment of railway sleepers. Initially, foresters tried to completely ban the practice of annual firing by placing large tracts of forests under protective measures. These operations enjoyed mixed success in the early years of forest administration. The figures given in Table 3.5 highlight the fluctuating rates of success in the Kumaun circle. Both 1916 and 1921 were exceptionally dry fire seasons,

[44] Brahmawar, *Garhwal WP*, p. 57. Cf. also R. S. Troup, *The Silviculture of Indian Trees*, p. 1123, and Tullock, *Tehri Garhwal WP*, p. 7.
[45] See C. G. Trevor and E. A. Smythies, *Practical Forest Management* (Allahabad, 1923), pp. ix–xi.
[46] N. Hearle, *WP for the Deoban Range, Jaunsar For. Div., NWP* (Allahabad, 1889), p. 22.
[47] E. A. Smythies, 'Some Aspects of Fire Protection in Chir Forests', IF, vol. 37 (1911), p. 59.

TABLE 3.5

*Fire Protection in Kumaun Circle 1901–1921**

Year	Area attempted (acre)	Area burnt	Success (per cent)
1909–10	186,117	49,008	73.67
1910–11	247,637	479	99.81
1911–12	269,772	6,179	97.71
1912–13	330,770	4,830	98.45
1913–14	397,409	7,800	98.04
1914–15	375,187	9,567	97.45
1915–16	533,638	192,400	63.95
1916–17	371,113	239	99.94
1917–18	377,263	1,484	99.61
1918–19	395,660	3,673	99.07
1919–20	401,451	33,769	91.59
1920–21	404,455	272,865	32.54

*Kumaun Circle did not exactly correspond with Kumaun Civil Division.
SOURCE: Computed from C. G. Trevor and E. A. Smythies, *Practical Forest Management* (Lucknow, 1923).

coinciding with outbreaks of 'planned incendiarism'.[48]

The major disasters of 1916 and 1921 led to considerable rethinking among scientific forestry experts on the desirability of extensive fire-protection measures. Incendiarism 'left a deep and lasting impression on the mind of the silviculturist, compelling him to think on new lines about ways and means of preventing the recurrence of such wholesale destruction, past methods of placing excessive trust in the people having conspicuously failed.'[49] In Kumaun fire protection was verily 'the stumbling block of [forest] management'.[50] Areas that had been protected for many years accumulated much grass and

[48] For details see chapter 5. Arson was usually directed at carefully chosen targets, e.g. chir forests worked for commercial purposes and resin depots.
[49] J. E. C. Turner, 'Slash in Chir Pine Forests: Causes of Formation, Its Influence and Treatment', IFR, vol. XIII, pt VII (Calcutta, 1928), pp. 22–3.
[50] See review of APFD, 1922–3, in IF, vol. 50 (1924), pp. 265–6.

debris; here, regeneration was totally wiped out by unforeseen outbreaks of fire. And where trees were being tapped for resin, fire ignited the open resin channels and consequently the tree itself.[51] An additional fire hazard was the large amounts of waste wood that accumulated in forests newly felled for railway sleepers.[52] Several years earlier, similar operations in the foothills of Punjab had conclusively proved that the

> Forest Department is quite helpless to cope with a serious outbreak of incendiarism. Fire lines, fire guards, special night patrols, etc. have been tried in vain and there is no doubt that once the villagers have made up their minds to burn the forests the Forest Department is powerless to prevent them.[53]

As a result, the inspector-general of forests and other senior foresters convened several meetings that investigated proposals for the firing of forests by the agency of the department itself, combined with regeneration operations which could be concentrated in specific areas—to aid protection—rather than widely dispersed.

The results of these investigations were summarized in a lengthy monograph authored by R. S. Troup. Troup's proposals showed a remarkable grasp not merely of silviculture but of the social and cultural environment in which the workings of colonial forestry science were predicated. Departmental firing, he pointed out, was advocated not 'as a measure directly beneficial to the forests, but as the lesser of two evils, in cases where universal fire protection endangers the area under regeneration' —indeed, 'regulated burning may be absolutely necessary to save the area under regeneration.'[54] Troup's detailed prescriptions, which are widely in operation even today, envisaged a system of controlled burning. Thus, areas under regeneration were divided into blocks and separated from the rest of the forest by 'fire lines' of a width of up to 100 feet. These lines were cleared of tree growth and burned annually, under depart-

---

[51] H. G. Champion, 'Observations on Some Effects of Fires in the Chir Forests of the West Almora Division', IF, vol. 45 (1919), pp. 353–63.

[52] See Turner, *Slash in Chir Pine Forests*, for details.

[53] H. M. Glover, 'Departmental Firing in Chir Forests in the Rawalpindi Division, Punjab', IF, vol. 39 (1913), pp. 568–71.

[54] R. S. Troup, '*Pinus longifolia roxb*: A Silvicultural Study', *The Indian Forest Memoirs*, silvicultural series, vol. 1, pt 1 (Calcutta, 1916), p. 72.

mental control, during winter or early spring, preferably after a spell of rain. When this had been successfully accomplished, villagers were allowed to burn the rest of the open forest—subject to certain controls—before the end of March and the onset of summer. Occasionally, supplementary narrow lines of up to 15 to 20 feet in width were cleared of grass; in the event of a fire these were employed as bases for counter-firing. The size of the fire lines and the blocks which they protected would, Troup emphasized, have to vary with local conditions; for 'where incendiarism is common, broad cleared lines merely reduce the forest area without affording any real safeguard; under such conditions narrow lines as counter-firing bases are equally effective.'[55]

These proposals soon gained acceptance among foresters. Departmental burning which 'reduced the damage done to forests... and rendered the villagers more contented with forest management' spread to Tehri Garhwal and is in fact widely in operation even today.[56] Troup's manual on fire protection strikingly reflected the environment of popular resistance in which colonial forestry operated, and which it tried with varying success to overcome. Before outlining the prescribed techniques, which embodied decades of research in the hill forests of Punjab and Uttar Pradesh, Troup observes: 'In forest administration generally, and in fire protective operations in particular, the value of enlisting the sympathies of the local population and the undesirability of imposing irksome restrictions of an unnecessary character are matters of common knowledge.' In districts

> where the population is particularly truculent, any degree of success in universal fire protection is now recognized after years of fruitless endeavour, to be unattainable, and the concentration of protective measures on blocks under regeneration, with careful annual or periodic burning of the remaining areas, is considered to be the only possible means of effecting successful reproduction.[57]

Clearly, the concentration of regeneration operations and adoption of a flexible attitude towards grazing, lopping and fire protection were informed by the silviculturist's perennial fear of popular protest. At the level of forestry ideology 'grazing and

[55] Ibid., p. 73. [56] Bahuguna, *Tehri WP*, p. 61. [57] Troup, *Pinus*.

lopping are declared enemies of the forest'.[58] Working among a peasant population implacably opposed to commercial forestry, colonial silviculturists quickly rejected a total ban on customary use, adopting instead strategies of manipulation and control which minimized the threat to rationalized timber production. Summarizing the experience of a century, the official manual of silviculture remarks that foresters have, over time, learnt 'to turn to good effect the various destructive [*sic*] influences threatening the forest', the essential point 'being that the silviculturist shall have them under his control instead of having to fight them as declared enemies'.[59]

Alienation of humans from nature

What, one may now ask, was the cumulative impact of these strategies of management and control on the relationship between humans and forest in Uttarakhand? At the most obvious level the reservation of large tracts of forest meant an effective loss of control over their habitat for forest-based communities. Inevitably, an increased pressure was felt on the forests that did remain open to villagers, in many cases hastening their destruction.

A more fundamental change was the reorientation in agrarian relations induced by scientific forestry. In response to peasant protest, state forestry evolved a set of strategies, described earlier, that could manipulate the customary use of the forest in order to enable sustained timber production. An underlying principle of these techniques was that individual use of the forest represented a lesser threat to commercial forestry than the collective use sanctioned by custom. Accordingly, and through the mechanisms of the forest act, the state preferred to deal directly with individual households rather than with village communities as such.

This transition from collective to individual use of the forest bespoke a fundamental change in the agrarian life of Uttarakhand. For the loss of community ownership had effectively broken the link between humans and the forest. Although the government had, in certain areas, made over limited tracts of

[58] F. C. Ford Robertson, *Our Forests* (Allahabad, 1936), p. 28.
[59] H. G. Champion and S. K. Seth, *A General Silviculture for India* (New Delhi, 1968), pp. xix–xx.

forests to the villages (the so-called 'third class' or 'village' forests) the proviso in the forest act that these forests must first be declared 'reserved' strengthened suspicion of the state's true intentions.[60] Many officials were convinced that if villagers were assigned a proper legal title to forest land and assured both of the products grown and the management, they would continue to preserve tree growth as zealously as before.[61] In the absence of such assurances Garhwali peasants, apprehensive that the demarcation of reserved forests would be followed by the government taking away other wooded areas from their control, were in certain cases deforesting woodland.[62] In the ecologically comparable pargana of Jaunar Bawar which bordered Tehri Garhwal on the west, a similar process followed settlement operations. Thus, 'not altogether without reason, the villagers believe that any self-denial or trouble they may exercise in preserving and improving their third class forests will end in appropriation of the forests by the [forest] department as soon as they become commercially valuable.'[63]

The erosion of the social bonds which had regulated the customary use of the forests thus led to what can be described as an alienation of humans from nature. The concept of alienation used here draws directly from the work of Marx on the alienation of the worker under conditions of industrial capitalism.[64] While the application of Marx's theory, formulated in an entirely different context, must be done with some degree of caution, I would argue that in both instances we are dealing with the growth of a social system (industrial capitalism/colonialism) that replaced another (craft production/subsistence agriculture) whose social relations did not produce conditions of alienation and estrangement.[65]

[60] See B. Ribbentrop, *Forestry in British India* (Calcutta, 1900), p. 126.
[61] W. H. Lovegrove, 'The Formation of Communal Forests', IF, vol. 34 (1908), pp. 590–1; notes by J. K. Pearson and V. A. Stowell in FD file 83/1909, UPSA.
[62] T. D. Gairola to secy to govt, UP, 8 January 1918, in FD file 83/1909, UPSA.
[63] Supdt, Dehradun, to comm., Meerut division, dated 22 May 1897, in file no. 244, list no. 2, RAD.
[64] The classic text is Karl Marx, 'Economic and Philosophical Manuscripts' (hereafter EPM), in Lucio Colletti (ed.), *Karl Marx: Early Writings* (Harmondsworth, 1975), pp. 280–400.
[65] Cf. Lewis Feuer, 'What is Alienation? The Career of a Concept', in Maurice Stein and Arthur Vidich (ed.), *Sociology on Trial* (Englewood Cliffs, 1963).

Capitalism produces an atomized society, one that is in conflict with communal activity and communal consumption—defined by Marx as 'activity and consumption that confirm themselves directly in *real association* with other men'.[66] By analogy, state control was a negation of the communal appropriation of nature in Uttarakhand. Not only did forests constitute an important means of subsistence, but their products were treated, as in other peasant societies, as a free gift of nature to which all had equal access. The assertion of state monopoly ran contrary to traditional management practices. These practices were at once an affirmation of communal action oriented towards production and of the unity between humans and nature. Colonial forest law, which recognized only individual rights of user (this was true of Tehri Garhwal as well), initiated the fragmentation of the community and erosion of social bonds, processes hastened by the commercialization and capitalist penetration of later years. Further, the produce of the forests no longer belonged to the hill villagers but was appropriated by the state for the use of the classes it represented. Despite the spatial gulf, the interests of these classses were sharply opposed to those of a peasantry alienated from the forest growth it had helped to nurture.

Other writers have, in different cultural and historical contexts, commented on similar processes of the alienation of humans from nature. Verrier Elwin has talked of the 'melancholy' effect forest reservation had on the tribals of Central India, for whom nothing aroused more resentment than the taking away of the forests they regarded as 'their own property'.[67] Indeed, the Gonds, although they possessed an extensive medical tradition, were convinced that these remedies did not operate in this age of darkness, Kalyug, which began when the government took away their forests.[68] In Europe, too, the takeover of woodland for hunting or for timber production was deeply resented by the peasantry, for whom 'the law, almost any law but forest legislation particularly, appeared alien and destructive'. Resorting to extensive forest fires at state incursion into their rights, the French peasantry 'had come to hate the

---

[66] Marx, EPM, p. 350.
[67] V. Elwin, *A Philosophy for NEFA* (Delhi, 1960), pp. 86 f.
[68] V. Elwin, *Leaves in the Jungle* (1936; rpt. London, 1968), p. 57.

forests themselves, and hoped that if they ravaged them enough they would get rid of their oppressors.'[69]

As this last citation makes evident, in its extreme form alienation occasionally forced peasants to degrade the surroundings with which they once lived in symbiosis. The lack of interest that has, at times, been exhibited by forest communities in preserving vegetation on land that is no longer vested in them may be traced to the loss of community control consequent on state intervention. In Uttarakhand such alienation took various forms. In eastern Kumaun the reservation of large tracts of forests adjoining cultivation, and the constant harassment by forest patrols, had even led to villagers losing interest in their cultivation.[70] Elsewhere, forest reservation evoked a fear that if the villagers looked after the forests as of yore, 'a passing forest official will say—here is a promising bit of forest—government ought to reserve it. If on the other hand, they ruin their civil forest, they feel free from such reservation.'[71] Today, in an ironic but entirely predictable development, villagers in parts of Garhwal look upon the reserved forest as their main enemy, harbouring the wild animals that destroy their crops.[72] This is of course a classic form of alienation wherein the forest now appears as an entity *opposed* to the villager. Above all, alienation signifies a mode of life in which circumstances distort the innate qualities of human beings, compelling them to act in a self-destructive fashion.[73]

[69] Eugene Weber, *Peasants into Frenchmen* (Stanford, 1976), pp. 59–60. Cf. George Perkins Marsh on the period immediately following the French revolution: 'In the popular mind, the forest was associated with all the abuses of feudalism, and the evils the peasantry had suffered from the legislation which protected both it and the game it sheltered blinded them to the still greater physical mischiefs which its destruction was to entail upon them. No longer protected by the law the crown forests and those of the great lords were attacked with relentless fury, unscrupulously plundered and wantonly laid waste, and even the rights of property in small private woods were no longer respected.' David Lowenthal (ed.), *Man and Nature* (1864; rpt. Cambridge, Mass., 1967), p. 244.

[70] S. D. Pant, *Social Economy of the Himalayans* (London, 1935), p. 86.

[71] Note by H. S. Crosthwaite, secy to govt, to governor, UP, 2 April 1922, in FD file 109/1921, UPSA.

[72] P. H. Gross, *Birth, Death and Migration in the Himalaya* (Delhi, 1982), pp. 174–5.

[73] Feuer, 'What is Alienation?', p. 131. As an indication of how far alienation has proceeded in some areas, I recall a conversation with the Chipko leader Chandi Prasad Bhatt in October 1983. When I told him that colonial administrators in the

THE AGENDA OF SCIENTIFIC FORESTRY

The analysis of scientific forestry presented in this chapter points to its context-laden character. Predicated on the ideological setting in which they operate, the techniques of scientific forestry are, as it were, designed to reorder both nature and customary use in its own image. Clearly, the need to develop such strategies arose from the historical circumstances in which state forestry was first imposed on Uttarakhand. Having disrupted traditional forms of resource utilization, scientific forestry had to contend with the simmering discontent, occasionally breaking out into open revolt, that accompanied the takeover of the Himalayan forests. In the event, both legislation and silvicultural technique were designed to facilitate social control. Here, the evolution of colonial silviculture mirrored the history of German forestry, from which it claimed a direct lineage, where the 'development of scientific sylviculture and of positivist criminology were two sides of the same coin: one studying sustained yield and the other the endemic ('moral' as they would say) obstacles to that yield.'[74]

The silvicultural agenda of colonial foresters working in the Himalaya was the transformation of mixed forests of conifers and broad-leaved species into pure stands of commercially valuable conifers. This manipulation of a delicate and imperfectly understood ecosystem was further complicated by the competing demands exercised on the forest by the peasantry. Even if the usurpation of the forests by the state redefined customary use as forest 'crime', it could not, within the framework of colonial administration, completely eliminate 'illegal' use by peasants. Like their German counterparts, colonial foresters had therefore to overcome the social obstacles to sustained yield. Faced with a set of constraints that were both eco-

---

1920s had singled out Chaundkot pargana for its well-tended oak groves, he remarked that this part of southern Garhwal was now notable only for its lack of tree cover.

[74] Peter Linebaugh, 'Karl Marx, the Theft of Wood, and Working Class Composition: A Contribution to the Current Debate', *Crime and Social Justice*, no. 6, Fall–Winter 1976, p. 14. On the worldwide influence of German forestry, see Bernard Fernow, *A History of Forestry* (Toronto, 1902), and Franz Heske, *German Forestry* (New Haven, 1937).

logical as well as social, British foresters arrived at two mutually reinforcing solutions. At an instrumental level they carefully regulated peasant access by restricting it to areas of forest not deemed commercially profitable. While completely forbidden to enter areas under commercial working, peasants were by no means at liberty to use the rest of the forest at will. The detailed provisions of the 1878 act sharply defined (and delimited) the amount of fuel, fodder, etc. each family was allowed to take from the forest. At the same time, the punitive sanctions of the act were a strong deterrent to its transgression. At a deeper epistemic level the language of scientific forestry worked to justify the shift towards commercial working. The terms 'valuable' and 'desirable' and the prefix 'inferior', used mainly to refer to oaks, bear no relation to the ecological and other functions the species thus described may perform for the surrounding countryside. By a similar act of redefinition, one that rested on a prior usurpation of 'legal' rights of ownership by the state, many users of the forest were designated its enemies. Thus the management profile of each forest division, the so-called 'working plans', while indicating possible sources of injury to the forest crop, includes men in the same category as natural hazards and wild animals.

These strategies were developed to enable the sustained reproduction of favoured species of trees while minimizing the threat to state monopoly that peasant protest entailed, ends which could be achieved only through the skilful manipulation and redefinition of customary practices of forest use. In the application of these techniques, considerations of control were paramount. The strategies forged by forestry science and legislation manipulated agrarian practices by carefully regulating the intrusion and exclusion of 'man', classified in the terminology of forestry science as one of the 'enemies' of the forest. Not surprisingly, the dislocation of agrarian practices that followed the imposition of state monopoly was to have far-reaching consequences.

This manipulation of ecological systems and human beings was deemed necessary to maintain a permanent supply of marketable forest produce. Given its poor statistical base and scanty knowledge of the Himalayan ecosystem, 'scientific' forestry was not able to fulfil even its primary objective. Recent research by Indian ecologists—ironically enough, commissioned by the forest department—has clearly demonstrated the yawning gulf between, on the one hand, the ideology of 'sustained yield' that is the *sine qua non* of scientific forestry, and, on the other, the actual operations of timber harvesting wherein the output of logged material often exceeds the increment to forest stock.[75] What is more relevant to our concerns, however, are the processes of social change that came in the wake of the commercialization of the forest. By introducing a radical shift in the management priorities of the Himalayan ecosystem, commercial forestry came into sharp conflict with a system of management that pre-dated it by several centuries, and whose priorities could hardly have been more dissimilar. It is to this conflict, between the imperatives of scientific forestry and the economic and cultural values of the hill peasantry, that we shall now turn.

[75] M. Gadgil, R. Ali and S. N. Prasad, 'Forest Management and Forest Policy in India: A Critical Review', *Social Action*, vol. 27, no. 2, 1983.

CHAPTER 4

Rebellion as Custom

The institution of monarchy seemed to satisfy certain eternal needs in the societies of old, needs which were entirely real and essentially human. The societies of today are equally aware of [these needs] yet are usually content to satisfy them in other ways. But in the eyes of his faithful subjects, a king was, after all, something very different from a mere high official. He was surrounded by a 'veneration', which did not simply originate in the services he performed. How can we understand this feeling of loyalty which was so strong and so specific at certain periods in our history, if, from the outset, we refuse to see the supernatural aura which surrounded these crowned heads?

—Marc Bloch

[Hegemony] does not entail any acceptance by the poor of the gentry's paternalism upon the gentry's own terms or in their approved self-image. The poor might be willing to award their deference to the gentry but only for a price. The price was substantial. And the deference was often without the slightest illusion: it could be seen from below as being one part necessary self-preservation, one part the calculated extraction of whatever could be extracted. Seen in this way, the poor imposed upon the rich some of the duties and functions of paternalism just as much as deference was in turn imposed upon them. Both parties to the equation were constrained within a common field of force.

—E. P. Thompson

RAJA AND PRAJA IN TEHRI

The peasant political ideal, in which the peasantry and the king are the only social forces, came as close as is historically possible to being realized in Tehri Garhwal. Here the social structure was polarized between the raja (king) on the one hand, and his *praja* (citizenry), organized in strong and remarkably egalitarian village communities, on the other. Although the unification of Garhwal was completed only in the fourteenth century, the ruling dynasty could trace its lineage to Kanak Pal, a

REBELLION AS CUSTOM 63

Panwar Rajput of Malwa who took over the throne of Garhwal around AD 688. With the ruling dynasty having enjoyed over 1200 years of continuous rule, broken only by the eleven-year Gurkha interregnum, the kingdom of Garhwal was by far the oldest in north India. Its isolated status and secure boundaries undoubtedly helped the maintenance of Panwar rule. According to the Mughal historian Ferishta, the ruler of Garhwal 'commanded great respect from the emperors of Delhi'.[1]

Although in theory the sovereign possessed proprietary rights in the soil, the cultivating body which formed the bulk of the population enjoyed all privileges of ownership except for the right to alienate land (cf. chapter 2). Even artisan castes often cultivated a portion of land which yielded enough for their subsistence.[2] This relative autonomy (and prosperity) was strengthened by several factors, chief among which was the absence, over most of the kingdom, of an intermediary rentier class between the peasantry and the monarch. Land revenue demand, too, was extraordinarily light, lower than in the neighbouring British territory. Cultivators had the right to extend their fields during the period intervening between two successive land-revenue settlements without incurring the liability of enhanced assessment.[3] British travellers were apt to comment on the low incidence of land revenue, one 'wholly disproportionate to the extent of the [Tehri] Raj'.[4] As in other agrarian societies largely governed by customary law, the monarch would grant remission of revenue in years of distress. Occasionally, when crops failed, substantial amounts of money were advanced for the procurement of grain.[5]

The king as 'Bolanda' Badrinath

The exalted status of the monarch may be viewed in the context of these two factors, namely the durability of the Garhwal

[1] Quoted in S. S. Panwar, 'Garhwalis: The Warrior Race of the North', *The Commentator* (Dehradun), 16 August 1971.
[2] 'Mountaineer', *A Summer Ramble in the Himalaya* (London, 1860), p. 165.
[3] No. 1885/XVI-63, 17 January 1914, from comm., KD, to CSG, UP, in GAD 398/1913, UPSA.
[4] W. Moorcroft and G. Trebeck, *Travels in Hindusthan* (1837; rpt. Delhi, 1971), p. 15.
[5] See, for example, T-G Report, 1892-3, in nos. 267-9, Progs, January 1894, Internal B, foreign dept, NAI.

kingdom and the comparative autonomy enjoyed by the agrarian population—the latter a consequence of the low level of revenue demand imposed by the state. This was strengthened by the quasi-divine status enjoyed by the king in the eyes of his subjects, which stemmed from the historical connection between the throne of Garhwal and the sacred shrine of Badrinath. Located in the interior hills a few miles from the source of the Alakananda (one of the two rivers that form the Ganga), the Badrinath temple is perhaps the holiest shrine for Hindus. It is believed that Kanak Pal helped Adi Shankara in expelling Buddhism from the hills and in erecting the Badrinath temple. His successors assumed the responsibility for the management of the temple, endowing it with the revenue of a large number of villages (*gunth*) to meet its expenses. In addition, another set of villages en route was designed as *sada bart* villages, their income set aside to feed and house pilgrims. Over time, the Panwar rulers acquired the title of 'Bolanda Badrinath', i.e. Speaking Badrinath, or the deity personified. The Garhwal rulers enjoyed the religious title of 'Shri 108 Basdrischarayaparayan Garhraj Mahimahendra, Dharmabaibhab, Dharma Rakshak Sirmani', a title used as the form of address in all petitions to the monarch.[6]

The throne (*gaddi*) of Garhwal was commonly referred to—after its ruling deity—as the gaddi of Badrinath, on which state officials would take the oath of office.[7] The raja 'being from time immemorial the *religious* head of the temple',[8] pilgrims traditionally made ritual obeisance to him before proceeding to the shrine, a practice that continued at least until the late nineteenth century.[9] For the peasantry the king was the very

[6] Memorandum to the secretary, Indian States Committee, sd Chakradhar Juyal, home member, in file no. 122-P/1931, F&P dept, NAI. This was a rather modest list when compared to that used by the tsar of Russia, who was at once the 'Emperor and Autocrat of all Russias, Moscow, Kiev, Vladimir and Novgorod, Tsar of Kazan, Tsar of Poland, Tsar of Siberia, Tsar of Kherson in the Tavrida, Tsar of Georgia, Grand Duke of Finland...' See Teodor Shanin, *Russia as a 'Developing' Society* (New Haven, 1986), vol. 1, p. 34. (Full citation in Bibliography.)

[7] *Garhwali Visheshank* (special number), 4 October 1919; H. K. Raturi, *Narendra Hindu Law* (Lucknow, 1918), pp. 72–3.

[8] 'Notes on the Badrinath Temple', 6 July 1914, in 'Tour Diary of Pt. Keshavanand Mamgain [forest member, T-G state] for 1914–15', S. S. Panwar collection, emphasis added.

[9] See file no. 306-P of 1931, F&P dept, NAI.

incarnation of the deity, and Garhwali soldiers during the world wars went into battle with the slogans 'Bolanda Badrinath' and 'Jai Badri Vishal' on their lips. The birthday of the raja, 'Shri 108 Maharaj', was celebrated throughout the kingdom at religious shrines, where priests urged devotees to celebrate the birthday of 'their compassionate lord' (*apne dayalu prabhu*) with great gusto.[10]

After the bifurcation of Garhwal in 1815 the Badrinath temple lay in British territory. The Tehri raja, however, continued to be the chairman of its managing committee and the choice of the new *rawal* (head priest) fell to him. Every year a priest was deputed by the king to open the temple gates at the start of the pilgrim season. The exercise of the rawal's authority was subject to the general supervision of the durbar.[11] Like his predecessors, Narendra Shah was aware, none the less, that the lack of territorial control over the shrine undermined the social basis of his legitimacy. Arguing that the temple and the Tehri durbar 'are inseparable' the king offered,[12] in exchange for the four square miles on which the temple stood, to relinquish control over the hill station of Mussoorie (leased to the British) and to forgo the claim to seven hundred square miles of disputed land lying between Garhwal and Tibet.[13] In view of the strategic location of the town of Badrinath, en route to the Niti and Mana passes, and the opposition anticipated from certain Hindu organizations, the request was not acceded to.[14] The persistence with which Narendra Shah pursued the matter underlines the significance of traditional claims to legitimacy exercised by the king of Garhwal.[15]

The motif of the wicked official

A recurring feature of peasant and tribal revolts has been attacks on functionaries of the state. The state, or the monarch, appears as an abstract entity far removed from the scene of

[10] *Garhwali*, hereafter GRH, 25 August 1928.
[11] 'Notes on the Badrinath Temple'.
[12] Maharaja Narendra Shah to pvt. secy to viceroy, 9 December 1930, in file no. 122-P of 1931, F&P dept.
[13] See file no. 102-P of 1933, F&P dept.
[14] File nos 415-P/1933, 556-P/1933, 608-P/1934, all in F&P dept, NAI.
[15] See *Annual Administrative Report of the Tehri Garhwal State for 1935–36* (Tehri, 1936) (hereafter T-G Report), p. 5.

exploitation, while its functionaries become the targets of popular uprisings. The situation of the actual exploiter—the state and the interests which the state represents—is obscured in the minds of rural communities, and surrogate officials are perceived as the true exploiters. The notion of a 'just' government, integral to the Hindu tradition, is another factor which influences popular perceptions; thus, tyrannical officials are seen as breaching the ethical code of justice governing relations between ruler and ruled.[16]

The king's concern for the welfare of his subjects is, therefore, contingent on the degree of competence of his officials. Without competent officials (*yogya karamchari*) the king was helpless. The lofty ideals of Raja Narendra Shah were circumscribed, according to his subjects, by the highhandedness and unconcern of the high officials of the durbar, notably the new dewan (chief minister) Chakradhar Juyal.[17] Juyal, it was alleged, had achieved high office not by virtue of competence but through flattery and other devious machinations.[18] The king was constantly enjoined to be aware of the troubles of his subjects and not place sole faith on officials like the present dewan.[19] His 'duty was to protect his subjects from the oppression and cruelty of his officials.'[20]

The tension to which this relationship was subject was particularly manifest in periods of the king's minority, when administrative responsibility vested exclusively in a council of regency and no direct channel of communication existed between raja and praja. During the minority of Kirti Shah, who took over the gaddi in 1892, the desire was persistently expressed that the councillors should be removed and the young prince left to rule entirely on his own.[21] In the absence of an independent sovereign, complaints against the council were routed by villagers to the British government. The inefficiency and extravagance of the councillors in the period before

[16] Dharampal, *Civil Disobedience and Indian Tradition* (Delhi, 1971), Introduction; S. Devadas Pillai, *Rajas and Prajas* (Bombay, 1976), pp. 36–8.
[17] See letter by 'ek Tehri niwasi' (one resident of Tehri), GRH, 19 May 1928.
[18] GRH, 19 October 1929 and 2 November 1929.
[19] See Nardev Shastri, *Dehradun aur Garhwal mein Rajnaitik Andolan ka Itihas* (Dehradun, 1932).
[20] *Indian States Reformer* (hereafter ISR), 22 February 1932.
[21] Letter from S. C. Ross, comm., KD, and pol. agent to T-G state, 15 July 1887, in reply to petition from Assamees of Patti Ramoli, T-G, S. S. Panwar collection.

REBELLION AS CUSTOM 67

Narendra Shah's accession were similarly criticized, and their replacement by the acting maharani urged.[22] On his accession the king promised to 'discard and punish the vicious and immoral and to always have at heart the policy of promoting the happiness and welfare of my people, who were so long naturally anxious to see me invested with ruling powers, which is . . . an unerring indication of their loyal devotion to my house'.[23]

The dhandak

In the ruling ideology of kingship, the harmonious relationship between raja and praja was complicated in this manner by officials to whom the king had delegated administrative powers and the day-to-day functioning of the state. These powers were always liable to be misused. While this was not an infrequent occurrence, there existed in the moral order of society mechanisms whereby the peasantry could draw the attention of the monarch to the wrongdoings of officials.[24] Traditionally, peasant protest in Uttarakhand took the form of individual and collective resistance to tyranny by officials with a simultaneous call to the monarch to restore justice. This form of protest was known as the dhandak, derived from 'dand kiye gi', the admonition used by Garhwali mothers to hush troublesome children.[25] Dhandaks were never directed at the king or at the institution of kingship; rather, they emerged in response to what was perceived as oppression by subordinate officials and/or the introduction of new taxes and regulations. On punishments being inflicted upon the erring officials, the dhandak invariably died down, only to flare up again when fresh cases of tyranny occurred.

The dhandak typically encompassed two major forms of protest. First, peasants refused to co-operate with new rules and the officials who enforced them. Alternatively, when the demands grew excessive and were backed by force, villagers fled to the jungles or across political frontiers into British territory—a classic form of protest.[26] Occasionally, peasants

[22] See file no. 332/1916, GAD, UPSA.
[23] Speech by Narendra Shah on his investiture ceremony, in GRH, 6 December 1919.
[24] Cf. A. M. Hocart, *Kingship* (1927; rpt. Chicago, 1970), *passim*.
[25] Personal communication from S. S. Panwar.
[26] Shekhar Pathak, 'Uttarakhand mein Coolie Begar Pratha: 1815–1949', unpublished Ph.D. thesis, Department of History, Kumaun University, 1980,

caught hold of the offending official, shaved off his hair and moustaches, blackened his face, put him on a donkey with his face towards the tail, and turned him out of the state. Such non-co-operation at a local level was often accompanied by a march to the capital. A mass gathering would be proclaimed by the beating of drums, and peasants from surrounding villages would gather at an appointed spot, often a shrine. Here they would decide not to cultivate their fields or pay revenue and march to the capital demanding an audience with the king. On the king appearing in person and promising redress, the crowd would disperse.[27]

In the dhandak the absence of physical violence, barring isolated attacks on officials, was marked. The moral and cultural idiom of the dhandak was predicated firstly on the traditional relationship between raja and praja, and secondly on the democratic character of these peasant communities. The rebels did not mean any harm to the king, whom they regarded as the embodiment of Badrinath. In fact they actually believed they were helping the king restore justice.[28]

Interestingly, the officials, particularly those deputed from British India, who were often the targets of such revolts were unable to comprehend the social context of the dhandak. They invariably took any large demonstration to be an act of hostile rebellion. Keshavanand Mamgain, financial member of the regency council, viewed articles in the *Garhwali* criticizing the council as having

for their object the creation of discontent and unrest in the minds of the ill-informed subjects of the state leading ultimately to disturbances and riots (dhandaks) which the malcontents of the town of Tehri have in the past found a ready means of bringing the management into contempt and disrepute.

He went on to compare the impending dhandak with the Sinn Fein movement, then at its height in Ireland.[29] And in 1925

---

appendix III, hereafter Pathak; Tejram Bhatt, 'Tehri Niwasi aur Kranti', *Yugvani* (hereafter YV), 1 September 1947.

[27] J. M. Chatterjee, 'Popular "Risings" among Hill Tribes', ISR, 22 March 1931.

[28] 'Mass Demonstrations in the Hills', ISR, 22 March 1931.

[29] Financial member to president, council of regency, 23 May 1916, in GAD, 332/1916, UPSA.

C. D. Juyal described the people of the pargana of Rawain as being able to 'reap the pleasures of Heaven on this earth merely for their extreme religious devotion and unequalled loyalty towards your highness'. But a mere five years later, following the 1930 dhandak in which he figured prominently, Juyal thought the rebels 'a formidable and strongly armed gang of outlaws', and the Rawain people 'professionally freebooters'.[30] Actually Juyal himself, who was later to epitomize the callous and wicked official, had at one time been praised by his fellow hillmen for his administrative abilities in British India.[31] This hiatus between the self-perceptions of dhandakis and the views of targeted functionaries may be traced to the theme of the wicked official as one who disturbs the traditional relationship between raja and praja.

The dhandak essentially represents a right to revolt traditionally sanctioned by custom. Hindu scriptures urged obedience to the sovereign, subject to the right to revolt when the king failed to protect his people.[32] In the trans-Yamuna Simla states a form of protest called the *dum* or *dujam*, not dissimilar to the dhandak, was widely prevalent. Such revolts were not directed at the monarch, the peasantry being convinced of his divine origins. In order to draw the king's attention to some specific grievance the cultivators would abandon work in the fields and march to the capital or to other prominent places. As the suspension of farm work affected revenue collection, the king would usually concede the demands of the striking farmers.[33]

EARLY RESISTANCE TO FOREST MANAGEMENT

The changes in agrarian practices consequent on the imposition of forest management (chapter 3) had far-reaching consequences for the life of the hill peasant. With their traditional rights severely curtailed, the villagers regarded state forestry as

[30] Speech by C. D. Juyal on 15 December 1925, and letter by Juyal, both in ISR, 11 January 1931.

[31] Cf. GRH, 27 March 1920.

[32] K. M. Panikkar, *The Ideas of Sovereignty and State in Indian Political Thought* (Bombay, 1963), pp. 22, 54.

[33] 'Mass Demonstrations in the Hills'; nos. 40–2, Internal A, Progs, March 1908, foreign dept, NAI; Ranbir Sharma, *Party Politics in a Himalayan State* (Delhi, 1977), p. 31 and *passim*.

an incursion not sanctioned by custom or precedent. In the forests leased by the British, where the raja had no control, the 'people [had] become the slaves of the Forest Department, the lowest ranger or patrol having more power for good or evil than the Raja and all his councillors.'[34]

While 'powerless' to stop such oppression, Pratap Shah had taken back part of the leased forests in 1885. However, forest management, whether under the British or the aegis of the raja himself, produces uniform results with regard to peasant access to forest produce and pasture. Rationalized timber production can only be ensured—as the preceding chapter argues —by the regulation of traditionally exercised rights. As over time the greater part of the revenue of the Tehri durbar came to be realized from its rich forests, the raja steadily introduced a policy of stricter forest conservancy modelled on the system prevailing in British territory. This met with stiff resistance from villagers who 'began to look on the demarcation boundary pillars with suspicion often developing into positive hostility'. From its early years forest restrictions were 'much disliked and utterly disregarded by villagers and led to cases of organised resistance against authority'.[35] In response to the difficulties created by the reservation of forests, 2500 people of Rawain— a pargana in the north-western part of the state—marched to Tehri to demand an audience with their sovereign. Meanwhile, Pratap Shah died and, according to one chronicler, the peasants took pity on the widowed maharani. Deeming it unjust to put pressure on her, they returned to their homes.[36] Soon afterwards, during the minority of Kirti Shah, the peasants of Patti Ramoli submitted a long list of grievances to the political agent. These included complaints at the extent of begar taken by officials, restrictions on the collection of grass and leaves, and various other taxes levied on land and buffaloes.[37] Elsewhere, resentment was expressed at the policy of allowing

[34] No. 1139/XXII-29, 25 May 1886, from pol. agent, T-G state, to CSG, foreign dept, in nos. 72–9, Internal A, Progs, September 1886, foreign dept, NAI.
[35] P. D. Raturi, *WP for the Jamuna For. Div.*, *T-G State 1932–33 to 1952–53* (Tehri, 1932), pp. 11, 50.
[36] Shyamcharan Negi, 'Tehri Jan Andolan Zindabad', YV, 11 February 1947.
[37] File no. 332/1916, GAD, UPSA.

Gujars (nomadic graziers) to graze large numbers of buffaloes in forest pastures.[38]

The next recorded dhandak concerning forests occurred around 1904 in the patti of Khujni, lying to the south of the capital, Tehri. This was a consequence of the repeated demands for bardaish made by the conservator of forests, Keshavanand Mamgain, and his staff, and the new taxes levied on cattle for which the forests were the main source of fodder. When villagers refused to meet what they regarded as excessive and unjustified levies, the forest staff entered their homes, broke vessels, and attempted to arrest the strikers. Peasants resisted and beat up Mamgain's men; meanwhile some men fled to Tehri. In an affirmation of solidarity and their democratic spirit, the village councils of Khujni resolved that whosoever did not join the rebels would be expelled from the community.[39] Kirti Shah sent a high minister, Hari Singh, to pacify the rebels, who put him under arrest. Like peasant rebels in Russia seeking the tsar's intervention, they were not satisfied with the king's emissary—they needed an assurance from the monarch himself.[40] Ultimately, the new taxes had to be lifted and Mamgain's men were withdrawn from forest work in Khujni.[41]

The man who succeeded Mamgain as conservator, Pandit Sadanand Gairola, was to suffer a worse fate at the hands of enraged villagers. Gairola was directing forest settlement operations in the patti of Khas. Subsequent developments have been described by the official report on the dhandak:

On December 27th, 1906, the forests surrounding the Chandrabadni temple about 14 miles from Tehri town were being inspected, preparatory to their being demarcated and brought under reservation. It is reported that the villagers both then and previously had taken exception to the reservation of these forests, but it was not supposed that their objections would extend beyond the refusal of supplies and petty obstructions. On the morning of the 28th December, however, about 200 villagers armed with sticks assembled at the camping

[38] P. D. Raturi, *WP for the Uttarkashi For. Div., T-G State 1939–40 to 1959–60* (Tehri, 1938), p. 37.

[39] For similar coercion used by village communities on reluctant rebels in revolutionary France, see Georges Lefebvre, *The Great Fear* (rpt. Princeton, 1982), p. 33.

[40] See Daniel Field, *Rebels in the Name of the Tsar* (Boston, 1976), pp. 46–7.

[41] Pathak, p. 462.

ground where the officials' tents were pitched and objected to *any* state interference with forests over which they claimed *full* and *exclusive* rights. They attacked the Conservator against whom they are alleged to have had a special grudge as a *foreigner* to the state, introducing *unaccustomed* forest customs and regulations. It is reported that they beat him, branded him with a hot iron, tore down his tents, pillaged his baggage and took away and broke his guns. He is represented as having escaped with much difficulty into Tehri.

Next day, the Raja sent out his brother, with an armed force to quell the disturbance and arrest the ringleaders. The attempt failed. The people gathered from the villages over a considerable tract of country to a number reported to be about 3000, opposed the Magistrate and began to collect arms. The Raja thereupon applied to Government for assistance.[42]

Unnerved by the strength of the opposition to forest conservancy, the raja resorted to a show of force and, when that failed, asked the British for assistance. Clearly, the recurring dhandaks had forced the sovereign to consider new methods—apart from those socially sanctioned—to contain discontent.

Two aspects of the repeated protests against state forestry need mention: (*i*) their localized nature, and (*ii*) the total isolation from political developments elsewhere in India.[43] The Khas patti dhandak became especially famous for the act of branding the conservator's face with an iron, an act symbolizing a decisive triumph over the inimical powers of forest officials. The incident has passed into legend and different versions are recounted throughout Garhwal even today. Peasants in the Alakananda valley believe that it occurred during the 1921 forest movement in British Garhwal (chapter 5), the officials involved being the British conservator of forests and the commissioner of Kumaun division, Percy Wyndham.[44]

THE DHANDAK AT RAWAIN, 1930

The decisive breakdown of traditional methods of conflict resolution was yet to come. This followed a dhandak in Rawain

[42] No. 46, 16 January 1907, from CSG, UP, to secy to GOI in the foreign dept, in nos. 37–9, Internal B, Progs, October 1907, foreign dept, NAI ('Report on a disturbance which broke out in December 1906 in the native state of Tehri'), emphasis added.
[43] P. N. Painuli, *Deshi Rajyaun aur Jan Andolan* (Dehradun, 1948), pp. 11–12.
[44] Interview with Alam Singh Rawat, Gopeshwar, May 1982.

in opposition to the revision of the forest settlement based on the recommendations of the German expert Franz Heske. The case has, for various reasons, become a *cause célèbre* in Garhwal. What follows is a reconstruction, based on a variety of sources, of the dhandak and its aftermath. With the interpretations of the conflicting parties widely varying, my account is necessarily selective. It is, however, based on a careful consideration of the available evidence.

The parganas of Rawain and Jaunpur lie at the western extremity of Tehri and share certain distinctive cultural traits. Unlike other parts of Uttarakhand, where the consumption of alcohol was unknown till a few decades ago, here liquor was brewed in every household, a practice that met obvious functional needs in the bitter cold. Home brewing had been banned by Dewan Chakradhar Juyal, when, in a bid to augment the state's coffers, liquor contractors had been asked to open shops.[45] Another measure which evoked resistance was the ban on poppy cultivation, imposed by the British government in accordance with their international obligations.[46]

Nor was the revision of the forest settlement, carried out by Padma Dutt Raturi, taken lightly. Villagers contrasted the restrictions over customary rights in forests with the extravagant spending of the Tehri durbar and its officials.[47] Under the new settlement forest concessions were said to have been considerably reduced. It was rumoured that the prescriptions of the settlement could disallow each family from keeping more than ten heads of sheep, one cow and one buffalo—this in an economy largely dependent on sheep and cattle rearing. Villagers were to be levied taxes on herds exceeding the prescribed limit. Peasants complained, too, that very little waste land had been left outside the reserved forests. They were also no longer allowed to cut or lop *kokat* (hollow) trees without a permit. Villagers sent several representations to the durbar; when these elicited no response they resorted to the time-honoured means of obtaining redress—the dhandak.[48]

[45] GRH, 25 April (?) 1931.
[46] No. 256/C, 19 June 1930, from pol. agent, T-G state, to CSG, UP (hereafter Stiffe's Report), in file no. 458-P/1930, NAI acc. no. 22 (microfilm), Crown Representative Records (CRR), NAI.
[47] GRH, 19 April 1930.
[48] T. D. Gairola, 'The Disturbance in Rawain (Tehri)', *Leader*, 3 August 1930,

The dhandak soon spread from Rawain to the neighbouring pargana of Jaunpur. P. D. Raturi's house was surrounded and a portion of the state reserves set on fire.[49] The resisters sent a telegram demanding the king's personal intervention. As the monarch had gone to Europe, the durbar sent Harikrishna Raturi, the former dewan, 'as the man most likely to establish confidence'.[50] Raturi, an old official of the state who first codified its law, was well acquainted with dhandaks. Apprising the peasants of the king's absence, he asked them to stay quiet till his return. They agreed on condition that the durbar stayed the new forest restrictions in the mean time.[51]

Raturi's agreement was, however, not ratified by the dewan. Instead, Juyal conveyed orders to the local magistrate, Surendra Dutt Nautiyal, to arrest the leaders. Nautiyal asked two of them, Rudra Singh and Jaman Singh, to proceed to Barkot on the banks of the Yamuna, where their grievances were to be heard. In Barkot the two, along with Ramprasad (a prominent shopkeeper of the village) and Dayaram, were handcuffed and sent onwards to Tehri. Nautiyal and P. D. Raturi escorted the prisoners part of the way and then left them in the custody of the police. While returning to Barkot the two officials were accosted by a group of peasants who were taking food for the arrested men. In the ensuing quarrel Raturi fired on the group, killing two men and wounding two others. Mounting a horse, Raturi escaped to Tehri. Meanwhile the police supervisor had released the handcuffed men. Nautiyal was captured and interned in a house by the rebels.[52]

The Padma Dutt Raturi episode provided an additional impetus to the dhandak. It began to spread rapidly. In a manner characteristic of peasant upsurges, rumours circulated

---

on microfilm at Nehru Memorial Museum and Library (NMML); GRH 3 May 1930.

[49] Bhaktdarshan, *Garhwal ke Divangat Vibhutiyan* (Dehradun, 1980), p. 342 (hereafter Bhaktdarshan); GRH, 3 May 1930.

[50] Stiffe's Report. In medieval Europe, too, 'sympathetic' officials were used in the not always successful attempt to pacify lower-class rebels. See Emmanuel Le Roy Ladurie, *Carnival in Romans* (New York, 1980), p. 111, and Lefebvre, *Great Fear*, pp 103-4.

[51] GRH, issues of 10 May and 24 May 1930.

[52] GRH, 31 May 1930; 'Rawain ki Chitti' (letter from Rawain), GRH, 28 June 1930.

to the effect that the raja had not gone to Europe but had been held in internment by the present dewan, a foreigner to the state. The dhandakis appointed Hira Singh, padhan of Nagangaon, as their head. He, along with the shopkeeper Ramprasad and Baijram of Khamundi village, assumed leadership of the movement. Villagers were asked to endorse blank papers called *dharmpattas* affirming their support. Village headmen received notices that unless they joined the dhandak within a specified time they would be robbed and beaten up.[53] As an official, posted immediately afterwards to Rawain, recalled, Hira Singh designated himself prime minister of the 'Shri 108 Sarkar'. The appellation clearly indicates the king's continuing legitimacy in the eyes of his subjects, who believed that through their actions they were helping him regain his lost powers. Meetings of this independent authority or Azad panchayat were convened at Tiladi, a vast expanse of level ground overlooking the Yamuna.[54]

Alarmed at the rapid turn of events, Juyal moved to Nainital to confer with N. C. Stiffe, commissioner of Kumaun division and political agent to Tehri Garhwal state. Undoubtedly influenced by the civil disobedience movement then at its height in British India, Stiffe advised Juyal to take punitive action. Juyal returned to Narendranagar on 26 May and ordered the state forces to march the same day. When the troop commander, Colonel Sunder Singh, refused to march on his kinsmen, the dewan removed him from the post and externed him from the state. Juyal personally assumed charge of the troops and marched to Rawain, covering seventy miles in two and a half days. Hoping to impede the army's progress, villagers dropped logs on the road and set fire to them.[55] The dewan sent two villagers to the dhandakis, asking them to surrender. Their response was that when their president (presumably Hira Singh) returned, he would send a reply if he so wished.[56]

Instead, on the 30th the troops marched to Tiladi, where

[53] Report by dewan, 12 June 1930, addressed to vice-president, executive council (hereafter Juyal's Report), in file no. 458-P/1930, NAI acc. no. 22 (microfilm), CRR, NAI.
[54] Personal communication from S. S. Panwar.
[55] S. C. Dabral, *Uttarakhand ka Itihas* (Dugadda, n.d.) (hereafter Dabral) vol. 8, pt 1, p. 235; H. S. Panwar, 'Tiladi ka Hatyakand', YV, 26 May 1949.
[56] Juyal's Report.

the villagers had gathered. Juyal's men fired several rounds and an indeterminate number of peasants was killed (estimates vary from four to two hundred). Others frantically jumped into the Yamuna and were drowned. Many villagers fled to the jungles or into British-ruled Jaunsar Bawar.[57] The army also indulged in looting; 164 people were later arrested and confined in Narendranagar jail. Of these, 80 were freed and the remaining awarded sentences ranging from one day to twelve years in jail.[58] The extent of mass support for the revolt can be judged from the fact that of those who died in the incident and its aftermath, one was a Dom—Bhagirath Mistri—and another a kinsman of the raja, Thakur Gulab Singh, representing the two extremes of the social hierarchy of Garhwal.[59]

In his report the dewan portrayed the striking peasants as a gang of outlaws engaged in dacoities and murders throughout the state. He did not explain how a band of outlaws chose as their rendezvous a virtually defenceless field enclosed on three sides by hills. If the villagers had been as well equipped as Juyal made believe, it is difficult to comprehend how the army did not suffer any casualties. Clearly, the dewan was hoping to gain the support of the higher authorities for his attack on unarmed villagers.[60] But his distortion of events was only in part a wilful one; it was also informed by his lack of acquaintance with the cultural idiom of the dhandak. As a police officer from British India, his training equipped him to view any sign of popular unrest with suspicion. In a fashion typical of functionaries of the raj, Juyal blamed urban politicians for fomenting trouble to undermine his authority. He accused Bishambar Datt Chandola, editor of the *Garhwali*, and Pandit Bhawani Dutt, the ex-dewan, of inciting the 'credulous' Rawain folk.[61] This conspiracy theory was also advanced in the communiqué issued by the Tehri durbar shortly after the incident.[62] Although Chan-

[57] GRH, 2 June 1930.
[58] GRH, 25 July 1931.
[59] Shyamcharan Negi, 'Tehri Garhwal ke Shahid', YV, 23 January 1977.
[60] See the two telegrams sent by Juyal and the villagers, respectively, in DO no. 1159, 9 June 1930, from CSG, UP, to pol. secy, GOI, in file no. 458-P/1930, NAI acc. no. 22 (microfilm), CRR, NAI.
[61] Juyal's Report.
[62] 'Tehri Durbar Communiqué', sd D. D. Raturi, chief secy, T-G state, 23 June 1930, in ISR, 1 February 1931.

dola was in close contact with the peasantry during and after the dhandak and did publish their reports in his paper, there is no evidence that he or Bhawani Dutt actually influenced the course of the dhandak.[63] As Stiffe reported, when 'Swarajists' entered the area the local people had no use for these intruders and 'promptly handed them over to the local magistrate'.[64] Evidently, the rebels believed it to be a personal affair between them and their ruler and would brook no outside interference.

On the king's return from Europe the dewan was able to convince him that the gravity of the situation called for a punitive expedition. Despite several representations, the people of Rawain were unable to acquaint the king with their version of events.[65] Shortly afterwards, Narendra Shah deplored the outbreak, criticizing the Rawain folk for deviating from their peaceful ways. Pinning the blame on 'unworthy' headmen, the sovereign asserted that as villagers were ignorant of forest conservancy, he had called in a foreign expert to advise him. In a conciliatory gesture the king promised to end utar by building better roads.[66] In response, the *Garhwali* agreed that while forest management was necessary the present commercial orientation left the wants of peasants unfulfilled. The continuing burden of utar and the ban on private distillation also came in for criticism.[67]

Narendra Shah's failure to dismiss Juyal and make amends epitomized the changing relations between the peasantry and the monarch. In two earlier dhandaks, H. K. Raturi told Stiffe, the outbreaks had been 'quelled by the personal presence of the then Raja, to whose side most of the people gathered'.[68] Constrained by the imperatives of scientific forestry, and wary of the political movements in British India, the administration of Tehri Garhwal began to exhibit a visible strain: inevitable because an increasingly bureaucratic system impinged on the highly personalized structure of traditional authority. Simultaneously, the continuing protests forced the king to adopt a

[63] Personal communication from Smt. Lalita Devi Vaishnav, daughter of the late B. D. Chandola.
[64] Stiffe's Report.
[65] GRH, 25 April 1931.
[66] Speech by maharaja, reproduced in GRH, 2 May 1931.
[67] Reply to above speech in GRH, issues of 2, 9, 16 and 23 May 1931.
[68] Stiffe's Report.

more autocratic style of rule, one reinforced by his closer contacts with British colonialism. Thus, Raja Narendra Shah's approval of the Rawain firing, it was later alleged, stemmed from a belief that, unlike his predecessors, he saw himself not as one of his people but as 'the *ruler* of the Garhwalis'.[69] It was, however, the dewan and his rapacious behaviour which figured prominently in the popular consciousness. Wild rumours began to circulate that the all-powerful Juyal had proposed new taxes on women and drinking water and an enhanced tax on potato cultivation.[70] His attack on the Rawain peasant lives on in peasant folksongs which recount the awesome terror of the dewan's rule.[71] As one contemporary observer put it, living in Tehri Garhwal after Rawain *kand* (firing) was like living in a jail.[72]

Unprecedented in the history of the state, the Rawain kand was graphically described as an arrow that pierced the heart of the Garhwali motherland (*gadmata*).[73] One writer, shocked that the house of Bolanda Badrinath could sanction such a gruesome act, asked the king:

These people [of Rawain] resorted to the only method known to them of making their grievances known to the Ruler, who, to them is the incarnation of Badrinath. Your illustrious ancestors never had to resort to firing on such occasions. Why? They treated them like children. But why red-hot bullets on this occasion?[74]

However, this writer's indignation apart, the breakdown of authority was a partial and fragmented one. Half a century later peasants believed that the raja had appropriately rewarded Chakradhar by gouging out his eyes.[75] While the Panwar house lost only some of its enormous prestige, the Rawain kand does mark an important watershed in the social

[69] T. R. Bhatt, 'Affairs of Tehri (Garhwal)', *National Herald* (AISPC), file no. 165 of 1945–6, NMML.
[70] Juyal's Report.
[71] Cf. D. S. Manral, *Swatantra Sangram mein Kumaun–Garhwal ka Yogadan* (Bareilly, 1978), p. 110.
[72] GRH, 13 June 1931.
[73] Govind Chatak, *Garhwali Lokgeet* (Dehradun, 1956), pp. 266–7.
[74] Open letter to His Highness of Tehri, by J. M. Chatterjee, ISR, 22 February 1931. See also Prayag Joshi, 'Tiladi: Murdon ki Ghati', YV, 28 May 1967.
[75] Interview with Jamansingh, Badyar village, January 1983.

history of Tehri Garhwal. This breakdown of traditional authority—however partial—had important consequences in the peasant movements of the 1940s.

THE KISAN ANDOLAN, 1944-8

These intermittent and localized protests were to crystallize into a widespread movement, engulfing large areas of the state, that culminated in the merger of Tehri Garhwal with the Indian Union. Resembling the archetypal peasant movement far more than the dhandak, the Tehri kisan andolan was nevertheless composed of different strands. On the one hand the spread of the nationalist movement into princely India led to the formation of the Tehri Rajya Praja Mandal at Dehradun in 1939. On the other the growing incorporation of the Tehri peasants into the market economy rendered them more vulnerable to its fluctuations, notably during the depression and World War II. The situation engendered by the loss of control over forests, by now almost complete, was further aggravated by the new taxes the durbar imposed on an unwilling peasantry. The intervention of the Tehri Praja Mandal (itself no replication of the Congress, with its activists rooted in the cultural milieu of the state) was, therefore, mediated through a peasant uprising whose idiom was determined rather more directly by a distinctive social history of protest.

The oppressive forest rules continued to be met with suspicion. The rates at which villagers could buy timber in excess of their allotment far exceeded those at which the durbar sold wood to outside agents. In 1939 the forests between the Bhilagna and Bhageerathi rivers caught fire. Many heads of cattle perished, as did nine peasants who attempted to extinguish the blaze. The durbar refused to award any compensation. Outside the forest restrictions, Juyal had introduced a new tax called *pauntoti*, a form of customs duty levied on the belongings of subjects as and when they entered the state. As a greater number of Garhwalis were now dependent on outside employment, this levy was the cause of much resentment. So was the cess on potatoes, one of the state's chief crops.[76]

[76] Dabral, vol. 8, pt II, pp. 271, 320, etc.; A. S. Rawat, 'Political Movements in Tehri Garhwal State', *Uttarakhand Bharati*, vol. II, no. II, 1977, pp. 31-2.

The Praja Mandal (Citizens' Forum), established on 3 January 1939, took up the issues of begar and pauntoti. Its outstanding leader, Sridev Suman, was born in Jowal village of Baimund patti in 1916. A member of the Congress since his youth, Suman played an important part in the activities of its wing, the All India States People's Conference (AISPC). Determined to set up an organizational forum to mediate between raja and praja, Suman wrote articles and delivered speeches on both local and national struggles. He invoked the spirit of Bhagat Singh and B. K. Dutt, and praised Chandra Singh Garhwali, the hero of the soldiers' mutiny in Peshawar in 1930, as a 'glowing example' of a non-violent revolutionary. In and out of the state Suman had a strong influence on the students of the college in Tehri. In 1940, in an unprecedented act, students went on strike. Several were expelled. They continued to be in close touch with Suman and with Garhwali students at the Banaras Hindu University, whose mentor was the respected socialist and doctor from Badyargarh, Khuslanand Gairola. Postal employees in Tehri, who sympathized with Suman, were able to sabotage the censorship enforced by the authorities. On 21 July 1941 Suman embarked on a hunger strike outside the Tehri police station; this continued for several days, and attracted much attention and support.[77]

Externed from the state, Suman continued his work in British India. On his release from a spell of imprisonment in Agra jail, he re-entered Tehri state and began to tour villages and organize meetings. He was arrested and lodged in Tehri jail. Here he embarked on an indefinite hunger strike, appealing that: (*i*) the Praja Mandal should be recognized and allowed to work in the state; (*ii*) the cases against him should be personally heard by the maharaja; (*iii*) he should be allowed contact with the outside world. When these demands went unheeded, Suman succumbed to pneumonia and heart failure after a fast that lasted eighty-four days.[78]

[77] D.O. no. 433-SC/MISE-13/4, 17 September 1941, from resident, Punjab states (RPS), to secy to crown representative (CR), in file no. 449-P(S)/31, pol. dept, pol. branch, NAI acc. no. 15, CRR, enclosing reports by Suman's agent, NAI.

[78] See fortnightly reports on the political situation in the Punjab states (hereafter FR) for the year 1944, in NAI acc. no. 7, CRR.

Despite being labelled (by the British) a follower of Lenin 'who uses Lenin's method of outwardly constitutional agitation combined with secret revolutionary groups of terrorists', Suman's aims were far more restricted in their scope.[79] According to a close associate, Suman's campaign was directed at the officials of the durbar and not at the king, whom he venerated and respected. His ultimate aim was to reach an agreement between the Praja Mandal and the durbar, whereby the former could engage in constructive work under the guidance of the king. In his last declaration in court Suman averred that opposition to the maharaja, to whom he professed total devotion, ran counter to the principles by which he lived.[80]

Suman's supreme sacrifice (*balidan*) was to be of immense propaganda value in the years to come. In the year of his death the durbar embarked on a fresh land survey and settlement, in revision of the settlement operations of 1917–26. The king hoped to take advantage of the incarceration of Suman and other activists in British India. The resident however prophetically warned him that 'unless he could obtain the services of energetic revenue officers he would be asking for trouble.'[81] The extensive operations, carried out under the supervision of the settlement officer, Ramprasad Dobhal, involved the measurement of land and fixation of the new (enhanced) rates of revenue. Immediately, surveying officials had to contend with non-co-operation by peasants who refused to submit to the survey.[82]

Sustained opposition to the settlement followed the submission of interim reports by the *amins* and patwaris, when the settlement officer himself held court to ratify the survey. Dobhal's large entourage, which included his guests and dancing parties, claimed *bara* (services) and begar as a matter of course. Despite rules prescribing payment for rations and transport, officials were taking services at nominal rates and claiming receipts for the full amount. Complaints were made about

[79] Report by Suman's agent in ibid.
[80] Bhaktdarshan, pp. 255–6, 282.
[81] Note on the visit of RPS to T-G, 21 to 23 March 1944, in file no. 347-P(S)/44, pol. dept, pol. branch, NAI acc. no. 7, CRR.
[82] Personal communication from Acharya Gopeshwar Narain Kothiyal, hereafter Kothiyal.

the arbitrary manner in which *nazrana* (revenue) rates were fixed and impediments put on the breaking of fresh ground for cultivation. Peasants also demanded the right to alienate land enjoyed by their counterparts in British Garhwal. Simultaneously, the forest department's highhandedness came in for sharp criticism. One incident was reported of peasants being tied up and stones loaded on their head when a forest fire occurred in their vicinity. Legitimate requests for building timber went unheeded as well.[83]

The first meeting to oppose the settlement, attended by about a thousand peasants, was held on 21 April 1946. The movement, one largely autonomous of the Praja Mandal, was led by a retired employee of the postal department, Dada Daulatram. It spread rapidly to Barjula, Kadakhot, Dangchaura and Akhri pattis. Refusing to supply bara and begar, peasants forced Dobhal's entourage to cook and clean utensils themselves. Nor could they move camp without hiring costly coolies. Refusing to submit to intimidation, villagers desisted from attending *muqabala* (settlements) in Dobhal's court. Instead, the relevant cases were decided in the village panchayat.[84] In some localities peasants tore up the settlement papers which attempted to codify the state's demands, an action characteristic of rural jacqueries throughout the world.[85] Under Daulatram's leadership a *jatha* (group) of peasants marched to Narendranagar, the new capital, raising slogans against begar and nazrana. Daulatram and his associates were arrested and jailed on 21 July 1946.[86]

On hearing of their leader's arrest another jatha proceeded to Tehri. Led by Lachman Singh Bist, an ex-soldier of the Indian National Army, this party had the object of releasing

[83] Typed report by Jainarayan Vyas (secy, AISPC), on a visit to Garhwal, in AISPC, file no. 165/1945–6.

[84] 'Report on movement against Nazrana and Land Settlement excess in Tehri State', unsigned, undated, in ibid.

[85] Sher Singh Mewar, 'Tehri Garhwal ka Krantikari Itihas' (handwritten manuscript at present in my possession), p. 5. Cf. Le Roy Ladurie on the burning of land registers in sixteenth-century France: 'the land registers represented the intrusion of the written word and modern method of calculation into the casual archaism of the seigneurial system. The peasants considered them efficient, therefore highly dangerous.' *Carnival in Romans*, p. 137.

[86] Bhaktdarshan, pp. 479–83.

the prisoners from jail and proceeding to Narendranagar to celebrate '1942 day' on 9 August. In the ensuing scuffle several peasants were arrested but the rest, including Lachman Singh, evaded arrest. Meanwhile, Daulatram and several colleagues, including the young communist Nagendra Saklani, went on a hunger strike in protest against the durbar's actions.[87]

At this juncture the Congress stepped in to mediate between the peasantry and the durbar. The party's traditional suspicion of peasant movements over which it did not exercise control was perhaps reinforced in this case by the immediacy of the interim government in which it was to hold power.[88] Accordingly, a delegation led by Jainarayan Vyas and Khuslanand Gairola visited Tehri Garhwal between 10 and 20 August. An agreement was reached with the durbar whereby the Praja Mandal was registered and allowed to hold processions and meetings. The pact also envisaged the release of those activists in jail.[89] Under its new constitution the 'ultimate object' of the Praja Mandal was the 'achievement of responsible government under the aegis of His Highness ... by constitutional, legitimate and peaceful means'.[90] Triumphantly, the resident proclaimed that this article constituted 'a very considerable success for the Darbar'.[91]

The terms of the pact were, however, not adhered to by the durbar. While several prisoners were released on furnishing personal bonds, others including Daulatram and the Praja Mandal president, Paripurnanand Painuli, were still in jail and being tried. Daulatram had also been refused defence counsel. On 13 September Painuli, labelled a 'communist' by the authorities, and several other prisoners commenced an indefinite hunger strike, demanding a repeal of the Registration of Associations act under which the Praja Mandal had been derecognized.[92]

[87] D.O. no. XP G-2-5/46, from RPS to secy to CR, 16 August 1946, in file no. 347-P(S)/44, NAI acc. no. 7, CRR.
[88] Cf. Sumit Sarkar, *Modern India* (Delhi, 1983).
[89] Press statement, 26 August 1946, sd J. N. Vyas, in AISPC, 165/1945-6, NMML.
[90] Article II, constitution of Tehri Rajya Praja Mandal, in ibid.
[91] See file no 347-P(S)/44, NAI acc. no. 7, CRR.
[92] Letters to J. N. Vyas from Praja Mandal Karyalaya, Tehri, 20 October 1946, and from Shyamcharan Negi, 14 October 1946, both in AISPC, 165/1945-6.

In the circumstances, there was a growing perception among the Tehri villagers that the Congress signatories of the pact had 'totally forgotten those leaders of theirs who are rotting in jails for the simple crime that they wanted to establish Prajamandal in the state boundaries'.[93] Strongly protesting the durbar's actions (which included the arrest of Suman's brother) the hero of Peshawar, Chandra Singh Garhwali, accused Jainarayan Vyas of deliberately allowing the durbar to sabotage the pact. A professed anti-communist who had purged the AISPC of leftist elements, Vyas suspected their involvement in the kisan andolan. But, as Garhwali pointed out, the solitary communist involved in the movement was Nagendra Saklani, and in his case too the peasantry was unacquainted with his political beliefs.[94]

In December 1946 Painuli effected a dramatic escape from Tehri jail. Donning the robes of a sadhu, he trekked westwards until he reached the Tons valley and British territory. From there he proceeded to Dehradun. He had been presumed dead by the AISPC, who had passed a condolence resolution following his disappearance.[95] On 9 February 1947 Daulatram and five fellow prisoners went on a fast, demanding that they be re-tried in a British Indian court. Using the occasion of the birth of a son, the maharaja released political prisoners on 23 February. Shortly afterwards, Daulatram was rearrested after an altercation with a police constable.[96]

The Praja Mandal had its first open meeting in Tehri on 26 and 27 May 1947, and Daulatram was chosen its head for the next year. On 14 August Painuli sent a wire to the maharaja, warning him of his intention to enter the state on Independence Day. He was promptly arrested on arrival.[97] Gathering momentum, the movement had spread to Saklana, the only muafi in the state.[98] In Saklana, a major potato pro-

[93] Letter from Dr Gairola to J. N. Vyas, undated, in ibid.
[94] Letter from Chandra Singh Garhwali to J. Nehru, 27 November 1946, in AISPC, file no. 242 of 1946–7, NMML.
[95] Interview with Shri Painuli, Dehradun, May 1983.
[96] See FR for 1947, file no. 5(1)-P(S)/47, pol. dept, NAI.
[97] Ibid.
[98] The Saklana muafidars were responsible for revenue collection and enjoyed IIIrd-class magistrate's powers; other affairs of government, including forests, were controlled by the Tehri durbar.

ducing area, peasants had been protesting extortion by the potato 'syndicate' to whom the durbar had accorded sole rights of collection and sale. Muletteers were also desisting from paying the tax levied on transport. When the police arrested striking peasants, the refusal to pay taxes became more widespread. Some villagers fled to Dehradun district. The police also raided houses and beat up the inhabitants. Angered, the kisans encircled durbar officials and forced them to leave Saklana. The *muafidars* voluntarily abdicated and left for Dehradun. In the last week of December victorious peasants formed an *azad* panchayat which abolished taxes and declared that each cultivator had ownership rights.[99]

As news of the development at Saklana spread, azad panchayats were formed in several other pattis.[100] In Badyargarh events took a dramatic turn at the Dhadi Ghandiyal *jath*. At this fair, held every twelve years, peasants paid homage to the local deity of Ghandiyal. Shrewdly utilizing this opportunity, Daulatram and his colleagues arranged to address the crowd on the Saklana and Kadakhot dhandaks. The gathering was informed of the impending march on Kirtinagar, where peasants from different parts of the state were expected to congregate.[101]

Following the Dhadi jath, activists fanned out into the villages. In several places *chowkis* (offices) were captured and their patwaris replaced by men chosen from among the peasantry. Survey officials were made to return bribes extorted from villagers. Occasionally, liquor contractors were beaten up and their stills smashed.[102]

Jathas of around fifty peasants each were rapidly sent onwards to Kirtinagar. On 30 December policemen came searching for Daulatram. The constables were arrested by the villagers and asked by Daulatram to report at the court at Kirtinagar. The next day, when the police fired on a crowd at Jakhni village, angry peasants captured the court and police station at Kirtinagar. The police inspector's house, where the

[99] Girdhar Pandit, 'Saklana Andolan: Tehri Jankranti ka Pratam Charan', *Parvatiya Times* (Annual), 30 March 1983.
[100] YV, 15 January 1948.
[101] Interviews in Badyargarh, January 1983.
[102] Govind Negi, 'Tehri Riyasat Mukti Sangarsh: Ek Romanchkari Adhyay',* YV, issues of 15 August, 22 August, 5 September and 12 September 1976. Hereafter G. Negi.

deputy collector was also taking refuge, was surrounded. When the officials refused to surrender, the crowd collected kerosene preparatory to burning the house. The deputy collector was caught while trying to escape and taken across the Alakananda river to Srinagar. The police party who had fired at Jakhni on the 31st were found tied up on the road. They were taken to the office of the District Congress Committee at Pauri and made to sign letters of resignation. In Devprayag, too, the court had been captured by the dhandakis. The same night Daulatram and Painuli were spirited away to Narendranagar for negotiations with the durbar.[103]

Meanwhile, thousands of peasants had collected at Kirtinagar. Daulatram himself returned on 9 January. The town had initially been cleared of all officials and an azad panchayat had been proclaimed.[104] In response, the durbar sent an armed force led by Baldev Singh Panwar, a close kinsman of the raja. This force arranged a meeting with Daulatram in the local court. However, as soon as Daulatram returned, soldiers fired teargas shells and bullets at the waiting crowd. When fire was set to the building, senior officials tried to flee. The crowd chased them, whereupon one officer fired several bullets, killing the young communist Saklani.[105]

The next day the crowd took the bodies of Saklani and Moluram (a peasant killed in the firing outside the court) and proceeded to Tehri via Devprayag. En route the jatha exhibited the corpses in different hamlets. A second jatha, led by Daulatram and including the captured officials, proceeded directly to Tehri. On 14 January the two jathas met and immersed the martyrs in the confluence of the Bhageerathi and Bhilagna rivers. The army having fled, an azad panchayat took over Tehri under its padhan, Virendra Dutt Saklani.[106]

Hoping to win over the people through his presence, the raja rushed to Tehri from Narendranagar. His attempt to enter Tehri was foiled when the bridge across the Bhageerathi was

---

[103] Balkrishna Bhatt, 'Tehri mein Kya Hua', YV, 15 February 1948; D. Ghildiyal, 'Kirtinagar ka Andolan', YV, 1 March 1948.

[104] Letter from Nagendra Saklana to P. N. Painuli, 10 January 1948, in YV, 11 January 1970.

[105] G. Negi.

[106] Bhaktdarshan, pp. 484–5; YV, 15 January 1948.

shut. The physical gulf that separated him from his people became invested with a deeper meaning: as one peasant recounted, on one bank were the massed subjects, on the other their ruler ('*Us taraf raja, is taraf praja*').[107] The raja had now lost control. Thousands of peasants from Jaunpur and Rawain gathered at Bhavan and handcuffed police inspector Baijram, the man responsible for Suman's arrest. Functionaries of the police, revenue and forest departments were forced out of the locality and an azad panchayat established.[108] In defeat, the raja called in the Praja Mandal leaders for negotiations. A ministry headed by Dr Gairola was established, which held office till the state's merger with Uttar Pradesh the following year.

Peasants and parties

The kisan andolan differed from the preceding dhandaks in two major respects, one of which was in its spread. The initial confluence of several local movements gained an additional impetus with the Kirtinagar kand (firing) and came to cover much of the state. Secondly, this movement had an organizational forum in the shape of the Praja Mandal. The dyadic relationship between raja and praja was therefore complicated by the presence of Congress-inspired nationalists. The specific linkages between the Praja Mandal and the praja it claimed to represent thus need to be examined.

The relationship between the Praja Mandal and the peasantry can be viewed at several levels, each invested with different layers of meaning. The Praja Mandal's aims initially encompassed the reformation of an administration viewed through the prism of modern nationalism as *samantshahi* (feudal). In fact, in the early part of the movement there were reports that the peasant leader Daulatram had 'been disowned by the Praja Mandal'.[109] As we have seen, the AISPC was keen on a settlement with the raja, bypassing the kisan andolan that had enabled its intervention in the first place.

On assuming power on 15 August 1947 the Congress attitude towards the Tehri movements underwent a major shift.

[107] Interviews in Badyargarh, January 1983.
[108] YV, 21 January 1948.
[109] FR for first half of July 1946, in NAI acc. no. 7, CRR.

The desire to integrate princely states with the Indian Union, coupled with the growing pressure of the peasant movement itself, led the Congress to view Daulatram and his associates in a more favourable light. Now the Praja Mandal agitation imperfectly merged with the kisan andolan in a movement that generated its own dynamic: the outcome perhaps exceeding what either the Praja Mandal or the peasantry had envisaged.

The hiatus between the Praja Mandal and those it professed to represent remained, at the level of perception, a considerable one.[110] As a young activist later recounted, the attempt to popularize the slogan 'Inquilab Zindabad' (associated with the Punjabi revolutionary Bhagat Singh) at village meetings met with a miserable failure. As the slogan was raised along with the national tricolour, peasants interpreted it in a manner more representative of their feelings. They responded by shouting 'Yanno Khala Jandabad' (this is the way we will bring about the rule of the flag). Although the Praja Mandal attempted to explain the original slogan and its significance, the same misperception repeated itself at the next village.[111]

Interestingly, whereas Praja Mandal activists explained the origins of the Kirtinagar 'satyagraha' in terms of India having won freedom while Tehri was in bondage, peasants were emphatic that their struggle was against the oppressive taxes and the settlement operations that came in their wake. But it was not merely at the level of perception that this duality persisted; it was imbricated in the significance attached to different actions. Thus, peasant participants recounted, with evident satisfaction, how patwaris had been overthrown and symbolically replaced by their own men, adding that their nominees continued to hold office for some time. (In using a time of social instability to replace state officials with their own nominees, Garhwali peasants were in honourable company; very similar acts attended the peasant revolutions in Russia in 1905 and Mexico in 1919.[112]) On the other hand, Praja Mandal

[110] It must, however, be added that many of the Tehri Praja Mandal activists had a far more positive view of the kisan andolan than the AISPC bosses.

[111] G. Negi.

[112] Shanin, *Russia as a 'Developing' Society*, II, pp. 108–11; John Womack, *Zapata and the Mexican Revolution* (New York, 1969), p. 225.

activists emphasized the formation of the interim ministry as a major fulfilment of their goals.[113]

Peasants were also insistent that the king did not himself know of the injustice (*anniyayi*) being perpetrated in his name. As the AISPC peace mission observed, 'villagers were not found disloyal to the maharaja or the gaddi and had a feeling that all that was being done was not in the knowledge of the maharaja.' The fear of retribution from the police was adduced as an important factor which dissuaded peasants from approaching the king.[114] For its part, the Praja Mandal had a far more ambivalent attitude. Its eagerness to share power with the durbar was nevertheless accompanied by an ideology which was implicitly anti-monarchical.

ELEMENTARY ASPECTS OF CUSTOMARY REBELLION

'I obey, but do not comply.'
—Puerto Rican peasant saying

As we have seen, in Tehri Garhwal the mechanisms of social protest drew heavily on the indigenous tradition of resistance known as dhandak. Yet, for all its distinctiveness, the dhandak is representative of a type of rebellion widely prevalent in pre-industrial and pre-capitalist monarchies. Variations on the dhandak theme have been reported from other parts of Asia, and Africa and Europe as well. The dhandak is a sub-type of what one might call 'customary' rebellion: a form of rebellion that draws its legitimacy from custom and does not seek to overthrow the social order. As Max Weber commented, here 'opposition is not directed against the system as such—it is a case of "traditional revolution" '[115]—peasants' accusations against the ruler being that he or his officials failed to observe the traditional limits to their power. In the classic formulation of Max Gluckman, custom 'directs and controls the quarrels through conflicts and allegiances so that despite rebellions, the same social system is re-established over wider areas of com-

[113] Interviews in Badyargarh and Dehradun, January and April 1983.
[114] Typed report, untitled, prob. by J. N. Vyas, n.d. (probably June 1946), in AISPC, 265/1945–6.
[115] Max Weber, *Economy and Society*, translated by Guenther Roth and Claus Wittich (Berkeley, 1978), volume II, p. 220.

munal life and through longer periods of time.'[116] In this perspective customary rebellion is seen as central to the coherence and persistence of a society, a functional safety valve that allows for the periodic and constructive release of discontent. While Gluckman's interpretation has been very influential, I believe it is both partial and inadequate. A comparative analysis of the 'elementary aspects' of customary rebellion—with the Tehri Garhwal case very much in the foreground—may help reveal this, as may an alternative interpretation of the significance of customary rebellion as a form of social protest.

Typically, the origins of rebellion in traditional chiefdoms and monarchies stem from a perceived breach of the covenant between ruler and ruled. This covenant between high and low, or patron and client, is normally couched in the idiom of father and son. Being by definition the ruler *par excellence*, the monarch patronizes his subjects not only in the economic sphere but in the socio-political and judicial spheres as well. According to the dominant ideology, the peasantry looks to the king for impartial arbitration and social justice. On his accession to the throne of Garhwal in 1919, the young prince Narendra Shah was exhorted to live up to the traditions of his ancestors: the main elements of princely rule being designated as justice (*nyaya*) and protection of subjects (*praja ki raksha*).[117] When, in 1946, Narendra Shah abdicated for reasons of ill health, he invoked 'the Shastric maxim of Raja and Praja conceived as Pita (father) and Putra (son) [which] has always been the guiding principle of the patriarchs who occupied this gaddi'.[118] The symbolism of father and son well epitomized the essentially patriarchal style of domination, where 'protection' of the peasantry harmonized with the kingly ideal of benevolent rule. A similar idiom was skilfully used by German and British colonialists in Africa, with the all-powerful Kaiser, or the English king, symbolizing the head of a large family,

---

[116] Max Gluckman, *Custom and Conflict in Africa* (Oxford, 1956), p. 47. Cf. also his *Order and Rebellion in Tribal Africa* (London, 1963), and *The Ideas in Barotse Jurisprudence* (New Haven, 1965).

[117] *Garhwali Visheshank* (special number), 4 October 1919.

[118] Statement by Narendra Shah, addressed to 'my beloved Praja', in file no. 49-P(S)/46, pol. dept, NAI.

REBELLION AS CUSTOM

consisting of the various nationalities under European domination.[119]

This covenant, while indicating the limits of arbitrary action by both rulers and subjects, is continually under threat. For, intermediate between the king and the peasantry are myriad laws relating to the land, the forests, and the waters of the kingdom, and myriad officials to enforce these laws. And in the eyes of the peasantry officials are invariably tyrannical and high-handed; moreover, they tend to pervert the king's commands and interpret laws in their favour and against the interests of the peasants. 'In its simplest and most common expression', observes Daniel Field in his fine study of customary rebellion in Russia, 'popular monarchism took the form of the adage, "the Tsar wants it, but the boyars resist." '[120] Often ethnically and economically distinct from the peasant masses, these officials are both despised and feared. In times of revolutionary change (e.g. Tehri Garhwal in 1948 or Russia in 1905), peasants seize the opportunity to appoint their own men in place of officials deputed from outside. Yet this opportunity very rarely presents itself: more frequently peasants follow the Russian Peasant Union in petitioning the king to 'free us from officials . . . who cost a lot and do not give us order, only disturb our life and work and offend us daily . . . understanding nothing of our problems.'[121] If these pleas are unheeded, peasants take matters into their own hands, physically attacking officials even as they break the new laws. In this act of trespass peasants could cry, as in nineteenth-century France,

[119] See Terence Ranger, 'The Invention of Tradition in Colonial Africa', in Eric Hobsbawn and Terence Ranger (eds), *The Invention of Tradition* (Cambridge, 1983).

[120] Daniel Field, *Rebels in the Name of the Tsar* (Boston, 1976), p. 14. Cf. also Philip Longworth, 'Peasant Leadership and the Pugachev Revolt', *Journal of Peasant Studies*, vol. 2, no. 2, January 1975, pp. 187–8. A fascinating parallel is found in the slave societies of North America. Here, while plantation owners also used a patriarchal ideology which claimed the slaves as children under their protection, the white overseer who actually supervised day-to-day operations was the obvious target of attack, slaves often complaining of his tyrannies to the master. See Eugene Genovese, *Roll, Jordan Roll: The World the Slaves Made* (New York, 1973).

[121] Quoted in Teodor Shanin, *Russia as a 'Developing' Society* (New Haven, 1986), vol. II, p. 112.

'long live the king, down with the Forest Administration'; or, as Balzac puts it, shout 'long live the king, with enthusiasm, to avoid shouting, "long live the count".'[122] Alternatively, as they sometimes did in Garhwal, they could march to the capital demanding an audience with the king—as did the peasants in early Meiji Japan who went to Tokyo hoping to get justice from the central authority 'because they were unable to get a fair hearing from their prefecture'.[123]

Such appeals to the king were made in the name of 'custom' —namely the argument that the new laws were contravening time-honoured social (and natural) arrangements. Custom, as Marc Bloch observed many years ago, is a 'double-edged sword', serving both peasants and their overlords in turn. If French peasants could claim that enclosure violated their hitherto unrestricted access to common land, their lords could insist on the prompt payment of taxes and tithes even in bad crop years.[124] But in the transition to capitalism it is peasants who have more frequently invoked custom, for it is they who stand to lose most from enclosure, state forest management, or the mechanization of agricultural work. European peasants were known to invent king's charters which variously exonerated them from taxes or gave them the run of forests and pasture; they accused officials of 'concealing the king's orders' while insisting that their own actions were perfectly in accord with the wishes of the monarch.[125] In Tehri Garhwal, several centuries later, custom was often the most effective weapon for a peasantry facing the onslaught of a 'modernizing' state. For, 'the ideological struggle to define the present is a struggle to define the past as well', and, like the poor peasants of the Malay village of Sedaka, those left behind by capitalism have no option but to collectively create a 'remembered village and remembered economy that serve[s] as an effective ideological

[122] John Merriman, 'The Demoiselles of the Ariege, 1829–31', in Merriman (ed.), *1830 in France* (New York, 1975), p. 94; Henri Balzac, *The Peasantry* (New York, 1900), p. 311.
[123] William Kelly, *Deference and Defiance in Nineteenth Century Japan* (Princeton, 1985), pp. 205–6.
[124] Marc Bloch, *French Rural History* (rpt. London, 1978), pp. 70–1.
[125] Ladurie, *Carnival in Romans*, pp. 43–7; Lefebvre, *The Great Fear*, pp. 30 ff., 95–7.

backdrop against which to deplore the present'.[126] Of course in Tehri Garhwal the remembered village and remembered economy were not merely figments of the imagination: things were far better before the coming of the forest department, and to that extent Garhwali peasant appeals to the monarch rested on a solid core of truth.

Yet such invocations are not merely tactical; the opposition to new laws and their enforcing officials has often been strengthened, as in eighteenth-century France, by the 'profound conviction that the king was on their side'.[127] In general, appeals to the monarch rested on two core assumptions: that the king symbolized the spirit of the collectivity and that, as the temporal and spiritual head, he was the very fount of justice.[128] The monarch is the head of an 'imagined community'.[129] Unlike the political overlords of contemporary imagined communities like the nation-state, however, his persona is avowedly sacred, not secular.[130] Traditional societies experience life as an ever-expanding web of connections which reaches beyond local and national communities into the depths of nature. It is the function of the monarch to maintain the harmony of this integration between society and nature, between the microcosmos of human beings and the macrocosmos of gods. As the mediating link between the sacred and the profane, the king takes on

[126] J. C. Scott, *Weapons of the Weak: Everyday Forms of Peasant Resistance* (New Haven, 1986), p. 178.

[127] Lefebvre, *Great Fear*, p. 42.

[128] In some modern societies a supreme religious figure could have a very similar symbolic function. Thus the noted Chilean author Ariel Dorfman, commenting on the sense of anticipation with which his countrymen awaited the visit of the Pope, says: 'The despair has been such that now [Chileans] believe that the Pope will fix everything. He represents a figure from the outside who is pure and immaculate and not part of the everyday bickering and horror.' See *Christian Science Monitor*, 30 March 1987, p. 9.

[129] The phrase is from Benedict Anderson, *Imagined Communities: Reflections on the Origins and Spread of Nationalism* (London, 1985). Anderson sees the nation, replacing societies centred around kingship and religion, as the major form of the imagined community in modern times.

[130] The boundaries of such communities are not geographical—as are those of nation-states—but cultural. Thus, even peasants in the British-ruled portion of Garhwal thought of themselves as 'Garhwalis', acknowledging the Tehri monarch as their temporal and spiritual head.

some of the attributes of the gods: he is quasi-divine:

Sovereigns are the kinsmen, the homologues or the mediators of the gods. The closeness of the attributes of power and of the sacred indicates the link that has always existed between them—a connection that history has tended to pull apart but has never broken.[131]

The divinity of kingship is further heightened in isolated and protected tracts, such as Garhwal, where the tranquillity of the cosmic order and its integration with society remain relatively undisturbed by cataclysmic social or natural events.[132]

In his mediating role the king must faithfully observe the rituals of investiture, symbolically undertake the first annual ploughing, and enact the other societally varying magico-religious ceremonies which are believed to constitute royal power and assure social harmony. Failure to do so may bring the wrath of his subjects upon him or his office. In the Bemba kingdom of Central Africa the chief was blamed for the economic distress of the 1920s, his subjects believing it to be caused

[131] George Balandier, *Political Anthropology* (London, 1970), p. 99. Evans-Pritchard says: 'In my view kingship everywhere and at all times has been in some degree a sacred office. This is because a king symbolises a whole society and must not be identified with any part of it. He must be in the society and yet stand outside it and this is only possible if his office is raised to a mystical plane.' E. E. Evans-Pritchard, 'The Divine Kingship of the Shilluck of the Nilotic Sudan' (Frazer Lecture, 1948), in his *Social Anthropology and Other Essays* (New York, 1962), p. 210. On divine kingship in Africa, see also the classic collection edited by Meyer Fortes and Evans-Pritchard, *African Political Systems* (London, 1940).

[132] Cf. Henri Frankfort, *Kingship and the Gods* (1948; rpt. Chicago, 1978), Introduction. The divinity of the Panwar kings seriously calls into question the thesis of 'secularization' of Hindu kingship—in which the Brahmin is held to have exclusive control over the sacred realm—advanced by Louis Dumont and Romila Thapar in their enormously influential works. See Dumont, 'The Conception of Kingship in Ancient India', in his *Religion, Politics and History in India* (Paris, 1970); idem, *Homo Hierarchicus* (London, 1970); Thapar, *A History of India*, vol. 1 (Harmondsworth, 1966). Derived largely from scriptural sources, the Dumont–Thapar thesis does not stand up to the scrutiny of anthropological studies from different parts of India, which conclusively demonstrate that divinity is intrinsic to the Hindu conception of kingship. See, *inter alia*, Frederique Apffel Marglin, *Wives of the God-King* (Delhi, 1985); R. K. Jain, 'Kingship, Territory and Property in Pre-British Bundelkhand', *Economic and Political Weekly*, 2 June 1979; S. C. Sinha, 'State Formation and Rajput Myth in Rajput Central India', *Man in India*, vol. 42, no. 1, 1982; and, for Nepal, R. Burghart, 'Hierarchical Models of the Hindu Social System', *Man*, n.s., vol. 13, no. 4, December 1978.

by the monarch's failure to build, as custom demanded, a new capital upon his accession.[133] Apart from the correct observance of traditional rituals, the physical presence of the king is required—especially at crucial times like the harvest. In the state of Bastar in Central India peasants revolted in 1876 when the king left the state to pay his respects to the Prince of Wales, 'leaving the ryots to the tender mercies of [cruel officials like] Gopinath and Adit Pershad'.[134] Likewise, the Garhwali king's visit to Europe coincided with the Rawain uprising of 1930; and his physical removal from the scene undoubtedly led to the tragedy whereby a routine dhandak ended in an unprecedented massacre.

As the embodiment of the spirit of the collectivity, the protector of his subjects and the fountain of justice, the monarch is the ultimate court of appeal for rebels claiming the sanction of custom. Here lies one major difference between the idiom of customary rebellion in small, relatively homogeneous and well integrated states like Tehri Gahrwal, and in states organized according to different political and economic principles. In large monarchies, for example, one important variant on the theme of customary rebellion is the appearance of a 'pretender'. This phenomenon normally occurs in the far-flung corners of a huge kingdom, where peasants are far removed from the centre of authority and are unlikely to have ever seen a member of the royal family. A pretender comes among the villagers, claiming to be the true monarch (the just tsar in Russia, Ratu Adil in Java); he asks, and frequently gets, their support in a social movement directed against corrupt officials.[135] The dhandak

---

[133] Karen Fields, *Revival and Rebellion in Colonial Central Africa* (Princeton, 1985), p. 57. 'A legend recorded in the thirteenth century *Heimskringla*', observes Bloch, 'relates that Halfdan the Black, king of Norway, had been "of all kings the one who had brought most success to the harvests". When he died, instead of burying his corpse entire and in one single piece, his subjects cut it into four pieces, and buried each portion under a mound in each of the four principal districts of the country; for "the possession of the body"—or one of its fragments—"seemed to those who obtained it to give hope of further good harvests".' Marc Bloch, *The Royal Touch: Sacred Monarchy and Scrofula in England and France*, trans. J. E. Anderson (1923; English edition, London, 1973), p. 32.

[134] See foreign dept, pol. agent, Progs, August 1876, nos. 163-72, NAI.

[135] For Russia, see Philip Longworth, 'The Pretender Phenomena in Eighteenth Century Russia', *Past and Present*, no. 66., Feb. 1975; *idem*, ' "The Pugachev Revolt", the Last Great Cossack-Peasant Uprising', in H. A. Landsberger (ed.),

can also be distinguished from the phenomenon of regicide found in the segmentary states of Africa, where disaffected subjects can call upon a chief to replace the incumbent to whose inadequacies are attributed current economic and political tensions.[136] In Tehri Garhwal, loyalty was owed to the person occupying the throne, not simply to the institution of kingship; there was no question of the rebels calling upon another person to replace the one in power.

Paternalism from above and from below

> [T]he slaves found an opportunity to translate paternalism itself into a doctrine different from that understood by their masters and to forge it into a weapon of resistance... [T]hey acted consciously and unconsciously to transform paternalism into a doctrine of protection of their own rights.
>
> —Eugene Genovese

The religious idiom of divine kingship tends to obscure the mundane and practical ends to which it was put. As Marc Bloch observes, 'the miraculous power attributed to their kings by the "primitives" is generally conceived as employed for collective ends which are intended to serve the well-being of the whole group...'.[137] To an outside observer a peasant rebellion calling upon an omnipotent and quasi-divine monarch may smack of naïvety; yet it is striking how often peasants have used the idiom of divine kingship to advance their own interests. Tehri villagers may have looked upon their monarch as Bolanda Badrinath, the deity personified, but they usually called upon his miraculous powers in support of their traditional rights in the forest and in opposition to increases in land tax. This central feature of customary rebellion is captured well by Daniel Field:

Naïve or not, the peasants professed their faith in the Tsar in forms, and only in those forms, that corresponded to their interests... [The]

Rural Protest: Agrarian Movements and Social Change (London, 1974). For the Ratu Adil phenomenon in Java, see Sartono Kartodirdjo, *Protest Movements in Rural Java* (Singapore, 1973).

[136] See the works by Gluckman cited in note 116 above; Evans-Pritchard, 'Divine Kingship', and Gillian Feeley-Harnuk, 'Issues in Divine Kingship', *Annual Review of Anthropology*, vol. 14, 1985.

[137] Bloch, *Royal Touch*, p. 33.

goals peasants pursued under the aegis of the myth [of the divine king] were eminently practical: more land, tax relief, and self-rule. Their means were draped in mystery, but their ends were worldly.[138]

Peasants in Tehri, as in Russia, twisted the myth of divine kingship to serve utterly mundane and practical ends. The abolition of the Panwar monarchy was beyond their powers; in the circumstances the dhandak, like the French Carnival, 'used the most effective or most audible means of agitation possible, considering the culture and psychology of the times',[139] to wrest concessions from their superiors. This suggests that far from being a society's safety valve, a functionalist device to maintain the integration and coherence of a society (as some anthropological accounts suggest), customary rebellion is more appropriately viewed as a shrewd and effective tactic used by peasants to exploit the inherent ambiguities of the dominant ideology. Indeed—

> The most common form of class struggle arises from the failure of a dominant ideology to live up to the implicit promises it necessarily makes. The dominant ideology can be turned against its privileged beneficiaries not only because subordinate groups develop their own interpretations, understandings and readings of its ambiguous terms, but also because of the promises that the dominant classes must make to propagate it in the first place.[140]

And so, through a lengthy detour into the indigenous idiom of domination and resistance, we come back full circle to Weber:

> experience shows that in no instance does domination voluntarily limit itself to the appeal to material, affectual or ideal motives as a basis for its continuance. In addition, every such system attempts to establish and to cultivate the belief in its legitimacy.[141]

Weber yes, but with more than a dash of Marx. For what is viewed from above as a justification of elite domination is

---

[138] Field, *Rebels*, pp. 209–10.
[139] Le Roy Ladurie, *Carnival in Romans*, p. 321. Cf. Eugene Genovese: 'The practical question facing the slaves was not whether slavery itself was a proper relation but how to survive it with the greatest degree of self-determination'. *Roll, Jordan, Roll*, p. 125.
[140] J. C. Scott, *Weapons of the Weak*, p. 338.
[141] Max Weber, *Economy and Society*, vol. 1, pp. 55, 213.

reinterpreted from below as a mandate to rebel against attempts to change, even in the slightest, the relative balance of power between elite and subaltern classes. Thus the legitimizing belief that underlay the eighteenth-century food riot in England serves just as well in explaining the moral idiom of the dhandak. 'By the notion of legitimation', writes E. P. Thompson,

> I mean that the men and women in the crowd were informed by the belief that they were defending traditional rights and customs, and in general that they were supported by the wider consensus of the community. On occasion this popular consensus was endorsed in some measure by license afforded by the authorities.[142]

The dominant ideology, therefore, while serving in a general way to consolidate elite rule, also constricts in some significant respects its room for manoeuvre, just as it necessarily has within it a certain ambiguity and openness that allow for lower-class resistance. Embedded in every ideology that legitimizes domination there is a sub-text, a legitimizing ideology of resistance. The contradiction between the claims of the ruling ideology and the actual state of affairs in any society is, as Scott implies, a most frequent cause of resistance. The central argument of this work is that forms of domination structure forms of resistance. While protest normally arises in response to domination and attempts to resist it, most forms of domination actually enable resistance. Thus the hiatus between the rhetoric of liberal democracy and living conditions in southern United States produced the civil rights movement, and the denial of workers' rights in an avowedly 'socialist' state led to Solidarity. In the same manner, the failure to meet the promise of protection held out by the quasi-divine monarch enabled peasant rebels in Garhwal to claim the sanctity of custom.

---

[142] E. P. Thompson, 'The Moral Economy of the English Crowd in the Eighteenth Century', *Past and Present*, no. 50, 1970–1, p. 78.

CHAPTER 5

Rebellion as Confrontation

God sent Gandhi in the form of a Bania [merchant] to conquer Bania government.

—Kumaun peasant leader, 1921

This chapter examines the trajectory of social protest in Kumaun division during the early decades of this century. While the absence of popular protest in the first century of British rule had given rise to the stereotype of the 'simple and law abiding hillman',[1] the reservation of the Kumaun forests between 1911 and 1917 'met with violent and sustained opposition',[2] culminating in 1921 when, within the space of a few months, the administration was paralysed first by a strike against utar (statutory labour) and then through a systematic campaign in which the Himalayan pine forests 'were swept by incendiary fires almost from end to end'.[3]

This transformation in peasant consciousness and peasant revolt was closely related to the more subtle but equally enduring changes in the structure of colonial administration. As chapter 2 documents, in view of the strategic location of Kumaun the demands of the state on the peasantry were extraordinarily light; moreover, the style of rule was a typically paternalist one, exemplified in the person of Henry Ramsay, commissioner from 1856 to 1884. It was the advent of forest management—with the hill conifers being arguably the most valuable forest 'property' in India—that indicated a growing intervention of the state in the day-to-day life of the peasantry. The workings of scientific forestry, in particular, by curtailing

[1] P. Mason, *A Matter of Honour* (London, 1975), p. 451; cf. also T. W. Webber, *The Forests of Upper India and Their Inhabitants* (London, 1902), p. 39.
[2] E. P. Stebbing, *The Forests of India*, 3 volumes (London, 1922-6), III, p. 258.
[3] E. A. Smythies, *India's Forest Wealth* (London, 1925), p. 84.

customary rights, drastically affected the mode of peasant social and economic organization. At the same time, the imperatives of exercising effective control led to a more general bureaucratization of state authority. This transition was succinctly expressed by a district officer in Almora in the late 1930s who recalled Ramsay's rule 'as a benevolent despot who could do as he liked and [which] would always remain an envious [sic] example to the present generation of civilians who are so much bound by red tape and the bulky Manual of Government Order'.[4]

The trajectory of social protest in British Kumaun was intimately connected with the changes in administrative structures and styles. The early phase of resistance to forest management and the begar system lay, in various ways, in a direct path of continuity with traditional methods of peasant resistance. As this resistance crystallized into a more widespread movement, it began to use new mechanisms of protest—chiefly in response to forest management—in addition to those traditionally used. These changes in the method of protest were matched by concomitant changes in peasant consciousness, both reflecting the rapidly fading legitimacy of the colonial state. Transformations in peasant ideology and forms of resistance, and their interrelationship with changing structures of power and authority, are vividly illustrated by the history of social protest in colonial Kumaun.

EARLY RESISTANCE TO FORCED LABOUR

The incidence of utar was comparatively slight in the first century of British rule. Nevertheless, its impressment was resisted in various ways. The village *pradhan* (himself exempt) occasionally concealed some of the hissedars in his village;[5] alternatively, travellers who indented for coolies found the headman being 'openly defied' by his villagers, who refused to supply labour or provisions.[6] When census returns from Garhwal reported a large excess of males over females in the ten to

[4] M. S. Randhawa, *The Kumaun Himalayas* (Delhi, 1970), p. 12.
[5] J. H. Batten, 'Final Report on the Settlement of Kumaun', in Batten (ed.), *Official Reports on the Province of Kumaun* (1851; rpt. Calcutta, 1878), p. 270.
[6] 'Mountaineer', *A Summer Ramble in the Himalaya* (London, 1860), p. 167.

fourteen age group, this discrepancy was traced to the age (sixteen years) at which men were called upon to carry loads or furnish bardaish. Thus, all those whose age could possibly be understated were reported to be under sixteen.[7] Officials commented too that the hillman's aversion to being made to work under compulsion had led to his earning an undeserved reputation for indolence. While he worked hard enough in his fields, coolie labour—especially during the agricultural season—was performed in a manner that made his resentment apparent.[8] Travellers and soldiers often found themselves stranded when villagers failed to oblige in carrying their luggage. White mountaineers on expedition found that villagers on begar duty, when pushed too hard, either refused requests to prolong the duration of the expedition or expressed their resentment by taking an 'unconscionable time' over meals.[9] It is reported that Henry Ramsay, the long-time commissioner of Kumaun, had once to levy a fine of Rs 500 on a village near Someshwar in Almora district which struck against utar. Another strike in 1903 led to the imprisonment of fourteen villagers of Khatyadi.[10] Concurrently, opposition to the begar system was expressed in newspapers, edited by nationalists of the Gokhale school, from Almora, Nainital and Dehradun. The Kumaun Parishad, based in Almora, took up both the begar and forest issues, asking the forest department to hire its own coolies and build more roads.[11]

With the advent of the forest department the burden of these services on the Kumaun villager dramatically increased. The reservation of the forests and their future supervision

[7] Census of India, 1891, vol. 16, pt 1, NWP & O, General Report, pp. 29–30.

[8] V. A. Stowell, *A Manual of the Land Tenures of the Kumaun Division* (1907; rpt. Allahabad, 1937), pp. 150–6; H. G. Walton, *British Garhwal: A Gazetteer* (Allahabad, 1911), pp. 68–9.

[9] Thomas Skinner, *Excursions in India, Including a Walk over the Himalaya Mountain to the Sources of the Jumna and Ganges* (London, 1832), volume 1, p. 307; A. M. Kellas, 'The Mountains of Northern Sikkim and Garhwal', *The Geographical Journal*, vol. 40, no. 3, September 1912, p. 257.

[10] See Shekhar Pathak, 'Uttarakhand mein Coolie Begar Pratha: 1815–1949', unpublished Ph.D. thesis, Kumaun University, 1980; idem, 'Kumaun mein Begar Annulan Andolan', paper presented at Jawaharlal Nehru University, October 1982, pp. 4–14. Hereafter Pathak (1) and (2).

[11] See letter from comm., KD, to chief secretary, UP, 18 September 1916, in FD file 164/1916, UPSA.

involved extensive touring by forest officials who took utar and bardaish as a matter of course. Coming close on the heels of the demarcation of the forest, the additional burdens which the new department had created evoked a predictable response. Forest officers touring in the interior of Garhwal were unable to obtain grain as villagers, even where they had surplus stock, refused to supply to a department they regarded 'as disagreeable interlopers to be thwarted if possible'.[12] Utar, in the words of the Kumaun Forest Grievances Committee, was 'one of the greatest grievances which the residents of Kumaun had against the forest settlement'.[13] When coupled with the abbreviation of customary access to the forest, it represented an intervention unprecedented in its scope and swiftness. Villagers looked back, not altogether without justification, to a 'golden age' when they had full freedom to roam over their forest habitat, and state interference was at its minimum. These emotions were poignantly expressed by a government clerk who applied for exemption from begar and bardaish:

In days gone by every necessities of life were in abundance to villagers than to others [and] there were no such government laws and regulations prohibiting the free use of unsurveyed land and forest by them as they have now. The time itself has now become very hard and it has been made still harder by the imposition of different laws, regulations, and taxes on them and by increasing the land revenue. Now the village life has been shadowed by all the miseries and inconveniences of the present day laws and regulations. They are not allowed to fell down a tree to get fuels from it for their daily use and they cannot cut leaves of trees beyond certain portion of them for fodder to their animals. But the touring officials still view the present situation with an eye of the past and press them to supply good grass for themselves and their [retinue] without even thinking of making any payment for these things to them who after spending their time, money and labour, can hardly procure them for their own use. In short all the privileges of village life, as they were twenty years ago, are nowhere to be found

---

[12] DO no. 10x, 6 February 1917, from DFO, North Garhwal, to conservator of forests (CF), Kumaun circle, GAD file 398/1913, UPSA.
[13] *Report of the Kumaun Forest Grievances Committee* (thereafter KFGC), in Progs A, June 1922, nos. 19–24, file no. 522/1922, dept of rev. & agrl. (forests), p. 2, NAI.

now, still the officials hanker after the system of yore when there were everything in abundance and within the reach of villagers.[14]

As one can discern from this petition, the new laws and regulations were already beginning to threaten the considerable autonomy enjoyed by the Khasa community. Here, as in other colonial societies, unusual extractions and other forms of state encroachment upon the privileges of individuals or communities were regarded as transgressing the traditional relationship between ruler and ruled. By clashing with his notions of economic and social justice, increased state intervention breached the 'moral economy' of the peasant.[15] Anticipating that the hillman would react by 'throwing his forest loads down the khud and some day an unfortunate Forest Officer may go after them', Wyndham, commissioner of Kumaun, believed that the only way to prolong the life of the utar system would be for forest officials to use pack ponies. Government could hardly defend the use of utar by a money-making department which, if it continued to avail of begar, would hasten the end of the system.[16] Echoing the commissioner's sentiments, the Garhwal lawyer and legislative council member Taradutt Gairola pleaded for a 'vigorous policy of reform' failing which 'trouble [would] arise' at the revision of the revenue settlement.[17]

These warnings were to prove prophetic, but in the meantime the state hoped to rely on a series of ameliorative measures. The lieutenant-governor had in 1916 rejected the possibility of the utar system itself being scrapped; while it had caused 'hardship' in certain areas, the government, he emphasized,

[14] Petition to Sir James Meston, L-G, UP, by Pandit Madan Narayan Bist (village Ulaingad, patti Wallawigad, Almora), clerk on duty at the office of the director-general of archaeology at Ootacumund, 17 May 1913, GAD file 398/1913. Grammar and punctuation as in original.

[15] J. C. Scott, *The Moral Economy of the Peasant* (New Haven, 1976).

[16] 'Note on transport of Forest officials by Utar and pack ponies' by comm., KD, 17 August 1919, in file no. 21 of 1918–19, dept xv, Regional Archives, Nainital (RAN).

[17] 'Report of the Kumaun Sub Committee of the Board of Communications of coolie utar and bardaish in Kumaun', sd P. Wyndham, chairman, 9 October 1919; note on above report by T. D. Gairola, 17 October 1919, GAD file 739/1920, UPSA.

was concerned merely 'with checking any abuse of the system'.[18] In a move initiated by Gairola, coolie agencies were started in parts of Garhwal: by paying money into a common fund from which transport and supplies were arranged, villagers were not required to perform these tasks themselves.[19] In other parts registers were introduced to ensure that the utar burden did not fall disproportionately on any individual or village. Officers were advised to camp only at fixed places and procure grain from merchants subsidized by the government. Rules were framed prescribing what kinds of supplies could be indented for, and loads restricted to twelve pounds per coolie.[20] In a bid to 'raise the status of the soldier', retired and serving members of the Garhwal regiments were granted personal exemption from utar in 1900, although they were required to provide a substitute.[21] This was extended during World War I into an unconditional exemption for all combatant members of the 39th Garhwalis, and for the direct heirs of soldiers killed in battle.[22] The introduction of these 'palliatives which afford a considerable measure of relief', it was hoped, would ensure the continuance of the system itself.[23]

EARLY RESISTANCE TO FOREST MANAGEMENT

It is important to reiterate the dislocations in agrarian practices consequent on the imposition of forest management. The working of a forest for commercial purposes necessitates its division into blocks or coupés, which are completely closed after the trees are felled to allow regeneration to take place. Closure to men and cattle is regarded as integral to successful reproduc-

[18] Speech by Sir James Meston at durbar held in Nainital on 30 September 1916, GAD file 108/1918, UPSA.
[19] See, for example, 'Annual Report of the Coolie Agencies in Garhwal District for 1911–12', in GAD file 398/1913.
[20] No. 6544/xv/50, 10 October 1916, from comm., KD, to chief secretary, UP; 'Rules for touring officials in the hill pattis of the Kumaun Division', sd comm., 18 October 1916, both in ibid.
[21] No. 6056/xvi-19, 19 June 1900, from comm., KD, to chief secretary, NWP & O; no. 2503/1-303B, 4 August 1900, from chief secretary, NWP & O, to deputy adjutant general, Bengal, both in file no. 19 of 1899–1900, dept xvi, RAN.
[22] No. 1156/iii/398, 5 June 1916, from chief secretary, UP, to officers commanding 1st and 2nd 39th Garhwal Rifles, GAD file 398/1913.
[23] See note by under secretary to chief secretary, UP, 17 August 1913, in ibid.

tion, and grazing and lopping, if allowed, are regulated in the interests of the reproduction of favoured species of trees. Further, protection from fire is necessary to ensure the regeneration and growth to maturity of young saplings. Thus, the practice of firing the forests had to be regulated or stopped in the interests of sustained production of chir pine. While the exercise of rights, where allowed, was specified in elaborate detail, rightholders had the onerous responsibility, under section 78 of the act, of furnishing knowledge of forest offences to the nearest authority and of extinguishing fires, however caused, in the state forests. In general, as endorsed by the stringent provisions of the forest act, considerations of control were paramount (see chapter 3 for details).

We find evidence of protest at the contravention of traditionally held and exercised rights well before the introduction of forest management. Charcoal required for smelting iron in the mines of Kumaun was brought from neighbouring forests. Where these forests lay within village boundaries, villagers prevented wood being cut without the payment of malikhana.[24] And in the years following the constitution of the DPF in 1893, the deputy commissioner (DC) of Garhwal reported that 'forest administration consists for most part in a running fight with the villagers.'[25]

Even where discontent did not manifest itself in overt protest, the loss of control over forests was acutely felt. The forest settlement officer of British Garhwal commented thus at the time of the constitution of the reserved forests:

The notion obstinately persists in the minds of all, from highest to the lowest, that Government is taking away their forests from them and is robbing them of their own property. The notion seems to have grown up from the complete lack of restriction or control over the use by the people of waste land and forest during the first 80 years after the British occupation. The oldest inhabitant therefore and he

[24] J. O. B. Beckett, 'Iron and Copper Mines in the Kumaun Division', report of 31 January 1850, in *Selections*, vol. II, pp. 31–8. 'There is *not a single* malgoozar of any of the villages in the neighbourhood of the iron mines who has not at one time or other endeavoured to levy a tax on *all* the charcoal burners...' Ibid., 36, emphasis added.

[25] 'Note on forest administration for my successor', by McNair, DC, Garhwal, Feb. 1907, in FD file 11/1908, UPSA.

naturally is regarded as the greatest authority, is the most assured of the antiquity of the people's right to uncontrolled use of the forest; and to a rural community there appears no difference between uncontrolled use and proprietary right. Subsequent regulations—and these regulations are all very recent—only appear to them as a gradual encroachment on their rights, culminating now in a final act of confiscation . . . [My] best efforts however have, I fear, failed to get the people generally to grasp the change in conditions or to believe in the historical fact of government ownership.[26]

This brings out quite clearly that the root of the conflict between the state and hill villagers over forest rights lay in differing conceptions of property and ownership. There did not exist a developed notion of private property among these peasant communities, a notion particularly inapplicable to communally owned and managed woods and pasture land. In contrast, the state's assertion of monopoly over forests was undertaken at the expense of what British officials insisted were *individually* claimed rights of user. With the 'waste and forest lands never having attracted the attention of former governments',[27] there existed strong historical justification for the popular belief that all forests within village boundaries were 'the property of *the villagers*'.[28]

Discontent with the new forest regulations manifested itself in various other ways. The option of flight was considered by a group of villagers belonging to Tindarpur patti in Garhwal, who approached an English planter for land 'as the new forest regulations and restrictions were pressing on them so severely that they wished to migrate into another district and climate rather than put up with them any longer.'[29] Another time-honoured form of protest—non-compliance with imposed regulations—was evident when villagers gave misleading information at the time of fixation of rights.[30] As villagers were 'not

[26] J. C. Nelson, *Forest Settlement Report of the Garhwal District* (Lucknow, 1916), pp. 10–11.
[27] E. K. Pauw, *Report on the Tenth Settlement of the Garhwal District* (Allahabad, 1894), p. 52.
[28] T. D. Gairola, *Selected Revenue Decisions of Kumaun* (Allahabad, 1936), p. 211.
[29] District and sessions judge, Moradabad, to pvt. secretary to L-G, UP, 2 March 1916, in FD file 163/1916 (Forest Settlement Grievances in the KD), UPSA.
[30] According to the settlement officer, 'much was omitted and much exag-

in a frame of mind to give much voluntary assistance', one divisional forest officer (DFO) accurately predicted 'active resentment' at the fire protection of large areas and their closure to grazing and other rights.[31]

The year 1916 witnessed a number of 'malicious' fires in the newly constituted reserved forests. In May the forests in the Gaula range of Nainital division were set ablaze. The damage reported was exclusively in chir forests; 28,000 trees which were burnt had to be prematurely felled. For the circle as a whole it was estimated that at least 64 per cent of the 441 fires which burnt 388 square miles (as against 188 fires that had burnt 35 square miles in the preceding year) were 'intentional'.[32]

The 'deliberate and organized incendiarism' of the summer of 1916 brought home to the state the unpopularity of the forest settlement and the virtual impossibility of tracing those who were responsible for the fires. Numerous fires broke out simultaneously over large areas, and often the occurrence of one fire was the signal for general firing in the whole neighbourhood: 44 fires occurred in North Garhwal division, almost all in order to obtain a fresh crop of grass. In Nainital and in the old reserves of Airadeo and Binsar of Almora district—areas which had been fire-protected for many years—an established crop of seedlings was wiped out. The area chosen for attack had been under both felling and resin-tapping operations.[33] In Airadeo the fire continued for three days and two nights, with 'new fires being started time after time directly a counterfiring line was successfully completed'.[34] As a result of such 'in-

---

gerated, much extenuated and much set down in malice', while quarrels over rights 'were unfortunately always very bitter.' Nelson, 'Forest Settlement Report', pp. 2–4, 13, 25.

[31] A. E. Osmaston, *WP for the North Garhwal Forest Division, 1921–22 to 1930–31* (Allahabad, 1921), p. 67.

[32] *Report on the Administration of the United Provinces of Agra and Oudh, 1915–16* (Allahabad: Government Press, 1916), p. viii.

[33] *Annual Progress Report of the Forest Administration of the United Provinces* (hereafter APFD), 1915–16, p. 7.

[34] H. G. Champion, 'Observations on Some Effects of Fires in the *Chir* (*Pinus longifolia*) Forests of the West Almora Division', *Indian Forester*, vol. 45 (1919), pp. 353–63.

cendiarism' several thousand acres of forest were closed to all rights for a period of ten years.[35]

The protests against the forest settlement were viewed with apprehension in Lucknow, where the lieutenant-governor, anticipating the conclusion of World War I, observed that 'it would be a pity for the 39th Garhwalis to come home and find their villages seething with discontent.' Reporting on the situation the DC of Garhwal concluded, somewhat self-evidently, that government could not but affect village life in every patti by taking over the forests. The people's 'dislike of the forest department and the horde of new underlings let loose on the district' was shared by the soldiers, one of whom stated that if the war had ended before they left Europe they could have petitioned the king to rescind the settlement. The soldiers' discontent was evidently disturbing, for, as the district officer put it, 'if we can get them on our side it will be a great thing ... They are already a power in the land and will be still more a power after the war.'[36] The forest department continued to be complacent about the possibilities of such discontent blowing over when the villagers had 'greater familiarity with the true aim of the department'.[37] Alternatively, they pointed to the strategic and financial results obtained in a few years of commercial working.[38] Percy Wyndham, as the commissioner of Kumaun the senior official entrusted with law and order, was considerably less sanguine. He preferred that the hills continue to provide 'excellent men for sepoys, police and all such jobs'— a situation jeopardized by the forest department which had demarcated the 39th Garhwali villages as if 'the world were made for growing trees and men were vermin to be shut in'. In a situation where 'the Revenue Department holds the whole country by bluff', without the help of regular police, Wyndham was clearly not prepared to enforce new rules on a 'dissatisfied

[35] H. G. Champion, *WP for the Central Almora For. Div.* (Lucknow, 1922), pp. 13–14.

[36] J. C. Meston (lieutenant-governor) to comm., KD, 5 March 1916; DC, Garhwal to L-G, 27 March 1916; 'Note on the Forest Settlement and the Garhwali Officers of the Regiment', by DC, Garhwal, 20 March 1916, all in FD file 163/1916.

[37] GO no. 197/XIV/163, 14 February 1918, appended to APFD, 1916–17.

[38] See GO no. 114/XIVA/172 of 1918, 4 February 1919, appended to APFD, 1917–18.

people', preferring to do away with forest rules and staff altogether.[39]

Contravention of the new regulations concerning lopping, grazing and the duties of rightholders was, as Table 5.1 indicates, perhaps the most tangible evidence of the continuing friction. Figures from other forest circles are given by way of comparison. While the number of yearly convictions in the Kumaun circle far exceeded those obtained elsewhere, a comparison with 'criminal justice' in Kumaun itself is no less revealing. Over a ten-year period (1898–1908) an average of only

TABLE 5.1

Breaches of Forest Law in UP, 1911–22

Circle Year	Western circle A**	B**	Eastern circle A	B	Kumaun circle* A	B
1911–12	786	1798	1167	2306	958	2159
1912–13	881	2182	1230	2424	1203	3374
1913–14	1006	2091	1365	2905	1309	3864
1914–15	1248	2681	1646	3293	1671	5857
1915–16	1401	2662	1514	3029	1610	5796
1916–17	1368	2517	1636	2944	2023	10264
1917–18	1242	2364	1530	2777	2197	11046
1918–19	1153	2058	1723	3167	2167	11024
1919–20	1162	2120	1378	2773	2136	13457
1920–21	926	1618	901	2154	1723	10328
1921–22	1248	2437	1622	839	2070	3799***

* The total area of reserved forest in UP equalled 4.32 million acres, of which 1.91 million acres lay in the Kumaun circle.
** A = cases; B = convictions (persons).
*** Cases dropped due to the recommendation of the Kumaun Grievances Committee.
SOURCE: APFD, relevant years.

[39] Wyndham to Meston, 26 June 1916; *idem*, 3 July 1916; 'Subjects for discussion at the conference of selected officers to be held at Government House, Nainital at 10.30 a.m. on the 28th August 1916', sd P. Wyndham, 14 August 1916, all in FD file 163/1916.

416 persons was convicted annually in Almora district, on account of cognizable crime of all kinds, ranging from non-payment of excise to murder.[40] Indeed, with the absence of an adequate patrolling staff, many breaches of the forest law went undetected.[41] Underlying the stiff resistance to the regulations of the forest department was a tradition of hundreds of years of unrestricted use.[42]

The continuing opposition to forest administration bore a strong similarity to traditional methods of social protest in Kumaun and Garhwal. The forms of protest—flight, strikes, occasional attacks on officials, marches—as well as its moral idiom, which reflected the state's failure to meet traditional obligations, were integral to the indigenous form of collective resistance known as the dhandak (see chapter 4). As the distinctive form of social protest specific to this area, the dhandak continued to be used, albeit with variations, in both the colonial territory of British Kumaun and the princely state of Tehri Garhwal.

THE UTAR AND FOREST MOVEMENTS OF 1921

Meanwhile, village opposition to the begar system was matched organizationally by the establishment of the Kumaun Parishad in 1916. This association of local journalists, lawyers and intellectuals, chaired in its initial years by Rai Bahadurs professing loyalty to the King Emperor, underwent a rapid transformation with the setting up of the forest department and the increased requirement of customary services. The impact of village-level protest and, indirectly, of upsurges elsewhere in India, contributed to a growing radicalization of the Parishad, best exemplified in the person of Badridutt Pande of Almora. As Shekhar Pathak has compellingly shown, Pande, far more than other Kumaun nationalists (such as Govind Ballabh Pant), was acutely aware of the growing discontent amongst the peas-

[40] Figures calculated from H. G. Walton, *Almora: A Gazetteer* (Allahabad, 1911), appendix.
[41] See, for example, GO no. 123-XIV-209, 2 November 1922, appended to APFD, 1921-2.
[42] See APFD, 1919-20, p. 8; Osmaston, 'North Garhwal WP', p. 89.

antry.[43] Convinced of the futility of memoranda presented to government by a few individuals based in Almora, Pande and his associates sought to establish branches of the Parishad in the villages of Kumaun. Simultaneously, his weekly, *Shakti*, published from Almora, became an important forum in which the begar system and forest rules were made the butt of strident criticism.[44]

In 1920 *Shakti* reported a strike against utar by villages in patti Kairaro, with villagers refusing to pay the fine levied on them. At the annual session of the Kumaun Parishad, held at Kashipur in December 1920, a major conflict arose between those who still hoped to negotiate with the state and village representatives who pressed for direct action. After the reformists had walked out the latter urged Badridutt Pande and other Parishad leaders to come to the Uttaraini fair.[45] Held in mid January at Bageshwar, the temple town at the confluence of the Saryu and Gomati rivers, this fair annually attracted fifteen to twenty thousand pilgrims from all over the hills.

Here, matters came to a head. In early January the conservator of forests was refused coolies at Dwarahat and Ganai, and, anticipating a strike, the DC of Almora, W. C. Dible, urgently asked government for a declaration of its future policy —a request summarily dismissed.[46] At Bageshwar a crowd of over ten thousand heard Badridutt pass on a message from Mahatma Gandhi that 'he would come and save them from oppression as he did in Champaran.' When almost everyone responded to a call to raise their hands to show that they would refuse utar, Pande continued: 'After abolishing coolie utar they would agitate for the forests. He would ask them not to extract

[43] However, most Parishad leaders were small landholders, like the majority of their kinsmen, and perhaps less alienated from the villages than urban nationalists in many other parts of India. See G. B. Pant's evidence to the *Royal Commission on Agriculture in India* (London, 1927), vol. III, p. 360.

[44] Shekhar Pathak, *Badridutt Pande aur Unka Yug* (Lucknow, 1982), pp. 12–24. Hereafter Pathak (3).

[45] Pathak (2), pp. 22–4. Prominent among the village activists was Mohan Singh Mehta of Katyur.

[46] HC no. C.3, Bageshwar, 17 January 1921, from DC, Almora, to comm., KD; extract from confidential fortnightly report of comm., KD, 10 January 1921, both in police department (PD) file 1151/1921, UPSA.

resin, or saw sleepers, or take forest contracts. They should give up service as forest guards which involves insulting their sisters and snatching their sickles.' Slogans in praise of Mahatma Gandhi and 'Swatantra Bharat' and cries that the government was 'anniyayi' (unjust) filled the air.[47] In a dramatic gesture, village headmen flung their coolie registers into the Saryu.[48]

In the weeks following the fair, several officials were stranded when the villages neighbouring Bageshwar declined to supply coolies. Elsewhere, only *khushkharid* (on payment) coolies were available, at extraordinarily high rates. With schoolmasters and other government functionaries extending their support to the movement, Dible hastily summoned the regular police.[49] Pathak has uncovered evidence of at least 146 anti-begar meetings in different villages of Garhwal and Kumaun, held between 1 January and 30 April 1921.[50] When the DFO of Almora complained of the continuing difficulties faced by touring officials, he was tersely told that the district administration was not in a position to 'give you or your department one utar coolie'.[51] Requests for utar were not made in tracts when they were likely to be refused.[52] In a matter of weeks the state's determination not to dispense with the system itself had broken down, and its abolition followed. In the following year over 1.6 lakh rupees were spent by the exchequer on the transport and stores of touring officials in the hills.[53]

The resistance to utar mirrored similar opposition in parts of Java, Africa and New Guinea, where attempts by colonial regimes to extract corvée labour were often met with sullen resentment. As in Kumaun, peasants sometimes expressed the

[47] Summary of Badridutt Pande's speech at Bageshwar, by S. Ijaz Ali, deputy collector, Almora, in ibid.

[48] Pathak (2), p. 28.

[49] DC, Almora, to comm., KD, no. C.3, 17 January 1921; *idem*, no. C.4, 20 January 1921; no. 43, CL.21, 29 January 1921, from comm., KD, to chief secretary, UP, all in PD file 1151/1921.

[50] Pathak (1), appendix III.

[51] No. 42, C.I.21, 28 January 1921, from comm., KD, to DFO, Almora, in PD file 1151/1921.

[52] Comm., KD, to secretary to government, UP, 4 March 1921, in GAD file 739/1920.

[53] Resolution passed by UP legislative council on 5 March 1921; table on transport of officers in camp, 1921-2, enclosed with DO no. 215, 17 June 1922, from comm., KD, to deputy secretary, GAD, UP, both in ibid.

REBELLION AS CONFRONTATION 113

wish that whites should carry their own loads, and in extreme cases, by striking, made this inescapable. The sentiments of Sindano, a Watchtower-movement preacher in Zambia during World War I, could serve equally well as an expression of the anti-utar campaign conducted around the same time in Kumaun and Garhwal: 'There they are, they who overburden us with loads, and beat us like slaves, but a day will come when they will be the slaves.'[54] However, in the Himalayan case resistance to corvée labour was greatly intensified by its association with the major indignity peasants had to suffer at the hands of colonial rulers: the loss of control over forests. And, as the press communiqué issued by the UP government emphasized, the growth of the forest department, with all that this implied for the social and economic life of the hill peasant, was at the root of the anti-begar movement.[55]

Peasant opposition to utar was conducted at a different level and for quite different reasons from that symbolized by the periodic memoranda—appealing to the instincts of a benign and civilized government—that liberal nationalists continued to submit to the state.[56] An English planter based in Kausani reported that while Hargovind Pant, an Almora lawyer, was asking that coolies be not supplied for utar, village leaders were prepared to go even further. Thus, local activists insisted that no coolies should be supplied at all, i.e. they were against khushkharid coolies as well.[57] After Bageshwar, the DC of Almora was tersely informed by a group of padhans that they had refused to supply coolies in order to compel attention to their grievances, chief among which was the taking away of their forests. Dible reported that proposals for closure to grazing had much to do with this intense feeling. A fund had

[54] Karen Fields, *Revival and Rebellion in Colonial Central Africa* (Princeton, 1985), p. 135; see also S. Moertono, *State and Statecraft in Old Java* (Ithaca, 1968), p. 75; Peter Worsley, *The Trumpet Shall Sound* (London, 1957), pp. 104–6.

[55] 'In recent years, mainly owing to the rapid expansion of the Forest Department, the demands for utar have greatly increased and the obligations of furnishing utar has caused growing resentment.' Press communiqué, 1 February 1921, sd H. S. Crosthwaite, secretary to government, UP, in GAD file 739/1920.

[56] See memorandum on coolie utar submitted by Kumaun Association (Ranikhet branch) to L-G, UP, 16 October 1920, in ibid.

[57] Letter from R. G. Bellaire, colonization officer of Soldier Settlement Estates, Kausani, to DC, Almora, 1 February 1921, in PD file 1151/1921.

been created by the villagers—anticipating punitive action—for defending anyone against whom the state had initiated proceedings, and for paying fines where they were inflicted.[58] While this unity and sense of purpose necessarily made their actions political, the politics of the peasantry was clearly not derivative of the politics of urban nationalism. Apart from a hazy perception of Gandhi as a saint whose qualities of heroic sacrifice were invoked against the inimical powers of government,[59] the utar movement had little in the nature of an identification with the Congress as such.

The Forest Movement of 1921

Following Uttaraini, Pande and his colleagues toured the different pattis of Almora, establishing local *sabhas* of the Parishad. Inspired by the success of the anti-utar campaign, Pande urged in his speeches the need for direct action in order to recover lost rights over forests. For, the 'government that sells the forest produce is not liable to be called a real government' —indeed, it was precisely these mercenary motives which had made God send Gandhi 'as an incarnation in the form of Bania to conquer Bania government'.[60] As the reference to Gandhi's caste indicates, the term 'bania' evoked images of power as well as deception; by selling forest produce the state was hastening the erosion of the legitimacy it had earlier enjoyed in the eyes of the peasantry. At Bageshwar Badridutt had depicted this transition in tellingly effective symbols. When forest resources and grass were plentiful and easily available, villagers had an abundance of food and drink. But now, he said, 'in place of tins of ghee the forest department gives them tins of resin.'[61]

---

[58] DC, Almora, to comm., KD, 17 January 1921; *idem*, no. C.15, 24 January 1921, both in ibid.; Wyndham was clear that 'the root of the whole evil and discontent is our d——d forest policy': no. 2, C.11.21, 1 February 1921, from comm., KD, to chief secretary, UP, in ibid.

[59] Cf. Govind Chatak, *Garhwali Lok Geet* (Dehradun, 1956), pp. 261–2.

[60] 'Report of Pandit Badridutt Editor's Speeches to Villagers in Almora District', in PD file 1151/1921.

[61] See criminal case no. 7 of 1921, *King Emperor vs. Motiram, Budhanand and Badridutt* of Totashiling, at police station Palla Boraraw, in the court of W. C. Dible, district magistrate, Almora, 7 July 1921, in FD file 157/1921 ('Forest fires in Kumaun'), UPSA. The implication, if it needs to be spelled out, was that while the forests had earlier supplied products like ghee and thus contributed to the

Sensing the peasantry's mood after the utar strike, Dible had with uncanny prescience predicted the shape of the impending agitation: '[The] next move will be against the Forest Department. Agitators will make a dead set for resin coolies and contractors' coolies engaged in sleeper work, and try to drive them from this work. The people will be incited to commit Forest offences and we shall have serious trouble with fires.' In the coming months breaches of the forest law increased daily. These included not merely the firing of forests for grass but also 'wholesale cutting of trees'.[62] In British Garhwal, too, the popular feeling against the forest policy continued to be 'very bitter'.[63]

The summer of 1921 was one of the driest on record. The failure of the winter rains had contributed to a poor *rabi* crop and money was sanctioned as subsistence *taccavi* in the hill districts.[64] In Totashilling, where the campaign was to be at its most intense, the local branch of the Kumaun Parishad passed a resolution that the people were themselves to decide whether or not to set fire to forest land falling within 'san assi' boundaries.[65] From the last week of April a systematic campaign, especially in Almora district, had been launched for firing the forest. When called upon (under section 78 of the forest act) to assist in extinguishing these blazes, villagers instead directed their energies towards helping the fire to spread. As a consequence the attempted fire protection by the forest department of commercially worked areas was a major failure. Of 4 lakh acres of forest in which fire protection was attempted, 2.46 lakh acres were burnt over.[66] The machinery

---

local economy, now they were used to produce resin which was of no use to villagers. The use of such a metaphor, it may be added, reiterates the strong emphasis placed on village autonomy.

[62] DC, Almora, to comm., KD, no. C.15, 24 January 1921; *idem*, no. C.63, 2 March 1921, both in PD file 1151/1921.

[63] Extract from fortnightly DO from comm., KD, for second half of March 1921, FD file 157/1921.

[64] See file no. 56 of 1921, A. Progs, nos. 1–2, May 1921, dept of revenue and agriculture (famine), NAI.

[65] See resolution printed in the *Shakti* of 12 April 1921 (extract found in FD file 157/1921). All archival sources in the rest of this chapter, unless mentioned otherwise, are from this source.

[66] Fortnightly DO no. CY.21, 23 May 1921, from comm., KD, to chief

for control of forest offences 'more or less broke down', and an estimated total of 819 offences occurred, of which 395 were definitely known to be 'incendiary'.[67]

Several features of a form of social protest summarily labelled 'incendiarism' by the state merit comment. On the one hand incendiarism represented an assertion of traditionally exercised rights—the annual firing of the forest floor—circumscribed by the state in the interests of commercial forestry. On the other the areas burnt over were almost exclusively chir pine forests being worked for both timber and resin, this wholesale burning of the chir reserves representing, as Wyndham acknowledged, a 'direct challenge to government to relax their control over forests'.[68] The intensification of the campaign in Almora and Nainital was confined to those areas well served by a network of roads that had been under commercial working for some time. When fires swept through nearly all the areas being logged, young regeneration was wiped out. Covering nearly 320 square miles of forest, these fires destroyed 11.5 lakh resin channels and 65,000 maunds of resin.[69] At the same time, there is no evidence that the vast extent of broad-leaved forests, also under the control of the state, was at all affected. As in other societies in different historical epochs, this destruction by arson was not simply a nihilistic release, but carefully selective in the targets attacked. As Eric Hobsbawm has argued, such destruction is never indiscriminate, for 'what is useful for poor men'—in this instance broad-leaved species far more than chir—is spared.[70]

A striking analogy with the burning of resin depots comes from nineteenth-century France, when peasants' rights in the forest were curtailed in favour of producing wood for iron forges. Believing that the 'wood supplying the forges was in the domain of their traditional rights of usage', villagers burnt the

---

secretary, UP; DO no. 348, 28 May 1921, from chief conservator of forests (CCF), UP, to governor, UP; no. 53-CC/xiv-1, 2 June 1921, from offg CF, Kumaun circle, to CCF, UP.

[67] APFD, 1921–2, pp. 7–8.

[68] DO no. 31.C.vi.21, 9 June 1921, from comm., KD, to home member, UP.

[69] S. B. Bhatia, *WP for the East Almora Forest Division 1924–25 to 1933–34* (Allahabad, 1926), p. 41.

[70] See his *Primitive Rebels* (3rd edn, Manchester, 1974), pp. 25–6.

forges to the ground.[71] Iron forges in nineteenth-century France, and resin depots in Kumaun a century later, both represented commercial uses of the forest that were taking priority over earlier subsistence-oriented uses. In either case this change, fostered from above, was fiercely resisted by peasants denied traditional rights of access and use. Indeed, as the analysis of court cases by the collector of Almora indicates, the act of burning the chir forests represented a direct confrontation with the colonial authorities. The decision to burn the commercially worked areas was predicated not merely on their containing the locally almost useless (in comparison with oak) chir pine. As Badridutt Pande well understood, the export of forest produce by the state clashed strongly with the subsistence orientation of the hill peasant. In the collector's classification—typical in its detail of the concern of the colonial state to understand, with a view to suppressing, any sign of protest—the fire cases were broken down into the headings shown in Table 5.2.[72]

Further details which may reveal more about the nature of protest can be gleaned from summary accounts of court cases. Gangua, aged sixteen, was one of the several youths 'put up by non-co-operators' to destroy 'valuable regeneration areas' by fire. Nor was participation restricted to men: thus, one Durga was sentenced to a month in jail when she 'deliberately set fire to Thaklori forest'. In at least four different instances, witnesses set up by the prosecution were 'won over' by non-co-operators and the cases had to be dropped. Chanar Singh and four others of the Tagnia clan of Doba Talla, Katyur, were 'affected by lectures' by 'Non-cooperators and a Jogi' and set fire to regeneration areas. This tantalizingly brief reference to the yogi, who was later prosecuted, leads one to speculate that the peasantry sought, as in the Uttaraini mela, a moral/religious sanction for their acts. No such sanction was required by Padam Singh and Dharam Singh of Katyur, awarded the

---

[71] John Merriman, 'The Demoiselles of the Ariege, 1829–1831', in Merriman (ed.), *1830 in France* (New York, 1975), pp. 102–3.

[72] This extremely revealing classification and the following paragraph are taken from the two 'Statements on fire cases in Almora', W. C. Dible, 23 July 1921 and 3 November 1921, respectively. Unfortunately, similar details could not be traced for Nainital and Garhwal.

TABLE 5.2

Fire Cases in Almora, 1921

Head	No. of cases	No. of persons involved
I. INTENTIONAL		
(A) To paralyse forest department (FD) by destroying valuable areas	8	21
(B) To cause loss to FD by way of revenge due to hatred	26	45
(C) To have good grass for cattle	11	17
(D) To cause loss to resin mates out of enmity	2	3
(E) To spite another out of enmity	3	5
(F) Whose agitation was direct cause of fire	NA	13
TOTAL	50	104
II. ACCIDENTAL (This includes smoking or carrying fire within the reserves, the spread of fire from cultivated fields or waste and not under government, etc).	23	45

SOURCE: Forest department (FD), file 157/1921, UPSA.

maximum sentence of seven years rigorous imprisonment, who expressed their opposition to state monopoly in no uncertain terms. In the words of the magistrate: 'The compartment fired was near the village and used by them. They resented the work of the Department in this compartment since it interfered with their use of the compartment. Therefore they set fire to it deliberately.'[73]

The firing of pine needles for grass occurred in Garhwal as well. With commercial forestry and the protection of regeneration areas from grazing and fire as yet restricted in their operations, the damage to the state-controlled forests was not as widespread as in Almora. Yet the DC had convicted 549 persons, 45 for 'direct or indirect incendiarism' and 504 for

[73] Cf. Eric Hobsbawm on the Luddites: 'In some cases, indeed, resistance to the machine was quite consciously resistance to the machine in the hands of the capitalist.' See his *Labouring Men* (London, 1964), p. 10.

refusing to extinguish fires, before the recommendations of the grievances committee led to all pending cases being dropped. Fires were reported to be most acute in the areas bordering Almora, and in the southern pattis of Lansdowne subdivision in the outer hills. With resin-tapping in its infancy, fires were most often started with a view to obtaining fresh grass.[74]

While all social groups participated, the involvement of soldiers in the forest movement of 1921—in the same way as the participation of village headmen in the utar campaign— bore witness to the failure of the attempt by the colonial state to create an indigenous collaborating élite. Like leaders of cargo cults in Melanesia, these soldiers were not always leaders in the old authority structure. However, they had a special experience of white rule, one that enabled them to exercise a moral claim on the rulers. When this claim was ignored and the forest regulations not withdrawn, expectation quickly turned to outrage; in consequence, soldiers were in the forefront of the opposition to commercial forest management. Like the demobilized soldiers who led their fellow peasants in the Mexican Revolution, these hill soldiers were 'proud veterans now and still full of fight, their revolutionary consciousness ironically enhanced by the official discharge papers they carried, [who] went back home as missionaries of the new unruliness'.[75] Thus, in Garhwal the fires were most often started by soldiers on leave, but as '99% of the population sympathized with them', their apprehension by the authorities became an impossible task.[76] After the Uttaraini mela, ex-soldiers were active among those who helped the Kumaun Parishad form sabhas in the villages of the Kosi valley. One soldier said in his speeches that 'Government was not a Raja, but a Bania and Rakshasi Raj and the King Emperor was Ravan.' Recounting his experiences in Europe, where he was wounded, the pensioner described the visit of the King Emperor to his hospital bedside. Asked to state his grievances, 'he complained against *Patwaris* and forest

[74] 'Fire cases in Garhwal district', sd P. Mason, DC, Garhwal, 9 September 1921; DC, Garhwal, to secretary, government of UP, 29 December 1921; DO no. 31.C.v.21, 9 June 1921, from comm., KD, to home member, UP.

[75] Worsley, *Trumpet*, p. 69; John Womack, *Zapata and the Mexican Revolution* (New York, 1969), p. 101.

[76] DC, Garhwal, to secretary to government, UP, 7 September 1921.

guards but all that has been given is the Rowlatt Act and Martial Law.'[77] No longer was the king perceived as being bestowed with the quasi-divine powers of intervening to restore justice and a harmonious relationship between the state and the peasant. As expressed through the symbolism of the epics, the government now embodied not merely the rapacious bania but the evil-intentioned demons of Hindu mythology. Ravan, the very personification of evil, was equated with the King Emperor, whose failure (or inability) to stem the expansive growth of the forest department and its minions had led to a rapid fall from grace.

SOCIAL PROTEST: 1921-42

The constitution of the Kumaun Forest Grievances Committee in the wake of the 1921 movement evoked mixed reactions in the hill districts. Meetings held at different villages expressed dissatisfaction at the composition of the committee. Soldiers who had voiced their resentment while fighting in Europe and figured prominently in the 1921 movement continued to be in the forefront of the opposition to forest policy. While the committee had only one non-official member, Jodh Singh, he too was regarded as being more on the side of the government than the people.[78] The chairman, Commissioner Wyndham, also came in for criticism for his attempts to drive a wedge between the two dominant communities in the hills, Rajputs and Brahmins. A famed shikari, Wyndham was held to be ignorant of 'true justice' (*asli-nyaya*). An example of his insensitivity to public opinion was provided by the 1918 report on qulibardaish, which he framed without asking the opinion of the inhabitants of Kumaun. As a consequence, the people had to take the initiative in stopping utar.[79]

As the committee did not contain any representative of the people, several villages resolved to boycott its sittings. A form was circulated, to be filled in by different villages in Garhwal and submitted to the KFGC. The form provided for the designation of different plots of forest near every village, over each of

[77] FD file 156/1921 ('Forest fires in Kumaun'), UPSA.
[78] *Garhwali* (hereafter GRH), 7 May and 21 May 1921.
[79] A. P. Bahuguna, 'Kumaun aur Janglat ki Committee', GRH, 21 May 1921.

which peasants would have exclusive rights of fuel, fodder, building timber and wood for agricultural implements, bamboos for basket-making and other crafts, and so on. It asked for villages to be given full rights over nearby forests, which would be managed by the panchayats. Further, it designated forests where afforestation could be carried out by the villagers themselves. Finally, the form asked the government to provide a forest patrol to each village to aid in protection.[80]

The committee itself toured the three hill districts in May–August 1921, examining 5040 witnesses in all. A particular source of bitterness related to the treatment of women and children who committed the bulk of the forest 'offences', but who did not appear in court as per custom. Attempts by forest officials to prevent them from lopping and cutting grass were greatly resented. Complaints were also made against the reservation of temple trees and oak groves which villagers had conserved for their own use. In some instances, forest boundary pillars were placed too close to cultivation, while 'in other cases the outcry against the forest pillars had been caused by a desire to get a freedom from the rules and restrictions which these pillars represent rather than by an existing need for more land.' The oft repeated act of the removal of these pillars symbolized the perceived threat to peasant autonomy and sovereignty that forest reservation represented.[81] In the circumstances, the committee concluded that 'any attempt to strictly enforce these [forest] rules would lead to riot and bloodshed.' It recommended the division of the existing reserved forests into two categories:

(1) Class I—containing forests of little or no commercial importance; (2) Class II—containing forests stocked with chir, sal, deodar, kail and other commercially exploitable species. In Class I reserves, management was to be almost nominal.[82] Of the existing forests, 1986 square miles were covered by Class II and 1090 square miles by Class I forests, respectively.

Table 5.3 gives details regarding breaches of forest rules during 1926–33, i.e. after the recommendations of the KFGC had taken effect. Several features merit comment. Forest

[80] 'Garhwal Janta ki Janglat Sambandi Mang', GRH, 18 June 1921.
[81] See Bhatia, 'East Almora WP', for details.
[82] KFGC, pp. 2–10.

TABLE 5.3

Breaches of Forest Law in UP, 1926-33

Year	Kumaun circle Cases	Convictions	Eastern circle Cases	Convictions	Western circle Cases	Convictions
1926–27	1919	3661	1470	3078	1440	2646
1927–28	1992	3786	1435	3167	1568	2809
1928–29	2545	5482	1418	2740	1334	2323
1929–30	2675	6019	1457	3148	1531	2600
1930–31	2511	4500	1705	3821	1299	2226
1931–32	2534	5514	1621	3170	1524	2629
1932–33	2629	5968	1928	3085	1681	2871

SOURCE: APFD, relevant years.

offences in Kumaun circle still consistently exceeded those in the two other circles of UP. Although the area under which the old restrictions operated fell away sharply, better supervision was possible in the commercial Class II forests to which attention was now confined. A comparison with Table 5.1 is instructive, as summarized below:

Period	Cases per year	Convictions per year
1916–22	2053	9986
1926–33	2401	4990

While there is an increase to the order of 17 per cent in cases per year, there is a corresponding decrease in the latter period of 40 per cent in convictions obtained. A plausible inference one can make is that while better supervision enabled detection of individual cases of infringement, such as fuel and fodder collection, collective or group infringement was no longer so common. The latter would typically include collective grazing of village cattle, burning of the forest floor, and failure to inform the authorities when a forest fire occurred. With the large area of Class I under light supervision, these activities were no longer as liable to be deemed infringements of the law. Another contributory factor was the introduction of controlled departmental burning (cf. chapter 3). In 1928-9, for example, 81,000 acres were departmentally burnt in Kumaun circle, of which 35,000 acres were burnt with unpaid voluntary labour.[83]

An outbreak of what the state still preferred to call 'incendiarism' or 'malicious firing' did, however, take place in both 1930 and 1931. In the summer of 1930 a large number of fires occurred in regeneration areas of Almora district, notably within a few miles radius of Bageshwar, venue of the historic Uttaraini mela. Interestingly, the burning of the forest was contrary to the wishes of the Congress leaders. Of 63 fires that burnt 15,591 acres, 58 occurred in the two forest divisions of East and West Almora. As in 1921, peasants concentrated on the most vulnerable state-held areas—thus 21 per cent of the area under chir regeneration was burnt.[84] According to a later estimate the reserved forests were fired 157 times, with 37,000 acres of chir regeneration (or 50 per cent of the total) being destroyed.[85]

The campaign in 1931 was more widespread, with the abnormally hot weather favouring the spread of fires. It was observed that 'burning the hill forests in a dry year is so easy and the results obtained with the minimum of exertion so large that it is one of the first ways in which any general feeling of unrest manifests itself.' Not so localized, the campaign spread to the Kosi, Gaula and Ladhia valleys of Nainital, apart from Almora and some parts of Garhwal. Of 89 fires that burnt 38,512 acres, 34 occurred in Nainital, 49 in the two Almora divisions, and 6 in Garhwal.[86]

The year 1931 witnessed a burst of nationalist activity, coinciding with the Civil Disobedience movement. A procession bearing the national tricolour made its way from one end of the Nainital lake to the other. In Almora, on 25 May, an attempt to hoist the flag on the municipal board building was foiled by the police. The next day there was a lathi charge when a crowd tried again to mount the tricolour at the same venue.[87] In

[83] See APFD, 1928-9, pp. 5-9.
[84] APFD, 1929-30, pp. 8-9.
[85] See F. C. Ford Robertson, *Our Forests* (Allahabad, 1936).
[86] APFD, 1931-2, pp. 4-6, etc.
[87] D. S. Manral, *Swatantra Sangram mein Kumaun-Garhwal ka Yogdan* (Bareilly, 1978), pp. 70-4.

Garhwal shops were closed in several towns when Mahatma Gandhi was arrested upon the completion of the Dandi march.[88] The incarceration of the popular local leader Anusuya Prasad Bahuguna in August provoked a *hartal* or general strike in Badrinath town. A half mile long line of demonstrators hoisted the tricolour on the highest point of the Badrinath temple. Unnerved, the rawal or head priest sent telegrams to both the Tehri raja and the commissioner of Kumaun.[89]

Simultaneously, there was opposition by villagers to the new land settlement, which had enhanced revenue by as much as 30 per cent. In Salt patti of Almora district, labourers were asked not to work for forest contractors. Several hundred villagers went to the forest to enforce a collective decision to excommunicate anyone who did work. This culminated in a scuffle with the police and many arrests. In Garhwal telegraph wires were cut in Dontiyal and protests organized in Dugadda.[90]

The next major wave of protest occurred during the Quit India movement of 1942, when Almora was perhaps one of the most active districts in the state. Several strikes were organized in the towns. In Deghat police fired and killed two members of a crowd protesting the arrest of their leader. When the patwari of Salem, one of the most active pattis, fled, villagers burnt his records. A force sent to quell them was repulsed by the villagers, who confiscated their weapons. Another force comprising white soldiers was dispatched, but this force too was engaged by the villagers using sticks and stones. Two villagers were killed in the battle. In Salem's neighbouring patti of Salt, police fired on satyagrahis, prompting Gandhi to call the patti India's second Bardoli.[91]

A favourite target of the 1942 rebellion continued to be the forest department. Totashiling in Katyur, one of the most active localities in 1921, witnessed the burning of a resin depot. In Nainital district youths cut telephone wires and burnt the Mangoli forest rest house and the dak bungalow at Ramnagar.

[88] GRH, 17 May 1930.
[89] GRH, 9 August 1930.
[90] Manral, *Swatantra Sangram*, pp. 75–7; S. C. Dabral, *Uttarakhand ka Itihas*, vol. 8, pt 2 (Dugadda, n.d.,) pp. 251–3.
[91] Manral, *Swatantra Sangram*, pp. 85–93.

The office of the conservator of forests also went up in flames. In Garhwal the forest bungalow in Siyasen and the post office at Chamoli were burnt. Telegraph wires were also cut. An elaborate plan, never carried out, was framed to burn all the timber godowns from Hardwar in the west to Ramnagar in the east.[92]

The relative freedom enjoyed by the peasantry following the recommendations of the KFGC undoubtedly contributed to the diminution of social protest in the years following 1921. At the same time, Kumaun was more fully incorporated in the orbit of colonial capitalism, as males migrated outwards to be employed in the British Indian Army and in the lower echelons of the colonial administration. Yet the specific episodes mentioned above do exhibit a marked continuity with the rather more concentrated activity of 1916-21. Arson, neither haphazard nor indiscriminate, continued to be aimed at symbols of authority, such as forest offices or rest houses, or at points where the state was most vulnerable, e.g. chir areas under regeneration or, latterly, channels of communication. No less striking was the refusal of the peasantry to merge fully with the structured and highly restrictive stream of Congress nationalism. While the spread of Congress activities played a role in the 1930 and 1942 movements, the defiance of orders from 'above' during 'incendiary' campaigns and the violent episodes of 1942 —which, it must be admitted, were in conformity with the countrywide character of Quit India[93]—testify to the imperfect control exercised by the Congress over peasant protest.

FROM CUSTOM TO CONFRONTATION

In their recent work, the Americans Michael Adas and James Scott have made a powerful case for the systematic study of forms of protest that minimize the element of confrontation between the peasantry and instituted authority. What Scott calls 'everyday forms of peasant resistance' and Adas 'avoidance protest' embrace a wide variety of protest forms, all of which

[92] Ibid; Dabral, *Uttarakhand*, pp. 288-90.
[93] See C. S. Mitra, 'Political Mobilization and the Nationalist Movement in Eastern Uttar Pradesh and Bihar 1937-42', unpublished D.Phil. thesis, Oxford University, 1983.

stop short of directly challenging the legitimacy of the rulers.[94] Clearly, as the extraordinarily rich material collected by Scott in rural Malaysia suggests, avoidance protest is more easily discerned through ethnographic research in contemporary societies. However, while the archival record may obscure, it can never completely eliminate evidence of everyday resistance. As elaborated in this chapter, many of the weapons of the weak described by Scott for Malaysia—including foot-dragging, false compliance, feigned ignorance, migration, breaches of the law, and social appeals to 'custom'—were effectively used by Himalayan villagers in thwarting the aims of colonial forestry. Yet my evidence also suggests that, over a period of time, peasants tended to discard these weapons in favour of more open and confrontational forms of protest: attacks on channels of communication, on state buildings, and most frequently on commercial forests and resin depots. This transformation in strategies of resistance was accompanied by a radical change in cultural perceptions of the overlord. Undoubtedly, the first century of British rule and the paternalist style of officials like Henry Ramsay may have seen a partial transference of an allegiance earlier owed to native kings. If early resistance drew on the dhandak tradition, by 1921 hill villagers were viewing the British authorities in distinctly unfavourable terms, equating the King Emperor with the very personification of evil, Ravan.

Nowhere was this transformation in rebel consciousness and forms of resistance more explicitly manifested than in the radicalization of an organization originally set up to mediate between the state and the peasantry. Established in the afterglow of the Coronation Durbar of 1911, the Kumaun Parishad initially swore undying loyalty to George Pancham (George V).[95] But the pressure from below, as it were, egged the Parishad leaders, and most noticeably among them Badridutt Pande, to adopt a more directly confrontationist position. By July 1921 their philosophy was being described as 'the anarchist doctrine

---

[94] Michael Adas, 'From Avoidance to Confrontation: Peasant Protest in Precolonial and Colonial South-east Asia', *Comparative Studies in Society and History (CSSH)*, vol. 23, no. 2, 1981; J. C. Scott, *Weapons of the Weak: Everyday Forms of Peasant Resistance* (New Haven, 1986).

[95] The Coronation Durbar was a lavish spectacle held in Delhi to commemorate the accession of George V.

of direct action, which has been attempted in England by Labour Revolutionaries'.[96] Clearly, such a situation had been brought about by the 'inherent' elements of folk or popular ideology impinging upon, and transforming in the process, the 'derived' elements originating in the sphere of organized politics.[97] In this instance, at least, 'primitive' rebellion proved to be several steps ahead of 'modern nationalism', the rationale of its acts and the success which attended them being attested by the rapidity with which the state capitulated on both the begar and forest issues.

What are the sociological factors that explain the transition from custom to confrontation in the social history of protest in Kumaun? While early resistance may have utilized the idiom of the dhandak, Kumaun peasants later displayed, like their counterparts in Tokugawa Japan, 'the capacity, language and organisational ability to create a new world view when the old was inconsistent with reality'.[98] Evidence from other societies suggests that the fabric of customary rebellion normally contains within it the latitude for rebels to step outside the traditional relationship of dominance and subordination and challenge the very foundations of authority. Thus,

to express rebellion against a lawful master the Javanese used the words *mbalik* (lit. to turn around and stand face to face), *mbeka* (to be recalcitrant), *mbalka* (to revolt), and the phrase *madeq kranan*, which can be translated as 'to set up one's own government', obviously with the purpose of establishing a new and independent territorial power or even a new government challenging an existing one.[99]

Closer to Kumaun, in the Hindu kingdom of Kathiawad in western India, peasants would resort to one of two kinds of protest against the government: (*i*) *risaaman*, indicating 'the

---

[96] Dible to Wyndham, DO no. C355, 24 July 1921, in FD file 157/1921, UPSA.

[97] These terms have been used by George Rudé, following Gramsci, in his *Ideology and Popular Protest* (London, 1980). Rudé, like some other historians, is rather more conscious of instances where 'derived' elements transform folk ideology.

[98] Irwin Scheiner, 'Benevolent Lords and Honorable Peasants: Rebellion and Peasant Consciousness in Tokugawa Japan', in Tetsuo Najita and Irwin Scheiner (eds), *Japanese Thought in the Tokugawa Period, 1600–1868* (Chicago, 1978).

[99] S. Moertono, *State and Statecraft in Old Java* (Ithaca, 1968), pp. 78–9, emphasis added.

temporary severing of relations between intimate friends or family members in order to emphasize one's grievances which, when applied to politics, led to peaceful protest and petition'; and (ii) *baharvatiya*, literally going outside the law—this implied the use of violence or other confrontational forms of protest.[100]

Its flexible 'repertoire of contention', to use Charles Tilly's phrase, throws further doubt on the interpretation of customary rebellion as a periodic release of discontent crucial to the integration and persistence of a society. What is more germane to our purposes, perhaps, is that the transition from 'avoidance' to 'confrontational' resistance in Kumaun followed a pattern quite similar to that observed in other colonial contexts. In Cochin China, for example, resistance to French colonialism in the early decades of this century 'passed from deferential petitioning in the tradition of Confucianism to an insurrection along anarchist lines'.[101] In Kumaun, as in Vietnam, Burma, Indonesia, and other parts of India, the imposition of colonial rule represented, in the Weberian sense, a transfer from traditional to legal/rational structures of authority. Traditional patterns of authority had, on the one hand, been flexible in their claims on peasant subsistence, and, on the other, bound by a cultural and personalized idiom of reciprocity. Under colonialism, however, a centralized and bureaucratic state apparatus increasingly impinged on village life; the rationalized and uniform tax structure, and the takeover of forests and other natural resources, rendered villagers far more vulnerable to economic fluctuations. As in Dutch-ruled Java, therefore, peasant risings in Kumaun 'can be regarded as protest movements against intruding Western economic and political control which were undermining the fabric of traditional society.'[102]

---

[100] Howard Spodek, 'On the Origins of Gandhi's Political Methodology: The Heritage of Kathiawad and Gujarat', *Journal of Asian Studies*, vol. 30, no. 2, February 1971.

[101] Scott, *Moral Economy*, p. 125.

[102] See Sartono Kartodirdjo, *The Peasant Revolt of Banten in 1888* (The Hague, 1966), pp. 3, 21–2, 28, 67, 94, 106, 321–2, etc. The framework of this fine work anticipates both the neo-Weberianism of Scott and Adas and the 'history from below' of the Subaltern Studies school; despite its unfortunate neglect by later scholars, it is a germinal contribution to the sociology of peasant resistance under colonialism.

REBELLION AS CONFRONTATION

The vantage point from which peasant rebels challenged the legitimacy of the colonial rulers in Kumaun provides an interesting twist to the following claim by Barrington Moore:

> Only when the obsolete character of a dominant group becomes blatantly obvious through *failure in competition with another society and culture* is it liable to lose its legitimate right to appropriate the surplus extracted from the underlying population. This is what happened to the Tsarist bureaucracy, the scholar gentry of China, and the armed knights of medieval Europe.[103]

In the examples advanced by Moore, the claim of the ruling class to rule was challenged from the perspective of the future, of a society in the making—state socialism in the case of Russia and China, capitalist democracy in the case of Europe. Colonialism, however, was challenged from the vantage point of the past, of the society which it had superseded. When the white rulers were deemed unfit to rule, their performance was compared not to the authority of a future millennium, nor to the ruling class in an adjoining state, but to the traditional rulers of the *same* society. Moreover, the persistence of customary forms of protest in the adjoining state of Tehri Garhwal must have acted as a reference point by which Kumaun peasants judged the responsiveness (or lack of it) of British officials to their demands.

While representing, as I have argued, a direct challenge to state authority, the actions of the Kumaun peasant do not conform to the picture of violence drawn by scholars reporting tribal and peasant revolts in peninsular India. The methods of resistance characteristically used by the hill peasant were strikes and the burning of the forest floor; physical violence was very rarely resorted to. In this connection one might refer again to the unusual political and economic structure of Kumaun, where the state dealt directly with the relatively egalitarian village communities without the help of an intermediary class enjoying a vested interest in land. The dreaded triad of 'Sarkar, Sahukar and Zamindar [which was] a political fact rooted in the very nature of British power in the subcontinent', was here conspicuous by its absence, as indeed was the 'total and integrated

---

[103] Barrington Moore, *Injustice: The Social Bases of Obedience and Revolt* (White Plains, NY, 1978), p. 43, emphasis added.

violence' of rebellion observed elsewhere.[104] Although 'impatient of control',[105] the hillman enjoyed an autonomy rarely found in other parts of India, as this description of the 'Garhwal village *paharee*' testifies:

> I suppose it would be difficult to find any peasantry in the world more free from the *res angustae domi* [i.e. straitened circumstances at home]: he is the owner of a well built stone house, has as much land as he wants at an easy rental, keeps his flocks and herds, and is in every sense of the word, an independent man.[106]

The absence of a culturally distinct buffer class between the body of cultivating proprietors and the state, and the relative autonomy these proprietors continued to enjoy, are germane to the particular forms assumed by the conflicts between the peasantry and the state, and the manner in which these conflicts were represented in popular consciousness. Thus, in Kumaun the absence of violent protest may be related to the structure of domination in hill society—this being one that did not quite correspond to the forms of domination in other parts of India—as well as to the distinctive tradition of peasant protest embodied in the dhandak. Moreover, while Adas is correct in suggesting that '*most forms* of the protest of retribution represent very limited responses that flaunt laws and threaten individuals ... [but] have little lasting impact on existing systems of peasant elite exchange and social control',[107] this was certainly not the case in Kumaun in 1921. Given the strategic importance of the hill forests to colonial rule, and their vulnerability to fire, the forest movements left the state with no effective response but to abandon control over large areas of woodland. Likewise, labour strikes in an inaccessible and poorly connected region crippled the administration, forcing it to end

---

[104] Ranajit Guha, *Elementary Aspects of Peasant Insurgency in Colonial India* (Delhi, 1983), pp. 27, 157, etc.

[105] *Report of the Kumaun Forest Grievances Committee*, Progs A, June 1922, nos. 19–24, file no. 522/1922, dept of rev. agl. (forests), p. 2, NAI.

[106] Dr F. Pearson, 'Report on Mahamurree and Smallpox in Garhwal', in *Selections from the Records of the Government of the Northwestern Provinces*, vol. II (Allahabad, 1866), p. 300.

[107] Michael Adas, 'From Footdragging to Flight: The Evasive History of Peasant Avoidance Protest in South and South-east Asia', pp. 81–2.

the begar system. Clearly, the extent of violence will vary with different forms of domination. And in Kumaun the peculiar social structure, cultural history of resistance, and the relative efficacy of different methods of protest, all favoured the eschewing of physical violence on the part of agrarian rebels.[108]

NATIONALISM AND THE VANGUARD PARTY

The history of social protest in the Indian Himalaya also calls into question the received wisdom on the participation of the peasantry in anti-colonial movements in the Third World. The literature on Indian nationalism, in common with that on the Vietnamese and Chinese Revolutions, has focused on the role of the vanguard party—in this case, the Indian National Congress—in agrarian movements.[109] While this bias is in part a function of the historical record—namely the accessibility of source materials on organized nationalist campaigns—it is also informed by a scepticism of the power of the peasantry to act independently in defence of its interests. According to a prominent Indian historian, nationalism as represented by the Congress party 'helped to arouse the peasant and awaken him to his own needs, demands and above all the possibility of any active role in social and political development.'[110]

This perspective on the possibilities of peasant protest lies much in the tradition of social analysis that I called, in chapter 1, the S–O paradigm for the study of lower-class resistance. It posits a linear transition from unorganized to organized forms of resistance, with the former doomed to hopeless defeat, and the latter, by virtue of its association with an

[108] The violence/non-violence debate acquires a particular significance in the context of Indian nationalism, with Marxist writers often accusing Gandhi of adopting non-violence to wean the masses away from the revolutionary path. See, for the classic statement, R. Palme Dutt, *India Today* (Delhi, 1948). For a different reading of Gandhi's methods, which stresses their roots in Indian political tradition, see Dharampal, *Civil Disobedience and Indian Tradition* (Varanasi, 1971).

[109] Cf. Sumit Sarkar, *Modern India, 1885–1947* (Delhi, 1983); idem, *Popular Movements and Middle Class Leadership in Late Colonial India* (Calcutta, 1983).

[110] Bipan Chandra, *Nationalism and Colonialism in Modern India* (Delhi, 1979), p. 345. For another commentator, 'the patronage of politics from above helped agrarian discontent to get organized [and] it was in that sense a child [sic] of the politics of Indian nationalism.' Majid Siddiqi, *Agrarian Unrest in the United Provinces, 1918–22* (Delhi, 1978), pp. ix–x.

organized party, having a fair chance of success. A Korean scholar has this to say on the links between the peasantry and communists in his country:

If traditional peasant uprisings can be characterized as unorganized, amorphous and spontaneous, then modern peasant uprisings can be said to be more organized, systematic and contrived. The traditional uprising was a more or less natural [sic] phenomenon arising in the face of possible starvation; economic factors played a decisive role. The modern peasant uprising, in contrast, possesses a relatively clear goal as well as calculated strategies; political factors such as leadership and ideology play a decisive role.[111]

In this vision peasants stand closer to nature than to culture; it takes the intervention of urban intellectuals, whether nationalist or communist, to transform elemental peasant needs into a social movement worthy of the name. Curiously enough, scholars of diametrically opposed political persuasions are apt to overestimate the influence of the vanguard party. For their own very different reasons intellectuals of the Rand Corporation and party historians would tend to magnify the role (conspiratory in one version, emancipatory in the other) of the Communist Party in the Vietnamese nationalist movements. Similarly, apologists of the British imperium as well as official Indian histories have, by and large, uncritically accepted the Congress party's projection of itself as the initiator, director, and guarantor of Indian nationalism. As Richard Cobb not unfairly observes, these party-centred perspectives assume 'that a popular movement cannot be self-led and that the common people are too stupid to look after things for themselves. It is a thesis that, for obvious reasons, has always had an appeal to the right wing mind and to the intellectual, two studies in arrogance.'[112]

There are at least three ways in which historical research has begun to challenge theories of peasant nationalism centring on a 'hegemonic' party. First, a reinterpretation of historical source material is shedding more light on the everyday forms of

[111] Se Hee Yoo, 'The Communist Movements and the Peasants: The Case of Korea', in J. W. Lewis (ed.), *Peasant Rebellion and Communist Revolution in Asia* (Stanford, 1974), pp. 75–6.

[112] Cobb, *The Police and the People: French Popular Protest, 1789–1920* (Oxford, 1970), p. 78.

peasant resistance, the 'prosaic but constant struggle between the peasantry and those who seek to extract labour, food, taxes, rent and interest from them'. For, 'to understand those commonplace forms of resistance is to understand what much of the peasantry does "between revolts", to defend its interests as best as it can.'[113] Second, scholars have been recovering the numerous peasant revolts in the nineteenth and early-twentieth centuries (well before 'modern' nationalism penetrated the countryside), reconstructing the world view of the rebels and their own radical rejection of colonial rule.[114] Third, and perhaps most significant, recent work has stressed the relative autonomy of peasant participation in later movements formally led and directed by a nationalist party. While the rural masses joined the national movement for reasons of their own—which often did not coincide with the charter of demands laid down by the Congress Working Committee—on many occasions peasants on their own initiative adopted forms of struggle that broke the narrow confines of Congress-directed non-co-operation.[115] My own research strongly suggests that peasants joined nationalist movements only when such participation could redress local grievances. Finally, the linkages between the educated leaders and the rank and file were by no means as one-sided as some party histories suggest. In many parts of India, and clearly so in Kumaun, the leaders of the Congress, like the leaders of the Indochinese Communist Party in another context, were 'overwhelmed by their subordinates'.[116]

One could even argue that far from being stirred from their 'apathy' by larger political developments, peasants have historically seen these forces as an opportunity to settle old scores with their local oppressors. Within the restricted sphere of the conflict over forest rights, ample confirmation is provided by evidence from three continents of the links between political upheavals at the national level and the assertion of peasant claims at the local level: witness the massive invasions of forest

[113] Scott, *Weapons of the Weak*, p. 29.
[114] The major work for India is Ranajit Guha, *Elementary Aspects*. See also A. R. Desai (ed.), *Peasant Struggles in India* (Delhi, 1979).
[115] The pioneering regional studies are G. Pandey, *The Ascendancy of the Congress in Uttar Pradesh, 1926–34* (Delhi, 1978); D. Hardiman, *Peasant Nationalists of Gujarat: Kheda District, 1917–34* (Delhi, 1981).
[116] Morche Commission Report, quoted in Scott, *Moral Economy*, p. 149.

and grazing lands during the Russian Revolution of 1905–7, and the affirmation of peasant (as opposed to landlord or state) control over forests during the Mexican Revolution, the latter occurring almost simultaneously with the movements in Kumaun.[117] Indeed, as far back as 1688 the Glorious Revolution was a signal for English villagers to mount a 'general insurrection against the deer' protected in royal hunting preserves.[118] Perhaps the best documented of all such cases concerns the French Revolutions of 1830 and 1848, which the French peasantry welcomed as a golden opportunity to recover their lost rights in the forest.[119] This is precisely how the villagers of Kumaun seem to have viewed the nation-wide campaigns of 1919–22; in fact, peasants and tribals of other forest regions of India also rode the impetus of the Non-Cooperation movement and the promise of 'Gandhi raj' in pursuance of strikingly similar ends.[120] Larger historical forces—democracy in nineteenth-century France, mass nationalism in twentieth-century India—served to legitimize protests oriented towards forest rights, enabling peasants to claim these rights more insistently and with greater militancy.

As the comparative history of peasant resistance so abundantly illustrates, there is often a yawning gap between the concrete reasons for which peasants join larger revolts, and the more abstract goals of 'democracy' and 'nationalism' invoked

[117] Teodor Shanin, *Russia as a 'Developing' Society* (New Haven, 1986), vol. II, pp. 36, 84, 90–1, etc.,; Oscar Lewis, *Pedro Martinez: A Mexican Peasant and His Family* (New York, 1964).

[118] E. P. Thompson, *Whigs and Hunters* (Harmondsworth, 1975), p. 41.

[119] A mayor in Ariege during the 1830 Revolution wrote thus: 'The liberty which his majesty Philippe I [sic] has just given the French nation has been misinterpreted by our mountain peasants, who now believe themselves authorized to violate the laws, in delivering themselves, without any limit, to all the disorders that they can commit against the forest administration.' Thus, 'liberty in the Ariege did not mean the "essential political liberties", the *charte*, or an extended electoral franchise . . . it primarily meant the return of traditional rights of usage in the forest.' Merriman, *Demoiselles*, pp. 104–5. In 1848, at the first sign of the republic, peasants in the Var marched on a forest newly enclosed by a landlord, destroying his wall and uprooting newly planted fruit trees—'the idea was to regain the forest for the community . . . since "now we are a Republic".' Maurice Agulhon, *The Republic in the Village* (Cambridge, 1982), p. 172.

[120] See Ramachandra Guha and Madhav Gadgil, 'Forestry and Social Conflict in Colonial India', *Past and Present*, no.123, May 1989.

by the articulate leadership. Thus in rejecting the idea that the national assembly and the urban bourgeoise organized the rural jacquerie at the time of the French Revolution, Georges Lefebvre comments sharply: 'The peasants had their own reasons for joining the conflict, and these reasons were more than sufficient.' Likewise, when Madeiro initiated the Mexican Revolution in November 1910, rural leaders in the province of Morelos 'did not flock to his cause without weeks of hard reckoning and calculation. And when they did join him, it was for conscious, practical reasons—to recover village lands and establish security.' Half a century later, peasants gleefully recalled a conversation between Madeiro and their leader Zapata. When Madeiro says he is 'fighting for Effective Suffrage, No Reelection [for the strongman Porfirio Diaz]', Zapata replies that he, on behalf of the poor, is fighting for 'Water, Land and Justice'.[121]

These complex and often unexpected interconnections between organized nationalism and lower-class resistance are sufficiently illustrated in the trajectory of social protest in British Kumaun. For the Himalayan peasant the cohesion and collective spirit of the village community, and not the organized resources of urban nationalism, provided the mainspring of political action. Congress leaders in the towns of Almora and Nainital very likely believed themselves to be fighting for the nation-wide goal of Purna Swaraj (complete independence), yet peasants used the vehicle of nationalism to, more effectively reclaim their lost rights in the forest. For forest administration had introduced a notion of property, one integral to colonial rule but previously foreign to Kumaun, which ran contrary to the experience of the Khasa village communities in which different jatis shared a 'remarkable amity', symbolized by their sharing of the common *hookah*.[122] Thus, the wide-ranging campaign of 1921, though differing from a modern social movement in its aims and methods, was far from being the spontaneous outburst of an illiterate peasantry, representing a blind reaction to the expropriation of a resource crucial to their subsistence. It expressed, albeit in a far more heightened

---
[121] Lefebvre, *Great Fear*, p. 99; Womack, *Zapata*, p. 220; Lewis, *Pedro Martinez*, p. 88.
[122] G. R. Kala, *Memoirs of the Raj: Kumaun* (Delhi, 1974), p. 20.

way, the motivations which underlay the sporadic and localized protests in the early years of forest administration. Expressed through the medium of popular protest were conflicting theories of social relationships that virtually amounted to two world views. One can meaningfully contrast state monopoly right with the free use of forest by members of the village community as sanctioned by custom, a pattern of use, moreover, regulated by the community as a whole. The exploitation of the pine forests on grounds of commercial profitability and strategic imperial needs was at variance, too, with the use of natural resources in an economy wholly oriented towards subsistence. The invocation of the symbols of Bania and Rakshas, with all that they stood for, was a natural consequence of this discrepancy. As the paternalist state transformed itself into an agency intruding more and more into the daily life of its subject population, so its claim to legitimacy floundered. Peasant opposition to this encroachment took the form of consciously determined actions that were incomprehensible to an observer unfamiliar with the social and cultural heritage of the Kumaun peasant. But set in their socio-historical context, these actions become intelligible and are seen to represent a frontal challenge to state authority. The seemingly docile peasantry had been thought incapable of this.

From the perspective of the sociology of domination, we can observe considerable differences between popular perceptions of an ancient dynasty and of a government alien in terms of both race and language. In Tehri Garhwal the king, sanctified as Bolanda Badrinath, enjoyed a status denied to representatives of the colonial state. The latter's workings were far more impersonal and lacked the sanctity of tradition. In Tehri it was the motif of the 'wicked official' that symbolized the impediment between raja and praja. As a consequence, peasant protest was directed exclusively at officials and the laws they implemented, not at the king as such. Rather, the monarch was required to restore justice by dismissing tyrannical officials or repealing unjust laws. Even the kisan andolan, which covered large parts of the state and led to the eventual fall of the monarchy, was not really anti-monarchical in its popular ideology. In Kumaun division, on the other hand, the social idiom of protest clearly revealed a growing separation of the state from the peasantry. Thus, the state was depicted as a Bania government, the caste appellation evoking images of power as well as deception. On another occasion it was called a Rakshas (demoniacal) government. As such, if the quasi-divine Tehri monarch exemplified the continuity—sometimes threatened but never fully breached—between the state and the people, in Kumaun division there had occurred by 1921 a near total rupture between the colonial state and its subject population.

CHAPTER 6

The March of Commercial Forestry

> It is strictly forbidden for us to go into the [state] forests to cut lumber or firewood, but those who have money are free to exploit the biggest forests.
> —A Mexican peasant, c. 1960

The rapid growth in forest industries, in consonance with the greatly expanded nature of industrialization since Independence, has necessitated an increased cut from the Himalayan forests. To facilitate increased extraction the building of roads into hitherto inaccessible forests became necessary. The relative isolation of many hill areas was ended as major highways and all-weather roads were built to transport timber and other forest produce to urban markets. Along with the communications network came the ubiquitous contractor whose job was to transport the produce to be processed by large-scale industries in the private sector.[1] In official circles the need was long felt for better communications, the lack of which was an impediment to greater exploitation of the hill forests. Though a rail line to the Alakananda valley, planned as early as 1920,[2] did not materialize, since 1947 road building in the hills has occurred at a rapid pace, especially after the creation of three new border districts in 1962. A Rs 56 million World Bank project was started in 1972 for the construction of 1330 kilometres of new roads and 16 new bridges, and the renovation of 620 kilometres of existing roads in the UP Himalaya. This project was initiated on the grounds that past road construction represented but a 'nominal fraction of the total requirements for the full

---

[1] Cf. Sunderlal Bahuguna, *Uttarakhand mein Ek Sau Bis Din* (Dehradun, 1974).
[2] Cf. R. N. Brahmawar, *WP for the Garhwal For. Div., 1930-31 to 1939-40* (Allahabad, 1938).

exploitation and proper development of these [hill] forests'.[3] The building of roads into interior areas was viewed with satisfaction as a development which would enable the sale of hitherto untapped oak forest.[4] Now, the clear felling of oak and its replacement with planted conifers was being envisaged. However, road building, by opening up virgin forests for use as industrial raw material elsewhere, has failed to materially help the hill economy. The net benefits to the hill people have been 'starvation' wages as forest labour, while the fragile mountain ecosystem has deteriorated further through imperfect alignment and hasty construction of roads.[5] In addition, improved communications have made penetration by urban pleasure-seekers possible; and with the Himalaya 'being sold as a Mecca for climbers, adventurers and tourists', deforestation and allied ecological degradation to meet their needs for firewood has proceeded apace.[6]

Table 6.1 gives some details of the increased pressure on the forest department. The dramatic expansion of resin-tapping operations was a further burden, not reflected in the table. In the Alakananda and Bhageerathi valleys, this was greatly helped by road-building operations. Resin outturn after reaching a peak of 4.18 lakh quintals in 1974–5 (valued at Rs 74.8 million) averaged 1.30 quintals in 1978–9.[7]

These pressures of rising commercial and industrial demand called for a significant intensification of commercial forest operations. Important modifications introduced in forest working were the reduction in the diameter at which resin tapping was commenced, and the lowering of the age at which chir trees were cut. Incentives such as the awarding of bonus to resin mates who exceeded their targeted yield were also

[3] Uttar Pradesh Forest Department, 'Forest Development Project, Uttar Pradesh, India', mimeo, n.d. (1971?), pp. 117–21.
[4] Introduction by B. P. Srivastava in V. P. Singh, *WP for the West Almora For. Div., Kumaun Circle, 1966–67 to 1975–76* (Nainital, 1967).
[5] Madhav Gadgil, 'Towards an Indian Conservation Strategy', paper presented at the Workshop on a New Forest Policy, Indian Social Institute, New Delhi, 12–14 April 1982, p. 26.
[6] G. D. Berreman, *Himachal: Science, People and 'Progress'*, IWGIA document no. 36 (Copenhagen, 1979), p. 19 f.
[7] See *Uttar Pradesh Forest Statistics 1978–79* (Lucknow, n.d.), for details.

TABLE 6.1

Outturn of Selected Species in Uttarakhand
(cu. m. sawn wood)

Year	Deodar	Fir & spruce	Kail	Chir
1930–31	2,917	—	14,191	31,885
1934–35	4,333	—	—	30,299
1948–49	7,561	4,616	595	59,041
1950–51	9,542	10,987	5,135	87,415
1955–56	9,316	14,923	—	99,761
1960–61	9,571	39,502	5,380	1,07,435
1965–66	10,531	20,010	4,727	1,34,587
1970–71	11,612	39,766	5,166	2,00,030
1971–72	67,379	29,722	8,362	1,59,930
1972–73	48,623	60,106	5,162	2,06,645
1973–74	10,830	28,926	8,983	2,30,787
1974–75	15,464	37,463	9,742	1,86,114
1975–76	29,971	71,493	10,896	2,95,745
1976–77	14,712	37,980	5,632	2,67,458
1977–78	8,863	67,682	5,077	2,64,509
1978–79	7,965	84,954	6,023	3,19,081

SOURCE: *UP Forest Statistics, 1978–79* (Lucknow, n.d.).

suggested.[8] Meanwhile, the sale of chir wood was given a considerable fillip when laboratory trials of the Forest Research Institute (FRI) revealed that the utilization of chir waste (i.e. material left after the conversion of chir to sleepers) for paper making was a viable proposition.[9] With a view to selling the waste and utilizing the considerable areas of chir affected by twist (and hence unsuitable for sleepers) the forest department entered into a contract with Star Paper Mills of Saharanpur, owned by the Bajoria family. Under the terms of this contract, effective from 1 October 1961 to 30 September 1981, the mill

[8] See, for example, N. K. Agarwala, 'WP for the Kedarnath For. Div., Garhwal Circle, 1972–73 to 1981–82', mimeo (Nainital, 1973), pp. 168, 339–40.

[9] S. R. D. Guha, 'Chemical Pulps and Writing and Printing Papers from *Chir (Pinus longifolia Roxb)*', *Indian Forester*, vol. 84 (1958), pp. 235–40.

would be sold waste timber and twisted chir trees at ridiculously low prices.[10] Approximately 15 to 20 thousand tonnes of pulpwood were supplied annually to the mill.[11] When further research at the FRI established that ash and hornbeam could be used in the manufacture of sports goods, the Symonds Company of Allahabad were granted access to the high-level broad-leaved forests.[12]

The state's eagerness to further commercial working inevitably entailed further restrictions on village use. Cases were reported of the misuse of timber for their own use by high officials of the forest department. The high rates at which forest produce was sold to the surrounding population (as compared to the rates existing before 1947) and the takeover of disputed land by the department were also the subject of complaint. The department was widely believed to be in connivance with timber thieves.[13] In a bid to tighten control, the government had given the department extensive powers in the management of forest panchayats. Under the new rules, panchayats could only fell trees marked by the department. Local sale of slates and stones (used for housing) and export of resin were only allowed with the permission of specified senior forest officials who also directed the quantum of extraction and its destination. Finally, panchayats could retain only a fixed share (40 per cent) of any royalty on the sale of produce from their forests.[14]

More crucial, however, was the wilful neglect of the local population in the extraction and processing of forest produce. Initial hopes that road building would lead to industrialization and generation of local employment were belied by government policy which consistently favoured the export of raw materials to be processed by large industry in the plains. A sizeable proportion of the resin extracted—estimated at 85–90 per cent of the total output—was dispatched to the Indian Turpentine and Resin Co. (ITR) near Bareilly, in which government had the majority shareholding. Of the remainder, some was allotted to

[10] For details, see N. K. Agarwala.
[11] Estimated from figures given in different working plans; 1 tonne of paper requires 2 tonnes of pulpwood.
[12] Agarwala, 'Kedarnath WP', pp. 78–9.
[13] See *Yugvani* (YV), issues of 17 July 1960, 21 July and 18 December 1966, 4 October and 18 October 1970, and 18 April 1971.
[14] Agarwala, 'Kedarnath WP', pp. 28–30.

local co-operative societies and the rest sold by open auction. Initially, ITR and the co-operatives were sold resin at the same rates. This policy was changed in the 1970s, with ITR being supplied at the earlier (subsidized) rates, while local units had to buy resin at open auctions. In any case, these units were often allotted inaccessible forests where tapping was not economically feasible. As a result of such neglect, they rarely operated at more than 50 per cent capacity.[15] Requests to lower prices by Rs 15 per quintal to meet the costs of transporting processed resin to railheads were also not acceded to.[16]

Discrimination against small units by the government was matched by its refusal to end the contractor system of forest working. While policy documents recognized the need to do away with the intermediaries who, it was admitted, exploited both their labour and the forests, in practice the system continued to be patronized.[17] Under the initiative of Sarvodaya workers, forest labour co-operatives (FLCs) were started in different parts of Garhwal and Kumaun. Repeated pleas to the government to allot them blocks of forest at concessional rates went unheeded.[18] In fact, the chief conservator of forests had himself suggested at one stage that the department actively promote the working of FLCs in the hills. He was, however, tersely informed by the governor that 'since the forest department is a sort of commercial department, it cannot be expected to extend concession in the transaction of its business, even to co-operative societies.' The official was referred to the experience of Bombay state, where such a scheme had cost the government 'quite dearly and considerable amounts were lost to the exchequer'.[19] Apparently, the role played by contractors

[15] V. P. S. Verma, 'WP for the Tehri For. Div., Garhwal Circle, 1973-74 to 1982-83', mimeo (Nainital, 1973), pp. 44, 55; National Council of Applied Economic Research, *Growth Centres and Their Industrial Potential: Chamoli* (Delhi, 1975). Interview with C. P. Bhatt, May 1981.

[16] See YV, 17 February 1974.

[17] Cf. Ramachandra Guha, 'Forestry in British and Post-British India: A Historical Analysis', *Economic and Political Weekly* (in two parts), 29 October 1983 and 5 November 1983.

[18] YV, issues of 30 October 1960 and 14 June 1970.

[19] GO no. VOB 289/XIV-378-56, 23 July 1960, from assistant secretary, UP government, to chief conservator of forests, UP (office of the conservator of forests, Tehri circle, Dehradun).

(almost all of whom belonged to the plains) as political patrons stood in the way of the implementation of stated policy objectives.

Several features testify to the marked degree of continuity between colonial and post-colonial forest policies. While the pressure of industrial and commercial classes may have replaced strategic imperial needs as the cornerstone of state forestry practices, in both periods 'successful' implementation of policy has been at the expense of the hill peasantry and their life support systems. The use of silvicultural and other strategies of manipulation and control, designed to limit and carefully regulate the access of the surrounding population to the forest, has been remarkably invariant throughout this time span. Finally, the forest department, assigned the role of a revenue generating organ by both the colonial state and the Tehri durbar, has continued to be a veritable money-spinner for the government of Uttar Pradesh. Between 1967–8 and 1978–9 forest revenue from the hill region increased from Rs 962 to 2020 lakhs.[20]

ECOLOGICAL CHANGE AND THE MONEY-ORDER ECONOMY

In chapter 2 I had argued that in the period before commercial forestry, hill peasants were able quite comfortably to meet their subsistence requirements and have, occasionally, a surplus of grain for export. The egalitarian structure of the village community, the abundance of forests and other natural resources, and its insulation from the political instability of the Indo-Gangetic plain all contributed to the autonomy and relative prosperity of hill society. This depiction found verification from the numerous accounts of European travellers and officials, which repeatedly contrasted the fine, upstanding hill peasantry of the nineteenth century with poverty-stricken villagers in other parts of India and even in Europe.

The picture drawn in chapter 2 is, in fact, considerably at variance with the situation as it exists today. An element of continuity, no doubt, is provided by the continued dependence on agriculture. While population pressure has led to the

[20] See *UP Forest Statistics, 1978–79* (Lucknow, n.d.).

fragmentation of holdings, there exists little opportunity for the emergence of a class of capitalist farmers. Thus, in terms of the indices of 'modernization', for example the use of improved seeds, irrigation, commercial crops, etc., hill agriculture fares poorly.[21]

Table 6.2 presents data on the occupational structure of six exclusively hill districts in 1971, or just prior to the Chipko movement. The overwhelming importance of agriculture obscures one crucial fact: that while farming systems in the Himalaya continue to be subsistence-oriented, cumulative social and environmental changes have undermined the hill society's capacity to feed itself. Foodgrain output is no longer adequate for subsistence. Whereas for most families it was a point of pride not to purchase food from the market, declining yields and an increased population have forced a majority of peasant families to buy a significant portion of their grain requirements.[22] The substantial deficit between production and

TABLE 6.2
Percentage Distribution of Work-force, 1971

District	Cultivators	Agricultural labourers	Animal husbandry/ forestry	Agriculture as percentage of total population
Pithoragarh	78.01	1.30	1.62	80.93
Almora	80.51	1.99	1.02	83.52
Uttarkashi	85.90	1.00	1.55	88.45
Pauri	82.97	1.03	0.73	84.73
Tehri-Garhwal	90.96	0.55	0.68	92.19
Chamoli	86.52	0.49	0.19	87.15

SOURCE: Computed from 1971 census, in G. C. Tewari, *An Economic Profile of the Hill Region of Uttar Pradesh*, Occasional Paper No. 10, G. B. Pant Social Science Institute, Allahabad, 1982.

[21] Cf. Waheeduddin Khan and R. N. Tripathy, *Plan for Integrated Rural Development in Pauri Garhwal* (Hyderabad, 1976).

[22] Marcus Moench, 'Resource Utilization and Degradation: An Integrated Analysis of Biomass Utilization Patterns in a Garhwal Hill Village, Northern Uttar Pradesh, India', MS thesis, University of California, Berkeley, 1985, p. 22.

consumption—estimated at around 160 kgs of grain per person per annum—can only be met through purchase in the market.[23]

In order to keep pace with rising population, hill peasants have adopted two adaptive strategies. First, they have increased their holdings of livestock. The density of livestock has increased from an earlier estimate of 342 animals/km² to 474 animals/km² in 1980. This is because animal manure is the key input for arresting the decline in yields. Peasants have also colonized new lands. However, while the population has increased by 119 per cent in the last eighty years, cultivated area has increased only by 54 per cent, and cropping intensity has barely crept up by 14 per cent. At the same time, as Table 6.3 suggests, the yields of major agricultural crops have actually fallen.[24]

TABLE 6.3

Estimated Yields of Agricultural Crops in Uttarakhand (kg/ha)

Crop	1896	1979	Percentage of gross cropped area (1979)
Rice	1120	1133	17.6
Wheat	898	538	25.4
Barley	NA	362	5.7
Mandua	1120	924	24.6
Jhangora	1100	924	13.4

SOURCE: William Whittaker, 'Migration and Agrarian Change in Garhwal District, Uttar Pradesh', in T. P. Bayliss-Smith and Sudhir Wanmali (eds), *Understanding Green Revolutions: Agrarian Change and Development Planning in South Asia* (Cambridge, 1984).

Declining agricultural productivity can be directly attributed to the deterioration of the hill ecosystem, in particular

[23] S. C. Joshi, D. R. Joshi and D. D. Dani, *Kumaun Himalaya* (Nainital, 1983), p. 233.
[24] W. Whittaker, 'Migration and Agrarian Change in Garhwal District, Uttar Pradesh,' in T. P. Bayliss-Smith and Sudhir Wanmali (eds), *Understanding Green Revolutions: Agrarian Change and Development Planning in South Asia* (Cambridge, 1984), p. 125.

the degradation of the hill forests. Recent satellite data shows that of the 34,042 square kilometres of land declared as forests in Uttarakhand, good tree cover exists only on 6.6 per cent of the forest land, while another 22.5 and 13.8 per cent can be classified as medium and poor forests, respectively. According to satellite imagery, therefore, over half the land officially classified as forest has no tree cover at all: even allowing for the areas above the tree line and snowy peaks, this is an alarming figure.[25] There is a direct and reciprocal relationship between the loss and degradation of forests and the decline of hill agriculture. On a healthy vegetative slope a dynamic balance exists between the rate of erosion and soil formation. As the expansion of cultivable land in the hills can only take place at the expense of forests or on excessively steep slopes, this in itself increases the rate of soil erosion. Meanwhile, the increasing transfer of leaf manure to farms to maintain soil fertility for human consumption impairs the forests' regenerative capacity. Simultaneously, commercial forestry is radically altering the ecology of natural forests. The removal of large volumes of timber without the replenishments of nutrients—normally accomplished through the decay of wood and litter—also increases soil loss, especially in the monsoon season. These cumulative pressures lead to the impoverishment of the ecosystem, and hill agriculture enters a downward spiral from which there is seemingly no escape.[26]

Neither intensification nor expansion of agriculture, therefore, offers a viable solution to the growth of human population and the loss of control over forest resources. Faced with multiple environmental hazards, Uttarakhand society is in a 'state of continuing economic deterioration'.[27] A second and more widespread adaptive strategy is to look for alternative sources of employment. As these do not exist within the Himalaya, Uttarakhand peasants have no option but to emulate their counterparts from Nepal and 'follow their soils down the slopes'.[28] While this process was set in motion during

[25] N. C. Saxena, 'Social Forestry in the U.P. Himalayas', mimeo, ICIMOD (Kathmandu, 1987), p. 7.
[26] Whittaker, 'Migration and Agrarian Change', pp. 114–17.
[27] P. H. Gross, *Birth, Death and Migration in the Himalayas* (Delhi, 1982), p. 184.
[28] Cf. Eric Eckholm, *Losing Ground* (New York, 1976).

the colonial period, male migration out of the hills has greatly increased since 1947. These migrants work mostly in the armed forces, the police, and as clerical workers and menial servants in the towns and cities of northern India. Village studies have reported that over half of the adult male population does not reside in the village for most of the year, being forced to seek employment elsewhere. On my visits to hill villages I observed a preponderance of children, women and old men, testifying to the absence of able-bodied males. In some parts more than 60 per cent of the family income is generated outside by male migrants who remit a major portion of their earnings (by 'money order') to the village.[29] Uttarakhand now has, therefore, a dual economy—based partially on remittances and partially on the eroding basis of subsistence agriculture.[30]

In the absence of alternative energy sources, deforestation and the money economy have placed an additional strain on the women, left in the village to pick up the pieces of farm life. The customary tasks of fuel and fodder collection now require far more time and effort than they did earlier. Increasingly charged, too, with agricultural tasks, the woman's lot is a miserable one, poignantly captured in the writings of local activists.[31] Yet the malaise of hill society is by no means restricted to one section of its population. The processes of environmental change that came in the wake of commercial forestry have had a devastating impact on the social fabric of Uttarakhand: fragmentation of the family, erosion of local authority structures and co-operating institutions, and a crisis of confidence resulting from the decline and fall of a once prosperous system of agrarian production. As the commercial sector of the plains begins to cast a covetous eye on other natural resources of the hills (e.g. water and minerals), we begin to see a strong parallel with the exploitation of mountain peoples in other parts of the globe. Kai Erikson's description of Appalachia serves in its

[29] See 'Report of the Task Force for the Study of Eco-Development in the Himalayan Region', mimeo, Planning Commission (New Delhi, March 1982).
[30] Cf. Whittaker, 'Migration and Agrarian Change', p. 129.
[31] See, inter alia, Bahuguna, 'Uttarakhand'; Sarala Devi, 'A Blueprint for Survival of the Hills', supplement to *Himalaya: Man and Nature*, vol. 4, no. 6, November 1980; and for a treatment in liction, C. P. Bhatt, *Pratikar ke Ankur* (Gopeshwar, 1979).

essentials, if not in fine detail, in capturing the economic and ecological exploitation of the Himalayan villagers:

[The] men and women of Appalachia are among the most truly exploited people to be found anywhere. In the beginning, they had rights to good land. It was covered with timber; rich seams of coal ran under its crust. It had soil fertile enough for the modest uses to which it was put and its forests were alive with fish and game. In the course of a few decades, however, dating from the last years of the nineteenth century, almost all of these valuable resources were cut or scraped or gouged away [by outsiders]; and when the land lay bruised and exhausted from the punishment it had received, the people of the region had virtually nothing to show for it.[32]

FRAGMENTS OF A PRISTINE CONSCIOUSNESS: 'COMMUNITY' MANAGEMENT

At the time of the reservation of the hill forests, settlement officers, in the belief that the management of the forests not reserved would be made over to the villages, restricted rights in many cases.[33] In anticipation of protest, villagers were in fact told that while the reserved forests would be in the strict control of the forest department, 'they would be given complete freedom of operation in the remaining areas...'[34] Although proposals were mooted at various times, there was no concerted attempt to establish village forests on land not vested with government. In British Kumaun, after the forest movement of 1921, the Grievances Committee did consider the establishment of village forests on land taken away from the forest department. An official sent to Madras to examine the system of communal management there strongly recommended the creation of similar reserves, to be controlled by villagers, in Kumaun. In face of the active opposition of forest officials, who argued quite falsely that village management of forests reflected a lack of concern for the needs of future genera-

[32] Kai Erikson, *Everything in Its Path: Destruction of Community in the Buffalo Creek Flood* (New York, 1976), p. 68.
[33] No. 3681/XXVI-2, 4 May 1915 from comm., KD, to chief secy, UP, in FD file 83/1909, UPSA.
[34] See note by J. R. W. Bennett, 26 August 1919, in ibid.

tions,[35] these proposals were implemented only in piecemeal fashion.

Despite official apathy, foresters, in both the colonial and post-colonial periods, have admitted that the panchayat forests in Garhwal, though small in extent as a consequence of government policy, were often well maintained,[36] with many having done 'exemplary work in connection with forest protection and development'.[37] Where ownership was still vested in the community, forests continued to be well looked after—such as the twenty-mile stretch between Rudraprayag and Karanprayag in the Alakananda valley, where the government had explicitly made over the forests to the neighbouring villages.[38] In Tehri Garhwal, too, informal management practices continued to prevail over forests not taken over by the durbar. A recent survey concluded that while some panchayat forests there are in better condition than the reserved forests in the area, they are uniformly better maintained than forests under the jurisdiction of the civil administration.[39] During fieldwork in the valley of Badyar, a tributary of the Alakananda, I came across a panchayat forest containing both banj and chir, with profuse regeneration of the two species coming up side by side. A village schoolteacher explained how extraction was carefully regulated, with monetary fines being levied on offenders. Exceptions were made only in the case of religious festivals, or when the timber was required for community purposes such as the construction of the panchayat *ghar* or a school.

In Uttarakhand the age-old panchayat system had been accustomed to handling diverse issues of which forest matters, though undoubtedly very significant, were only one aspect.[40] The partial breakdown of traditional mechanisms of allocation and control has been a consequence of the commercial penetra-

[35] Cf. A. E. Osmaston, 'Panchayat Forests in Kumaun', IF, vol. 58 (1932), pp. 603–8.

[36] C. M. Johri, *WP for the Garhwal For. Div.* (Allahabad, 1947), p. 20; D. N. Lohani, *WP for the North and South Garhwal Divisions, UP, 1958–59 to 1972–73* (Allahabad, 1962), p. 35.

[37] *Report of Kumaun Forest Fact Finding Committee* (Lucknow, 1960), p. 37.

[38] Note by D. Joshi in FD file no. 83/1909, UPSA.

[39] Personal communication from Madhav Gadgil, 25 July 1981.

[40] Cf. *Garhwali*, 14 February 1920.

tion of hill economy and society that followed in the wake of state forestry. Yet cases continued to be reported of the *lath panchayat* of the village (an institution not recognized by law) managing small blocks of forest 'for the common welfare of the village community as a whole'.[41] More rarely, it was individuals rather than the community that took the lead, a notable example being Vishveshwar Dutt Saklani, brother of the peasant leader Nagendra Saklani (martyred in the 1948 movement), who has over a period of forty years planted and raised to maturity thousands of broad-leaved trees in the Saklana area of Tehri Garhwal. As forest officials were constrained to admit, when oak forests were entrusted to nearby villages who appointed their own *chaukidars*, lopping was done systematically and the trees well protected.[42] And in Kumaun numerous instances were reported of panchayat land being closed to grazing by common consent, the copious regeneration in these forests presenting a 'striking contrast' to the heavily browsed reserved forests.[43] A recent study of the Aglar valley in Tehri Garhwal reports the existence of a large community grassland used equitably and without friction by the inhabitants of as many as seventeen villages.[44] In Ranikhet subdivision of Almora district, a civilian reported in the 1960s that there were a 'large number of successful forest panchayats'; and in certain localities the only forests that existed belonged to them.[45]

Admittedly, there are variations. In Kumaun, where commercialization had penetrated earlier, the experience of forest panchayats is far more mixed. Yet, whether judged on its own terms or against the manifest failures of state forestry, the fine performance of *van* panchayats in parts of Garhwal and Kumaun is instructive. This situation has prevailed where cohesive and largely egalitarian village communities have retained some control over their forest habitat. It also testifies

[41] Census of India 1961, vol. xv, pt vi, Village Survey Monograph, no. 5, *Village Thapli, Tehsil Pauri, District Garhwal*, p. 2.

[42] Uttarkashi Working Plan, quoted in Sunderlal Bahuguna, 'The Himalaya: Towards a Programme of Reconstruction', in K. M. Gupta and Desh Bandhu (eds), *Man and Forest* (Delhi, 1979).

[43] V. P. Singh, *WP for the West Almora For. Div., Kumaun Circle, 1966–67 to 1975–76* (Nainital, 1967), pp. 109–10.

[44] Cf. Moench, 'Resource Utilization', pp. 106–7.

[45] Prakash Kishan, *The Broad Spectrum* (Delhi, 1973), p. 58.

to a reservoir of local ecological knowledge that has managed to persist amidst a century of alienation and protest. It was left to the Chipko movement to awaken and crystallize this fund of local knowledge in the hill peasantry's latest and most sustained challenge to the march of commercial forestry.

CHAPTER 7

Chipko: Social History of an 'Environmental' Movement

As a popular movement that has focused worldwide attention on the environmental crisis in the Himalaya, the Chipko andolan provided the point of entry for the present work. In this chapter I explore the major dimensions of Chipko as a social movement. Essentially, a sociological study of the Chipko andolan must grapple with three sets of issues.

First, there is the understanding of the movement in its historical dimension. On the one hand, we need to interpret the social idiom of Chipko in the context of earlier movements (described in chapters 4 and 5) centring around the question of peasant access to forests. On the other hand, we need to examine the interconnections between Chipko and different aspects of state intervention, both scientific forestry in particular and, more generally, the administrative policies followed by different governments. In keeping with the overall emphasis of this work, both social participation in Chipko and its reflection in popular consciousness are sought to be depicted in terms of the changing relationship between the state and the peasantry.

Second, the links between specific forms taken by Chipko and its relationship to the social structure of Uttarakhand need to be spelt out. Here, one must emphasize the social changes that have created a 'money-order' economy and a lopsided demographic profile in the villages of Uttarakhand. Thus, Chipko can be read as a response to the fragmentation of the village community in recent decades. Again, women have always played an important role in economic life (chapter 2), and this structural constant may explain the widespread participation of women—marking an important departure from the pre-Independence period—in contemporary social movements.[1] At the same time, the participation of women in Chipko and its associated movements has been influenced by the impact of recent economic changes in intensifying their traditional dependence on the natural environment.

Finally, while Chipko lies in a direct path of continuity with an earlier history of social protest, as an organized and sustained social movement, at the same time, it represents an expansion in the scale of popular mobilization and the development of popular consciousness. This extension has two distinct aspects. First, the enduring nature of Chipko and its assumption of an organizational form has raised major questions: the nature of leadership, the ideological clashes between different subcultures of the movement, and the redefinition of the relations between the sexes. These were absent from many of the earlier, largely 'unorganized', movements of social protest in Uttarakhand. Second, notwithstanding its internal schisms, as an extension of popular consciousness Chipko attempts to combat the growing social and ecological disintegration of hill society. This attempt consists, on the one hand, of an expansion of the movement to embrace other social issues, and, on the other, of the presentation to the state and the general public with alternative strategies of resource use and social development.

CHIPKO: ITS ORIGINS AND DEVELOPMENT

The background

Not surprisingly, the continuation by the government of independent India of forestry practices inimical to local needs generated a certain amount of discontent. In 1958 a committee was formed to 'investigate ... the grievances of the people' of Uttarakhand concerning forest management. It deplored the situation in the hill tracts where, even after the

[1] The narrative of social movements in chapters 4 and 5 mentions women only in passing. This fact should be taken only as indicative of the biases of the sources used. It is very likely that women played a key supporting role in the peasant movements in both Tehri Garhwal and Kumaun divisions, by keeping the household and farm economy going in periods of social conflict with the state, and perhaps even by aiding rebel movements. The sources are obviously biased towards reporting the activities of men, who, unlike women, came into repeated contact with the state and its officials.

attainment of independence, 'not only great discontent against the Forest Department prevails at several places, but it is also looked upon with extreme suspicion and distrust.' While recognizing the need to locally develop the resources of the hills, the committee considered as inevitable the continuance of restrictions viewed by the people as a 'forfeiture of their hereditary natural rights'. Its typically non-specific recommendations gave priority to the 'preservation, development and extension of the forests' and to meeting the 'genuine needs of the local people'. It also asked for a declaration from the government that it would respect village rights over forests and that, along with forest preservation, 'it would provide every opportunity for the economic progress of the people'.[2] In the absence of concrete programmes, local legislators warned, there was every chance of a popular upsurge in the tradition of movements against the British and the Tehri durbar.[3] In fact, Communist Party of India activists in the Yamuna valley had organized several satyagrahas against the highhandedness of different state agencies.[4] Great resentment continued to be expressed against the practice of large timber coupés being sold to 'outside' contractors. Villagers also refused to help the forest staff extinguish fires, as they were bound to do under the forest act.[5]

The undercurrent of protest against forest management was combined with opposition to other facets of commercialization and the continuing underdevelopment of the hills. Led by Sarvodaya workers, thousands of villagers, mostly women, opposed the widespread distillation and sale of liquor. Processions and the picketing of liquor stills were organized in different districts of Garhwal. In Tehri the prominent Sarvodaya leader Sunderlal Bahuguna and several women were arrested for defying prohibitory orders.[6] A partial prohibition was imposed on the occasion of the centenary of Gandhi's birth;

[2] *The Report of the Kumaun Forest Facts Finding Committee* (Lucknow, 1960), esp. pp. 26 ff.

[3] Speech by Ramachandra Uniyal in Vidhan Sabha, reported in YV, 3 April 1960.

[4] See YV, 20 November 1966.

[5] See Gopal Singh, 'WP for the Nainital For. Div., Kumaun Circle, 1968–69 to 1977–79', mimeo (Nainital, 1969).

[6] YV, issues of 2 April and 9 July 1967, 22 May 1970, etc.

when this was successfully challenged by liquor contractors in the high court, sale was recommenced. This led to a fresh wave of *dharnas*, with Bahuguna embarking on an indefinite hunger strike. Thirty-one volunteers were arrested in Tehri for picketing liquor shops.[7]

Meanwhile the demand for a separate hill state gathered momentum. Students went on strike demanding the establishment of universities in the hills. *Bandhs* were successfully organized in several towns. In a metaphor reminiscent of the forest movement of 1921 (chapter 5), the government was termed 'Bania', a government which yielded only under coercion. Consciously seeking to establish a continuity with earlier protest movements, the Uttarakhand Rajya Sammelan had organized a meeting at Bageshwar on the sacred occasion of the Uttaraini mela. Here, speakers stressed the looting of natural resources from the hills, the growing unemployment, and the cultural similarities between Garhwal and Kumaun. The government responded by setting up universities and autonomous development corporations in both Garhwal and Kumaun divisions.[8]

The 1970 flood

The unusually heavy monsoon of 1970 precipitated the most devastating flood in living memory. In the Alakananda valley, water inundated 100 square kilometres of land, washed away 6 metal bridges and 10 kilometres of motor roads, 24 buses and several dozen other vehicles; 366 houses collapsed and 500 acres of standing paddy crops were destroyed. The loss of human and bovine life was considerable. The Gauna lake, formed by the Alakananda flood of 1894, was filled with debris. Apart from the tributaries of the Alakananda, the Kali and Bhageerathi rivers also spilled their banks. Houses in Rishikesh, where the Ganga enters the plains, were also destroyed. Due to the blockage of the Ganga canal, 95 lakh acres of land in eastern UP went unirrigated.[9]

[7] YV, issues of 14 November, 21 November and 28 November 1971.

[8] See YV, issues of 13 June, 15 July, 29 July, 5 September, 12 September, 19 September, 26 September and 3 October 1971, 24 December and 31 December 1972, and 28 January 1973.

[9] C. P. Bhatt, *Eco-system of the Central Himalayas and Chipko Movement* (Gopeshwar, 1980), pp. 11–13.

The 1970 flood marks a turning-point in the ecological history of the region. Villagers, who bore the brunt of the damage, were beginning to perceive the hitherto tenuous links between deforestation, landslides and floods. It was observed that some of the villages most affected by landslides lay directly below forests where felling operations had taken place.[10] Preceding official initiative, 'folk sense was the only body that surveyed the grim scene and drew conclusions. The causal relationship between increasing erosivity and floods on the one hand, and mass scale felling of trees on the other, was recognized by [it].'[11]

The villagers' cause was taken up by the Dashauli Gram Swarajya Sangh (DGSS), a co-operative organization based in Chamoli district. Organized by several local youths in the mid 1960s, the DGSS had as its major objective the generation of local employment. Despite serious obstacles it operated a small resin and turpentine unit, manufactured agricultural implements, and organized the collection and sale of medicinal herbs.

On 22 October 1971 the DGSS organized a major demonstration in Gopeshwar, the district town of Chamoli. The demonstrators called for an end to liquor sale and to untouchability, and for giving priority to the local use of forests. Arguing that they had nurtured the forest growth themselves, villagers demanded that local units be given preference in the allotment of raw material. Led by Sarvodaya workers, such as Gandhi's English disciple Sarla Devi (who had set up an ashram in Almora district in the 1940s) and the leading local activist Chandi Prasad Bhatt, the procession was of a size never before seen in Chamoli district.[12] In the following year major public meetings were held at Gopeshwar and Uttarkashi, which demanded the replacement of the contractor system with forest

[10] S. Bahuguna, 'Uttarakhand mein Mrityu aur Tabahi ki Janam key Liye Jangalon ka Janaja Zimmedar', YV, 4 October 1970.

[11] C. P. Bhatt, 'Eco-development: People's Movement', in T. V. Singh and J. Kaur (eds), *Studies in Ecodevelopment: Himalaya: Mountains and Men* (Lucknow, 1983), p. 475.

[12] YV, 31 October 1971; *Uttarakhand Observer* (in Hindi), 25 October 1971, in Chipko file, Centre for Science and Environment, New Delhi (hereafter CSE file). The DGSS is now known as DGSM (M for Mandal). However, I shall continue to refer to it as DGSS.

labour co-operatives (FLC's) and the setting up of small-scale industries.[13]

Mandal[14]

In early 1973 the DGSS had asked for an allotment of ash trees in order to make agricultural implements. The forest department refused to accommodate this request. Instead, they asked the DGSS to use chir trees, totally unsuitable for the purpose. However, the Symonds Co. was allotted ash trees in the forest of Mandal, barely several miles from Gopeshwar. This blatant injustice inspired the DGSS to organize several meetings in Mandal and Gopeshwar to discuss possible action. Two alternatives presented themselves: (i) to lie down in front of the timber trucks; (ii) to burn resin and timber depots as was done in the Quit India movement. When Sarvodaya workers found both methods unsatisfactory, Chandi Prasad Bhatt suddenly thought of embracing the trees. Thus 'Chipko' (to hug) was born. Led by their headman, Alam Singh Bist, the villagers of Mandal resolved to hug the trees even if axes split open their stomachs. Young men cemented the oath with signatures of blood.

The birth of Chipko preceded the actual advent of Symonds Co. in Mandal. Hearing of the villagers' plan, the district magistrate wired the UP government, who responded by calling Bhatt for negotiations to Lucknow. A compromise was suggested, whereby the government would allot the DGSS ash trees on condition that the sporting goods firm could take away its quota. Despite raising its offer from one ash tree to five, the authorities could not break down the stiff resistance. The labour and agents of Symonds Co. were forced to turn away from Mandal without felling a single tree.

In June Symonds was allotted trees near the village of Phata in the Mandakini valley, en route to the shrine of Kedarnath.[15]

[13] See YV, 24 June 1973.
[14] This account is based on A. Mishra and S. Tripathi, *Chipko Movement* (Delhi, 1978), pp. 7–12, supplemented by S. Bahuguna, 'Uttarakhand ka Chipko Andolan', YV, 24 June 1973; news report in YV, 6 May 1973; interview with Alam Singh Bist (ex-pradhan, Mandal village), Gopeshwar, May 1982.
[15] The villagers rendered the firm's name as 'Simon Co.' Interestingly, the firm has been referred to as 'Simon Co.' in all subsequent literature on the Chipko andolan.

When the news reached the DGSS, they were able to contact (the late) Kedar Singh Rawat, a prominent social worker of the area. Despite heavy rainfall a huge demonstration was organized on 24 June. Dismayed, the company's agents returned to Gopeshwar, where they complained at the forest office that even after depositing the guarantee money they were unable to fell the trees marked for them.

Reni[16]

Despite these early protests, the government went ahead with the yearly auction of forests in November. One of the plots scheduled to be assigned was the Reni forest, situated near Joshimath, in the Alakananda valley—a locality affected by landslides in the recent past. Reni itself was a village inhabited by members of the Bhotiya community who had abandoned nomadic pastoralism in favour of settled agriculture.

Hearing of the auction, DGSS workers contacted the block *pramukh* of Joshimath, Govind Singh Rawat of the Communist Party of India. While trekking through the area they noticed that over 2000 trees had already been marked for felling. Ironically enough, the labour for marking had been provided by the villagers themselves. Meetings were organized at which the tragic 1970 flood was remembered, and the possible consequences of felling the marked trees highlighted. Bhatt suggested to the villagers that they adopt the Chipko technique. The village women huddled some distance from the meeting were clearly amused at the thought of 'Chipko'.

The fellings were scheduled for the last week of March 1974. On the 25th a massive demonstration was organized in Joshimath where college students from Gopeshwar threatened to embark on a Chipko andolan unless the fellings were called off. Fearing opposition to the felling operations, the forest department resorted to subterfuge. The conservator of forests, who was based at Pauri, hoping that Chandi Prasad Bhatt could be persuaded to stay on in Gopeshwar, arranged to visit the DGSS

[16] Based on Mishra and Tripathi, 'Chipko', pp. 16–18, 21–30; J. C. Das and R. S. Negi, 'The Chipko Movement', in K. S. Singh (ed.), *Tribal Movements in India*, volume II (Delhi, 1983), pp. 383–92; poster issued by Zila Chamoli Sangharsh Samiti, Joshimath, in CSE file; interviews with C. P. Bhatt, Gopeshwar, May 1982, and Pithoragarh, October 1983.

premises on the 26th. Bhatt stayed on to receive him. The same day the men of Reni and neighbouring villages were called to Chamoli to receive the compensation long overdue for lands appropriated by the Indian army after the Chinese invasion of 1962.

With both DGSS workers and local men out of the way, the lumbermen proceeded to the forest on the 26th. The same evening Govind Singh Rawat phoned Bhatt with news of the department's deceit. Now it was believed to be too late. A plan to *gherao* the conservator was foiled when the official fled from Gopeshwar.

At Reni events had taken a dramatic turn. The contractors' men who were travelling to Reni from Joshimath stopped the bus shortly before Reni. Skirting the village, they made for the forest. A small girl who spied the workers with their implements rushed to Gaura Devi, the head of the village Mahila Mandal (Women's Club). Gaura Devi quickly mobilized the other housewives and went to the forest. Pleading with the labourers not to start felling operations, the women initially met with abuse and threats. When the women refused to budge, the men were eventually forced to retire.

The government steps in

Reni's importance in the saga of the Chipko andolan is twofold. It was the first occasion on which women participated in any major way, this participation, moreover, coming in the absence of their own menfolk and DGSS activists. As Gaura Devi recounted,

it was not a question of planned organization of the women for the movement, rather it happened spontaneously. Our men were out of the village so we had to come forward and protect the trees. We have no quarrel with anybody but only we wanted to make the people understand that our existence is tied with the forests.[17]

Secondly, no longer could the government treat Chipko merely as the reaction of motivated local industry deprived of raw material. For, until then, Reni was an archetypal hill village isolated from the market and dependent on the forests only as an input for subsistence agriculture. From now on Chipko was

[17] Das and Negi, 'Chipko', p. 390.

to come into its own as a peasant movement in defence of traditional forest rights, continuing a century-long tradition of resistance to state encroachment. The chief minister of UP, H. N. Bahuguna, who himself hailed from Garhwal, had earlier told the Chipko leaders that he could not meet their demands as he was 'the chief minister of the entire state, not only of the hill districts'.[18] After the Reni incident he conferred with them and agreed to set up a committee to investigate the incident. Headed by a botanist, Virendra Kumar, the members of the committee included Bhatt and secretaries of several government departments. Later, its terms of reference were extended to include the entire upper catchment of the Alakananda. The committee concluded that one important reason for the 1970 flood was the widespread deforestation in the Alakananda catchment. Accordingly, commercial fellings were banned for a period of ten years in the upper catchment of the river and its tributaries.[19]

A second government committee, headed by K. M. Tewari of the forest department, was formed to investigate the existing practices of resin tapping.[20] The Tewari Committee found that tapping rules were rarely followed. In the several forest divisions toured by it, irregularities concerning the width, depth and length of cuts were observed to be widespread. Such maltreatment had made the trees particularly vulnerable to lightning.[21]

The UP government also promised to review the lease granted to Star Paper Mills. Proposals to set up units in the hills were examined by another committee, headed by a paper technologist from the FRI, and included Bhatt. The latter proposed that a number of small units, spread over the entire hill region, should be set up. Although eight sites were identified for the purpose, the scheme was found economically unviable. However, the committee found two sites suitable for the siting of units of a capacity of 25 tonnes per day, and where infrastructural and raw material facilities were available.

---

[18] Interview with C. P. Bhatt, Gopeshwar, May 1981.

[19] YV, issues of 17 November 1974 and 7 August 1977; Bhatt, *Eco-system*, p. 18.

[20] V. P. S. Verma, 'WP for the Tehri For. Div., Garhwal Circle, 1973-74 to 1982-83', mimeo (Nainital, 1973), p. 377.

[21] B. Dogra, *Forest and People* (Delhi, 1983), pp. 38-40; S. Bahuguna, 'Let the Himalayan Forests Live', *Science Today*, March 1982, pp. 41-6.

Although detailed project reports were prepared, these recommendations were never implemented by the government.[22]

One proposal that did materialize in response to Chipko was the constitution of a forest corporation or Van Nigam, to take over all forms of forest exploitation. As originally envisaged, the auction system would be abolished and a large proportion of forest lots were to be allotted to FLC's by the corporation. Over time, however, the corporation reverted to the old system wherein outside agents were subcontracted the task of felling.[23]

Chipko spreads to Tehri

Following Reni, forest auctions were opposed in different parts of Garhwal. In Dehradun the auction of the Chakrata division forests had to be called off following protests led by local students. At Uttarkashi's Hanuman Mandir, Sunderlal Bahuguna underwent a two-week fast in October 1974, calling for a change in the existing forest policy.[24] That summer youths from both Kumaun and Garhwal had embarked on a 700 kilometre trek from Askot village—the eastern extremity of Kumaun—to Arakot on the borders of Himachal Pradesh. The marchers traversed the breadth of Uttarakhand in forty-four days. They were accompanied for part of the distance by Bahuguna.[25]

The lack of co-operation between the newly constituted Van Nigam and labour co-operatives, coupled with the damage done to chir trees, was central to the next major form the movement was to take. On the occasion of Van Diwas (30 May, the anniversary of the Tiladi firing), Chipko activists in Tehri district informed the forest department that the resin-scarred chir trees would be bandaged. When the department did not respond to the call to save the trees, a direct action programme was commenced on another historic day, the anniversary of Sridev Suman's death (25 July). Villagers of Khujni patti started pulling out the iron leaves inserted to extract resin. In Advani forest, close to the Hemval river, the Sarvodaya

---

[22] File no. 15 (25), cellulose and paper branch, FRI, Dehradun.
[23] See YV, 5 September 1976.
[24] YV, issues of 20 October and 10 November 1974.
[25] Dogra, *Forest and People*, pp. 46–7; Shekhar Pathak, 'Chipko Andolan ki Nayi Lahr', *Dharmayug*, August 1977.

worker Dhum Singh Negi went on a fast which was called off when villagers assured him that they would save the marked trees. Signifying their close relationship with trees, women tied 'raakhees' around the wounded spots. A reading of the Bhagavad Gita was also organized.[26]

The monsoon of 1978 saw another major flood, this time in the Bhageerathi valley. The immediate cause was a blockage in the Kanodia Gad, a tributary of the Bhageerathi. The financial loss due to the flood was estimated at Rs 25 crores.[27] Despite the flood, forest auctions were held at Nainital under heavy police protection. Opposition to forest felling also took place in the Chamyala forest, near Bahuguna's ashram at Silyara.[28] Elsewhere, people's committees were formed which successfully opposed felling at Loital and Amarsar. Now Chipko moved on to Badyargarh, where over 2300 trees had been marked for felling by the forest corporation.[29]

Chipko in Kumaun

In Kumaun the Chipko andolan had first been introduced during the Nainadevi fair at Nainital in 1974, following which forest auctions were opposed at several places.[30] However, it gathered momentum following the major landslides at Tawaghat, a village situated close to the India-Nepal border, in 1977. In the landslide 45 men and 75 heads of cattle perished. Young activists of the Uttarakhand Sangharsh Vahini (USV) opposed the auctions that were scheduled despite the Tawaghat disaster. In October 1977 large demonstrations were organized in Nainital. When several leaders of the USV were arrested, a crowd of a thousand people surrounded the Rink Hall, where the auctions were being held. The auctions were rescheduled for November. This time too section 144 had to be enforced. In the presence of the police and the provincial armed constabulary, protesters sang the songs of the legendary folk poet, Gaurda. Again, the leaders were arrested. Some rowdies,

---

[26] Dogra, pp. 52–3; YV, issues of 14 August and 18 December 1977.
[27] YV, issues of 13 August and 27 August 1978.
[28] YV, 8 October 1978.
[29] YV, 17 December 1978; Dogra, *Forest and People*, pp. 53–4.
[30] YV, 29 September 1974.

probably not connected with Chipko, then set fire to the Nainital Club.[31]

In the following months different Chipko agitations were organized by the USV. On 15 December Chipko activities were commenced in the Hat forest of Almora, where 5000 chir trees had been marked for felling. The USV demands included the revision of the forest settlement and a ban on the export of raw material from the hills.[32] In Chanchridhar forest, situated in the sensitive catchment area of the Gagas river, protesters marched into the block where the forest corporation planned to fell 6000 trees. They camped in the forest for over a week till the foresters had to admit defeat. Later, fellings scheduled by the corporation were successfully stalled at Janoti Palri and at Dhyari on the Almora–Pithoragarh road.[33]

Chipko returns to Chamoli

Chipko witnessed a resurgence in Chamoli, when, despite its early successes, commercial fellings continued to threaten the ecological stability of different habitations. In the Bhyunder valley, adjoining the famous Valley of Flowers, oak trees were marked to meet the fuelwood needs of Badrinath town. In Badrinath, an important pilgrim centre, the temple alone consumed over 1000 quintals of wood between May and November every year, during the pilgrim season. The total fuelwood consumption of the town was estimated at 2500 quintals. When trees were marked near Pulna village, the village panchayat wrote to the divisional forest officer and the district magistrate. Officials replied that 250 villagers could not get precedence over 1.5 lakh pilgrims. On the second day of felling operations (5 January 1978) the women of Pulna, despite 40 centimetres of snow, surrounded the labourers, took away their implements, and gave them a receipt for the tools. In this manner 621 trees were saved.[34]

---

[31] *Dinman*, issues of 23–29 October and 18–24 December 1977 (CSE file); interview with G. B. Pant of the USV, Nainital, May 1983.

[32] *Janpath*, 15 December 1977, CSE file.

[33] Dogra, *Forest and People*, p. 60–1.

[34] Rosalyan Wilson, 'Phulon ki Ghati mein Chipko Andolan', *Dainik Nayi Duniya*, 1 March 1978, CSE file.

One of the more significant agitations occurred in the Pindar valley, near the village of Dungri-Paintoli. Here the men of the village wanted to sell their oak forest to the horticulture department, which intended to establish a potato farm on the land. If the forest, the only good one for miles around, had been cut, the women would have had to walk a long distance every day to collect fuel and fodder. When the women voiced their opposition, it went unheeded. At this juncture Chipko activists intervened and, helped by the district administration, ensured that the forest area remaining (some forest had already been cleared) was saved.[35] Angered at the women's success, the village headman threatened Bhatt and his colleague Ramesh Pahari with dire consequences if they came back to the area.[36]

The significance of Dungri-Paintoli lies in the open conflict of interest between the men and women of the village. Lured by promises of better communications and other 'modern' facilities, the men hoped to make some quick money. The women, for their part, 'raised some fundamental questions challenging the system. In their opinion, agriculture and animal rearing was entirely dependent upon them, both closely related to the forest, and yet they were not consulted with regard to any [decisions] taken relating to forestry.'[37]

The next Chipko agitation took place at Parsari, near the army encampment of Joshimath. Here, kharsu and *moru* (high-level oak) trees were being felled to meet the fuel requirements of Joshimath town. The appointed forest provided fuel and fodder to four villages nearby which had appointed a watchman to guard it. In fact, the Kumar Committee had recommended that there be no felling in this area. A people's committee headed by Narendra Singh and Narayan Singh organized the village opposition, which refused to allow the fellings.[38]

[35] Gopa Joshi, 'Men Propose, Women Dispose', *Indian Express*, 14 January 1982.
[36] Interview with C. P. Bhatt, Gopeshwar, May 1982.
[37] C. P. Bhatt and S. S. Kunwar, 'Hill Women and Their Involvement in Forestry', in S. S. Kunwar (ed.), *Hugging the Himalayas: The Chipko Experience* (Gopeshwar, 1982), p. 84.
[38] C. P. Bhatt, 'Joshimath mein "Chipko" Andolan', CSE file.

THE BADYARGARH ANDOLAN

Thus far, I have presented a broad overview of the major Chipko agitations that have occurred since the movement's inception. Let us now look more closely at one particular Chipko mobilization in order to properly appreciate its social and cultural idiom. The Chipko agitation that occurred in the Badyargarh patti of Tehri Garhwal district in the winter of 1978-9 forms the focus of the section, and my analysis of it is based largely on fieldwork conducted in early 1983. I present here an internal analysis of the movement, i.e. its patterns of mobilization and type of organization, the participation of different social groups, its ideology and methods, and the relationship between the leadership and the rank and file. I also highlight the changing perceptions of the state which has replaced the Tehri durbar as the unit of legitimate authority. The fundamental characteristics of Chipko, as the movement is conceived by its participants, may thereby become clearer.

The patti of Badyargarh is situated between the Bhageerathi and Alakananda rivers, about 130 kilometres north-east of Rishikesh. The social structure, in conformity with the rest of Uttarakhand, is built around relatively homogeneous and cohesive village communities. For the past few decades, however, grain production has been inadequate to sustain the population. In this money-order economy, women labour hard to perform household and agricultural tasks.

Badyargarh is a relatively prosperous patti, containing a large number of retired and serving army personnel. The growing opportunities offered to individuals by commercialization, education, government employment, etc. have definitely contributed to the erosion of the community co-operative spirit. The possibility of individual social mobility that the outside world offers is reflected in the village by the return of successful individuals to build cement structures. Although the community spirit is still present, as shown by Chipko, there is, simultaneously, a slowly growing differentiation within the village due to the impact of commercialization. There is, too, a sense of disruption of the traditional social fabric that the opening out of Garhwal has brought, as well as anger at the comparative underdevelopment of the hills.

Commercial forestry in the region started only around 1965, with the building of a motor road into the area. In the following years the extraction of resin and turpentine was commenced, alongside the felling of chir trees. In 1979 the Van Nigam gave out a big contract for the felling of chir pine in the area. The felling, which went on for several months, was, according to villagers, very destructive, with young regeneration being removed in addition to the logged trees. Several dozen trucks came and went daily, taking away all the wood, including the branches of trees. As people later reminisced, the contractor replied to early signs of protest by remarking that he would not leave any part of the tree behind (*'Hum ped ka koi hissa nahin choddenge'*).

The andolan

Following upon this activity and just prior to the proposed logging in the Malgaddi forest, Sarvodaya workers, trusted associates of the Chipko leader Sunderlal Bahuguna, came to Badyargarh to enquire into the people's grievances. These leaders, Dhum Singh Negi, Kunwar Prasun, Pratap Shikhar and Vijay Jardari, among others, went from village to village informing people of the proposed felling and its harmful ecological consequences. At the same time Bahuguna's wife, Vimla, and other ladies mobilized the village women on the issue.

The andolan started on 25 December 1978 but acquired momentum only after Bahuguna went on a hunger fast from 9 January 1979. Conducted in a disused shepherd's hut in the forest, and in the middle of winter, the fast was a rallying point for people of the surrounding villages. Thus, over three thousand men, women and children participated, 'one for every chir tree in the forest'. An attempt at cutting by night was foiled by villagers taking night duty by turns. Classic non-cooperation tactics were adopted, there being no question of any violence used (*'himsa ka koi saval nahin tha'*). Bahuguna was carried away by the police on the night of 22 January and interned in Tehri jail, where he continued his fast. Meanwhile, a reading of the Bhagavad Gita was started on the 26th. Meeting determined resistance from the villagers even after the removal of their leader from the scene, the contractor and forest officials had to admit defeat and abandon felling.

Participation: A feature of the andolan was the active participation of all social groups. This was explained by the evident fact that all were equally affected by deforestation. The Bajgis, a caste of musicians, were solicited to mobilize villagers through their *dholaks* (drums). Women played a prominent part, as did government servants and defence personnel, though their support could only be covert.

Children too joined in a movement which recreated the atmosphere of joyous celebration in a fight against injustice. When police camped in Dhadi Ghandiyal High School, children went on strike in protest at the invasion of a 'temple of knowledge' (Vidya Mandir). While the strike itself lasted four days, all through the andolan students skipped school with the connivance of the teachers. As the principal recounted, he was placed in an awkward position, with the police harassing him on the one hand and, on the other, villagers imploring him to let his wards come to the forest. The schoolteacher, highly respected in Garhwal, symbolized in his person the conflict between government and people. As a figure of authority the state expected him to control the people, while the people wanted sanction for their acts by that very same authority.

The moral content of Chipko: Two further incidents that occurred after the successful completion of the andolan serve to illustrate the strong moral content of Chipko. When the contractor abandoned his labour, the locals fed them from village ration shops and petitioned officials to alleviate their plight. Only with the arrival of the labour commissioner could the grievances be redressed and the labour sent home to Himachal.

The second incident relates to the wood felled prior to Chipko, which was not allowed to be carried away for conversion to sleepers. The Badyargarh Van Suraksha Samiti (BVSS) resolved to release the wood only after the local people had fulfilled their needs. This entailed that the first claim would be exercised by those individuals and villagers who had not been granted timber rights, following which the requirements of the other inhabitants of Badyargarh and its neighbouring pattis would be met on payment of nominal rates. It was proposed that the income so generated would be used to regenerate the deforested areas of Badyargarh. Despite stern official warnings the BVSS stuck to their stand.[39]

[39] *Chipko Samachar*, datelined Badyargarh, 4 February 1979, in file of the Badyargarh Van Suraksha Samiti (BVSS).

Chipko and popular consciousness

There are several important characteristics of Chipko as the movement relates to popular perceptions.

The link between forests and humans: During my fieldwork I found that almost everyone I interviewed was aware of the importance of forest cover in regulating soil and water regimes. Chipko has contributed to a heightened awareness—the interesting question (to which chapter 2 provides one answer) is the extent to which this ecological consciousness predates Chipko. Thus, in Badyar village no grass cutting has traditionally been allowed on the steep hill overlooking the settlement. The cliff has a thick crop of grass and shrubs, in the absence of which boulders would come tumbling down the hill during the monsoon—hence the ban. As I argued in chapter 3, the link between humans and forests that existed before the inception of commercial forestry has been eroded by the loss of community control. In this context Chipko aims at halting the growing alienation of humans from nature, an alienation with potentially damaging consequences.

Chipko and community solidarity: An ecological consciousness, however attenuated, and the manifold benefits of forest cover to the hill economy (and ecology) can explain Chipko's success in mobilizing all sections of hill society. In response to criticism that the andolan depended largely on Bahuguna's appeal, the BVSS pointed out that if the movement did not enjoy popular support it would have terminated with Sunderlal's arrest and removal. As villagers see it, efforts to put out forest fires, which they are obliged to do under the settlement, are made in the belief that their property was being destroyed. Thus, when the government started indiscriminate felling (*andhadhun katai*) it was keenly resented.

Attitude towards officials: The lack of fulfilment of the basic needs of education, health and employment found the accumulated grievances being crystallized in Chipko. One BVSS activist put it thus:

> *Humme thoda sa anaaz mila, jab usse bhi*
> *nahin paka sake, tho andolan karna pada.*[40]

[40] Freely translated: 'when we could not obtain the wood to cook even the little grain we get, we had to resort to a movement.'

The implacable hostility towards state officials, particularly those belonging to the forest department, can be read as a symbol of such disillusionment. Chipko participants expressed delight in recalling the impotence of high officials (*ucchadhikari*) in the face of the andolan. Senior officials of the civil and forest administration, as well as the police, arrived but were powerless to resume felling operations ('*Ucchadhikari pahunch gaye, lekin kuch nahi kar paye*').

Women and Chipko: It has been stressed that hill women have agricultural tasks. This situation is further aggravated, in Badyargarh and elsewhere, by the absence of adult males. Some analysts see a direct causal link here. According to Bahuguna himself,

Due to washing away of fertile soil, the menfolk were compelled to leave their families and wander in search of employment, thus making the women bear all the responsibilities, collecting fodder, firewood and carrying water, which form the main chores besides farming.[41]

This interpretation can be disputed: for, as I show in chapter 2, the important economic role of women is culturally specific to the hill family and not merely a result of changed ecological or economic conditions. Can one then relate the subordinate position of women in Uttarakhand to the enthusiastic support given by them to the Chipko andolan?

An interesting conversation at a teashop in Badyar village brought out the conflicts inherent in such a situation. One retired army man was strongly of the opinion that women's participation in Chipko was a consequence of their inferior position in hill society. Observing the men gathered around the shop, he asked rhetorically, 'We men are sitting drinking tea, but can we see any woman here? Why not?' A look at the far hillside, where women were gathering firewood, provided the answer: 'They are not here for they have work to do.' This feminist stand brought forth jeers from fellow villagers, who later advised me not to take him seriously.[42] Nevertheless, the local women's leader, Sulochana Devi, was emphatic that the success of Chipko depended on women. The movement,

[41] S. Bahuguna, *Chipko* (Silyara, 1980), p. 5. Emphasis added.
[42] This is in keeping with the tendency, often reported by anthropologists, to minimize internal criticism in the presence of outsiders.

she argued, was only the first step; women needed to be educated and dowry banned in order that others did not fritter away women's wealth (*'ladkiyon ka dhan na khoya jaye'*).

Chipko in a history of protest

Badyargarh was the scene of a wide-ranging peasant movement in 1948 that culminated in the merger of Tehri state with the province of UP (see chapter 4). Protesting against extortion of money by the king's officials, villagers gathered at a religious fair at Dhadi Ghandiyal, marched towards the capital, Tehri, capturing outposts on the way and symbolically replacing corrupt patwaris by their own men.

The 1948 dhandak remains vividly in the collective memory of the peasants of Badyargarh and their heroism then was invoked by the Chipko leaders in 1979. Apart from the participation of many in both, the movement itself has strong similarities—such as the identification of officials as the main exploiters, the belief that justice was on their side, and the forms of protest itself. In both instances the act of protest was seen as having a moral–religious sanction. While in 1948 the peasantry was mobilized on the occasion of a religious fair held once in thirteen years, an important event in Chipko was the reading of the Gita. Camped in the forests, Chipko volunteers commenced the reading of the epic and the rendition of folk songs. The conservator of forests who opposed the ceremony was firmly told that all the Vedas were written in the forest. And when the patwari threatened one of the priests with arrest the priest replied: 'Arrest me under any section of law, but what are the rules for the Nigam people?'

Bahuguna and the idiom of protest: The idiom of Chipko, then, can be understood in terms of the 'moral economy' of the Garhwal peasant, who could readily comprehend the tactics of the charismatic leader of the Badyargarh andolan, Sunderlal Bahuguna. Bahuguna concentrates his fire on the officials of the forest department who, in league with contractors, 'do not leave a splinter of wood in the forests'.[43] The call to forest officers to change their ways and serve local communities evokes a positive reaction from a people exposed to extortion by officials during earlier regimes.

[43] S. Bahuguna, 'Her Story: Women's Non-violent Power in the Chipko Movement', *Manushi*, no. 6 (1980), p. 31.

Bahuguna's method of functioning is far removed from that of self-seeking politicians. A non-political person, he was able to strike a chord in the hearts of those disenchanted with the hypocrisy of politicians and the electoral process. Gandhian methods of non-violence and Bahuguna's personal asceticism were appreciatively responded to by the predominantly Hindu peasantry. The capacity for physical suffering (vide the hunger fast in the bitter cold) and spirit of sacrifice (*tyaga*) in an age of selfishness were constantly marvelled at by villagers who read into these acts the renunciation of worldly ambition as exhorted by Hindu scriptures.

Sunderlal's charisma is undoubted and his deeds are still an object of wonder in Badyargarh. His success is clearly related to the distinctive character of social protest in Tehri Garhwal. The attacks on forest officials can be understood in the context of dhandaks aimed at the raja's minions. Sunderlal's remarkable physical endurance and sage-like appearance make him a natural leader whose followers look to him to restore a pristine state of harmony and just government. In fact, Bahuguna records that his life was changed by a chance encounter with Sridev Suman when he was a schoolboy. He 'proudly refers to Sridev Suman as his guru in all respects'—a theme he stresses repeatedly in his speeches.[44] Here one finds a striking parallel with other agrarian movements, where too the invocation of the spirit and memory of peasant martyrs is a primary 'means by which a sense of the past is revived, codified, and used'. References to predecessors like Suman reinforce Bahuguna's own credentials, as a notable ascetic of his time, to be the undisputed leader of the peasantry of these districts. The Tehri Garhwal case provides yet another illustration of what is a much more pervasive phenomenon so far as lower-class movements are concerned, for, as Eugene Genovese has pointed out,

from the peasant revolts of medieval Europe, to revolutionary Puritanism, to the early working class organizations, to the great revolutionary movements of our own time, asceticism has provided a decisive ingredient in the mobilization of popular risings.[45]

[44] Interview in *The Telegraph*, 6 August 1983; S. Bahuguna, *Van Shramik* (Silyara, 1977).

[45] See Anne Walthall, 'Japanese *Gimin*: Peasant Martyrs in Popular Memory', *American Historical Review*, vol. 91, no. 5, December 1986; Eugene Genovese, *Roll, Jordan, Roll: The World the Slaves Made* (New York, 1973), p. 276.

For its practitioners, asceticism is a potent vehicle of cultural communication. Even as Bahuguna's own lifestyle evokes a sympathetic response among peasants, his message is conveyed through a local cultural idiom, both by his own acts and those of his followers—for example the noted folk-singer Ghanshyam Sailani, who has played a central role in the Chipko movements of Tehri Garhwal.

What is distinctive about Sunderlal Bahuguna's asceticism is that it is accompanied by a call to higher authority to side with the suffering peasants. During the course of the Badyargarh andolan, Sunderlal assured the villagers that even if the forest department was opposed to the movement, the prime minister, Morarji Desai, and Lokanayak Jayaprakash Narayan were on their side. While breaking the fast he commenced in Badyargarh in Dehradun jail Bahuguna said he did so only due to a request from 'JP', whom he called his general (*senapathi*). He recalled Suman's historic eighty-four-day fast in Tehri jail and also mentioned the support of home minister H. M. Patel for his *dharmayuddha* (holy war) to save the Himalayan forests.[46] After the victory of the Congress party in the elections of 1980 he invoked the support of the prime minister, Indira Gandhi, citing her concern at the situation in the Himalaya.[47] In this invocation leading politicians assume a role not dissimilar to that of the Tehri maharaja in earlier days. While their functionaries are viewed as being in league with corrupt contractors, those in power are believed to sympathize with the oppressed. Chipko then becomes, in a strikingly similar fashion to the dhandak, the only possible means to obtain justice by bringing the wrongdoings of officials to the notice of heads of government.

CUSTOM AND CONFRONTATION IN CHIPKO

As an organized movement of both national and international significance, Chipko can be analysed from the perspective of the sociology of social movements. In this study, too, I have highlighted several classic themes in the literature: the pattern of leadership, the forms of mobilization, the emergence of a

[46] S. Bahuguna, 'Badyargarh mein Itihas Ban Raha Hai', YV, 7 January and 21 January 1979. Cf. also YV, 4 February 1979.
[47] Cf. S. Bahuguna, *Walking with the Chipko Message* (Silyara, 1983).

codified ideology, and the relationship between leader and led.[48] I would, however, stress that this analysis of the formal characteristics of Chipko as a social movement must be supplemented by a study of its less formal features. Moving away from the public arena of Chipko and its popular stereotypes, through a case study of the Badyargarh movement I have tried to understand the transformations of meaning it has brought in the lives of its participants. An exploration of the less structured aspects of the movement reveals the existence of certain tenaciously held values, adhered to by village participants. The ideology that can be inferred from peasant actions is not entirely consistent with the formal ideology of Chipko as presented to the outside world. Finally, one of Chipko's central features is its historicity—i.e. its relationship with past movements which raised similar questions concerning the relationship between the state and the peasantry.

Locating Chipko culturally and historically provides a long overdue corrective to the popular conception of Chipko, which is that of a romantic reunion of humans, especially women, with nature. The dramatic act—often threatened but rarely brought into play—of hugging the tree to save it from the contractor's axe is the chief characteristic with which the movement is identified. Some writers have seen Chipko as having its origins in an incident believed to have occurred in Rajasthan in 1763, when members of the Bishnoi sect laid down their lives to protect trees being felled under orders from the maharaja of Jodhpur.[49] Within the movement, Sunderlal Bahuguna's writings and lectures have done much to propagate this view of Chipko.[50] Other writers have stressed the role of women, as the sex crucially affected by deforestation. It has even been suggested that Chipko is a 'feminist' movement.[51]

It will be clear from our study that the above stereotypes are

[48] Cf. J. R. Gusfield, 'Social Movements and Social Change: Perspectives of Linearity and Fluidity', in Louis Kriesberg (ed.), *Research in Social Movements, Conflict and Change*, volume 4 (Greenwich, Conn., 1981); J. C. Jenkins, 'Resource Mobilization Theory and the Study of Social Movements', *Annual Review of Sociology*, no. 9, 1983.

[49] Richard St Barbe Baker, 'Chipko—Hug to the Tree People', in S. Bahuguna, *Chipko* (Silyara, 1981), pp. 1–4.

[50] See, for example, S. Bahuguna, *Paryavaran aur Chipko Yatra* (Silyara, 1983).

[51] Centre for Science and Environment, *The State of the Environment: A Citizen's Report* (Delhi, 1982), pp. 42–3.

seriously inadequate in interpreting the origins, idiom and trajectory of the movement. The analogy with the incident involving the Bishnoi community obscures Chipko's origins, which are specific to the conditions of Uttarakhand. Chipko is only one, though undoubtedly the most organized, in a series of protest movements against commercial forestry dating from the earliest days of state intervention. Different Chipko agitations have invoked the spirit and memory of past upsurges against the curtailment of customary rights. This continuity is also strikingly manifest in the moral idiom in which protest has been expressed. Similar notions of morality and justice have permeated movements against the durbar and the colonial state as well as Chipko. As this case study of the Badyargarh andolan reveals, the peasantry was protesting against the denial of subsistence rights which state policy has wrought. Essentially, the movement was in response to a perceived breach of the informal code between the ruler and the ruled known as the 'moral economy' of the peasant.

Clearly, this continuity is more marked in the case of Tehri Garhwal. Here, Bahuguna's personal acquaintance with later movements against the durbar as well as the distinctive flavour of the dhandak has informed a movement whose contemporary character cannot be adequately grasped without reference to its historical context. The identification of officials as oppressors, the belief that Indira Gandhi or other high-level politicians— the contemporary equivalent of sovereigns—could intervene and dispense justice, and Bahuguna's own asceticism, which is reminiscent of Suman, all testify to this continuity.

In so far as Chipko constitutes a part of an overall tradition of protest, this continuity is present, albeit in an attenuated form, in other parts of Uttarakhand as well. Thus, certain variations in the different subcultures of Chipko can be explained with reference to the different socio-political structures in which they operate. Bhatt's identification of macro forces, such as overall state policy, as the major cause can perhaps be related to the rather different political history of the Alakananda valley, where, much earlier, the rupture between the state and the people had occurred as a result of British colonialism. Similarly, the adherence of the USV to a more radical posture may in part be a consequence of the earlier, and deeper, penetration of 'modern' political ideologies into Kumaun.

In Uttarakhand the participation of women in popular movements dates from the anti-alcohol agitations led by Sarvodaya workers in the 1960s. However, despite the important role played by women, it would be simplistic to characterize Chipko as a feminist movement. In several instances, especially the early mobilizations at Mandal and at Phata, it was men who took the initiative in protecting forests. Women came to the fore in Reni, when in the contrived absence of menfolk they unexpectedly came forward to thwart forest felling. In other agitations, such as Badyargarh, men, women and children have all participated equally. Dungri-Paintoli is the only instance of an overt conflict between men and women over the management and control of forest resources. As such, even at the level of participation Chipko can hardly be said to constitute a women's movement. Undoubtedly, the hill women have traditionally borne an extraordinarily high share of family labour—and their participation in Chipko may be read as an outcome of the increasing difficulty with which these tasks have been accomplished in the deteriorating environment. Interestingly, Chandi Prasad Bhatt does believe that women are capable of playing a more dynamic role than the men who, in the face of growing commercialization, are apt to lose sight of the long-term interests of the village economy.[52] On the other hand, it has been suggested that while they are the beasts of burden as viewed through the prism of an outside observer, hill women are in fact aware that they are the repository of local tradition. In the orbit of the household women often take decisions which are rarely challenged by the men. In the act of embracing the trees, therefore, they are acting not merely as women but as bearers of continuity with the past in a community threatened with fragmentation.[53] The conflict between men and women has surfaced much more sharply in other social movements in the hills, most notably in the anti-alcohol movement organized by the USV in 1984.[54]

Another possible source of confusion lies in the important

[52] Speech at a village meeting at Bakarkhatia, district Pithoragarh, October 1983.

[53] This is the position (as expressed in personal communications) of two scholars with an intimate knowledge of Uttarakhand, Shekhar Pathak and Jean Claude Galey.

[54] See Shekhar Pathak, 'Intoxication as a Social Evil: The Anti-Alcohol Movement in Uttarakhand', *Economic and Political Weekly*, July 1985.

role played by leaders owing an allegiance to the Sarvodaya movement. Gandhian institutions have been quick to hail Chipko as a modern example of satyagraha, calling it 'direct action in the best Gandhian spirit'.[55] In so far as the personal commitment and personal lifestyle of activists like Bhatt and Bahuguna exemplify the highest traditions of Gandhian constructive work, the characterization is not altogether incorrect. However, both Bhatt and Bahuguna, like the Praja Mandal activists of an earlier era, are anything but alienated from the historical and contemporary specificities of village life in Garhwal. Their involvement in Chipko is crucially informed, albeit in quite different ways, by a sharp historical sense and the experience gleaned from years of social activism in the hills. At the level of popular participation the Gandhian label is even less appropriate. It seems clear from the description of different Chipko agitations that the role played by external ideologies is a severely limited one. Villagers see Chipko as a fight for basic subsistence denied to them by the institutions and policies of the state. Although Chipko, like many Gandhian movements, has an important ethical dimension, its underlying notions of morality and justice are intrinsic to a history of protest against state restrictions on peasant access to forest produce. Nor should superficial similarities in methods of protest lead one to designate Chipko as 'Gandhian', its 'nonviolent' method being an inspired and highly original response to forest felling rather than ideologically motivated.

At the same time, the Gandhian association may actually have helped Chipko in its largely successful bid to stop the onslaught of commercial forestry in the Himalaya. It is noteworthy that while the last decade has seen the emergence of several forest-based movements in peninsular India, none of these movements has had a comparable success in attracting public support or influencing the direction of government policies.[56] Indeed, they have on occasion been crushed with a brutality

[55] Foreword by Radhakrishna of the Gandhi Peace Foundation, in A. Mishra and S. Tripathi, *Chipko Movement*.

[56] For an analysis of these movements see, *inter alia*, Peoples Union for Democratic Rights, *Undeclared Civil War* (Delhi, 1982); Nirmal Sengupta (ed.), *Jharkhand: Fourth World Dynamics* (Delhi, 1982); G. De Silva, *et al.*, 'Bhomi Sena: A Struggle for People's Power', *Development Dialogue*, no. 2, 1979.

that has been notably absent in the state's attempt to deal with Chipko. Several factors account for the relative lack of success which these movements have enjoyed. First, the regions in which they have arisen have undergone rapid economic differentiation; wracked by internal contradictions, these struggles are unable (unlike in single-class hill society) to present a united front in opposition to forest policies. These movements have also tended to be more violent. Second, the cultural composition of forest dwellers in peninsular India is overwhelmingly non-Hindu. Chipko, on the other hand, located as it is in an area of enormous religious significance for the majority Hindu community, has struck a sympathetic chord in the heart of the Indian public. Finally, there is the veneer of Gandhianism with which Chipko is cloaked, a matter of some embarrassment for a state claiming to be the rightful successor of the freedom struggle and upholding Gandhi as the Father of the Nation. In this manner Chipko has, knowingly or unknowingly, successfully exploited the ambiguities in the dominant ideology of the Indian state. While this ideology is avowedly non-religious in its actions, the state goes to considerable lengths not to offend the Hindu sentiments of the majority of its subjects; and while its development policies are a strong repudiation of Gandhian economics, by paying daily obeisance to the Mahatma in its official rituals the state tries to symbolically appropriate the enormous prestige associated with his name. Faced with a popular movement which originated in the watershed of the holy Ganga, used techniques of non-violence and was led by Gandhians, the state has been hoist with its own petard.[57]

CHIPKO AS AN ENVIRONMENTAL MOVEMENT

I have repeatedly emphasized the fact that Chipko lies in a path of continuity with earlier peasant struggles in Uttarakhand; at the same time, as an organized and sustained social

[57] A relevant analogy within Uttarakhand is with the massive anti-alcohol campaigns organized by the Uttarakhand Sangharsh Vahini (USV) in 1984. Divorced from the Gandhian movement, the USV leaders do not enjoy the kind of access both Bhatt and Bahuguna have to several high officials. This element, and the more militant nature of their struggle, clearly played a role in the state's punitive response and its reluctance to concede the long-term demands of the movement.

movement it promises to go beyond them. Here it is useful to distinguish between the 'private' face of Chipko, which is that of a quintessential peasant movement, and its 'public' profile as one of the most celebrated environmental movements in the world. Thus, while the last Chipko agitation in Uttarakhand occurred in 1980, the movement's activists have since been tirelessly propagating its message. Within the Himalaya, footmarches and environmental camps are organized at regular intervals. There has also been a significant attempt to contribute to the environment debate in India and abroad.

The widening of Chipko

In April 1981 Sunderlal Bahuguna went on an indefinite fast, urging a total ban on green felling in the Himalaya above an altitude of 1000 metres. In response the government constituted an eight-member 'expert' committee to prepare a comprehensive report on Himalayan forest policy. Although the thrust of the committee's report was to exonerate the forest department and 'sustained-yield' forestry, the government agreed to allow a fifteen-year moratorium on commercial felling in the Uttarakhand Himalaya.[58] Well before the moratorium, however, there was little doubt that the Chipko movement had significantly slowed the march of commercial forestry. Thus the output of major forest produce from the eight hill districts had declined, in the decade 1971–81, from over 62,000 to 40,000 cubic metres per annum.[59]

By successfully bringing commercial forestry to a standstill, Chipko marks the end of an epoch for the people and landscape

[58] 'Report of the Experts Committee to Look into the Policy Regarding Fellings and Protection of Trees and to Bring Improvement in the Maintenance of Environmental Balance in the Himalayan Region of U.P.', mimeo, Uttar Pradesh Forest Department, Lucknow, March 1982. In Uttarakhand proper, Bahuguna's fast marks an end to the activist phase of Chipko and its shift towards both publicity and reconstruction work. While Chipko-style movements (for example, the Appiko movement in Karnataka) have emerged in other parts of India, one must not make the mistake of seeing these movements as merely derivative of Chipko. Appiko, like Chipko, must be studied in its local historical and cultural contexts; assimilating it to Chipko, as some writers have done, does it as much violence as assimilating Chipko itself to abstract ideas of feminism, environmentalism, Gandhianism, etc.

[59] N. C. Saxena, 'Social Forestry in the Hill Districts of Uttar Pradesh', mimeo, ICIMOD (Kathmandu, 1987), Table 22.

of the Indian Himalaya. However, state forestry is by no means the only threat to the ecological and social stability of the hills, for the past decades have witnessed a rapid expansion in the scale of commercial penetration in Uttarakhand. This is exemplified by the location of large dams, increasing mining operations and the spread of alcoholism. This intensification of resource exploitation has been matched almost step by step with a sustained opposition, in which Chipko has played a crucial role, in catalysing and broadening the social consciousness of the Himalayan peasantry. Thus, movements against big dams, unregulated mining and the sale of illicit liquor have been organized by all three wings of the Chipko movement. While a detailed description of these ongoing struggles is beyond the scope of this study, in such a widening of the movement's horizons changes in forest policy are conceived of as only one element in an alternative development strategy. Moreover, despite insinuations that Chipko has a localized frame of reference, the bid to rescue hill society from the ravages of capitalist penetration does not call for a narrow 'regionalism'. As the agriculture of the Indo-Gangetic plain depends heavily on an assured supply of water from the rivers that originate in the Himalaya, the stabilization of Uttarakhand ecology and society has far wider implications.

Three environmental philosophies

Drawing on the experience of years of social activism, the leaders of the different wings of the Chipko movement have put forward their own interpretations of local and national processes of environmental degradation. One of the most forceful statements has come from Sunderlal Bahuguna, perhaps the best-known Chipko leader. Bahuguna holds commercial forestry and the close links that exist between contractors and forest officials as responsible for the deteriorating Himalayan environment. However, shortsighted forest management is a symptom of a deeper malaise—the anthropocentric view of nature intrinsic to modern industrial civilization. Thus, 'the ecological crisis in Himalaya. is not an isolated event. It has its roots in the [modern] materialistic civilization, which makes man the butcher of Earth.'[60]

[60] Cf. Sunderlal Bahuguna, *Chipko Message*, p. 18.

While Bahuguna's group is active in the Bhageerathi valley, the wing of Chipko active in the Alakananda valley is associated with the name of Chandi Prasad Bhatt. Unlike Bahuguna, Bhatt does not deny the villagers' role in deforestation, stressing, however, that 'this has been a result of separating the local population from the management of the forest wealth.'[61] Further, Bhatt argues, both forest officials and commercial forestry are merely agents of a development process biased in favour of the urban–industrial complex and against local needs. He is also sharply critical of the growing separation between the state and the people, as clearly manifest in the framing of development schemes by urban-centred technocrats that have little relevance to the realities of rural India.[62]

Interestingly, the two leaders also affirm alternative systems of environmental activism. Bahuguna works in what one might call a prophetic mode: attempting to convert the uninitiated with a constant flow of articles, lectures and marches. In an inspired move, he undertook a 4000 kilometre foot march across the Himalaya, which was completed in April 1983, attracting wide coverage on the extent of environmental degradation in hill tracts outside Uttarakhand. Chandi Prasad Bhatt and his group work in what I would call the mode of reconstruction. Apart from several afforestation camps conducted yearly, they are also working on the installation of bio-gas plants and on other low-cost energy-saving devices. A remarkable fact about the afforestation camps organized by the DGSS has been the rate of survival of saplings (65 to 80 per cent)—the survival rate achieved in government plantations (around 10 to 15 per cent) seems pathetic by comparison.[63] Interestingly, the rate of survival showed a rapid rise following the greater involvement of women.[64]

The major differences between the perspectives of the two major leaders are presented in the chart on pp. 182–3. Here, the major schism in Chipko is interpreted along two separate

[61] Cf. C. P. Bhatt, 'Eco-Development: People's Movement'.

[62] C. P. Bhatt, 'Himalaya Kshetra ka Niyojan', mimeo, in Hindi (Gopeshwar, 1984).

[63] Personal communication to me from S. N. Prasad of the Indian Institute of Science, who conducted the study.

[64] See Anil Agarwal and Sunita Narain (eds), *India: The State of the Environment 1984–85: A Citizen's Report* (New Delhi, 1985).

but interlinked axes: historically, with reference to the earlier division of Uttarakhand into a traditional monarchy and a colonial bureaucratic regime; and ideologically, with reference to two distinct philosophies of development.

A third group, the Uttarakhand Sangharsh Vahini (USV), which is active in Kumaun, adheres to an ideology strongly influenced by Marxism. While attempting to move away from the public identification of Chipko with the two major leaders, USV insists that the human–nature relationship must not be viewed in isolation from existing relationships between humans. For the USV, social and economic redistribution is seen as logically prior to ecological harmony. It follows that the USV refuses to associate itself with state-sponsored development programmes, and in its own work it has occasionally come into sharp confrontation with the administration.[65]

These streams within Chipko reflect, in microcosm, different strands in the modern environmental debate. In his rejection of industrial civilization Bahuguna comes strikingly close to the American historians Lynn White and Theodor Roszak who stressed the role of religious beliefs in determining human attitudes towards nature. Modern science and technology are largely informed, in this perspective, by Judaeo-Christian ideals of human transcendence and rightful mastery over nature. This ethos is contrasted with the value systems of so-called primitive societies which, unlike Western science, viewed the ecosystem in its totality, thereby ensuring a rational and sustainable use of resources.[66] While accurately pinpointing the inability of Western science to come to grips with the eco-crisis, the alternative proposed by this school implies a return to pre-industrial modes of living—a vision perhaps as elusive as Western science's claim to bring material prosperity for all.

While acknowledging the alienation of modern science from the true needs of the people, Bhatt places a far greater emphasis on alternative technologies that could be more environmentally

[65] This paragraph is based on interviews with USV activists in Nainital and Pithoragarh, in May and October 1983.

[66] Cf. Lynn White, 'The Historical Roots of Our Ecologic Crisis', and Theodor Roszak, 'The Sacramental Vision of Nature', both in Robin Clarke (ed.), *Notes for the Future* (London, 1975). Cf. also John Passmore, *Man's Responsibility for Nature* (2nd edition: London, 1980).

CHART

Bahuguna versus *Bhatt: Personality and Ideology*

THEME	BAHUGUNA	BHATT
Historical influences	Specific to Tehri Garhwal—uses the symbols and targets of dhandaks. Invokes past protests and heroes like Suman. Sees high-level politicians as supporting movement (analogue with sovereign?)	Less specific—but recognizes and stresses overall history of deprivation of forest rights and protest in Uttarakhand
Identification of agents of deforestation	Representatives of forest dept in league with timber contractors	Forest policy influenced by commercial interests—villagers alienated from forest growth they helped to nurture
Broader underlying causes	Modern industrialization in which man is the Butcher of Nature	Development policy biased towards city and big industry and against local economic and ecological self-reliance
Methods of working	A prophetic mode—articles, lectures, pada-yatras, fasts—of late mostly outside Garhwal	Localized reconstruction work and appropriate technology of various kinds—in small industry, mini hydel plants, and bio-gas plants. Also the occasional article or lecture
Personal style	Ascetic, charismatic and all-inclusive. Relation with others in the movement more in the guru–shishya or master–disciple mould	Relatively low-keyed. More democratic—works closely alongside others in the DGSS. Ascetic, but less consciously so

Relation to Gandhian movement	Idealism, invocation of scriptures reminiscent of Vinobha Bhave, to whom he was close both personally and ideologically	Synthesis of Gandhianism and Western socialism—ideologically closer to J. P. Narayan and R. M. Lohia
Solution: local	Total ban on green felling—forests to revert to villagers. Trees for fuel, fodder, fertilizer, fruit and fibre to be propagated	Ban felling in sensitive areas. Large-scale afforestation drives involving state and villagers. Judicious extraction for local use only—aimed at generating employment through ecologically sound technology
Solution: global	Not specified—but a return to pre-industrial economy implied	Alternative path of industrialization—with political and economic decentralization. Based on technologies that promote self-reliance, social control and ecological stability

conscious as well as socially just. In this respect his views are similar to the pioneer formulations of the technologist A. K. N. Reddy, who emphasizes the role of appropriate technology in an environmentally sound development policy. The criteria of technological choice advocated by Reddy are, briefly: technologies that are employment generating, ecologically sound, which promote self-reliance (both in terms of invoking mass participation and using local resources), which tend to reduce rather than reinforce inequalities, and which build upon rather than neglect traditional skills.[67]

While the USV does share with the DGSS this vision of an ecologically oriented socialism, the two groups differ in their relative emphasis on political activism. The USV clearly prefers organizing social movements that confront the state to grassroots reconstruction work such as afforestation, arguing that it is the responsibility of the state to reverse the processes of capitalist penetration and environmental degradation. It does not share, either, the doctrinal emphasis on non-violence espoused by both Bahuguna and Bhatt.

In their own very different ways the three wings of Chipko have questioned the normative consensus among Indian intellectuals and political élites on the feasibility of rapid industrialization and technological modernization. Of course the environment debate is, worldwide, as yet in its very early stages. The linkages between technology and ecology, and politics and culture, will undoubtedly undergo significant changes in the years ahead. In the Indian context the Chipko movement and its legacy have helped define these issues with particular clarity and sharpness. It is likely that the continuing evolution of Chipko and of its three contending subcultures will help define the outcomes as well.

---

[67] See A. K. N. Reddy, 'An Alternative Pattern of Indian Industrialization', in A. K. Bagchi and N. Banerjee (eds), *Change and Choice in Indian Industry* (Calcutta, 1982).

CHAPTER 8

Peasants and 'History'

THE UNQUIET WOODS: FOREST CONFLICTS
IN TWO CONTINENTS

Liberty and Forest Laws are Incompatible.
—An English country vicar, c. 1720

Prior to the reservation of forests, hill society could be described as a conglomeration of village communities, with control over the means of production and over the resources needed to reproduce itself. In the ecological setting of Uttarakhand, forest management struck at the very root of traditional social and economic organization. Moreover, it operated on radically different principles from the customary use of forests by surrounding villages. This underlying conflict manifested itself, in a variety of forms, in virtually all the forest movements in Uttarakhand, including Chipko. The clash of two sharply opposed perceptions of the forest was captured in an insightful remark made by the commissioner of Kumaun during the 1921 movement. As Percy Wyndham saw it, the recurrent conflicts were a consequence of 'the struggle for existence between the villagers and the Forest Department; the former to live, the latter to show a surplus and what the department looks on as efficient forest management.'[1]

In its most elementary form, then, social protest was aimed at the restrictions on customary patterns of use entailed by scientific forestry. The takeover of the hill forests and their subsequent management on commercial lines were at once a denial of the state's traditional obligations and a threat to the 'subsistence dilemma' of the peasantry.[2] In response, peasant resistance to the new regulations typically made two claims. First, it unequivocally asserted continuing rights of control and

[1] DO no. 67/II/21 dt. 21 February 1921, from Percy Wyndham, comm., KD, to H. S. Crosthwaite, secy to govt, UP, in FD file 109/1921, UPSA.
[2] Cf. J. C. Scott, *The Moral Economy of the Peasant* (New Haven, 1976).

use. As the frequent attacks on forest officials in Tehri Garhwal showed, peasants objected to 'any state interference with the forest over which they claimed full and exclusive rights'.[3] In Kumaun, the idiom of agrarian protest similarly reflected the contending claims of villagers and the state. Here arsonists chose as their target blocks of forest and resin depots especially valuable for the administration, and official buildings that were the most visible symbol of alien rule. Second, the opposition to state management also contrasted the subsistence orientation of village use with the commercial orientation of the new forest regime. By initiating the commercial exploitation and export of forest produce earlier under the exclusive control of village communities, the governments of Tehri Garhwal, Kumaun division and independent India were, albeit in very different ways, placing at peril the legitimacy of their rule.

In this manner, protest has brought to the fore, on the one hand, alternative conceptions of property and ownership, and, on the other, alternative conceptions of forest management and use. The social idiom of protest in Uttarakhand bears a striking resemblance to the conflicts over forest rights that were an important feature of the transition to industrial capitalism in Europe.[4] The slow but steady growth of state forestry in Western Europe and the enclosure of communal forests by large landowners also substituted a uniform and rationalized system of forest administration in place of a flexible and informal system of customary use. As in Uttarakhand, this transition was neither smooth nor harmonious, with the peasantry protesting bitterly at the deprivation of their traditional rights of access and use.[5] In the mountainous region of Ariege in France,

[3] For the often violent conflict between state/commercial forestry and village use of common lands in Mexico, see Oscar Lewis, *Pedro Martinez: A Mexican Peasant and His Family* (New York, 1964).

[4] There is one notable difference, though. In the feudal system of Europe, peasants were continually fighting a battle for control of common property resources—thus, 'claim and counter-claim had been the condition of forest life for centuries.' See E. P. Thompson, *Whigs and Hunters* (Harmondsworth, 1975), p. 35. In Europe the commercial working of the forest under state auspices, which accompanied the rise of capitalism, was the final but decisive blow to customary rights. In Uttarakhand, by contrast, there was no ambiguity about who controlled the forest in pre-colonial (and pre-capitalist) times. Here the takeover of the forests by more powerful economic forces came through a sudden usurpation, not a gradual process of encroachment. [5] See chapters 4 and 5.

for example, the development of the metallurgical industry in the second half of the eighteenth century initiated radical changes in the management priorities of crown forests and private forests. Landlords and the state came down heavily on peasant user rights, introducing in 1827 a forest code of 225 articles that forbade grazing in many areas and sharply limited supplies of fuel and timber to small agriculturists. In response, some peasants 'desperately searched for old deeds granting them rights of usage, checking the basements of deserted churches and going as far to look as [the town of] Montauban.' There was a rapid rise in forest offences, while groups of armed men disguised as women ('Demoiselles') attacked forest guards and the police—strangers to the region who symbolized the new and oppressive forest regime.[6] Elsewhere in France breaches of the forest law were by far the most common form of rural 'crime' in the early part of the nineteenth century.[7] Public records, especially those pertaining to the forest code, were burnt by angry peasants. Their rage was directed both at the state and at landlords; indeed, 'wherever landlords enclosed meadows and woods, they faced the rage and subversion of poor people who now had no place to pasture their animals.'[8] The villagers, Balzac observed in a thinly fictionalized account of this process, 'behaved as if they had an established right to cut wood in the forests.' As one woman defiantly says in *Le Paysans*, 'my man has sworn, I know, by all that's sacred, that we shall get our firewood and that all the gendarmerie on earth shall not hinder us, and that he will do it himself, and so much the worse for them.'[9]

In other parts of Europe as well, the battle for the forest was a central feature of the larger confrontation between an advancing capitalism and the peasant community. As in France, the development of the metallurgical industry in Germany and the growth of an urban market for fuelwood

[6] John Merriman, 'The *Demoiselles* of the Ariege, 1829–1831', in Merriman (ed.), *1830 in France* (New York, 1975), pp. 87–118.

[7] Maurice Agulhon, *The Republic in the Village: The People of the Var from the French Revolution to the Second Republic* (Cambridge, 1982), pp. 21–37.

[8] Charles Tilly, *The Contentious French* (Cambridge, Mass., 1986), pp. 15–16, 198–9, 214.

[9] Honore de Balzac, *The Peasantry*, volume xx of *The Works of Honore de Balzac* (New York, 1900), p. 170.

provoked landlords to enclose forests which were earlier open to the poor for grazing and fuel collection. Again, convictions for stealing wood and other forest offences showed an extraordinary rise in the first half of the nineteenth century. As Marx, commenting on the rash of forest 'crime', put it, a 'customary right of the poor' was, through force and fraud, transformed 'into a monopoly of the rich'.[10] Elsewhere, forests which provided fodder were taken over by the state for commercial timber production, forcing peasants to change grazing practices and rely on the cultivated meadow rather than the forest. Moreover, the relative valuation of different species was strikingly similar to Uttarakhand, with the state preferring species not especially favoured by villagers. Thus, in the state-owned forests, deciduous trees used for fuel and fodder were gradually replaced by conifers valued for commercial purposes. Inevitably, such changes met with opposition.[11]

As in the Himalayan villages covered by this study, in Europe too peasant protest was informed by alternative conceptions of property and use. What is common to the resistance to scientific forestry in nineteenth-century Europe and twentieth-century Uttarakhand is that in both cases it represented a defence of a traditional economic and social system, which afforded the peasantry some measure of stability, against the forces of a rising and expansionist capitalism. The spread of capitalism has everywhere radically redefined property relations and forms

[10] Peter Linebaugh, 'Karl Marx, the Theft of Wood, and Working-Class Composition: A Contribution to the Current Debate', *Crime and Social Justice*, Fall–Winter 1976, pp. 5–16; Karl Marx, 'Debates on the Laws on Thefts of Woods', *Rheinishche Zeitung*, 1842, reprinted in Karl Marx and Frederick Engels, *Collected Works*, volume I (Moscow, 1975), p. 235. As early as 1525 free access to the forests was a major demand of rebels in the German War. See F. Engels, *The Peasant War in Germany* (1850; English translation Moscow, 1956), pp. 51, 80, 88, 110. The conflicts over peasants' rights in royal hunting preserves, described both in E. P. Thompson, *Whigs and Hunters*, and several of the essays in *Albion's Fatal Tree* (Harmondsworth, 1975), are not strictly comparable. Although here too peasants were denied traditional use-rights, in so far as the forests were enclosed for pleasure (exclusive hunting by nobles) and not for profit (commercial forestry) one might say that these conflicts were more characteristic of feudalism than of the transition to capitalism.

[11] M. M. Postan (ed.), *The Cambridge Economic History of Europe: Volume I—The Agrarian Life of the Middle Ages* (2nd edition: Cambridge, 1966), esp. pp. 172–4; Franz Heske, *German Forestry* (New Haven, 1937).

of productive enterprise; just as inevitably, it has met its alter ego in the form of a *'rebellious* traditional culture'. A fine description of this culture is provided by E. P. Thompson in his study of eighteenth-century English society:

> The conservative culture of the plebs as often as not resists, in the name of 'custom', those economic innovations and rationalizations (as enclosure, work-discipline, free market relations in grain) which the rulers or employers seek to impose. Innovation is more evident at the top of society than below, but since this innovation is not some normless and neuter technological/sociological process ('modernization', 'rationalizing') but is the innovation of capitalist process, it is most often experienced by the plebs in the form of exploitation, or the expropriation of customary use-rights, or the violent disruption of valued patterns of work and leisure. Hence the plebeian culture is rebellious, but rebellious in defence of custom.[12]

In analysing the elements of a rebellious traditional culture, whether in Uttarakhand, France, Germany or England—and whether the genesis of rebellion is due to land tax, food prices, or forest rights—we must recognize that lower-class resistance typically has both instrumental and expressive dimensions. Faithfully reflecting disciplinary and ideological boundaries, anthropologists as well as Weberians are prone to emphasize the latter, while political economists and Marxists stress the former. However, lower-class rebels, whether in their actions or in their ideology, are not themselves inclined to strictly separate economic and cultural realms. The characteristic interpretation of utilitarian and symbolic elements in peasant revolt is clearly evident in the widespread opposition to scientific forest management in Uttarakhand; for the clash between scientific forestry and village management has not been merely an economic one. The conflicting perspectives rest on fundamentally different conceptions of the forest, on radically different systems of meanings. As chapter 2 documents, through a mix of religion, folklore and tradition the peasants of Uttarakhand had drawn a protective ring around the forest. As with other forest-dwelling communities, the continuity of their world rested on continuity in their relationship with the forest.[13]

---

[12] E. P. Thompson, 'Eighteenth Century English Society—Class Struggle without Class?', *Social History*, vol. 3, no. 2, May 1978, p. 154.

[13] For fine anthropological studies in the cosmology of forest-dwelling communi-

Scientific forestry threatened to disrupt this continuity, most obviously by denying villagers physical access, but perhaps more significantly by imposing an alien system of management on the forest. Thus the social idiom of agrarian protest has strongly reflected the threat to traditional cultural and communal values represented by scientific forestry. Most strikingly, there has been a close association of protest with folk religion: an association that was at once formal and informal, organizational and symbolic. The religious milieu of everyday peasant existence has influenced peasant resistance in two distinct ways. Protesters have, for one, sought a moral–religious sanction for their acts. This was accomplished either by involving priests and *sadhus* (ascetics), who enjoyed enormous prestige and influence locally, or in a more institutional form by using religious networks as means of communication. Thus, both temples and fairs have frequently served as locations where support was canvassed, or from which activities were co-ordinated.[14] Second, the ideology of peasant protest is heavily overlaid with religious symbolism. In the Kumaun movement of 1921, for instance, peasants invoked symbols from the Hindu epics while characterizing the colonial government as evil and demonic.

While the participation of priests testified to the involvement of figures of spiritual authority in social movements, holders of temporal authority were also prominent in the communal resistance to forest management. Both the colonial state and the Tehri Garhwal durbar tried without success to woo village leaders, especially headmen and retired soldiers. Almost without exception, the latter rejected these overtures and played a leading role in the mobilization and organization of the peasantry. In the Chipko movement too, retired schoolteachers, ex-soldiers and government officials—all prominent in the village authority structure—have played key leadership roles.

---

ties in peninsular India, see Verrier Elwin, *The Baiga* (London, 1939); Savyasachi, 'Fields and Farms: Shifting Cultivation in Bastar', mimeo (World Institute of Development Economic Research, Helsinki, July 1987).

[14] For examples of religious events turning into protest gatherings in early modern Europe, see Emmanuel Le Roy Ladurie, *Carnival in Romans* (New York, 1980); Georges Lefebvre, *The Great Fear* (rpt. Princeton, 1982); Paul Slack (ed.), *Rebellion, Popular Protest and the Social Order in Early Modern Europe* (Cambridge, 1984).

By choosing to cast their lot with their kinsmen, religious and community leaders have upheld their symbolic status as representatives of social continuity. The use of a religious idiom and of primordial networks of community solidarity suggests that the culture of resistance in Uttarakhand is simultaneously instrumental and symbolic. For if, as I have argued, scientific forestry represented a threat to the economic as well as cultural survival of the village communities, opposition to its workings has necessarily to invoke an alternative system of use *and* of meanings.[15]

AGAINST EUROCENTRICISM

> The blood of the villages is the cement by which the edifice of the cities is built.
> —Mahatma Gandhi

Reflecting on the century of social protest culminating in the Chipko andolan, what is especially striking from the perspective of the sociology of peasant protest is the persistence of conflicts over forest rights in India. The forest conflicts in Europe just described were representative of a particular historical epoch, when the rise of capitalism undermined the basis of subsistence agriculture. Bitter as these struggles were, they greatly diminished in scope and intensity with the maturing of the Industrial Revolution and the absorption of surplus workers in the cities or through emigration to the colonies. Simultaneously, the intensification of agriculture at home and the widening of the food production base through colonization greatly reduced the dependence of farming and stock-rearing on the forest. Subjected to commercial exploitation under sustained-yield silviculture, the forest has itself been transformed into an industrial enterprise run on capitalist lines. Of

---

[15] Although most accounts are silent on this score, the culture of peasant resistance to commercial forestry in Europe is likely to have invoked religious and cultural symbols in defence of the earlier system of forest use. A hint is provided by Linebaugh, who comments, apropos of German folklore, that 'the legends and stories of the forest testified to the fact that poor woodspeople and the peasants of the purlieus could find friends in the densest regions of the forest against the oppressions not only of princes and seigneurs, but also of their more recent enemies—the tax collector, the forest police, and the apostles of scientific forest management.' Linebaugh, 'Karl Marx', p. 13.

course, the forest continues to be an arena of conflict in Europe, as the labour force engaged in timber harvesting seeks to improve its wages and working conditions. The battle *for* the forest, however, between commercial forestry and the rural community, has, with the victory of industrial capitalism, been transformed into a battle *in* the forest. Although commercial forestry in India has created its own tensions between contractors and labourers, these conflicts pale into insignificance when compared with the continuing struggle between peasants and the state over control and use of the forest. The battle for the forest remains a very visible part of the social and ecological landscape. Thus the nature of social conflict in the transition to industrial capitalism in Europe differs greatly from the endemic conflict over forest rights in ex-colonial countries like India. B. H. Baden-Powell, one of the architects of Indian forest policy, had pointed to this distinction when he observed that in Europe, 'in a more advanced state of social life and occupation it has become more and more easy to alter an occupation that could not be continued if a forest right was taken away.'[16] The contrast with Europe holds good for peasant movements in general. Struggles over land and its produce continue to be very widespread in India, long after they have ceased to be significant in Europe.[17]

The continuing importance of peasant movements in the Third World challenges some of the basic assumptions of left-wing scholarship. In European historical writing, peasant movements are often treated as antiquarian, as pre-modern phenomena fated to disappear with the rise of modernity. As captured in the title of Eric Hobsbawm's classic work on the subject, these rebellions are 'primitive' and 'archaic', in effect against history.[18] This perspective on the historical significance of peasant movements makes a sharp distinction between spontaneous and 'organized' movements, viewing the latter as a *sine qua non* of the incorporation of the peasantry into the

[16] B. H. Baden-Powell, *Memorandum on Forest Settlements in India* (Calcutta, 1892), p. 5.

[17] See A. R. Desai (ed.), *Agrarian Struggles in India after Independence* (Delhi, 1986). For outstanding reportage on agrarian conflicts in India, see *Economic and Political Weekly* (EPW), Bombay, and *Frontier*, Calcutta.

[18] Eric Hobsbawm, *Primitive Rebels: Studies in Archaic Forms of Social Movements in the Nineteenth and Twentieth Centuries* (3rd edition, Manchester, 1974).

modern state and the march towards industrialization. A typical statement comes from the pen of a leading German scholar of the peasant war of 1525:

[A] peculiarity of traditional peasant movements in Europe is their general freedom from ideology. They were for the most part spontaneous movements with few informing ideas, characterized instead by concrete goals. Some historians have tried to raise the cry for the 'old law' to the level of a social idea, but such an expression is in reality not much more than a simple conservatism. Modern associational movements, however, do need an ideology, precisely because the actors do not interact personally and they do act over time. Of course, traditional types of movements take place constantly in modernizing societies. In such cases the peasant remains acted upon; the dynamic element is external to him. A modern movement makes the peasant part of the process of change as he expresses his demand for participation in the polity. In this transformation, however, he probably determines his own disappearance *qua* peasant.[19]

The thrust of this work has been towards challenging such simple-minded contrasts between unorganized, non-ideological, 'spontaneous' peasant protests on the one hand, and organized, ideological, 'modern' movements on the other. It is time to challenge, too, the theory of history that underlies the structural–organizational paradigm for the study of lower-class resistance. As the latter part of Sabean's statement makes evident, this paradigm confidently predicts the disappearance of the peasant from the modern world. Basing itself on what is arguably a narrow reading of European history, it further attempts to extend the lessons of that experience to the non-European world. It is imbued with a view of history in which the victory of capitalism, by allegedly preparing the way for industrial socialism, marks a major step in the march of human progress. The disappearance of the peasant, as a class that looks backwards rather than forward, is then accepted as axiomatic; its loss is indeed a precondition for the making of the modern world.

There is, however, another tradition of left-wing scholarship, one that is notably sensitive to peasant culture and ideology. Unburdened with a pejorative view of the peasantry but shar-

[19] David Sabean, 'The Communal Basis of Pre-1800 Peasant Uprisings in Western Europe', *Comparative Politics*, vol. 8, no. 3, 1976, p. 364.

ing nonetheless a teleological view of history based on the European experience, Barrington Moore could write:

The chief social basis of radicalism [in the early modern world] has been the peasants and the smaller artisans in the towns. From these facts one may conclude that the wellsprings of human freedom lie not only where Marx saw them, in the aspirations of classes about to take power, but perhaps even more in the dying wail of a class over whom the wave of progress is about to roll.[20]

In much of the Third World the 'wave of progress' has not yet rolled over the peasantry. In the incompleteness of this transition some scholars see a glimmer of hope. Concluding his fine study of Adivasi movements in western India David Hardiman writes: 'As yet, full fledged capitalism represents in these regions only a possibility, not an achievement. The adivasis' values have deeper roots with a resilience which provides us with at least some source of hope.'[21] In much the same vein, James Scott comments on the resistance to mechanization in rural Malaysia: 'The delaying of the complete transition to capitalist relations of production is in itself an important and humane accomplishment. It is often the only accomplishment within reach of a beleaguered peasantry.'[22]

This defence of traditional peasant values is of course based on a radically different interpretation of capitalism as a world historical process. Unlike in the paradigm case of Europe, in the Third World capitalism has been imposed from without, accelerating, even if not originating out of, the consolidation of the European imperium. Conceived by Europeans as essentially an extractive process, colonial capitalism greatly altered agrarian structure through the imposition of new taxes,

[20] Barrington Moore, Jr, *Social Origins of Dictatorship and Democracy* (Harmondsworth, 1966), p. 505.

[21] David Hardiman, *The Coming of the Devi: Adivasi Assertion in Western India* (Delhi, 1987), p. 217. In his last days, Marx himself seems to have gone back on one of his most cherished beliefs—namely the inevitably 'progressive' nature of capitalism. Through his correspondence with Russian revolutionaries who invoked the *mir* as an example of rural solidarity, Marx concluded that non-industrial societies could use their traditions of collective organization as a vehicle for a direct transition to socialism, bypassing capitalism. See Teodor Shanin (ed.), *Late Marx and the Russian Road* (London, 1983).

[22] J. C. Scott, *Weapons of the Weak: Everyday Forms of Peasant Resistance* (New Haven, 1986), p. 235.

landholding patterns and cash farming. More recently, the policies of post-colonial regimes have followed one of two paths. Where they are weak they have continued to exploit the predatory nature of colonial capitalism, which has now assumed grotesque and brutal forms unheard of in its original European home. Where they are strong they have embarked upon an ambitious programme of planned economic development, attempting to achieve in decades what it took the West centuries to accomplish. In this strategy small and landless peasants, and women and tribal minorities, are expected to bear the brunt of the forced march to industrialization. In either case post-colonial policies have continued to undermine the social, economic and ecological basis of peasant agriculture, without replacing it with a more viable or prosperous system of production. The familiar ills of Third World societies—land hunger, food scarcity, disease, urban decay, rising crime rates, civil strife and warfare—all testify to the cumulative impact of this process. In the ex-colonial world the ship of capitalism has finally run aground.

Third World capitalism, then, is a gross caricature of European capitalism, reproducing and intensifying its worst features without holding out the promise of a better tomorrow. Not surprisingly, scholars have seen in peasant resistance to its expansion a cause for celebration. There is another reason, barely hinted at even by writers as sympathetic as Scott and Hardiman, to see in such resistance 'the wellsprings of human freedom'. For if the transition to both industrialism and capitalism must necessarily remain incomplete in most of the Third World, the primary reason for this is *ecological*. The European miracle of successful industrialization was born out of a unique set of circumstances. The naïveté of both socialist and capitalist regimes notwithstanding, it is impossible to replicate that experience through the rest of the globe. Prior to the advent of colonialism most Third World societies consisted of a mosaic of long settled and sophisticated agrarian cultures which had a finely tuned but delicately balanced relationship with their natural environment. Colonial and post-colonial capitalism has disrupted this relationship in many ways. While the social consequences of this disruption are widely documented, what is less often observed are the devastating ecological consequences. In the absence of a 'frontier' such as was available to European colonists, even state-planned industrialization has to contend with a limited resource base and rapid environmental degradation. In most countries, and certainly in India, progress as conceived of in the energy-intensive, capital-intensive, western industrial model has already begun to meet with diminishing returns. Urban and industrial development, while not even successful on its own terms, has wreaked tremendous havoc on the countryside, pauperizing millions of people in the agrarian sector and diminishing the stock of plant, water and soil resources at a terrifying rate.[23]

From an ecological perspective, therefore, peasant movements like Chipko are not merely a defence of the little community and its values, but also an affirmation of a way of life more harmoniously adjusted with natural processes. At one level they are defensive, seeking to escape the tentacles of the commercial economy and the centralizing state; at yet another level they are assertive, actively challenging the ruling-class vision of a homogenizing urban–industrial culture. It is this fusion of what I have termed the 'private' (peasant movement) and 'public' (ecological movement) profiles that has lent to Chipko a distinctive quality and strength.[24] Far from being the dying wail of a class about to drop down the trapdoor of history, the call of Chipko represents one of the most innovative responses to the ecological and cultural crisis of modern society. It is a message we may neglect only at our own peril.

[23] For a fine documentation and analysis of environmental degradation in India, see Agarwal and Narain, *India: The State of the Environment 1984–85*. Cf. also Ramachandra Guha, 'Ecological Roots of Development Crisis', EPW, 12 April 1986.

[24] Within Western (especially American) environmentalism, there is, by contrast, a marked disjunction between intellectual prophets of doom, who point unerringly to the earth's inability to sustain infinite economic expansion, and popular environmentalism, which views nature primarily in aesthetic terms as a good to be 'consumed'. For the former, see, for example, the famous Club of Rome study—Donnella Meadows, *et al.*, *The Limits to Growth* (New York, 1971); for the latter, Samuel Hays, *Beauty, Health and Permanence: Environmental Politics in the United States, 1955–85* (New York, 1987).

EPILOGUE (1998)
The After-lives of Chipko

APPROPRIATIONS AND ASSIMILATIONS

Social movements have a pre-history, and also an after-life. Many popular struggles are kept alive long after they become inactive, their memory and myth continuing to inspire later generations. As a movement of the Himalayan peasantry against commercial forestry, Chipko was active from 1973 to 1981. Thereafter, it has faded away in the hills, but its echoes and resonances can still be picked up in places far distant from its original home.

The Unquiet Woods was first published in 1989. The research had commenced in the summer of 1981, coinciding with the movement's formal demise. Taking Chipko as its point of departure, the book filled in the historical context, narrating the stories of prior protests that were largely forgotten within the hills and completely unknown outside them. It sought also to provide a reasonably complete account of the development of the andolan itself. One hoped thus to rescue Chipko from the master narratives of feminism, Gandhism, and environmentalism, and to firmly place it within the social history of Uttarakhand.

But the Chipko movement was simply too evocative and too glamorous to be contained by fact or history. Especially outside Uttarakhand, it is a case of 'every man his own Chipko', and quite often every woman too. People in general, and environmentalists in particular, have put their own interpretations on the movement, regardless of whether these interpretations can bear up to historical truth or scholarly scrutiny. The Chipko andolan remains possibly the best-known and certainly the most widely misrepresented ecological movement in the world.

This epilogue deals with aspects of Chipko's 'post-history'. Let me begin with an invocation from London, made by Survival International, an organization that campaigns for the rights of indigenous people. In a booklet issued to commemorate its silver jubilee, Survival International printed a 'Dateline' of the milestones in the past twenty-five years. One entry reads as follows

1972: India: tribal women in the Himalayas revive the ancient custom of hugging trees to protect them from the axe. This movement, known as 'Chipko', inspires similar protests around the world.[1]

How many errors can one make in a single sentence? The year the movement began was 1973, not 1972; Chipko's pioneers were caste Hindu men, not tribal women; their method was innovated on the spot rather than being a harking back to an 'ancient custom' (nor, it must be said, did they actually hug the trees.) Move on now, from the campaigners for cultural survival to a philosopher in the academy. 'Ecofeminism', writes Karen Warren, 'builds on the multiple perspectives of those whose perspectives are typically omitted or undervalued in dominant discourses, for example Chipko women, in developing a global perspective on the role of male domination in the exploitation of women and nature.'[2]

The problems here are interpretative rather than narrowly factual. What is glossed over in this wish to build a global theory of ecofeminism are the deeply local roots of Chipko, and more seriously, the role played by men in the movement, sometimes with women, sometimes without them. Consider, finally, this use of Chipko by Western environmentalists seeking to save a Malaysian forest:

On the morning of 5 July 1991, a group of eight individuals from the US, UK, Germany and Australia—most of whom had never met each other until just a few days before—walked onto the grounds of a timber camp at the mouth of the Baram River in Sarawak, East Malaysia, climbed up the booms of several barges, and chained themselves there. They hung

---

[1] See *Survival*, newsletter of Survival International, no. 33, 1994.
[2] Karen Warren, quoted in Carolyn Merchant, *Radical Ecology: the Search for a Livable World* (New York 1992), p. 185.

banners from their perches and ignored the entreaties of officials who asked them to come down. After some eight hours they were brought down by police and arrested. To the great frustration of authorities, they gave their names as *Chipko Mendes Penan, Stop the Logging, Save the Forests*, and so forth. When subsequently their identities were established, they were tried and most were sentenced to 60 days in prison. They were there to protest the destruction of Sarawak's forests by timber companies, and the effects of that destruction on a small group of hunter-gatherers, the Penan.[3]

Chipko is now clubbed with the struggle of Brazilian rubber-tappers (led by the late Chico Mendes), these two unrelated movements drawn in to service a campaign in a third place still, among the Penan of Sarawak. One sees here, more clearly even than in the claims of Survival International or Karen Warren, how for Western environmentalists the historical specifics of Chipko are largely irrelevant. Disenchanted with the mores and values of the society they live in, they take Chipko (and Chico, and the Penan) to be signs of a hopeful alternative. To locate this generalized and abstracted love for a social movement that took place thousands of miles away, one needs to go back to that famous essay by the California historian Lynn White. White, we may recall, had argued that the roots of the ecological crisis lay in the Judeo-Christian ethos, which prescribed man's domination of nature. In Eastern religions, he had then suggested, possibly lay the roots of an ethic of respect for nature.[4] In the Chipko andolan the alienated Westerner has at last found the alternative. The message s/he takes from this movement is simple: Good Hindu women protect and reverence nature, just as surely as bad Christian men destroy and devastate it. More generally, 'primal' and 'indigenous' people (Amazonians, Himalayans, the Penan) are praised as protectors of nature, while 'modern' and 'industrial' people (with whom the Chipko admirers are, unfortunately, compelled to live) are condemned for destroying the environment.[5]

[3] J. Peter Brosius, *Arresting Images: Post-Colonial Encounters with Environmentalism in Sarawak, East Malaysia* (Manuscript, Department of Anthropology, University of Georgia, 1996). I am grateful to Professor Brosius for allowing me to quote from this paper.

[4] Lynn White Jr., 'The Historical Roots of our Ecologic Crisis' (1967), reprinted in Robin Clarke (ed.), *Notes for the Future* (London 1975).

[5] Although grossly vulgarized, this reading of Chipko can be traced, at one or more remove, to Sunderlal Bahuguna. Especially in the West, where

Though the disregard for the truth can be irritating, the attractions of a certain reading of Chipko in the West do not come as a surprise. Indian environmentalists also tend to be worshipful of Chipko, if slightly better informed of the facts. For them Chipko fulfils the function of a myth of origin. This is where their movement began. Before Chipko, political and popular discourse was dominated by an ideology of resource-intensive, socially disruptive and environmentally destructive pattern of development. After Chipko, opposition to this model crystallized. It became possible to talk of alternate ways of relating to the poor and to nature. The baton has now passed to the movement against the Narmada dam, which has been for some time now the most influential environmental campaign in the country. But Chipko shall always occupy a distinctive place as the originator of environmental concern in contemporary India.[6]

One expects greens in New Delhi or San Francisco to go to town on Chipko. More startling is the praise for the movement expressed by its historic enemies. In 1995 I attended a national workshop on 'Joint Forest Management' in New Delhi. In his inaugural address, the Inspector General of Forests—the most powerful forestry official in the country—spoke generously of the contribution of the Chipko movement towards the growing concern with the fate of India's forests. 'Women are the real conservators', he said, 'they are the embodiment of service and sacrifice'. To take forward the programmes of joint forest management, one needed to marry 'ancient wisdom and modern ecological knowledge'.[7]

In the last decade, forest policy in India has taken a decided turn away from the past. There is, on the one hand, a greater

---

he frequently travels and lectures, his is the name most readily identified with the movement. In any case his cultural-religious 'spin' on Chipko would resonate easier with foreign audiences than Chandi Prasad Bhatt's more materialist interpretation. The bias is made more pronounced because Bhatt travels little outside Uttarakhand and, unlike Bahuguna, does not speak English.

[6] See, as one example among many, the homage to Chipko in the dedication and text of Anil Agarwal and Sunita Narain (eds.), *India: the State of the Environment 1984-5: the Second Citizens' Report* (New Delhi 1985).

[7] Address by M. A. Ahmed, National JFM Workshop organized by the Society for Promotion of Wastelands Development, New Delhi, 29th November 1995.

appreciation of the value of species diversity—no longer are monocultures of commercially valued trees assiduously promoted. On the other hand, the pressures of popular movements have forced the state to move, at least on paper, towards a more decentralized and participatory form of management. In this ecological and social reorientation of forest policy the heritage of Chipko has played more than a walk-on part. Its own criticisms of commercial forestry and authoritarian forest officials have become the conventional wisdom, accepted not just by activists elsewhere in India but also by bureaucrats and donor agencies.[8]

Possibly the most innovative recent initiative in the forest sector is the programme of Joint Forest Management, or JFM. In different parts of India the Forest Department has signed agreements with individual village councils, making them the chief beneficiaries of forest working and consulting them in management decisions. There are now tens of thousands of village forest committees, helping take care of land previously guarded strictly by the state. This turn-around is a product not so much of rethinking within the forest bureaucracy as of continuing social conflict between communities and the state. That is to say, the concessions to local use and village right have not been granted from above but wrested from below.[9]

The demands now codified in the JFM policies were made, implicitly by numerous Himalayan struggles, and explicity in representations made to the Kumaun Forest Grievances Committee of 1921 (cf pp 120–1, above). These demands were, of course, made most forcefully and repeatedly by the Chipko andolan itself. It is, therefore, a curious irony that the state of Uttar Pradesh lags far behind other parts of India in the spread of JFM. In states such as West Bengal the Forest Department has genuinely taken aboard the message of 'participatory management'. By contrast, UP forest officials have, with only the

[8] Cf Madhav Gadgil and Ramachandra Guha, *Ecology and Equity: the Use and Abuse of Nature in Contemporary India* (London 1995), chapters III and VII.
[9] Cf Mark Poffenberger and Betsy McGean (eds.), *Village Voices, Forest Choices: Joint Forest Management in India* (New Delhi 1996); Sarah Jewitt and Stuart Corbridge, 'From Forest Struggles to Forest Citizens? Joint Forest Management in the Unquiet Woods of India's Jharkhand', *Environment and Planning A*, volume 29, number 12, 1997.

odd exception, continued to prefer the old-fashioned methods of policing and exclusion. The principal reason for this divergence lies perhaps in administrative history, in the continuation in northern India of older, more feudalistic styles of governance.

Be this as it may, the woods of the Himalaya are not quiet. The conflicts persist. When, under the guise of felling 'dead' trees, contractors are allowed by the forest officials of Uttarkashi Division to clear whole areas, village women preempt them by tying protective threads around the marked trees.[10] Likewise, in Kumaun there is considerable resentment over the curbs placed on the autonomous functioning of van panchayats. Though technically under the control of the villagers, the Forest Department can veto schemes for improvement, while of the revenue generated, 40 per cent is swallowed by the state exchequer. 40 per cent of the rest is by law granted to the village, but this money too first finds its way into a 'consolidated fund' controlled by the District Magistrate, to which individual panchayats have then to apply.[11] There are signs of an emerging movement to do away with these constricting rules. A chronicler of this discontent writes that 'those who know the history of forest struggles say that after Chipko the Van Panchayat andolan will be the biggest such movement in the hills'.[12] To Khas Patti (1906), Bageshwar (1921), Rawain (1930), Totashiling (1942), Mandal (1973), Reni (1974), and Badyargarh (1979) might yet be added other milestones in the history of forest movements in Uttarakhand.

HISTORY ENDS, HISTORY CONTINUES

There is a clever remark, attributed to John F. Kennedy, that 'success has many fathers but defeat is an orphan.' This is at

[10] Suresh Bhai and Manoj Bhai, 'Van Kataan ke Virudh "Raksha Sutra" Andolan', *Himalaya: Man and Nature*, volume 18, number 6, October–December 1995.

[11] Cf E. Somanathan, 'Deforestation, Incentives and Property Rights in Central Himalaya', *Economic and Political Weekly*, 26 January 1991.

[12] Jai Prakash Pawar, 'Chipko ki Parampara mein ab Van Panchayatain Janta ko Andolit kar Rahi Hain', *Naini Tal Samachar*, 1 September 1994 (my translation).

best a half-truth. Success, especially runaway success, certainly has its snipers and detractors.

A massive prick in the Chipko bubble came in the form of a cover story in the New Delhi fortnightly, *Down to Earth*. The magazine's editor, Anil Agarwal—one of the world's most highly regarded environmentalists—had often emphasized his own debt to Chipko.[13] On the movement's twentieth anniversary, in April 1993, he dispatched a reporter to Uttarakhand to find out what remained. The question that the magazine posed was: 'Chipko influenced the world, but have its local objectives been met?' The answer was an unequivocal 'no'. The reporter found former participants bitter about the consequences of Chipko. They had fought for their livelihood, but the portrayal and acceptance of the andolan as pre-eminently an 'environmentalist' movement had seriously backfired. In Uttarakhand the 'state used the environmental concern that was first enunciated in the country by Chipko to centralise forest management, instead of decentralising'. Under the Forest Conservation Act of 1980, numerous development projects—schools, bridges, roads, hospitals—had been stalled. If these projects required even a tiny plot of land legally designated as 'forest', and even if this land actually had no trees under it, the central government had to grant clearance, leading to unconscionable delays. The state's new-found enthusiasm for 'conservation' had led also to the constitution of new National Parks, where traditional activities of grazing, fuel and herb collection were prohibited.

Down to Earth also criticized the later work of the two major Chipko leaders. Other observers had praised Chandi Prasad Bhatt and his Dashauli Gram Swarajya Mandal for their afforestation drives, with their creative release of the energies of women. In villages around Gopeshwar, the DGSM has successfully mobilized women in the protection and plantation of forests, encouraging them also to take control of the village panchayats.[14] But *Down to Earth* suggested that by taking grants for this work, Bhatt had 'governmentalized' Chipko. Bahuguna,

---

[13] Cf Anil Agarwal, 'An Indian Environmentalist's Credo' (1985), reprinted in Ramachandra Guha (ed.), *Social Ecology* (New Delhi 1994).

[14] See Mukul, 'Villages of Chipko Movement', *Economic and Political Weekly*, 10 April 1993.

meanwhile, was chastised for having 'internationalised' Chipko by putting it at the service of the world conservation community.[15]

Six months later, another funeral oration was printed in the pages of the Kathmandu periodical *Himal*, also a respected voice in sub-continental journalism. Chipko, it complained, might thrive elsewhere but it was dead and buried in Uttarakhand. The movement 'has migrated from the hills of its origins to seminars and conferences further south and overseas. It lives in university courses, academic tomes and in articles like this one, which keep the controversy, but not the issues alive'. Once again, the torchlight was made to shine fiercely on the icons of Chipko. 'Bhatt's DGSM', wrote Himal's lady on the spot, 'is now a more passive NGO than a grassroots initiative taking organisation'. If 'Bhatt's organisation is but a ghost of Chipko', Bahuguna too 'seems today a holdover from a more involved past'. In a sharp reference to Bahuguna's solitary fasts against the Tehri hydroelectric project, the journalist wrote that 'one cannot help feeling that without the dam he would be a man without a cause, a following, and an audience'. The skepticism was reinforced by a photograph of Bahuguna posing for the Smithsonian magazine, hugging a pipal tree. The verdict, overall, was harsh and unforgiving: 'Chipko as a definable movement got wound up too quickly, its energies sapped by excessive adulation. While study of the movement has become *de rigeur* in universities in India and abroad, within Uttarakhand itself Chipko is spoken of in the past tense'.[16]

In some circles in India and abroad, the story of Chipko is told principally as '*our* story', the narrative of the coming of age of a dissident tradition, namely, environmentalism. Within the movement, however, there has long been a tussle for control over the history of Chipko. Chandi Prasad Bhatt, and his supporters, claim that he should be seen as the principal figure, for having founded the andolan. Sunderlal Bahuguna's camp claim, to the contrary, that only he made Chipko a properly

---

[15] Amit Mitra, 'Chipko: An Unfinished Mission', *Down to Earth*, 30 April 1993.

[16] Manisha Aryal, 'Axing Chipko', *Himal*, January-February 1994.

'environmentalist' movement.[17] The attempt in each case is to construct the story as '*My* Story', or more accurately perhaps, as '*Not*-His story'. A further complication is provided by the ecofeminists, who seek to diminish the role of both Bhatt and Bahuguna, and of Chipko men in general. Here, if a story is to be told, it is, emphatically, of the Chipko andolan as 'Her Story'.

Our Story, My Story, Her Story. It was left to *Down to Earth* and *Himal* to impartially but comprehensively rubbish these competing narratives of Chipko. It seems the story was that were was *no* story. The movement was dead, finished. The participants of Chipko had themselves put a final full stop to it. It remained only for the scribes to write an epitaph to the End of History.

This writer believes that both magazines were deeply unappreciative of what it takes to start and build a social movement. Indeed, before they came to Chipko, Bhatt and Bahuguna had spent years in the service of their people. From social workers they became, for a while, leaders of a popular struggle. After some years of intense activity, the movement exhausted itself—as movements will. When Chipko ended, Bhatt and Bahuguna had already entered late middle age. But they did not renounce the world, or take *sannyas* as a tired Hindu would. Bhatt has encouraged villagers to take care of their forests, and also written perceptively on the larger ecological problems of the region.[18] Bahuguna has risked his life in three long fasts against the Tehri dam project.[19]

Instead of respecting Bhatt and Bahuguna for what they have done, the journalists complain that they haven't done enough. 'Bahuguna's public relations ability and international appeal and Bhatt's organizing ability, put together', comments *Himal*, 'might have taken the people of Uttarakhand further than where they are today'. *Down to Earth* writes that 'a

---

[17] See, respectively, Anupam Mishra and Satyendra Tripathi, *Chipko Movement* (New Delhi 1978); Bharat Dogra, *Forests and People* (Rishikesh 1980); also the exchange cited in footnote 2 of the preface to the first edition of this book.

[18] Cf Chandi Prasad Bhatt, 'Uttarakhand mein bade Jalashyon va Vidyut Pariyojanaon ka Bhavishya', *Pahad I* (Nainital 1983), revised and translated as *The Future of Large Projects in the Himalaya* (Nainital 1992).

[19] See Praveen Swami, 'Blundering Progress: The Tehri Project and Growing Fears', *Frontline*, 30 June 1995.

movement that could have given the world its most powerful green party with village self-governance at its heart, fell apart'.[20] The lack of sympathy is manifest, and unfortunate. This is a classic case of the projection of the hopes of the middle-class intellectual onto the 'people'. The intellectual seeks total, systemic change, but the task of bringing this about is always left to others, in this case, Bhatt, Bahuguna and the like. These agents do mobilize mass energies and, for a time, bring about significant social change. But the intellectual chooses only to remembers what they have not done.

History has ended for some analysts of Chipko, but history continues for the people of Uttarakhand. The summer after the latter of these two stories was printed, the hills were lit alight by a massive popular upsurge. In a region not unfamiliar with social movements, the struggle for a separate state of Uttarakhand was unprecedented in its scope, spread and scale of participation. In July and August 1994, there were a series of strikes, lock-outs, processions and demonstrations. These were held in all eight districts of Uttarakhand, in all of its towns and many of its villages too. The unity and sense of solidarity was noteworthy. In both Nainital, towards the eastern end of the region, and Mussoorie, towards the western end, public meetings were held daily, where news of the struggle in other parts was collated and conveyed. As one local newspaper commented, this was 'an expression of popular sentiment such has never been seen or heard of before'.[21] Or, as a more dispassionate observer remarked, 'no movement in contemporary Indian politics has been able to muster so much popular support, that too in such a short time-span, as the movement for a separate hill state of Uttarakhand in Uttar Pradesh'.[22] The authorities were worried enough to send seventy battalions of the Central Reserve Police to keep the 'peace'.[23]

[20] Aryal, op. cit., p. 19; Mitra, op. cit., p. 36.

[21] In the more expressive Hindi, 'Ek aisa jan ubhaar jaisa na kabhi dekha, na kabhi suna'. 'Andolith Uttarakhand', *Nainital Samachar*, 1 September 1994.

[22] Pradeep Kumar, 'Uttarakhand Movement: Areas of Peripheral Support', *Mainstream*, 9 August 1997.

[23] A good account of the protests in July-August 1994 is provided by Jagdish Chandra Bhatt, in his reports printed in the Delhi edition of the *Times of India*.

The demand for a separate hill province was first clearly enunciated at a public meeting in Haldwani in 1946. The prime mover was our old friend Badridutt Pande, *Kumaun Kesari* and leader of the begar and forest movements of 1921.[24] It was argued that the hills were distinct from the rest of Uttar Pradesh—distinct geographically, socially, culturally, economically, and linguistically. The argument continued to be made over the years, as the costs of being part of UP became more apparent. It seemed clear that Uttarakhand remained poor largely because its natural resources—forests, water, minerals, herbs—were diverted for use elsewhere. By some calculations, this expropriation of resources was ten times more than the budgetary allocation for the region made by the Central and State Governments.

Over the years, as the resentment built up, the Uttarakhand demand took organizational shape. Various fora and fronts were floated to take it forward: one such, the Uttarakhand Yuva Morcha, organized a *padayatra* from Badrinath to New Delhi in 1978. The Uttarakhand Kranti Dal (UKD) was formed in the following year. The UKD set up successful candidates in the legislative elections of 1980 and 1985. On 23 November, 1987, it led a large procession in Delhi, culminating in a petition offered to the President of India. Critical support for such activities was provided by the 'prabasi', the migrant from the hills working in the cities and towns of the plains.

The upsurge of 1994 was, however, of a different order of magnitude. It was sparked by the decision of the Uttar Pradesh government to extend its new reservation policy to the hills. This mandated that 27 per cent of all government jobs and, in time, of all seats in state-funded colleges would be reserved for candidates belonging to the 'Other Backward Classes', or OBCs. Now the social structure of Uttarakhand (see Chapter 2) is polarized between Bith and Dom, between high caste Brahmins and Rajputs on the one side and the so-called Scheduled (or 'untouchable') castes on the other. The OBCs constitute less than

---

[24] This and the subsequent paragraph are largely based on the information contained in Govind Pant (ed.), *Aaj ka Uttarakhand, Kal ka Uttarakhand Rajya?*, (special number of *Nainital Samachar*, August 1989).

2 per cent of the population of the hills. Thus the implementation of the new policy would lead inevitably to an inflow of outsiders from the plains, to take up jobs in a region already marked by scarce employment opportunities.

The Uttarakhand movement is an illustration of 'nonseccessionist regionalism'.[25] Like the Vidarbha and Jharkhand movements, but unlike the Kashmir insurgency or the (now suppressed) Khalistan struggle, it does not wish to secede from the Indian Union. Its demand, rather, is for a separate province, to be hived off from the larger province of which it is presently part. Both leaders and supporters take inspiration from the ecologically comparable state of Himachal Pradesh. Himachal was given separate status in 1972; till then it was part of Punjab, a state otherwise dominated by *maidani* (plains) economy and *maidani* culture. Since its separation Himachal has steadily progressed, economically as well as socially. The Uttarakhandis likewise believe that a state of their own will allow them to more constructively use their natural bounty and generate revenue through tourism. Rule by their own politicians and administrators will also, they hope, be more conducive to the provision of desperately needed social services such as health and education.

In a recent essay, Emma Mawdsley has pointed to several areas of overlap between the Chipko and Uttarakhand movements. Both have identified the problem in terms of exploitation by external agencies of the patrimony of the hills. Both also criticize an imported culture of administration that has, over the decades, facilitated this exploitation. Both see the solution as, broadly, local control over natural and political resources. One important point of divergence is the attitude towards the state. Past movements, including Chipko, had defined themselves in opposition to the state. The Uttarakhand struggle, however, seeks not to reject the state but to capture it.[26]

The creation of a new province in the hills might be seen perhaps as the logical culmination of a century of popular

---

[25] The term used in Emma Mawdsley, 'Nonseccessionist Regionalism in India: the Uttarakhand Separate State Movement', *Environment and Planning A*, volume 29, number 12, 1997.

[26] Emma Mawdsley, 'After Chipko: From Environment to Region in the Uttaranchal', forthcoming in the *Journal of Peasant Studies*.

struggle against forms of rule and types of rulers inimical to the autonomous social development of the hills. That conclusion will not be inaccurate, but it is safe to say that the formation of Uttarakhand will not lead to the end of social protest. Warnings have already been issued that if the new state merely repeats the politics of capitalism and cronyism, or if it continues the rapacious and shortsighted exploitation of nature, then it will not be welcomed.[27] For the administration of Uttarakhand to continue the practice of previous governments is to encourage the revival of protest and struggle, to see the birth of new movements against what its participants shall perceive to be unjust and insensitive governance. Indeed, the history of peasant protests in Tehri Garhwal suggests that the expectations placed on 'indigenous' rulers can be higher still.

At the time of writing (October 1998), Uttarakhand stands tantalizingly close to being formed. The Uttar Pradesh Assembly has formally ratified its creation, and successive Prime Ministers have promised their support. A bill has been drafted, and at some stage will be tabled in Parliament. Although all major parties are committed to its creation, differences have arisen on terminology—the Bharatiya Janata Party, currently in power in both Lucknow and Delhi, prefers 'Uttaranchal' to 'Uttarakhand—and over territory, with regard to the extent of the Terai to be included along with the strictly mountainous regions. I must admit here to a vested interest in the creation of the new state. I support it for political reasons, as a critic of the excessive centralization of the Indian polity. But there is also a personal stake, for the Uttarakhand movement has inadvertently—but emphatically—'proved' a major thesis of the present work, as this last vignette explains.

A leading part in the upsurge of the summer of 1994 was played by the students of Garhwal University, based in the old town of Srinagar, on the Alakananda. Students of both sexes participated with equal fervour. Now the boys organized themselves as a 'Chandra Singh Garhwali dal', naming their group after the hero of the Peshawar mutiny of 1930, who later became something of a father confessor for the activists in the

---

[27] See, in this connection, the articles and reflections in Govind Pant, op. cit.

Tehri peasant movement of the forties. The girls, for their part, called their group the 'Gaura Devi dal', invoking the memory of the Bhotiya from Reni who first brought women into the Chipko Andolan. Far more effectively than an academic work, the students of Garhwal had rescued their struggle from the dominating discourses of the outside world. Chipko was returned to where it originally belonged, put back in the social history of Uttarakhand, back in the history of social movements in Uttarakhand.

APPENDIX
Indian Environmental History (1989–1999)

SOCIAL INFLUENCES ON SCHOLARSHIP

New fields of historical research emerge in one of two ways; by questioning from within or by pressure from without. For instance, the development of environmental history in the United States has been hugely influenced by the modern environmental movement. Most practitioners have been partisans, their research aiding or responding to the agenda set by social activists. A counter-example comes from France, which among the countries of Western Europe probably has the least active environmental movement, yet whose historians have for a very long time been interested in the influence of ecology on social life. In France, history and geography enjoy an intimate relationship, best exemplified in the work of the *Annales* school. For scholars such as Marc Bloch and Lucien Febvre or, more recently, Emmanuel Le Roy Ladurie and Georges Duby, the incorporation of nature as a key variable is a way of expanding the reach of history, not a moral obligaton imposed by allegiance to a social movement.

In this respect, the writing of environmental history in India follows the American rather than the French pattern. In their work earlier generations of Indian historians had been indifferent to the natural context. Traditions of social and economic history, well developed in themselves, paid little attention to the role played by natural resources such as water and forests in rural life. Left to themselves, academic historians might never have come round to the study of the relations over time between humans and nature. They were only alerted to the significance of these relations by signals sent their way by society. The Chipko Andolan was the first such 'wake-up' call, followed through the seventies by a series of struggles over forest rights in other parts of India.

In retrospect, the aborted Forest Bill of 1982 might be regarded as a landmark in the emergence of environmental history as a distinct sub-field. Before that Bill was introduced in Parliament, it found its way into the hands of activists, who were appalled by its clauses. These sought to strengthen the state's already firm grip on the 23 per cent of India's land area legally designated as 'forest'. Under the new Act, traditional rights provided for by the forest settlement could be extinguished at any time, the amount of compensation to be decided by the state. Fresh powers in the hands of forest officials included the power to arrest without trial. 'Offences' coming under the purview of the new clauses included the collection of fuel, fodder, or herbs—what millions of Indians were obliged daily to do. It would now be illegal to be found in the possession of such locally essential produce as mahua seeds and tendu leaves. Fines were enhanced for all offences, as were periods of imprisonment. There was only one exception—the punishment handed out to forest officers for 'wrongful' seizure, where the fine stayed static, refusing even to keep pace with inflation. Indeed, a hallmark of the new Bill was the consolidation of the powers of the forest department *vis-a-vis* other arms of the state and the citizenry as a whole.

The government of India's rationale for the new Bill was the clear evidence of deforestation in recent decades. Some surveys suggested that almost half the official 'forest' area was actually without any tree cover. The consquences of habitat destruction—soil erosion, floods, the loss of biodiversity and the like—were also being documented. Without denying this, the activists argued that the social costs of deforestation were as significant as the ecological costs. Moreover, their burden was chiefly borne by the rural poor, who were faced with increasing shortages of forest produce that were crucial to their subsistence. There were also fears that greater state control would be used to meet commercial demands of plywood and paper factories while putting curbs on local use. All in all, the new Bill was a slap in the face of the social movements calling for a less authoritarian, villager-friendly style of forest management.[1]

In the forefront of the opposition to the Bill were two Delhi groups, the Peoples Union for Democratic Rights (PUDR) and the Indian Social Institute (ISI). The ISI organized a convention of activists working in different forest regions, whose resolutions were then used to lobby Members of Parliament. The PUDR produced an impressive critical study of the provisions of the proposed legislation.[2] In the face of such sustained pressure, the Government of India was forced to drop the Bill.

The forestry debate of the seventies and eighties encouraged young historians to take up what was previously uncharted territory. Inspired by the controversy over the draft Act, they began to look more closely into the colonial origins of forest legislation. The more left-oriented among them began digging in the archives for a prehistory of forest struggles to complement the already well documented prehistory of peasant and working class struggles. Those who had come from the environmental movement initiated studies of cultural processes in different forest zones. Economic historians came to understand, for the first time, the significance of biomass in the village economy of India.

Forest history is, without question, the real growth area of environmental history in India. The past decade has seen the completion of almost a dozen monograph-length works on the history of forest use and abuse. These have showcased different production systems as well as different ecosystems. There have been studies of the place of forests in the social life of pastoralists, swidden cultivators, artisans and plough agriculturists. All these works have, to a lesser or greater degree, focused on conflicts over access to and use of state forests. In terms of geographical coverage, scholars have ranged from the Himalaya in the north to the Nilgiris in the south, from Bengal in the east to the Dangs of

---

[1] Cf Ramachandra Guha, 'Forestry in British and Post-British India: A Historical Analysis', in two parts, *Economic and Political Weekly*, 29 October and 5-12 November 1983.

[2] PUDR, *Undeclared Civil War* (New Delhi, 1982).

Gujarat in the west. Several have worked in the tribal heartland of Madhya Pradesh, right in the centre of India.[3]

Environmental historians in India tend, like their counterparts in the United States, to be committed to the goals of the environmental movement. It must be stressed however that as these goals vary so do the concerns and research strategies of the historian. A dominant interest of American environmentalism has been in the protection of wilderness. In response, historians have abundantly documented the devastation of the wild over the centuries; they have also recovered and sought to honour the voices of those individuals who defended the rights of threatened species or habitats. By contrast, the 'environmen-

[3] Dhirendra Dangwal, 'Forests and Social Change in Tehri Garhwal, 1850-1950', unpublished Ph D thesis, Jawaharlal Nehru University, New Delhi, 1996; Vasant K. Saberwal, *Pastoral Politics: Shepherds, Bureaucrats and Conservation in the Himachal Himalaya* (New Delhi, 1999); Chetan Singh, *Natural Premises: Ecology and Peasant Life in the Western Himalaya, 1800-1950* (New Delhi, 1998); R. Prabhakar, 'Resource Use, Culture and Ecological Change: A Case Study of the Nilgiri Hills of Southern India', unpublished Ph D thesis, Indian Institute of Science, Bangalore, 1994; K. Sivaramakrishnan, *Modern Forests: Statemaking and Environmental Change in Colonial Eastern India* (New Delhi and Stanford 1999); Archana Prasad, 'Forests and Subsistence in Colonial India: A Study of the Central Provinces, 1830-1945', unpublished Ph D thesis, Jawaharlal Nehru University, 1994; Ajay Pratap, 'Paharia Ethnohistory and the Archaeology of the Rajmahal Hills: Archaeological Implications of a Historical Study of Shifting Cultivation', unpublished Ph D thesis, University of Cambridge, 1987; Mahesh Rangarajan, *Fencing the Forest: Conservation and Ecological Change in India's Central Provinces, 1860-1914.*(New Delhi, 1996).

These works were all conceived as explicitly environmental histories. Other studies that pay attention to the forests in the course of a more general socio-economic analysis include Ajay Skaria, *Hybrid Histories: Forests, Frontiers and Wildness in Western India* (New Delhi 1999); Nandini Sundar, *Subalterns and Sovereigns: An Anthropological History of Bastar* (New Delhi, 1997); and M. S. S. Pandian, *The Political Economy of Agrarian Change* (New Delhi, 1989). See also Purnendu S. Kavouri, *Pastoralism in Expansion* (New Delhi, 1999).

The focus on forests is also revealed by an examination of the two collections of essays published on South Asian environmental history. Six out of eleven essays are devoted to forests/pasture in David Arnold and Ramachandra Guha (eds.), *Nature, Culture, Imperialism: Essays in the Environmental History of South Asia* (New Delhi, 1994), while the proportion is even higher (twenty-three out of thirty-one) in Richard H. Grove, Vinita Damodaran and Satpal Sangwan (eds.), *Nature and the Orient: the Environmental History of South and South-east Asia* (New Delhi 1998).

talism of the poor' in India has been more centrally concerned with questions of human rights and social justice. Environmental historians have been concerned less with the wild *per se* as with the impact on tribal and peasant livelihoods of environmental destruction and/or state expropriation.

THE GREAT 'ECOLOGY AND COLONIALISM' DEBATE

A notable feature of the outcrop of works on forest history is their rather limited time frame. Most scholars have focused on the heyday of British colonialism, which ran, roughly, from 1858 to 1947. One reason for this is the greater abundance of source material. For pre-colonial times the sources get progressively scarce. The British Raj, as we know, produced tonnes of written material on the people and resources of India, material which was (for the most part) very well maintained. But while Indian historians had industriously mined British records, their ecological blindness had kept one crucial set of documents outside their purview. These were the records of the Forest Department, which didn't interest them because (as pointed out above) forests themselves didn't interest them.

When younger scholars began to do 'environmental' history, in the eighties, they seized with relief and not a little glee on the mountain of material their seniors had turned their backs on. For the records of the Forest Department constituted a very rich vein for historians. From them one could reconstruct the legal history of the forest, the techniques of forest use as they had evolved over time, and—more tentatively—the changing species composition of the forest. Moreover, with customary use representing a threat to commercial forestry, the state was obliged to study and monitor many aspects of agrarian life. These records were a privileged window into environmental history, but also an indispensable source for social history as well.

But it was not merely methodological convenience that lay behind this emphasis on the colonial period. British rule was also of interest to the historian for the rapid, widespread, and in some respects irreversible, changes it introduced. Once again, these changes had both an ecological as well as a social dimension. Previous historians had told the story of the new laws and cultural patterns, the ideas and ideologies brought to India by the British. They had documented the changes that resulted, and offered a balance sheet of colonial rule. The younger generation now took it upon itself to study the changes in humannature interactions, of how British policies had transformed existing patterns of resource use and initiated fundamental alterations in the natural environment.

Early writings in forest history, mine included, were strongly critical of colonial environmental policies. They were shown to be socially unjust, ecologically insensitive, and legally without basis in past practice. Colonialism, it was argued, constituted an 'ecological watershed' in the history of India.[4] For the partisan scholar it became imperative that the injustices of the past be corrected by the undoing of colonial laws and policies. Forest communities had themselves believed that freedom would mean a repeal of British forest laws, an opening out to them of woods previously policed by the state. But the government of independent India had only strengthened the structure it inherited, now using it to favour the new wood-based industries that mushroomed after independence. The historian as citizen allied with those who urged a change in forest laws whose undoing became, so to say, part of the 'unfinished' business of Indian independence.

The thesis that the coming of British rule was a watershed in the ecological history of India has not gone uncontested. Perhaps the most vigorous denial can be found in the writings of the Cambridge scholar Richard Grove. Grove argues that British forest officials were not as vulgarly commercial as some Indians scholars suggest. In fact, quite a few of them demonstrated a precocious environmental consciousness, alerting their bosses to the impact on soil erosion and climate change of the massive clearing of forests in the early phase of colonial rule. Grove also argues that state intervention and environmental destruction were not the monopoly of the British alone. The clearing of the forest in pre-colonial times shows that Indians

---

[4] Madhav Gadgil and Ramachandra Guha, *This Fissured Land: An Ecological History of India* (New Delhi and Berkeley, 1992), Chapters V to VIII.

were not exactly incapable of ecological profligacy. He also claims that state control over woodlands was a feature of many Indian political regimes.[5]

Grove's work ranges widely over the sites of British colonialism. Three long chapters of *Green Imperialism*, his major work, concentrate on India; others on Mauritius and the Caribbean (he has also written, elsewhere, on colonial conservation in southern Africa). As an adventure in the history of scientific ideas it is certainly impressive. His research into old journals has brought to light a fascinating discourse on 'dessication' among now forgotten figures. But as a history of policy his work is less reliable. As with some other intellectual historians, Grove strongly identifies with the individuals he writes about. He is sometimes prone to 'modernize' their ideas according to prevailing standards of political correctness, and to exaggerate their influence on colonial rule. The claim that these eco-conscious naturalists exercised 'disproportionate influence' is assumed, not demonstrated. For India, at least, Grove has not examined the archival records of the state. It is only through a close study of these records that one can see how (or if at all) ideas offered in scientific journals come to permeate official discourse or become codified in law and policy.

As one leading historian of Empire has remarked, 'it is all too easy to exaggerate the degree of autonomy scientists enjoyed or to attribute to them present-day values and thereby ignore the almost overwhelming power of the imperial ethos'.[6] Let me move on, however, from the limitations inherent in Grove's method to the substance of his larger arguments. Was colonialism an ecological watershed? Grove questions this claim on two major grounds: first, that there are many examples of forest destruction in the pre-colonial period, and second, that there are, equally, many examples of state forestry systems which predate the British. No one, still less an Indian conversant with the Mahabharata, would dispute that forests were indeed cleared

---

[5] Richard H. Grove, *Green Imperialism: Colonial Expansion, Tropical Island Edens and the Origins of Environmentalism, 1600-1860* (Cambridge 1995).

[6] David Arnold, *The Problem of Nature: Environment, Culture and European Expansion* (Oxford 1996), p. 168 (commenting on the work of Richard Grove).

in the pre-colonial period. The burning of the Indo-Gangetic forest and its conversion to agro-pastoral production was one major watershed in the ecological history of the sub-continent. But following this great clearing a reasonably secure relationship was established between areas under cultivation and areas outside it, between the arable which raised the crops and the pasture and woodland which provided so much of the input to make food production possible.

These interrelationships between arable and woodland were undermined by British rule. In the intervening centuries, forests were felled here and there, principally to make way for the extension of cultivation. However, there is little evidence either of ecological collapse or of social conflict over forest resources. The British brought in new technologies of social control and resource extraction that altered the balance between state and subject with regard to access to the fruits of nature. New species were brought in and old ones exterminated. Now the peasantry was faced, if not for the first time, then for the first time in a very long while, with shortages of forest resources. No longer could the peasant so easily escape through migration to areas uncolonized by the plough. The discomfort was acute, as evident in the numerous popular struggles against state forest management.

When it took over the forests of India under the Acts of 1865 and 1878, the colonial state advanced, in justification, the example of previous states that had arrogated to themslves the right to forests or forest produce. That Tipu Sultan reserved the sandalwood tree for royal use or that the Amirs of Sindh reserved the right of shikar for themselves over certain areas constituted convenient precedent for the unprecedented usurpation by the state of massive areas of forests after 1865. A century later, Grove likewise claims that what the British did was to merely base themselves 'firmly on an indigenous system, from which the installed colonial forestry system differed little in detail'.[7] However, he omits to tell us that in precolonial times state

---

[7] Richard H. Grove, 'Conserving Eden: the (European) East India Companies and their Environmental Policies on St. Helena, Mauritius and in Western India, 1600 to 1854', *Comparative Studies in Society and History*, volume 35, number 2, April 1993, p. 348.

intervention was infrequent and localized, or that the new rulers brought in technologies of extraction, conversion and transportation of forest resources that were completely unknown to India, as indeed were the elaborate and detailed forest codes contained in the 1878 Act. In scope, style, reach, and outcome, the colonial forestry system differed massively in detail from what preceded it.

Contemporary observers well understood how colonial rule marked a radical break in the history of Indian forestry. In 1869, the government of India sent the Madras government a draft forest bill. They, in turn, invited comments from various of its officers. The views of one such, Narain Row, Deputy Collector of Nellore, are completely representative. The proposed legislation, he said, had no historical precedent, for 'there were originally no Government forests in this country. Forests have always been of natural growth here; and so they have been enjoyed by the people'.[8] After many such responses came in, the Madras Board of Revenue told the Government of India that the claim of the state to uncultivated forests and wastes was vitually non-existent. For

There is scarcely a forest in the whole of the Presidency of Madras which is not within the limits of some village and there is not one in which so far as the Board can ascertain, the state asserted any rights of property unless royalties in teak, sandalwood, cardamoms and the like can be considered as such, until very recently. All of them, without exception are subject to tribal or communal rights which have existed from time immemorial and which are as difficult to define as they are necessary to the rural population.... [In Madras] the forests are, and always have been common property, no restriction except that of taxes, like the Moturpha [tax on tools] and Pulari [grazing tax] was ever imposed on the people till the Forest Department was created, and such taxes no more indicate that the forest belongs to the state than the collection of assessment shows that the private holdings in Malabar, Canara and the Ryotwari districts belong to it.[9]

---

[8] 'Memorandum on the Forest Bill', dated Nellore, 8 May 1871, in Board of Revenue Proceedings Nos 5739 to 5789, Tamil Nadu State Archives, Chennai.

[9] 'Remarks by the Board of Revenue, Madras', dated 5 August 1871, in A Proceedings Nos 43-142, March 1878, Legislative Department, National Archives of India, New Delhi.

In disregarding such evidence, the government of India relied heavily on the odd instance where precolonial Rulers had 'asserted any right of property' in the forest. One case which was often cited by the colonial state, as it is indeed by Grove, was that of the Amirs of Sindh who had enclosed forests for hunting. When B. H. Baden-Powell of the Indian Civil Service invoked the case of the Sind *shikargahs* in support of government takeover of forests without compensation, the first Inspector General of Forests responded that

> ... the fact that the former Rulers have extinguished such customary use of the forest in a summary manner and without compensation is hardly an argument in point, for these were cases of might versus right. As against other individuals and communities the customary rights to wood and pasture have as a rule been strenuously maintained.[10]

The best case that colonial forestry was a force both qualitatively and quantitatively new was made by its victims. The people of Uttarakhand were not alone in thinking that the new laws and policies were without precedent in Indian history and devastating in their effects. These policies greatly accelerated deforestation in the subcontinent, created serious resource shortages, and sparked bitter and endemic conflict between the peasantry and the state. The works cited in footnote 3 provide abundant evidence of the ways in which rural communities, *all over* the subcontinent, repeatedly made clear their understanding of colonial rule as a watershed in the ecological history of India.[11]

BOOM AND BUST IN HISTORICAL RESEARCH

It is my belief that environmental history in India will continue to take its inspiration from the environmental movement. Thus,

---

[10] D. Brandis, *Memorandum on the Forest Legislation Proposed for British India (Other than the Presidencies of Madras and Bombay)* (Simla 1875), pp 13-4.

[11] And not just India. As an agent of ecological destruction European colonialism exercised an unparalleled influence in many other regions of the world. The literature on this topic is so large (and so conclusive) that any selection will be arbitrary. However, two works whose analyses exhibit strong parallels with South Asian developments are William Cronon, *Changes in the Land: Indians, Colonists and the Ecology of New England* (New York 1983), and Nancy Peluso, *Rich Forests, Poor People: Resource Control and Resistance in Java* (Berkeley 1992).

in the eighties and nineties conflicts over water have become more visible than conflicts over forests. Inspired by such movements as the Narmada Bachao Andolan, historians have begun systematic research into the history, organization, technology and socio-ecological outcomes of different forms of water management—large dams, small dams, tanks, wells, and canals.[12] The history of wildlife destruction and preservation is also attracting its chroniclers. Urban history is being given an ecological twist, through the mapping of resource flows between city and hinterland and the investigation of health and living conditions within cities. Intellectual historians are exhibiting an interest in the work of early environmental thinkers, such as the dissident Gandhians who unsuccessfully advocated that India take to a rural-based, resource-conserving pattern of development after 1947. In another decade, as these works are disseminated in the form of dissertations, books, and articles, forest history will no longer so grossly dominate the landscape of Indian environmental history.

One incidental achievement of environmental historians has been the breaking down of one of the most sacred boundaries within the Indian academy. In strict disciplinary terms, history ends at midnight on August 14/15 1947, with sociology and anthropology taking over thereafter. But Nature itself did not stop to take account of 'freedom at midnight'. The continuities between the colonial and postcolonial regimes are manifest most clearly in the institutional frameworks which govern the management—and mismanagement—of forests, water, wildlife, minerals and other resources. The environmental historian cannot, therefore, stay on one side of the divide only. Much more so than the social or economic or political historian, s/he has been inclined to disregard what in social or economic or political terms is treated as a definitive break in the history of modern India, that is, the achievement of national independence.

Even its practitioners would not, perhaps, have anticipated the rapid rise of environmental history in India. When *The*

---

[12] Nirmal Sengupta has been a pioneer in this field. See, among other works, his essay 'Irrigation: Traditional *versus* Modern', *Economic and Political Weekly*, Special Number, August 1985.

Unquiet Woods was first published, there were no courses being taught or theses being written on the subject. So far as Indian historians and history departments were concerned, environmental history did not exist. However, the other body of work to which this book addressed itself, the study of lower-class resistance, was then very much in fashion. The early volumes of Subaltern Studies had enthused fresh life into a 'history from below'. But that particular project has since meandered into the dreary desert sand of deconstruction. Subalternists have, for the most part, lost interest in the experience of peasants and workers; the dissection of colonial and elite discourse is now the rage. Subaltern Studies, properly so called, might not yet be bust, but it has unquestionably gone into a steep decline.[13] In contrast, the sub-discipline of environmental history is booming. Ten years is a short time in 'history', but not, it seems, for historical scholarship.

---

[13] Cf my articles, 'Subaltern and Bhadralok Studies' and 'Beyond Bankim and Bhadralok Studies', *Economic and Political Weekly*, 19 August and 23 December 1995, respectively. See also Sumit Sarkar, *Writing Social History* (New Delhi 1998), where one of the founders of the Subaltern Studies Collective pungently criticizes the descent into discourse of his former comrades.

Bibliography

A. ARCHIVAL SOURCES

National Archives of India, New Delhi
Files of the following departments:
  Foreign Department
  Foreign and Political Department
  Department of Revenue and Agriculture (Famine and Forests)
  Political Department
  Crown Representative Records (microfilm)

Uttar Pradesh State Archives
Files of the following departments:
  Forest Department
  General Administration Department
  Police Department
  Political Department

Regional Archives, Dehradun and Nainital
Miscellaneous files

Nehru Memorial Museum and Library, New Delhi
All India States' People's Conference Papers

B. OTHER MANUSCRIPT SOURCES

Records of the S. S. Panwar Collection, Dehradun
Miscellaneous files at the office of the Conservator of Forests, Tehri Circle, Dehradun
'Chipko' file, Centre for Science and Environment, New Delhi
File of the Badyargarh Van Suraksha Samiti, Badyar, Tehri Garhwal
Sher Singh Mewar, 'Tehri Garhwal ka Krantikari Itihasa' (handwritten manuscript at present in my possession)

C. PERIODICALS

The following periodicals have been extensively used:
  Indian Forester, Dehradun, 1883–1958
  Garhwali, Dehradun, 1918–31
  Yugvani, Dehradun, 1948–79
  Indian States Reformer, Dehradun, 1931–2

I have also used itinerant issues of the following periodicals: *Empire Forestry, Hindustan Times, Illustrated Weekly of India, Indian Express, Leader, Parvatiya Times, The Statesman*

D. GOVERNMENT DOCUMENTS

I. *Periodical Reports*

Annual Progress Report of the Forest Department of United Provinces, various years

Report on the Administration of the United Provinces and Oudh, for 1915–16 only

Annual Administrative Report of the Tehri Garhwal State, various years

Census of India, 1891, 1901, 1911, 1921 and 1931, volumes for the United Provinces

II. *Documents pertaining to Forest Management*

Agarwala, N. K., *WP for the Kedarnath Forest Division, Garhwal Circle, 1972–73 to 1981–82* (Nainital, 1973)

Anon., *A Manual of Forest Law compiled for the use of students at the Imperial Forest College* (Dehradun, 1906)

———, *The National Forest Policy of India* (New Delhi, 1952)

———, 'A Note on the UP Hill Forests', typewritten copy submitted to the Kaul Committee on the UP Hill Forests (Lucknow, 1981)

———, *The Report of the Kumaun Forest Fact Finding Committee* (Lucknow, 1960)

———, *Report of the National Commission on Agriculture: Volume IX: Forestry* (Delhi, 1976)

Baden-Powell, B. H., and Gamble, J. S. (eds), *Report of the Proceedings of the Forest Conference, 1873–74* (Calcutta, 1874)

Bahuguna, M. N., *WP for the Tehri Forest Division, Tehri Garhwal State, 1939–40 to 1969–70* (Tehri, 1941)

Bhatia, S. B., *WP for the East Almora Forest Division, UP, 1924–25 to 1933–34* (Allahabad, 1926)

Brahmawar, R. N., *WP for the Garhwal Forest Division, 1930–31 to 1939–40* (Allahabad, 1938)

Brandis, Dietrich, *Memorandum on the Forest Legislation Proposed for British India (Other than the Presidencies of Madras and Bombay)* (Simla, (1875)

———, *Review of the Forest Administration in the Several Provinces under the Government of India for the year 1877–78* (Simla, 1879)

———, *Suggestions Regarding Forest Administration in the Northwestern Provinces and Oudh* (Calcutta, 1882)

———, and Smythies, A. (eds), *Report of the Proceedings of the Forest*

Conference held at Simla, October 1875 (Calcutta, 1876)

Champion, H. G., and Seth, S. K., *General Silviculture for India* (Delhi, 1968)

Ford, Robertson F. C., *Our Forests* (Allahabad, 1936)

Hearle, N., *WP for the Tehri Garhwal Leased Forests, Jaunsar Forest Division* (Allahabad, 1888)

——, *WP of the Deoban Range, Jaunsar Forest Division, NWP* (Allahabad, 1889)

Imperial Institute, Indian Trade Enquiry, *Report on Lac, Turpentine and Resin* (London, 1922)

Johri, C. M., *WP for the Garhwal Forest Division, Kumaun Circle, UP, 1940–41 to 1954–55* (Allahabad, 1940)

Kaul Committee, *Report of the Experts Committee to look into the Policy Regarding Felling and Protection of Environmental Balance in the Himalayan Region of UP* (Lucknow)

Lohani, D. N., *WP for the North and South Garhwal Divisions, UP, 1958–59 to 1972–73* (Allahabad, 1962)

Ministry of Agriculture, *India's Forests and the War* (Delhi, 1948)

Mobbs, E. C., *WP for the Tons Forest Division, Tehri Garhwal State, 1925–46* (Allahabad, 1926)

Nelson, J. C., *Forest Settlement Report of the Garhwal District* (Lucknow, 1916)

Osmaston, A. E., *WP for the North Garhwal Forest Division, 1921–22 to 1930–31* (Allahabad, 1921)

Pant, K. P., *WP for the Tons Forest Division (Old Leased Forests), Tehri Garhwal State, 1945–46 to 1964–65* (Dehradun, 1948)

——, *WP for the Tons Forest Division (Non-Leased Forests), Tehri Garhwal State, 1939–40 to 1969–70* (Dehradun, 1948)

Pearson, R. S., 'Note on the Antiseptic Treatment of Timber in India, with special reference to Railway Sleepers', *Indian Forest Records* (IFR), vol. III, pt 1 (Calcutta, 1912)

——, 'A Further Note on the Antiseptic Treatment of Timber with Results obtaining from Past Experiments', IFR, vol. VI, pt 9 (Calcutta, 1918)

Raturi, P. D., *WP for the Jamuna Forest Division, Tehri Garhwal State, 1932–33 to 1952–53* (Tehri, 1932)

——, *WP for the Uttarkashi Forest Division, Tehri Garhwal State, 1939–40 to 1959–60* (Tehri, 1938)

Ribbentrop, B., *Forestry in British India* (Calcutta, 1900)

Singh, Gopal, *WP for the Naini Tal Forest Division, Kumaun Circle, 1968–69 to 1977–78* (Nainital, 1969)

Singh, Puran, 'Note on the Distillation and Composition of Turpentine Oil from the Chir Resin, and the Clarification of Indian Resin', IFR, vol. IV, pt 1 (Calcutta, 1912)

Singh, V. P., *WP for the West Almora Forest Division, Kumaun Circle, 1966–67 to 1975–76* (Nainital, 1967)
Smythies, E. A., 'The Resin Industry in Kumaun,' *Forest Bulletin No. 26* (Calcutta, 1914)
Smythies, A., and Dansey, E. (eds), *A Report on the Proceedings of the Forest Conference held at Dehradun* (Simla, 1887)
Trevor, C. G., and Smythies, E. A., *Practical Forest Management* (Allahabad, 1923)
Troup, R. S., *A Note on Some European Silvicultural Systems with Suggestions for Improvements in Indian Forest Management* (Calcutta, 1916)
——, 'Pinus Longifolia Roxb: A Silvicultural Study', *The Indian Forest Memoirs*, Silvicultural Series, vol. 1, pt 1 (Calcutta, 1916)
——, *The Work of the Forest Department in India* (Calcutta, 1917)
Tulloch, J. C., *WP for the Leased Deodar Forests in Tehri Garhwal* (Allahabad, 1907)
Uttar Pradesh Forest Department, *Forest Development Project, Uttar Pradesh, India* (Lucknow, n.d.)
——, *Uttar Pradesh Forest Statistics* (Lucknow, n.d.)
Verma, V. P. S., *WP for the Tehri Forest Division, Garhwal Circle, UP, 1973–74 to 1982–83* (Nainital, 1973)

III. *Other Government Documents*

Anon., *Report of the Royal Commission on Agriculture in India*, volume III, Evidence (London, 1927)
——, *History of Indian Railways* (Delhi, 1964)
——, *Report of the Scheduled Areas and Scheduled Tribes Commission, Volume I 1960–61* (Delhi, 1967)
Atkinson, E. T., *The Himalayan Districts of the Northwestern Provinces*, 3 volumes (Allahabad, 1884–6)
Batten, J. H., 'Report on the Settlement of the District of Garhwal', in *idem* (ed.), *Official Reports on the Province of Kumaun* (1851; rpt. Calcutta, 1878)
——, 'Final Report on the Settlement of Kumaun', in ibid.
British Parliamentary Papers, vol. 59 (1890–2)
Chopra, P. N. (ed.), *The Gazetteer of India*, vol. III (Delhi, 1975)
Census of India, *Village Thapli, Tehsil Pauri, District Garhwal*, vol. 15, pt 6, Village Survey Monograph no. 5, 1961
Gairola, T. D., *Selected Revenue Decisions of Kumaun* (Allahabad, 1936)
Pauw, E. K., *Report on the Tenth Settlement of the Garhwal District* (Allahabad, 1896)
Planning Commission, *Report of the Task Force for the Study of Eco-development in the Himalayan Region* (Delhi, 1982)
Selections from the Records of the Government of the North Western Provinces,

first series, volumes 2, 3 and 5; second series, volumes 2 and 3 (Allahabad, 1866–70)

Stowell, V. A., *A Manual of the Land Tenures of the Kumaun Division* (1907; rpt. Allahabad, 1937)

Walton, H. G., *Almora: A Gazetteer* (Allahabad, 1911)

———, *British Garhwal: A Gazetteer* (Allahabad, 1911)

E. SECONDARY WORKS : BOOKS, ARTICLES, THESES

Adas, M., 'From Avoidance to Confrontation: Peasant Protest in Precolonial and Colonial South East Asia', *Comparative Studies in Society and History* (CSSH), vol. 23, no. 2, 1981

———, 'From Footdragging to Flight: The Evasive History of Peasant Avoidance Protest in South and South-East Asia', *Journal of Peasant Studies*, vol. 13, no. 2, 1986

Agarwal, Anil, 'An Indian Environmentalist's Credo', in Ramachandra Guha (ed.), *Social Ecology* (New Delhi 1994)

Agulhon, Maurice, *The Republic in the Village* (Cambridge, 1982)

Anderson, Benedict, *Imagined Communities: Reflections on the Origin and Growth of Nationalism* (London, 1983)

Arnold, David, 'Rebellious Hillmen: The Gudem Rampa Risings, 1839–1924', in Ranajit Guha (ed.), *Subaltern Studies I* (Delhi, 1982)

———, 'Industrial Violence in Colonial India', CSSH, vol. 23, no. 2, 1981

———, *The Problem of Nature: Environment, Culture and European Expansion* (Oxford, 1996)

———, and Ramachandra Guha, (eds.), *Nature, Culture, Imperialism: Essays on the Environmental History of South Asia* (New Delhi, 1994)

Aryal, Manisha, 'Axing Chipko', *Himal*, January-February 1994

Baden-Powell, B.H., *The Land Systems of British India*, vol. II (1892; rpt. Delhi, 1974)

Bahuguna, Sunderlal, *Uttarakhand mein Ek Sau Bis Din* (Dehradun, 1974)

———, *Van Shramik* (Silyara, 1977)

———, 'The Himalaya: Towards a Programme of Reconstruction', in K. M. Gupta and Desh Bandhu (eds), *Man and Forest* (Delhi, 1979)

———, *Chipko* (Silyara, 1980)

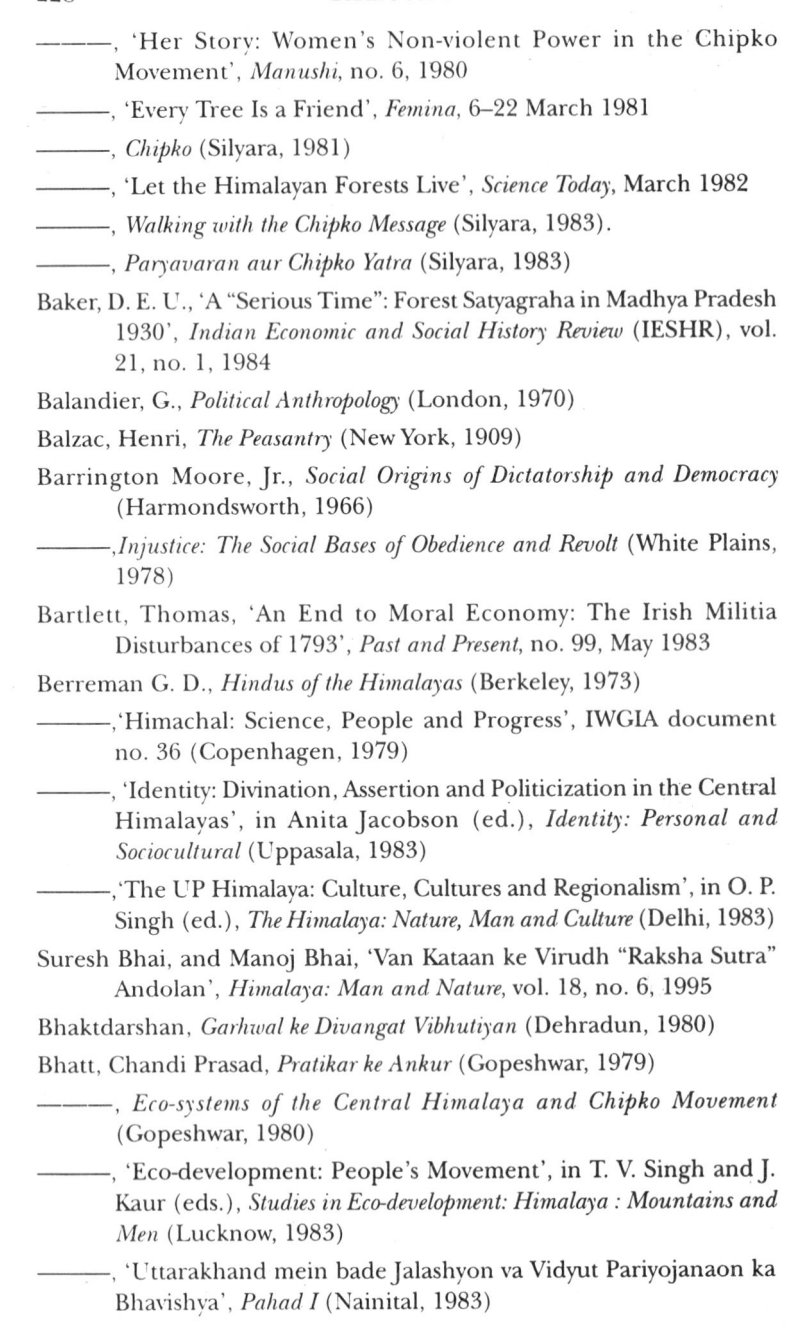

———, 'Her Story: Women's Non-violent Power in the Chipko Movement', *Manushi*, no. 6, 1980

———, 'Every Tree Is a Friend', *Femina*, 6–22 March 1981

———, *Chipko* (Silyara, 1981)

———, 'Let the Himalayan Forests Live', *Science Today*, March 1982

———, *Walking with the Chipko Message* (Silyara, 1983).

———, *Paryavaran aur Chipko Yatra* (Silyara, 1983)

Baker, D. E. U., 'A "Serious Time": Forest Satyagraha in Madhya Pradesh 1930', *Indian Economic and Social History Review* (IESHR), vol. 21, no. 1, 1984

Balandier, G., *Political Anthropology* (London, 1970)

Balzac, Henri, *The Peasantry* (New York, 1909)

Barrington Moore, Jr., *Social Origins of Dictatorship and Democracy* (Harmondsworth, 1966)

———, *Injustice: The Social Bases of Obedience and Revolt* (White Plains, 1978)

Bartlett, Thomas, 'An End to Moral Economy: The Irish Militia Disturbances of 1793', *Past and Present*, no. 99, May 1983

Berreman G. D., *Hindus of the Himalayas* (Berkeley, 1973)

———, 'Himachal: Science, People and Progress', IWGIA document no. 36 (Copenhagen, 1979)

———, 'Identity: Divination, Assertion and Politicization in the Central Himalayas', in Anita Jacobson (ed.), *Identity: Personal and Sociocultural* (Uppasala, 1983)

———, 'The UP Himalaya: Culture, Cultures and Regionalism', in O. P. Singh (ed.), *The Himalaya: Nature, Man and Culture* (Delhi, 1983)

Suresh Bhai, and Manoj Bhai, 'Van Kataan ke Virudh "Raksha Sutra" Andolan', *Himalaya: Man and Nature*, vol. 18, no. 6, 1995

Bhaktdarshan, *Garhwal ke Divangat Vibhutiyan* (Dehradun, 1980)

Bhatt, Chandi Prasad, *Pratikar ke Ankur* (Gopeshwar, 1979)

———, *Eco-systems of the Central Himalaya and Chipko Movement* (Gopeshwar, 1980)

———, 'Eco-development: People's Movement', in T. V. Singh and J. Kaur (eds.), *Studies in Eco-development: Himalaya : Mountains and Men* (Lucknow, 1983)

———, 'Uttarakhand mein bade Jalashyon va Vidyut Pariyojanaon ka Bhavishya', *Pahad I* (Nainital, 1983)

———, 'Himalaya Kshetra ka Niyojan', mimeo (Gopeshwar, 1984)

———, *The Future of Large Projects in the Himalaya* (Nainital 1992)

———, and Kunwar, S. S. (eds), 'Hill Women and Their Involvement in Forestry', in S. S. Kunwar (ed.), *Hugging the Himalaya: the Chipko Experience* (Gopeshwar, 1982)

Bloch, Marc, *The Royal Touch: Sacred Monarchy and Scrofula in England and France* (rpt. London, 1973)

———, *French Rural History* (rpt. London, 1978)

Blunt, E. A., *The Caste System of Northern India* (1931; rpt. Delhi, 1969)

Bor, N. L., *A Manual of Forest Botany* (Oxford, 1953)

Brandis, D., *Indian Forestry* (Woking, 1897)

Brosius, J. Peter, 'Arresting Images: Post-Colonial Encounters with Environmentalism in Sarawak, East Malaysia', unpublished ms., Department of Anthropology, University of Georgia, Athens (1996)

Burghart, R., 'Hierarchical Models of the Hindu Social System', *Man*, n.s., vol. 13, no. 4, December 1978

Centre for Science and Environment, *The State of India's Environment 1982: A Citizen's Report* (Delhi, 1982)

———, *The State of India's Environment 1984–5: A Citizen's Report* (Delhi, 1985)

Chandra, Bipan, *Nationalism and Colonialism in Modern India* (Delhi, 1979)

Chandra, Ramesh, 'Sex Role Arrangements to Achieve Economic Security in North West Himalayas', in C. von Fürer Haimendorf (ed.), *Asian Highland Societies in Anthropological Perspective* (Delhi, 1981)

Chatak, Govind, *Garhwali Lokgeet* (Dehradun, 1956)

Chatterjee, P., 'More on Modes of Power and the Peasantry', in Ranajit Guha (ed.), *Subaltern Studies II* (Delhi, 1983)

Cobb, Richard, *The Police and the People: French Popular Protest, 1789–1820* (Oxford, 1970)

Corbett, Jim, *My India* (Bombay, 1952)

Cronon, William, *Changes in the Land: Indians, Colonists and the Ecology of New England* (New York, 1983)

Dabral, S. C., *Uttarakhand ka Itihas*, vol. 8 (Dugadda, n.d.)

Dangwal, Dhirendra, *Forests and Social Change in Tehri Garhwal, 1850–1950*, unpublished Ph D thesis, Jawaharlal Nehru University, New Delhi, 1998

Das, J. C. and Negi, R. S., 'Chipko Movement', in K. S. Singh (ed.), *Tribal Movements in India*, volume II (Delhi, 1983)

Desai, A. R. (ed.), *Agrarian Struggles in India since Independence* (Delhi, 1987)

Devadas Pillai, S., *Rajas and Prajas* (Bombay, 1976)

Dharampal, *Civil Disobedience and Indian Tradition* (Varanasi, 1971)

Dogra, B., *Forests and People* (Rishikesh, 1980)

Dumont, L., 'The Concept of Kingship in Ancient India', in *Religion, Politics and History in India* (Paris, 1970)

———, *Homo Hierarchicus* (London, 1970)

Eckholm, Erik, *Losing Ground* (New York, 1976)

Elwin, Verrier, *The Baiga* (London, 1939)

———, *Leaves in the Jungle* (1936; rpt. London, 1968)

———, *A Philosophy for NEFA* (Delhi, 1960)

Engels, F., *The Peasant War in Germany* (1850; English translation, Moscow, 1956)

Erikson, Kai, *Everything in Its Path: Destruction of Community in the Buffalo Creek Flood* (New York, 1976)

Faith, Rosamund, 'The Great Rumour of 1377 and Peasant Ideology', in T. H. Ashton and R. H. Hilton (eds), *The English Rising of 1381* (Cambridge, 1984)

Febvre, Lucien, *A Geographical Introduction to History* (1925; rpt. London, 1950)

Feeley Harnuk, Gillian, 'Issues in Divine Kingship', *Annual Review of Anthropology*, vol. 14, 1985

Fernow, Bernhard, *A History of Forestry* (Toronto, 1902)

Feuer, Lewis, 'What is Alienation? The Career of a Concept', in Arthur Stein and Maurice Vidich (eds), *Sociology on Trial* (Englewood Cliffs, N. J., 1963)

Field, Daniel, *Rebels in the Name of the Tsar* (Boston, 1976)

Fields, Karen, *Revival and Rebellion in Colonial Central Africa* (Princeton, 1985)

Fortes, M. And Evans-Pritchard, E. E. (eds), *African Political Systems* (1940; rpt. Oxford, 1964)

Frankfort, H., *Kingship and the Gods* (1948; rpt. Chicago, 1978)

Gadgil, M., 'Towards an Indian Conservation Strategy', paper presented at the workshop on a New Forest Policy, Indian Social Institute, New Delhi, 12–14 April 1982

———, 'Forestry with a Social Purpose', in W. Fernandes and S. Kulkarni (eds), *Towards a New Forest Policy* (Delhi, 1983)

———, Prasad, S. N. and Ali, R., 'Forest Management and Forest Policy in India: A Critical Review', *Social Action*, vol. 33, no. 2, 1983

———, and Ramachandra Guha, *This Fissured Land: An Ecological History of India* (New Delhi and Berkeley, 1992)

———, *Ecology and Equity: The Use and Abuse of Nature in Contemporary India* (London and New Delhi, 1995)

Geertz, Clifford, *The Interpretation of Cultures* (New York, 1973)

———, *Local Knowledge* (New York, 1980)

Genovese, Eugene, *Roll, Jordan, Roll: The World the Slaves Made* (New York, 1973)

Gluckman, Max, *Order and Rebellion in Tribal Africa* (London, 1963)

———, *Politics, Law and Ritual in Tribal Society* (Oxford, 1965)

———, *The Ideas of Barotse Jurisprudence* (New Haven, 1965)

———, *Custom and Conflict in Africa* (1956; rpt. Oxford, 1966)

Gross, P. H., *Birth, Death and Migration in the Himalayas* (Delhi, 1982)

Grove, Richard H., *Green Imperialism: Colonial Expansion, Tropical Island Edens and the Origins of Environmentalism, 1600–1860* (Cambridge 1995)

———, 'Conserving Eden: the (European) East India Companies and their Environmental Policies on St. Helena, Mauritius and in Western India, 1600 to 1854', *Comparative Studies in Society and History*, vol. 35, no. 2, 1993

———, Vinita Damodaran and Satpal Sangwan (eds.), *Nature and the Orient: The Environmental History of South and South-east Asia* (New Delhi, 1998)

Guha, Ramachandra, 'Forestry in British and Post-British India: A Historical Analysis', *Economic and Political Weekly* (EPW), 29 October and 5–12 November 1983

———, and Gadgil, Madhav, 'State Forestry and Social Conflict in British India: A Study in the Ecological Bases of Agrarian Protest', *Past and Present*, no. 123, May 1989

Guha, Ranajit (ed.), *Subaltern Studies*, volumes I to IV (Delhi, 1982–5)

———, 'The Prose of Counter-Insurgency', *in Subaltern Studies II*

―――, *Elementary Aspects of Peasant Insurgency in Colonial India* (Delhi, 1983)

Gupta, R. K., *The Living Himalaya, Volume I: Aspects of Environment and Resource Ecology of Garhwal* (Delhi, 1983)

Gusfield, J. R., 'Social Movements and Social Change; Perspectives of Linearity and Fluidity', in Louis Kriesberg (ed.), *Research in Social Movements, Conflict and Change*, vol. 4 (Greenwich, Connecticut, 1981)

Haimendorf, C. von Fürer, *Himalayan Barbary* (London, 1955)

Hardiman, D., *Peasant Nationalists of Gujarat: Kheda District, 1917–34* (Delhi, 1981)

―――, *The Coming of the Devi: Adivasi Assertion in Western India* (Delhi, 1987)

Hardwicke, T., 'Narrative of a Journey to Shrinagar', *Asiatic Researches*, vol. 6 (1809; rpt. Delhi, 1979)

Harris, Marvin, *Cows, Pigs, Wars and Witches: The Riddles of Culture* (New York, 1974)

Hay, Douglas, 'Poaching and the Game Laws on Cannock Chase', in *Albion's Fatal Tree* (Harmondsworth, 1976)

Hays, Samuel, *Beauty, Health and Permanence: Environmental Politics in the United States, 1955–85* (New York, 1987)

Heim, A., and A. Gansser, *Central Himalaya* (1939; rpt. Delhi, 1975)

―――, *The Throne of the Gods: An Account of the first Swiss Expedition to the Himalayas* (London, 1939)

Heske, Franz, 'Problem der Walderhaltung in Himalaya', *Tharandter Forstlichien Jahrbuch*, vol. 82, no. 8, 1931

―――, *German Forestry* (New Haven, 1937)

Hilton, Rodney, *Bond Men Made Free* (London, 1973)

―――, *The English Peasantry in the Later Middle Ages* (Oxford, 1975)

Hobsbawm, Eric, *Bandits* (1969; rpt. Harmondsworth, 1972)

―――, *Primitive Rebels* (3rd edition, Manchester, 1974)

Hocart, A. M., *Kingship* (1972; rpt. Oxford, 1969)

Hodgson, B., *Essays on the Languages, Literature and Religion of Nepal and Tibet* (1874; rpt. Varanasi, 1971)

Jain, R. K., 'Kingship, Territory and Property in Bundelkhand', EPW, 2 June 1979

Jenkins, J. C., 'Resource Mobilization Theory and the Study of Social Movements', *Annual Review of Sociology*, no. 9, 1983

Jewitt, Sarah, and Stuart Corbridge, 'From Forest Struggles to Forest Citizens? Joint Forest Management in the Unquiet Woods of Jharkhand', *Environment and Planning A*, vol. 29, no. 12, 1997

Jones, E. C., 'The Environment and the Economy', in P. Burke (ed.), *The New Cambridge Modern History*, vol. XIII (Cambridge, 1979)

Joshi, B. K., 'Underdevelopment of Hill Areas of UP', mimeo, GIDS, Lucknow, 1983

Joshi, Gopa, 'Men Propose Women Dispose', *Indian Express*, 14 January 1982

Joshi, L. D., *The Khasa Family Law* (Allahabad, 1929)

Joshi, S. C., D. R. Joshi, and D. D. Dani, *Kumaun Himalaya* (Nainital, 1983)

Kala, G. R., *Memoirs of the Raj: Kumaun* (Delhi, 1974)

Kartodirdjo, Sartono, *The Peasants' Revolt in Banten in 1888* (The Hague, 1966)

——, *Protest Movements in Rural Java* (Singapore, 1973)

Kavouri, Purnendu S., *Pastoralism in Expansion* (New Delhi, 1999)

Kelly, William, *Deference and Defiance in Nineteenth Century Japan* (Princeton, 1985)

Kennedy, James, *Life and Work in Benares and Kumaun 1839–1877* (London, 1884)

Kern, Fritz, *Kingship and the Law in the Middle Ages* (Oxford, 1956)

Khan, W., and Tripathy, R. N., *Plan for Integrated Rural Development in Pauri Garhwal* (Hyderabad, 1976)

Kishan, Prakash, *The Broad Spectrum* (Delhi, 1973)

Kumar, Pradeep, 'Uttarakhand Movement: Areas of Peripheral Support', *Mainstream*, 9 August 1997

Kunwar, S. S. (ed.), *Hugging the Himalaya: The Chipko Experience* (Gopeshwar, 1982)

Ladurie, Emmanuel Le Roy, *Carnival in Romans* (New York, 1980)

Lall, J. S. (ed.), *The Himalaya: Aspects of Change* (Delhi, 1981)

Lefebvre, Georges, *The Great Fear* (rpt. Princeton, 1982)

Lewer, J.C.G., *The Sowar and the Jawan* (Ilfracombe, Devon, 1981)

Lewis, Oscar, *Pedro Martinez: A Mexican Peasant and His Family* (New York, 1964)

Linebaugh, Peter, 'Karl Marx, the Theft of Wood and Working Class Composition: A Contribution to the Current Debate', *Crime and Social Justice*, no. 6, Fall-Winter 1976

Longworth, Philip, 'The Pugachev Revolt: The Last Great Cossack-Peasant Uprising', in H. A. Landsberger (ed.), *Agrarian Movements and Social Change* (London, 1974)

Low, D.A. (ed.), *Congress and the Raj* (London, 1977)

Manral, D. S., *Swatantra Sangram mein Kumaun-Garhwal ka Yogdan* (Bareilly, 1978)

Marglin, F. A., 'Kings and Wives: The Separation of Status and Royal Power', *Contributions to Indian Sociology*, n.s., vol. 15, nos. I and 2, December 1981

Marsh, G. P., *Man and Nature* (1864; rpt. Cambridge, Mass., 1967)

Marx, Karl, 'Debate on the Law on Thefts of Wood' (1842), in Karl Marx and Frederick Engels, *Collected Works*, volume I (Moscow, 1975)

———, 'Economic and Philosophical Manuscripts of 1844', in Lucio Colletti (ed.), *Karl Marx: Early Writings* (Harmondsworth, 1975)

Mason, P., *A Matter of Honour* (London, 1975)

Mawdsley, Emma, 'Nonseccessionist Regionalism in India: The Uttarakhand Separate State Movement', *Environment and Planning A*, vol. 29, no. 12, 1997

———, 'After Chipko: From Environment to Region in the Uttaranchal', forthcoming in the *Journal of Peasant Studies*

Meadows, Donella, et al., *The Limits to Growth* (New York, 1971)

Merchant, Carolyn, *Radical Ecology: the Search for a Livable World* (New York, 1992)

Merriman, John, 'The Demoiselles of the Ariege, 1829–1831', in Merriman (ed.) *1830 in France* (New York, 1971)

Mishra, A., and S. Tripathi, *Chipko Movement* (Delhi, 1978)

Mitra, Amit, 'Chipko: An Unfinished Mission', *Down to Earth*, 30 April 1993

Mitra, C. S., 'Political Mobilization and the Nationalist Movement in Eastern Uttar Pradesh and Bihar, 1937–42', unpublished D. Phil. thesis, Oxford University, 1983

Moench, Marcus, 'Resource Utilization and Degradation: An Integrated Analysis of Biomass Utilization Patterns in a Garhwal Hill Village, Northern Uttar Pradesh, India', M. S. thesis, University of California, Berkeley, 1985

Moertono, S., *State and Statecraft in Old Java* (Ithaca, 1968)

Moorcroft, W., and Trebeck, G., *Travels in Hindusthan* (1837; rpt. Delhi, 1971)

'Mountaineer', *A Summer Ramble in the Himalaya* (London, 1860)

Mukul, 'Villages of Chipko Movement', EPW, 10 April 1993

Mumm, A.L, *Five Months in the Himalayas* (London, 1909)

Netting, R.M., *Balancing on an Alp* (Cambridge, 1981)

Painuli, P. N., *Deshi Rajyaun aur Jan Andolan* (Dehradun, 1948)

Pandey, G., *The Ascendancy of the Congress in Uttar Pradesh, 1926–34* (Delhi, 1978)

Pandian, M. S. S., *The Political Economy of Agrarian Change* (New Delhi, 1989)

Panikkar, K. M., *The Ideas of State and Sovereignty in Indian Political Thought* (Bombay, 1963)

Pannalal, *Hindu Customary Law in Kumaun* (1921; rpt. Allahabad, 1942)

Pant, G. B., *The Forest Problem in Kumaun* (Allahabad, 1922)

Pant, Govind, (ed.), *Aaj ka Uttarakhand, Kal ka Uttarakhand Rajya?* (Naini Tal, 1989)

Pant, S.D., *Social Economy of the Himalayans* (London, 1935)

Panwar, S. S., 'Garhwalis: The Warrior Race of the North', *The Commentator* (Dehradun), 16 August 1971

Passmore, J., *Man's Responsibility for Nature* (2nd edn, London, 1980)

Pathak, Shekhar, 'Uttarakhand mein Coolie Begar Pratha, 1815–1949', unpublished Ph.D. thesis, History Dept, Kumaun University, 1980

———, 'Kumaun mein Begar Anmulan Andolan', paper presented at seminar on Peasant Movements in UP, Jawaharlal Nehru University, 19–20 October 1982

———, *Peshawar Kand ki Yad* (Almora, 1982)

———, *Badridutt Pande aur Unka Yug* (Lucknow, 1982)

———, 'Anti-Alcohol movement in Uttarakhand', EPW, 28 July 1985

———, *Uttarakhand mein Kuli Begar Pratha* (Delhi, 1987)

Patiram, *Garhwal: Ancient and Modern* (Simla, 1916)

Paul, G. P., *Felling Timber in the Himalayas* (London, 1871)

Pawar, Jai Prakash, 'Chipko ki Parampara mein ab Van Panchayatain Janta ko Andolit kar Rahi Hain', *Naini Tal Samachar*, 1 September 1994

Peluso, Nancy, *Rich Forests, Poor People: Resource Control and Resistance in Java* (Berkeley, 1992)

Polanyi, Karl, *The Great Transformation* (1944; rpt. Boston, 1968)

Poffenberger, Mark, and Betsy McGean, (eds.), *Village Voices, Forest Choices: Joint Forest Management in India* (New Delhi, 1996)

Postan, M. M. (ed.), *The Cambridge Economic History of Europe. Volume I: The Agrarian Life of the Middle Ages* (2nd edn, Cambridge, 1966)

Prabhakar, R. *Resource Use, Culture and Ecological Change: A Case Study of the Nilgiri Hills of Southern India*, unpublished Ph D thesis, Indian Institute of Science, Bangalore, 1994

Prasad, Archana, *Forests and Subsistence in Colonial India: A Study of the Central Provinces, 1830–1945*, unpublished Ph D thesis, Jawaharlal Nehru University, 1994

Pratap, Ajay, *Paharia Ethnohistory and the Archaeology of the Rajmahal Hills: Archaeological Implications of a Historical Study of Shifting Cultivation*, unpublished Ph D thesis, University of Cambridge, 1987

Raha, M. K., 'Forest in Tribal Life', *Bulletin of the Cultural Research Institute*, vol. 2, no. 1, 1963

Randhawa, M. S., *The Kumaun Himalayas* (Delhi, 1970)

Rangarajan, Mahesh, *Fencing the Forest: Conservation and Ecological Change in India's Central Provinces, 1860–1914.* (New Delhi, 1996)

Ranger, Terence, 'The Invention of Tradition in Colonial Africa', in Eric Hobsbawm and Terence Ranger (eds), *The Invention of Tradition* (Cambridge, 1983)

Raturi, H. K., *Garhwal Varnan* (Bombay, 1910)

———, *Garhwal ka Itihas* (1927; rpt. Dehradun, 1980)

Rawat, A. S., 'Political Movements in Tehri Garhwal State', *Uttarakhand Bharati*, vol. 2, no. 2, 1977

———, 'Administration of Land Revenue in British Garhwal (1856–1900)', in *Quarterly Review of Historical Studies* (Calcutta), vol. 21, nos. 2 and 3, 1981–2

Reddy, A. K. N., 'An Alternate Pattern of Indian Industrialization', in A. K. Bagchi and N. Banerjee (eds), *Change and Choice in Indian Industry* (Calcutta, 1982)

Roszak, T., 'The Sacramental Vision of Nature', in R. Clarke (ed.), *Notes for the Future* (London, 1975)

Rude, G., *The Crowd in History* (New York, 1964)

———, *Ideology and Popular Protest* (London, 1980)

Sabean, David, 'The Communal Basis of Pre-1800 Peasant Uprisings in Western Europe', *Comparative Politics*, Vol. 8, no. 3, 1976

Saberwal, Vasant, *Pastoral Politics: Shepherds, Bureaucrats and Conservation in the Himachal Himalaya* (New Delhi, 1999)

Saksena, B. P. (ed.), *Historical Papers Relating to Kumaun, 1809–1842* (Allahabad, 1956)

Sanwal, R. D., 'Social Stratification in the Hill Region of Uttar Pradesh', in Indian Institute of Advanced Studies, *Urgent Research in Social Anthropology* (Simla, 1969)

———, *Social Stratification in Rural Kumaun* (Delhi, 1976)

Sarkar, S., *Modern India, 1885–1947* (Delhi, 1983)

———, *Writing Social History* (Delhi, 1998)

Savyasachi, 'Fields and Farms: Shifting Cultivation in Bastar', mimeo, World Institute of Development Economies Research, Helsinki, 1987

Saxena, N. C., 'Social Forestry in the Hill Districts of Uttar Pradesh', mimeo, ICIMOD, Kathmandu, 1987

Scheiner, Irwin, 'Benevolent Lords and Honorable Peasants: Rebellion and Peasant Consciousness in Tokugawa Japan', in Tetsuo Najita and Irwin Scheiner (eds), *Japanese Thought in the Tokugawa Period, 1600–1868* (Chicago, 1978)

Scott, J. C., *The Moral Economy of the Peasant* (New Haven, 1976)

———, 'Protest and Profanation: Agrarian Revolt and the Little Tradition', *Theory and Society*, vol. 4, nos. 1 and 2, 1977

———, *Weapons of the Weak: Everyday Forms of Peasant Resistance* (New Haven, 1986)

Sengupta, Nirmal, 'Irrigation: Traditional *versus* Modern', EPW, Special Number, August 1985

Shanin, Teodor, *The Roots of Otherness: Russia's Turn of Century; Volume I: Russia as a 'Developing Society'; Volume II: Russia, 1905–7: Revolution as a Moment of Truth* (New Haven, 1986)

Sharma, R., *Party Politics in a Himalayan State* (Delhi, 1977)

Shastri, N., *Dehradun aur Garhwal mein Rajnaitik Andolan ka Itihas* (Dehradun, 1932)

Sherring, C. A., *Western Tibet and the Indian Borderland* (1916; rpt. Delhi, 1974)

Shipton, Eric, 'More Explorations Around Nanda Devi', *The Geographical Journal*, vol. 90, no. 2, 1937

Siddiqi, M. H., *Agrarian Unrest in North India: The United Provinces, 1918–22* (Delhi, 1978)

Singh, Chetan, *Natural Premises: Ecology and Peasant Life in the Western Himalaya, 1800–1950* (New Delhi, 1998)

Sinha, S. C., 'State Formation and Rajput Myth in Tribal Central India', *Man in India*, vol. 42, no. 1, 1962

Sivaramakrishnan, K., *Modern Forests: Statemaking and Environmental Change in Colonial Eastern India* (Delhi and Stanford, 1999)

Skaria, Ajay, *Hybrid Histories: Forests, Frontiers and Wildness in Western India* (Delhi, 1999)

Skinner, Thomas, *Excursions in India, Including a Walk over the Himalaya Mountain to the Source of the Jumna and the Ganges*, volumes 1 and 2 (London, 1832)

Slack, Paul (ed.) *Rebellion, Popular Protest and the Social Order in Early Modern Europe* (Cambridge, 1984)

Smythe, F. S., 'Explorations in Garhwal around Kamet', *The Geographical Journal*, vol. 79, no. 1, 1932

Somanathan, E., 'Deforestation, Incentives and Property Rights in Central Himalaya', EPW, 26 January 1991

Sundar, Nandini, *Subalterns and Sovereigns: An Anthropological History of Bastar* (Delhi, 1997)

Swami, Praveen, 'Blundering Progress: The Tehri Project and Growing Fears', *Frontline*, 30 June 1995

Sopher, D. E., 'Rohilkhand and Oudh: An Exploration of Social Gradients Across a Political Barrier', in R. G. Fox (ed.), *Realm and Region in Traditional India* (Delhi, 1977)

Spodek, H., 'On the Origins of Gandhi's Political Methodology: The Heritage of Kathiawad and Gujarat', *Journal of Asian Studies*, vol. 30, no.2, February 1971

Srivastava, R. P., 'Tribe/Caste Mobility in India and the Case of the Kumaun Bhotias', in C. von Fürer Haimendorf (ed.), *Caste and Kin in Bengal, India and Ceylon* (Bombay, 1966)

Stebbing, E. P., *The Forests of India*, 3 volumes (London, 1922–7)

Strachey, R., 'On the Physical Geography of the Provinces of Kumaun and Garhwal in the Himalaya', *Journal of the Royal Geographical Society*, vol. 21, 1851

Swaminathan, M., 'A Study of Energy Use Patterns in Garhwal Himalaya', in Kunwar (ed.), *Hugging the Himalaya*

Tewari, G. C., 'An Economic Profile of the Hill Region of Uttar Pradesh', occasional paper no. 10, G. B. Pant Social Science Institute, Allahabad, 1982

Thapar, R., *A History of India*, vol. 1 (Harmondsworth, 1966)

Thompson, E. P., 'The Moral Economy of the English Crowd in the Eighteenth Century', *Past and Present*, no. 50, 1970–1

———, 'The Crime of Anonymity', in *Albion's Fatal Tree* (Harmondsworth, 1976)

———, *Whigs and Hunters* (Harmondsworth, 1977)

———, Eighteenth Century English Society: Class Struggle without Class?', *Social History*, vol. 3, no.2, 1978

Thorner, Daniel, 'Peasant Economy as a Category in Economic History', in T. Shanin (ed.), *Peasants and Peasant Societies* (Harmondsworth, 1972)

Tilly, Charles, *From Mobilization to Revolution* (Reading, Mass., 1978)

———, *Big Structures, Large Processes, Huge Comparisons* (New York, 1985)

———. *The Contentious French* (Cambridge, Mass., 1986)

Traill, G. W., 'Statistical Sketch of Kumaun', *Asiatic Researches*, vol. 16 (1828; rpt. Delhi 1980)

Troup, R. S., *Silviculture of Indian Trees* (Oxford, 1921)

Walthall, Anne, 'Japanese *Gimin*: Peasant Martyrs in Popular Memory', *American Historical Review*, vol. 91, no. 5, 1986

Webber, T. W., *The Forests of Upper India and their Inhabitants* (London, 1902)

Weber, Max, *Economy and Society*, two volumes, translated and edited by Güenther Roth and Claus Wittich (Berkeley, 1968)

Weber, Eugene, *Peasants into Frenchmen* (Stanford, 1976)

White, Lynn, 'The Historical Roots of our Ecologic Crisis', in Clarke (ed.), *Notes for the Future*

Whittaker, William, 'Migration and Agrarian Change in Garhwal District, Uttar Pradesh', in T. P. Bayliss-Smith and Sudhir Wanmali (eds), *Understanding Green Revolutions: Agrarian Change and Development Planning in South Asia* (Cambridge, 1984)

Wolf, Eric, *Peasant Wars of the Twentieth Century* (New York, 1969)

Womack, John, *Zapata and the Mexican Revolution* (New York, 1969)

Yoo, Se Hee, 'The Communist Movements and the Peasant: The Case of Korea', in J. W. Lewis (ed.), *Peasant Rebellion and Communist Revolution in Asia* (Stanford, 1974)

Index

Adas, Michael, 125, 128n, 130
Agarwal, Anil, 203
agrarian relations, 6, 14–21; and subsistence, 2, 15, 24–5, 56, 79; *see also* village community; women
alienation from nature, 55–8, 168; *see also* community forest management; conservation: traditional systems of
All India States Peoples Conference, 80, 84, 87, 89; *see also* Congress Party; Praja Mandal
animal husbandry, 28, 145; and forests, 31–2, 49–50, 54–5, 70–1, 73, 113, 150
Appiko movement, 178n
Arnold, David, 217n
arson, 3, 52n, 82n, 123–5; in Kumaun division, 107–8, 115–19; in Tehri Garhwal, 82; *see also* fire protection; forest fires; protest: mechanisms of
artisans, 12, 13–14, 63
authority: bureaucratic, 7, 99–100, 128; legitimate, 3, 7, 97–8; traditional, 7, 77, 128

Baden-Powell, B. H., 192, 220
Bahuguna, Sunderlal, 154, 161–2, 166, 169–72, 174, 176–80, 182–4, 203–6; *see also* Chipko Andolan

Bahuguna, Vimla, 166
Balzac, Honore de, 1, 35, 92, 187
Barrington Moore, 4, 5n, 129, 194
begar system, 16, 25–7; abolition of, 112, 120; and forest department, 71, 101–3; opposition to, 70–1, 77, 81–2, 99–104, 111–15
Bhatt, Chandi Prasad, 58, 59n, 1566–60, 164, 174–6, 177n, 180–4, 203–6; *see also* Chipko Andolan
Bhotiya, 14, 158
Bist, Alam Singh, 157
Bloch, Marc, 62, 92, 95n, 137, 211
Brandis, Dietrich, 220

capitalism, 1–2; and alienation, 56–7; peasant resistance to, 92, 186n, 187–9, 193–5, 209
caste, 11–14, 207–8
children (in Chipko), 166–7
Chipko Andolan, vii, viii, 8, 144, 150, 151–84, 185, 190, 196, 197–206, 208–10, 212; and environment debate, 178–84, 195–6, 200–01, 203; and Gandhians, 176–7, 197; and women 159, 163–4, 169–70, 172, 174, 177, 182, 198–9, 200, 210; background, 153–7; development, 157–72; in a history of protest, 152–4, 159–61, 170, 172, 174, 177, 182, 208–10; three wings of,

172–84; misrepresentations of, viii, 197–9, 203–6; see also Sarvodaya workers; women; resistance: ideologies of chir forests, 29, 36, 51, 53, 123, 149, 163; burning of, 107, 116; see also arson; resin tapping
Cobb, Richard, 132
colonialism, 1–2, 6, 192; and alienation, 56–7; and ecological decline, 194–6, 215–20; peasant resistance to, 128, 133, 136–7
community forest management, 40, 55–8, 148–51, 200–02; see also alienation from nature; conservation: traditional systems of
Congress Party, 6, 131–3, 172; in Kumaun division, 123, 125, 135; in Tehri Garhwal, 79, 81, 83, 86, 88; see also All India States Peoples Conference; political organizations; Praja Mandal
conservation: traditional systems of, 29–34; breakdown of, 57–8; sacred groves in, 29–31; communal institutions in, 31–2; see also community forest management
contractor system, 45n, 138, 142–3, 154, 156, 161, 166–7
customary rebellion, 8, 71, 89–98, 110, 127–9; in Tehri Garhwal, 67–79, 87; see also divine kingship; protest: mechanisms of; Tehri Garhwal maharaja

Dashauli Gram Swarajya Sangh, 156–9, 180, 184, 203–4
Daulatram, Dada, 82–8
deodar forests, 30, 37–40
dhandak, see customary rebellion

divine kingship, 62, 93–8; see also customary rebellion; Tehri Garhwal maharaja
Dom, 12–14, 21, 76
ecofeminism (also feminism)–see Chipko Andolan; women
ecological change, 9–7
ecological decline, 8; and agrarian economy, 144–8, 212; and floods, 155–6, 160, 162; and outward migration, 146–7; see also forest destruction
ecological determinism, 6
ecological succession, 36–7
ecological zones, 14
Elwin, Verrier, 57
environmental history, vii–xi, 5–8, 211–12; development of, in India, 211–15, 220–2
Erikson, Kai, 148

Febvre, Lucien, 34, 211
Field, Daniel, 91, 137
fire protection, 51–4, 105, 107, 115, 122–3
forest conflicts: European, 8, 91–2, 116–17, 133–4, 186–8, 192
forest destruction: and ecological decline, 146, 216–18; and fire, 51–2; and industrialization, 138–9; and railways, 37–8; and scientific forestry, 60–1; and villagers, 107, 115–16; and World Wars, 42–3, 47–8
forest fires, 79, 99, 107–8, 115–19, 123; and pasture, 29, 49, 51, 115, 118; see also arson; fire protection
forest labour co-operatives, 142–3, 156–7
forest law: breaches of, 48–9, 51–2, 59, 70, 109–10, 115–16, 121–

3; *see also* arson; forest conflicts: European; protest: mechanisms of
forest management: and agrarian economy, 104–5, 121, 185–6, 203, 212–14, 215, 219; and imperial needs, 39, 48; commercial orientation of, 40–2, 45, 48, 50, 60–1, 70, 77, 108, 114, 117, 136, 138–9, 143, 216; concessions to industry, 139–41; in Europe, 49–50, 57–9; peasant resistance to, 69–76, 79, 99, 105–10, 114–25, 220; *see also* Chipko Andolan
Forest Research Institute, 41, 140–1
forest rights: restrictions on, 39–41, 43–5, 60, 69–70, 79, 141, 143, 212–13, 219–20
forests, 35–7; and subsistence agriculture, 6–7, 28–9, 57, 114–15, 117, 135–6, 213; loss of community control over, 55, 57–8; takeover by state, 6, 38–48, 57

Gairola, Khuslanand, 80, 83, 87
Gairola, Taradutt, 26n, 103–4
Gandhi, Mahatma, 11–12, 114, 124, 131n, 134, 154, 176–7, 191
Garhwali, Chandra Singh, 80, 84, 209
Gaura Devi, 159
Geertz, Clifford, 6n,
Genovese, Eugene, 96, 171
Gluckman, Max, 8, 89–90
Grazing, *see* animal husbandry
Grove, Richard, 216–17, 218, 220
Gujars, 71
Gurkhas, 10–11

Hardiman, David, 194–5
Hobsbawm, Eric, 4n, 116, 192

Indo-Gangetic plain, 9–10, 27, 179
industrialization: Euro-American and Indian compared, 191–6; ecological limits to, 195–6

Jardari, Vijay, 166
joint forest management–*see* community forest management
Juyal, Chakradhar, 69, 73–8

Kartodirdjo, Sartono, x, xi, 128n
Kennedy, John F., 202
Khasa, Khasiya, 11–13
Kumar, Virendra, 160
Kumaun Forest Grievances Committee, 48, 102, 120–1, 125, 148, 201
Kumaun Parishad, 101, 110–11, 114–15, 119, 126

land revenue, 23–5, 27, 63
land-tenure system, 16–21
land settlement, 81; opposition to, 81–9, 124
Lefebvre, Georges, 135
lopping, 50, 54–5

Madras Board of Revenue, 219
Marsh, George Perkins, 58n
Marx, Karl, 5, 56–7, 97, 194n
Marxism, 1, 4, 131n, 181, 189
Mawdsley, Emma, 208
Mendes, Chico, 199
'money-order' economy, 147, 152, 165

Narmada Bachao Andolan, 200, 221
nationalism, 6, 8, 131–5; *see also* political organizations
Negi, Dhum Singh, 162

INDEX

oak forests, 28, 36–7, 48, 51, 60, 121, 139, 149, 163
officials: popular opposition to, 65–8, 91, 95, 168–9, 170, 172; in Tehri Garhwal, 71–2, 74, 85–8; *see also* customary rebellion

Painuli, Paripurnanand, 83–4, 86
panchayats, 14, 141, 149–50; and protest, 71, 75, 86, 202; *see also* village community
Pande, Badridutt, 110–11, 114, 117, 126, 207; *see also* Kumaun Parishad
Pant, Govind Ballabh, 110
Pant, S. D., 22
Panwar kings, 63
paternalism, 62, 90–1, 96–9, 136; *see also* customary rebellion; divine kingship
Pathak, Shekhar, viii, 110, 112
Penan, 198–9
Political–Cultural (P–C) paradigm, 2–5
political organizations: and the peasantry, 2–3, 8, 131–5, 171, 192–3; in Kumaun division, 113–14, 123, 127–8; in Tehri Garhwal, 87–9; *see also* Congress Party; Praja Mandal
population pressure, 143–5
Praja Mandal: Tehri Rajya, 79–84, 87–9, 176; *see also* All India States Peoples conference; Congress Party
Prasun, Kunwar, 166
protest: mechanisms of, 3–4, 49, 125–33, 185–6, 206–7; and fairs, 85, 111–12; and lack of violence, 68, 129–31, 177; boycott, 120–1; dissimulation, 100–1, 106; hunger fasts, 80, 83, 166, 171;

migration, 67, 76, 106; refusal to pay taxes, 69, 85; shutdowns, 124, 155; *see also* arson; customary rebellion

Ramsay, Henry, 15, 24, 99–101, 126
Rawain firing, 75–6, 78, 95, 161
Rawat, Govind Singh, 158–9
Rawat, Kedar Singh, 158
Reddy, A. K. N., 184
Redfield, Robert, 33
resin tapping, 43–7, 116, 139, 141–2, 160
resistance: ideologies of, 3, 6–7, 117–18, 136–7, 170–3, 177, 190–1; in Chipko, 166–8; in Kumaun division, 100, 103, 114–15, 119–20, 126–9; in Tehri Garhwal, 92–3, 97–8; *see also* customary rebellion; protest: mechanisms of
Roszak, Theodor, 181
Row, Narain, 219
Rude, George, 4n, 127n,
rumours, 74–5, 78

Sailani, Ghanshyam, 172
Sabean, David, 193
Saklani, Nagendra, 83–4, 86, 150
Saklani, Virendra Dutt, 86
Saklani, Vishveswar Dutt, 150
Sarla Devi, 156
Sarvodaya workers, 142, 154, 156–7, 161–2, 176; *see also* Chipko Andolan
scientific forestry, 53,–5, 59–60; and agrarian economy, 49–51, 54–5, 99–100; ecological characteristics of, 59–61; *see also* forest management
Scott, J. C., 4, 98, 125–6, 128n, 194–5

Shikhar, Pratap, 166
Skinner, Thomas, 15–16
sociology of social movements, 1–4, 172–3, 189
soldiers, 22–5, 104, 125, 209; participation in social movements, 82, 108, 120, 165, 190
statutory labour, *see begar* system
Structural–Organizational (S–O) paradigm, 2–6, 131
Subaltern Studies, viii–ix, 4, 6, 128n, 222
Sulochana Devi, 169
Suman, Sridevi, 80–1, 84, 87, 161, 171
Symonds Co., 157–8

tea cultivation, 24
Tehri Garhwal maharaja, 20–2, 62, 69–71, 75, 77–8, 80–1, 83–4, 86–7, 90, 172; links with Badrinath temple, 7n, 63–4, 68, 78, 96, 124, 136; quasi-divine status of, 63, 89, 136–7; *see also* customary rebellion; divine kingship
Thompson, E. P., 4n, 62, 98, 189
Thuljat, 12–13
Tilly, Charles, 2, 4–5, 128
Troup, R. S., 53–4

Uttarakhand: compared with other mountain societies, 28, 33–4

Uttarakhand movement, vii, 216–10
Uttarakhand Sangharsh Vahini, 162–3, 174–5, 177n, 181, 184

Van Nigam (forest corporation), 161, 166, 170
village community, 9, 16, 21; egalitarian nature of, 20–1, 27–8, 33–4, 62–3, 68, 73, 129–30, 135–6, 143, 150; frangmentation of, 147, 149–50, 165
village forests, *see* community forest management; conservation: traditional systems of
village headmen, 14, 16, 73, 77, 100, 112, 190

Warren, Karen, 198, 199
Weber, Max, 7, 89, 97
White, Lynn, 181, 199
Wolf, Eric, 4
women, 21–2, 147, 152; participation in social movements, 117, 152–4, 158–9, 163–4, 166–7, 169–70, 175, 202, 203, 210; *see also* agrarian relations; Chipko Andolan
Wyndham, Percy, 72, 103, 108, 116, 120, 185

Zapata, 135

Environmentalism

A Global History

RAMACHANDRA GUHA

for
Bill Burch, internationalist

Series Editor's Preface

Of the several processes that all human societies in all ages have had in common, none has been more fundamental than their continual interaction with their natural environment. In fact, more than any other aspect of human endeavor, the diverse modes of human societal interaction with the larger ecological setting provide the basis for a genuinely global history of humanity. But, unlike so many of the other themes and patterns from which world history can be constructed, environmental history transcends the human experience. Due to the profound technological and scientific transformations that have occurred over the past millennium, it has come to effect—often fatally in recent centuries—every species of living creature on earth.

In view of its centrality, it is rather remarkable that serious work on the global dimensions of the history of human responses to and impact upon their environments has, with important exceptions, been undertaken only in the last three or four decades. There were, of course, important ecological dimensions to the patterns of societal development that Ibn Khaldun delineated in his fourteenth-century treatise *The Muqaddimah*, especially in his stress on the ebb and flow of pastoral nomadic and sedentary adaptations in the history of North Africa and the Middle East. And George Perkins Marsh's magisterial meditation on *Man and Nature* was published nearly a century and a half ago. But it is only since the 1960s, that world and cross-cultural historians, led by William H. McNeill, Alfred Crosby, and more recently John McNeill, have embarked on sustained and thoroughly documented explorations of the diverse patterns of social and environmental interactions over time.

Thus far, much of the research and writing that these pioneering historians have inspired has been focused on specific ecosystems or regional complexes of environmental patterns. And almost all of the work done thus far, including that of more globally-oriented pioneers like McNeill and Crosby, has concentrated on actual processes of human interventions into the natural world and their consequences for both human societies and affected plant and animal species. Though a considerable amount has been written on the attitudes towards the natural world exhibited by specific cultures or civilizations, little work has yet appeared that attempts to study these cross-culturally or from a global perspective. The most important exception to this general trend is Clarence Glacken's massive *Traces on the Rhodian Shore*, which surveys responses to the environment from ancient times to the modern era. But Glacken's work is oriented to European thinkers and civilizations and to the ancient Mediterranean milieux that give rise to them.

Given this situation, Ramachandra Guha's *Environmentalism: A Global History* is an especially welcome addition to the Longman World History series. Guha's incisive and wide-ranging survey of environmental thinking and the movements it has spawned is genuinely cross-cultural and global in scope. His focus is environmentalism in the modern age, but he delineates and explores in depth a multiplicity of approaches to those issues, with particular emphasis on the often variant currents of the latter half of the twentieth century. Ideas about the environment and movements aimed at focussing attention on the causes of its degradation and the ways to protect it are set in the different socioeconomic and political contexts which gave rise to them. But Guha is also sensitive to the ways in which thinking about ecology is reworked or transformed when it is exposed to international or intercultural influences. He seeks to identify the commonalities and differences in environmental thinking and activism through case studies drawn from the experience of areas as diverse as the United States, the former Soviet Union, China, India, Africa and Brazil. Guha candidly assesses the strengths and shortcomings of each of these strands of environmentalism as well as their contributions to the coalescence of a global environmental consciousness.

In many ways Ramachandra Guha is the ideal person to author the first genuinely global history of environmentalism. Over the past two decades, his many fine books and articles have earned him the reputation as one of the foremost thinkers on ecological issues relating to South Asia, historically one of the pivotal regions in environmental history for reasons he elucidates in the study that follows. In recent years, building on his regional expertise, Guha has become one of the more provocative and perceptive commentators on environmentalism in its cross-cultural and global dimensions. He has made a convincing case for the importance of understanding the often fundamental differences that separate Euro-American environmental activists and theorists and those who argue from the perspective of the post-colonial societies, where the great majority of humanity lives. He has placed great emphasis on the critical distinctions between strains of ecological activism based on preservationist, conservationist, earth first, and human accomodationist priorities. His capacity to identify and analyze the central precepts of these different strands of environmentalism, in combination with his well-informed critiques of each of them in the larger context of the current global predicament, render *Environmentalism: A Global History* a lively and engaging study of ideas and debates that all of us will find central to our lives in the twenty-first century.

MICHAEL ADAS
Series Editor
Rutgers University at New Brunswick

Author's Preface

The roots of this book go back to two gloriously happy years I spent working at Yale University in the mid 1980s. On the basis of my own work in India I had imagined environmentalism to be principally a question of social justice, of allowing the poor to have as much claim on the fruits of nature as the powerful. But living and teaching in the United States I was to come face-to-face with a rather different kind of environmentalism, which shifted attention away from humans towards the rights of plants, animals and wild habitats. I have ever since been fascinated by the diversity within the global environmental movement. This book explores the part played by different cultural and national traditions in the making and shaping of that diversity.

I returned to India from the USA in 1987, but have gone back several times since, to renew acquaintance with and deepen my understanding of American environmentalism. More recently, I spent the academic year 1994–95 in Germany, a country that is unquestionably the leader within Europe in matters environmental, and is home also to the German Greens, the protest movement which became a political party. Briefer trips to Latin America in 1994, to Russia in 1996, and to Southern Africa in 1997, allowed a glimpse of the problems and possibilities of environmentalism in those territories.

These forays, short and long, have been paid for by hospitable universities and indulgent foundations who have helped me challenge one of the unacknowledged taboos of international scholarship. For the way that the world is structured, Brazilians may write about Brazil, Nigerians about Nigeria, Bangladeshis about Bangladesh. But broader works of contrast and comparison, books that are not restricted to one country but which take the world as their oyster, are written from the comfortable citadels of a great and prosperous university in Europe or the United States. This prejudice is not cultural or racial, but merely geographical. Global histories, be they of environmentalism, feminism, liberalism or fundamentalism, are generally the handiwork of people working and teaching in the northern half of the globe. It is as difficult for a scholar of British origin to

Author's Preface

write a global history living in Bogota as it is easy for an Indian while based in Indianapolis.

My thanks then, first of all, to the School of Forestry and Environmental Studies at Yale University. Two colleagues at Yale, Bill Burch and Joe Miller, and two students, Mike Bell and Joel Seton, encouraged me to move beyond what had been, until then, a nearobsessive concern with the history and politics of my own country. Next in chronological order comes the University of California at Santa Barbara, whose invitation in 1989 to deliver the Ninth Steven Manley Memorial Lecture forced me to think more seriously about the comparative aspects of the environmental question. The arguments of that lecture were given a firmer empirical basis in the year I spent at the Wissenschaftskolleg zu Berlin, whose magnificently efficient library staff chased and procured dozens of obscure references and out-of-print books. Other institutions that have helped materially include the University of California at Berkeley; the Harry and Frank Guggenheim Foundation, New York; the Social Science Research Council, New York; and the Nehru Memorial Museum and Library, New Delhi: my thanks to all of them.

The themes and arguments of this book have been shaped by numerous conversations across the continents. I have learnt much from three scholars whose interests exemplify the cross-cultural character of the environmental movement: from Juan Martinez-Alier, a Spaniard most at home in Ecuador and Cuba; from Mike Bell, a Rhode Islander who happily mixes with Little Englanders; and from Wolfgang Sachs, a Bavarian radical with a keenly developed insight into the practice of the Gujarati Mahatma, Gandhi. There are other friends in Europe and American with whom I have argued fiercely or gently but always (to me, at any rate) productively, and yet others who have passed on valuable tips and sources. I thank here William Beinart, David Brokensha, J. Peter Brosius, Louise Fortmann, Andrew Hurrell, Arné Kalland, Margit Mayer, Arné Naess, Paul Richards, David Rothenberg, Katherine Snyder, Carol Warren and Donald Worster. I owe a particular debt to K. Sivaramakrishnan (of Yale, again), the source of a steady stream of books and articles impossible to get hold of in India.

To come home now, to the students and scholars of the Indian environmental movement, the college of colleagues to whom I perhaps owe most of all. Discussions over many years with Anjan Ghosh, Madhav Gadgil and Shiv Visvanathan have helped me more clearly see India in the cold light of the world, and the world through the warm glow of India. I have also been challenged and inspired by the verse and zest of younger colleagues such as Amita Baviskar, Ashish Kothari, Mahesh Rangarajan and Nandini Sundar. André Béteille, a distinguished senior scholar, and Keshav Desiraju, an experienced environmental administrator, read and helpfully commented on an earlier draft. For valuable comments on the manuscript I am indebted to the following reviewers: Randall Dodgen (Sonoma State University); Robert Entenmann (St. Olaf College); Vera Reben (Shippensburg University); Cathy Skidmore-Hess (Georgia Southern University); Tracey Steele (Sam Houston State University). I would also to thank my editors, Pam Gordon at Addison Wesley Longman (New York) and Rukun Advani at Oxford University Press (New Delhi) for their critical support to the project.

But it is, of course, the editor of this series who made the book possible, who gently nudged all that talking and listening towards the more reliable medium of print. Michael Adas invited me to write on global environmentalism, waited trustingly as I missed one deadline after another, and then, when the draft chapters finally began to arrive, sent them back with meticulously detailed comments. It is a pleasure to thank him for all this, and a delight to remember those happy days at Yale when Michael and I first met.

Contents

PART I: ENVIRONMENTALISM'S FIRST WAVE

Chapter 1   GOING GREEN   1
The movement's two waves; environmentalism and industrialization; the varieties of environmentalism

Chapter 2   BACK TO THE LAND!   10
The English Love of the Country—Wordsworth, Ruskin and company; *Were the Nazis Green?*—environmentalism and nationalism in Germany; *The Gandhian View of the Simple Life*—early environmentalists in India

Chapter 3   THE IDEOLOGY OF SCIENTIFIC CONSERVATION   25
Conservation Internationalism—The wider significance of George Perkins Marsh; *The Global Reach of Scientific Forestry*—German science in Asia and America; *The Balance Sheet of Scientific Forestry*—the social and ecological costs of state forest management

Chapter 4   THE GROWTH OF THE WILDERNESS IDEA   44
Conservation in the Colonies—the crisis of African wildlife; *Wilderness Thinking in America*—the work of John Muir and Aldo Leopold

Afterword   SOME WHO DON'T FIT   59
'Trans-disciplinary' environmentalists—Patrick Geddes, Lewis Mumford, and Radhakamal Mukerjee

PART II: ENVIRONMENTALISM'S SECOND WAVE

Prologue   THE AGE OF ECOLOGICAL INNOCENCE   63
The decades of development and the making of the 'affluent' society; some

dissenters—Carl Sauer, E. F. Schumacher, Lewis Mumford, and Mira Behn

Chapter 5 THE ECOLOGY OF AFFLUENCE   69
The Significance of Silent Spring—how a book by a woman scientist changed the world; *The Environmental Debate*—science and the discourse of ecological crisis; *The Environmental Movement*—environmental action in Europe and the United States; *Radical American Environmentalism*—the competing claims of Deep Ecology and environmental justice; *The German Greens*—how a protest movement became a political party

Chapter 6 THE SOUTHERN CHALLENGE   98
The postmaterialist hypothesis challenged; *The Environmentalism of the Poor*—social action among the desperately disadvantaged in the Third World; *An India/Brazil Comparison*—ecological degradation and environmental protest in two large and important countries; *A Chipko/Chico Comparison*—the parallels between two famous forest movements; *Redefining Development*—bringing back nature and the people

Chapter 7 SOCIALISM AND ENVIRONMENTALISM   125
Early Soviet Environmentalism—the life and death of a dissident tradition; *The Three Gorges Project*—destructive development in China; *Democracy and Environmentalism*—how the political system facilitates or suppresses environmental action

Chapter 8 ONE WORLD OR TWO?   138
The Earth Summit and North-South conflicts; unity and division among the environmental movement

BIBLIOGRAPHIC ESSAY   146

INDEX   155

1

Going Green

The environmental movement is a child of the sixties that has stayed its course. Where other manifestations of that decade of protest—pacifism, the counter-culture and the civil rights struggle—have either lost out or lost their way, the green wave shows no sign of abating. The environmental movement has refused to go away and, some would say, refused to grow up, retaining the vigor and intensity but also the impatience and intolerance of an ever-youthful social movement. Alone among the movements of the sixties, it has gained steadily in power, prestige and, what is perhaps most important, public appeal.

Popular support apart, the success of the environmental movement is also reflected in the forests and wild areas it has helped set aside, as well as in the laws it has repealed or got enacted, nowhere more effectively than in the United States of America. In this country the pressures of environmentalists, rather than autonomous government action, have created an extensive and for the most part well managed system of national parks. Having protected large chunks of wilderness from the threat of 'development,' the American environmental movement has increasingly turned its attention to controlling the hazardous byproducts of industrialization: air and water pollution, and the production of toxic or radioactive wastes. Here too it has been conspicuously successful, forcing Congress to enact over seventy environmental measures into law. Among these is the National Environment Protection Act of 1969, a comprehensive piece of legislation and the envy of environmentalists in other countries who struggle to enforce minimum standards on their own governments.

While opinion polls consistently show over two-thirds of the public in support of even stricter environmental measures—and willing to part with some hard-earned dollars in the cause—the green agenda is also influencing the outcome of local, state and federal elections. Politicians from both parties assiduously project a green image and cultivate a green constituency. It was a Republican President, George Bush, who famously remarked, 'We are all environmentalists now.' The Democrats, not to be outdone, sent forth as Vice-President the author (Al Gore) of a respectably thorough and best-selling survey of the environmental dilemma, entitled *Earth in the Balance*. As the political scientist Richard Andrews points out, the influence of the environmental movement is 'demonstrable in all levels of government in extraordinary quantities of legislation, regulations and budgetary allocations, as well as in continuing media attention.' Or as John Oakes, an editor at the *New York Times*, writes of the movement's most cherished achievement, 'The national parks are as sacred to most Americans as the flag, motherhood and apple pie.'

Like apple pie, but unlike the flag, national parks are distinctively but not uniquely American. For the beauty and diversity of its resident species and habitats, Serengeti in Tanzania is probably more celebrated than Yellowstone in Wyoming, Manas in eastern India at least as remarkable as Yosemite in California. Indeed, environmentalism is by now a genuinely international movement, occurring with lesser or greater intensity in a variety of countries around the globe. Nor do these national movements necessarily work in isolation. In the age of e-mail and the fax machine, information generated in one country can be instantaneously transmitted to another. Environmentalism has thus come to constitute a field-of-force in which different individuals and organizations, far removed in space, collaborate and sometimes compete in forging a movement that often transcends national boundaries.

II

Moving outwards from the American experience, this book presents a global history of the environmental movement. Its focus is not on the nature and extent of environmental degradation; thus it has little to say about the rates of tropical deforestation, the extinction of species, or the build-up of carbon in the atmosphere. Those facts are properly the preserve of the scientist. Rather, this is a historical account and analysis of the origins and expressions of environmental concern, of how individuals and institutions have perceived, propagated, and acted upon their experience of environmental decay. This

Chapter 1: Going Green

is a book, in sum, of the environment as a spur to human reflection and human action, rather than a scientific study of the state of nature or a balance sheet of the impact of human beings on the earth.

As a program of political reform, articulating concrete policies for states and societies to adopt, environmentalism needs to be distinguished from a more narrow aesthetic or scientific appreciation of the natural world. Classical literary traditions manifest an abiding concern with natural landscapes: in writing of the beauty of birds, animals, rivers and farms, both the Roman poet Virgil (c. 70–1 BC) and the Sanskrit dramatist Kalidasa (c. AD 375–415) would qualify as 'nature-lovers'. Moving on to the late Middle Ages, the exploration by European travellers of Asia and the Americas also kindled a keen interest in the richness and diversity of nature. The exuberance of plant and animal life in the tropics was documented by a whole array of European scientists, of whom the Englishman Charles Darwin (1809–82) is perhaps the best known and most influential.

However, as understood in this book environmentalism goes beyond the literary appreciation of landscapes and the scientific analysis of species. I argue that environmentalism must be viewed as a *social* program, a charter of action which seeks to protect cherished habitats, protest against their degradation, and prescribe less destructive technologies and lifestyles. When then did the environmental movement begin? Most accounts of the American movement date its beginnings to Rachel Carson's book on pesticide pollution, *Silent Spring*, published in 1962 and variously described as the 'bible' and 'founding event' of modern environmentalism. It is true that it is only in the sixties that environmentalism emerges as a popular *movement*, successfully influencing public policy through a mixture of protest in the streets and the lobbying of legislators in the corridors of power. However, an intellectual concern for the protection or conservation of nature goes back at least to the last decades of the eighteenth century. This precocious interest rapidly grew in the nineteenth century, its votaries seeking to influence the modernizing governments of North America and Europe. Without always commanding a mass base, this earlier generation of environmentalists initiated wideranging programs of forest and water conservation and also helped set up the first national parks.

The history of environmentalism in most countries has followed a broadly similar pattern; an early period of pioneering and prophecy, culminating in recent decades in a widespread social movement. We might thus speak of a *first wave* of environmentalism, the initial response to the onset of industrialization, and a *second wave*, when a largely intellectual response was given shape and force by a groundswell of public support. Environmentalism thus has a rather longer and more distinguished lineage than is sometimes allowed for. In its contemporary forms it is certainly a child of the nineteen sixties, but also, as this book shows, perhaps a grandchild of the eighteen sixties.

The first wave of environmentalism proceeded step-by-step with the Industrial Revolution, itself the most far-reaching process of social change in human history. The industrialization of the world dramatically altered the natural world through new methods of resource extraction, production, and transportation. The scale and intensity at which nature was used (and abused) increased manifold. Simultaneously, advances in medical technology led to a steady increase in human populations. More humans producing more and consuming more led axiomatically to greater pollution and habitat degradation. The pace of environmental destruction greatly accelerated. Nature became a source of cheap raw material as well as a sink for dumping the unwanted residues of economic growth. Open-cast mining and the ever-growing appetite of industry decimated forests and wildlands. New and dangerous chemicals were excreted into rivers and the atmosphere.

The industrialization of Europe led also to major changes in the rural economy. The factories and cities needed materials to process and consume, these demands leading to a transformation of agriculture through the adoption of more capital-intensive, market-oriented methods of production. Pastures and hedgerows and small farms with mixed crops gave way to a more monotonous landscape, of large, continuous holdings dominated by crop monocultures. Further afield, European economic growth also impacted the natural environments of Asia, Africa and North America. Industrialization had an organic connection with imperial expansion, as white colonists took possession of large parts of the globe, re-orienting local economies towards the demands of the metropolis. British ships were built of Burma teak, their sailors wearing clothes of cotton grown in India, drinking Kenyan coffee sweetened with sugar planted in the Caribbean. Decimating the forests of north-eastern United States, southern Africa and the Western Ghats of India—to name only three such regions—the British were, through the eighteenth and nineteenth centuries, unquestionably the world leaders in deforestation. Emulating them in lesser or greater degree were the Dutch, the Portuguese, the French, the Belgians and the Germans, European powers who were to all become prime agents of ecological destruction in their colonies.

Environmental *problems* were certainly not unknown in the past, but possibly for the first time in human history there was now the perception of an environmental *crisis*. This was the perception seized upon by the first wave of environmentalism, which asked whether the great increases in wealth and prosperity brought about by modern industrialization were in fact sustainable. Notably, while the industrial city was the prime generator of ecological degradation, much of the burden of this degradation was felt in the country and the colony. As we shall see in this book, in the vanguard of the first wave of environmentalism were residents of the countryside, such as William Wordsworth, as well as unwilling subjects of colonialism, such as Mohandas Karamchand 'Mahatma' Gandhi.

As a dynamic social response to the Industrial Revolution, environmentalism bears comparison with three other movements of the modern world—democracy, socialism, and feminism. Defined in opposition to absolutism, democracy calls for a greater voice of ordinary citizens in decisions that affect their lives. Defined in opposition to both feudalism and capitalism, socialism calls for a more equitable distribution of wealth and productive resources. Defined in opposition to patriarchy, feminism calls for the granting of greater political and economic rights to women. Meanwhile the environmental movement has expanded human understandings of 'rights' and 'justice', calling for greater attention to the rights of nature as well as for sustainable lifestyles. Its agenda has sometimes been complementary to the agendas of other movements—at other times, in competition with them. These connections, between environmentalism on the one side and democracy, socialism or feminism on the other, shall be made explicit throughout this book.

Like all social movements, the environmental movement has within its fold different individuals, trends, traditions, and ideologies. Just as they are varieties of feminism, there have been varieties of environmentalism as well.

The first part of the book explores three such varieties, each a distinctive response to the emergence and impact of industrial society:

1. We have, first of all, the moral and cultural critique of the Industrial Revolution, here termed *back-to-the-land*. For the great romantic poets like Blake and Wordsworth, the 'dark, satanic mills' of the industrial age threatened to obliterate for ever their green and pleasant land, the pastoral idyll of rural and traditional England. Novelists like Charles Dickens and political thinkers like Friedrich Engels wrote critically of the inhuman working and living conditions of the time, the bleak

homes and the dark, damp and polluting factories. Others, like the Indian saint-politician Mahatma Gandhi, combined a moral critique with a simple lifestyle, living gently on the earth while deploring the multiplication of wants that modern civilization had brought about.

2. The second strand, that of *scientific conservation*, chose not to turn its back on industrial society, but to work instead on taming its excesses. Based on careful research in the empirical mode, rather than on a purely artistic or affective response, this variety of environmentalism argued that without careful guidance by experts industrialization would rapidly use up resources and pollute the environment. Conservation was the 'gospel of efficiency,' the use of science to manage nature and natural resources efficiently and in the long run. Crucial here is the idea of 'sustained yield,' the belief that human use of fish or forest, water or wildlife, should not dip into the capital stock, restricting itself to the annual increment of the resource in question. By the late nineteenth century, scientific conservation had emerged as a global movement, with foresters taking the lead in establishing resource management agencies run on scientific lines in Asia, Africa, Europe and North America.

3. The third strand of environmentalism, which combines elements of morality, science, and aesthetics, is what has come to be known as the *wilderness idea*. The industrialization of Europe, and the settlement and spread of European populations in the New World, devastated large areas of forest and wilderness. There arose in response a movement of artists and scientists which aimed to lock up areas still untouched, to keep them free of human disturbance. Sometimes the motivation was the protection from extinction of endangered species like the grizzly bear, at other times the saving of scenic habitats like Yosemite. Although it has its outposts in other corners too, the wilderness movement has flowered most vibrantly in the United States, as discussed in the pages of this book.

Back-to-the-land, *scientific conservation* and the *wilderness idea* constitute three generic modes of environmentalism. Part I of this book defines and documents these modes, tracing their evolution and expressions across the centuries and continents. In Part II we move forward to the second wave of environmentalism, its transformation from intellectual response to mass movement. Here we study the resurgence of the three distinctive strands in the 1960s and thereafter, and also explore the new dimensions brought to global environmentalism by the fears of a population explosion, the claims and assertions of women, and, especially, the divide between the rich countries of the North and the mostly poor countries of the South. We show how, in one country after another, there has arisen a vibrant and popular social movement dedicated to protecting or replenishing nature. Readers will note that while Part I starts with an examination of British traditions, Part II begins with an analysis of American trends. This choice is in keeping with our emphasis on industrialization as the generator of environmentalism. For the United Kingdom was the home of the original Industrial Revolution, while the United States has led the world in later elaborations of the industrial way of life. One country, consequently, pioneered the first wave of environmentalism; the other country showed the way in the second. Both parts of the book thereby uses an exemplary country as a springboard, to set off the subsequent discussion of environmentalism in other cultures. Our focus is as much on the differences as the similarities, for these 'national' movements have varied widely among themselves with regard to their tactics of protest and their ideas of what constitutes a worthwhile environment for us to nourish and live in.

III

To write a global history of anything, let alone a complex and widespread phenomenon such as environmentalism, is to be savagely selective. Inevitably, some of the more telling illustrations come from the histories of the two countries I am myself most familiar with, India and the United States. But I have tried to cast my net wider, to pick up examples and exemplars from times past and distant places. Where the Indian and American materials come from my own research, I have distilled from other peoples' writings and experiences the history of environmentalism in the countries of Asia and Latin America, as well as of Africa and Europe. Even so, some readers will complain that I have omitted their favourite country, others that I have not honored their favourite environmentalist.

There have been millions of words written on the history of American environmentalism, by historians and journalists, scientists and sociologists—all American. Following their lead, scholars elsewhere have written on the history of environmentalism in their own country. Studies of the United States still dominate the shelf of the library marked 'The Environmental Movement', but these are now being rapidly joined by works on the history of German, Swedish, British or Brazilian environmentalism. This book breaks with an established pattern, providing not another national history but a *trans*-national perspective on the environmental debate, by comparing and contrasting historical processes in six continents. By bringing in the experience of other cultures, and juxtaposing it with a fresh reading of environmentalism in the United States, the book hopes to set the American experience more properly in its global context.

A second aim of the book is to document the flow of ideas across cultures, the ways in which the environmental movement in one country has been transformed, invigorated and occasionally distorted by infusions from outside. Let me quickly run through some examples developed at length later. The founder of the United States Forest Service, Gifford Pinchot, honored as his mentor and prime inspiration a German botanist, Dietrich Brandis; it was Brandis who had previously set up the Forest Department in India, perhaps the largest and most influential of natural resource bureaucracies; this debt was returned with interest a century later when the ideas of Mahatma Gandhi were freely borrowed by the German Green Party, the most potent political expression of contemporary environmentalism. Gandhi himself is sometimes regarded as a quintessentially Indian, even Hindu thinker, yet he was deeply influenced by Russian populism (via the novelist, Leo Tolstoy, with whom he had been in correspondence); and by American radical individualism via Henry David Thoreau, whose essay on civil disobedience he regarded as his own political testament; and most significantly by English anti-industrialism via the works of the critic John Ruskin. Or take, finally, the movement of Deep Ecology, the leading edge of the American environmental movement today, which fights for 'biocentric equality,' that is, the placing of humans on par with and not above other species. While most of its adherents are to be found on the west coast of the United States, the ideas of Deep Ecology were first formulated by a Norwegian philosopher, Arné Naess, who once wrote a dissertation on—Gandhi!

The divides this book spans are, however, as much temporal as spatial. In the academy's division of labor, wherein historians study the past and sociologists and anthropologists study the present, earlier works have tended to concentrate on either the first or the second wave of environmentalism, rarely both. By contrast, this book locates the present in the past, showing the influence on contemporary movements of patterns and processes that have persisted over the years, or gone underground only to resurface once more. In this it draws inspiration from the Stanford poet, Wallace Stegner, who remarks that

> The tracing of ideas is a guessing game. We can't tell who first had an idea; we can only tell who first had it influentially, who formulated it in some form, poem or equation or picture, that others could stumble upon with the shock of recognition. The radical ideas that have been changing our attitudes towards our habitat have been around forever.

I would wish only to substitute, for the poet's 'forever', the less evocative but historically more precise phrase, 'at least for a hundred years'.

2

Back to the Land!

THE ENGLISH LOVE OF THE COUNTRY

In the eighteenth and nineteenth centuries the landscape of England was reshaped by the Industrial Revolution. Coal mines, textile mills, railroads and shipyards were the visible signs of an enormous expansion of industry and trade which made England the foremost economic power in the world. Industrialization was accompanied by rapid urbanization; between 1801 and 1911 the proportion of the British population living in cities increased from 20 per cent to 80 per cent. But the countryside was also being transformed, with a new breed of landowners producing wool, cotton and grain for the urban market. Peasants, shepherds and artisans, who had formed the backbone of the rural economy in medieval times, increasingly joined the ranks of the dispossessed, flocking to the cities in search of employment.

England was the home of industrialization, but also of opposition to it. The anthropologist Alan Macfarlane has captured this paradox well. In the mid-nineteenth century, he writes,

> England was the most urbanized country in the world, yet one where the yearning for the countryside and rural values was the most developed. Its strangely anti-urban bias was shown in the prevalence of parks, the ubiquity of flower gardens, the country holiday industry, the dreams of retirement to a honeysuckle cottage and the emphasis on 'nature' and rural values in the Romantic and pre-Raphaelite movements.

This affirmation of country life, in direct opposition to the emerging urban-industrial culture, was perhaps most eloquently expressed in a

Chapter 2: Back to the Land!

rich literary tradition, flowering in some of the finest works in the English language.

An early exemplar of this tradition was William Wordsworth (1770–1850), whose poetry expresses an intimate affinity with the natural world. During his lifetime Wordsworth walked some 175,000 miles through England, and, as the literary historian Jonathan Bate remarks, he taught his readers 'how to walk with nature' too. In his travels Wordsworth saw only 'the darker side of the great change' wrought by the Industrial Revolution: the 'outrage done to nature' by the cities and factories, such that the common people were no longer 'breathing fresh air' or 'treading the green earth.' The poet was profoundly out of sympathy with the mores of city life, with its impersonality and its elevation of money-making above all other values. In the country, and only there, lay 'the secret spirit of humanity,' which, despite war, revolution and economic change,

> 'mid the calm oblivious tendencies
> of nature, 'mid her plants, her weeds and flowers,
> And silent overgrowings, still survived.

Underlying Wordsworth's poetry and philosophy was a defense of the organic union with nature of the peasant and shepherd, a way of life that the deadly combination of industrialization and market farming wished to obliterate. Although village folk were illiterate and inarticulate, they were in closer touch with nature than the city dweller. 'And grossly that man errs,' he wrote, 'who should suppose'—

> That the green Valleys, and the Streams and Rocks
> Were things indifferent to the Shepherd's thoughts.
> Fields, where with cheerful spirits he had breath'd
> The common air; the hills which he so oft
> Had climb'd with vigorous steps; which had impress'd
> So many incidents upon his mind
> Of hardship, skill or courage, joy or fear;
> Which like a book preserv'd the memory
> Of the dumb animals, whom he had sav'd,
> Had fed or shelter'd . . .
>   these fields, these hills
> Which were his living Being, even more
> Than his own Blood—what could they less? had laid
> Strong hold on his affections, were to him
> A pleasurable feeling of blind love,
> The pleasure which is there in life itself.

This is from a poem about the shepherds of the Lake District, the region with which Wordsworth is most closely identified. He even wrote a guide to the people and scenery of the Lakes: a book now forgotten, but a bestseller in its day, which earned him more money than his most celebrated poems. Indeed, in the last years of his life Wordsworth was moved to begin a public campaign against the extension of the railway to the Lake District, a development he feared would disrupt the beauty and integrity of the region.

Wordsworth's book on his favorite place was published in various editions, under various titles. The 1842 version had an expansive title, redolent of the nineteenth century: it was published as *A Complete Guide to the Lakes, Comprising Minute Directions for the Tourist, with Mr Wordsworth's Description of the Scenery of the Country, etc. And Three Letters on the Geology of the Lake District, by the Rev. Professor Sedgwick, Edited by the Publisher*. By any name it was rather more than a brochure, and little less than a summation of the poet's natural credo. In his book *Romantic Ecology*, Jonathan Bate nicely places Wordsworth in the context of his own time and ours. The values of the Guide, he says, were

> the maintaining of the place for the benefit of the whole nation; the conception of landscape beauty, with a particular emphasis on wild (sublime) country; the belief in the importance of the open air; the respect for buildings that have a history in the place; and the recognition that traditional agricultural practices are integral to the identity of the place. Wordsworth would have been pleased that shepherds still work on the hills of Westmorland and Cumberland, since, in contrast to the American model, the English and Welsh National Parks do not consist of enclosed areas owned by the government; the land in them remains privately owned ... Conservation is sought by means of planning rather than possession.

One of Wordsworth's junior contemporaries was John Clare (1793–1864), a poet from farming stock. Clare's best-known verses deal with the impact of the enclosure, by rich landowners, of village common land to raise crops for the urban market. Enclosure threw the rural poor out of work and destroyed the diversity of life-forms that had long been a feature of the English landscape. Clare's poem *The Village Ministrel* speaks of how—

> There once were lanes in nature's freedom dropt,
> There once were paths that every valley wound—
> Inclosure came, and every path was stopt;
> Each tyrant fix'd his sign where paths were found,
> To hint a tresspass now who cross'd the ground:

Justice is made to speak as they command;
The high road must now be each stinted bound:
—Inclosure, thou'rt a curse upon the land,
And tasteless was the wretch who thy existence plann'd . . .
. . . Ye fields, ye scenes so dear to Lubin's eye,
Ye meadow-blooms, ye pasture-flowers, farewell!
Ye banish'd trees, ye make me deeply sigh,
Inclosure came, and all your glories fell.

Next in the English tradition of romantic environmentalists lies John Ruskin (1819–1900), artist, art critic, sometime Professor of Poetry at the University of Oxford. Ruskin thought modern towns 'little more than laboratories for the distillation into heaven of venomous smokes and smells, mixed with effluvia from decaying animal matter, and infectious miasmata from purulent disease.' The air was foul, and the water too, for every river in England had been turned 'into a common sewer, so that you cannot so much as baptize an English baby but with filth, unless you hold its face out in the rain, and even that falls dirty.' This destruction, he thought, owed itself to the fact that modern man had *desacralized* nature, viewing it only as a source of raw materials to be exploited, and thus emptying it of the mystery, the wonder, indeed the divinity with which pre-modern man saw the natural world. Observe the contrast at work through Ruskin's luminous prose:

> Whereas the mediaeval never painted a cloud, but with the purpose of placing an angel in it; and a Greek never entered a wood without expecting to meet a god in it; we should think the appearance of an angel in the cloud wholly unnatural, and should be seriously surprised by meeting a god anywhere. Our chief ideas about the wood are connected with poaching. We have no belief that the clouds contain more than so many inches of rain or hail, and from our ponds and ditches expect nothing more divine than ducks and watercresses.

Unlike Wordsworth, Ruskin focused closely on the physical consequences of the industrialization of England: the befouling of the air and of the waters, as well as the impact of this pollution on human health and the landscape. But the influence of the poet on his work is manifest, never more so when, in 1876, he launched a fresh campaign (see *box*) to prevent the extension of the railroad into the Lake District. Ruskin believed that the trains, and the hordes of tourists they might bring, would destroy the District. As with Wordsworth, Ruskin's love of the land was inseparable from his love of the rustic who dwelled in it. In opposing the railways he wished as much to protect

RUSKIN OPPOSES THE RAILWAYS, DEFENDS THE LAKES

In John Ruskin the passion of the environmentalist fused with the eloquence of a great prose stylist.

When the frenzy of avarice is daily drowning our sailors, suffocating our miners, poisoning our children, and blasting the cultivable surface of England into a treeless waste of ashes, what does it really matter whether a flock of sheep, more or less, be driven from the slopes of Helvellyn, or the little pool of Thirlmere filled with shale, or a few wild blossoms of St. John's vale lost to the coronal of English spring? Little to any one; and—let me say this, at least, in the outset of all saying—*nothing to me*. No one need charge me with selfishness in any word or action for defence of these mossy hills. I do not move, with such small activity as I have yet shown in the business, because I live at Coniston (where no sound of the iron wheels by Dunmail Raise can reach me), nor because I can find no other place to remember Wordsworth by than the daffodil margin of his little Rydal marsh. What thoughts and work are yet before me, such as he taught, must be independent of any narrow associations. All my own dear mountain grounds and treasure-cities, Chamouni, Interlachen, Lucerne, Geneva, Venice, are long ago destroyed by the European populace; and now, for my own part, I don't care what more they do; they may drain Loch Katrine, drink Loch Lomond, and blow all Wales and Cumberland into a heap of slate shingle; the world is wide enough yet to find me some refuge during the days appointed for me to stay in. But it is no less my duty, in the cause of those to whom the sweet landscapes of England are yet precious, and to whom they may yet teach what they taught me, in early boyhood, and would still if I had not to learn,—it is my duty to plead with what earnestness I may, that these sacred sibylline books may be redeemed from perishing.

... I have said I take no selfish interest in this resistance to the railroad. But I do take an unselfish one. It is precisely because I passionately wish to improve the minds of the populace, and because I am spending my own mind, strength, and fortune, wholly on that object, that I don't want to let them see Hellvellyn while they are drunk. I suppose few men now living have so earnestly felt—none certainly have so earnestly declared—that the beauty of nature is the blessedest and most necessary of lessons for men; and that all other efforts in education are futile till you have taught your people to love fields, birds, and flowers. Come then, my benevolent friends, join with me in that teaching.

Source: 'The Extension of Railways in the Lake District' (1876), in *The Works of John Ruskin, Volume XXXIV*, edited by E. T. Cook and Alexander Wedderburn (London: George Allen, 1908), pp. 137–8, 142.

Chapter 2: Back to the Land!

nature as the moral fibre of the villagers whose strength and virtue yet survive to represent the body and soul of England before her days of mechanical decrepitude and commercial dishonour.'

His writings apart, Ruskin also worked to build institutions which would recapture the flavor of a world rapidly being lost. He set up a guild, named for St. George, that ran farms and craft shops which stressed self-sufficiency and simplicity, producing food and weaving cloth for their own use. The revival of handicrafts was also vigorosly promoted by his disciple William Morris (1834–96), likewise a man mostly out of step with his times, a man who—as the writer Jan Marsh points out—'wished as far as possible to live in the fourteenth rather than the nineteenth century.'

Poet, prophet, designer, architect and socialist, William Morris lived a life of many parts; he has since been claimed as an ancestor by numerous artistic and political movements. But the environmental movement has as good a claim as any. A native Londoner, Morris deplored the city's growth, its 'swallowing up with its loathsomeness field and wood and heath without mercy and without hope, mocking our feeble attempts to deal even with its minor evils of smoke-laden sky and befouled river.' Morris wished to turn England 'from the grimy backyard of a workshop into a garden,' from which factories would disappear, with town and country resuming a relation of harmony and mutual benefit. His long narrative poem 'The Earthly Paradise' begins by asking the reader to—

> Forget six counties overhung with smoke,
> Forget the snorting steam and piston stroke,
> Forget the spreading of the hideous town;
> Think rather of the pack-horse on the down,
> And dream of London, small, and white, and clean,
> The clear Thames bordered by its gardens green . . .

We move on, finally, to Edward Carpenter (1844–1929), an associate of Morris with whom the English back-to-the-land movement finally turned international. Trained as a mathematician, ordained as a priest, Carpenter resigned holy orders and a prestigious Cambridge fellowship to move back to the land. With some friends he set up a commune on a hill above the factory town of Sheffield, offering a union of manual labor and clean air as an alternative to industrial civilization. In this he was influenced by Morris, but also by the Americans Walt Whitman and Henry David Thoreau, whose message of the simple life he enthusiastically embraced. The commune grew its own food and vegetables and baked its own bread; its members, who included men from working class backgrounds, discarded most of their clothing as superfluous. Their farm has been described as 'a true Arcadia; three fields running down to a brook, a wooded valley below and the moors above.' The contrast with Sheffield could be sharply etched, and looking down on the town in May 1889, Carpenter saw—

> only a vast dense cloud, so thick that I wondered how any human being could support life in it, that went up to heaven like the smoke from a great altar. An altar, indeed, it seemed to me, wherein thousands of lives were being yearly sacrificed. Beside me on the hills the sun was shining, the larks were singing; but down there a hundred thousand grown people, let alone children, were struggling for a little sun and air, toiling, moiling, living a life of suffocation, dying (as the sanitary reports only too clearly show) of diseases caused by foul air and want of light—all for what? To make a few people rich!

The writings of Wordsworth, Ruskin, Morris and Carpenter helped inspire the establishment of an array of environmental societies in the late nineteenth century. These included the Commons Preservation Society, begun in 1865 to prevent the encroachment of cities on woodland and heath used by communities for recreation; the Society for the Protection of Ancient Buildings, founded by William Morris himself in 1877; the Lake District Defence Society, stoutly in the Wordsworth–Ruskin lineage, which was formed in 1883; the Selborne League, created in 1885 for the protection of rare birds, beautiful plants, and threatened landscapes, and named for the great eighteenth-century naturalist Gilbert White of Selbourne; and the Coal Smoke Abatement Society, influenced by Edward Carpenter's writings, and started in 1898 as an independent pressure group to make the government enforce pollution control laws on errant factories. Preceding all of these was the Scottish Rights of Way Society, formed in 1843 to protect walking areas around the city of Edinburgh.

One of the most influential of these societies has been the National Trust, which was created in 1895. A prime mover behind the setting up of the Trust was Octavia Hill (1838–1912), quite possibly the first woman environmentalist of significance. A friend of Ruskin, Hill, like her compatriots, coupled environmental protection with social reform and was a pioneer in establishing clean and congenial dwellings for the urban poor. She was active in many environmental campaigns: she organized the first anti-smoke exhibition in London and, as a member of the Commons Preservation Society, helped protect numerous areas of the city from encroachment or deterioration. As the *Dictionary of National Biography* notes, 'it was largely due to her efforts that Parliament Hill and many other large and small open spaces were secured for public use and enjoyment.' Octavia Hill also helped define the objectives of the National Trust, which were outlined in its first annual report:

> to promote the permanent preservation, for the benefit of the Nation, of land and tenements (including buildings) of beauty or historic interest; and as regards lands, to preserve (so far as practicable) their natural aspects, features, and animal and plant life; and for this purpose to accept from private owners of property, gifts and places of interest or beauty, and to hold the lands, houses and other property thus acquired, in trust for the use and enjoyment of the nation.

These aims are much broader than the protection of old buildings and stately homes, the activities for which the National Trust is now chiefly known. At the same time, they were much narrower than the aims of John Ruskin or Edward Carpenter, which were to turn the clock back, to restore England as a country of cozy villages and manageable small towns nestling within a landscape of pretty pastures, luxuriant oak forests, and clean swift-flowing rivers. Indeed, throughout history visionary aims have served as the source of more modest or, one might say, *piecemeal* reform. By setting aside forests and wetlands, or preserving historic buildings and parks, the environmental societies begun in the late nineteenth century have saved at least some parts of England from the contaminating effects of urban-industrial civilization. This represents the tangible fruits of the back-to-the-land movement, the putting into practice, albeit in a limited way, of the ideas and aspirations of Ruskin and company. The international influence of these English visionaries will be explored later in the chapter. But we must first take a small detour.

A DETOUR: WERE THE NAZIS GREEN, AND ARE GREENS NAZIS?

By the late nineteenth century, Germany had surpassed England as the front-runner in technological and industrial development. Here too, poets and writers were in the vanguard of the movement to keep their land rural and their forests virgin, uncontaminated by the greed of the cities and the excrement of their factories. Consider these lines from a poem published in 1901 by Rainer Maria Rilke:

> Everything will again be great and mighty,
> The land simple and the water bountiful,
> The trees gigantic and the walls very small.
> And in the valleys strong and multiformed,
> A nation of shepherds and peasant farmers.

A nation of peasants and shepherds, not of factory workers and entrepeneurs, which was in fact what Germany was fast becoming. In the Rilkean vision peasants were celebrated as the backbone of the nation, but the forests were more important still, as the repository of German culture, the inspiration for its poets, musicians, and artists. The self-proclaimed sociologist 'of field and forest,' William Heinrich Reill, wrote in 1861 that the woods 'were the heartland of [German] folk culture . . . so that a village without a forest is like a town without any historical buildings, theater or art galleries. Forests are games fields for the young, feasting-places for the old.' But by making the peasant into a market-driven farmer, and by destroying forests or converting then into timber plantations, industrialization was undermining the very basis of 'German-ness.' In the German romantic tradition environmentalism was united with patriotism, such that peasants, forests and the nation came to constitute an organic whole. 'The German people need the forest like man needs wine,' wrote a nineteenth-century theologian, adding: 'We must preserve the forest, not simply so that the oven does not grow cold in winter but also in order that the pulse of the national life continues to beat warm and happy [in order that] Germany remains German.'

Of course, in England as much as in Germany, rural romantics were in a distinct minority. The dominant industrial culture of the two countries met in the First World War, a conflict which first revealed the awesome destructive power of modern technology. To some observers the costs of war—some ten million dead—were the consequence wholly of industrialization and capitalist development, through the hunger for territory and the forces of avarice that they had unleashed. Indeed no sooner had the conflict ended that there occurred a revival of the agrarian ideal throughout Europe. This took various forms: the establishment of a Council for the Protection of Rural England in 1928; the growth of agrarian parties in Eastern Europe to defend the peasant from exploitation by the city dweller; and the spread of ruralist ideas in Scandinavia through the work of the novelist Knut Hamsun, who spent his Nobel Prize money on restoring an old farm.

In Germany the reassertion of peasant environmentalism in the 1920s was accompanied by the rise of the National Socialists. There was unquestionably, at times, a congruence between the views of environmentalists and Nazis. Some Nazi thinkers also emphasized a mystic unity between the peasant, the forest, and the national spirit. Others railed against the growth of the cities. The party's newspaper worried in 1932 that 'the influence of the metropolis has grown

Chapter 2: Back to the Land!

overwhelmingly strong. Its asphalt culture is destroying peasant thinking, the rural lifestyle, and [national] strength.' Leading Nazis were prominent in environmental causes. The Minister for Agriculture, Walter Darré, was an enthusiast for organic farming. Herman Göering, second only to Adolf Hitler in the party hierarchy, strongly supported nature protection, appointing himself Master of the German Hunt as well as Master of the German Forests.

The apparent affinity between Nazism and green ideology has led some commentators to claim that environmentalism is conducive to authoritarian thinking. When the German Green Party was formed in the 1970s (a development explored in Chapter Five), some of its opponents darkly suggested that the National Socialists were the first 'Green party.' The historian Raymond Dominick, after a careful study of the subject, points out, however, that 'although several substantial areas of agreement drew National Socialism together, to cross over into the Nazi camp a conservationist had to accept blatant racism.' In the Nazi slogan of 'Blut und Boden' (Blood and Soil) many environmentalists identified only with the latter part. Moreover, in practice the Nazis built an industrial economy—in part to ready themselves for war—that was totally at odds with the peasant ideology they sometimes claimed to uphold. The journalist Sebastian Haffner, who was forced into exile by Hitler's regime, wrote in 1944 that as 'soon as the Nazis took over in Germany they began feverishly to build. First came technical construction work, motor roads, aerodromes, armanent factories, fortifications:' scarcely the agenda of environmentalists. As one of their leading architects, with a sheaf of commissions in hand, put it, the Nazis wished to give 'permanent evidence in concrete and marble of the greatness of our time.' They also vigorously promoted consumerism; Hitler once promised every German citizen a Volkswagen car and built in anticipation highways to drive them on. In the wry judgement of the Spanish scholar Juan Martinez Alier, the reality of Nazi rule was not *Blut und Boden* but rather *Blut und Autobahnen*.

Some Nazis were indeed Green, but most were not. In any event, to be Green—then or now—is not connected with being Nazi.

THE GANDHIAN VIEW OF THE SIMPLE LIFE

In 1889 Edward Carpenter published *Civilization: Its Cause and Cure*, a book which has been termed a 'kind of text for the back-to-the-land movement.' One of its early and admiring readers was a twenty-year-old Indian who had recently arrived to study law in London.

The Indian did not know Carpenter, but soon became intimate with his disciple Henry Salt, a pacifist and animal rights activist who likewise preached a return to nature and praised the simplicity of rural life. It was in Salt's *Journal of the Vegetarian Society* that the young man published his first writings, the beginnings of an oeuvre that came to comprise ninety closely printed volumes.

The Indian was Mohandas Karamchand Gandhi, a political and spiritual leader of consummate skill and considerable achievement, regarded by the *International Herald Tribune*, and by countless other organizations and individuals, as the greatest person of the twentieth century. Mahatma Gandhi is celebrated as a doughty opponent of racism in South Africa, where he lived, and struggled, for over twenty years; as an Indian freedom fighter whose opposition to British rule helped inspire numerous anti-colonial movements in Asia and Africa; and as the perfector of a technique of non-violent protest that has since been used in a variety of contexts, from the civil rights movement in the United States to Solidarity in Poland. All this notwithstanding, he was also an early environmentalist who anticipated the damaging effects on nature of the industrial economy and the consumer society.

In his autobiography, Gandhi recalled that of the books he read in his youth, 'the one which brought about an instantaneous and practical transformation in my life was [John Ruskin's] *Unto This Last*.' John Ruskin and Edward Carpenter are both acknowledged in Gandhi's first book, *Hind Swaraj* (Indian Home Rule), published in 1909. In this work Gandhi decisively rejects industrialization as an option for India, then a colony struggling to free itself from British rule. For industrial society, as Gandhi had observed it in the West—in person and through the writings of Ruskin and company—was selfish, competitive, and grossly destructive of nature. He thought that 'the distinguishing characteristic of modern civilization is an indefinite multiplication of wants,' to satisfy which one had to forage far and wide for raw materials and commodities. Gandhi believed that by contrast preindustrial civilizations were marked by an 'imperative restriction upon, and a strict regulating of, these wants.' In uncharacteristically intemperate tones, he spoke of 'wholeheartedly detest[ing] this mad desire to destroy distance and time, to increase animal appetites, and go to the ends of the earth in search of their satisfaction. If modern civilization stands for all this, and I have understood it to do so, I call it satanic.'

Gandhi offered, as an alternative, a code of voluntary simplicity that minimized wants and recycled resources—his own letters were

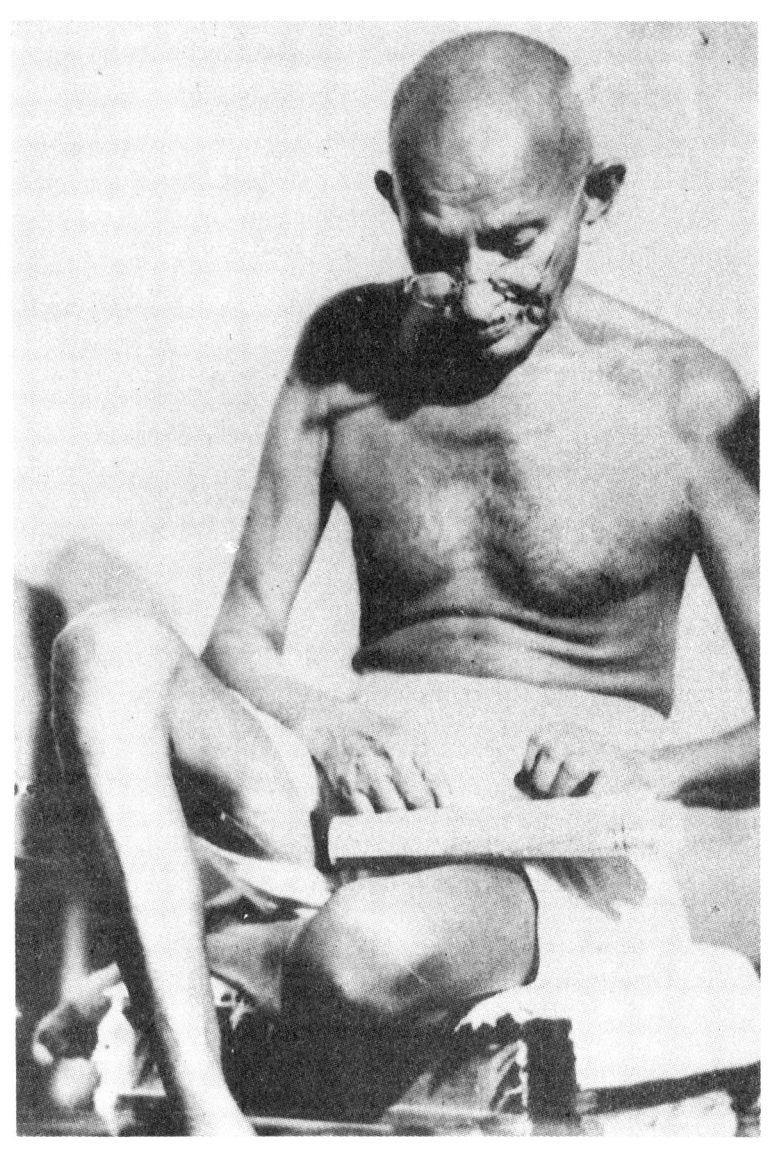

Mahatma Gandhi, at his spinning wheel, circa *1946.*
SOURCE Unidentified Photographer.

written on the back of used paper. One of Gandhi's best known aphorisms is: 'The world has enough for everybody's need, but not enough for one person's greed:' an exquisitely phrased one-line environmental ethic. It was an ethic he himself practised; when he died in January 1948 this man, whose followers were reckoned in the tens of millions, and who helped bring down one of the most powerful empires in history, had possessions that could fit in a small box: two or three changes of clothes, a clock, a pair of spectacles, and a few other odds and ends.

Gandhi's broader vision for a free India was a rural one. He worked for the renewal of its villages, in defiance of the worldwide trend towards industrialization and urbanization. The reasons for this were moral as well as ecological—namely, that there were natural limits to the industrialization of the whole world, as distinct to the industrialization of one country. As he wrote in December 1928: 'God forbid that India should ever take to industrialization after the manner of the West. The economic imperialism of a single tiny island kingdom [England] is today keeping the world in chains. If an entire nation of 300 million [India's population at the time] took to similar economic exploitation, it would strip the world bare like locusts.'

For Gandhi, as for Ruskin and Morris, the growth of cities and factories was possible only through a one-sided exploitation of the countryside. 'The blood of the villages,' he wrote in July 1946, 'is the cement with which the edifice of the cities is built.' He himself wished to see that 'the blood that is today inflating the arteries of the cities runs once again in the blood vessels of the villages.'

Gandhi also opposed the industrialization of agriculture, that is, the replacement of the plough by the tractor and the spread of chemical fertilizers, measures which undeniably increased productivity in the short term but which created unemployment and depleted the soil of its nutrients. He warned that 'trading in soil fertility for the sake of quick returns would prove to be a disastrous, short-sighted policy.' He promoted instead the use of organic manure, which enriched the soil, improved village hygiene through the effective disposal of waste, and saved valuable foreign exchange. But the revitalization of the rural economy also depended on the revival of craft industry (see *box* for his vision of village renewal). India's once vibrant traditions of weaving and other handicrafts had been largely destroyed under British rule, and to restore them Gandhi created two organizations: an All India Village Industries Association and an All India Spinners' Association.

These organizations were run by one of Gandhi's close followers, J. C. Kumarappa, an economist to whom he entrusted the work of village reconstruction. Kumarappa had studied accountancy in London and economics at Columbia University in New York, before joining the Indian nationalist movement in the 1920s. Working with Gandhi, Kumarappa explored the relation between peasant agriculture and the natural world. For Indian peasants the cultivation of the soil was made possible only by the flow of nutrients from outside: water from ponds and rivers, and manure from cattle dung and from the forest. This meant that the careful management of common property resources, such as irrigation tanks and grazing grounds, was as important to agricultural production as the management of privately owned plots of farmland. There had once existed vigorous village-level institutions for this purpose, which had decayed under British rule. Water and pasture were gifts of nature that were central to peasant farming in India: and in Kumarappa's view, the revival of collective institutions for their management was an important task for economic policy in free India.

AN IDEAL VILLAGE

Gandhi's prosaic, down-to-earth description of his ideal Indian village, offered in January 1937.

It will have cottages with sufficient light and ventilation, built of a material obtainable within a radius of five miles of it. The cottages will have courtyards enabling householders to plant vegetables for domestic use and to house their cattle. The village lanes and streets will be free of all avoidable dust. It will have wells according to its needs and accessible to all. It will have houses of worship for all, also a common meeting place, a village common for grazing its cattle, a co-operative dairy, primary and secondary schools in which industrial [i.e. vocational] education will be the central fact, and it will have Panchayats [village councils] for settling disputes. It will produce its own grains, vegetables and fruit, and its own Khadi [hand-spun cotton]. This is roughly my idea of a model village . . .

Source: *Collected Works of Mahatma Gandhi, Volume LXIV* (New Delhi: Publications Division, 1976), p. 217.

Like his master, Kumarappa believed that an 'economy of permanence' could be founded only on agriculture. 'There can be no industrialization without predation,' he observed, whereas agriculture is, and ought to be, 'the greatest among occupations,' in which 'man attempts to control nature and his own environment in such a way as to produce the best results.' This contrast could be expressed in terms of their relative impact on the natural world. Thus—

in the case of an agricultural civilization, the system ordained by nature is not interfered with to any great extent. If there is a variation at all, it follows a natural mutation. The agriculturist only aids nature or intensifies in a short time what takes place in nature in a long period … Under the economic system of [industrial society] … we find that variations from nature are very violent in that a large supply of goods is produced irrespective of demand, and then a demand is artificially created for goods by means of clever advertisements.

Comparing the philosophies of Ruskin and Gandhi, the eminent Indian economist M. L. Dantwala has remarked that for both thinkers 'industrialization was the culprit which destroyed their idyll of a peaceful self-sufficient rural society, in which workers bought their own raw materials, spun and wove them and sold their finished goods to the rural community.' The Gandhian version of the simple life did indeed follow the English model in several respects: in its focus on manual labor, in its elevation of the village as the supreme form of human society, in its corresponding rejection of industrial culture as violent, competitive and destructive of nature and thus unsustainable in the long run. To quote Dantwala once more, the work of Gandhi and Ruskin is best understood as 'a reaction to the egregious excesses of adolescent industrialization.' Nonetheless, the Indian tradition is to be distinguished from the English in at least two respects. First, the Gandhian vision was a severely practical one, ridding itself of the lyric romanticism of Wordsworth and company. Gandhi had little time for art or poetry or music; his concerns were resolutely focused on the economic and the political, the restoring of the livelihoods and dignity of villagers subjugated by the cities and by British colonial rule. Second, in the England of the nineteenth century peasants and craftsmen had been more or less extinguished by the Industrial Revolution; going back-to-the-land was in this sense an act of defiance, quite out of step with the dominant ethos. It might, through pressure groups and environmental societies, moderate the progress of industrialization, but it could scarcely hope to halt it. By contrast, while Gandhi and Kumarappa worked and wrote India was a land of 700,000 villages whose traditional methods of farming, pastoralism and craft production still had a fair chance of withstanding competition from factory-made products. The agrarian ideal for Ruskin was just that—an ideal; whereas for Gandhi it might just conceivably have formed the basis for social renewal in a free India.

3

The Ideology of Scientific Conservation

CONSERVATION INTERNATIONALISM

In May 1864 the well-known New York firm of Charles Scribners published a volume called *Man and Nature: Or, Physical Geography as Modified by Human Action*. The book was based on years of careful study and reflection, but the author, a Vermont scholar and diplomat named George Perkins Marsh, expected it to have little impact. So doubtful was Marsh of the book's sales that he donated the copyright to the United States Sanitary Commission. Thoughtful friends purchased the copyright and gave it back to the author; a prudent move, for, contrary to Marsh's expectations, *Man and Nature* was to achieve canonical status as the book that sparked the first wave of American environmentalism. As the historian and critic Lewis Mumford once remarked, Marsh's opus was the 'fountainhead of the conservation movement,' a 'comprehensive ecological study before the very word ecology had been invented.'

In the same year as Marsh's book first appeared, a German botanist employed by the government of British India was invited to head a newly created, countrywide, Forest Service. This man, Dietrich Brandis, knew and corresponded with Marsh; he shared with the American a concern with the pace of deforestation and an abiding faith in the powers of scientific expertise to reverse it. The Indian Forest

Department, which Brandis headed for close on two decades, has been one of the most influential institutions in the history of conservation. Established in 1864, by the turn of the century it came to control a little over a fifth of India's land area. It was by far the biggest landlord in a very large country, a status it continues to enjoy to this day.

Although separated by some 10,000 miles, the American publication of *Man and Nature* and the formation of the Indian Forest Department should be viewed as part of the same historical process. From the late eighteenth century, Western scientists had begun exploring the links between deforestation, desiccation, and drought. The rapid clearance of forests, due to agricultural colonization and industrial development, contributed to accelerated soil erosion, and even, some scientists argued, to a decline in rainfall. In North America as well as in the Continent, the growth of human populations and the expansion of trade and industry led to a crisis in the availability of wood products and a steep rise in their price. In Africa and Asia too, the dynamic forces unleashed by European colonialism led to massive environmental degradation, as rainforests in the hills were converted to tea plantations and pastures in the plains replaced by commercial crops such as cotton and sugarcane.

A pioneering analyst of global deforestation was the German scientist and explorer Alexander von Humboldt (1769–1859). From a study of the fluctuating levels of a Venezuelan lake he drew these general conclusions:

> The changes which the destruction of forests, the clearing of plants and the cultivation of indigo have produced within half a century in the quantity of water flowing in on the one hand, and on the other the evaporation of the soil and the dryness of the atmosphere, present causes sufficiently powerful to explain the successive diminution of the lake of Valencia . . . By felling the trees that cover the tops and sides of mountains, men in every climate prepare at once two calamities for future generations, the want of fuel and the scarcity of water. . . . When forests are destroyed, as they are everywhere in America by the European planters, with an improvident precipitation, the springs are entirely dried up, or become less abundant. The beds of rivers, remaining dry during a part of the year, are converted into torrents, whenever great rain falls on the heights. The sward and the moss disappearing with the brushwoods from the sides of the mountains, the waters falling in rain are no longer impeded in their course, and instead of slowly augmenting the level of the rivers by progressive filtrations, they furrow during heavy showers the sides of the hills, beat down the loosened soil and

Chapter 3: The Ideology of Scientific Conservation 27

form these sudden inundations that devastate the country. Hence it results that the destruction of forests, the want of permanent springs and the existence of torrents are three phenomena closely connected together. Countries that are situated in opposite hemispheres, Lombardy bordered by the chain of the Alps and Lower Peru inclosed between the Pacific Ocean and the Cordillera of the Andes, exhibit striking proofs of the justness of this assertion.

The British historian Richard Grove correctly observes that these observations of 1819 'have not been superseded by more recent findings'. But Humboldt was, as Grove further reminds us, but the most sophisticated among a group of like-minded conservationists. In both metropolis and colony, the process of habitat destruction was viewed with horror by these conservation-minded scientists. Where private greed—notably, the pioneer's plow and the lumberman's axe—had contributed to deforestation, scientists believed that prompt intervention in the form of public ownership of forests and other natural resources might arrest environmental decline and provide a basis for steady economic growth. Crucial here was the idea of *sustained yield*, based on the belief that scientists could accurately estimate the annual increment of renewable natural resources like wood and water, fish and wildlife. Scientists prescribed that utilization stayed within this increment, thus maintaining nature's capital and ensuring a yield capable of being 'sustained' in the long term.

George Perkins Marsh in North America, and Dietrich Brandis in South Asia, were in the vanguard of what was to emerge as a scientific movement of truly global consequence. By the middle of the nineteenth century, the centralization of political authority and the formation of nation-states allowed experts to intervene more broadly, on a national scale, in the planning and management of natural resources. It began to make sense to speak of 'national forests,' or of 'rivers as the property of the nation,' where previously these resources were recognized largely as being locally owned and controlled, by villages, tribes, or municipalities. The growing prestige of science, and its ever closer alliance with the state, helped foresters and irrigation engineers, soil conservationists as well as wildlife managers, build numerous institutions based on sustained-yield principles in different parts of the world. Some of the more extensive and powerful of these institutions were to be found in the European colonies of Asia and Africa, where authoritarian state systems allowed for the exercise of scientific conservation unconstrained by parliaments, a free press, or the practice of democracy more generally.

To locate scientific conservation in its international context, let us consider the following developments, all of which occurred ten years either side of the publication of G. P. Marsh's *Man and Nature*. In 1859, a Forest and Herbiage Protection Act was passed by the Government of the Cape Colony of Southern Africa, allowing the state to intervene and take over areas of veld and forest threatened with destruction. The next year, 1860, the governor-general of colonial Java formed a committee to plan forest legislation for the island, the epicenter of the Netherlands' overseas empire. Laws protecting Java's forests and affirming state control over them were passed in 1865, also the year of the first Indian Forest Act. Already in 1862, the French had promulgated the first of a series of ordinances designed to create forest reserves in their colonies in Cochinchina (present-day Vietnam). Further east, the 1870s witnessed a flurry of forest-related activities in the British colony of Australia. Thus the province of Victoria appointed a Royal Forestry Commission in 1871, while South Australia passed a Forest Tree Act two years later. Australian forest enthusiasts frequently used Marsh's findings as supporting evidence (see *box*); meanwhile, at the other end of the world, *Man and Nature* was acquiring belated attention at home. The book stimulated the American Association for the Advancement of Science to submit a petition to Congress in 1873, urging the establishment of a national forestry system and the creation of forest reserves.

As these examples illustrate, foresters were unquestionably in the lead of a scientific movement that also counted, among its constituents, votaries of sustained-yield soil, water, wildlife and fisheries management. This movement was held together by a set of beliefs that was remarkably invariant across the continents and across the different sectors in which it was applied. In the phrase of the South African scholar William Beinart, scientific conservation was an ideology of 'doom and resurrection,' predicting that agricultural and industrial expansion would destroy the environment unless replaced, forthwith, by more rational and far-seeing forms of resource use. Here the conservationist singled out the pioneer farmer for special attention, or, should one say, special condemnation. Thus, one colonial soil scientist remarked in 1908 on the tendency of European settlers in African colonies to 'scoop out the richest and most beautiful valleys, leaving them dry and barren.' Or, as a Scottish forester working in the same continent put it: 'Is it not the case that the history of civilized man in his colonisation of new countries has been in every age substantially this—he has found the country a wilderness; he has cut down trees, and he has left it a desert.' Again, the head of the

Chapter 3: The Ideology of Scientific Conservation

United States Soil Conservation Service wrote in 1935 that 'the ultimate consequence of unchecked soil erosion when it sweeps over whole countries as it is doing today must be national extinction.'

SCIENTIFIC CONSERVATION IN AUSTRALIA

A year after the publication of George Perkins Marsh's Man and Nature, *a Melbourne newspaper reprised the book's message for its own readers. Note the global reach of the discussion, the cautionary tales as well as the positive lessons gleaned from the experience of other lands.*

Over and over again we have urged that steps should be taken to protect our forest lands, not only because extravagance will lead to scarcity, but also because the local climate will be affected in all those places where the forests are removed. In protecting the forests we do more than increase the growth of timber—we prevent waste of soil, we conserve the natural streams, it is not improbable that we prevent decrease in the rainfall, and it is certain that we largely affect the distribution of storm waters. A covering of shrubs and grasses protects the loose soil from being carried away by floods ... The Italian hydrographers have made mention very often of the disastrous results attendant on destruction of forests—Frisi relates that when the natural woods were removed from the declivities of the Upper Val d'Arno, in Tuscany, the soil of the hills was washed down to the Arno in vast quantities, to the great injury of the riparian proprietors. Some districts of Catalonia have suffered even more by the incautious operations of man; and, on the other hand, we know by what has been done in Italy, in France, in Germany and in Algeria, how much the local climate may be ameliorated, and the fruitfulness of gardens and fields increased by judicious planting.

... The reservation of large tracts of forests is our first duty. By keeping the hills clothed we may make fruitful the valleys, and provide stores of moisture for the parched plains. ... Carefully managed, we have much wealth in our forests. The miner, the agriculturalist, and the housebuilder, notwithstanding that their demands are large, can be fully supplied if extravagance be checked and waste be prevented. As the old trees are removed others should be planted. We may with advantage take a lesson from Mehemet Ali and Ibrahim Pacha, who planted more than 20 million of trees in Egypt ... The conservation of the forest lands, and the extension and improvement of them, concern alike the landholder and the miner, and should occupy the attention of everyone who has leisure and means to become a co-worker with nature.

Source: *The Argus*, Melbourne, 16 October 1865, quoted in J. M. Powell, *Environmental Management in Australia, 1788–1914* (Melbourne: Oxford University Press, 1976), pp. 61–2.

Strikingly, this hostility extended to indigenous forms of land use, that is, to the varieties of pastoralism and cultivation practised by African and Asian communities in territories recently colonized by Europeans. Pastoralists were accused of over-stocking and careless grazing practices, peasants of short-sightedness in their use of water and timber, but particular opprobrium was reserved for swidden or shifting agriculturists. Swidden farmers worked forest areas in rotation, burning and felling a patch of woodland before cultivating the soil for a few years, then moving on to the next patch: returning to the area originally felled once it had been fully reclaimed by forests, to start afresh this rotational cycle of fire, cultivation and fallowing. Although it had been successfully practised for generations, and sustained the economy of hill communities across large parts of Africa and Asia, to the European eye swidden cultivation epitomized indolence, instability and especially wastefulness, intensifying soil erosion and destroying forest areas that could perhaps be put to better use. Representative here are these remarks, dating from the 1860s, of a British forest officer on the Baigas of central India, a tribe that lived in valuable forests that the newly established Forest Department wished to take over. The officer wrote of this community of swidden farmers that they were 'the most terrible enemy to the forests we have anywhere in the hills.' It was sad 'to see the havoc that has been made among the forests by the Baiga axes.' In some areas 'the hills have been swept clean of forests for miles; in others, the Baiga marks are tall, blackened, charred stems standing in hundreds among the green forests'—it was 'really difficult to believe that so few people could sweep the face of the earth so clear of timber as they have done.'

However, scientific conservation was an ideology that was at once apocalyptic and redemptive. It did not hark back to an imagined past, but looked to reshape the present with the aid of reason and science. For rational planning would ensure that the 'great error' of waste—whether caused by settlers, native farmers, or industrialists—could be done away with, and a more efficient and sustainable system put in place. This could only be brought about by the state, the one body capable of taking a long-term view. For the profit motive was incompatible with conservation; with both individuals and enterprises being notoriously short-sighted, the state had to assume the responsibility for managing resources such as forests and water. Individuals and corporations came and went but the government, wrote the founder of the United States Forest Service, Gifford Pinchot, 'is not mortal. Men die but the Government lives on. The forests, like the race, must

Chapter 3: The Ideology of Scientific Conservation

live on also. And the government alone can have, and does have, the continuity of purpose without which, in the long run, the forests cannot be saved.'

The opposition to private control was by no means an argument for locking up resources. It was, rather, a precondition for wise use. To quote Pinchot again, 'the job was not to stop the ax, but to regulate its use.' Likewise, the first head of the U.S. Bureau of Fisheries noted that 'while we are aiming to prevent the depletion of the great resources with which our country has been blessed, it follows logically that these resources must not be permitted to lie in a state of unproductive idleness.' The 'real problem of conservation,' he continued, 'is plainly a problem of efficient development and utilization.' That was a specific aim baldly stated: but men like Gifford Pinchot were also prone to identify their ideology with all that was good and noble in the human condition. In an essay published in the magazine *American Forests*, Pinchot wrote that Conservation

> is the wise and far-sighted use of all the things—natural, artificial, and spiritual—which men require upon this earth. . . . Conservation is as wide as the earth itself, as inclusive as the needs and interests of humanity upon the earth. It is far too great a question, therefore, to be included within the bounds of any single government department . . . It is the background, the spirit, and the strength of the progressive movement in American public life. It is the forward-looking point of view. It is the signboard on the road to a greater and better America.

Other conservationists were generally less lyrical, defining their faith more modestly in terms of its abhorrence of waste and its emphasis on wise use. These were embodied in the definition of conservation as 'the greatest good of the greatest number *for the longest time*,' this last phrase giving a distinctive twist to the ideals of utilitarian philosophy. The credo of scientific conservation was early and authoritatively expressed in George Perkins Marsh's *Man and Nature*, a book which drew upon the author's varied professional experience—as farmer, timber merchant, fish commissioner, plenipotentiary and Congressman—and his wide travels through North America and Europe. Recent scholarship has suggested that the strong and at times almost hysterical condemnation of peasants and pioneers by foresters and soil conservationists stemmed in good part from a competition for territory, with the conservationist aiming to take over, under state auspices, land or forests controlled by rival groups. Marsh himself was not interested in power; his language was sober rather than choleric, but his conclusions were equally disturbing. Taking a global view, he remarked that

Man has too long forgotten that the earth was given to him for usufruct alone, not for consumption, still less for profligate waste . . . There are parts of Asia Minor, of Northern Africa, of Greece, and even of Alpine Europe, where the operation of causes set in action by man has brought the face of the earth to a desolation almost as complete as that of the moon . . . The earth is fast becoming an unfit home for its noblest inhabitant, and another era of equal human crime and human improvidence . . . would reduce it to such a condition of impoverished productiveness, of shattered surface, of climatic excess, as to threaten the deprivation, barbarism, and perhaps even extinction of the species.

David Lowenthal, Marsh's biographer, writes that through the Vermonter's studies 'History revealed man as the architect of his own misfortune, but when the processes of nature were better understood, foresight and technical skill might reverse the decline.' In Marsh's view man was an agent of destruction as well as regeneration, with the potential, as he so beautifully put it, to be a 'restorer of disturbed harmonies.' For the history of early modern Europe had shown quite clearly that judicious intervention and systematic management could rehabilitate degraded forests, thereby arresting soil erosion, helping to regulate the flow of streams and rivers, and (not least) assuring a steady supply of wood for the economy. As Marsh wrote in the preface to his great work, 'my purpose is rather to make practical suggestions than to indulge in theoretical speculations.' Pre-eminent here was the need for public ownership of forests and water, resources so vital to the social and economic life of the nation. In his view, concessional grants to individuals and companies, while an attractive option in the short term, 'may become highly injurious to the public interest for years later:' an outcome he thought unlikely were these resources securely under state control. Marsh's insights, writes Lowenthal, were to 'become the guiding principles behind American conservation policy,' to be embodied, in time, in such institutions as the United States Forest Service and the Bureau of Reclamation.

The poet and critic Matthew Arnold said of Marsh that he was 'that *rara avis*, a really well-bred and trained American,' the characteristically English note of condescension barely masking what was well-considered and well-merited praise. But Marsh was also a genuine internationalist, who sought to influence the New World through the example of the Old, and whose work, in turn, was read and admired as far afield as India and Australia (and also in Russia, where his book had appeared in translation as early as 1866). Appositely, the Vermont conservationist spent his last days in a forestry school in the mountains above Florence, talking with students and walking

Chapter 3: The Ideology of Scientific Conservation

among the firs. When he died there, on July 23, 1882, his body was draped in an American flag, but his coffin was carried down the hill by the Italian students, to be finally buried in a Protestant cemetery in Rome. In life, as in death, George Perkins Marsh epitomized the internationalism of scientific conservation, the movement of which he was such an outstanding exemplar.

THE GLOBAL REACH OF SCIENTIFIC FORESTRY

Scientific forestry, the oldest and most influential strand in the conservation movement, had its origins in late medieval Europe. By the end of the nineteenth century, however, it had moved steadily outward to embrace much of the globe. France was a pioneer, introducing a Forest Code in the fourteenth century and a stricter forest ordinance in 1669, both initiatives aimed at regulating wood production for the navy. But by the eighteenth century, Germany had clearly emerged as the front-runner in the field.

The ascendancy of German forest science was a consequence of the quantitative methods developed there to estimate growing stock and yield. In large, powerful kingdoms such as Frederick the Great's Prussia, forestry officials reaped the benefits of a centralized administration which enabled the close supervision of state forests. In refining techniques of sustained-yield management, foresters moved from an area-based approach to a more reliable yield-based system. In the former case, foresters estimated the mature age of a tree species, then divided up the forest into areas whose number equalled this age (in years): on the assumption that equal areas yielded equal amounts of wood, the harvest of one patch annually would not dip into forest capital. Over time, this was replaced by a system based more directly on estimates of the volume and weight of trees of different ages. By carefully studying growth patterns on experimental plots, silviculturalists developed standard 'yield tables' for different species which computed, with a fair degree of accuracy, the wood mass of individual trees as well as of whole stands. These numbers, adjusted for varying soil and moisture conditions, then formed the basis of sustained-yield forestry.

To quote the historian Henry E. Lowood, 'Theories, practices and instructional models from Germany provided the starting point for every national effort in forest science and management until the end of the nineteenth century.' German foresters were mercenaries as well as missionaries, enthusiastically traveling abroad to promote and propagate methods that had successfully stabilized the forest economy of their land. Throughout Europe, in Austria, Poland, Russia, Finland, Sweden, even in France—close neighbor, old enemy, and forestry pioneer itself—forest schools and departments were established on the German model and very often with German technical support.

German experts also set up forestry establishments in their own colonies and, perhaps more surprisingly, in colonies controlled by rival European powers as well. When the Dutch wished to systematically exploit the teak forests of Java, they could only turn to Germans for advice. From 1849 till the early decades of this century, a stream of German experts arrived to help the Dutch colonies institute a forest regime, based on strict state control. The foresters' brief was to harvest teak for the construction of roads, railways, and for the growing export trade—teak being a high-quality wood plundered for making furniture to adorn European drawing rooms. Likewise, the Indian Forest Department was serenely guided, for its first half century, by three successive German Inspectors General of Forest: Dietrich Brandis, Wilhelm Schlich, and Bertold von Ribbentrop. The Germans took on a wide array of tasks seen as essential for successful forest administration: the reservation of forest areas to the state, by curtailing or extinguishing rights exercised by village communities; dividing up these reserves into territories controlled by individual officers; identifying valuable species and studying their growth curves; and finally, establishing schools and laboratories for furthering research and education. In time, British officers trained by Brandis and company emerged as forest internationalists in their own right, with officials of the Indian Forest Service helping to set up forest departments in West and East Africa, in South East Asia, and in New Zealand.

One of the most remarkable of these German forestry missionaries was Ferdinand Müeller, a graduate of the University of Kiel appointed Government Botanist of the Australian province of Victoria in 1852. Over a forty-year period Mueller used the varied fora of the government commission, the scientific seminar and the newspaper column in awakening the Australian public to the destruction of forests which provided pit props for their mines, charcoal for their railway engines and, indirectly, water for their rivers. Unusually for a forester, Mueller used ethical and esthetic arguments in conjunction with the more familiar utilitarian ones. In an address of June 1871 to the Technological Museum in Melbourne, he urged that the forest be seen

Chapter 3: The Ideology of Scientific Conservation

as an heritage given to us by nature, not for spoil or to devastate, but to be wisely used, reverently honoured, and carefully maintained. I regard the forests as a gift, entrusted to any of us only for transient care during a short space of time, to be surrendered to posterity again as an unimpaired property, with increased riches and augmented blessings, to pass as a sacred patrimony from generation to generation.

The German experience also deeply stamped the evolution of North American forestry. A Prussian forester, Bernhard Fernow, was in 1879 appointed the first chief of the Division of Forestry in the Federal Government; he went on to set up forestry schools at the universities of Cornell and Toronto. When a full-fledged forest service was created in 1900, its first head was a home-grown American, Gifford Pinchot, the scion of a distinguished Pennsylvania Republican family who ended up as governor of his home state. But Pinchot himself always maintained that his mentor was Dietrich Brandis, the German scientist who set up the Indian Forest Department. When, in the 1880s, the American decided to make a career in forestry, he made a pilgrimage to Bonn, where Brandis lived in retirement. Brandis took charge of Pinchot's education, continuing to advise him after his return to the United States. In his autobiography, *Breaking New Ground*, Pinchot generously acknowledged this debt. 'Measured by any standard, Brandis was the first of living foresters,' he wrote, who 'had done great work as a pioneer, and had made Forestry to be where there was none before. In a word, he had accomplished on the other side of the world [in India] what I might hope to have a hand in doing in America.' The impact of Brandis on Pinchot, and the more general influence of German forestry on American forestry, are illustrated in the *box*.

Gifford Pinchot also helped found a forestry school at Yale University which rapidly established itself as a world leader in forestry research and education. Fittingly, it was the Yale University Press which, in 1938, published the first historical survey of the significance and impact of German forestry. The author, a reputed German silviculturist named Franz Heske, celebrated his country's experience as a 'shining example for forestry in all the world.' After having transformed their 'depleted, abused woods' into 'well-managed forests with steadily increasing yields,' German foresters, working at home and overseas, had made it

> considerably easier for the rest of the world to pursue a similar course, because the attainable goal is now known, at least in principle. The sponsors of sustained-yield in countries where forestry is still new can find in the results of this large-scale German experiment a strong support

in their battle with those who know nothing, who believe nothing, and who wish to do nothing [to protect forests]. This experiment and its outcome have rendered inestimable service in the cause of a regulated, planned development and use of the earth's raw materials, which will be an essential feature of the coming organic world economy.

AMERICA LOOKS TO EUROPE

Two Chiefs of the United States Forest Service outline their country's debt to Germany and Germans.

1. We see the need of curbing individualistic exploitation and we are looking towards the future with justified apprehension. In this situation we instinctively turn to the experience of older countries. . . . In Germany the conflict between public interest and private right is resolved by the concept of the dependence of the individual on the nation as a whole, '*Gemeinnutz geht vor Eigennutz.*' In no other framework could the crowded nations of Europe maintain their national well-being. This tenet of totality is the growth of centuries of sacrifice and struggle. It has gained a perspective in which the future becomes a fixed reality. In German forestry policy this concept is expressed in what foresters call sustained-yield management. It is what Dr Heske calls it, an example for all the world.

2. His connection . . . with the English students led Sir Dietrich [Brandis] very naturally to take charge of American students who came to Europe to study. Taking charge of a student meant with him not merely to advise as to the general course of study, but also to require bi-weekly reports, and to read and to criticize them, to send long letters written in longhand to each of us from time to time, and in every detail to try, with a never-ending patience, enthusiasm and generosity, to see that each of us got from his work exactly what he came for. This was done for me, then for Graves, then for Price, Olmsted, Sherrad and many others. Sir Dietrich thus had a guiding hand in shaping many of the men whose fortune it became afterwards to shape the general policy of forestry in the United States.

Source: 1. Henry S. Graves, 'Preface,' in Franz Heske, *German Forestry* (New Haven: Yale University Press, 1938), pp. xvii–xviii.
2. Gifford Pinchot, 'Sir Dietrich Brandis,' *Proceedings of the Society of American Foresters*, volume 3, number 1, 1908, pp. 58–9.

A forestry pioneer trained in France rather than Germany was the Mexican Miguel Angel de Quevedo. Born in 1862, Quevedo took a bachelor's degree in Bordeaux before moving to the Ecole Polytechnique in Paris to study hydraulic engineering. Here one of

Chapter 3: The Ideology of Scientific Conservation

his teachers told him that an engineer not instructed in forestry was 'deficient, an ignoramus who will make grave mistakes.' The lesson came home most forcefully when Quevedo returned to Mexico in 1887, and began work as a hydraulic engineer. Supervising a drainage project outside the capital, Mexico City, he came to understand the impact of deforestation in the hills on flooding in the plains below. He then spent a decade as a consultant to various hydro-electric companies, studying afresh how forest cover, or its disappearance, had an impact on water flow and rates of sedimentation.

Quevedo's public debut as a forestry campaigner came at a 1901 conference on climate and meteorology. Here he spoke out on the need for a nation-wide law to protect and replenish Mexico's fast-depleting forests. He then started a lobbying group, the Junta Central de Bosques: this promoted parks and tree nurseries in the cities, and compiled inventories of forest cover in different districts. In 1917 he persuaded the new post-revolutionary government to insert a clause in the Constitution, which read: 'The nation shall always have the right to impose on private property the rules dictated by the public interest and to regulate the use of natural elements, susceptible to appropriation so as to distribute equitably the public wealth and to safeguard its conservation.'

In 1922 Quevedo founded the Mexican Forestry Society to more effectively 'clamor against the silence of our country against the national suicide that signifies the ruin of the forest and the scorn of our tree protector.' Quevedo and his society were instrumental in the passing, at last, of a national forest act in 1926. By now, his work had come to the attention of Mexico's new President, Lazaro Cardenas, a progressive reformer already known for his interest in land reform and workers' rights. In 1935 Cardenas created a Department of Forestry, Fish and Game. Quevedo was appointed its first commissioner, an appointment, as one of his followers remarked, which 'constituted the synthesis and crowning achievement of the great work in defense and propagation of our natural resources that the wise investigator, the noble apostle, the pure spirit, Miguel Angel de Quevedo has undertaken during his life.'

Quevedo's recent biographer, Lane Simonian, likewise refers to him as 'Mexico's apostle of the tree.' He was certainly a remarkable man, in energy and foresight fully the equal of other and, thus far, better-known conservationists from other lands. Quevedo shared with these contemporaries a hostility to peasants, whom he held to be chiefly responsible for the destruction of his country's forests. He also tended to oscillate between exuberant optimism, foreseeing a future when scientists would finally be in charge, and bleak pessimism, in case his technically equipped visionaries were not placed in positions of power and influence. The following quote, from 1939, captures him in the latter mood, in despair after forty years of mostly unsuccessful preaching and proselytizing:

> Each day the Mexican forest problem becomes graver: the large woods are being depleted at an alarming rate, the production of chicle diminishes notably year by year, the hardwoods and even firewood cannot be obtained in regions once classified as heavily forested. Everywhere one observes forests impoverished and ruined by greed and thoughtfulness and almost we can claim that Mexico is heading for drought.
>
> [translated by Lane Simonian]

THE BALANCE SHEET OF SCIENTIFIC FORESTRY

The actual experience of scientific forestry was quite often at odds with its professed aims and supposed achievements. Especially in the colonies, it followed a 'custodial' approach, with the strengthening of state control having as its corollary the denial of customary rights of user exercised by peasant and tribal communities. For the acres and acres of woodland taken over by the state were by no means pristine, untouched forests; rather, they had been controlled and used by humans down the centuries. Peasants and pastoralists, swidden cultivators and wood-working artisans, all looked upon the forest as a provider of their basic means of subsistence: the source of fuel for cooking, grass for livestock, leaf for manure, timber for homes and plows, bamboos for baskets, land for extending cultivation, herbs for curing ailments, and so on. When access to these resources was restricted by the creation of strictly protected government reserves, escalating conflict between local communities and forest departments was the inevitable outcome.

In South Asia, where the history of scientific forestry has perhaps been most fully documented, the forest department quickly became a reviled arm of the colonial state. When a comprehensive Indian Forest Act was enacted in 1878—to supersede a preliminary Act of 1865—the government was warned, by a dissenting official, that the new legislation would leave 'a deep feeling of injustice and resentment amongst our agricultural communities;' indeed, the act might 'place in antagonism to Government every class whose support is desired and essential to the object in view [i.e. forest conservation], from the Zamindar [landlord] to the Hill Toda [tribal].' These words were far-sighted, for once the act was in place, peasant and tribal groupings resisted the operations of the Forest Department in all kinds of ways: through arson, breaches of the forest law, attacks on officials and on government property, and quite often, through co-ordinated and collective social movements aimed at restoring local control over forests. These rebellions formed part of broader nationalist upsurges; sometimes engulfing thousands of square miles, they were quelled only by the superior firepower of the colonial army and police.

A flavor of the sentiments behind these militant and enduring protests is contained in some remarks of the nineteenth-century social reformer, Jotiba Phule. Writing in 1881, Phule captured the transformations that the forest department had wrought in the Indian countryside. 'In the old days,' remarked the reformer,

> small landholders who could not subsist on cultivation alone used to eat wild fruits like figs and [berries] and sell the leaves and flowers of the flame of the forest and the mahua tree. They could also depend on the village ground to maintain one or two cows and two or four goats, thereby living happily in their own ancestral villages. However, the cunning European employees of our motherly government have used their foreign brains to erect a great superstructure called the forest department. With all the hills and undulating areas as also the fallow lands and grazing grounds brought under the control of this forest department, the livestock of the poor farmers do not even have place to breathe anywhere on the surface of the earth.
>
> [translated from the Marathi by Madhav Gadgil]

These contemporary *social* criticisms of scientific forestry (see also quotes in *box*) have now been joined by retrospective *environmental* ones. Recent work by ecologists suggests that, at least in the tropics, sustained-yield forestry has been honored mostly in the breach. Tropical forests are very diverse in their species composition, quite unlike the species-poor temperate woodlands where scientific forestry was first formulated and, for the most part, successfully applied. In Northern Europe, a single species of pine might dominate large areas of forest; a situation far removed from the tropical humid forests of Asia and Africa, in one acre of which dozens of tree species co-exist along with hundreds of plant varieties in the understorey, not to speak of thousands of micro-organisms and animals of many shapes and sizes. In South and South-east Asia, an additional complicating factor is the monsoon, the two or three months of torrential rain which quickly wash away soil exposed by logging, thus rendering regeneration extraordinarily difficult. In such circumstances, it is

The long straight lines of scientific forestry: an eucalyptus plantation in Goa, Southern India.

SOURCE Photo by M. D. Subhas Chandran

Chapter 3: The Ideology of Scientific Conservation

highly questionable whether sustained-yield forestry on the European model can be successfully practised, a skepticism that is borne out by the record. In India, for instance, 130 years of state forest management have left the forests in much poorer condition than they were when scientific forestry first made its appearance. Twenty-two per cent of India's land mass is still controlled by the forest department, but less than half of this has tree cover on it: proof of the failures of German forestry to successfully replicate itself in the tropics.

PEASANTS VERSUS THE FOREST DEPARTMENT

In 1913 the Government of Madras appointed a Commission to investigate grievances against the forest administration. Offered here are two exchanges with the Commission, one with a group of ryots (peasants), the other with an individual landholder identified by name. The conversations reveal the sharp opposition between scientific foresters and the interests of the rural community.

Committee	:	What is your next grievance?
Ryots	:	We have no firewood; and are not given permits for them.
Committee	:	Are you willing to pay for permits for firewood?
Ryots	:	No; it has not been the custom up till now. There are only three or four rich ryots and all the rest are poor and cannot pay for fuel. We pray that we may be given the grants.
Committee	:	At present what do you burn?
Ryots	:	We use cow-dung cakes . . . We want more manure leaves.
Committee	:	Do you always use them?
Ryots	:	When the land was a [commons], we used to get leaves for manure, sixteen years ago.
Committee	:	You do not get them now?
Ryots	:	Occasionally one or two men who can afford it send their men to distant places to get leaves.
Committee	:	What are your difficulties about the forests?
Timma Reddy	:	There are two temples on the top of the hill . . . There is worship there every week. There are many devotees. If ryots go there, the forest subordinates trouble them and they do not go even to the temple. If we do not worship in any year, tanks will not get supply of water.

Committee	:	Did you worship this year?
Timma Reddy	:	Yes. A case was also made against us. While the God was being taken along the path, some trees were said to have been injured and the District Forest Officer inquired and let us off. . . . We worship every year. Instead of worshipping the God there, the ryots have to worship the forest subordinates.
Committee	:	Did you not represent to the District Forest Officer?
Timma Reddy	:	Once we went to worship the God and a case was made against my brother that he went for hunting. The District Forest Officer charged us for trial in the Taluk Magistrate's Court. There we were acquitted. Even if we go to the D.F.O., we thought we will not have justice. So we do not go to him.

Source: Atluri Murali, 'Whose Trees? Forest Practices and Local Communities in Andhra, 1600–1922,' in David Arnold and Ramachandra Guha, editors, *Nature, Culture, Imperialism: Essays on the Environmental History of South Asia* (New Delhi: Oxford University Press), pp. 106, 110.

One Asian country that has not followed European models—in this as in so many other respects—is Japan, also, and not coincidentally, a country that never came under colonial rule. Independent of, and at least as early as in Germany, Japanese scientists had developed skilled methods of regenerative forestry that helped stabilize the forest cover and mountain slopes of their islands. The historian Conrad Totman notes that between 1590 and 1660 Japanese farmers and timber merchants 'devastated much of their forest land and seemed to be in the process of pressing the archipelago beyond endurance.' Disaster was forestalled by a mix of negative and positive interventions; the former aimed at restricting and regulating tree-felling so as to assist natural regeneration, the latter at more actively enhancing tree cover through plantations, especially of conifers. Large tracts of woodland owned by temples and shrines were also sequestered by the central government, to be worked on rotations of a hundred years and more. Meanwhile, a proliferation of books and pamphlets authored by officials and intellectuals urged the public to help the government protect forests and pass on their patrimony to later generations. As Totman observes, the concerns of these writers were emphatically practical, affirming not a mystic ecological consciousness—of the kind looked for by recent Western enthusiasts of Japanese Zen Buddhism—but, rather, highlighting the very real dangers of soil erosion and resource shortages that deforestation would give rise to. An official of the Akita district wrote, in the early seventeenth century, that 'The treasure of the realm is the treasure of the mountains [i.e. soil and water]. When all the trees are cut and gone, however, their value will be nil. Before all is lost, proper care must be taken. Destitution of the mountains will result in destitution of the realm.' This is a succinct statement of the ideology of scientific conservation, apocalyptic at one level, holding out the hope of redemption at another.

4

The Growth of the Wilderness Idea

I shift now to a third variety of environmentalism, the conservation of wild species and wild habitats. The formal history of wilderness conservation is little more than a century old, but viewed more broadly this movement has an ancient lineage. On the one side are popular traditions of 'sacred groves,' patches of forest worshipped as the home of deities and protected from human interference, that are to be found in all non-Christian cultures: Hindu Nepal, Buddhist Thailand, those parts of Africa that retain their ancestral religions. On the other side were elite feudal traditions of 'hunting preserves'—prevalent in Norman England, Qing China and Mughal India—where animal species such as the tiger and the deer were reserved for the exclusive pleasure of lords and kings, with peasants and commoners banned from the hunt and sometimes from the preserve itself. However, my focus here is on the distinctively modern traditions of nature conservation, the growth of the wilderness idea in the decades since the establishment of the first national park in the western United States during the latter half of the nineteenth century.

CONSERVATION IN THE COLONIES

We live in a time of international environmental conferences: seminars of atmospheric scientists, struggling to make sense of the dynamics of climate change; meetings of heads of state, putting their signatures

Chapter 4: The Growth of the Wilderness Idea

to this or that treaty to protect biodiversity; communions of social activists, exchanging notes on how best to mobilize public opinion to resist environmental degradation.

These meetings have become more frequent in recent years, with the revolution in communications and the growing ease with which people now talk or move back and forth across the continents. But which was the first-ever 'international' environmental conference? It took place in the distant year 1900, in the city of London, and its topic was the protection of the wildlife of Africa. Characteristically for the times, there were no Africans present, the delegates to the meeting being the foreign ministers of the European colonial powers who then controlled the continent: France, Germany, Belgium, Italy, Spain, Portugal, and pre-eminently, Great Britain.

Convened by the British Foreign Office, the London conference was spurred by the massive destruction of African wildlife by European hunters in the preceding decades. For young men serving in the outposts of empire, hunting was the preferred form of recreation, offering trophies scarcely to be found at home. As one colonial official candidly remarked in 1857, 'the main attraction of India lay in the splendid field it offered for the highest and noblest order of sport, in the pursuit of the wild and savage denizens of its forests and jungles, its mountains and groves:' hunting here was, indeed, a 'welcome change from the boredom of shooting seals in the Shetland Isles.' India boasted the tiger and the Asian elephant, but Africa offered greater opportunities still. Through the nineteenth century, European soldiers, officials, missionaries and travellers relentlessly hunted anything that moved: elephant, lion, leopard, cheetah, zebra, antelope, or wildebeest. By the turn of the century, as *The Times* of London recorded, it was

> necessary to go far into the interior to find the nobler forms of antelope and still further if the hunter wants to pursue the elephant, the rhinoceros, or the giraffe. It is perfectly clear that very soon those animals, unless something is done to prevent their extermination, will be stamped out as completely as the dodo.

The parties to the London conference of 1900 signed a 'Convention for the Preservation of Animals, Birds and Fish in Africa.' Although the title indicates a grand sweep, in point of fact the conservation measures introduced were rather modest. Only a few endangered species were accorded complete protection: these included the gorilla, the giraffe, and the chimpanzee. For some other threatened species, such as the elephant and the gazelle, hunters were given licenses which limited the numbers that could be shot and prohibited the shooting of infants and pregnant females. Ironically, some species were classified as 'vermin,' deemed dangerous to men and cattle, and their killing was expressly encouraged. Bounties were thus offered for the shooting of the lion and the leopard—among the most cherished of wild animals from today's vantage point.

The London meeting was soon followed by the establishment of the first multinational conservation society. This was the 'Society for the Preservation of the Fauna of the Empire,' started in 1903 to halt the destruction of wild animals in the British colonies. The Society had local chapters across a wide swathe of Asia and Africa: dominated everywhere by hunters turned conservationists, it was known 'on account of its nucleus of elderly big game hunters as the Repentant Butchers Club.'

Through the colonies, wildlife conservation followed a set pattern. The first step was to moderate demand by specifying closed seasons when animals could not be shot, and issuing licenses, the possession of which alone allowed hunting. The second step was to designate particular species as 'protected.' The third step was to designate specified territories as 'game reserves' meant exclusively for animals, where logging, mining and agriculture were prohibited or restricted. The final and most decisive step was the establishment of national parks, which gave sanctity to entire habitats, not merely to animal species dwelling within them (see *box*).

In Southern Africa, the progress of conservation was linked to the development of a distinct settler identity. As English and Dutch colonists settled in for the long haul, identifying with Africa and turning their backs on their country of origin, the preservation of landscapes became synonymous with the preservation of the national spirit. Prominent Afrikaaner politicians, such as Paul Kruger and Jan Smuts, called for the creation of parks and sanctuaries so that the children and grandchildren of the pioneers could see the veld 'just as the Voortrekkers saw it.' The creation of reserves was thus dictated by sentiment as well as science, to simultaneously allow space for wild species and to affirm a shared human past. In neighboring Southern Rhodesia, where the English dominated, the grave in the Matopos hills of the great imperialist Cecil Rhodes became the nucleus of a national park extending over 45,000 acres.

Where did the African fit into all this? To be precise, nowhere. The white settler identified with the land but not with the men and women who had dwelt there long before their arrival. As the historians Jane Carruthers and Terence Ranger have pointed out, wildlife conservation cemented a union between the Dutch and the English in southern Africa, but it also consolidated, on the whole, white domination over the majority black population. In game reserves Africans were barred from hunting, while in national parks they were excluded altogether, forcibly dispossessed of their land if it fell within the boundaries of a designated sanctuary. Conservation was even viewed as 'part of the white man's necessary burden to save the nation's natural heritage from African despoilation.' But this was a conveniently ahistorical belief which glossed over the butchery of European hunting in the early decades of colonialism. If there was indeed a 'crisis of African wildlife,' this crisis had been created by the white man's gun and rifle, not the native spear and sling shot.

AND WHY A NATIONAL PARK?

In 1916 a Games Reserves Commission outlined the reasons for the creation of National Parks in South Africa. Note however that terms such as 'the general public' and 'the town dweller' refer exclusively to one race only, that is, white, and for the most part also to one sex, that is, male.

We think that . . . greater facilities should be offered to scientists, naturalists, and the general public to make themselves acquainted with a portion of their country which should be of the greatest natural interest for the following reasons:

(i) Here one may view and study conditions once generally obtaining throughout large areas of the Union, but which, owing to the advance of civilisation, are now rapidly disappearing and must eventually disappear altogether.

(ii) As a training ground for the scientific student, whether in botany, zoology, or other directions, the area is unequalled.

(iii) It is becoming more and more difficult for the town dweller to gain knowledge of the natural conditions of the country, and with the gradual extinction of game and other animals that is steadily going on, even to see the fauna of the country other than in the sophisticated surroundings of a zoological collection.

(iv) Here and nowhere better can the natural surroundings and habits of South African fauna be really studied, unaffected as the animals are by the instinctive dread of the huntsman, which in other parts of the country tend completely to alter their habits.

Source: Jane Carruthers, *The Kruger National Park: A Social and Political History* (Pietermaritzburg: University of Natal Press, 1995), p. 56.

Poster encouraging visitors to a national park in South Africa.
SOURCE Jane Carruthers, The Kruger National Park *(University of Natal Press.)*

WILDERNESS THINKING IN AMERICA

The first national park created anywhere was Yellowstone, in 1872. By now there are a thousand such parks spread across the globe. The United States has itself created what is generally regarded to be the best-managed system of national parks in the world. It is also in the U.S. that intellectuals and thinkers have pondered most deeply on what the wilderness has meant for the nourishment of the human spirit.

The background to wilderness conservation was the despoliation of the American continent by the westward movement of European settlers. In an essay published in the July 1897 number of the *Atlantic Monthly*, the California writer John Muir captured the environmental destruction caused by the pioneer's axe and fire, his corn fields and his cattle and sheep herds. Muir wrote stirringly of the past, present and possible future of the

> American forests! the glory of the world! Surveyed thus from the east to the west, from the north to the south, they are rich beyond thought, immortal, immeasurable, enough and to spare for every feeding, sheltering beast and bird, insect and son of Adam; and nobody need have cared had there been no pines in Norway, no cedars and deodars on Lebanon and the Himalayas, no vine-clad selvas in the basin of the Amazon. With such variety, harmony, and triumphant exuberance, even nature, it would seem, might have rested content with the forests of North America, and planted no more.
>
> So they appeared a few centuries ago when they were rejoicing in wildness. The Indians with stone axes could do them no more harm than could gnawing beavers or browsing moose. Even the fires of the Indian and the fierce shattering lightning seemed to work together only for good in clearing spots here and there for smooth garden prairies, and openings for sunflowers seeking the light. But when the steel axe of the white man rang out in the startled air, the doom [of the forest] was sealed. Every tree heard the bodeful sound, and pillars of smoke gave the sign in the sky.
>
> I suppose we need not go mourning the buffaloes. In the nature of things they had to give place to better cattle, though the change might have been made without barbarous wickedness. Likewise, many of nature's five hundred kinds of wild trees had to make way for orchards and cornfields. In the settlement and civilization of the country, bread more than timber or beauty was wanted; and in the blindness of hunger, the early settlers, claiming Heaven as their guide, regarded God's trees as only a larger kind of pernicious weed, extremely hard to get rid of.

Accordingly, with no eye to the future, these pious destroyers waged interminable forest wars; chips flew thick and fast; trees in their beauty fell crashing by millions, smashed to confusion, and the smoke of their burning has been rising to heaven [for] more than two hundred years. After the Atlantic coast from Maine to Georgia had been mostly cleared and scorched into melancholy ruins, the overflowing multitudes of bread and money seekers poured over the Alleghanies into the fertile middle West, spreading ruthless devastation ever wider and further over the rich valley of the Mississippi and the vast shadowy pine region about the Great Lakes. Thence still westward the invading horde of destroyers called settlers made its fiery way over the broad Rocky Mountains, felling and burning more fiercely than ever, until at last it has reached the wild side of the continent, and entered the last of the great aboriginal forests on the shores of the Pacific.

This is a crisp if starkly chilling summation of the ecological history of eighteenth- and nineteenth-century America. Fortunately, by the time Muir penned these words public opinion had been sufficiently stirred to try and protect the 'aboriginal forest' that remained. As he noted with relief and pleasure, lovers of the landscape, 'bewailing its baldness, are now crying aloud, "Save what is left of the forest!" Clearing has surely now gone far enough; soon timber will be scarce, and not a grove will be left to rest in or pray in.'

John Muir himself was one who shouted loudest, longest, and most effectively. Born in the Scottish town of Dunbar in 1838, he moved with his family to Wisconsin when a young boy. Here he grew up on a pioneer's farm, with an interest in botany and geology and an aptitude for things mechanical. After a desultory year or two at the University of Wisconsin, he left his home for the road, travelling through Canada before walking a thousand miles down to the Gulf of Mexico. Reaching San Francisco in March 1868, he settled in California, making repeated and extended forays into the Sierra mountains. Within a decade he had become known as a writer and lecturer, speaking out on the need to save what remained of the Western wilderness. In 1892 he founded the Sierra Club, which has since been the most influential conservation society in the career of American environmentalism.

Like Mahatma Gandhi, John Muir was not a systematic thinker: his ideas are scattered through his articles and speeches; they are not to be found in one, single, authoritative text. Yet there is no question that—like Gandhi—he was a thinker far ahead of his time. He knew well the economic rationale for forest protection—to supply a steady supply of timber, to prevent soil erosion, and to regulate the flow of

Chapter 4: The Growth of the Wilderness Idea

John Muir, at his desk, c. 1897.
SOURCE *Muir Papers, University of the Pacific, Stockton, California, here taken from Stephen Fox*, The American Conservation Movement *(University of Wisconsin Press.)*

water in the rivers—yet he also believed passionately in an independent, non-utilitarian rationale for preserving the wild. In an early meeting of the Sierra Club, he pointed out that

> any kind of forest on the flank of the Sierra would be of inestimable value as a cover for the irrigating streams. But in our forests we have not only a perfect cover, but also the most attractive and interesting trees in every way, and of the highest value, spiritual and material, so that even the angels of heaven might well be eager to come down and camp in their leafy temples!

Brought up a devout Christian, the son of an evangelical preacher, Muir came to embrace a mystical pantheism somewhat at odds with his received religious tradition. Christian doctrine puts man in a position of dominance over the rest of creation, but for Muir, as one admirer noted, 'cliff, air, cloud, flower, tree, bird and beast—all these were manifestations of a unifying God.' For him every species had its own honored place in the scheme of Nature. Man thought himself the master of the Universe, but Muir insisted that

> Nature's object in making animals and plants might possibly be first of all the happiness of each one of them, not the creation of all for the happiness of one. Why should man value himself as more than a small part of the one great unit of creation? And what creature of all that the Lord has taken the pains to make is not essential to the completeness of that unit—the cosmos? The universe would be incomplete without man; but it would also be incomplete without the smallest trans-microscopic creature that dwells beyond our conceitful eyes and knowledge.

Muir wrote evocatively of landscapes, and lovingly of individual species too. The Sierra bear was for him 'the sequioa of the animals,' a fellow rambler in the forest who was 'everywhere at home, harmonizing with the trees and rocks and shaggy chapparal.' The water ouzel was a 'brave little singer on the wild mountain streams;' to see this bird and love him was 'to look through a window into Nature's warm heart.' To the city-dweller nature was distant at best, terrifying at worst, but to Muir the forest and its diverse inhabitants were always welcoming. When the philosopher Ralph Waldo Emerson visited Yosemite, Muir tried in vain to take him to the wild. He wanted to show Emerson the 'Sierra manifestations of God,' but the great man's hangers-on, full of the 'indoor philosophy of Boston,' held him to the hotels and approved trails. However, towards the end of his life Muir was heartened to see growing numbers of city folk come out to

Chapter 4: The Growth of the Wilderness Idea

savor the glories of the Sierra. He saw that 'thousands of tired, nerve-shaken, over-civilized people are beginning to find out that going to the mountains is going home.' To Muir this was proof that 'wildness is a necessity; and that mountain peaks and [forest] reservations are useful not only as fountains of timber and irrigating rivers, but as fountains of life.'

In contrast to John Muir, for whom the Sierra was a second and occasionally a first home, these 'over-civilized' folk lived the year round in the cities and only seasoned their lives, a week at a time, with the wild. By the early twentieth century, growing urbanization had spawned a leisure industry which created a powerful social force for the preservation of wild areas. Muir might have wanted to protect Nature for its own sake, but the more humdrum pleasures of weekend camping and trekking played as influential a part in the creation of a national park system. As the historian Alfred Runte points out, the first reserve established on purely ecological grounds was the Everglades national park, created in 1934. Runte suggests that in fact several of the early national parks were created specifically to meet a rising surge of cultural nationalism. The apparent agelessness and sheer size of their mountains and forests provided, for the American intelligentsia, a substitute for the rich traditions of art and architecture that their country so conspicuously lacked. Unlike Europe, where the farmer and the shepherd carried in themselves the continuity of an ancient culture, there was no authentic heritage here of peasant life and traditions. Meanwhile, this land's indigenous inhabitants, the Native Americans, had been decimated in numbers and become degenerate in spirit. Into this void stepped the wilderness, which became, so to speak, *America's past*—a past to be mighty proud of. For if the Sierra redwoods had begun to grow before the birth of Christ, if the Rockies were twice as high as the Alps, and if compared to the Mississippi the Danube was a mere ditch, then this new nation could boast of a series of natural wonders vastly superior to the man-made artefacts, the churches, forts and paintings of Europe. In this sense, the monumental and unsurpassed scenery of the West provided American patriots with a way to answer Europe, the ancient civilization with respect to which they had a marked inferiority complex.

John Muir was himself a kind of ecological patriot, who believed that American forests were second to none: in their 'variety, harmony and triumphant exuberance' superior to the cedars of Lebanon, the deodars of the Himalaya, the selvas of the Amazon. But it is the ecological sensitivity rather than the patriotism which makes his a distinctive voice. Muir is rightly honored for his consideration for species other than the human, for his dogged insistence (see *box*) that nature had a right to be cared for regardless of any man's bank balance or any country's gross national product. He has become something of a cult figure for latter-day environmentalists, who worship him as a bearded prophet, alone in the wild, embattled and beleaguered, crying out against the forces of commerce and industry that would devastate nature. Just adjacent to John Muir in the pantheon of the wilderness movement is the man we now come to, Aldo Leopold.

HOW AND HOW NOT TO REVERENCE NATURE

John Muir on the threats to nature, and how to forestall or work around them.

1. Travellers in the Sierra forests usually complain of the want of life. 'The trees,' they say, 'are fine, but the empty stillness is deadly; there are no animals to be seen, no birds. We have not heard a song in all the woods.' And no wonder! They go in large parties with miles and horses; they make a great noise; they are dressed in outlandish, unnatural colors; every animal shuns them. Even the frightened pines would run away if they could. But Nature lovers, devout, silent, open-eyed, looking and listening with love, find no lack of inhabitants in these mountain mansions, and they come to them gladly.

2. The battle we have fought, and are still fighting, for the forests [of the Sierra] is a part of the eternal conflict between right and wrong, and we cannot expect to see the end of it.... The smallest forest reserve, and the first I ever heard of, was in the Garden of Eden; and though its boundaries were drawn by the Lord, and embraced only one tree, yet even so moderate a reserve as this was attacked. And I doubt not, if only one of our grand trees on the Sierra were reserved as an example and type of all that is most noble and glorious in mountain trees, it would not be long before you would find a lumberman and a lawyer at the foot of it, eagerly proving by every law terrestrial and celestial that the tree must come down. So we must count on watching and striving for these trees, and should always be glad to find anything so surely good and noble to strive for.

Sources: 1. 'Among the Yosemite,' *The Atlantic Monthly*, December 1898, p. 751. 2. 'Address on the Sierra Forest Reservation,' *The Sierra Club Bulletin*, volume 1, number 7, 1896, p. 276.

Leopold was born in January 1887 into a family of cultured and highly educated German immigrants. He grew up amidst books and

Chapter 4: The Growth of the Wilderness Idea

music, but also acquired an interest in the outdoors, inspired by his father, a keen hunter himself. Aldo went on to obtain a degree at the Yale School of Forestry, before joining the United States Forest Service in 1909. He worked in the Forest Service for a quarter of a century, mostly in the south-west. In 1933 he moved to a Professorship at the University of Wisconsin, dividing his time between the college campus and a small farm he had bought in the country.

In his career Leopold was to shift allegiance from one variety of environmentalism to another. Long years in the Forest Service, that showcase of scientific conservation, prepared him for a late emergence as a philosopher of nature, as what one colleague termed 'the Commanding General of the Wilderness Battle.' Posted in forest areas with plentiful populations of wild animals, Leopold developed a philosophy of 'game management' modelled closely on the principles of scientific forestry, with game replacing timber as the product which needed to be harvested on a 'sustained-yield' basis. But in time he came to appreciate the cultural and ecological significance of the wild, and from promoting 'game refuges' began urging that a portion of the National Forests be set aside as fully protected wilderness.

Leopold's move from the Forest Service to the University of Wisconsin was also a move from the tradition of Gifford Pinchot to the tradition of John Muir, and beyond (see quotes in *box*). In January 1935 he helped found the Wilderness Society, an autonomous pressure group that embraced both a philosophical credo—'an intelligent humility towards man's place in nature'—and a practical program, the setting aside for posterity of wild areas as yet untouched by mining, industry, logging, roads and other such threats. Later the same year, Leopold went on a study tour of Germany, where he was dismayed by the artificialized systems of forest and game management, which had reduced the diversity found in nature in favour of a few select species. He remarked, of the mania for spruce, that 'never before or since have the forests of a whole nation been converted into a new species within a single generation.' The Germans, wrote Leopold in disgust, had 'taught the world to plant trees like cabbages.'

In *A Sand County Alamanac*, his chronicle of life on a Wisconsin farm, Leopold offered moving descriptions of the coming and passing of the seasons, the changes through the year in plant and animal life. The land he tilled formed part of the prairie where the buffalo had once roamed in large numbers. Characteristically, Leopold mourned not so much the great buffalo as the lowly Sulphium, a native weed being exterminated by the plow and the lawn mower. The disappearance of Sulphium, he remarked, was 'one little episode in the funeral of the native flora, which in turn is one episode in the funeral of the floras of the world.'

> ### ALDO LEOPOLD CHANGES ALLEGIANCES
> *Aldo Leopold moved from being a hard-nosed utilitarian conservationist to a philosopher of ecological harmony and interdependence. These quotes help mark the shift:*
>
> 1. A harmonious relation to land is more intricate, and of more consequence to civilization, than the historians of its progress seem to realize. Civilization is not, as they often assume, the enslavement of a stable and consistent earth. It is a state of mutual and interdependent cooperation between human animals, other animals, plants and soils, which may be disrupted at any moment by the failure of any of them.
>
> 2. The emergence of ecology has placed the economic biologist in a peculiar dilemma: with one hand, he points out the accumulated findings of his search for utility, or lack of utility, in this or that species; with the other he lifts the veil from a biota so complex, so conditioned by interwoven cooperations and competitions, that no man can say where utility begins or ends.
>
> Source: 1. 'The Conservation Ethic,' *Journal of Forestry*, volume 31, number 6, 1933, p. 635. 2. 'A Biotic View of Land,' *Journal of Forestry*, volume 37, number 9, 1939, p. 727.

Leopold has been the most influential wilderness thinker since Muir, and the Californian is indeed the authority most often cited in *A Sand County Almanac*. But where Muir had been a pioneer plowman himself, Leopold came from a more pedigreed background. Moreover, by the time he grew up, America had become a technologically advanced and urbanized society. These differences in biography and context might explain why Leopold's was an urbane, reflective approach, lacking the sheer *rawness* of Muir's engagement with nature. John Muir, one might say, was a moralist and self-taught scientist, Leopold a trained ecologist turned ethicist.

While Leopold and Muir both celebrated the wild, they are divided in their attitude to what happened outside it. For Muir displayed in abundance the siege-like mentality of the wilderness lover; he was hostile to any force or form that might disturb the integrity of nature. Thus his deep aversion to the 'marauding shepherds' who grazed their flocks of 'hoofed locusts' in the national parks: these, along with miners and timber contractors, were to him 'the Goths and vandals

Chapter 4: The Growth of the Wilderness Idea

of the wilderness, who are spreading black death in the fairest woods God ever made.' Muir thought the parks must be guarded by the military, for him the 'only effective and reliable arm of the government.' Soldiers with guns might make sure that 'not a single herd or cow be allowed to trample in the Yosemite garden,' a garden 'given to the State for a higher use than pasturage.'

In the view of Aldo Leopold, however, responsible human behavior *outside* the national parks was perhaps even more important than the protection of wild species within them. He urged private landowners to promote a mix of species on their holdings, thereby enhancing soil fertility and maintaining a diverse flora and fauna. Strict control of wild areas by the state mattered little unless individuals and communities moderated their consumption and respected nature. 'We need plants and birds and trees restored to ten thousand farms,' he wrote, 'not merely to a few paltry reservations.' As the Harvard historian Donald Fleming has remarked, for Leopold

> The virtue of small farms and rural living was the homely private transactions with nature to which they lent themselves, the untremendous and unpremeditated encounters knit into the fabric of daily life. National parks and national forests were seen as the goal of a pilgrimage, holy places set apart under the care of a jealous priesthood of conservationists, against the day when a lay believer, once in a lifetime, would conform to the faith in some cathedral-of-pines. This was the core of Leopold's objections to the Transcendentalists posture towards nature. It was irrevocably coupled to the idea of retreats from practical life, and worse still, to a corresponding devaluation of the workaday world as an appropriate arena for cherishing the natural environment. Leopold's own purpose was exactly the opposite. He wanted to strip the conservation ideal of its remote and sacred aspects and make the cultivation of a loving and wondering attitude toward other organisms and toward the land itself a matter of voluntary daily practice in modest contexts, particularly when men were unobserved and unintoxicated by the gigantic and patently sublime.

Aldo Leopold differed not only from John Muir but from dozens of wilderness thinkers before or since, who have had time only for spectacular habitats like the seas and the mountains, and for charismatic animals such as the tiger and the whale. These thinkers have focused narrowly, too narrowly perhaps, on the creation of parks and sanctuaries policed from within and protected by walls and fences from without. Leopold's was a more inclusive approach, and this in more than one respect. Ecologically, he moved from the protection of species to the protection of habitats and on toward the protection of all forms of biological diversity. Socially, he recognized that wild areas could hardly be saved without a wider reorganization of the economy on ecological principles, so that the fruits of nature's use could be more equitably distributed among humans. Ethically, he hoped that an attitude of care and wonder towards nature would not be expressed only on occasional excursions into the wild, but come to be part of the fabric of our daily lives, so that on weekdays, as much as on weekends, we would come to tread gently on this earth.

AFTERWORD

Some Who Don't Fit

Scientific conservation, back-to-the-land, and wilderness thinking have been the most influential ideologies of the first wave of environmentalism. Into one or other of these three modes would fit numerous thinkers and strands across the continents, by no means all of whom have been featured in this narrative. Rather than add to the list of representative thinkers, I shall in conclusion consider a trinity of environmentalists who cannot be easily slotted into any of these categories. Analytical rather than argumentative, reflective rather than passionate, this trio is remembered for helping build bridges between the natural sciences and the social sciences, as forerunners of the 'inter-disciplinary' and 'trans-disciplinary' intellectual movements of the present day.

The first of these unclassifiable environmentalists is the Scotsman Patrick Geddes (1854–1932), an admirer of John Ruskin and George Perkins Marsh but withal an original thinker in his own right. In a long and colorful career Geddes taught botany at Dundee and sociology in Bombay, ran a museum in Edinburgh and established a college in the south of France. 'By both training and general habit of mind,' wrote one of his students, Geddes was 'an ecologist long before that branch of biology had obtained the status of a special discipline.' However, Geddes was not so much a biological ecologist as a *social* ecologist, a scholar who sought to understand the dynamic interrelationships between human societies and their natural environments.

Geddes' most significant work, in an intellectual as well as practical sense, was in the field of town and city planning. He was one of the first thinkers to highlight the parasitism of the modern city, its

Book of correspondence between Patrick Geddes and Lewis Mumford, Scottish environmentalist and his Manhattan disciple.
SOURCE *Frank G. Novack, Jr.*, Lewis Mumford and Patrick Geddes: The Correspondence *(Routledge)*

exploitation of the rural hinterland through its voracious appetite for energy and materials. The dependence of the industrial city on fossil fuels, and the tremendous pollution this engendered, were captured in his evocative phrase, 'carboniferous capitalism.' Geddes wrote dozens of plans for cities in Europe and Asia, each of which aimed at harmonizing urban living with the values and virtues of the countryside. He thus called for 'a return to the health of village life, with its beauty of surroundings and its contact with nature,' but 'upon a new spiral turning beyond the old one, which, at the same time, frankly and fully incorporates the best advantages of town life.' Town planning, in his view, should aim above all at 'the Conservation of Nature and for the increase of our accesses to her.' His own plans—which, alas, were rarely followed or implemented—stressed the creation of open spaces and parks, the planting and protection of trees, and the conservation of water and water bodies.

Geddes' ideas were carried forward by two of his outstanding disciples, the American historian Lewis Mumford (1895–1986) and the Indian sociologist Radhakamal Mukherjee (1889–1966). Active as a writer and thinker for over fifty years, Mumford spanned the two waves of the environmental movement, and made notable contributions to both. Like Muir and Gandhi before him, Mumford did not have a college education: his own university, he liked to say, was the city of Manhattan, where he grew up and in whose streets and parks and libraries he learnt of life. He was to write insightfully on this and other cities, on the environment within them and on the region of which they formed part. Mumford's published works include a couple of dozen books and a couple of hundred essays, all of which owed as much to his own lived experience as to book learning.

Mumford argued that the organic unity between the city and the hinterland, characteristic of medieval Europe, had been disturbed by the coal-and-iron based industrialization of the nineteenth century, whose most distinctive features were the polluting factory and the unhygienic slum—indeed, it was 'plain that never before in recorded history had such vast masses of people lived in such a savagely deteriorated environment.' But Mumford looked forward, not backwards, hoping for the emergence of a new, post-industrial phase of economic development, based on non-polluting sources of energy, such as solar power and hydroelectricity, and on long-lasting alloys. The society he wished for would restore three disturbed equilibria: the equilibrium between the city and the village; the equilibrium in population, by balancing birth and death rates; and, most vital of all, the equilibrium between humans and nature.

As a historian, Mumford studied dispassionately the emergence of the 'money economy of destruction;' while as a citizen he worked actively for 'the future life economy of renewal.' The roles of scholar and activist were also combined in the person of Radhakamal Mukherjee, a sociologist who fell under Geddes' sway when the latter lived in India, between 1915 and 1922. Where other social scientists studied humans in isolation from nature, Mukherjee insisted that any social group must be considered in relation to 'the interwoven chain of biotic communities to which it is inextricably linked, the plants it cultivates, the animals it breeds, and even the insects which are indigenous to a region.' In the region that he most closely studied, the Indo-Gangetic plain, he found 'exhaustion and depletion' everywhere—in the form of deforestation, soil erosion, and declining yields—this in place of the 'renewal and enrichment of nature' which should legitimately be man's goal. He thus called for an 'alliance with the entire range of ecological forces' through the 'imparting of new values—the thought for tomorrow, the sacrifice for the inhabitants of the region yet unborn.'

Combining reason with passion, the Geddes-Mukherjee-Mumford tradition of social ecology goes beyond the partial visions of other traditions of environmentalism. Its key analytical category, 'the region,' brings together the three realms—of the wilderness, the countryside, and the city —which other schools tend to view in isolation. For a regionalist program works simultaneously for the preservation of the primeval wild, the restoration of a stable rural community, and for an urban-industrial complex that is sustainable without being parasitical. In 1938, Louis Mumford demarcated this approach from the mainstream environmental movement. Mumford wrote that

> originating in the spectacle of waste and defilement, the conservation movement has tended to have a negative influence : it has sought to isolate wilderness areas from encroachment and it has endeavoured to diminish waste and prevent damage. The present task of regional planning is a more positive one: it seeks to bring the earth as a whole up to the highest pitch of perfection and appropriate use—not merely preserving the primeval, but extending the range of the garden, and introducing the deliberate culture of the landscape into every part of the open country.

The next year the world was at war, and environmentalism in all its varieties was relegated to the margins of public life.

PROLOGUE

The Age of Ecological Innocence

However appealing it might seem to some today, the 'green agenda' with which we ended Part I found few takers at the time. The reason for this was not its intrinsic weaknesses but rather its overshadowing by an event of truly global consequences, known appropriately as the Second *World* War. The human costs of the holocaust of 1939–45 were to exceed those of the battles of 1914–18, yet the outcome was very different. The First World War had cast a pall of gloom over the thinkers of Europe, a good many of whom sought imaginative refuge in a pre-industrial past when war between neighbors did not seem to exact such a terrible price. In contrast, the Allied victory in 1945 was to fuel a visible optimism with regard to the future of humanity.

Unlike its predecessor, World War II was more readily understood as a struggle of good against evil, the freedom-loving democracies of Britain and the U.S.A. versus the authoritarian and Fascist states of Italy and Germany. Moreover, the 'right' side won. No such clear-cut identification of virtue and vice was possible with respect to World War I, which was merely a conflict between rival imperialists over materials and territories. The moral salience of World War II was underscored when its end was quickly followed by the granting by Britain of independence in 1947 to the 'jewel in the crown' of its empire, India. The Western powers, it appeared, were affirming their commitment to democracy by getting rid of their colonial possessions. Other nations were to follow the British example, although political independence was in most countries an outcome as much of militant nationalism as of the benevolence of departing colonialists. The Dutch left Indonesia in 1948, the Americans gave up the Philippines the next year, while Britain progressively withdrew from its numerous colonies in Asia and Africa. Most reluctant to go home were the French and the Portuguese, who had to fight bitter and bloody wars—in Algeria and Indo-China in the óne case, in Angola and Mozambique in the other—before finally conceding that the epoch of white rule over colored peoples had irrevocably passed.

The consequences of peace in Europe/America and decolonization in Asia/Africa were in one crucial respect the same. In both contexts, the supreme task of governments was now to fulfil, and if possible to exceed, the *economic* expectations of their citizens. In the North, intellectuals and politicians alike believed that the generation and distribution of wealth, more than anything else, would help wipe away the memories of war. For the victory achieved in the far-flung battlefields of the Second World War was widely perceived to be a victory for technology as much as for democracy. The conflict ended, the route to future salvation seemed to lie in the fruitful application of technology to the production process. As President Truman insisted in his inauguration speech of January 20, 1949, 'greater production is the key to prosperity and peace.'

The 'preoccupation with productivity and production' which the economist John Kenneth Galbraith was to see so manifest in post-War America was in fact quite characteristic of post-War Europe as well. The population in these societies had for the most part been adequately housed, clothed, and fed; now they expressed a desire for 'more elegant cars, more exotic food, more erotic clothing, more elaborate entertainment.' When Galbraith termed 1950s America the 'affluent society' he meant not only that this was a society most of whose members were hugely prosperous when reckoned against other societies and other times, but also that this was a society so dedicated to affluence that the possession and consumption of material goods became the exclusive standard of individual and collective achievement. This was a culture, remarked the anthropologist Geoffrey Gorer, in which 'any device or regulation which interfered, or can be conceived as interfering, with [the] supply of more and better things is resisted with unreasoning horror, as the religious resist blasphemy, or the warlike pacifism.' While addressing Congress in 1941, one of the greatest of American presidents, Franklin Roosevelt, had looked forward to a 'world founded upon four essential freedoms:' the freedom of expression and of worship, and the freedom from

Prologue: The Age of Ecological Innocence

want and from fear. A decade later, with the war in a safely forgotten past, it seemed as if the four freedoms most cherished by the affluent society were the freedom to produce, to consume, to get rich, and to get richer.

The newly independent nations of Asia and Africa were also preoccupied with productivity and production, but with the removal of poverty rather than the generation of greater affluence as their goal—this corresponding to the third of Roosevelt's original list, the 'freedom from want everywhere in the world.' Nationalists like Nehru in India, Sukarno in Indonesia, and Nasser in Egypt were united by the belief that imperialism had only been made possible by the economic and technological superiority of the colonial powers. Decolonization had opened up the possibility of these previously 'underdeveloped' nations 'developing' along the same lines as the West. Rapid industrialization, it was thought, would end poverty and unemployment and make for a strong and self-reliant society.

Now, when there is so much cynicism abroad about the very idea of 'development', it is good to remember the deeply humane and democratic sensibilities that underlay its original formulation. The age of empire had been governed by the belief that white was superior to brown and black, but the idea of development implied that people *everywhere* had equal rights and capabilities. Inequalities between or within nations were not natural or pre-ordained; rather, they could be removed (or at least mitigated) by concerted social action. Modern science and technology, theoretically within reach of all, provided one plank of this equalizing effort; the other was the new nation-state, often headed by a charismatic leader embodying the hopes and aspirations of millions of ordinary people. In India, for example, the state, as well as the process of economic development itself, was ruled over by a Prime Minister (Nehru) whose personal popularity surpassed that of Mahatma Gandhi at the height of his fame; while behind him stood a Congress party which had led a multi-class freedom movement and since come to power through the ballot box rather than the bullet.

The sincerity and legitimacy of the 'developers' duly noted, one must nonetheless recognize that the times were scarcely propitious for the formulation or advancement of an environmentalist agenda. With the overwhelming focus on production, environmentally oriented thinking—in the domains of the city, countryside, or forest—could find little play. For opinion-makers in the 'affluent society' and in the 'developing country' likewise called for a more intensive use of nature and natural resources. The twenty years after World

War II are known as the 'development decades,' but they might more accurately be termed the 'age of ecological innocence.' In the U.S. as much as in India, in Britain as well as in Brazil, talk of ecological constraints to economic growth was regarded as irrelevant at best, and at worst as a dangerous deviation from the primary national task, defined in one context as the generation of affluence and in the other as the lessening of the gap between rich and poor nations. The air was suffused with optimism; especially the optimism of the technologist. Characteristic here are some remarks of the U.S. secretary of the treasury, Henry Morgenthau, offered at the founding of the International Bank for Reconstruction and Development (the World Bank) in 1945. The Bank, wrote Morgenthau confidently, would help create 'a dynamic world economy in which the peoples of every nation will be able to enjoy, increasingly, the fruits of material progress on an earth *infinitely* blessed with natural riches.'

In this manner, the prospect of unending economic growth was held out to the people of the North, the prospect of becoming exactly like America, and living like Americans, offered to the underdeveloped world. Science was said to be the 'endless frontier,' technology the 'inexhaustible resource;' working in harness, they would dispel any thoughts of resource shortages, temporary or permanent. Such was the view of the men who both defined and deified the age of ecological innocence, for instance Vannevar Bush of NASA or the geologist Kirtley F. Mather of Harvard University, who believed that Mother Earth herself had 'enough and to spare.'

To be sure, there was the odd discordant voice. One was the great Berkeley geographer Carl Sauer, who located the current of buoyant optimism firmly in time and place. He remarked that 'the doctrine of a passing frontier of nature replaced by a permanent and sufficiently expanding frontier of technology is a contemporary and characteristic expression of occidental culture, itself a historical-geographical product.' This frontier attitude, he went on, 'has the recklessness of an optimism that has become habitual, but which is residual from the brave days when north-European freebooters overran the world and put it under tribute.' Warning that the surge of growth at the expense of nature would not last indefinitely, Sauer—speaking for his fellow Occidentals—noted wistfully that 'we have not yet learned the difference between yield and loot. We do not like to be economic realists.'

A second dissident was E. F. Schumacher, a German economist who had fled Nazism to settle in England. Schumacher believed that

Prologue: The Age of Ecological Innocence

the 'economic expansion [which] is the common ideology of all mankind today' had legitimized the rapacious exploitation of non-renewable resources such as coal and oil. 'We forget that we are living off capital in the most fundamental meaning of the word,' he wrote in 1954, adding: 'Mankind has existed for many thousands of years and has always lived off income. Only in the last hundred years has man forcibly broken into nature's larder and is now emptying it out at a breathtaking speed which increases from year to year.' Yet another prescient voice was Lewis Mumford, who was more concerned with the instruments by which nature was being ravaged. Writing in 1955, he warned that the 'awful omniscience and the omnipotence of our science and technology' might 'turn out to be more self-destructive than ignorance and impotence.' He deplored the rule of 'power, prestige and profit,' insisting that 'only when love takes the lead will the earth, and life on earth, be safe again.'

Sauer, Schumacher and Mumford are all recognizably part of the history of Western environmentalism. Let us now consider a dissenter unknown to that history. Mira Behn—her real name was Madeleine Slade—was the daughter of an English admiral who joined Mahatma Gandhi in 1927 and spent the next thirty years in the service of her teacher and his land. Shortly after the war she moved from Gandhi's ashram in central India to a village in the Himalaya, seeking to understand the rhythms of nature and the relation of peasant life to it. Her primary concern, as befitting a Gandhian, was with the rehabilitation of the village economy, but at times, as befitting an Englishwoman, she expressed an almost Wordsworthian affinity with nature. Herself a 'devotee of the great primeval Mother Earth,' she complained in April 1949 that

> The tragedy today is that educated and moneyed classes are altogether out of touch with the vital fundamentals of existence—our Mother Earth, and the animal and vegetable population which she sustains. This world of Nature's planning is ruthlessly plundered, despoiled and disorganized by man whenever he gets the chance. By his science and machinery he may get huge returns for a time, but ultimately will come desolation. We have got to study Nature's balance, and develop our lives within her laws, if we are to survive as a physically healthy and morally decent species.

As it happens, Mira Behn could hardly have been less in tune with the society in which she lived, and in later life she settled near Vienna to seek out the spirit of Beethoven—yet another dedicated German nature-lover. Meanwhile independent India was restless, on the move, determined to conquer and master nature rather than submit silently to its laws. This called for the construction of steel mills and atomic power plants, not the organic farms and village woodlots which the Gandhians advocated. Likewise, Lewis Mumford's regionalist program, which had found ready adherents in the 1930s, had no place in an America that now took the globe as its oyster. E. F. Schumacher was also to battle unsuccessfully against 'a vision of a future when technology would ensure that there was plenty for all'—as his biographer tells us, 'no one was [then] interested in listening to an economist who told them that [their] future was built on dreams.' Incomprehension, indifference and hostility were what faced those who dared challenge the age of ecological innocence, a phase which stretched from the end of the Second World War to the last quarter of 1962. It was in that year that the second wave of environmentalism announced itself through the unlikely medium of a newly published book.

5

The Ecology of Affluence

THE SIGNIFICANCE OF *SILENT SPRING*

Put two historians in a room and you have a debate; put a couple more and you have a cacophony of discordant voices. In a tribe notorious for disputation and disagreement, there is a surprising unanimity on what begat modern environmentalism. 'The landmark book *Silent Spring*,' writes Ralph H. Lutts, 'played a vitally important role in stimulating the contemporary environmental movement.' Stephen Fox goes further: *Silent Spring*, he says, 'became one of the seminal volumes in conservation history: the *Uncle Tom's Cabin* of modern environmentalism.' Kirkpatrick Sale is more categorical still; he quotes a stirring paragraph from the preface of the book in question, and adds: 'With those angry and uncompromising words, it can be said that the modern environmental movement began.'

Silent Spring was the work of Rachel Carson, a biologist who had worked for years with the U.S. Fish and Wildlife Service, and was the author previously of two best-selling but non-controversial books on the sea. The influence of her third book might be judged by numbers: by the fact that *Silent Spring* sold half-a-million copies in hard cover, the fact that it stayed thirty-one weeks on the *New York Times* bestseller list, the fact that it was quickly published, in English or in translation, in some two dozen countries. The book's impact is also measured, in the historians' accounts, by the controversies it generated in the media, in corporate boardrooms, in scientific journals and within government departments.

The curious thing, however, is that *Silent Spring* is apparently not much read any more. Historians of the environmental movement have dwelt at length on its impact, a few among them have offered potted biographies of the author, yet one is hard put to find in the published literature an intelligent summary and assessment of the book itself. And that is a pity, for *Silent Spring* is a truly remarkable work, a contribution to science that is worth reading—and re-reading—for its literary qualities alone.

For Rachel Carson the 'central problem of our age' was the 'contamination of man's total environment with substances of incredible potential for harm.' These were the new chemicals patented during and after the war, such as dicholoro-diphenyl-trichloroethane (DDT), an insecticide that had found wide favor among farmers and scientists. DDT was only the most prominent of an array of pesticides synthesized by chemists for use on the farm and in the factory. Between 1947 and 1960, the output of pesticides in the U.S. jumped from 1.24 to 6.37 million pounds; moreover 'in the plans and hopes of the industry this enormous production [was] only a beginning.' Used for a worthy purpose—to increase food production by eliminating pests—these manipulated chemicals had become, in Carson's colorful language, 'elixirs of death,' a 'battery of poisons of truly extraordinary powers.' As she explained, chemicals applied to plants and trees slowly leached into the soil and water, thereupon entering the food chain. Passing from one organism to another, from insects and birds to fish and animals, they went on to enter the bodies of humans in repeated small doses. These chemicals, modeled in the laboratory with little regard to their impact on the natural world, thus constituted an ever-present if insidiously invisible danger to diverse forms of life.

The early chapters of *Silent Spring* describe these new chemicals, their applications and impact on soil, water, and forests. The book then moves on to a defense of nature against these modern and, in the author's view, unwarranted intrusions. A chapter on wildlife is followed by one on birds, centered on deaths of robins in parts of New England, poisoned by eating worms contaminated by insecticides sprayed on the elm tree—a perfect example of how the poisons worked their way up the food chain. It was this threat to a loved and familiar bird that the book's title evoked: 'the sudden silencing of the song of birds, the obliteration of the color and beauty and

Chapter 5: The Ecology of Affluence

interest they lent to our world,' such that 'spring now comes unheralded' by their return, with 'the early mornings strangely silent where once they were filled with the beauty of bird song.' This was certainly the reality in a few villages and towns here and there, but the work's power lay in its suggestion that this could become the norm *throughout* North America, unless humans worked quickly to control pesticides.

Only a little less loved than the robin was the eagle, America's national bird, and the salmon, that sprightly fish so lovingly memorialized in poetry and myth. Carson provides accounts of eagle kills and salmon deaths, before arriving finally at the threat to human life through chemical ingestion, most dramatically illustrated by the increasing incidence of cancer. Here too the narrative is full of foreboding—Carson herself was diagnosed as suffering from cancer while working on *Silent Spring*—but the book ends with an offering of hope, the hope that biological methods of pest control would give humans a last chance to 'reach a destination that assures the preservation of our earth.' Biological methods had been tested in other countries; Carson quotes the distinguished Dutch entomologist C. J. Brejér in support of her own view that scientists had to commence

> some very energetic research on other control measures, measures that will have to be biological, not chemical. Our aim should be to guide natural processes as cautiously as possible in the desired direction rather than to use brute force . . . Life is a miracle beyond our comprehension, and we should reverence it even when we have to struggle against it. . . . Humbleness is in order; there is no excuse for scientific conceit here.

Silent Spring is a marvel of popular and partisan science, rich in well chosen examples and carefully detailed case studies drawn from specialized scientific works, here arranged and presented to the public in beautifully crafted prose. Beneath and beyond the facts lay a deeper philosophical argument, to the effect that nature was to be respected as a 'complex, precise and highly integrated system of relationships between living things which cannot safely be ignored any more than the law of gravity can be defied with impunity by a man perched on the edge of a cliff.'

Environmentalists had for some time been concerned with the protection of endangered species or beautiful habitats; it was *Silent Spring* which helped them move further, to an appreciation that 'in nature nothing exists alone,' that 'there are intimate and essential relations between plants and the earth, between plants and other plants, between plants and animals:' that nature was, in sum, 'an intricate web of life whose interwoven strands lead from microbes to man.' The interconnectedness of all life called for a modest, gentle and cautious attitude toward nature, rather than the arrogant, aggressive and intrepid route taken by synthetic chemistry and its products. Otherwise the web of life could very easily become the web of death.

Silent Spring's impact was not, of course, contingent on an acceptance of this philosophy of nature, for the facts of pesticide abuse and its consequences for wildlife and humans spoke for themselves. The book, noted a historian twenty years after its publication, found a constituency broader 'than that enjoyed by any previous environmental issue. Never before had so diverse a body of people, from bird watchers, to wildlife managers and public health professionals, to suburban homeowners, been joined together to deal with a [common] threat.' Early admirers of *Silent Spring* included the secretary of the interior, Stewart Udall, and President John F. Kennedy himself, whose Scientific Advisory Committee put out a report endorsing Carson's conclusions.

The consequences of the book were far-reaching. In the wake of *Silent Spring* towns 'reconsidered their foolish herbicidal assaults' on avenue shrubs and trees; citizens and officials became more alert to potential fish kills in rivers; senators and congressmen were energized to make pesticide production a subject for political debate and legislative enactment; a federal committe on pest control was established to scrutinize new products; the U.S. department of agriculture, once a keen enthusiast for synthetic pesticides, outlawed several dangerous chemicals; dozens of states and the Federal Government outlawed the use of the most deadly of them all, DDT; and finally, a Pesticide Control Act of 1972 and a Toxic Substances Control Act of 1974 gave legal teeth to attempts to more closely control and monitor chemicals. Not since the appearance of John Maynard Keynes' *General Theory of Employment, Interest and Money*—which was published in England in 1937—did a single book have such a dramatic and simultaneous impact on public opinion, scientific research, and state policy.

The impact of *Silent Spring* was by no means restricted to the United States. Carson herself acknowledged foreign influences on her work; on the scientific side, the Dutch entomologist C. J. Brejér provided some key arguments, while the concept of 'food chain,' used in the book to such telling effect, had first been elaborated by the great Oxford ecologist Charles Elton, an authority several times quoted respectfully by the author. The book was dedicated to the Alsatian doctor Albert Schweitzer, begetter of the philosophy of 'reverence for life,' while its epigraph came from the English poet John Keats: 'The sedge is wither'd from the lake, And no birds sing'—words which provided the book with its title and its most effective image.

Rachel Carson was no narrow nationalist, yet her debts to other cultures were to be duly returned, with interest. Translated into twelve languages, *Silent Spring* had a striking impact on the resurgence of environmentalism throughout Europe. A historian of Germany explains how in that country 'the translation of [this] landmark polemic stood as a best-seller for many months,' its 'echo seen in the sharp upsurge' of membership of conservation organizations. A sociologist of Sweden writes that in his country 'it was Carson's book that served to usher in the modern era of environmentalism.' In Britain, the publication of the book provoked a furious debate in the House of Lords; outside that august body, it came to the attention of the biologist Julian Huxley. Through reading *Silent Spring* Huxley realized that in Britian too the new insecticides and herbicides were decimating plant and animal life; when he communicated this to his brother Aldous, the famous writer remarked that 'we are losing half the subject-matter of English poetry,' a comment that—had it reached her—would have greatly pleased Carson.

In the American context, *Silent Spring* is best compared to George Perkins Marsh's monumental *Man and Nature*, likewise a model of scientific clarity and exhaustiveness, and likewise a call to action aimed at scientists as well as to the public at large. It is unlikely that Rachel Carson herself thought of this comparison. For the author of *Silent Spring* wrote as if unaware of the first wave of environmentalism, as if there did not exist an authentically American tradition of respect and reverence for the integrity of nature. John Muir admired George Perkins Marsh, Aldo Leopold honored Muir, but Carson does not mention any of the great trio that preceded her. Her book did not go back beyond the Second World War, the event which set in motion the production and dissemination of the chemicals which were her immediate concern. This focus was understandable, but it is notable nonetheless that she fails to acknowledge that her nature philosophy had such a distinguished pedigree. Her silence in this regard is testimony perhaps to the hold of the Age of Ecological Innocence, which seems to have so effectively wiped away the memory and heritage of the first wave of environmentalism.

WAVES WITHIN THE WAVE

The Environmental Debate

Early in her book, Rachel Carson identified two reasons for the lack of awareness with regard to the new chemicals. 'This is an era of specialists,' she explained, 'each of whom sees his own problem and is unaware of or intolerant of the larger frame into which it fits. It is also an era dominated by industry, in which the right to make a dollar at whatever cost is seldom challenged.'

Carson herself was more concerned with the specialists, her book an extended polemic against narrow-minded chemists by one who was obliged on account of her own training to be always mindful of the 'larger frame.' Chemical controls, she wrote, 'have been devised and applied without taking into account the complex biological systems against which they have been blindly hurled.' Her remarks are laced with sarcasm—e.g., 'the chemists' ingenuity in devising insecticides has long ago outrun biological knowledge of the way these poisons affect the living organism'—and her book ends with an utter condemnation of the science of specialists:

> The concepts and practices of applied entomology for the most part date from the Stone Age of science. It is our alarming misfortune that so primitive a science has armed [itself] with the most modern and terrible weapons, and that in turning them against the insects it has also turned them against the earth.

This theme was underlined by Julian Huxley in his foreword to the British edition of *Silent Spring*. Pest control, he wrote, 'is of course necessary and desirable, but it is an ecological matter, and cannot be handed over entirely to the chemists.' Like Carson, Huxley was a biologist, schooled in a science that in three major respects differs from the disciplines of physics and chemistry. First, biologists are taught to look for interdependence in nature, viewing individual life forms not in isolation but in relation to one another. Ever since Darwin, biologists have also been oriented toward a longer time frame, thinking in aeons and generations rather than months and years. Finally, biologists have a direct professional interest in species other than humans; as ornithologists, botanists and zoologists, they are, willy-nilly, more alert to the interests of bird, plant or animal life.

Inspired by Carson, though sometimes following lines tangential to hers, other biologists also came to play a disproportionate role in shaping the environmental debate of the sixties and seventies. Environmental 'classics' that appeared in the decade following *Silent*

Chapter 5: The Ecology of Affluence

Spring include Raymond Dasmann's evocation of the threatened beauty of a great American state; Paul Ehrlich's grim prediction of collective human suicide through over-breeding; Garret Hardin's equally despairing parable of how human society would self-destruct through aggressive competition over nature and natural resources; and Barry Commoner's urbane extension of Carson's attack on one-eyed science, where atomic physics was placed alongside synthetic chemistry. All these works were written by biologists, and all had apocalyptic titles: *The Destruction of California* (Dasmann); *The Population Bomb* (Ehrlich); *The Tragedy of the Commons* (Hardin); *The Closing Circle* (Commoner).

These works were closely followed in Europe, but in that continent too home-grown biologists were to emerge as major spokesmen for the new environmentalism. In Sweden the microbiologist Bjorn Gillberg and the biochemist Hans Palmstierna came to prominence in the late sixties as authors of scholary studies on chemical hazards as well as of numerous popular articles in the press. Their counterpart in the Netherlands was C. J. Brejér, a friend of Carson who in 1967 produced his own influential version of *Silent Spring* entitled *Zilveren Sluiersen Verborgen Sevaren* (Silver Veils and Hidden Dangers). Among the first to ring the alarm bells in the United Kingdom were Eric Ashby, F. Fraser Darling, C. H. Waddington and Julian Huxley, all eminent biologists with a more than professional interest in protecting the environment.

This is not to say that only biologists contributed to the burgeoning literature and intensifying public debate. E. F. Schumacher, still a dissident among economists, found his moment had arrived in 1973 when he published *Small is Beautiful*, a book much admired for its espousal of a 'Buddhist' economics based on 'appropriate' technology—that is, machines and production processes that would be cheap, decentralized, use little energy, and be sensitive to the environment. Schumacher had been deeply influenced by Gandhi, and by a trip he made to India in the early sixties (see *box*). Important contributions also came from the California historian Lynn White Jr. and the Norwegian philosopher Arné Naess, both concerned with the ethical and religious aspects of our relations with nature. More influential than these single-authored works was the collaborative *Limits to Growth*, a study commissioned by the Club of Rome which argued on the basis of computer simulations that current trends in population growth, energy demand and resource consumption were pressing hard on the carrying capacity of the earth. Published in 1972, *Limits* appeared in thirty languages and sold some four million copies in all.

One man who saw his life's work vindicated by the new environmental consciousness was Lewis Mumford. Born in 1895, Mumford had lived long enough to influence the first wave of environmentalism, to welcome the second, and, not least, to protest vigorously against the age of innocence which came in between. In October 1962, weeks after Rachel Carson's book appeared, Mumford was due to speak at the Davis campus of the University of California. Although I have no conclusive proof, he must already have read *Silent Spring*—if not the whole book, at least the extracts that had appeared previously in the *New Yorker* (a magazine he too wrote for). In any

---

ECONOMICS AS WISDOM

The German-British scholar E. F. Schumacher explains what he means by an 'economics of permanence;' he invokes Gandhi, but not his follower J. C. Kumarappa, who back in 1945 had written a book with a tantalizingly similar title, 'The Economy of Permanence.'

From an economic point of view, the central concept of Wisdom is Permanence. We must study the Economics of Permanence. Nothing makes economic sense unless its continuance for a long time can be projected without running into absurdities. There can be 'growth' towards a limited objective, but there cannot be unlimited, generalized growth. It is likely, as Gandhi said, that 'Earth provides enough to satisfy every man's need, but not for every man's greed.' Permanence is incompatible with a predatory attitude which rejoices in the fact that 'what were luxuries for our fathers have become necessities for us.'

... The Economics of Permanence implies a profound re-orientation of science and technology, which have to open their doors to Wisdom ... Scientific or technological 'solutions' which poison the environment or degrade the social structure and man himself, are of no benefit, no matter how brilliantly conceived or how great their superficial attraction. Ever bigger machines, entailing ever bigger concentrations of economic power and exerting ever greater violence against the environment do not represent progress: they are a denial of Wisdom. Wisdom demands a new orientation of science and technology towards the organic, the gentle, the non-violent, the elegant and beautiful. . . . We must look for a revolution in technology to give us inventions and machines which reverse the destructive trends now threatening us all.

Source: E. F. Schumacher, 'The economics of permanence,' *Resurgence*, volume 3, number 1, May/June 1970, reprinted in Robin Clarke, editor, *Notes for the Future: An Alternative History of the Past Decade* (London: Thames and Hudson, 1975).

Chapter 5: The Ecology of Affluence

event, his message was entirely consistent with Carson's. Mumford first outlined the history of ecological abuse on the American continent, beginning with the pioneers and culminating in the polluting epoch of what he, following Patrick Geddes, liked to call 'carboniferous capitalism.' He asked his student audience to replace the reigning myth of the machine with 'a new myth of life, a myth based upon a richer understanding of all organic processes,' a myth that would help humans work 'in co-operative relation with all the forces of nature.' Three years later, addressing a conference of ecologists, he urged scientists to place their particular concerns in a broader frame. 'When we rally to preserve the remaining redwood forests or to protect the whooping crane,' he said, 'we are rallying to preserve ourselves, we are trying to keep in existence the organic variety, the whole span of natural resources, upon which our own further development will be based.'

The historian Donald Fleming once remarked that the resurgence of environmentalism in the sixties allowed Mumford to 'reconstruct and amplify the themes of a lifetime.' The themes were the same, but a new urgency had now manifested itself in the sage's pronouncements. As he wrote in 1973, 'the chief effect of the regressive transformations that have taken place in the last quarter of a century [i.e. since the end of World War II] has been to change my conclusions from the indicative to the imperative mood; not "we shall" achieve a dynamic equilibrium [between humans and nature] but *"we must"*—if we are not to destroy the ecological balance upon which all life depends.'

In both Europe and North America, then, there was a prolific outcrop of environmentalist tracts in the years following the appearance of *Silent Spring*. Some of these works were sober and scholarly, others passionate and polemical. Several carried forward traditions characteristic of the movement's first wave. Thus the heritage of wilderness thinking was manifest in 'Neo-Malthusians' such as Garret Hardin and Paul Ehrlich, who worried that exploding human populations were dangerously encroaching on the living space of other species. It was also manifest in the ideas-centered work of Arné Naess and Lynn White, who like Muir and Leopold before them complained that most of their fellow humans sought to tame and dominate nature rather than understand or cherish her. Likewise, the traditions of scientific conservation were reinvigorated by the technocrats—as for instance the members of the Club of Rome—who sought to moderate world economic development toward a sustainable path, and by the more radical 'eco-socialists,' like Barry Commoner, who called for alternate, non-polluting technologies and welcomed greater state control over the processes of production. Least visible of the older trends was 'Back-to-the-Land,' for by the 1960s peasants were no longer around in most of Europe to be defended or identified with. Yet the voices of Ruskin and Carpenter do resonate with Schumacher's *Small is Beautiful*, and with the *Blueprint for Survival*, issued in 1972 by the London-based *Ecologist* magazine: both works that not so much defended nature as mounted a wholesale attack on the excesses of industrial civilization. 'The principal defect of the industrial way of life,' announced the authors of *Blueprint*, 'is that it is not sustainable. Its termination within the lifetime of someone born today is inevitable—unless it continues to be sustained for a while longer by an entrenched minority at the cost of imposing great suffering on the rest of mankind.'

These modern manifestations of older traditions disagreed bitterly amongst themselves, but they are to be collectively distinguished from their common enemy, the ruling ideology of the age of innocence. Thinkers of the latter persuasion turned on environmentalists of all stripes, calling them 'backward-looking reactionaries,' 'prophets of doom,' and worse. It was not unknown for an environmentalist to be termed a CIA plant behind the Iron Curtain and a KGB agent in the free world. Socialists accused greens of deviating attention from the class struggle, capitalists accused them of seeking to impede the working of the market. The counterattack was led by economists who believed that the market and technology would find substitutes for any resource that went short or for rivers that ran dry. Paul Samuelson of the Massachussets Institute of Technology, a future Nobel Prize winner, reacted sharply to the Club of Rome report, insisting that the 'wonders of the Industrial Revolution are not over.' Across the Atlantic, Wilfrid Beckerman of London University went so far as to predict that 'economic growth will continue uninterrupted for 2,500 years.'

Economists measure growth by aggregate statistical measures such as Gross National Product or Per Capita Income—numbers that often conceal a multitude of sins. Ecologists are more keenly interested in the components of growth, i.e. the technologies that produce goods, the processes by which these goods are consumed, the cumulative impact of production and consumption on the living systems of the earth. Their orientation made them less sanguine: where economists looked buoyantly forward to increases in GNP over the next thousand years, ecologists looked back critically at what had happened in the last twenty-five. And wherever they looked they saw or smelt danger, caused by the effluents of the dangerously novel technologies elaborated in the epoch of innocence. One such ecologist, Barry Commoner, wrote unambiguously that—

> It is economic motivation that has impelled the sweeping anti-ecological changes in the technology of production that have occurred since the Second World War. These changes have turned the nation's factories, farms, vehicles, and shops into seed-beds of pollution: nitrates from fertilizer; phosphates from detergents; toxic residues from pesticides; smog and carcinogenic exhaust from vehicles; the growing list of toxic chemicals and the mounds of undegradable plastic containers, wrappings, and geegaws from the petrochemical industry.

Here were listed some of the *effluents of affluence*, to use a term coined by the Spanish scholar Juan Martinez Alier. These effluents inspired the work of scientists such as Carson and Commoner, but they were also to generate a wider social response, an environmental *movement* in addition to an environmental *debate*.

THE ENVIRONMENTAL MOVEMENT: FROM IDEAS TO ACTIVISM

The University of Copenhagen, March 1969: a seminar on natural history is in progress, with some of Denmark's foremost scientists in attendance. A group of students enter the conference hall, lock the doors, and cut off the ventilation. Shouting slogans against pollution, they burn garbage they have brought with them, spray water from a polluted lake all over the participants, and hold aloft a duck doused with oil. 'Come and save it,' they scream at the scientists: 'You talk about pollution, why don't you do anything about it.' An hour of this hectoring and eerie symbolism elapses before the youths open the doors. But their protest is not finished: they drag the naturalists off to the next room. In this room was being held the founding meeting of NOAH, a body that would take Danish conservation beyond genteel discussion toward systematic social action.

This dramatic episode captures the distance between environmentalism's first wave and its second. Muir and Leopold, Marsh and Ruskin, were all 'activists' in their own way, yet their activism consisted for the most part in speaking and writing, in using the power of their words and the precision of their analyses to persuade others to join or follow them. Other conservationists worked closely with politicians and public officials, seeking to influence state policies toward forest protection or water management. Contemporary environmentalism has by no means eschewed these strategies of propaganda and advocacy, yet its potential has been greatly increased by its resort to more militant forms of action.

In this respect, of course, environmentalism has resembled other social movements of the late '60s and '70s. That was a time when the North Atlantic world was hit by a flurry of citizens' initiatives, exemplifying a new and participatory approach to politics. Willing on this process were several social movements that were to acquire distinct identities of their own: the feminist movement, the peace movement, the civil rights movement, and the environmental movement.

Environmentalism shared some tactics of protest with these other movements, but it was also to forge innovative methods of its own. Marches and processions in defense of the wild or in opposition to pollution were influenced by the civil rights struggle. The 'teach-in,' used to such good effect by the anti-war movement, was the model for a nation-wide effort, Earth Day, held on April 22, 1970, and described as 'the largest organized demonstration in human history.' In thousands of cities and towns spread across America, an estimated 20 million participants affirmed their commitment to a clean environment by planting trees, clearing up garbage, or silently protesting with placards outside polluting industries. Before and after Earth Day have occurred hundreds of more localized protests against more focused targets. Faced with a noxious chemical plant or an illegal toxic waste dump, with the coming in of chainsaws into their favorite forest or a dam being built on their favorite river, environmentalists took to the streets and increasingly to the courts to obtain redress. To 'Plant more Trees,' and 'Save the Grizzly' was added a more threatening slogan: 'Sue the Bastards.'

The Swedish sociologist Andrew Jamison has written of the new social movements that they were primarily the work of 'young people impatient with the political methods of their elders;' they represented, in effect, a 'revolt of the young.' With feminism and the peace movement, environmentalism was also driven by the energy and idealism of men and women in their twenties and thirties. But it did enjoy one clear advantage over the other movements: it was less divisive. Feminists would be accused of breaking up homes, civil rights workers of dividing black from white, peaceniks of ignoring the vital security interests of the nation. But in the U.S. at least, hundreds of thousands of citizens who suspiciously stayed away from those movements readily flocked to the green banner. When, after Earth Day 1970, the newsmagazine *Time* put Barry Commoner on its cover, it called him the 'Professor with a Class of Millions.' The mood of the times enabled scientists like Commoner and Ehrlich to command an

Chapter 5: The Ecology of Affluence

audience far greater than that of the university classroom. This wider support for environmenal concerns could lend itself to a cynical interpretation. Environmentalism, suggests the sociologist Denton E. Morrison, 'came as something of a relief to a movement-pummeled white, middle-class America and its representatives in the power structure. The environmental movement especially seemed to have potential for diverting the energies of a substantial proportion of young people away from more bothersome movements and into [groups] that seemed to stand for something close to Country, God, Motherhood and Apple Pie, and that, at worst, [was] clearly the safest movement in town.'

It is unquestionably true that of the 'new' social movements environmentalism alone has grown steadily in support and influence. Table I captures elements of this growth in statistical terms; it mentions but four conservation groups, but there are numerous others which have grown in membership strength in these past decades. An estimated 14 million Americans, or one in every seven adults, are members of one or other environmental organization. Likewise, in both Britain and Germany some 5 million people are now involved as citizens in environmental pressure groups. And in the Netherlands the foremost nature protection forum, the Vereniging tot Behoud van Natuurmonumented, has increased its membership from 235,000 to 700,000 between 1980 and 1992.

Table I

Membership of selected U.S. conservation organizations (in thousands)

Organization	1966	1970	1980	1985	1991
Sierra Club	39	113	165	350	650
Audobon Society	41*	120	400	450	600
Wilderness Society	27**	54	50	100	350
National Wildlife Federation	272	540	818	825	5600

* figure for 1962   ** figure for 1964

Sources: Stephen Fox, *The American Conservation Movement: John Muir and His Legacy* (1985); Kirkpatrick Sale, *Green Revolutions: the American Environmental Movement, 1962–92* (1993).

This impressively large constituency can hardly be explained by the theory that environmentalism represents a 'safety valve' to defuse more threatening forms of collective action. Rather, the expansion of the mass base of the environmental movement is more plausibly related to corresponding changes in economy and society. For as the affluent society grew more affluent still, its members yearned for more arresting goods to consume. By the mid-sixties, cars, refrigerators and washing-machines had become commonplace, but holidays in the wild were not. The shift to a five-day week meant that consumers had both money and the means to travel. They now wished to escape, if only for a weekend or two, from their everyday milleu of factory or farm, city or suburb. Nature, whether in the form of forests to walk through, beaches to swim from, or mountains to climb and recline upon, provided the perfect—since temporary—antidote to industrial civilization. In 1964 a German magazine captured these manifold attractions of nature to the city-dweller:

> Here in Nature's reposed and silent forest, where there are no rows of houses, no noise of motors, no advertising lights, no machines and bank books, here, where the day-in, day-out, nerve-deranging concatenation of all doing with money . . . lies far behind us, the deepest essence of man, his soul and his spirit steps into its own. This value is not to be measured by money, and moreover [it] is granted free, without price and service charge.
>
> [translated from the German by Raymond H. Dominick III]

This message had a captive audience; between 1957 and 1972 the proportion of Germans who took vacation trips of a week or more rose from 36 per cent to 53 per cent. Nor was Germany exceptional; in Sweden, the increase in free time meant that 'more Swedes wanted to hunt, fish, bird-watch and collect berries, mushrooms and wild flowers in the forest.' In a nation of only 8.5 million people, as many as 600,000 came to own country cottages. In their working life these Swedes were caught up in 'the landscape of industrial production,' ruled by 'rationality, calculation, profit and effectiveness,' escaping on holidays and weekends to 'another landscape of recreation, contemplation, and romance.' All over the industrial world, as the historian Samuel Hays points out, 'natural environments which formerly had been looked upon as "useless" waiting only to be developed, now came to be thought of as "useful" for filling human wants and needs. They played no less a significant role in the advanced consumer society than did such material goods as hi fi sets or indoor gardens.'

This last quote seems to point to an uncomfortable gap between

Chapter 5: The Ecology of Affluence

the environmental debate and the environmental movement. Scientists and ideologues were concerned with resource shortages and the disappearance of species. They were critical of the direction of economic growth and its impact on local, national or global ecosystems. Set against these prophets of doom was the growing popular interest in the wild and the beautiful, which not merely accepted the parameters of the affluent society but was wont to see nature itself as merely one more good to be 'consumed.' The uncertain commitment of most nature lovers to a more comprehensive environmental ideology is illustrated by the paradox that they were willing to drive thousands of miles, using up scarce oil and polluting the atmosphere, to visit national parks and sanctuaries; thus using anti-ecological means to marvel in the beauty of forests, swamps or mountains protected as specimens of a 'pristine' and 'untouched' nature.

The environmental groups fussed little about this gap betwen the prophets and the people. They were glad enough with the massive surge in their memberships, which gave them the finances and legitimacy to push for legislative and political change. In the '70s and '80s these groups moved from activism in the streets and courts toward a more accommodating incorporation in the structures of governance. Environmentalists began to rely heavily on the expertise of scientists and lawyers who could work with rather than work against industry and government. As legislation was drafted for protecting nature or controlling the effluents of affluence, these specialists collaborated with state officials in fixing the permissible standards for industrial emissions, and identified particular species and habitats for designation as 'protected' or 'endangered.' In preparing briefs for legislators and sending forth emissaries to sit on scientific committees, the environmental movement helped set up and (in time) staff government departments, most notably the Environmental Protection Agency, which with 18,000 employees is currently the largest civilian arm of the U.S. government.

The routinization and professionalization of the environmental movement has in recent years generated a counter-movement, a struggle to return environmentalism to its confrontational past. In the U.S. this radical reaction has been led by the group Earth First! The group's founder, Dave Foreman, remarked some years ago that 'too many environmentalists have grown to resemble bureaucrats—pale from too much indoor light; weak from sitting too long behind desks; co-opted by too many politicians.' Warning his colleagues against 'playing the games of political compromise the industrial power-brokers have designed for us,' Foreman thought the 'time has come to translate the non-violent methods of Gandhi and Martin Luther King to the environmental movement.' 'We must place our bodies,' he said, 'between the bulldozers and the rain-forest; stand as part of the wilderness in defense of herself; clog the gears of the polluting machine; and with courage oppose the destruction of life:' injunctions Foreman and his group have since carried out at different locations in the American West.

In Europe too, techniques of civil disobedience have come back into fashion among a section of environmentalists. An anti-road campaign in Britain, gathering momentum as I write, has protected old houses, forests and farms by blocking bulldozers and setting up protest camps. These militants seek to defend not an undisturbed wilderness but a composite rural culture remembered and honored in collective memory. But like Dave Foreman, anti-road protesters also acknowledge Gandhi to be a powerful influence—the 'fundamentals of his teachings form the backbone of my beliefs today,' to quote the British campaigner Chris Maile. Foreman and Maile are inspired by Gandhi, but we know that the Mahatma's strategies of civil disobedience were inspired in turn by an essay of Henry David Thoreau, and that his defense of the rural community drew abundantly on the works of John Ruskin and Edward Carpenter. The ideas and example of Gandhi have thus helped return these American and British radicals to their own half-forgotten traditions of dissent and moral authority: testimony, once more, to the global and cross-cultural character of the environmental movement.

RADICAL AMERICAN ENVIRONMENTALISM

In the lexicon of social movements, 'radical' is invariably opposed to 'reformist,' the latter standing for compromise and accommodation, the former for purity and militancy. The word is almost always used in self-definition by thinkers or activists who wish to distinguish themselves from trends they deride as less daring or more compromising than themselves.

In the context of American environmentalism, there are at least two legitimate claimants to the 'radical' label. The first is the strand in the wilderness movement known as 'Deep Ecology.' This dates its origins to an essay published in 1972 by the Norwegian Arné Naess, which called for environmentalists to embrace an ethic, termed *biospheric egalitarianism*, that would place humans on a more or less equal footing with other species. Biospheric egalitarianism would be a truly 'deep' ecology, in contrast to the 'shallow' ecology which

Chapter 5: The Ecology of Affluence

concerned itself merely with pollution or resource depletion without going to the deeper roots of the ecological crisis (see *box*). Recast in philosophical terms, this can be stated as the distinction between *anthropocentricism*, the belief that humans stand apart and above the rest of creation, and *biocentricism*, which rejects a human-centered perspective by looking at history from the perspective of other species and nature as a whole.

Naess' work has been controversial in his native Norway, where his campaign for the protection of wolves has angered farmers and his support for the ban on whaling alienated fisherfolk. Indeed, it

---

A PLATFORM FOR DEEP ECOLOGY

Arné Naess offers a set of eight principles for uniting deep ecologists: a platform first outlined by him in 1984 and revised several times since. This version is from 1993.

1. The flourishing of human and nonhuman living beings has intrinsic worth. The worth of nonhuman beings is independent of their usefulness for human purposes.
2. Richness and diversity of life forms on earth, including forms of human cultures, have intrinsic worth.
3. Humans have no right to reduce this richness and diversity, except to satisfy vital needs.
4. The flourishing of human life and cultures is compatible with a substantially smaller human population.
5. Present human interference with the nonhuman world is excessive, and the situation is worsening.
6. The foregoing points indicate that changes are necessary in the dominant way humans until now have behaved in their relation to the earth as a whole. The changes will, in a fundamental manner, affect political, social, technological, economic, and ideological structures.
7. The ideological change in the rich countries will mainly be that of increased appreciation of life quality rather than high material standard of living, in this way preparing [the way for] a global state of ecologically sustainable development.
8. Those who subscribe to the foregoing points have an obligation, directly or indirectly, to try to implement the necessary changes by nonviolent means.

Source: David Rothenberg, *Is it too Painful to Think? Conversations with Arné Naess* (Minneapolis: University of Minnesota Press, 1993), pp. 127–8.

might be said that the most faithful and energetic of his disciples are now to be found in and around the state of California. In the U.S., there already existed a tradition of reflection and activism in defense of the wilderness, a tradition that despite its submergence in the '40s and '50s was being discovered anew (see *box*). In 1967 Roderick Nash published his *Wilderness and the American Mind*, a book that re-presented the ideas of Muir and Leopold to a modern public. A steady stream of Muir biographies followed, and when Oxford University Press brought out a new edition of Leopold's *A Sand County Almanac* in 1973, it sold fifty times as many copies as had the original.

ON HOW THE FIRST WAVE OF WILDERNESS THINKING IS INTEGRATED WITH THE SECOND

A historical geographer's perceptive analysis of why Aldo Leopold's ideas resonate so deeply with the wilderness lovers of the present day:

Leopold's land ethic is immensely popular among purists because it successfully resolves four difficulties. First, the purist is encouraged to see himself as part of the advance guard for a higher level of civilization, which is a much more pleasant self-image than 'nature nut.' Second, Leopold's views on wilderness as a baseline fit very well with the axiom and corollaries of the wilderness ethic. Third, Leopold's fusion of the land ethic with the science of ecology lends the prestige of science to the purist's beliefs. Fourth and most important, geopietistic mystic experience gains a code of moral directives based on scientific fact ... Science is used to justify the purist's numinous experience and to interpret this experience as a useful, satisfying moral code.

Source: Linda H. Graber, *Wilderness as Sacred Space* (Washington, D.C.: The Association of American Geographers, 1976), p. 50.

Arné Naess' distinction between shallow and deep ecology fitted well with this rediscovery of John Muir and company. It seemed to give a firm philosophical basis to the belief, already widespread among wilderness lovers, that the presence of humans was always and invariably a threat to other species. Deep Ecology found adherents within the scholarly community, with fine-grained discussions of the anthropocentric/biocentric distinction appearing in the scholarly literature. A new and influential journal, *Environmental Ethics*, placed the debate squarely in the center of the academic discipline of philosophy. Beyond the university, Deep Ecology was enthusiastically taken up by activists disenchanted by the gentle lobbying

Chapter 5: The Ecology of Affluence

efforts of the Washington professionals. It influence is visible in the very title of Earth First!, the group that has most stridently captured this disaffection with incremental methods to protect nature. Elsewhere in the forests of North America, militant efforts to defend the wild have also been inspired by the tenets of Deep Ecology. One such place is the Canadian province of British Columbia where, as Catherine Caufield writes, radicals have

> blockaded logging roads with fallen trees, boulders and their own bodies; buried themselves up to their necks in the paths of advancing bulldozers, and suspended themselves from trees, dangling a hundred feet off the ground for days at a time. Less frequently, they have engaged in controversial acts of sabotage, ranging from pouring sugar into the gasoline tanks of logging trucks, to disabling bulldozers, to rendering trees worthless—and dangerous—for milling by driving six-inch-long iron spikes into them.

These actions are mandated by the ethic that the interests of nature are as important as the interests of humans: that to put yourself in the path of an advancing bulldozer is to invoke the most radical traditions of philosophical thought and environmental action. Deep Ecologists, whether within the academy or outside it, see themselves as the intellectual, spiritual and political vanguard of American environmentalism. But this self-definition has not gone uncontested. Its critics accuse it of misanthropy and of a peculiar blindness of its own, which ignores environmental degradation outside the wild and the human suffering that is its consequence. Deep Ecologists are charged, with some reason, for ignoring the problems of social inequality, both within the countries of the North and between the North and the South. Within the United States itself, the wilderness movement has scorned the city, which it sees as the source of all that is modern, industrial, man-made, and hence *un*natural. Indeed, as the sociologist Michael Meyerfeld Bell has pointed out, much of contemporary environmentalism derives from an 'ideology of urban abandonment and urban escape', resulting in a near-complete neglect of the ecological problems of city life. The critics of Deep Ecology draw attention to another and in their view more authentically radical strand, the *environmental justice* movement.

Where the nerve-centers of Deep Ecology are in the wild, environmental justice is firmly rooted in human habitations. The threats it fears are toxic waste dumps and landfills, the excretions of affluence that have to be disposed of somehow, and somewhere. An early and notorious case is of the unhappily named Love Canal in upstate

New York, the recipient of 43 million pounds of wastes produced by the firm of Hooker Chemicals.

Love Canal happens to pass through a white area, but other toxic waste sites have been overwhelmingly located in areas inhabited by minority communities. For example, more than 2 million tons of uranium tailings have been thrown onto Native American lands, in some cases causing rates of cancer twenty times the national average. Likewise, a study commissioned by the National Assocation for the Advancement of Colored Peoples estimates that almost 60 per cent of all African-Americans have been put at risk by hazardous waste dumps and landfills. The Alabama town of Emelle, whose population is four-fifths Black, receives wastes from all of forty-five states.

One of the first to blow the whistle on this process of effluent discrimination was the sociologist Robert Bullard. He found that in the city of Houston, where Whites comfortably outnumber Blacks, three out of four disposal sites had been placed in black neighborhoods. Bullard saw that 'the landfill question appears to have galvanized and politicized a part of the Houston community, the Black community, which for years had been inactive on environmental issues.' Indeed, movements of resistance to dangerous dump-sites have sprung up in numerous towns and counties across America. Lois Gibbs, who led the campaign to clean up Love Canal, helped set up a national co-ordinating body, the Citizens Clearinghouse for Hazardous Wastes (CCHW), which lists a staggering 4000 affiliated groups. Through demonstrations, press campaigns and lawsuits, these groups have worked to stop fresh sitings or have made industry and government accountable for the hazards posed by dumps that already exist.

These struggles are currently being chronicled by sociologists, but early reports from the battlefield all point to one striking feature: the leading role of women. The opposition to polluters has often been in the hands of housewives with no previous experience of social activism. Within the communities where wastes are being dumped, men are sometimes susceptible to blandishments of job or money, but women do not see the health of their children as a 'negotiable category.' A resister in southern Los Angeles explained her opposition to an incinerator thus: 'People's jobs were threatened, ministers were threatened, but, I said, "I'm not going to be intimidated." My child's health comes first; that's more important than a job.' Nor has this been purely a defensive operation; led by Lois Gibbs and the CCHW, the movement has also outlined, as alternatives to the production and dispersal of toxics, the 'four R's of recycling, reduction, reuse and reclamation.'

Chapter 5: The Ecology of Affluence   89

The struggles against hazardous wastes have contributed to a profound reorientation of American environmentalism. The political scientist Ken Geiser suggests that because the anti-toxics movement is 'so tightly rooted in the immediate experience of people's community and family life, it has an urgency and concreteness that is incredibly compelling.' The movement, he further notes, is composed largely of 'working-class and other lower-income people who would feel out of place at a meeting of a typical chapter of say, the Audobon Society or the Sierra Club.' For these 'new' environmentalists, the 'environment is not an abstract concept polluted and decreasing in beauty and scientific value. For many [of them] it is something which has already exposed them to hazards which are debilitating them and hastening their deaths.' Or, as an African-American activist more simply and sharply put it: 'The principle of social justice must be at the heart of any effort aimed at bringing Blacks into the mainstream of environmental organizations in the U. S. [We] must not misuse concern for endangered species as a way of diluting our responsibility to meet [the] basic need for human health care, food and shelter.'

THE GERMAN GREENS

Environmentalists of all kinds are now known as 'greens,' much as socialists of different tendencies were once known as 'reds.' The color has come to stand for nature, for life; its association with environmentalism so firmly rooted in the popular mind that in this book I have used it unselfconsciously and ubiquitously. Yet the usage is of surpisingly recent provenance. It dates to 1978, when a group of environmentalists taking part in local elections in Germany put forward candidates under the 'Green List,' *Grüne Liste Umweltschutz*. From that modest beginning arose a national party to which the label attached itself. It is this party and its later and conspicuous successes which have led to the identification of the color green with environmentalists in Germany, and everywhere else.

Formed in March 1979, the Green Party made a stunning entry into the Bundestag in the elections of 1983, the first new party to 'make it' to the German Parliament in sixty years. Its position was consolidated in the elections of 1987, and after a poor performance in the post-unification polls of 1990, in the 1994 elections as well. By this time Greens were also represented in most provincial parliaments, and even held office (in coalition with the social democratic party, the SPD) in one or two provinces. The German Greens offered a beacon for environmentalists in other European countries, who tried to form political parties of their own. It has been a hard act to follow, and although in Belgium, Italy and Sweden green parties have since entered Parliament, they have not had quite the same impact. In the history of modern environmentalism, the German Greens stand out for their political victories and for the moral challenge they offer to the governing beliefs of industrial civilization.

The origins of the Greens can be traced, at one remove, to the efflorescence all over the North Atlantic world of social movements in the 1960s. After the end of the Second World War the German people had turned inward, persuaded by the ruling Christian Democratic Union to forget their horrific immediate past and work collectively toward the good, i.e. affluent, society. Chancellors Konrad Adenauer and Ludwig Erhard ruled over a nationwide consensus to the effect that political stability would generate prosperity. In the late '60s, however, a militant student movement sprung up, which used the Vietnam war to mount a more general broadside against authority and the 'Establishment.' Simultaneous with the students' struggle were a series of citizens' actions, the so-called *Burger Initiativen* (BI), which for the first time in recent German history expressed an open skepticism of parties, politicians, and the state.

As in neighboring France and England, the protest of the students was at first captured in the number 1968, denoting a year, a mood, and a movement. The students' revolt played itself out in a while, but the BIs were rather more enduring. The Indian scholar Saral Sarkar, a longtime resident of Germany and a keen observer of its politics, suggests that the BIs passed through three distinct if chronologically overlapping phases. From 1969 to 1972 they operated mostly as 'one-point actions,' a multitude of local efforts to stop damaging industries, rehabilitate battered women and drug addicts, and construct playgrounds and schools without waiting for the government to do so. At this time the BIs took up a wide array of causes before finding 'its predominant theme in ecology.' This sharpening of focus was helped along by the formation, in Frankfurt in 1972, of a federal union of BIs, with more than a thousand registered groups and a membership of over 300,000 individuals.

The controversy over nuclear power emerged as central to this redefinition of a dispersed network of citizens' initiatives as the 'ecology movement.' Following the oil price hike of 1973, West Germany embarked upon an ambitious—but to many citizens reckless—expansion of its nuclear industry. New plants were feared for their contributions to pollution, for their links to the armaments industry, and

Chapter 5: The Ecology of Affluence

for the shroud of secrecy which surrounded them. Opposition to atomic energy as a 'sellout of the future' brought under one banner farmers whose lands and homes would have to make way for the new nuclear power plants with the educated middle-class of the cities, for whom this risky and potentially lethal technology became the 'very embodiment of socio-economic development gone wrong.' 'The fear of the people,' wrote a Hamburg correspondent in November 1973,

> is today ranged not only against the danger from nuclear power plants themselves, but primarily against the industrial concentrations which are necessarily connected with the massive energy production. . . . If the unrestrained industrial growth is not stopped, then in the course of the next few years we shall experience the destruction of our ecology and with it the poisoning of the water and air of Hamburg in an unprecedented and unimaginable scale. It would not suffice any more to see "environmental protection" in protests against carelessly thrown away banana skins.

As elsewhere, protesters against polluting industries took readily to the streets. The '70s in Germany were peppered with demonstrations and strikes against new nuclear plants and older chemical factories. Keeping pace with civil disobedience were the writings of intellectuals who promoted a society greener than the one they found themselves in. When the established political parties continued to keep their distance, environmentalists thought of directly representing themselves. From 1977 they began putting up candidates at local and municipal elections. These regional efforts crystallized in an 'alternative political alliance,' or what we now know as the Green Party.

In the new formation from the beginning was Petra Kelly, a young and highly personable woman of mixed German-American parentage. Kelly hoped the party would be 'a lobby for all those who have no lobby.' Others were more specific. The Green Member of Parliament Helmut Lippelt recalled the party as having

> attracted conservatives concerned about protection of the environment; Christians concerned about the destruction of creation; educated liberals who had learned about global ecology; technicians with knowledge of high-risk technologies; socialists concerned about the fallouts of capitalism; and, of course, the new Marxist-Leninists, waiting for the true-left party and examining whether perhaps they could educate *Die Grünen* to become just that party.

The journalist Werner Hülsberg provides another exhaustive listing, not necessarily incompatible with the first. The party drew into its fold, he writes, 'farmers whose existence was threatened, radical-democratic doctors, left-liberal school teachers, critical trade unionists, bored office workers, young people without any future, radicalized women, nature-lovers, freaked-out hippies, militant animal rightists and a whole host of mueslies (health-food addicts) . . .'

This mother-of-all-rainbow coalitions sent forth some of its members to the Bundestag in 1983, after the Greens had unexpectedly crossed the threshold 5 per cent of the popular vote which qualified them for representation. Their diversity marked them out from the dourly homogeneous parties which sat across them. The most charismatic of the Green MPs, Petra Kelly, thought this was their strength. 'The variety of currents enriches our party,' she remarked, for 'I don't want to exclude communists and conservatives, and I don't have to. One current learns from the other. There is no mutual destruction, but a convergence of views. That's what is new about our movement.'

These hopes were illusory, for a political party needs to be rather more single-minded than a social movement. When the party was faced with the prospect of forming provincial governments with the well-established SPD, the whiff of power brought to the fore an apparently irreconcilable opposition between two groups, dubbed in journalistic shorthand as the Fundis (fundamentalists) and the Realos (or realists). Where the Fundis rejected any thought of Green participation in government, seeing it as the final sell-out to the Establishment, the Realos believed they owed it to their voters to responsibly incorporate Green ideals in governance. The Fundis thought little of parliamentary work, preferring to canvass among local groups and the citizenry at large. The Realos on the other hand welcomed the attention paid by the media to their new and distinctive voice in parliament, and accordingly gave importance to televised speeches as well as to closed-door committee work. These differences in political tactics masked deeper ideological divisions too. Thus the Fundis were wholly opposed to the market, the epitome to them of greed and avarice; the Realos argued that since the market was here to stay the task was to tame and control it, not to turn one's back on it.

The Fundis were, and are, themselves of two kinds, each drawing on a rich historical tradition. On the one side were the socialists-turned-ecologists, colored reddish-green so to speak, contemporary carriers of the German brand of revolutionary communism once associated with such figures as Rosa Luxemburg and Karl Liebnecht. These eco-socialists rejected industrial capitalism but nourished the hope that a future socialist society would be more gentle on the environment (see *box*). On the other side were the agrarian romantics, colored deep green, who offered as their alternative to industrial society the decentralized rural utopia dreamt of by countless German poets down the centuries. But both types of Fundis stood, in the words of the philosopher Rudolf Bahro, for the 'radical reversal of

> ### SOME PRECONDITIONS FOR RESOLVING THE ECOLOGY CRISIS
>
> *In a talk at Freiburg in 1979, the philosopher Rudolf Bahro, an erstwhile East German dissident who became a leading member of the 'Fundi' faction of the West German Greens, outlined some pretty radical solutions to the ecology crisis. His list makes for an intriguing contrast with the principles outlined by Arné Naess, quoted earlier. While Naess lays more stress on ethical and value change, Bahro, and the German Greens generally, focus somewhat more on changes in existing patterns of production, consumption and distribution.*
>
> — The ecology crisis is insoluble unless we work at the same time at overcoming the confrontation of military blocs. It is insoluble without a resolute policy of detente and disarmament, one that renounces all demands for subverting other countries. . . .
>
> — The ecology crisis is insoluble without a new world order on the North-South axis. And we must realize that our entire standard of living [in the North] is largely based on the exploitation and suppression of the rest of humanity. . . .
>
> — The ecology crisis is insoluble without a decisive breakthrough towards social justice in our own country and without a swift equalisation of social differences throughout Western Europe. . . .
>
> — The ecology crisis is insoluble without progress in human emancipation here and now, even while capitalism still exists. It is insoluble without countless individuals managing to rise above their immediate and compensatory interests. . . .
>
> — If all this is brought to a common denominator, the conclusion is as follows: The ecology crisis is insoluble under capitalism. We have to get rid of the capitalist manner of regulating the economy, and above all of the capitalist driving mechanism, for a start at least bringing it under control. In other words, there is no solution to the ecology crisis without the combination of all anti-capitalist and socialist tendencies for a peaceful democratic revolution against the dominant economic structure. . . .
>
> Source: Rudolf Bahro, *Socialism and Survival* (London: Merlin Books, 1982), pp. 41–3.

the capitalist industrial system,' a perspective from which Green participation in government was merely to 'clean the dragon's teeth and freshen its breath.'

The Fundis gave powerful stimulus to the Green party in its early years, but over time they found themselves increasingly at odds with the rank-and-file. An estimated 80 per cent of Green voters wanted their party to work with the SPD in bringing about legislation to check pollution and moderate energy use. The Realos found their most effective spokesman in Joschka Fischer, Green Minister of Environment in Hesse between 1985 and 1987, a votary of 'qualitative growth' who sought to temper and redirect industrial society toward a greener path. 'I am no longer motivated by utopias,' remarked Fischer in 1985, 'but by the description of existing conditions. The ecological crisis, the arms race, the rise in criminality—those are more than enough for me. I am no missionary with a promise of a new tomorrow . . . If we can take one step in the right direction, one step which moves us away from the abyss, then that is sufficient justification for the existence of the [party].' The language, consciously or unconsciously, is reminiscent of Mahatma Gandhi's, likewise a politician who combined a utopian vision with shrewdly practical ends, who liked to speak of the 'beauty of compromise' and of 'taking one step at a time.'

At the time of writing the Realos reign triumphant, with Fischer himself being one of the best-known and popular German politicians. Knowledgeable analysts accurately predicted the prospect of a SPD–Green coalition capturing the Bundestag in the 1998 election, thus ending nearly twenty years of rule by the conservative Christian Democratic Union. Three Greens have joined the Cabinet, with Joschka Fischer appointed the new Foreign Minister of the most populous, most prosperous and most influential country in Europe. This surely marks the highest point of a journey already singular in the history of global environmentalism. But let me conclude this assessment by asking, first: Why did the Greens rise to prominence in Germany and nowhere else? And second, what in the ideas of the German Greens is of real and lasting significance?

Why is there no Green party in my country, the American reader will ask. In fact there is one, founded in Minneapolis in 1984, but with little to show in the thirteen years it has been around. One hurdle the American Green Party faces is the vibrant presence of apolitical environmental groups such as the Sierra Club and the Wilderness Society, who seem already to have captured the loyalty of the environmentalist constituency. Another is the entrenched two-party system, in which better equipped 'third' parties—the Socialists of Norman Thomas, the Progressives led by Henry Wallace, the Populists of George Wallace, and most recently Ross Perot's Reform Party—have failed to make a dent. The Federal Republic of Germany also has two dominant parties of its own—the CDU and the SPD—but smaller parties are given a decent chance by the system of proportional representation, through which a group commanding more than 5 per cent of the vote can enter Parliament. Proportional representation has allowed environmentalists to take the political route in Germany, an option foreclosed by the constituency-based system prevalent in countries such as the U.S. and the U.K.

To this political difference one must add a geographical one, viz. that West Germany was a front-line state in the Cold War. It faced the massed might of the Soviets across the Iron Curtain and was the unwilling home of thousands of NATO troops and their nuclear weapons. Germans were hence able to more starkly perceive the destructive power of industrial society—as compared, for instance, to isolated Canadians or insulated residents of the state of California—and to more readily embrace a caring attitude towards the earth. Not to be discounted either was the Nazi past, which has fostered a massive guilt complex among the ordinary and especially the educated German, an urgent and overpowering desire to atone for the crimes of a previous generation. This has unquestionably heightened their sense of responsibility to other cultures and later generations. Taking the idea of 'Limits to Growth' seriously, they have turned the searchlight inward, illuminating the ways in which their society sets an unworthy example to the rest of the world. 'The key to a sustainable development model worldwide,' writes Helmut Lippelt, 'is the question of whether West European societies really are able to reconstruct their industrial systems in order to permit an ecologically and socially viable way of production and consumption.' That Lippelt does not include the U.S. or Japan is noteworthy, an expression of his, and his movement's, willingness to take the burden upon themselves. West Europeans should reform themselves, rather than transfer their existing 'patterns of high production and high consumption to eastern Europe and the "Third World" [and thus] destroy the earth.'

For the German Greens, economic growth in Europe and North America has been made possible only through the economic and ecological exploitation of the Third World. Rudolf Bahro is characteristically blunt: 'the present way of life of the most industrially advanced nations,' he says, 'stands in a global and antagonistic contradiction to the natural conditions of human existence. We are eating up what other nations and future generations need to live on.' From this perspective, indeed—

> The working class here [in the North] is the richest lower class in the world. And if I look at the problem from the point of view of the whole of humanity, not just from that of Europe, then I must say that the metropolitan working class is the worst exploiting class in history... What made poverty bearable in eighteenth or nineteenth-century Europe was the prospect of escaping it through exploitation of the periphery. But this is no longer a possibility, and continued industrialism in the Third World will mean poverty for whole generations and hunger for millions.

Even the most hardheaded Realo acknowledges the unsustainability, on the global plane, of industrial society. Joschka Fischer, asked by a reporter where he planned to spend his old age, replied: 'In the Frankfurt cemetry, although by that time we may pose an environmental hazard with all the poisons, heavy metals and dioxin that we carry around in our bodies.' Or as a party document more matter-of-factly put it: 'The global spread of industrial economic policies and lifestyles is exhausting the basic ecological health of our planet faster than it can be replenished.' This global view, coupled with the stress on accountability, calls for 'far-reaching *voluntary* commitments to restraint by wealthy nations.' The industrialized countries, which consume three-fourths of the world's energy and resources, and who contribute the lion's share of 'climate-threatening gaseous emissions,' must curb their voracious appetite while allowing Southern nations to grow out of poverty. The Greens ask for the cancellation of all international debt, the banning of trade in products that destroy vulnerable ecosystems, and, most radical of all, for the freer migration of peoples from poor countries to rich ones.

Attentive to the rights of other nations and future generations, the Greens have also taken aboard the claims of the most disadvantaged section of their own society: women. By party mandate, fully 50 per cent of all officers and parliamentarians have to be women. During meetings and congresses, the roster alternates men and women speakers, rather than simply leave the floor open to those who are more aggressive or have louder voices (who would most likely be men). These policies had immediate results, with the number of women who voted for the Party increasing six-fold between 1980 and 1987. But Green feminism is not restricted to public fora: thus a 'Mothers' Manifesto' presented to the party has urged that the traditional concern with equal pay for equal work be enlarged to properly

Chapter 5: The Ecology of Affluence

compensate housewives who contribute, unpaid, roughly half of all social labor. It is these mothers, moreover, who have taken the lead in organizing 'ecologically responsible households.'

Their feminism in theory and in practice adds to the list of what marks the Greens out as the most daring political experiment of our times. When they appeared on the German stage a decade or more ago, the famously conservative prime minister of Bavaria, Franz-Josef Strauss, dismissed them as 'the Trojan horse of the Soviet cavalry.' But now even Strauss' CDU party has borrowed elements of the Green program, proof of the party's impact on the most recalcitrant of its opponents. For all their 'various shortcomings and difficulties,' notes the political scientist Margit Mayer, the Green Party has

> transformed the political landscape of Germany. What used to be considered nonconventional, marginal and utopian demands of the Greens in the '70s—such as demands to end nuclear energy, end linear economic growth, bring about unilateral disarmament, or proportional representation of women in all spheres—are now discussed and even demanded by other parties in the political mainstream.

Mayer writes only of the impact in Germany, but of course the party has attracted considerable attention and acclaim all over the globe. It might justly be regarded as the finest achievement of the second wave of environmentalism, referred to by the respectful capital that sets it apart from its peers and contemporaries: the Greens, as distinct from all other kinds of greens.

6

The Southern Challenge

There is a widespread belief that environmentalism is a phenomenon peculiar to the rich nations of the North, a product of the move toward 'postmaterialist' values among the populations of North America and Western Europe. In a series of books and essays published over the last twenty years, the political scientist Ronald Inglehart has argued that environmentalism is central to this shift 'from giving top priority to physical sustenance and safety toward heavier emphasis on belonging, self-expression, and the quality of life.' A corollary of this thesis is the claim that poor countries cannot possibly generate environmental movements of their own. Consider these statements by three senior, serious scholars:

> If you look at the countries that are interested in environmentalism, or at the individuals who support environmentalism within each country, one is struck by the extent to which environmentalism is an interest of the upper middle class. Poor countries and poor individuals simply aren't interested. (Lester Thurow, *The Zero-Sum Society*, 1980).

> It is no accident that the main support for ecological policies comes from the rich countries and from the comfortable rich and middle classes (except for businessmen, who hope to make money by polluting activity). The poor, multiplying and under-employed, wanted more 'development,' not less. (Eric Hobsbawm, *The Age of Extremes*, 1994).

> Only the maligned Western world has the money and the will to conserve its environment. It is the 'Northern White Empire's' last burden, and may be its last crusade. (Anna Bramwell, *The Fading of the Greens*, 1994).

Chapter 6: The Southern Challenge

From this point of view, the expression of environmentalism in countries not previously marked by it is a sign that these societies have finally arrived at the threshold of modernity and affluence. When protests against pollution broke out near Seoul in 1991, the respected British weekly, the *New Scientist*, announced that South Korea had at last 'woken up to the environment.' Likewise, the steady growth of an environmental constituency in Taiwan has been interpreted as a consequence of the clear triumph, within that island nation, of modernity over tradition. The Taiwanese, writes Stevan Harrell, had come to—

> value nature because the city is polluted and noisy, and because nature is more accessible than it was. They go on [excursions on] weekends because their time, as industrial citizens, is structured in regular blocks. . . . There is nothing particularly Chinese about any of this, nor is there anything particularly Western or Westernized. There is something peculiarly modern, the self-critique of the social formation that has allowed all this leisure and luxury.

By equating environmentalism exclusively with affluence, scholars seem to posit an evolutionary sequence—of poor societies becoming prosperous before they can find green movements in their midst. But as Steven Brechin and Willett Kempton note, 'the conventional wisdom—that the citizens of developing countries do not or cannot care about the environment—has been broadly accepted by Western publics and the diplomatic community, with theoretical backing from the postmaterialist thesis but *with little data from those developing countries.*'

The consensus that *Silent Spring* begat the modern environmental movement might be allowed to stand; but the consensus that the societies of the Third World are too poor to be green shall not go undisputed. By bringing in 'data from those developing countries,' this chapter suggests that there does in fact exist a vibrant and growing environmental constituency in societies such as Brazil, India and Thailand, countries far-flung and richly varied among themselves but united nonetheless by the poverty of the masses of their peoples.

THE ENVIRONMENTALISM OF THE POOR

Let me offer five examples of poor peoples' environmentalism, taken from five recognizably less-than-wealthy societies of the globe.

1. The Penan are a tiny community of hunters and farmers who live in the forests of the Malaysian state of Sarawak. They number

less than 7000 individuals, and do not generally seek the limelight. In the late '80s, however, they became major players in a major controversy. For their forest home had been steadily encroached upon by commercial loggers, whose felling activities had fouled their rivers, exposed their soils and destroyed plants and animals which they harvested for food. Beyond this material loss was a deeper loss of meaning, for the Penan have a strong cultural bond with their river and forest landscape. Helped by Bruno Manser, a Swiss artist who then lived with them, the tribe organized blockades and demonstrations to force the chainsaws and their operators back to where they came from. The Penan struggle was taken up and publicized by the respected Penang-based group, Sahabat Alam Malaysia, and by transnational forums such as Greenpeace and the Rainforest Action Network.

2. The Sardar Sarovar dam, being built on the Narmada river in central India, shall stand as a showpiece of Indian economic development. Four hundred and sixty feet high when completed, the dam will provide much-needed irrigation and electricity, but it shall also submerge historic old temples, rich deciduous forests, and at least 250 villages. These potential 'oustees' have come together under the banner of the Narmada Bachao Andolan (Save the Narmada Movement), which is led by a forty-year-old woman, Medha Patkar. In their bid to stop dam construction, Patkar and her colleagues have fasted outside provincial legislatures, camped outside the Indian prime minister's house in New Delhi, and walked through the Narmada valley to raise awareness of the predicament of the to-be-displaced villagers.

3. Pressed to earn foreign exchange, the state forest department of Thailand initiated, in the late '70s, the conversion of acres and acres of natural forests into monocultural plantations of eucalyptus. The department hopes to thus plant up 60,000 square kilometres by the year 2020, to provide eucalyptus chips for paper mills, mostly owned by Japanese companies. While bureaucrats in Bangkok contemplated a rising intake of yen, peasants in the forests began opposition to the plantations. They believed that their rice fields would be affected by the proximity of the water-guzzling and soil-depleting Australian tree; they also mourned the loss of the mixed forests from which they harvested fodder, fuel, fruit and medicines. Peasant protesters are mobilized by Buddhist priests, who lead delegations to public officials and also conduct 'ordination' ceremonies to prevent natural forests being turned into artificial ones.

4. On November 10, 1995, the military dictatorship of Nigeria hung nine dissenters, the most prominent of whom was the poet and

Chapter 6: The Southern Challenge

Medha Patkar, leader of the Narmada Bachao Andolan (Save Narmada Movement), addressing a public meeting in Mumbai in 1992.
SOURCE Frontline *magazine.*

playwright Ken Saro-Wiwa. Their crime had been to draw attention to the impact on their Ogoni tribe of oil drilling by the Anglo-Dutch conglomerate, Royal Shell. Shell had been drawing some 25,000 barrels a day from the Ogoni territories. The federal government benefited from oil exploration in the form of rising revenues, but the Ogoni lost a great deal. They remained without schools, or hospitals; thirty-five years of drilling had instead led to death and devastation: 'a blighted countryside, an atmosphere full of . . . carbon monoxide and hydrocarbon; a land in which wildlife is unknown; a land of polluted streams and creeks, a land which is, in every sense of the term, an ecological disaster.' The Movement for the Survival of the Ogoni People, founded by Saro-Wiwa in 1991, had intensified the public opposition to Shell and its military backers. The generals in Lagos responded with threats, intimidation, arrest, and finally by judicially murdering Saro-Wiwa and his colleagues.

5. My final illustration is one of environmental reconstruction rather than protest. This is Kenya's Green Belt Movement, founded by Waangari Matthai, an anatomist schooled at the University of Kansas who became her country's first woman professor. In 1977 Matthai threw up her university position to motivate other, less-privileged women to protect and improve their environment. Starting with a mere seven saplings planted on June 5, 1977 (World Environment Day), the movement had by 1992 distributed 7,000,000 saplings, planted and cared for by groups of village women spread over twenty-two districts of Kenya. The Green Belt Movement, writes the journalist Fred Pearce, has 'arguably done more to stall the expansion of deserts and the destruction of soils in Africa than its big brother international body down the road, the United Nations Environmental Program [also headquartered in Nairobi] with its grand but largely unsuccessful anti-desertification programs.'

The cases I have chosen are all moderately well known among the environmental community. Medha Patkar was honored with the prestigious Goldman award (endowed by California philanthropists); the Penan have had films about their plight broadcast on British and German television; Saro-Wiwa's death even made it to the front page of the staid *New York Times*. I could certainly have chosen better known examples of the environmentalism of the poor: indeed two such, possibly the most famous of all, are examined later in the chapter. But I could also have chosen lesser-known examples, which number in the hundreds in the countries of the South. These include other movements that oppose commercial logging and industrial monocultures while defending traditional community rights and natural

Chapter 6: The Southern Challenge 103

Waangari Matthai, founder of the Kenyan Green Belt Movement.
SOURCE Photo by Runar Malkenes, here taken from Fred Pearce, The Green Warriors *(The Bodley Head)*.

forests; other struggles of dam-displaced people who do not wish to make way for expensive and destructive 'mega-projects;' movements of peasants whose crops and pastureland have been destroyed by limestone mines or granite quarries; movements of artisanal fisherfolk directed at modern high-tech trawlers that destroy their livelihood even as they deplete fish stocks; and movements against paper factories by communities living downstream, for whom chemical effluents destroy the beauty of the river as well as their sole source of drinking water. To these struggles against environmental degradation one must add struggles for environmental renewal, the numerous and growing efforts by rural communities in Asia and Africa to better manage their forests, conserve their soil, sustainably harvest their water or use energy-saving devices like improved stoves and biogas plants.

'The environmentalism of the poor' is a convenient umbrella term that I shall use for these varied forms of social action. The Peruvian activist Hugo Blanco has evocatively distinguished this kind of environmentalism from its better known and more closely studied Northern counterpart. At first sight, writes Blanco,

> environmentalists or conservationists are nice, slightly crazy guys whose main purpose in life is to prevent the disappearance of blue whales or pandas. The common people have more important things to think about, for instance how to get their daily bread. Sometimes they are taken to be not so crazy but rather smart guys who, in the guise of protecting endangered species, have formed so-called NGOs to get juicy amounts of dollars from abroad . . . Such views are sometimes true. However, there are in Peru a very large number of people who are environmentalists. Of course, if I tell such people, you are ecologists, they might reply, 'ecologist your mother,' or words to that effect. Let us see, however. Isn't the village of Bambamarca truly environmentalist, which has time and again fought valiantly against the pollution of its water from mining? Are not the town of Ilo and the surrounding villages which are being polluted by the Southern Peru Copper Corporation truly environmentalist? Is not the village of Tambo Grande in Piura environmentalist when it rises like a closed fist and is ready to die in order to prevent stripmining in its valley? Also, the people of the Mantaro Valley who saw their little sheep die, because of the smoke and waste from La Oroya smelter. And the population of Amazonia, who are totally environmentalist, and die defending their forests against depredation. Also the poor people of Lima are environmentalists, when they complain against the pollution of water in the beaches.
>
> [translated from the Spanish by Juan Martinez Alier]

One can identify some half-a-dozen distinguishing features of the environmentalism of the poor. First and foremost, it combines a concern for the environment with an often more visible concern for social justice. Through much of the Third World, writes David Cleary, 'reality is a seamless web of social and environmental constraints which it makes little sense to atomise into mutually exclusive categories.' Commercial forestry, oil drilling, and large dams all damage the environment, but they also, and to their victims more painfully, constitute a threat to rural livelihoods: by depriving tribals of fuelwood and small game, by destroying the crops of farmers, or by submerging wholesale the lands and homes of villagers who have the misfortune to be placed in their path. The opposition to these interventions is thus as much a defense of livelihood as an 'environmental' movement in the narrow sense of the term. This inseparability of social and environmental concerns is beautifully captured in a petition of December 1990, addressed to the President of Mexico by a community of Nahuatl Indians who were asked to make way for the proposed San Juan dam on the Balsa river:

> Mr President., we publicly and collectively declare our rejection of the San Juan Telecingo Dam because we cannot allow this project to destroy the economy, the historical and cultural heritage, and the natural resources on which [we] depend . . . This project, by flooding our villages and our lands, would cause great losses and hardships to us in every way: we would lose our houses, churches, town halls, roads, irrigation systems and other collective works that we have undertaken with great sacrifice over many years. We would lose the best farmland that we live from; we would lose the pastures that support our livestock; we would lose our orchards and our fruit trees; we would lose the clay deposits and other raw materials we use for our crafts; we would lose our cemeteries where our dead are buried, our churches, and the caves, springs and other sacred places where we make our offerings; we would lose, among others, Teopantecuanitlan, a unique archeological site of great importance . . .; we would lose all the natural resources we know and use for our sustenance as taught to us by our ancestors. We would lose so many things that we cannot express them all here because we would never finish this document.
>
> [translated from the Spanish by Catherine Good]

The fact that environmental degradation often intensifies *economic* deprivation explains the moral urgency of these movements of protest. The anthropologist Peter Brosius has seen in the Penan struggle an 'unambiguous statement of the rightness of one's case;' but similarly convinced that right—though not necessarily might—is on their side are the rural communities who oppose eucalyptus plantations, polluting factories, or soil-exposing mines. There too, a longstanding, *prior* claim to the resource in question—land, water, forests, fish—has been abruptly extinguished by profiteers working in concert with government, which has granted these outsiders oil, mineral or logging concessions. There is then manifest a palpable sense of betrayal, a feeling that the government, *their* government, has let down the poor by taking the side of the rich. For the Penan, notes Brosius, government officials have become 'men who don't know how to pity . . .;' men 'unfeeling about creating such hardship and disregardful of their concerns.'

There is, however, at first the hope that the government will come to see the error of its ways. These struggles thus most often begin by addressing letters and petitions to persons of authority, themselves in a position to bring about remedial action. It is when these pleas are unanswered that protesters turn to more direct forms of confrontation. Unlike in the North, where electronic media and direct mailers are intelligently used to canvass support, the channels of communication in the South rely rather more heavily on 'traditional' networks such as village and tribe, lineage and caste. Once a sufficient number of like-minded people have been gathered together, there unfolds a richly varied repertoire of collective action. In a study of popular environmentalism in India, I was able to identify seven distinct forms of social protest. These were the *dharna* or sit-down strike; the *pradarshan* or massed procession; the *hartal* or general strike (forcing shops to down shutters); the *rasta roko* or transport blockade (by squatting on rail tracks or highways); the *bhook hartal* or hunger fast (conducted at a strategic site, say the office of the dam engineer; and generally by a recognized leader of the movement); the *gherao*, which is to surround an office or official for days on end; and the *jail bharo andolan* or movement to fill jails by the collective breach of a law considered unjust.

Most of these methods were perfected by Mahatma Gandhi in his battles with British colonialism, but of course they have ready equivalents in other peasant cultures. Larry Lohmann, writing of the opposition to eucalyptus in rural Thailand, remarks on how—

> Small-scale farmers are weathering the contempt of bureaucrats and petitioning district officials and cabinet ministers, standing up to assassination threats and arranging strategy meetings with villagers from other areas. They are holding rallies, speaking out at seminars, blocking roads, and marching on government offices, singing songs composed

for the occasion. Where other means fail and they are well enough organized, they are ripping out eucalyptus seedlings, either surreptitiously or openly in large mobs, chopping down eucalyptus trees, stopping bulldozers and burning nurseries and equipment. At the same time, well aware of the need to seize the environmentalist high ground, many villagers are planting fruit, rubber, and native forest trees to preempt or replace eucalyptus and are explaining to sympathetic journalists the methods they have used to preserve local forest patches for generations.

These protests, singly and collectively, are sometimes underwritten by a powerful indigenous ideology of social justice. Gandhi, for instance, has given Indian environmentalists their most favored techniques of protest as well as a moral vocabulary to oppose the destruction of the village economy by industrialization. Thai peasants, likewise, take recourse to the Buddha and Buddhism to remind their rulers, who publicly profess the same religion, that their policies are a clear violation of the creedal commitment to justice, moderation and harmony with nature. It is notable that the anti-eucalyptus struggle has been led by Buddhist priests, known appositely as *phra nakanuraksa*, or 'ecology monks.' In Latin America, the ideology most conveniently at hand is popular Catholicism and its contemporary variant, 'liberation theology,' which makes clear the mandate of the clergy, and of the church as a whole, to redirect its energies towards the poor. Thus the resisters to the San Juan dam asked parish priests to hold nightly prayer meetings, walked with images of village patron saints to the site of the dam, and also marched to the cathedral in Mexico City in honor of the hallowed Virgin of Guadalupe.

One striking feature of the environmentalism of the poor has been the significant and sometimes determining part played by women. Women have effortlessly assumed leadership roles—as with Medha Patkar or Waangari Matthai, for example—and also contributed more than their fair share to making up the numbers in marches and demonstrations, strikes and fasts. They have been unafraid, in an often brutal political culture, of being harrassed, beaten or jailed. When a Venezuelan feminist writes that in her country 'today all women's groups are environmentalist regardless of whether they know what the environment means,' she could be speaking for women in India or Malaysia, Brazil, Kenya and Mexico.

Among women in the countryside, certainly, there is often a deep awareness of the dependence of human society on a clean and bountiful environment. A tribal woman in the Bastar district of central India, herself active in a forest protection campaign, puts it this way:

'What will happen if there are no forests? *Bhagwan Mahaprabhu* [God] and *Dharti Maata* [Mother Earth] will leave our side, they will leave us and we will die. It is because the earth exists that we are sitting here and talking.' Inspired by such remarks, some feminist scholars posit a near-mystical bond between women and nature, an intrinsic and proto-biological rapport which in their view is denied to men. Other feminists have argued, in my view more plausibly, that the participation of women in environmental movements stems from their closer day-to-day involvement in the use of nature, and additionally from their greater awareness and respect for community cohesion and solidarity. In the divison of labor typical of most peasant, tribal and pastoralist households, it falls on women (and children) to gather fuelwood, collect water, and harvest edible plants. They are thus more easily able to perceive, and more quickly respond to, the drying up of springs or the disappearance of forests. But it is also the case that women, more than men, are inclined to the long view, to sense, for example, that eucalyptus planted for industry might bring in some quick cash today but will undermine their economic security for tommorow and the day after (see *box*).

A GRASSROOTS 'ECO-FEMINISM'

The response of women in an Andean village to a proposal by male officials to plant eucalyptus:

in the community of Tapuc ... women vehemently said in Quechua that the transplanted eucalyptus in the parcels of *manay* must be immediately removed. *Manay* is an agricultural zone dedicated to the cultivation of root crops, in turns dictated by the system of sectoral flows, with years of rest in between. The community and individuals of the community exercise control together over the *manay*. Thus, the women, speaking for the community, insisted that these parcels had been inherited from their grandparents to supply root crops, they were not going to feed their children with the eucalyptus leaves. Moreover, where the eucalyptus grows, the soil is impoverished and it does not even grow onions.

Source: Enrique Mayer and Cesar Fonseca, *Comunidad y Produccion en el Peru* (Lima 1988), p. 187 (translated by Juan Martinez Alier).

AN INDIA/BRAZIL COMPARISON

I move on now to a comparison of the environmental movement as it has unfolded in two large, complex and vitally important Third World countries. Brazil and India have much in common: their sheer size in

Chapter 6: The Southern Challenge

geographical and demographic terms; the cultural diversity of their societies; the deep disparities between rich and poor; the history of ambitious and aggressive programs of state-sponsored industrialization; the appalling ecological and social costs of these programs; and last, the emergence of active environmental constituencies which have challenged the prevailing consensus on what constitutes proper development.

After World War II, politicians in both Brazil and India were in the vanguard of the movement among the poorer nations of the globe that sought to accomplish in a generation what had taken the affluent West centuries to achieve. The intelligentsia—scientists, technologists, civil servants, legislators—manifested an enormous sense of self-importance, viewing themselves as a chosen elite, leading their people out of darkness into light, or from disease-ridden poverty to prosperity. Pride of place was given to mammoth and pharaonic projects—steel mills, big dams, nuclear power plants and the like—which, it was hoped, would generate wealth and instil a sense of pride and self-worth among the public at large. These projects had their costs—thousands of people displaced, millions of hectares of forests felled and dozens of rivers fouled—but they were at first insulated from criticism by the prestige they enjoyed, the promise they held, and above all by the fact that they were initiated by a government which enjoyed a fair degree of popular support. Projects were legitimated by the ideal of national 'sacrifice:' when tribals had to hand over their forest to a paper mill, for example, or when peasants had to flee from the rising waters of a reservoir designed to inundate their lands, they were offered the solace that this often unwilling sacrifice of their livelihood was being made for the greater good of the nation, or more precisely for the happy augmentation of its Gross National Product.

In both the Brazilian and Indian models of development, the public sector was mandated to control the 'commanding heights' of the economy, with private capitalists assigned an important subsidiary role in generating wealth. Both public and private firms were, however, allowed the virtually free use of nature and natural resources: the state providing them timber, water, minerals, electricity, etc. at well below market prices, and also granting them what was, in effect, the right to freely pollute the air and the waters.

In Brazil the process of industrialization was perhaps more callous than in India. For one thing, the youthfulness of the national culture and the existence of an 'untapped frontier' in the form of the Amazon basin prompted a greater optimism about development and an acceleration of the pace at which it was to be carried out. For another, the country lacked a tradition of dissent such as Gandhism, which in India provided a cautionary voice to temper the impatience of the planners and developers, forcing them to make haste slowly and to take more account of the human costs involved. A vibrant multi-party system and multi-lingual press also gave freer play in India to a variety of voices. In Brazil, by contrast, an already fragile polity was captured in 1964 by a military dictatorship that simply wouldn't tolerate opposition to the highways it built or the licenses it gave on generous terms to industrial firms.

By the late sixties, however, the failures of state-sponsored industrialization lay exposed in both countries. Poverty refused to go away, the fruits of development, such as they were, being garnered by a minority of affluent urbanites and rural landlords. The latter drove cars, watched television, and used refrigerators like their Northern counterparts, while the majority of their countrymen and women continued to live in huts and shanty towns, cooking their meals with fuelwood or kerosene and relying on their own two feet for locomotion. At the same time, nature lay embattled and scarred, subject to levels of environmental degradation that were, in a word, horrific. The social and ecological costs are summed up in the following quotes, both pertaining to Brazil, but both equally true of India. First, some remarks of the sociologist Peter Berger, from his 1974 book *Pyramids of Sacrifice*:

> The overall picture that emerges is that of two nations, one relatively affluent, the other in various degrees of misery. Such a state of affairs, of course, exists in many countries of the Third World. The sheer size of Brazil, however, with its enormous territory and its population of about one hundred million, makes for a particular situation. Using reasonable criteria of differentiation, one may divide this population into about fifteen million in the sector of affluence and eighty-five million in the sector of misery. To see the economic import of these figures, one must focus on the fact that fifteen million is a very large number of people—indeed, it is the population of quite a few important countries with advanced industrial economies. As one commentator put it, Brazil is a Sweden superimposed upon an Indonesia.... In this way, the very size of Brazil contributes an additional dimension to the process of polarization. It also contributes a seeming plausibility to the rhetoric of the regime. With a little luck, a visitor may travel all over the country and see nothing but 'Sweden,' with some bits of 'Indonesia' either being absorbed into the former or serving as a colorful backdrop for it.
>
> This is the dry stuff of economics. Behind it lies a world of human pain. For a very large segment of the population, life continues to be a

Chapter 6: The Southern Challenge

grim struggle for physical survival . . . Millions of people in Brazil are severely undernourished, and some are literally starving to death. Millions of people in Brazil are afflicted with diseases directly related to malnutrition and lack of elementary public hygiene . . . It is on these realities that one must focus in relation to the economic data on unemployment, income distribution, and so on. The crucial fact is: These are realities that kill human beings.

Berger wrote at a time when environmental awareness was not a hallmark of the discipline of sociology; thus his diagnosis, accurate on its own terms, should be supplemented by these later observations of the ecologist Eduardo Viola:

> Uncontrolled exploitation of the forests and irrational monoculture are transforming important areas of the south, southeast, centre-west and Amazonic region into deserts . . . The debris of industrial production, the residues of toxics used in agriculture and the sewage dumped directly into rivers, have seriously endangered water resources. The quality of public water supplies consumed in the greater part of Brazil is dreadful when measured against internationally accepted standards. Industrial gases . . . have turned the atmosphere of Brazilian industrial cities into multipliers and generators of respiratory diseases. Cars produced in Brazil, with the exception of those made for export, are not installed with antipollution devices . . . On top of this, the general absence of sewers and inadequate treatment of refuse (aided and abetted by irresponsible sectors of the population who throw their rubbish anywhere, and also by public departments who rarely make provision for means of proper disposal and processing) transform cities into true 'minefields' from the point of public health. . . . Finally, to crown socioenvironmental degradation, the production of arms takes up a significant part of the industrial and scientific-technological effort of the country, making Brazil the fifth exporter of arms in the world league.

That ungainly term, socioenvironmental degradation, emphasizes how this litany of natural abuse, which could have come straight out of an Indian environmentalist tract, is as much a human as an 'ecological' disaster. The felling of forests destroys soils and biodiversity, but also throws gatherers and collectors out of work. Toxics kill fish and radically alter the p.h. count of rivers, but simultaneously expose communities to health hazards by contaminating their sole source of drinking water. Car emissions help make Sao Paulo and New Delhi among the ten most polluted cities in the world, but also further debilitate the ill-nourished among urban dwellers. However, this process operates differentially among social classes, for the rich are better insulated from the environmental degradation they cause, enjoy easier access to clean air and water, and can more easily move away from or withstand pollution.

At the first major United Nations environmental conference held in Stockholm in 1972, the governments of India and Brazil were vocal in their defense of development over environment. The Indian prime minister, Mrs Indira Gandhi, delivered a stirring speech to the effect that if pollution was the price of progress, her people wanted more of it; the Brazilian representatives hinted, in the same vein, at the conference being a sinister conspiracy to prevent the developing world from developing further. Whether these official voices accurately represented the views of citizens was already a moot question. A year before Stockholm, a group of professionals led by the respected agronomist José Lutzemberger had founded the Gaucho Association for the Protection of the Natural Environment, or AGAPAN. This is generally held to be the first important environmental initiative in Brazil, the direct analogue of India's Chipko or hug-the-tree movement, which began a year after that first U.N. conference.

In the decades since the founding of AGAPAN and Chipko, environmentalism in both nations has emerged as a genuinely popular movement, country-wide in its reach, and taking up a range of ecological and social concerns. Environmental struggles in Brazil and India have revolved around a shared set of issues: forests, dams, pollution, biodiversity. This is no 'elitist' environmentalism but a movement that has taken into its fold communities at the bottom of the heap. In Brazil the environmentalism of the poor emanates from urban squatters and indigenous people responding to swift and dramatic degradation (such as pollution and the burning of forests), whereas in India it has been the preserve of long-settled rural communities—farmers, fisherfolk, pastoralists, and swidden cultivators—responding to the takeover by the state or by private companies of the common property resources they depend on (see *box*). In both countries protesters have tended to take the militant route, preferring methods of direct action to the patient petitioning of government officials and the judiciary. Brazilian and Indian greens have both been supported by sympathetic coverage in the media. The movements are also united in what they neglect: most strikingly, the role of population growth in fuelling environmental degradation. Catholics in Brazil are temperamentally disinclined to talk of birth control; Gandhians in India dismiss talk of 'over-population' as 'Neo-Malthusianism;' both groups train their guns on social inequities, in their view more centrally responsible for the deterioration of the environment.

RENEWING THE LAND, AND THE PEOPLE TOO

In 1985 sixty scholars, journalists and social workers issued a 'Statement of Shared Concern on the State of India's Environment.' Excerpts:

The process of transforming India into a wasteland, which began under the British rule, has continued under post-independence governments. The most brutal assault has been on the country's common property resources, on its grazing lands, forests, rivers, ponds, lakes, coastal zones and increasingly on the atmosphere. The use of these common property resources has been organised and encouraged by the state in a manner that has led to their relentless degradation and destruction....

Nature can never be managed well unless the people closest to it are involved in its management.... Common natural resources were earlier regulated through diverse, decentralized, community control systems. But the state's policy of converting common property resources into government property resources has put them under the control of centralized bureaucracies, who in turn had put them at the service of the more powerful. Today, with no participation of the common people in the management of local resources, even the poor have become so marginalised and alienated from their environment that they are ready to discount their future and sell away the remaining natural resources for a pittance.

Indian villages have traditionally been integrated agrosylvopastoral entities, with grazing lands, agricultural fields, forests and groves, and water sources like ponds, wells and tanks. The state's development programmes have torn asunder this integrated character of the villages....

The process of state control over natural resources that started with the period of colonialism must be rolled back. The earlier community control systems ... were often unjust and needed restructuring. Given the changed socio-economic circumstances and greater pressure on natural resources, new community control systems have to be established that are more highly integrated, scientifically sophisticated, equitable and sustainable. This is the biggest challenge before India's political system—not just the politicians and their parties, but also citizens and social activists.... India can beat the problem of poverty, unemployment, drudgery and oppression only if the country learns to manage its natural resource base in an equitable and ecologically sound way....

Source: *India: the State of the Environment 1984–85: the Second Citizens' Report* (New Delhi: Centre for Science and Environment, 1985), pp. 394–7.

Brazil differs from India in at least three major ways, all of which are reflected in the manner in which its environmental movement has at times followed a somewhat divergent path. First, a much higher proportion of its population is based in the cities, where the living conditions—that is, the quality of housing, water, air, and sanitation—vary enormously from locality to locality. The struggle for a better environment in the shanty-towns of Sao Paulo, Rio and the like has been an important feature of the Brazilian green movement. But India is in demographic and cultural terms a more rural-oriented culture. It was Mahatma Gandhi who famously remarked that 'India lives in its villages.' Since most of his followers have followed him in turning their backs to the city, the problems of urban pollution and housing remain low on the environmental agenda. Indian greens have been more comfortable in the forest and countryside, working with peasants plagued by waterlogged soils or with tribals thrown out of their ancestral forest.

A second difference stems from the higher levels of literacy and education in Brazil. In the early seventies, while the military was still in power, the educated middle-class—scientists, lawyers, journalists, etc.—cautiously began advancing an environmental agenda, at first taking up relatively uncontentious issues such as pollution and the protection of green areas. The organization AGAPAN was in the forefront here; it was only with the withdrawal of the military in the late '80s that greens began to more directly challenge the 'system.' In India, on the other hand, environmentalism drew abudantly on traditions of peasant protest; in fact, it was these protests which first alerted the intelligentsia to the problems of forest loss, soil erosion and water depletion. One might say that in India the professional middle-class has been *reactive*, responding slowly and at times unwillingly to the environmentalism of peasants and tribals; whereas in Brazil it has been *proactive*, well-placed to collaborate with and publicize movements of the urban poor as well as of forest-dwellers and dam-displaced people.

Finally, it seems that Brazilian environmentalism has been more deeply influenced by Northern debates. While *Silent Spring* was translated into Portuguese the year it was first printed in English, trans-national bodies such as the International Union for the Conservation of Nature and Natural Resources have also had active and influential Brazilian chapters. American environmentalists, and to some extent the American public as well, have closely followed Brazilian developments and at times tried to influence them. Ecologically speaking, the destruction of the great Amazonian rainforest by settler agriculture and industrial mining has direct implications for life in the

Chapter 6: The Southern Challenge

North—through the loss of biodiversity and a sink to absorb carbon emissions—while, on the social side, the plight of indigenous people has played powerfully on the conscience of those whose forefathers ages ago decimated the native inhabitants of North America. Brazilian environmental problems thus have a high international visibility; further encouraged by the proximity—cultural, political and geographical—of the country to the United States of America.

In India, by contrast, neither Northern green classics nor Northern green bodies have had much of a presence. Again, the repercussions of environmental degradation—grave as they are—are contained largely within India, as are the agents of degradation, who are overwhelmingly government departments and private capitalists. In Brazil, however, both foreign firms and foreign aid agencies such as the World Bank have had a determining influence on the process of development through destruction.

These distinctions matter, but in the final reckoning it is the elements common to Brazil and Indian environmentalism that might matter more. In both countries the environmental movement has centrally contributed to a deepening of democracy, working toward a greater openness of decision making and a greater accountability for decision-makers. As José Lutzemberger put it in 1978, 'The citizen is realizing that he needs to participate in politics because if not the bureaucrats [and, I would add, the politicians] will steamroll right over him. He needs to participate to know what is happening and he needs to shout, even if it is in vain.' In both countries the environmental movement has moved beyond a concern with 'quality of life issues' to more directly challenging the official version of what constitutes welfare and prosperity. The politicians still urge citizens to make the necessary sacrifices for 'development;' the greens expose these claims for what they are, that is, as contributing to the persistence of social strife and ecological deterioration. Brazilian greens characterize development as it has unfolded in their country as 'predatory development;' their Indian counterparts replace 'predatory' with 'destructive,' but the meaning remains much the same.

A CHIPKO/CHICO COMPARISON

On March 27, 1973, in a remote Himalayan village high up in the upper Gangetic valley, a group of peasants stopped a group of loggers from felling a stand of hornbeam trees. The trees stood on land owned by the state forest department, which had auctioned them to a sports-goods company in distant Allahabad, on whose behalf the loggers had come. The peasants of Mandal—the name of the village which adjoined the forest patch—prevented felling by threatening to hug or 'stick' to (*Chipko*) the trees. The Mandal episode sparked a series of similar protests through the '70s, a dozen or more episodes whereby hill peasants stopped contractors from felling trees for external markets. These protests collectively constitute the Chipko movement, recognized as one of the most famous environmental initiatives of our times.

Chipko was representative of a wide spectrum of natural-resource conflicts that erupted in different parts of India in the 1970s and 1980s: conflicts over access to forests, fish and grazing resources; conflicts over the effects of industrial pollution and mining; and conflicts over the siting of large dams. One can understand each of these conflicts sequentially, as an unfolding of the processes of *Degradation—Shortages—Protest—Controversy (local)—Controversy (national)*. Applying this scheme to Chipko, for instance, we note that deforestation in the hills led on the one hand to shortages of fuel, fodder and small timber for local communities and on the other to shortages of raw material for wood-based industry (with Himalayan timber being especially prized as the only source of softwood in India). When the state inclined markedly in favor of one party to the conflict, namely industry, the other party, i.e. peasants, responded through collective action. Picked up by a press that is amongst the most voluble in the world, the protests then gave shape to a debate on how best the Himalayan forests should be managed—by communities, the state, or private capital; on what species should be planted and protected—conifers, broad-leaved, or exotics; and on what should constitute the forest's primary product—wood for industry, biomass for villagers, or soil, water and clean air for the community at large. Finally, this region-specific debate led in turn to a national debate on the direction of forest policy in the country as a whole.

Within India there have been numerous little Chipkos, so to speak, but in the broader global context this movement of Himalayan peasants is best compared to the campaign in the Brazilian Amazon associated with the name of Francisco 'Chico' Mendes. Chico Mendes was a labor organizer who achieved international fame for promoting the 'ecology of justice' in a region devastated by reckless economic exploitation. In the Amazon, a massive expansion of the road network—with some 8000 miles built between 1960 and 1984—opened the way for settlers from the south in search of quick fortunes. Roads brought in colonists and took away the timber of mahogany, rosewood, and other valuable trees. In thirty years almost 10 per cent of the territory, a staggering 60 million hectares of forest, or an area larger than France, had been logged or burnt over. An estimated 85 per cent of this had been converted into pastures for livestock; a most inappropriate form of land use on poor soils that were to be exposed and further impoverished by the next downpour of rain. All in all, this has been a colossal ecological disaster: in the words of one Brazilian scholar, 'the burning of the Amazonian forests represents the most intensive destruction of biomass in world history.'

Among the human communities affected by this devastation were collectors and harvesters of forest produce such as rubber, Brazil nuts, and the babasso palm. Unfortunately, these people often did not have firm legal titles to the land and forests they worked, whereas the ranchers and loggers had on their side the powers of a government determined to exploit and rapidly 'develop' the region. When the forests were taken over by ranchers—sometimes at gun-point—they lost their lands as well as their livelihoods. In the province of Acre, for example, ranchers bought 6 million hectares between 1970 and 1975, in the process displacing more than 10,000 rubber tappers. Aided by men such as Mendes, the tappers resorted to their own innovative form of protest: the *empaté* or stand-off. Men, women and children marched to the forest, joined hands, and dared the workers and their chain-saws from proceeding further. The first *empaté* took place on March 10, 1976—three years after the first Chipko protest. Over the next decade, a series of stand-offs helped save two million acres of forest from conversion into pastureland.

From the mid 1970s the rubber tappers have had a vigorous union of their own, and in 1987 they joined hands with the indigenous inhabitants of the Amazon to form a Forest Peoples' Alliance (see *box*). This alliance pledged to defend the forest and land rights of its members. It also worked for the creation of 'extractive reserves,' areas protected from the chain-saw where rubber tappers and others could sustainably harvest what they needed without affecting the forest's capacity for regenerating itself. But as the rubber tappers became more organized, 'the ranchers became more determined in their efforts to drive them off the land,' forming a coalition of their own, the Uniao Democratica Rural. In a region already scarred by high levels of violence, the conflict escalated in tragic ways. In 1980 ranchers and their agents had assassinated Wilson Pinheiro, a prominent union organizer. Eight years later, on December 22, 1988, they finally eliminated Chico Mendes, shot dead as he came out of his house.

There are striking similarities between the Chipko movement and the struggle of Chico Mendes and his associates. Both drew on a long history of peasant resistance to the state and outsiders: in the Himalayan case, stretching back a hundred years and more. Both thought up novel and nonviolent forms of protest to stop tree-felling; protest forms in which women constituted the front-line of defense, a tactical move that worked well in inhibiting loggers. In each case the leadership was provided not by city-bred or educated activists but by 'organic' intellectuals from *within* the community. Neither struggle was merely content with asking the loggers to go home: the Forest Peoples Alliance proposed sustainable reserves, whereas Chipko workers have successfully mobilized peasant women in protecting and replenishing their village forests. Both movements have

---

AMAZONIAN VOICES

In its second national meeting, held in 1989, the Rubber Tappers Council of Brazil offered its 'homage to all those in the struggle who gave their lives for the principles affirming our regional cultures. Especially we remember our most illustrious comrade Chico Mendes.' The Council then resolved to struggle for the following program:

POLICIES FOR DEVELOPMENT FOR FOREST PEOPLES

1. Models of development that respect the way of life, cultures and traditions of forest peoples without destroying nature, and that improve the quality of life.

2. The right to participate in the process of public discussion of all the government projects for forests inhabited by Indians and rubber tappers as well as other extractive populations, through the associations and entities that represent these workers.

3. Public guarantees to scrutinize and curb the disastrous impacts of projects already destined for Amazonia, and the immediate halt of projects that damage the environment and Amazonian peoples.

4. Information on policies and projects for Amazonia and any large projects to be subject to discussion in Congress, with the participation of the organizations that represent those people affected by these projects.

Based on these principles, the Council also outlined specific programs for agrarian reform, education and health, credit and marketing, and the protection of human rights.

Source: Susanna Hecht and Alexander Cockburn, *The Fate of the Forest: Developers, Destroyers and Defenders of the Amazon* (London: Penguin, 1990), Appendix E.

Chapter 6: The Southern Challenge

taken recourse to an ideology that carries wide appeal in their societies. The two best-known Chipko leaders, Chandiprasad Bhatt and Sunderlal Bahuguna, are lifelong Gandhians. Likewise, Catholic priests have supported the rubber-tappers; and as Chico Mendes recalled, when arrested after an *empaté* protesters would sing hymns en route to the police lock-up.

The Chipko movement and Chico Mendes's struggle are broadly comparable but not, of course, identical. While Himalayan deforestation has had disturbing ecological effects—in the shape of increased soil erosion and the incidence of floods—the clearing of the Amazon represents a much more serious loss of biodiversity, through the extinction of hundreds of species of insects, plants, birds and animals. (This is one reason why the Brazilian movement has attracted greater, and continuing, international attention than did Chipko). On the social side, forest conflicts in the Amazon have been characterized by a much higher level of violence. The traditions of democracy are rather less robust in Brazil than in India, and the expression of protest and dissent more likely there to be met with force. It is significant that while we tend to honor the Chipko movement for its *nonviolent* technique of protest, the Amazon struggle is more often remembered, at least outside Brazil, for the *violent* death of its leader.

One must note, finally, the prolific misrepresentations of both movements by the international media. The Amazon struggle is often reduced to the image of Chico Mendes as a 'green martyr' who died trying to 'save the Amazon' from its destroyers. Likewise, the most popular image of Chipko is of unlettered women 'saving the Himalaya' by threatening to hug the trees. There has arisen a mystique around Chipko and Chico that unfortunately obscures their real and deeper meaning, as struggles in which environmental protection has been inseparable from social justice.

REDEFINING DEVELOPMENT

Feeding on indigenous ideologies of justice—Gandhism, Buddhism or Catholicism—and emboldened by a more general assertion of 'ecofeminism,' the environmentalism of the poor has contributed to a profound rethinking of the idea of development itself. Intellectuals sympathetic to these movements have fashioned a critique of the industrial and urban bias of government policies, urging that it give way to a decentralized, socially aware, environmentally friendly and altogether more *gentle* form of development. These efforts have sometimes drawn explicitly on the ideas of the early environmentalists

Poster of Chico Mendes, leader of the Brazilian rubber-tappers, issued after the assassination of Mendes in December 1988.

SOURCE Susanna Hecht and Alexander Cockburn, The Fate of the Forest (Verso Books)

Chapter 6: The Southern Challenge   121

Poster of April 1989, demanding action against Mendes' alleged killers.
SOURCE Susanna Hecht and Alexander Cockburn, The Fate of the Forest (Verso Books)

discussed in Chapter II. But they have also been enriched by more contemporary thinking in ecology and the social sciences. Development as conventionally understood and practised has been attacked on a philosophical plane, but critics have been forthcoming with nose-to-the ground, sector-specific solutions as well. In the realm of water management, they have offered to large dams the alternative of small dams and/or the revival of traditional methods of irrigation such as tanks and wells. In the realm of forestry, they have asked whether community control of natural forests is not a more just and sustainable option when compared to the handing over of public land on a platter to industrial plantations. In the realm of fisheries, they have deplored the favors shown to trawlers at the expense of countryboats, suggesting that a careful demarcation of ocean waters, restricting the area in which trawlers can operate, might allow freer play to indigenous methods as well as facilitate the renewal of fish stocks.

As in the North then, in the South too there is an active environmental debate as well as environmental movement. To be sure, there are some salient differences to be noted. Where Northern environmentalism has highlighted the significance of value change (the shift to 'postmaterialism'), Southern movements seem to be more strongly rooted in material conflicts, with the claims of economic justice—that is, the rights to natural resources of poorer communities—being an integral part of green movements. This is why these movements work not only for culture change but also, and sometimes more directly, for a change in the production system (see *box*). And where Southern groups have tended to be more adversarial with regard to their government—opposing laws and policies deemed to be destructive or unjust—Northern groups have more often had a constructive side to their programs, working with their governments in promoting environmentally benign laws and policies.

In both contexts there has now accumulated a rich body of reflective work to complement direct action: although in the poorer countries the line of causation seems to run the other way, with intellectual reflection, for the most part, being prompted by or following popular protest (in contrast to the North, where books like *Silent Spring* might even be said to have sparked off the environmental movement). Finally, while Northern greens have been deeply attentive to the rights of victimized or endangered animal and plant species, Southern greens have generally been more alert to the rights of the less fortunate members of their own species.

One thing that brings together environmentalists in both contexts, however, is the anti-environmental lobby they have to contend

ENVIRONMENTALISM AND THE DEEPENING OF DEMOCRACY

Henry David Thoreau once remarked that 'In Wildness is the Preservation of the World.' The experience of modern Brazil seems to call for a postscript, that 'In Democracy is the Preservation of the Environment,' as these passages from a recent book explain:

The struggle against environmental degradation has increasingly come to be understood as a part of the democratic struggle to build and consolidate a new model for citizenship. Efforts to promote environmental rights have brought together numerous segments of the social movement, who have sought to ensure access to essential public goods such as water and air in adequate amounts and with sufficient quality to guarantee decent living standards; the use of collective goods needed for the social reproduction of specific socio-cultural groups such as rubber tappers, nut gatherers, fishermen, and indigenous people; a guarantee for the public use of natural resources such as green areas, waterways, headwaters and ecosystems, which have often been degraded by private interests that are incompatible with society's collective concerns....

... It [is] clear that in the Brazilian socio-environmental crisis, ecological degradation and social inequality are two branches stemming from the same root, namely, the specific ways in which capitalism has developed in Brazil by throwing peasants off their land, expanding the frontiers of agri-business, encouraging land speculation and deforestation, wearing out land and drying up rivers, making traditional fishing and forest extractivism unfeasible, adopting an environmentally harmful industrial standard, overloading urban structures, concentrating wealth, and marginalizing population groups....

... It is necessary to seek a kind of development that is not limited to preserving the supply and prices of natural resources as productive inputs. The majority of the Brazilian population is not interested in a kind of development that pretends to be 'sustainable' simply by technically reconverting productive systems and adopting a capitalist rationale in the use of natural resources. We should seek to change the determinant logic of development and make the environmental variable be incorporated as a component of the people's living and working conditions. This kind of change only depends secondarily on possibilities for technical progress. In fact, it depends primarily on the democratization of political processes.... To democratize control over natural resources, to deprivatize an environment that is common to society and nations, to introduce democracy into environmental administration, and to ensure the public character of common natural patrimony constitute the agenda of issues [for the environmental movement] ...

Source: Henri Acselrad, editor, *Environment and Democracy* (Botafogo: IBASE, 1992), Preface.

with. In countries such as the United States, businessmen and industrialists have been the most hostile critics of the greens. In India and Malaysia they are joined by state officials and technocrats, with both private and public promoters of development attacking environmentalists as motivated by foreigners, as creating law-and-order problems, or as wishing only to keep tribals and rural people 'backward,' placed in a museum for themselves and their fellow romantics to gawk at. The most famous and powerful of these anti-environmentalists has been the Prime Minister of Malaysia, Mahathir bin Mohammed. In 1990, he announced that he and his government did not

> intend to turn the Penan into human zoological specimens to be gawked at by tourists and studied by anthropologists while the rest of the world passes them by . . . It's our policy to eventually bring all jungle dwellers into the mainstream . . . There is nothing romantic about these helpless, half-starved and disease-ridden people.

Two years later, in a document specially prepared for the Earth Summit, Mahathir's government insisted that

> The transition from cave and forest dwelling to village and urban living is a phenomenon that has marked the transformation of human societies from time immemorial. The environmental activists have no right to stand in the way of the Penans in this process of change and human development.

Not only with regard to the Penan, not just in Malaysia, it has been the signal contributions of environmental activists to speak truth to power, to ask of politicians and other rulers the uncomfortable questions: Development at what cost? Progress at whose expense?

7

Socialism and Environmentalism (or the Lack Thereof)

EARLY SOVIET ENVIRONMENTALISM

The affluent societies of the Europe and North America, along with Japan, Australia, and New Zealand, are collectively known as the 'First' World; the poorer nations of the South, located in Africa, Asia, and Latin America, as the 'Third' World. This book has highlighted thinkers and movements from the First and Third Worlds, but has thus far left unmentioned the people and territories in between. It now arrives at the Second World, the countries behind the Iron Curtain which are neither rich nor poor and were distinguished, before the fall of the Berlin Wall in 1989, by their commitment to the ideology of state socialism. The discussion shall focus on the Soviet Union, the erstwhile superpower that was the Big Brother of the Second World.

The previous chapter has spoken of the obsession of Brazilian and Indian politicians with catching up with the affluent societies. This obsession in fact manifested itself much earlier in the Soviet Union, soon after the First rather than the Second World War. The leaders of the Bolshevik Revolution of November 1917 hoped to catch up in military as well as economic terms, for they believed that only breakneck industrialization would save their beleaguered country from being overrun by the capitalist powers. As Joseph Stalin once said, 'We are fifty to one hundred years behind the most advanced countries. We must close this gap in the span of ten years. Either we do that or they will sweep us away.' The worship of technology, the faith in industrial production as a means of solving social problems, the arrogant neglect of natural constraints, all helped shade the difference between Soviet communism and American capitalism. Writing in 1933, Aldo Leopold wrote insightfully of what worked to unite political systems apparently opposed to each other:

> As nearly as I can see, all the new isms—Socialism, Communism, Fascism ... outdo even Capitalism itself in their preoccupation with one thing: the distribution of more machine-made commodities to more people. Though they despise each other they are competitive apostles of a single creed: *salvation by machinery*.

Soviet programs of industrial reconstruction were buttressed by Marxism, an ideology which has an unshakeable faith in the powers of modern technology to tame and conquer nature. Marxists also believed that the abolition of private property leads automatically to a diminution of pollution, for the victory of communism would eliminate the capitalists who stoop to anything—putting untreated effluents into the water, for example—to protect their profits. In this view, any residual contamination of the environment would be taken care of by the all-seeing and all-knowing system of centralized planning.

With regard to philosophy and practice, then, Soviet Marxism was characterized, in the main, by a deep indifference to nature and natural limits. 'The proper goal of communism,' remarked Leon Trotsky in the early 1920s, 'is the domination of nature by technology, and the domination of technology by planning, so that the raw materials of nature will yield up to mankind all that it needs and more besides.' A decade later a Soviet scientist claimed that 'the history of humankind has been the road from slavery and blind subjection to the elemental forces of nature to the struggle [and] conquest of her ... In conditions of socialism ... the natural resource base for the economy is not contracting, but has all of the ingredients for limitless development.'

The signs were unpropitious, but as it happened in the first ten years of communist rule a fledgeling conservation movement was to take impressive strides. There already existed a rich pre-revolutionary tradition of natural history and nature protection societies which had helped set aside endangered habitats. In the first week of November 1917, concurrent with the Bolshevik assumption of power, a Conservation Conference in Petrograd discussed a proposal 'On the Types

Chapter 7: Socialism and Environmentalism 127

of Sites where it is Necessary to Establish *Zapovedniki* on the Model of the American National Parks.' In fact the Russian understanding of *Zapovedniki*, or protected areas, was more sophisticated than the American. National Parks in the U.S. had been established for cultural and nationalist reasons, whereas Soviet scientists were asking for sites of virgin nature to be selected on *ecological* criteria, to act as a 'baseline' from which to judge the suitability of human intervention in other, so to say unprotected areas.

LEON TROTSKY ON THE SOCIALIST CONQUEST OF NATURE

One of the architects of the Russian Revolution outlines his vision of socialist man's domination of nature.

The present distribution of mountains and rivers, of fields, of meadows, of steppes, of forests and seashores, cannot be considered final. Man has already made changes in the map of nature that are not few nor insignificant. But they are mere pupil's practice in comparison with what is coming. Faith merely promises to move mountains; but technology, which takes nothing 'on faith', is actually able to cut down mountains and move them. Up to now this was done for industrial purposes (mines) or for railways (tunnels); in the future this will be done on an immeasurably larger scale, according to a general industrial and artistic plan. Man will occupy himself with re-registering mountains and rivers, and will earnestly and repeatedly make improvements in nature. In the end, he will have re-built the earth, if not in his own image, at least according to his taste. We have not the slightest fear that this taste will be bad . . .

. . . Through the machine, man in socialist society will command nature in its entirety . . . He will point out places for mountains and passes. He will change the course of the rivers, and he will lay down rules for the oceans. The idealist simpletons may say that this will be a bore, but that is why they are simpletons . . .

Source: Leon Trotsky, quoted in C. Wright Mills, *The Marxists* (Harmondsworth: Penguin Books, 1963), pp. 278–9.

Indeed, in the early years of Soviet rule both scientific research and university education flourished. The historian Douglas Weiner speaks of the 1920s as 'a golden age' for the teaching of biology in Russia: No longer subject to the 'shackles of the obscurantist Romanov censors, biology was free to introduce the most advanced notions into the classroom. An entire generation of geneticists, ecologists, and experimental biologists of world rank was in formation.'

Some names might be offered here. Among biologists of world repute were N. I. Vavilov, the great student, collector and classifier of crop races; and G. F. Gauze, who pioneered the idea of the 'ecological niche' of a species. One must also mention V. I. Vernadskii, the scholar to whom we owe the terms 'biosphere' and 'geosphere:' it was Vernadskii who, forty years before the publication of the *Limits to Growth* report of the Club of Rome, pointed out that natural productive forces 'have limits and that these limits are real; they are not imaginary and they are not theoretical. They may be ascertained by the scientific study of nature and represent for us an insuperable natural limit to our productive capacity.' A fourth scientist of note was the entomologist A. P. Semenov-tian-shanskii, who combined laboratory expertise with a romantic love of nature. Semenov-tian-shanskii was to will his collection of 700,000 insects to the Zoological Museum in Moscow; this included specimens of 900 species which he had discovered and first described himself. Little wonder that he thought nature to be the 'great book of the existence of all things,' a museum 'indispensable for our further enlightenment and mental development, a museum which, in the event of its destruction, cannot be reconstructed by the hand of man.' Society, believed Semenov-tian-shanskii, had 'a great moral obligation toward Nature,' yet industrial man was showing himself to be a 'geological parvenu... disrupting the harmony of nature,' determined to destroy 'that grand tableau which serves as the inspiration of the arts.'

This efflorescence of scientific research was accompanied by the creation and consolidation of conservation societies. These included the Central Bureau for the Study of Local Lore (TsBK, in its Russian acronym), which worked for the protection of natural as well as cultural heritage; a regional body, the All-Ukranian Society for the Defense of Animals and Plants (ZhIVRAS); and the All-Russian Society for Conservation (VOOP), which drew into its fold some of the most distinguished Soviet scientists. By the late twenties TsBK boasted of 2000 branches and 60,000 members; the Ukranian society claimed a membership of 9000; VOOP had only 1400 paid-up members, but it brought out the influential journal *Okhrana prirody*, an illustrated bi-monthly with a circulation in excess of 3000.

Scientists and their societies were encouraged by the Soviet dictator Vladimir Illyich Lenin, who was the brother of a biologist and a trekker and nature lover himself. It was Lenin who signed, in September 1921, a new decree for the 'Protection of Monuments of Nature, Gardens and Parks,' which prohibited hunting and fishing in existing

Chapter 7: Socialism and Environmentalism 129

zapovedniki and encouraged the establishment of new ones. By 1929 there were 61 *zapovedniki* in the USSR, covering an area close to 4 million hectares. Woods falling outside these protected areas were governed by a Forest Code which was signed into law in July 1923: this promoted reforestation and sustained-yield logging while prohibiting clear-cutting in districts where forest cover was less than 8 per cent of the land area.

In retrospect the 1920s appear to have been a golden age for Soviet science and for Soviet environmentalism as well. 'Ecological conservation's moment in the Soviet sun,' remarks Weiner ruefully, 'was tragically brief.' There seem to be uncanny parallels between the defeat of Gandhism in India and the retreat of environmentalism in the USSR. Both streams, after promising beginnings, were vanquished by the rise to power of a philosophy of state-led industrialization that would not recognize natural constraints. But where the Gandhians merely went back to their *ashrams*, their Russian counterparts were less fortunate. Vernadskii, for example, spent many years in exile; Gauze was prohibited from designing new experiments; most tragic of all was the end of Vavilov, who, having crossed swords with the impostor Trofim Lysenko—Stalin's pet biologist—died in prison.

The demise of Soviet environmentalism was signalled by the first Five-Year Plan of 1929–34, which sought to radically alter production methods in agriculture and industry. The plan mandated an increase in timber production from 178 to 280 million cubic metres; other targets were equally far-reaching. There was now relentless pressure on ecologists to show 'results,' to make their research lead directly to the economic exploitation of natural resources. The collectivization of agriculture destroyed numerous protected areas on the steppes, converting natural biological communities into fields. Mining and logging were allowed in other wild areas. Where *zapovedniki* once covered 12.5 million hectares, by the early '50s this had declined to a mere 1.5 million hectares.

Ecologists and conservationists were on the defensive, in a professional as much as psychological sense. The attacks on them and their work were unforgiving. Commissars and communists thundered that there was no place any more for a 'saccharine-sentimental' approach to nature, for the 'naked idea of preservationism' which had, they thought, inhibited the further development of socialism. The TsBK was mocked as a 'Society for the Preservation of Antiquity,' a 'Society for Protection *from* the Revolution.' Scientific societies were compared to *zapovedniki* where protected professors roamed. The aim of

130   *Part II: Environmentalism's Second Wave*

the societies, it was said, was to 'save nature from the Five-Year Plan.' Respected scholars known for their conservationist views were dismissed as un-Marxist or anti-revolutionary, even as 'agents of the world bourgeoisie.'

Soviet conservation in its first and most fruitful phase had room for three distinct varieties of environmentalism: for ecologists who favored the protection of undisturbed wilderness; for those who combined careful science with rural romanticism; and for practitioners of sustained-yield management. By the late '30s the first two orientations had disappeared into near-oblivion. The third strand, of scientific conservation, still existed, but in an uneasy coalition with state-planned industrialization. A scientist who found himself on the winning side wrote that it was

> evident that the old theory of conservation of nature for nature's sake—a proposition that reeks of ancient cults of Nature's deification—stands in such sharp opposition to both our economic and our scientific interests that there is no place for it in our land of socialism-in-the-making... Not the preservation, come what may, of the existing state of nature, but the rational intervention, study, mastery, and regulation of natural productive forces—that is what should be emblazoned on the banners of our society.

When assessing the fate of Soviet environmentalism, the political climate in which it lived and died must never be overlooked. For the Russia of the 1930s and 1940s was the most totalitarian of societies, a place in which intellectual or political dissent was impermissible. N. I. Vavilov was one of an estimated 1,500,000 scholars, writers and revolutionaries who perished in the death camps for putting forward, however mildly, opinions that departed from the party line. Quite aside from the pressures of economics, then, there were very real constraints to the expression of environmentalist views that lay outside the narrow range of what was considered acceptable in Soviet Russia.

THE THREE GORGES PROJECT: A PROTEST THAT WASN'T

In 1956, the all-powerful Chairman of China's Communist Party took a swim in the great Yangtze river; coming out of the water, he looked forward to more spectacular demonstrations of man's powers over nature:

Chapter 7: Socialism and Environmentalism

SWIMMING
by Mao Zedong

Great plans are being made;
A bridge will fly to join the north and south,
A deep chasm will become a thoroughfare;
Walls of stone will stand upstream to the west
To hold back Wushan's clouds and rain,
Till a smooth lake rises in the narrow gorges.
The mountain goddess, if she is still there
Will marvel at a world so changed.
  [translated by John Gittings]

Great plans had first been made, in fact, in the 1920s, when the nationalist leader Sun Yat-Sen suggested the building of a dam across the Three Gorges, on the river's upper reaches. The idea was revived by Mao in the '50s, but it took another thirty years for it to move from the politician's poems to the engineer's sketches. As now proposed by China's planners, the Three Gorges Dam will be 185 metres (620 feet) high, generate 17,000 megawatts of electricity, take twenty years to build, and cost a staggering 50 billion U.S. dollars (224 billion yuan). It will be a feat of 'engineering giganticism,' the last defiant symbol of state planning, the last of the heroic projects, comparable in the country's history only to the Great Wall itself.

Communist China treats dissent with the same arrogance as did Soviet Russia, but in early 1989 a group of brave journalists and scholars came together to publish a book, *Yangtze! Yangtze!*, which took a cold and critical look at the Three Gorges project. Printed in February, the book was at first widely and sympathetically covered in the media. It formed part of the 'Peking Thaw,' the wider pro-democracy movement that reached its peak with the students' peaceful capture of the city's Tiannenmen Square. After the military fired on the demonstrators in June, the movement collapsed, and the state came down heavily on the opponents of the dam. Several were jailed; *Yangtze! Yangtze!* was banned soon after the bloodbath, its remaining copies recalled from stores and pulped.

The contributors to *Yangtze! Yangtze!* included some of China's most respected hydrologists, physicists, ecologists and planners. Their criticisms of the Three Gorges project focused on its techno-economic unviability. These scientists argued that the massive borrowing of funds would generate unacceptably high levels of inflation; that the project's promoters had grossly over-estimated benefits and under-estimated costs; that the dam would not help control floods; that it would seriously impede ship traffic on the Yangtze, which presently carried goods and passengers equivalent to fourteen railway lines; that it would increase sedimentation, leading to the decline of an important port, Chongquing; and that it would direct funds away from small-scale projects that were more practicable, less destructive and would produce quicker results.

These technical criticisms were accompanied by social, environmental and aesthetic ones. The dam would, when built, displace as many as 1.3 million people. Yet, as one scholar pointed out, for this 'massive population relocation' the planners offered a 'resettlement plan [which] is ridiculous.' The region, noted another expert, is 'already an overpopulated area where food is insufficient and the land depleted. To resettle a population as large as that of a small European country will certainly exceed the local environmental capacity of this mountainous region.' Most eloquent of all was the lament of the veteran botanist Hou Xueyu:

> Apart from irreparable damage to the soil, the natural beauty and cultural heritage of the area would be permanently damaged as well. I think the Three Gorges is the most beautiful of all the world's gorges. The surrounding areas have many national treasures, some more than 5,000 years old. These include the famous ruins of the ancient Daxi culture, and tombs from the Warring States period, the Eastern Han and the Ming and Qing dynasties ... Further, the Three Gorges has unique geological features that provide very important physical data for research. All this would be inundated if the reservoir were built, and tourism would suffer incalculable economic losses.

All over the world, large dams are being challenged as 'outdated monuments to an immodest era,' symbols of a centralizing, capital-intensive and environment-insensitive form of development that is no longer acceptable. The Chinese critics of the Three Gorges project are aware of, and take heart from, this world-wide movement. They grimly note that the construction of the Itaipu hydro-electric project—the grandest anywhere—was one of several such schemes that massively increased the Brazilian public debt, leading to an inflation rate of 365 per cent. They look hopefully across at the Silent Valley in south India and at the Franklin river in Australia, two instances where projected dams were called off after popular protest.

Tragically, the prospects of open and collective protest in China are close to zero. Elsewhere, in Brazil and India for example, people threatened with displacement have organized large processions, defiantly uprooted reservoir markers, marched on provincial and national capitals and burnt effigies of offending politicians and technocrats. These protests have not always been successful in stopping the dam; but at least they happen. In China, on the other hand, the million and more victims of the Three Gorges project must silently suffer as it is being built: criticisms being offered only by courageous scientists who were themselves swiftly silenced. In April 1992, a committee of the Communist Party finally voted to give the go-ahead to the dam. The next January, a Three Gorges Project Development Corporation was set up to oversee construction. An array of foreign firms, including Nippon and Merril Lynch, lined up to bid for contracts.

The conflict between environmental protection and authoritarian rule can only sharpen in China, a country which has liberalized its economic regime while remaining a one-party state. The industrial boom of the last decade has generated enormous amounts of pollution, but citizens are gravely inhibited from doing anything about it. In August 1993, villagers in Gansu Province protested against the contamination of their water by a chemical plant, leading to deaths of fish and livestock and an increase in respiratory illnesses. When the factory's managers, themselves well connected to the Communist Party, disregarded their complaints, peasants took to the streets. Riot police were called in; they killed two protesters and injured several others before restoring 'order.'

The Chinese government, indeed, will not even permit the formation of a non-political group of nature-lovers. A celebrated historian, Lian Congjie, applied in 1993 to register a society to be called the 'Friends of Nature,' which would 'work to educate China's populace about the importance of environmental conservation.' Permission was not refused but was not granted either, the application being ignored by officials. The editor of *Yangtze! Yangtze!*, Dai Qing, notes that 'even though Liang Congjie says "I'm not interested in politics; I only want to help the environment," the government doesn't believe him.'

DEMOCRACY AND ENVIRONMENTALISM, AND THE TIES THAT BIND THEM

The president of the Chinese Banking Association, Qiao Peixin, remarked that in the 'debate over the Three Gorges project, I am afraid that there has not been enough democracy; the affirmative voices are allowed to be heard but the negative voices are often suppressed.' The woman journalist who edited *Yangtze! Yangtze!* likewise observed, after the book was banned, that

Today, many Chinese and foreign newspapers and magazines have labeled me an 'environmentalist.' I am quite flattered by the title. Although I have a great deal of respect for the environmental movement, neither I nor my colleagues considered ourselves environmentalists when we were compiling and publishing *Yangtze! Yangtze!* Our goal was to push China a little bit further towards freedom of speech on the issue of government decision making.

The ideology of state socialism is antithetical to environmentalism on a number of grounds: in its worship of technology; in its arrogant desire to conquer nature; through its system of central planning in which pollution control comes in the way of the fulfilment of production targets. Most of all, though, state socialism has inhibited environmentalism by throttling democracy, by denying to those it rules over the basic freedoms of association, combination, and expression.

DARING TO HOPE, HOPING TO DARE

From an untitled poem by Bei Dao, translated by Geremie Barmé, and quoted at the very end of a book that presented the case against the mammoth Three Gorges dam project:

I do not believe that the Chinese will forever
 refuse to think for themselves;
I do not believe that the Chinese will never
 speak out through their writings;
I do not believe that morality and justice will
 vanish in the face of repression;
I do not believe that in an age in which
 we are in communication with the world,
'freedom of speech' will remain an empty phrase.

Source: Dai Qing, editor, *Yangtze! Yangtze!* (English edition: London: Earthscan, 1994), p. 265.

If in China protests against the Three Gorges dam surfaced in the brief thaw of 1988–89, elsewhere in the communist world environmental movements came to form part of a wider struggle for democracy. In Poland, where the trade union Solidarity led the opposition to Communism, it was also Solidarity which, through its local chapters, began studying and publicizing incidents of environmental abuse. All over Eastern Europe, as the struggle against totalitarianism gathered force in the 1980s, environmental groups began holding the state to account for its 'crimes against nature.' These crimes spoke for themselves: that in Poland the contamination of the environment had reduced life expectancy between 1970 and 1985; that in Czechoslovakia more than 50 per cent of the forest area had been damaged by acid rain; that in Romania an independent study identified a massive 625 centers of serious pollution; that in Russia the great Lake Baikal was dying a slow and painful death due to eutrophication.

Previously there had been little opportunity to speak out against all this, a state of affairs remedied by the rise to power, in 1985, of the Soviet leader Mikhail Gorbachev. Gorbachev's policies of *glasnost*, openness, quickly spilled over from the Soviet Union to its satelite states. People were now allowed to breathe more freely, indeed to demand cleaner air. The impetus for the new environmentalism came from a variety of sources: from Solidarity and the Catholic Church in Poland; from evangelical clergy in East Germany; from scientists in Hungary and Czechoslovakia; from plain old-fashioned democrats in Bulgaria and Rumania—home, respectively, to Todor Zhivkov and Nikolai Ceuceascu, the most tyrannical of the Communist tyrants. In these countries environmentalists played a not unimportant role in the revolutions of 1989 that consigned one-party states to oblivion. In the elections which followed, Green parties found parliamentary representation in Rumania, Bulgaria and Slovenia, while in Czechoslovakia environmentalists allied themselves to the victorious Civic Forum led by the green-minded playwright, Vaclav Havel.

In his own land Gorbachev's agenda also resonated nicely with an environmental constituency that had been making itself visible from about a decade before his arrival. One might speak here of two waves of Soviet environmentalism, interrupted of course by a long period of totalitarian rule. Although Joseph Stalin died in 1953 and his 'personality cult' was dramatically disavowed three years later, it took another twenty years for environmentalist writings to start finding a place in the newspapers and literary magazines. But from the mid '70s writers and scientists began gently criticizing the foul-smelling residues of unchecked industrialization. These criticisms became more strident in the mid '80s, following Gorbachev's ascent to power and the near-simultaneous accident at the Chernobyl nuclear plant, this the biggest disaster in a disaster-ridden history of 'planned' development. Numerous groups and societies began banding together— one such was the Ecology and Peace Association, whose President, S. P. Zalygin, offered the stirring motto, 'Only the Public can save Nature.' This public now bestirred itself to save beloved and beleaguered water bodies: which included the rivers Volga and Don, eyed by destructive dam-builders, and Lake Baikal, choked by the effluents of one of the world's biggest paper mills. Away from the great rivers and lakes, citizens came together to challenge polluting industries, forcing them to pay fines, to change over to cleaner processes, or to shut down altogether. By accident or design, many of the more dangerous factories had been sited outside Russia, in the subordinated republics of Estonia, Armenia, and Latvia. Here environmentalists allied themselves to nationalists, associating the offending factories with a Greater Russian Chauvinism, which they accused of craftily exporting polluting units to non-Russian areas.

But as Ze'ev Wolfson points out, this 'marriage of ecology and national history' has also been characteristic of 'a portion of Russia's [own] green movement.' Where Soviet novelists had once extolled steel mills and collective farms, there came to prominence, in the '70s and '80s, a school of writers which looked back lovingly to the peasants of the pre-revolutionary past. The best-known of these 'village' novelists, Valentin Rasputin, wrote a famous fictional defense of a rural community made to make way for a hydro-electric project. He also wrote feelingly of the threatened landscapes of his native Siberia and of Lake Baikal, near whose shores he lived. For Rasputin, as for his contemporary Vasiliy Belov, the village is 'the wellspring of morality, religious meaning, and harmony with the natural environment, and, moreover, the only reliable medium through which these values can be transmitted to future generations.' Or as Yuriy Bondarev put it,

> If we do not stop the destruction of architectural monuments, if we do not stop the violence to the earth and rivers, if there does not take place a moral explosion in science and criticism, then one fine morning, which will be our last and that of our funeral, we, with our inexhaustible optimism, will wake up and realize that the national culture of great Russia—its spirit, its love for the paternal land, its beauty, its great literature, painting, and philosophy—has been effaced, has disappeared forever, murdered, destroyed forever, and we, naked and impoverished, will sit on the ashes, trying to remember the native alphabet which is so dear to our hearts, and we won't be able to remember, for thought, and feeling, and happiness, and historical memory will have disappeared.
> [translated from the Russian by Robert G. Darst, Jr.]

This was spoken in 1986 at the annual Congress of the USSR Union of Writers, a body which would not have allowed, in 1966 or in 1946, such a forthright refutation of the economic ideology of communism, an ideology marked by disdain for the past and reverence for the mighty powers of the modern. But dissent is the life-blood of democracy, and it is not only in communist states that environmentalists have pushed back the limits of what has been considered politically acceptable. Thus in the Indonesian island province of Bali, where militant protests might be met with a hail of bullets, greens who oppose destructive development projects have shrewdly used petitions, poetry readings, prayers in temples and cartoons in the press. As the anthropologist Carol Warren remarks, in this one-party state 'environmental issues had become a vehicle for the expression of disaffection on broader social and political questions.' The connection between environmental reform and political reform more generally was also made manifest in a 1990 manifesto of a Bulgarian green organization. Where the state and party are one, it observed, 'we have privileged chiefs and unprivileged consumers.' And since 'those who make the strategic decisions are not the same people as those who have to face the consequences,' the 'degree of an individual's responsibility in decision-making is in inverse proportion to the actual suffering caused [to] him by environmental pollution.'

This Bulgarian group is called *Ecoglasnost*, a name which bears testimony to the inseparable link between democracy and environmentalism. For authoritarian states cannot permit the rise of green movements; conversely green movements might—as in 1970s Brazil and 1980s Eastern Europe—help move communist or military dictatorships in the direction of multi-party, so to say more open societies. It is no accident that one of the more robust green movements in the South is to be found in India, a democracy for all but two of its fifty-two years as an independent republic; or that environmentalism is most influential in the United States and Western Europe, where the commitment to political democracy runs deeper than in any other place or at any other time in human history.

8

One World or Two?

The world's largest conservation organization, the World Wildlife Fund, found a novel way to celebrate its twenty-fifth anniversary in September 1986. It brought together, at the small Italian town of Assisi, representatives of five of the world's great religions—Christianity, Islam, Hinduism, Buddhism and Judaism. Assisi is the birthplace of Saint Francis (1181–1226), the activist friar who was a lover of the poor and of nature, a precociously early environmentalist recognized by a papal bull of 1979 as the 'patron saint' of ecology. Now, some 650 years after his death, a congregation of spiritual leaders gathered at his basilica for a Religion and Nature Inter-Faith Ceremony to 'celebrate the dignity of nature and the duty of every person to live harmoniously within the natural world.' The ceremony started with sermons by leaders of the five faiths, explaining how their religious tradition could, and would, cope with the challenges of environmental degradation. These speeches were, in each case, accompanied by more evocative aspects of liturgy: Christian hymns, Buddhist chants, and Hindu temple dances. Time was also set aside for a ceremony of Repentance, where the seers asked forgiveness for harm that they or their fellow faithful had inflicted on nature.

The speakers at Assisi ranked high in the hierarchy of their faiths. They included an abbot of an ancient Buddhist shrine in north-eastern India, acting here as the personal representative of the Dalai Lama; the Minister-General of a leading Franciscan order; the Secretary-General of the Muslim World League; and the Vice-President of the World Jewish Congress. Also present were some powerful people from the secular world, such as the Italian Minister of the Environment, and Prince Philip, husband of the Queen of England and a

Chapter 8: One World or Two?

long-time patron of the WWF. Lis Harris, covering the event for the *New Yorker*, wrote that the organizers hoped to 'communicate the conservation message of the events in Assisi to the entire global network of local priests, mullahs, rabbis, lamas, and swamis who had intimate contact with that vast segment of the population which neither read papers nor watched television nor subscribed to magazines . . .' The idea behind the ecumenical service in Assisi was thus to harness these diverse and widespread energies towards a single collective goal: the protection of the One Earth which is the abode for us all.

By the 1970s, as this book has shown, environmentalism had emerged as a worldwide movement, with its chapters and outposts in all continents. In country after country, individuals and groups made manifest their concern at the deterioration of the environment in their own village, town, district, or province. By the 1980s, however, to these local and regional problems had been added a new class of problems that could only be described as global. These included the build up of carbon dioxide and other gases in the atmosphere, the so-called greenhouse effect; the hole in the ozone layer noticed over Anatartica, caused primarily by the emissions of chlorofluorocarbons or CFCs; and the rapid decline of biological diversity through the extinction of countless species of plants, insects and animals, and sometimes of the very habitats in which they had dwelt. These were considered to be global problems in so far as the terrain where they occured was property that could be claimed by everyone or by no one. They were global also in that no nation was so fortunate as to be insulated from their effects. With regard to the change in world climate or the loss of biological diversity, there was no telling, yet, which country would suffer first or suffer most.

The sentiment that there was only one world to share, or lose, was heightened by the pictures of the earth that started coming in from outer space. On the ground the earth's expanse seemed limitless; as did its capacity to sustain an infinite increase of human appetites and demands. But from the satelite the earth suddenly appeared vulnerable and fragile: a part of the universe small in itself but with a especial resonance for those who happened to live on it. The astronaut Edgar Mitchell, who flew aboard the spaceship Apollo 14, saw the planet as 'a sparkling blue-and-white jewel' which seemed 'like a small pearl in a thick sea of black mystery.'

In the first week of 1989, the popular newsmagazine *Time* authoritatively underwrote this emergence of a global environmental consciousness. It chose the earth as the 'Planet of the Year:' this was a striking departure from its usual practice of nominating a statesman, scientist, sportsman or rock star as its 'Man of the Year.' In his lead article, Thomas A. Sancton offered a listing of the previous year's environmental disasters—dust bowls, heatwaves, floods, species gone extinct, etc.—noting that

> Everyone suddenly sensed that this gyrating globe, this precious repository of all the life that we knew of, was in danger. No single individual, no event, no movement captured imaginations or dominated headlines more than the clump of rock and soil and water and air that is our common home.

Sancton quoted several respected American scientists in support of the view that 'both the causes and effects of the [environmental] problems that threaten the earth are global, and they must be attacked globally.' He then ended with a stirring exhortation of his own:

> Every individual on the planet must be made aware of its vulnerability and of the urgent need to preserve it. No attempt to protect the environment will be successful in the long run unless ordinary people—the California housewife, the Mexican peasant, the Soviet factory worker, the Chinese farmer—are willing to adjust their life-styles. Our wasteful, careless ways must become a thing of the past. We must recycle more, procreate less, turn off lights, use mass transit, do a thousand things differently in our everyday lives. . . . Now, more than ever, the world needs leaders who can inspire their fellow citizens with a fiery sense of mission, not a nationalistic or military campaign but a universal crusade to save the planet.

II

The convention at Assisi and the *Time* story both stressed the shared interest of all peoples in combating environmental stress. The newsmagazine approvingly quoted the Missouri botanist Peter Raven: '*All* nations are tied together as to their common fate. We are all facing a common problem, which is, how are we going to keep this single resource we have, namely the world, viable?' The priests and mullahs gathered at the WWF gathering would have endorsed this statement, only substituting 'religions' for 'nations.'

Possibly the first scientists to use this image of a common earth were Barbara Ward and René Dubos, one a London-based economist, the other a New York microbiologist, who together wrote a book for the first United Nations Conference on the Human Environment, held in Stockholm in 1972. Their study was called *Only One Earth: The Care and Maintenance of a Small Planet*, and the last line of its

Chapter 8: One World or Two? 141

introduction read: 'As we enter the global phase of human evolution it becomes obvious that each man has two countries, his own and the planet Earth.' This idea of a small, shared earth has provided the *raison d'etre* for the United Nations' continuing efforts to bring about international co-operation in the environmental field. In 1987, for example, it issued an influential report on sustainable development called *Our Common Future*, written by a transnational committee chaired by the Norwegian Prime Minister, Go Harlem Brundtland.

Following the Brundtland Report came the United Nations Conference on Environment and Development, known by the acronym UNCED. The UNCED was held at Rio De Janeiro in June 1992, as a somewhat delayed follow-up to the Stockholm meeting of twenty years earlier. One hundred and eighty countries participated in this 'Earth Summit;' represented in many cases by their heads of state. Alongside the official conference was held a parallel meeting of non-governmental organizations or NGOs, featuring talks and panel discussions by some of the best-known environmental activists of the globe. The Earth Summit was very likely the largest international conference ever held, and indisputably one of the most controversial. Where the spiritualists at Assisi and the scientists polled by *Time* magazine comfortably agreed on a 'common future,' the arguments at Rio suggested that while there might be one world, it was divided into two unequal halves.

The three major global problems discussed at Rio were deforestation, climate change, and the loss of biodiversity. UNCED had hoped that for each of these an inter-governmental treaty would be ratified by the participating nations. Draft treaties had already been circulated and discussed at a series of preparatory meetings in 1990 and 1991. At these 'prepcoms' two broad and generally opposing camps had emerged, whose disagreements spilled over into the discussions in June 1992. On the one side were placed the industrialized and mainly affluent countries of the North; on the other, the industrializing and mostly still-poor countries of the South.

The question of climate change emerged as the most contentious of all. To check the build up of greenhouse gases in the atmosphere, it was at first recommended that each country agree to stabilizing its carbon emissions by an agreed cut-off date, say 2015. This proposal, advanced by the Washington-based World Resources Institute (WRI), was bitterly attacked by Southern environmentalists. Anil Agarwal and Sunita Narain, of the Centre for Science and Environment, New Delhi, made a radical distinction between the 'survival emissions' of the poor and the 'luxury emissions' of the rich. They wondered how the WRI could 'equate the carbon dioxide contributions of gas guzzling automobiles in Europe and North America or, for that matter, anywhere in the Third World with the methane emissions of draught cattle and rice fields of subsistence farmers in West Bengal or Thailand?' It was known that the oceans and forests of the globe had a strictly limited capacity to absorb emissions, constituting as it were a 'carbon sink.' It was suggested that if there was now a dangerously high build-up of gases incapable of absorption, then the corrective action had first to come from the North. For if one were to allocate equal shares of the atmosphere to all living human beings, it was apparent that the North had more than used up its share of the 'sink,' whereas the emissions in countries like China and India were well within the limits of the share of the sink that was rightfully theirs.

At Rio was also circulated a forest convention which sought to strengthen global control over forest resources. Where Northern environmentalists wanted an international management regime to faciliate the growing of forests to serve as additional carbon sinks, their Southern counterparts insisted that national control must rather make way for local control, for forests were above all a community resource providing vital inputs for the survival of millions of forest dwellers in Asia, Africa and Latin America. A statement issued by activists from twelve Southern countries sharply asked why, if forests needed to be put under a system of global governance, natural resources coveted and controlled by the North should not be subject to the same. 'If forest management is of global consequence,' it asked, 'so is the management of the world's oil resources. Are we going to have a global oil convention for sustainable production, management and conservation of the world's oil resources?'

Dispute also ranged over a proposed biodiversity treaty, thought by Southern activists to be unduly biased in favor of Northern biotechnology companies. The draft treaty had not allowed for just compensation to be paid to the indigenous knowledge of local communities: knowledge that has in the past been used without payment, or even without acknowledgement, in the development of new and lucrative varieties of crops and medicinal drugs.

The Malaysian green activist Martin Khor Kok Peng has pointed out that UNCED seemed unable or unwilling to face up to two central questions: the fair assignation of responsibility for the degradation that had already taken place, and the extent to which the United Nations and other international fora really allowed an equal voice to all nations of the world. Many environmentalists, not all from the South, insisted that 'all available evidence shows that the environmental crisis has been precipitated almost exclusively by the wasteful and excessive consumption in the North. Indeed, roughly 80 percent of the resources of the planet as well as its sinks are being utilized by the 20 per cent of the population that lives in Europe, North America, Oceania and Japan.' Population growth in the Third World is sometimes held to be the prime cause of environmental degradation, but as the British writer Fred Pearce asked, 'Why is it that Western environmentalists worry so much about population growth in poor countries when each new child born in North America or Europe will consume 10 or 100 times as much of the world's resources and contribute many times as much pollution? A three-child American family is, in logic, many more times as dangerous to the planet than an eight- (or even an eighty-) child African family.'

To better understand the disputes at Rio, one needs to focus as much on the components as on the extent of this consumption. A prime contributor of chlorofluorocarbons are refrigerators; a prime contributor of greenhouse gases the emissions of automobiles. The possession of a car and a fridge have come to be regarded as the index of progress, of prosperity, sometimes of civilization itself. But the truth of the matter is that virtually all Americans, Japanese, Norwegians and Belgians already own a car and a fridge, whereas most Indians, Kenyans, Colombians and Rwandans don't, but *aspire to do so in the not-so-distant future*. To ask the countries of the South to 'cap' their emissions of CFCs and CO_2 is to deny to much of humanity the hope of ever possessing well-recognized artefacts of comfort and well-being such as automobiles and refrigerators.

In this respect the California housewife and Mexican peasant certainly do not share a common past or present—on what terms can they then come to share a common future? Only in a world where their voices carry equal weight, where there is put in place a genuinely participatory democracy at the global level. But as the Centre for Science and Environment complained in a 'Statement on Global Democracy' issued specially for the Earth Summit:

> There is no effort [at present] to create new levels of power that would allow all citizens of the world to participate in global environmental management. Today, the reality is that Northern governments and institutions can, using their economic and political power, intervene in, say, Bangladesh's development. But no Bangladeshi can intervene in the development processes of Northern economies even if global warming caused largely by Northern emissions may submerge half [their] country.

III

A thoughtful account of the divisions before and during the Earth Summit has been provided by the Pakistani sociologist Tariq Banuri. Differences between North and South, he suggests, were both conflicts based on economic interests and conflicts over meanings. The same event was thus viewed very differently, 'as though people sitting in the same theatre were to be seeing two different movies.' 'Where most Northerners,' remarked Banuri—

> see UNCED as the very welcome unfolding of collective action to save humanity, many southerners, government functionaries as well as NGO activists (albeit for different reasons) fear in it the emergence of a new imperialism, of new conditionalities, and of new obstacles to the alleviation of poverty and oppression. Northerners have lined up to take part in a movie of Noah building an ark to defend us against the deluge. But the south does not seem to belong in this story; it is in a theatre on the other side of the railroad tracks, where Jesus is being crucified to save humanity, where the poor have to suffer in their poverty so that the rich can enjoy their lifestyle.

In this context, one cannot but notice a vivid contrast between the 1986 meeting of religious leaders and the meeting of nations at Rio held six years later. The first was well-meaning and consensual, but also bombastic and vague, talking platitudinously of a shared responsibility mandated by all our faiths. The second was bitter and conflictual, but also concrete and precise, estimating culpability according to extent of emissions and arguing about each country's share of the biosphere.

This book has underlined the sheer variety of environmentalism, its rich and exuberant expression over the years and across the globe. In the past, as I have suggested, there have been distinct 'national' green traditions; but these have also creatively borrowed from one another. The battles of the Earth Summit seemed to presage another kind of encounter between environmentalists, one that might be destructive and disharmonious rather than mutually beneficial.

The residues of Rio will stay with us awhile, but beyond their real and basic differences there is something that unites different kinds of environmentalists. If there is indeed an idea that unites them, which brings together America's John Muir with India's Mahatma Gandhi, Kenya's Waangari Matthai with Germany's Petra Kelly, it is, I think, the idea of *restraint*. All through history those who have commanded power have shown a conspicuous disregard of limits on their behavior, whether toward the environment or towards other humans. Capitalists have exploited workers, socialists have suppressed citizens, both have dominated nature in the belief that it cannot speak back. In their own belief, and often in their practice, Greens are marked rather by restraint: as manifest in the wonder and reverence with which the wilderness thinker looks upon the wild, or the gentleness with which the rural romantic caresses the land, or, indeed, the statistical means by which the scientific conservationist seeks to maintain nature's capital by using only the incremental growth to its stock.

A clue to what brings together all shades of green, all varieties of environmentalism, is contained also in a remark of the Indian Sinologist, Giri Deshingkar. Deshingkar once observed that modern civilization has divorced us both from the past and from the future. By undervaluing traditional knowledge and traditional institutions, it has severed our links with our forefathers and our grandmothers. At the same time, by focusing on individual achievement and the here and now, it has radically discounted the future. 'In the long run we are all dead,' claimed the British economist John Maynard Keynes, a statement that might very well be the epitaph of the twentieth century.

The philosophy of 'in the long run we are all dead' has guided economic development in the First and Third Worlds, in both socialist and capitalist countries. These processes of development have brought, in some areas and for some people, a genuine and substantial increase in human welfare. But they have also been marked by a profound insensitivity to the environment, a callous disregard for the needs of generations to come. They have also perpetuated and in some cases intensified the divisions within human society, between the consuming classes and the working classes. It is what we know as the 'global green movement' that has most insistently moved people and governments beyond this crippling shortsightedness, by struggling for a world where the tiger shall still roam the forests of the Sunderbans and the lion stalk majestically across the African plain, where the harvest of nature may be more justly distributed across the members of the human species, where our children might more freely drink the water of our rivers and breathe the air of our cities. It is in this sense that the environmental movement has shown us a common future—and the multiple paths to get to it.

Bibliographic Essay

The scholarly works on environmentalism's first wave fall neatly into two categories: histories of the origins of environmentalism in different countries and biographical studies of key figures. Among the more important national histories are, for England, Jan Marsh, *Back to the Land: The Pastoral Impulse in England, from 1800 to 1914* (London: Quartet Books, 1982), Raymond Williams, *The Country and the City* (London: Chatto and Windus, 1973); and Keith Thomas, *Man and Nature: A History of the Modern Sensibility* (New York, Pantheon, 1982); for Germany, Raymond H. Dominick III, *The Environmental Movement in Germany: Prophets and Pioneers, 1871–1971* (Bloomington: Indiana University Press, 1992); for Australia, J. M. Powell, *Environmental Management in Australia, 1788–1914* (Melbourne: Oxford University Press, 1976) and for the U.S.A., where the literature is most copious, Roderick Nash, *Wilderness and the American Mind* (third edition: New Haven: Yale University Press, 1982), Samuel P. Hays, *Conservation and the Gospel of Efficiency: The Progressive Conservation Movement, 1880 to 1920* (Cambridge: Harvard University Press, 1958), Arthur Ekirch, Jr., *Man and Nature in America* (New York: Columbia University Press, 1963); William R. Burch, Jr. *Daydreams and Nightmares: A Sociological Essay on the American Environment* (New York: Harper and Row, 1971), and Alfred Runte, *National Parks: The American Experience* (second edition: Lincoln, University of Nebraska Press, 1984).

Much of the literature has focused on specific sectors in specific countries. Thus 'national' histories of the growth of scientific forestry published in the past decade include Conrad Totman, *The Green Archipelago: Forestry in Preindustrial Japan* (1989), Nancy Peluso, *Rich Forests, Poor People: Resource Control and Resistance in Java* (1992), Madhav Gadgil and Ramachandra Guha, *This Fissured Land: An Ecological History of India* (1993)—all three books published by the University of California Press, Berkeley—and Lane Simonian,

Defending the Jaguar: A History of Conservation in Mexico (Austin: University of Texas Press, 1995). Also worthy of note is Franz Heske's *German Forestry* (New Haven: Yale University Press, 1938), a celebratory account of how German forest science spread all across the world.

Another sector that has attracted the attention of historians is the history of widlife conservation, following upon the popular concern with the decline of wild species and habitats. Africa, with its endangered populations of spectacular mammals such as the elephant and the lion, has for good reason been the favorite stomping ground of historians so inclined. Recent and well-researched studies include Raymond Bonner, *At the Hand of Man: Peril and Hope for Africa's Wildlife* (New York: Alfred Knopf, 1993), and John M. Mackenzie, *The Empire of Nature: Hunting, Conservation and British Imperialism* (Manchester: Manchester University Press, 1988), as well as two essay-collections, David Anderson and Richard Grove, *Conservation in Africa: People, Parks and Priorities* (Cambridge: Cambridge University Press, 1987) and the special issue on 'The Politics of Conservation in Africa' of the *Journal of Southern African Studies* (volume 15, number 2, January 1989). Keeping in mind the ecological diversity of countries and continents, studies with a regional rather than national focus will form the next, or more specialized stage of research. Two such works are Mahesh Rangarajan's *Fencing the Forest: Conservation and Ecological Change in India's Central Provinces, 1860–1914* (New Delhi: Oxford University Press, 1996), and Jane Carruthers' *The Kruger National Park: A Social and Political History* (Pietermaritzburg: University of Natal Press, 1995).

Turning next to biographical studies, David Lowenthal's *George Perkins Marsh: Versatile Vermonter* (New York: Columbia University Press, 1958) stands out as an outstanding study of a great pioneering conservationist. Lowenthal's book, we may note, was published in the age of ecological innocence: he is now preparing a new edition more in tune with the temper of the times. Another thoroughly researched and well-written biography is Curt Meine's *Aldo Leopold: His Life and Work* (Madison: University of Wisconsin Press, 1988). John Muir completes the holy trinity of American environmentalists: and among the slew of modern works on or around Muir are Michael Cohen, *The Pathless Way: John Muir and American Wilderness* (Madison: University of Wisconsin Press, 1984), and Stephen Fox, *The American Conservation Movement: John Muir and His Legacy* (Madison: University of Wisconsin Press, 1985). There is also the valuable early study by Linnie Marsh Wolfe, *The Life of John Muir* (Madison:

University of Wisconsin Press, 1978—first published in 1945). In my analysis of Muir I have however relied directly on the prophet's writings in contemporary periodicals such as *Harper's* and *The Atlantic Monthly*, the articles through which he first alerted the public to the devastation of the American West.

Moving beyond America, the British have made the art of biography their own, as exemplified in E. P. Thompson's mammoth *William Morris: From Romantic to Revolutionary* (revised editon: London: Merlin Press, 1978) and in Jonathan Bate's much slimmer but no less provocative *Romantic Ecology: Wordsworth and the Environmental Tradition* (London: Routledge, 1991). A fine example of a 'cross-cultural' life is the Japanese scholar C. Tsuzuki's *Edward Carpenter, 1844–1929: Prophet of Human Fellowship* (Cambridge: Cambridge University Press, 1980). The environmental writings of some figures treated in Part I of this book, such as Mahatma Gandhi, J. C. Kumarappa, Patrick Geddes and Lewis Mumford, are treated at greater length in Ramachandra Guha and J. Martinez-Alier, *Varieties of Environmentalism: Essays North and South* (London: Earthscan, and New Delhi, OUP, 1997). But these writers must also be read in the original. Still valuable works include Patrick Geddes, *Cities in Evolution* (1915: reprint Williams and Norgate, 1949); J. C. Kumarappa, *The Economy of Permanence* (Wardha: All India Village Industries Associaton, 1945); Radhakamal Mukerjee, *Regional Sociology* (New York: Century Co., 1926) and *Social Ecology* (London: Longmans, Green and Co., 1942) and, especially, the two masterful ecological histories by Lewis Mumford, *Technics and Civilization* (1934) and *The Culture of Cities* (1938), both published by Harcourt, Brace and Jovanovich, New York. The American scholar Frank G. Novack Jr. has compiled a fascinating volume based on the letters between Geddes and Mumford—*Lewis Mumford and Patrick Geddes: The Correspondence* (London: Routledge, 1995).

The history of environmentalism/environmental thought in specific regions, time periods and contexts is also treated in a huge and ever-growing periodical literature. There are now two specialized journals on environmental history: the *Environmental History Review*, published in the U.S., and *Environment and History*, published in the U.K. Important essays on the subject also appear in more 'mainstream' journals such as the *American Historical Review* or the *Indian Economic and Social History Review*. Among the numerous periodical essays I have found useful let me mention only three: John Raslett, ' "Checking Nature's Desecration": Late-Victorian Environmental Organization,' in *Victorian Studies*, Winter 1983; William Beinart,

'Soil Erosion, Conservationism and Ideas about Development: a Southern African Exploration, 1900–60,' *Journal of Southern African Studies*, volume 11, number 1, 1984; and Donald Fleming, 'Roots of the New Conservation Movement,' in Donald Fleming and Bernard Bailyn, editors, *Perspectives in American History, Volume VI* (Cambridge, Mass: Charles Warren Center for Studies in American History, 1972).

Although no previous study has been so reckless as to attempt a global history of environmentalism, there is an increasing dissatisfaction with taking the nation as the framework of analysis. The links, positive and negative, between European colonial expansion and conservation are treated in Richard Grove's *Green Imperialism: Colonial Expansion, Tropical Edens and the Origins of Environmentalism* (Cambridge: Cambridge University Press, 1994), and in the essay-collection edited by Jacques Pouchepadass, *Colonisations et Environment* (Paris: Société Française d'Histoire d'Outre-Mer, 1993—orignially published as a special issue of the *Revue Française d'Histoire d' Outre-mer*.) A rich cultural history of representations of nature in the modern West is contained in Simon Schama's *Landscape and Memory* (London: HarperCollins, 1995). Another transnational study in Anna Bramwell's *Ecology in the Twentieth Century: A History* (London: Yale University Press, 1989), a comparative analysis of anti-industrial trends in Germany and Britain (despite its title, however, it is really restricted to these two countries, without a reference to Asia, Africa or Latin America and with but a few pages devoted to the U.S.).

Where works on environmentalism's first wave are generally able to maintain a critical distance from the people and processes they describe, those on the second wave are more insistently partisan, its writers influenced by events they have personally witnessed and sometimes even participated in. Nonetheless, we now have some important analyses of contemporary environmentalism that are likely to stand the test of time. Thus Philip Shabecoff's *A Fierce Green Fire: The American Environmental Movement* (New York: Hill and Wang, 1993) and Samuel P. Hays' *Beauty, Health and Permanence: The American Environmental Movement, 1955–85* (New York: Cambridge University Press, 1987), one by a journalist, the other by a veteran academic, provide authoritative analyses of a vibrant if internally divided movement. A wide-ranging anthology of writings on the wild and Deep Ecology is *The Great New Wilderness Debate* (Athens: University of Georgia Press), edited by J. Baird Callicott and Michael P. Nelson. The struggles for 'environmental justice' are the subject of Andrew

Szasz, *EcoPopulism: Toxic Waste and the Movement for Environmental Justice* (Minneapolis: University of Minnesota Press, 1994) and Robert D. Bullard, *Dumping in Dixie: Race, Class and Environmental Quality* (Boulder: Westview Press, 1990). The British movement is well covered in Philip Lowe and Jane Goyder, *Environmental Groups in Politics* (London: Allen and Unwin, 1983), the German (or West German) movement in Werner Hülsberg, *The German Greens: A Social and Political Profile* (London: Verso, 1988), in Margit Mayer and John Ely, eds, *Between Movement and Party: The Paradox of the German Greens* (Philadelphia: Temple University Press, 1997), and in Saral Sarkar's essay 'The Green Movement in West Germany,' *Alternatives*, volume 11, number 2, 1986.

Where these are all 'national' histories, a fine comparative analysis of environmental movements in three European countries small in size but precocious in civic action is contained in Andrew Jamison, Ron Eyerman, Jacqueline Cramer and Jeppe Lessøe, *The Making of the New Environmental Consciousness: A Comparative Study of Environmental Movements in Sweden, Denmark and the Netherlands* (Edinburgh: Edinburgh University Press, 1990). Also comparative in scope is the work of Ronald Inglehart. His thesis of environmentalism as a 'postmaterialist' movement is articulated in two books: *The Silent Revolution* (1977) and *Value Change in Industrial Societies* (1990), both published by Princeton University Press.

All this is to cite books only. The periodical literature is immense: it includes two valuable special issues showcasing country studies of environmentalism, viz. *International Journal of Sociology and Social Policy*, volume 12, numbers 4–7, 1992, and *Research in Social Movements, Conflicts and Change*, Supplement 2, 1992 ('The Green Movement Worldwide'). Among the specialized English-language journals on the environment are the American periodicals *Society and Natural Resources*, *Whole Earth Review*, *Environmental Ethics* and *Capitalism, Nature, Socialism*, and the British bimonthly *The Ecologist*—all of which regularly publish essays on environmental debates and movements.

One can also expect, in the years ahead, biographies of the key thinkers and activists of modern environmentalism. Those that already exist include Barbara Wood, *Alias Papa: A Life of Fritz Schumacher* (London: Jonathan Cape, 1984), a daughter's memoir, affectionate but also informative; Frank Graham, *Since Silent Spring* (Boston: Houghton Mifflin, 1970), this a biography of a book rather than author. Well worth reading too is the autobiography of Mira Behn (Madeline Slade), *A Spirit's Pilgrimage* (London: Longman, Green and Co., 1960), the story of the encounters of a British admiral's daughter with Gandhi and village India. In a class of its own is John McPhee's *Encounters with the Archdruid: Narratives about a Conservationist and Three of His Natural Enemies* (New York: Farrar, Strauss and Giroux, 1971), a characteristically urbane and witty account of life with David Brower, ex-President of the Sierra Club, founder of Friends of the Earth, and one of America's most influential and truculent conservationists. Also a biography, but of a village rather than individual, is Michael Meyerfeld Bell's ethnographic study of how English people perceive the environment: *Childerley: Nature and Morality in an English Village* (Chicago: University of Chicago Press, 1994).

Environmentalism's second wave has also spawned a rich outcrop of polemical and exhortative works on the human predicament. Preeminent here are the works of biologists, with their unique blending of science and prophecy. Numerous books by biologists are cited in the text: one which isn't, but which is worth consulting nonetheless, is René Dubos' *A World Within: A Positive View of Mankind's Future* (London: Angus and Robertson, 1973). Next in importance are the works of philosophers who have offered acute insights into the moral and social roots of environmental abuse. One such thinker is Rudolf Bahro, a East German dissident who later played a formative role in the founding of the Green Party. See Bahro's *From Red to Green: Interviews with New Left Review* (London: Verso, 1984), and his *Building the Green Movement* (Philadelphia: New Society Publishers, 1986). The idea of 'deep ecology,' as formulated by the Norwegian philosopher Arné Naess, is discussed in Naess' *Ecology, Community, Lifestyle*, translated from the Norwegian by David Rothenberg (Cambridge: Cambridge University Press, 1986). The relevance of different religions for comprehending or solving the environmental crisis is investigated in magisterial fashion by the Iranian philosopher Seyyed Hossein Nasr in his *Religion and the Order of Nature* (Oxford: Oxford University Press, 1996). The ideas of such influential thinkers as Carson, Commoner, Ehrlich and Mumford are treated in David Macauley, ed. *Minding Nature: The Philosophers of Ecology* (New York: The Guilford Press, 1996). Finally, a thoughtful and constructive agenda for moving Western society towards a more constructive path is contained in Wolfgang Sachs, Reinhard Loske, Manfred Linz et al., *Greening the North: A Post Industrial Blueprint for Ecology and Equity* (London: Zed Books, 1998).

In comparison to its Northern counterpart, the literature on Southern environmentalism is scarce. The very idea of the 'environmentalism of the poor' runs counter to the conventional wisdom of the social sciences. While movements in defense of forest rights and against 'destructive development' were common in the India of the seventies and the Brazil of the eighties, it has taken a while for their signals to be noticed in the academy. I have therefore relied heavily on my own research and on the ongoing research of friends and colleagues. The information on Bali comes from as yet unpublished papers by Dr Carol Warren of Murdoch University, while the account of the Penan case was enabled only by my access to a forthcoming book manuscript on the subject by Dr J. Peter Brosius of the University of Georgia. An even greater debt is owed to Professor Juan Martinez-Alier of the Autonomous University of Barcelona, from whose work on Latin American environmentalism I have freely borrowed.

The published work on Southern environmentalism is limited in extent and uneven in quality. The history of Brazilian environmentalism has however been analysed in two fine articles: Karl Goldstein's essay on 'The Green Movement in Brazil,' pp. 119–93 in Matthias Finger, editor, *Research in Social Movements, Conflicts and Change, Supplement 2: The Green Movement Worldwide* (Greenwich, Conn.: Jai Press, 1992), and Eduardo J. Viola's 'The Ecologist Movement in Brazil (1974–86): from Environmentalism to Ecopolitics,' *International Journal of Urban and Regional Research*, volume 12, number 2, November 1988. Also to be noted is W. E. Hewit's essay, 'The Roman Catholic Church and Environmental Politics in Brazil,' *The Journal of the Developing Areas*, volume 26, number 1, 1992. Amazonian deforestation and Chico Mendes' struggle are discussed in Susanna Hecht and Alexander Cockburn's *The Fate of the Forest: Developers, Destroyers and Defenders of the Amazon* (London: Penguin Books, 1990). Our understanding of Brazilian environmentalism will be enriched by the publication of two book-length studies currently under preparation: one by José Augusto Padua on early (eighteenth and nineteenth century) ecological thought, the other by Margaret Keck on the contemporary environmental movement.

The Chipko movement is the subject of my book, *The Unquiet Woods: Ecological Change and Peasant Resistance in the Himalaya* (New Delhi: Oxford University Press, 1989: second revised edition, 1999), while a broader analysis of Indian environmentalism is offered in Madhav Gadgil and Ramachandra Guha, *Ecology and Equity: The Use and Abuse of Nature in Contemporary India* (London: Routledge, 1995). The relationship between women and nature is explored in

Bina Agarwal's essay, 'The Gender and Environment Debate: Lessons from India', *Feminist Studies*, volume 18, 1992. Two seminal documents are the *Citizens Reports on the Indian Environment* published by New Delhi's Centre for Science and Environment (CSE) in 1982 and 1985. Informative essays on environmental issues in South Asia are carried in the *Economic and Political Weekly*, published in Mumbai, and the monthly *Himal*, printed in Kathmandu. The history of the CSE reports mentioned above is another tribute to the internationalism of the environmental movement. The title, as well as the format (with chapters devoted to different resource sectors or particular controversies) has been emulated in the highly successful *State of the World Reports* issued annually by the Washington-based Worldwatch Institute. As it happens, the Indian reports were themselves inspired by a slim *State of the Malaysian Environment Report* brought out by the Penang group Sahabat Alam Malaysia in 1980. But despite that country's leading role in articulating the 'voice' of the South, there are no reliable books or articles on the evolution of Malaysian environmentalism. Malaysia's neighbor, Thailand, has been better served in this respect. Useful essays on environmental conflict in that country include Larry Lohmann, 'Peasants, Plantations and Pulp: the Politics of Eucalyptus in Thailand,' *Bulletin of Concerned Asian Scholars*, volume 23, number 4, 1991; Jim Taylor, 'Social Activism and Resistance on the Thai Frontier: The Case of Phra Prajak Khuttajitto,' *Bulletin of Concerned Asian Scholars*, volume 25, number 2, 1993; and Philip Hirsh, 'What are the Roots of Thai Environmentalism?,' *TEI Quarterly Environmental Journal*, volume 2, number 2, 1994. There are, as yet, no authoritative works on African environmental conflicts, but an intimate first-hand account of the Ogoni struggle can be found in Ken Saro-Wiwa's *A Month and a Day: A Detention Diary* (London: Penguin Books, 1996).

Turning now to the socialist and ex-socialist world, one must mention first of all Douglas Weiner's comprehensive history of the forgotten past of Soviet conservation, *Models of Nature: Ecology, Conservation, and Cultural Revolution in Soviet Russia* (Bloomington: Indiana University Press). There is as yet no comparable book-length study of the 'second wave' of Russian environmentalism, but insightful accounts are available in Robert G. Darst, Jr., 'Environmentalism in the USSR: the Opposition to the River Diversion Projects,' *Soviet Economy*, volume 4, number 3, 1988; and in Ze'ev Wolfson and Vladimir Butenko, 'The Green Movement in the USSR and Eastern Europe,' in Matthias Finger, editor, *Research in Social Movements*,

Conflicts and Change, Supplement 2: The Green Movement Worldwide (Greenwich, Conn.: Jai Press, 1992).China, of course (and sadly), has had even less experience of environmental action and environmental debate than did Soviet Russia. The one exception was the debate over the Three Gorges Dam, summarized in Dai Qing and others, *Yangtze! Yangtze*, edited by Patricia Adams and John Thibodeau (London: Earthscan, 1994).

Index

Acselrad, Henri 123
Adenauer, Konrad 90
Africa 4, 6, 20, 26, 27, 30, 39, 44, 64;
  environmentalism in 34, 45–6; see
  also Kenya; Nigeria; South Africa
AGAPAN 112, 114
Agarwal, Anil 141–2
agriculture 12, 23–4, 46, 108;
  intensification of 4, 10, 11, 12–13,
  18, 26, 49; see also country life;
  peasants
Algeria 29
Amazon (region) 49, 109, 114–15,
  116–19
Andrews, R. L. N. 2
Armenia: environmentalism in
  136
Arnold, Matthew 32
artisans 10, 15, 22, 24, 38
Ashby, Eric 75
Audobon Society 81, 89
Australia 32; environmentalism
  in 28, 29, 34–5
Austria 34, 67

back-to-the-land movement 5–6, 78;
  in Great Britain 10–17, 18; in
  Germany 17–19, 92–3; in India
  19–24; in Russia 136
Bahro, Rudolf 93, 95–6
Bahuguna, Sunderlal 119
Banuri, Tariq 144
Bate, Jonathan 11, 12
Beckerman, Wilfrid 78
Beethoven, Ludwig von 67
Bei Dao 134
Beinart, William 28
Belgium 45; environmentalism in 90

Bell, Michael Meyerfeld 87
Belov, Vasiliy 136
Berger, Peter 110
Bhatt, Chandi Prasad 119
biodiversity 2, 3, 39, 52, 53–4, 62,
  71–2, 85, 128, 141, 142; decline/
  loss of 4, 6, 47, 49–50, 55–6, 67,
  83, 100, 111, 115, 119, 129, 132;
  conservation of 12, 16, 57–8, 77;
  see also national parks; wilderness
  thinking
Blake, William 5
Blanco, Hugo 104
Blueprint for Survival 78
Bondarev, Yuriy 136
Bramwell, Anna 98
Brandis, Dietrich 8, 25–6, 27, 34, 35,
  36
Brazil 66, 108–11; environmentalism
  in 112–21, 123, 132–3, 137
Brechin, Steven 99
Brejér, C. J. 71, 72, 75
Brosius, J. Peter 105–6
Brundtland Commission 141
Buddhism, see religion: and
  environmental concern
Bulgaria 135; environmentalism
  in 137
Bullard, Robert 88
Bush, George 2
Bush, Vannevar 66

Canada: environmentalism in 87
capitalism, see industrialization
Cardenas, Lazaro 37
Carpenter, Edward 15–16, 17,
  19–20, 78, 84
Carruthers, Jane 46–7

156 Index

Carson, Rachel 3, 69–77, 99, 114, 122
Caufield, Catherine 87
Centre for Science and Environment 113, 141–2, 143–4
Ceuceascu, Nikolai 135
China 44, 130–1; environmentalism in 131–3
Chipko movement 112, 115–19
Christianity, *see* religion: and environmental concern
cities 5, 10, 11, 13, 15, 19–20, 22, 52–3, 59–61, 87, 111, 114,
Clare, John 12–13
climate change 26, 29, 115, 139, 141–2
Club of Rome 75, 77, 78, 128
colonialism 20, 24, 27, 39, 63–4, 65; environmental impact of 4, 22, 26, 28, 34, 45–7, 49–50, 66, 113
common property resources 12, 16, 23, 38, 41, 112, 113
Commoner, Barry 75, 77–8, 79, 80–1
communism, *see* socialism; industrialization, socialist
consumerism 19, 64, 65, 82, 145; *see also* overconsumption
country life 10, 11, 13, 15, 16, 17, 18, 19, 23, 24, 57, 61, 67, 114; *see also* back-to-the-land movement
Czechoslovakia 135

Dai Qing 133–4
Dalai Lama 138
dams 80, 100, 104, 105, 107, 109, 122, 131–4, 135–6
Dantwala, M. L. 24
Darling, F. Fraser 75
Darré, Walter 19
Darwin, Charles 3, 74
Dasmann, Raymond 75
de Quevedo, Miguel Angel 36–8
Deep Ecology 8, 84–7; *see also* wilderness thinking
deforestation 4, 6, 13, 14, 18, 26–7, 28–9, 34, 37, 38, 41, 42, 43, 49–50,
62, 100, 111, 114–15, 116–17, 119, 123, 141; *see also* scientific forestry
democracy 5, 63, 64, 118, 119; absence of 110, 130, 131, 133, 143–4; and environmental concern 115, 123, 133–7
Denmark: environmentalism in 79
Deshingkar, Giri 145
dessication 26–7, 29, 38
development, *see* economic growth
Dickens, Charles 5
Dominick, Raymond 19
Dubos, René 140–1

Earth Day 80
Earth First! 83, 87
Earth Summit 141–4
ecofeminism, *see* women
Ecologist, The 78
economic growth 64–6, 76, 83, 90, 95, 109, 112, 115, 119; critiques of 66–7, 75, 76, 78, 95–6, 110–11, 119, 122–4, 128, 132, 145; *see also* industrialization
Egypt 65; environmentalism in 29
Ehrlich, Paul 75, 77, 80–1
Elton, Charles 72–3
Emerson, Ralph Waldo 52
energy consumption 38, 41, 61, 67, 75, 90–1, 94, 96, 100, 102, 104, 110
Engels, Friedrich 5
England, *see* Great Britain
Environmental Ethics 86
Environmental Protection Agency 83
environmental degradation, *see* biodiversity, loss of; climate change; deforestation; dessication; industrialization, environmental impact of; pollution; soil depletion; soil erosion; toxic wastes
environmental justice 5, 87–9, 105–6, 107, 119, 122; *see also* inequality; overconsumption
environmental protest 79–81, 83–4,

·87, 90–1, 100–4, 106–7, 112, 115–16, 117, 132–3
environmentalism 1–2, 59, 144–5; defined 3–9; of the poor 99–108, 112, 119; and electoral politics 89–90, 91, 92, 94, 95; as expression of nationalism 5, 17, 18, 31, 46, 53, 136; opposition to 54, 66, 68, 97, 112, 122, 124, 129–30; retreat of 63–6, 73, 78; comparative/international dimensions of 2, 6–8, 15, 24, 25–6, 28, 29, 32–3, 33–4, 35–6, 44–5, 59–62, 67, 72–3, 75, 76, 81, 82, 83–4, 85–6, 90, 94–5, 98–9, 102, 106, 108–19, 122, 127, 129, 132–3, 137, 139–44; *see also* back-to-the-land movement; Deep Ecology; environmental justice; environmental protest; scientific conservation; scientific forestry; wilderness thinking; and entries under different countries
equality/equity, *see* inequality
Erhard, Ludwig 90
Estonia: environmentalism in 136
Everglades 53

feminism 5, 7, 80; *see also* women
Fernow, Bernhard 35
Finland: environmentalism in 34
Fischer, Joschka 94, 96
fisherfolk, *see* fisheries
fisheries 6, 27, 31, 71, 85, 104, 111, 122, 123, 133
Fleming, Donald 57, 77
Forest Peoples Alliance 117–18
forests, *see* biodiversity; deforestation, scientific forestry
Fox, Stephen 69
France 28, 29, 45, 63, 64, 90; environmentalism in 33, 34, 36–7

Galbraith, John Kenneth 64
Gandhi, Indira 112
Gandhi, Mahatma 5, 6, 8, 19–24, 50, 65, 67, 75, 76, 84, 94, 106, 107, 110, 112, 114, 119, 129, 144

Gauze, G. F. 128, 129
Geddes, Patrick 59–62, 77
Geiser, Ken 89
Germany 26, 29, 42, 45, 63; environmentalism in 17–19, 33–6, 55, 73, 81, 82, 89–97
Gibbs, Lois 88
Gillberg, Bjorn 75
Göering, Herman 19
Gorbachev, Mikhail 135
Gore, Al 2
Gorer, Geoffrey 64
Graber, Linda H. 86
Graves, Henry S. 36
Great Britain 7, 22, 44, 63, 64, 66, 90; environmentalism in 10–17, 59–62, 73, 75, 81
Green Party (Germany) 8, 19, 89–97
Grove, Richard 27

Haffner, Sebastian 19
Hansen, Knut 18
Hardin, Garret 75, 77
Harrell, Stevan 99
Harris, Lis 139
Havel, Vaclav 135
Hays, Samuel P. 82
Heske, Franz 35–6
Hill, Octavia 16–17
Himalaya (mountains) 49, 67, 115–19
Hind Swaraj 20
Hinduism, *see* religion: and environmental concern
Hitler, Adolf 19
Hobsbawm, Eric 98
Hülsberg, Werner 91–2
Humboldt, Alexander von 26–7
Hungary 135
hunting 44, 45–6, 47; *see also* biodiversity; wilderness thinking; wildlife
Huo Xueyu 132
Huxley, Aldous 73
Huxley, Julian 74, 75

imperialism, *see* colonialism

India 4, 7, 26, 30, 45, 63, 65, 66, 75, 100, 108–10, 124; environmentalism in 19–24, 34, 38–42, 61–2, 67–8, 100, 107–8, 112–19, 132–3, 137
Indonesia 65, 110; environmentalism in 28, 34, 137
Industrial Revolution 4, 5, 7, 10, 11, 24; see also industrialization
industrialization 3, 17, 18, 19, 22, 68, 82, 108–11; capitalist 18, 61, 77, 92–4, 109, 125–6; socialist 92, 125–6, 129; environmental impact of 1, 4, 5–6, 11, 15, 20, 24, 61, 77, 78, 95–6, 107, 111; see also back-to-the-land movement; economic growth
inequality 5, 58, 65, 122; between nations 7, 87, 93, 96, 141–4; within nations 16, 87, 93, 109, 110–12, 123; intergenerational 95–6, 145; see also colonialism; environmental justice; overconsumption
International Union for Conservation of Nature 114
Italy 14, 29, 45; environmentalism in 32–3, 90, 138–9

Jamison, Andrew 80
Japan 95, 100; environmentalism in 42–3

Kalidasa 3
Keats, John 73
Kelly, Petra 91, 92, 144
Kempton, Willett 99
Kennedy, John F. 72
Kenya: environmentalism in 102–3
Keynes, John Maynard 72, 145
Khor Kong Peng, Martin 142–3
King, Martin Luther 84
Kruger, Paul 46
Kumarappa, J. C. 23–4, 76

Lake District 12, 13–14
Latvia: environmentalism in 136
Lebanon 49
legislation 1, 28, 37, 38, 83, 94
leisure: see recreation
Lenin, V. I. 128
Leopold, Aldo 54–8, 73, 77, 79, 86, 126
Lian Congjie 133
Liebnecht, Karl 92
Limits to Growth 75, 95, 128
Lippelt, Helmut 91, 95
Lohmann, Larry 106–7
Love Canal 87–8
Lowenthal, David 32
Lowood, Henry E. 33
Lutts, Ralph H. 69
Lutzemberger, Jose 112, 115
Luxemburg, Rosa 92
Lysenko, T. D. 129

Macfarlane, Alan 10
Maile, Chris 84
Malaysia: environmentalism in 99–100, 105–6, 124
Man and Nature, see Marsh, George Perkins
Manas 2
Manser, Bruno 100
Mao Zedong 130–1
Marsh, George Perkins 25–9, 31–3, 59, 73, 79
Martinez-Alier, Juan 19, 79
Marxism, see socialism
Mather, Kirtley F. 66
Matthai, Waangari 102, 103, 107, 144
Mendes, Chico 116–21
militarism, see warfare
mining 4, 14, 34, 104, 106, 129
Mira Behn (Madeleine Slade) 67–8
Mitchell, Edgar 139
Morgenthau, Henry 66
Morris, William 15, 16
Morrison, Denton E. 81
MOSOP 102
Müeller, Ferdinand 34–5
Muir, John 49–54, 55, 56, 57, 73, 77, 79, 86, 144
Mukherjee, Radhakamal 61–2

Index

Mumford, Lewis 61–2, 67, 68, 76–7

Naess, Arné 8, 75, 77, 84–6, 93
Narain, Sunita 141–2
Nash, Roderick 86
Nasser, Gamal Abdel 65
national parks 1, 2, 3, 12, 46, 47, 48, 49, 53, 83, 127, 128–9; *see also* biodiversity; wilderness thinking
National Trust 17–18
Nazis 18–19, 95
Nehru, Jawaharlal 65
Nepal 44
Netherlands 28, 34; environmentalism in 75, 81
New York Times, The 2, 69
New Yorker, The 76
New Zealand 34
Nigeria: environmentalism in 100, 102
Norway: environmentalism in 18, 84–5
nuclear power 90–1, 135

Oakes, John 2
overconsumption 20, 67, 75, 85, 93, 95–6, 143

Palmstierma, Hans 75
pastoralism 11, 12, 14, 17–18, 24, 38, 39, 108, 112, 117; blamed for environmental destruction 30, 49 56–7; *see also* back-to-the-land movement
Patkar, Medha 100, 101, 102, 107
Pearce, Fred 102, 143
peasants 10, 11, 17–18, 24, 38, 41, 67, 100, 108, 112, 123; blamed for deforestation 30, 31, 37; *see also* back-to-the-land movement
Phule, Jotiba 39
Pinchot, Gifford 8, 30–1, 35, 36, 55
Pinheiro, Wilson 117
Poland 20, 134, 135; environmentalism in 34
pollution 4, 6, 61, 80, 83, 90–1, 96, 99, 104, 111, 114, 126; of the atmosphere 1, 13, 16, 79, 102, 135; of water 1, 13, 79, 102, 133, 135, 136; by pesticides 3, 70–2, 73, 79; *see also* toxic wastes
population growth 4, 7, 26, 61, 75, 77, 85, 112, 132, 140, 143
Portugal 45, 64
postmaterialist hypothesis 98–9, 122
Powell, J. M. 29
Prince Philip 138–9

Quao Peixin 133

racism 46–7, 65, 88, 89
railways 10, 12, 13–14, 34
Rainforest Action Network 100
Ranger, Terence 46–7
Rasputin, Valentin 136
Raven, Peter 140
recreation 14, 53, 82, 83, 99
recycling 20–2, 88, 140
reforestation 29, 80, 102, 107, 129
Reill, W. H. 18
religion: and environmental concern 42–3, 44, 52, 75, 100, 107, 119, 135, 138–40, 144
resource scarcity 26, 29, 39, 41, 50, 66, 78, 83, 116
Ribbentrop, Bertold von 34
Rilke, Rainer Maria 17–18
rivers, *see* dams; pollution: water
Roosevelt, Franklin D. 64–5
rubber tappers 117–19, 123
Rumania 135
Runte, Alfred 53
Ruskin, John 8, 13–15, 16, 17, 20, 24, 59, 78, 79, 84
Russia 32, 95, 125–6; environmentalism in, 34, 126–30, 135–6

sacred groves 44; *see also* religion: and environmental concern
Sahabat Alam Malaysia 100
Saint Francis, of Assisi 138; *see also* religion: and environmental concern
Sale, Kirkpatrick 69

Salt, Henry 20
Samuelson, Paul A. 78
Sancton, Thomas A. 140
Sand County Almanac, A, see Leopold, Aldo
Sarkar, Saral 90
Saro-Wiwa, Ken 100, 102
Sauer, Carl 66, 67
Schlich, Wilhelm 34
Schumacher, E. F. 66–7, 68, 75, 76, 78
Schweitzer, Albert 13
scientific conservation 6, 25–6, 55, 77–8; ideology of 28–31, 43, 130; *see also* scientific forestry
scientific forestry 6, 8, 26, 27, 32, 36–8, 50–2; Germany as leader in 33–6; in the colonies 28, 29, 30, 34, 38–9; social and environmental costs of 38–42
Scotland, *see* Great Britain
Semenov-tian-shanskii, A. P. 128
Serengeti 2
shepherds, *see* pastoralism
Sierra Club 50, 52, 81, 89, 94
Silent Spring, *see* Carson, Rachel
Simonian, Lane 37, 38
Slovenia 135
Small is Beautiful, *see* Schumacher, E. F.
Smuts, Jan 46
socialism 5, 78, 92, 93, 125–6, 130, 131, 136–7; environmental arrogance of 126, 127, 134; *see also* China; Soviet Union
soil depletion 22, 100
soil erosion 26, 28, 29, 32, 39, 43, 50, 62, 117
Solidarity 20, 134, 135
South Africa: environmentalism in 28, 46–8
South Korea: environmentalism in 99
Soviet Union, *see* Russia
Spain 45
Stalin, Joseph 125–6, 135
Stegner, Wallace 9

Strauss, Franz-Josef 97
Sukarno, Ahmed 65
sustained yield 6, 27, 28, 33, 35–6, 39, 41, 55; *see also* scientific forestry
Sweden 82, 110; environmentalism in 34, 73, 75, 80, 90, 112
swidden cultivation 30, 38, 112
Switzerland 14

Taiwan: environmentalism in 99
Thailand 44; environmentalism in 100, 106–7
Thoreau, Henry David 8, 15, 84, 123
Thurow, Lester 98
Time 139–40
Tolstoy, Leo 8
Totman, Conrad 42–3
toxic wastes 1, 79, 87–9; *see also* pollution
Trotsky, Leon 126, 127

Udall, Stewart 72
UNCED, *see* Earth Summit
United Kingdom, *see* Great Britain
United Nations 112, 140–4
United States of America 1, 4, 7, 20, 63, 64, 66, 95, 124; environmentalism in 2, 3, 6, 8, 25–6, 29, 30, 31–3, 35, 49–58, 61–2, 69–75, 80–1, 83–4, 86–9, 137

Vernadskii, V. I. 128, 129
Vietnam 28, 64, 90
Viola, Eduardo 111
Virgil 3

Waddington, C. H. 75
Wales, *see* Great Britain
Ward, Barbara 140–1
warfare 18, 63, 64, 70, 90, 93, 94, 95, 111
Warren, Carol 137
waters, *see* dams; pollution: water
Weiner, Douglas 127, 129
whaling 85

Index

White, Gilbert 16
White, Lynn 75, 77
Whitman, Walt 15
Wilderness Society 55, 81, 94
wilderness thinking 6, 77; in the United States of America 49–56,, 86–7; in the Soviet Union 126–9; criticisms of 57, 62, 85, 87; *see also* biodiversity; Deep Ecology
wildlife 52, 57; destruction of 45, 49, 70–1, 102; *see also* biodiversity; national parks; wilderness thinking
women 90; in environmental movements 30, 88, 92, 96–7, 102, 107–8, 117, 118, 119; as environmental leaders 16–17, 91, 100, 102, 107; *see also* feminism
Wordsworth, William 5, 11–13, 14, 16, 24, 67
World Bank 66, 115
World Resources Institute 141–2
World Wildlife Fund 138–9

Yangtze! Yangtze 131–4
Yellowstone 2, 49
Yosemite 2, 6, 52

Zalygin, S. P. 135
Zhivkov, Todor 135

SAVAGING THE CIVILIZED
Verrier Elwin,
His Tribals, and India

RAMACHANDRA GUHA

Verrier Elwin, *c.* 1954 (Sunil Janah)

for Sujata

We tend to think of an Age in terms of the man we take as representative of it, and forget that equally a part of the man's significance may be his battle with his Age.

T. S. Eliot

What makes a man change his nationality, abjure civilization and, in the upshot, become a blend of Schweitzer in Africa and Gauguin in Tahiti?

W. G. Archer on Verrier Elwin

PROLOGUE

The Other Side of the Raj

In July 1943, as the Second World War was moving towards a climax, two American journalists raced each other deep into the Indian forest. They were Sonia Tamara of the *New York Herald Tribune* and Herbert Matthews of the rival *New York Times*, and their quarry was a forty-year-old Englishman, Verrier Elwin, an Oxford scholar and renegade priest who had made his home with the Gond tribals of the Maikal hills.

It was Sonia Tamara who reached Elwin first. She spent a week with him before rushing off to the nearest post office—in the town of Jabalpur, 150 miles from Elwin's own village of Patangarh. Her telegrams spoke of the scholar's 'simple, truthful manner' and of his work, amidst tigers, bears and malaria, for the 'primitivest, ancientest tribes' that offered 'one more aspect of the complexest Indian problem.' The man had gone native in the most emphatic sense, by marrying a 'pretty dark Gond girl with lithe limbs tiny hands everready smile,' their union confirmed by 'millenary old Gond rites.'

The American reporter found that these tribals spoke to the anthropologist without reticence, allowing him to record 'their lifestories their customs rites intimatest habits.' The affection the Gond and Baiga had for Elwin was manifest: when their car stopped in a village, wired Tamara, 'men women children outpoured talked volubly smiled babies put into his lap.'[1]

The breathlessness marks this out as an authentic scoop, the testimony of the 'first reporter whos reached Central Indias aboriginal tribes.' And yet, more sober commentators were equally impressed by the singularity of Elwin's life in the forest. They included the two greatest Indians of modern times, Jawaharlal Nehru and Mahatma Gandhi, and the French writer Romain Rolland. It was Rolland who wrote in 1936: 'In Africa, Albert Schweitzer, the philosopher; in India, Verrier Elwin, the poet'—a pairing that remains an intriguing one.[2] Fourteen years later, the *Times Literary Supplement* celebrated Elwin as a 'man of great culture and originality of thought,' a 'poet and translator as well as social worker, explorer and ethnologist, and in every branch of his work he is first-rate.' He was, it concluded, 'one of the best contributions this country ever made to India.'[3]

Thus the *TLS* in 1950; but I suspect few readers of that journal will recognize Elwin's name any more. For now, in the nineteen nineties, most British people know of their encounter with India mostly through books and films about sahibs and memsahibs. Their libraries are awash with studies of viceroys and explorers, of a Younghusband who was the first (white) man to reach Lhasa and a Mountbatten who gallantly lowered the Union Jack. Their television sets are peppered with retrospective celebrations of households, set in heat and dust, which defied death and disease to 'stay on.'

We Indians meanwhile know of our colonial experience through lenses tinted black. Our economists compute the drain of wealth to London and Manchester, our historians memorialize acts of resistance, big or small. An earlier generation of 'nationalists' wrote of campaigns visible and public, from the great revolt of 1857 down to Gandhi's triumphant satyagrahas of the thirties and forties. The present generation of 'subalternists' seek to recover voices silenced by the nationalists, the unnamed peasants and tribals whose protests against imperial authority were frequently more radical than the schemes of the Indian National Congress. But the new historians adhere likewise to the colour bar, the too easy division of the social world of colonial India between dominant whites and discontented browns.

Both British nostalgist and Indian nationalist cannot easily account for men like Verrier Elwin, or women like Annie Besant who was a socialist and suffragette in London before becoming a spiritualist and freedom-fighter in Madras. Elwin and Besant were exemplars of what the sociologist Shiv Visvanathan has called the 'other side of the Raj.' This other side also includes the saintly Charles Freer Andrews, the friend of Gandhi and of

PROLOGUE   vii

Indian plantation workers from Fiji to Guyana; the brilliant if inconstant Philip Spratt, a communist who came to blow up India in 1927 but ended up a passionate free-marketeer and analyst of the 'Hindu personality;' and the missionary Edward J. Thompson, biographer of Tagore, novelist of rural India and, in the words of his son, the great historian E. P. Thompson, 'a courier between cultures who wore the authorized livery of neither.'[4] Nor must one forget the women, who—judging by the readiness with which they changed their names—were more inclined to discard the culture they were born into. I think, for example, of Sister Nivedita (Margaret Noble), the Irishwoman who joined and led a Hindu religious order; and of Mira Behn (Madeleine Slade), the British admiral's daughter who adopted Gandhi and after years in his service left India to seek out the spirit of Beethoven in Austria.

In 1961 an American scholar published a study titled *The Nine Lives of Annie Besant*, comprising two 500-page volumes titled, respectively, *The First Five Lives* and *The Next Four Lives*. At about the same time Elwin was writing his autobiography. When he asked his publisher to suggest a title, the man came up with twenty-five alternatives. How could one adequately illustrate, in four or five words, a life so varied? 'From Merton to Nongthymai' would mark only the place he came from and the place he ended up in; 'Khadi, Cassock, and Gown' mechanically matched dress to vocation; 'Into the Forests, Over the Hills' said something of the terrain he went through on the way but nothing of what he did therein; 'Anthropologist at Large' and 'Philanthropologist' only indicated his last professional affiliation (and might invite unwelcome jokes about the 'philanderopologist'!); 'No Tribal Myth' and 'My Passage to Tribal India' focused only on the people with whom he had made his home.[5]

Verrier Elwin was as eccentric as Annie Besant, as inclined to rebel, as willing to throw up one career and campaign for another. He was also a better writer and, in the circumstances of his life, luckier. Besant, who came to Madras in 1893 and died there in 1932, knew only one kind of India; but Elwin, who came in 1927 and stayed on till his death in 1964, knew both the India of the Raj and the India of the Congress, and made notable contributions to both. We are fortunate, too, that the richness of experience is equalled by the richness of the oeuvre. For Elwin was a novelist, pamphleteer, poet, anthropologist, and autobiographer, an author in many genres of works that were influential in their day and are not unread in ours.

To write about Verrier Elwin is to throw fresh light on men of influence like Gandhi and Nehru, to focus once more on forgotten and oppressed peoples, to travel through all parts of India, to anticipate (by decades) current ideas of religious dialogue and cultural pluralism, to explore the practice of governments colonial and nationalist. In his life, and more so in his work, some of the great debates of the twentieth century find eloquent expression. A book on a man as public and controversial as Elwin shades the difference between self and society, biography and history. That said, this study stays close to its central character. I have not suppressed fact or been coy with opinion, but the interpretation is in the telling: for to intervene with currently fashionable theory would spoil the integrity of the narrative, indeed the integrity of life as it was lived by Verrier Elwin.

Contents

I	Evangelical Ghetto	1
II	Oxford Rebellion	13
III	Between Christ and the Congress	31
IV	Breaking Ranks	58
V	An Ashram of One's Own	78
VI	Defending the Aboriginal	103
VII	Going Gond	124
VIII	Anthropologist at Large	152
IX	Staying On	184
X	An Englishman in India	206
XI	A Sahib (Sometimes) in the Secretariat	234
XII	Nehru's Missionary	261
XIII	An Englishman for India	278
XIV	Outsider Within: The Worlds of Verrier Elwin	303
	Epilogue	315
	Appendices	335
	Acknowledgements	349
	Notes	353
	Index	387

List of Illustrations

Copyright owners have been credited below within brackets.

Frontispiece: Verrier Elwin, *c.* 1954 (Sunil Janah)

(between pages 148 and 149)
1. Baby Verrier with Bishop and Mrs Elwin (OUP)
2. Verrier, aged five (British Library)
3. Dean Close's prize student, 1919 (OUP)
4. A gent with a dog collar—the Vice Principal of Wycliffe Hall seminary, Oxford, 1926 (Wycliffe Hall)
5. Elwin with Gandhi, Sabarmati Ashram, 1931, the dutiful Mirabehn following (OUP)
6. Elwin with his fellow followers Jamnalal Bajaj and Pyarelal (in spectacles), Dhulia Jail, 1932 (OUP)
7. Mary Gillet, in the courtyard of the Ashram of St Francis, Tikeri Tola, 1933 (Verrier Elwin/British Library)
8. Shamrao Hivale, sometime in the mid nineteen thirties (Verrier Elwin/British Library)
9. Kosi Elwin, *c.* 1940 (Verrier Elwin/OUP)
10. A Baiga veteran (Verrier Elwin/OUP)
11. Muria chelik and motiari outside the ghotul (Sunil Janah/OUP)

(between pages 276 and 277)
12. The Deputy Director of the Anthropological Survey of India, on the balcony of his Calcutta home, 1949 (Sunil Janah)
13. Lila Elwin, *c.* 1963 (Sunil Janah/OUP)
14. Kumar Elwin, somewhere on the Frontier, *c.* 1960 (OUP)
15. The sahib and the scholar—Elwin with Professor C. von Fürer Haimendorf, Shillong, 1954 (OUP)
16. A Konyak Naga girl (Verrier Elwin/OUP)
17. Jawaharlal Nehru visiting Elwin's house and museum, Shillong, 1955, with Jairamdas Daulatram in the background (OUP)
18. Cover portrait of the Indian edition of the *Tribal World of Verrier Elwin* (OUP)
19. Elwin receiving the Padma Bhushan from the President of India, New Delhi, 1961 (Nehru Memorial Museum and Library)

CHAPTER ONE

Evangelical Ghetto

In fetid slums, in tiny hamlets, in fashionable watering-places, [late-nineteenth-century] Evangelicals were 'foremost in every scheme for propagating the gospel.' But their proselytism fell with greatest force on their closest relatives. Indoctrination, like philanthropy, began at home.

Clive Dewey

Verrier was the first of the Elwins to depart from the strict and narrow path of orthodoxy in religion and politics since the family began four hundred years ago.

Shamrao Hivale

Verrier Elwin's life was marked by a series of departures, by lively espousals and vigorous rejections of one way of life and belief for another. His first and in some ways most surprising move was away from the pious and resolutely imperialist background of the family into which he was born. The career of this rebel and controversialist begins in humdrum circumstances which are retrospectively interesting, so to say, inasmuch as they seem to contrast so precisely with the astonishing volcanic eruptions of his later life.

Harry Verrier Holman Elwin, to provide a full name he rarely used, was born in Dover on 29 August 1902. The Elwins were an Anglo-Saxon family of genteel but not aristocratic background, archetypes of what George Orwell once called the 'lower-upper-middle-class.' The men worked for the most part as solicitors, clergymen and officials. Two of Verrier's uncles, and two of his cousins, served in the Indian Civil Service.

Verrier's father, Edmund Henry Elwin, was born in 1871, the fifth son in a family of twelve. He studied at Merton College, Oxford, graduating in the summer of 1893 with a third-class honours degree in theology. He then joined the evangelical seminary, Wycliffe Hall, founded in 1877 to train graduates who wanted holy orders and be made 'God's men, Christian gentlemen in the finest and best sense of the word.'[1]

Ordained in 1894, E. H. Elwin was appointed curate of the Oxford parish of St Peter-le-Bailey. But Wycliffe Hall encouraged its men to take the gospel overseas, and in 1896 Elwin joined a party of Oxbridge men going out to the Church Missionary Society's station in Sierra Leone, a colony known with reason as the 'White Man's Grave.' In ninety years of work the CMS lost half its men to disease, but not before winning 50,000 converts in and around the capital, Freetown. The city was founded in 1787 by four hundred slaves dispatched to West Africa on a ship paid for by London philanthropists, who helpfully sent along 'eighty white women of loose character to keep them company.' The settlers, long since removed from their ancestral faith, were rich pickings for the missionaries. When the elder Elwin arrived in Freetown it already had a thriving Christian life: eighty working branches of a Bible-Reading Union, packed Sunday schools, churches with congregations of a thousand and more. Evangelical work now focused on an unclaimed and as yet largely unknown hinterland dominated by Muslim and 'heathen' communities.[2]

Edmund Elwin's first appointment was as vice-principal of Fourah Bay College, an institution affiliated to the University of Durham which allowed 'Africa's sons, without leaving African soil, [to] qualify for English degrees on equal terms with Englishmen.' On graduation most students of Fourah Bay were gathered into the fold of the CMS. The college sent forth a steady stream of pastors and teachers into the heart of West Africa, a territory that could scarcely be evangelized by Europeans alone.[3]

In the first months of 1898 Sierra Leone was convulsed by a popular rebellion. The immediate provocation was a new hut tax, to be paid in 'sterling coin' by every African who dwelt in his own home. The tax brought to a climax a more general disaffection with alien rule, and the response was explosive. As one eyewitness recalled, the uprising was 'really an attempt to cast off British rule, sweep away everything English, and drive the Sierra Leonean back to [Freetown]. There is not the slightest evidence that any discrimination was exercised, or any special spleen vented. Government quarters, trading centres, mission stations, were all equally assailed; and in every case where defense was inadequate, they raided, looted and murdered to their heart's content.'[4]

One victim of the rising was the principal of Fourah Bay, Reverend W. J. Humphrey, who was caught by the rebels and executed while on a tour of missions in the interior. Towards the end of the year, with the insurgency crushed and the hut tax withdrawn, pastors were allowed to return to their stations. In August 1899 their work was inspected afresh by Reverend Elwin, who had succeeded Humphrey both as principal of Fourah Bay and as secretary of the Sierra Leone Mission. In less than a week Elwin travelled 200 miles by row-boat, on horseback, and by foot, while plagued by rats and mosquitoes in the rudimentary dwellings where he passed the nights. Starting one afternoon from the college wharf, his boat reached Port Lokkoh after four hours of 'monotonous pulling of the oars.' The next day he set off with a colleague for the bush village of Funknin. Arriving at the mission after a twelve-hour trek, Elwin 'set to work, examined the log-book, the itinerating-book, the accounts, the service-book, and the school register; handed them a letter from the finance committee, talked it over and made suggestions:' an examination conducted at every station thereafter.

But routine was also accompanied by ritual, as the priest exhorted his juniors to claim Africans for their church. At Rogbere he assembled the pastors for Communion, and as they 'knelt round His Table right away in the heathen country, [they] learnt a little more really what Christ dying for the whole world meant, and what it means to follow in His steps as missionaries.' Victories were few and far between, but the evangelist hoped for the miraculous mass conversion, the single spark that would light a collective fire. A Temne youth in Makomp showed a striking interest in the Bible; prepared by a catechist, he was ready to be baptised by the visitor from Freetown. One morning Reverend Elwin led the boy down to the river and, in the presence of most of the village, baptised him in the water with the name of Yusufu Koma. 'It was a touching sight,' affirmed the priest:

> His father and mother were there and all his people, and it must have made an impression far more than baptism with sprinkling would have done to a people well trained in parables to see this boy thus saying good-bye to the past and rising to a new life in the risen Christ. I addressed the people after, and then Koma, telling him to be a brave 'krugba ka Christ' (warboy of

Christ). We had the Communion together, and then I started [back] for Port Lokkoh.[5]

E. H. Elwin's faith was described by his son, years later, as 'one of the dullest types of religion in the world.'[6] A student at Fourah Bay put it more neutrally; the principal, he said, 'forcibly emphasized the necessity for a life of saintliness and self-consecration to God.'[7] A photograph reproduced in the college jubilee volume shows the principal seated amidst his students: balding, bespectacled, an expression of grim resolution on his face. There is no gainsaying his commitment, for the number of graduates from Fourah Bay more than doubled during his tenure, while his energetic secretaryship helped restore the faith of a Mission badly shaken by the uprising of 1898. Hard work found its reward in preferment and in 1901, when the Bishop of Sierra Leone was appointed Chaplain-General of the British forces, Elwin was the obvious choice as his successor.

In the last week of December 1901 Edmund Elwin sailed with his wife for Liverpool. A month later, on 25 January 1902, he was consecrated along with the newly appointed Bishop of Likoma at a ceremony held at Westminster Abbey. The Archbishop of Canterbury, presiding, chose his text from the Book of Matthew: 'Lo, I am with you always, even unto the end of the world.' These words, said the archbishop, were 'especially appropriate for such an occasion as this, when they were sending forth ministers of the Gospel to preach the Word in distant parts, in countries which could not be called Christian, to heathens who knew nothing of the revealed word of God.' Even as he spoke, the spread of the Word was aided by the spread of the telegraph, the steamboat and the Union Jack. Characteristically, the Anglican pontiff saw the hand of providence in the consolidation of British imperialism. 'Not half the human race had yet learnt what the Gospel was,' he concluded, 'and the Lord was calling them. He was making it day by day easier to reach the places where His work was to be done wherever they might be on the whole surface of the globe.'[8]

An interested spectator at Westminster Abbey was the new bishop's wife: a disinterested one (so to say) was their son, a struggling foetus conceived, by my calculations, on the ship that carried his parents from Freetown to Liverpool. When the boy was born in August, the bishop was back at his post in West Africa, where he would be for most of Verrier's infancy. Growing up in a fatherless household, Verrier's first important relationships were with women. The family consisted of Verrier, his sister Eldyth, who was a year-and-a-half younger, and their brother Basil, who was four years younger still. Brother and sister were natural playmates, with the baby kept at a distance from the very beginning.[9] But it was their mother who was unquestionably the central figure in his early life. Verrier's portrait of his mother, in his later writings and especially in his memoirs, mixes genuine affection with a sardonic assessment of her fanatical faith. Evangelical families rested on a unanimity of opinion between husband and wife: no trouble here, for Minnie Elwin was devoted to the bishop and his religion. A renowned beauty (the looks were passed on to Verrier), she was also a forceful character, being described by one of her son's friends as 'the most powerful woman I have met,' by another as 'strongly Protestant and Fundamentalist,' by a third as 'a rather dominating possessive woman, but gracious in a distant missionary way.'[10]

To the Evangelical faith in the literalness of the Bible Minnie Elwin added a messianic belief in the Second Coming. The family, recalled Verrier, could not go 'to a theatre, cinema, circus or other place of entertainment, for it would have been rather embarrassing if Jesus had arrived in the middle of the programme.' God was the unseen member of the Elwin home, a more-than-adequate substitute for the father away in Africa. His Son, however, was the cause of sibling dispute. At the age of seven Verrier announced that he had given his heart to Jesus; when Eldyth insisted that she had done likewise, her brother hit her on the head with a celluloid doll, declaring: 'I am the only member of the family who has done it.'[11]

The renegade in the family was Minnie's mother, Flora Holman. She didn't go to church, never opened her Bible, and took regular swigs from a bottle of brandy hidden underneath her dress. Verrier and Eldyth knew Grandma Holman to be marked for Hell, but meanwhile she was the source of stories more fanciful than any to be found in the Bible. Her tales of northern India, where her father had been a soldier, began with Sitapur in Awadh, where 'wolves were very plentiful and very bold, and were accustomed to a good supply of Indian babies.' The canines came in search of a white baby, the Colonel's child, no less, to be thwarted by a devoted pie-dog who 'slept by the cot-side and accompanied the child everywhere.' At Agra, their next posting, thieves entered the house at night; by the time father emerged from the bedroom, sword in hand, the gang had made its getaway, leaving behind a 'grinning nude wretch' who tormented the soldier 'by playing around the dining-table in the most elastic and aggravating manner.' From Agra they moved on to Phillaur, a town (they had been warned) known for 'cholera, white ants, dust storms and a sprinkling of mad dogs.' What hit them instead was a terrific cyclone, with hailstones large enough to stun horses and kill crows. The wind 'lifted the tiles off the roof like biscuits,' their carriage was 'turned inside out and smashed to pieces, and our sleepy coachman was blown down a well.'[12]

Granny Holman's tales transported Verrier and Eldyth from the murky fog of England to the burning plains of India. Their father laboured on in Africa, confirming converts, raising money for a new cathedral in Freetown (left by his predecessor without a roof), rebuilding stations gutted in the 1898 rising and staffing them with fresh recruits. The policy of Africanization lay discredited after the troubles, but the bishop thought that only native pastors could be sent as 'pioneers to the unevangelized parts of our Hinterland' to meet the challenge of the other faith with universalist aspirations. 'It is high time,' remarked the bishop to a representative of the journal *Great Thoughts*, 'that the Christian Church everywhere awoke to the most earnest consideration of the question whether in the near future Africa is to be dominated by Islam or by Christianity.' He admitted that a pagan village won over to Islam exchanged 'its dirt and squalor for neatness and cleanliness,' he acknowledged that what 'it teaches of God is also a great advance on fetishism:' nonetheless, Islam encouraged polygamy and slavery, evils the African had to be delivered from. Islam, declared the bishop, 'cannot elevate any race beyond a certain level, and that a low one—higher than barbarism, it is true, but far below Christianity. Only the Gospel of Christ can bring hope to the Dark Continent.'[13]

This was spoken in April 1909; in November Bishop Elwin was dead, claimed, like so many of his fellows, by a deadly fever that ran its course within a week. He was buried at the Kissy Road cemetery in Freetown. One of Verrier's clearest childhood memories was news of his father's death reaching the family in England. Minnie Elwin shut herself in the lavatory but her son crept up to hear her weep.[14]

'Had the Bishop lived Verrier's life would have been very different,' remarks Elwin's early hagiographer;[15] but so of course would have been his mother's. E. H. Elwin was elevated to the episcopate at thirty, the minimum age: with years of service in the tropics he would assuredly have been rewarded with a sinecure at home, preparatory to a steady march up the hierarchy of the Church of England. Minnie Elwin might have anticipated becoming the wife of the Bishop of Durham or Norwich, opening fairs, awarding prizes, contentedly raising her children in a financially secure and stable home.

Her husband's death left a gap which Minnie Elwin filled with renewed devotion to her religion and her family. There was little money; where once they might have hoped to live in a spacious home in Cathedral Close, the Elwins now had to make do with tiny rented quarters: two rooms and a bathroom shared with other lodgers. Mrs Elwin fought continually with her landladies, the children grew up in 'an atmosphere of catastrophic rows with these formidable women.' The rows meant they were often on the move: between the ages of six and ten Verrier lived in and attended schools in the towns of Reigate, Eastbourne and London.

As the eldest child, a boy of precocious intelligence to boot, Verrier was the centre of his mother's affections and ambitions. Her family rallied around to help send him to a 'public' school: which one would it be? In their choice Mrs Elwin and her advisers were dominated, it seems, 'by the desire to keep [the boy] untainted by the Church of Rome and the infidelity which they believed to come from the application of modern scholarship to the Bible.' Westminster in London was a day school whose expenses could more easily be managed, but it was found to be soft on Catholicism. Rugby was considered next, but its headmaster was an admirer of Charles Darwin who admitted that he could think of the Book of Genesis as true only in a 'symbolic' sense. The choice finally settled on Dean Close Memorial School in Cheltenham, of a lineage scarcely as distinguished as the others but with a reassuringly Evangelical cast.[16]

The Cheltenham school was named for Francis Close, the Evangelical publicist and bitter opponent of the Anglo-Catholic or High Church faction in the Church of England. Born in 1797, Close was emphatically Low Church, a Tory who condemned Anglo-Catholics for their love of ritual and their greater tolerance of other religions. 'The Bible is conservative,' he said, 'the Prayer Book conservative, the Liturgy conservative, the Church conservative, and it is impossible for a minister to open his mouth without being conservative.' His dogmatism was awesome. The poet Alfred Tennyson spoke of Cheltenham as a 'polka, parson-worshipping place of which Francis Close is Pope,' while the London *Times* dismissed him as an 'ignorant, meddling claptrap preacher' who held in thrall an 'equally ignorant congregation.'[17]

Tennyson and *The Times* represented the intellectual party; however, the professionals and tradesmen who followed Francis Close were not lacking in number, money, influence or faith. In 1886 this supposedly ignorant congregation started a school in the preacher's name, choosing as its first headmaster a man of similar conviction and force of character. H. W. Flecker, born in 1859 into a family of Austrian Jewish converts, was a graduate of the University of Durham who had 'raised himself in the world solely by his brilliant intellectual gifts and his inexhaustible capacity for hard work.' Remembered by a younger colleague as a man of 'immensely strong will' who 'would not tolerate incompetence or halfheartedness,' Flecker created a school in line with the founders' intentions. His distrust of Anglo-Catholics would have pleased Close. As his grandson writes, 'A prayer book with a cross on the cover was disapproved of in the family as savouring of the near-idolatrous practices of the Ritualists.' Many of the students at Flecker's school were sons of Evangelical clergy. They could not have been left in safer hands, for (his biographer remarks) 'the great tradition of conversion, of bringing souls to God, lay behind—say within—the whole of Flecker's life and career.'[18]

Dean Close School was run more or less as a family enterprise. The headmaster taught mathematics and literature, his wife took on German and Hebrew, a son taught classics and a daughter science. The domination of the patriarch was confirmed by the layout of the place. The school is tiny in comparison with the typical English public school, its eight-acre campus built up with dorms and offices and classrooms and auditoria. This smallness might have fostered a feeling of intimacy, or more likely a sense of being closed in. The headmaster's study was at one end of the main corridor: when summoned, boys would walk nervously down the long passage, the door closing behind them as they entered to be spoken to, chastised or, as was sometimes the case, caned.

Verrier Elwin joined the school in September 1915 when Dr Flecker had been in control for almost thirty years. In that time he had made of Dean Close a respectable public school, if not yet of the first rank. But his powers were now on the decline. To the toll of age had been added the difficulties of war and the alienation of a greatly loved son. This was the poet James Elroy Flecker, author of *Hassan* and other works, and the only member of the family with no connection to Dean Close. Sent to another and better school, Uppingham, James Elroy had rebelled against his parents' faith, which he variously described as hypocritical, a farce, 'intolerably narrow,' merely a set of 'episcopal enlargements on Biblical platitudes.' At Oxford James Elroy fell in with the Anglo-Catholics, observing of the Evangelical undergraduates that their 'collective brain-power would not suffice to run a tuck-shop.' Before long he wrote to his father professing agnosticism, thus 'cutting the last thread of the double life.' On leaving university he married a Greek girl. His wife was never acknowledged by his parents, for whom the Greeks and their church were dangerously allied to Catholicism.[19]

James Elroy Flecker died of consumption in January 1915, unreconciled with his parents. In any case, the poet's spirit was quite alien to the atmosphere of their school. When Verrier arrived later in the year, militarism had been joined to Evangelicalism. With his Austrian ancestry, Dr Flecker had ambivalent feelings about the war, but he could not fight the mood of bellicose nationalism within and without the school. Afternoon games gave way to parades and marches conducted by a mock Officers Training Corps, in preparation for mass recruitment on graduation. A pacifist master remarked that 'the place isn't a school, it's a depot,' but his complaint went unacknowledged. The school magazine, the *Decanian*, printed with pride long lists of the serving and the dead. Some 700 Old Decanians enlisted in the army, of which as many as 120 perished in the trenches. A War Memorial Chapel was erected at the end of hostilities from a fund subscribed to by Old Boys and their parents, the impecunious Mrs Elwin contributing one pound, the minimum acceptable donation.

The war concluded, Dean Close returned with vigour to its principles. 'The evangelisation of the world in this generation' was a slogan on the lips of parents and teachers alike, and in the last weeks of 1919 the school was visited by a succession of missionaries working overseas. Verrier and his class heard the Reverend C. E. Tyndale-Biscoe speak on his work in Kashmir, Dr W. Miller on his school in northern Nigeria, and the Reverend J. A. F. Warner on missionary prospects in the United Provinces of India. The *Decanian* meanwhile was reproducing letters written to Dr Flecker by L. W. Smith, an old student currently working with the Punjab Government. Smith was viewing, from the sidelines, Gandhi's first non-cooperation movement against the Raj, which he thought a 'foolish thing altogether,' supplied 'with plenty of money and an unlimited quantity of ill-will.' In Gujranwala, where Smith was posted, a procession marched defiantly through the town, carrying an effigy of the king-emperor. This was then cremated according to Hindu rites, with the ashes immersed in the Chenab river. One of the Old Decanian's duties was to identify sites for punitive police pickets to forestall further trouble.

Two classes ahead of Verrier Elwin was Stephen Neill, regarded as the school's star student. The son of the vicar of St Mark's Church in Cheltenham, Neill had a phenomenal aptitude for languages and a near-photographic memory. He was also very pious. For years after he left school—with a scholarship to Trinity College, Cambridge—the Classics teacher would correct answers by saying 'Stephen Neill would never have written this.' In school Verrier shadowed Neill honour for honour, winning, like the elder boy, the three prestigious prizes for history, literature and scripture. But the divergences in their paths were also becoming apparent. When in 1918 a Crusaders Bible Class was founded by Neill (at the time Senior Prefect), Verrier was content to stay put in the Literary Society.[20]

Verrier's interest in English literature was kindled by Dr Flecker himself who, unusually for an Anglican, was an admirer of the poetry of John Donne. When a senior teacher left for the front the headmaster appointed two boys, Verrier being one, to look after the library. Other masters introduced him to Horace and Pope, and some writers he discovered on his own. A lasting recollection of life at school was of 'getting up at five in the morning to go in stockinged feet down the steps—put shoes on—and out into the grounds to read Wordsworth.'[21]

Verrier's wide and probably indiscriminate reading bore fruit in a series of papers read at the Lit. Soc. In three years his choice of subjects moved from the carefully conventional to the daringly heterodox. In 1919 he spoke on Hebrew poetry and on Thackeray; the next year on Swinburne and Tennyson, and more controversially on Wordsworth. *The Decanian* reported that 'H. V. Elwin read an enthusiastic, and in the opinion of many, a very misguided paper on Wordsworth. People who had preserved a dignified silence for terms, unlocked their hearts and expressed their utmost abhorrence of, or their entire agreement with, Wordsworth's nature-philosophy.' His advocacy of the poet's pantheism had divided the ranks, but Verrier was to go further still. In the summer of 1921 this secretary of the Literary Society brought his duties to a close by reading a paper on the anti-Christian thinker Samuel Butler. 'By his sympathetic treatment of the subject,' remarked *The Decanian*, 'H. V. Elwin showed us that he was not in complete disagreement with the rather grotesque views expressed in "Erewhon" and Butler's other works.'

Verrier Elwin left Dean Close in 1921. When I visited the school seventy-five years later I found it had diluted but by no means abandoned the principles on which it was founded. A kindly and helpful archivist, Humphrey Osmond, introduced me in the staff room as someone 'working on Verrier Elwin, a younger contemporary of Stephen Neill.' The headmaster, pleased, explained the credo of the school as 'trying to build on our traditions—the heritage of Stephen Neill and your chap.' The chaplain, more astute, seemed to have realized that mentioning Neill and Elwin in the same breath was an injustice to at least one of them, so after the formalities he put it this way: 'We have a tradition of producing rugged individualists—Richard St Barbe Baker (famous for planting trees to stop the spread of the African desert), George Adamson (the lion tamer, husband of Joy) and your chap.'

Stephen Neill is still venerated in Dean Close as the prize pupil whose future career most fully embodied the aspirations of the Evangelical party of the Church of England. Neill held high office—as Bishop of Tirunelvelli in southern India and Professor of Theology in Hamburg—and his contributions to scholarship include the standard histories of Anglicanism and of Christianity in South Asia. On returning to England he served for many years on Dean Close's board of governors. Neill, I was told, had donated a huge chunk of his book royalties to the school. He had also delivered the commemoration address before he died. Sadly, he didn't live long enough to write the foreword to the *Centenary Volume*. There now hangs a portrait of Stephen Neill in the school, the only Old Decanian so honoured, the pupil described by a loving *alma mater* as 'Evangelist, Missionary, Statesman, Scholar, Teacher and Benefactor.'

Anticipating my arrival, the archivist had taken out old issues of the *Decanian* with entries on Elwin already flagged. The photocopier was in the same room as the computers. At one terminal sat the chaplain, typing out the question paper for the 'Sykes and Charles and Elizabeth Prize,' the scripture prize once won both by my chap and theirs. As Mr Osmond photocopied the pages I slyly noted down the first and last questions of the question paper. The first was 'Write down Psalm 103 from memory;' the last: ' "Being a Christian at school is quite easy. But how will I manage when I leave?" Write a letter giving advice to an imaginary friend who has asked this question.'

The kind of letter Stephen Neill would have written Verrier Elwin, perhaps?

CHAPTER TWO

Oxford Rebellion

But in case you think my education was wasted
  I hasten to explain
That having once been to the University of Oxford
  You can never really again
Believe anything than anyone says and that of course is an asset
  In a world like ours;
Why bother to water a garden
  That is planted with paper flowers?

                        Louis Macniece (Merton 1925–8)

My path, thank God, led me through Oxford, but it also, thank God, led me away from it.

                        George Santayana

In the summer of 1921 Mrs Minnie Elwin acquired a new and semi-permanent home. For the not insubstantial sum of a thousand pounds she bought a two-storeyed house on Warnborough Road in north Oxford, just beyond the perimeter of what counts as university territory. The family were living in a rented cottage in the town of Worthing, but with Verrier's admission to Merton College his mother had thought to move closer. At Dean Close her son's education was reliably supervised by Dr Flecker, but it now seemed necessary to resume direct responsibility for his instruction.

Mrs Elwin's worries were not misplaced. The freedoms of the university are in contrast to the rule-bound regimen of an English public school—'the problems of life that confront one here,' wrote a Merton contemporary of Verrier, were: '1. How to find time to do any work. 2. How to get to bed before one . . . 3. How to get drunk cheaply. 4. How to be rude first. 5. How to sign one's name.' A typical day ran like this:

> Roll-call 5 to 8—bath after or before. Breakfast by fire 8.45. May or may not be lecture from 10 to 12. Lunch at 1.15. Afternoon spent in Darrell's motor or antique shops—I hope to play hockey occasionally. Tea at Fuller's or Ellison and Cavell's as cheap there as in college: may or may not be an hour's tutorial in the evening. Dine in hall at 7. 30—or dine out. Cinema or orgy afterwards. Gates shut at 12—a life, as you perceive, so fitted to prepare one for the thorny paths of the world. I am making the best of it and have bought some very nice suede shoes for 32/6. Never again, I am convinced, shall I have such comfort or such a beautiful room to live in—it is well then to enjoy it while one can.[1]

The freedoms of college are temporal, social, intellectual, spatial: the boy fresh from school is all at once free to do what he wants with his time, go where he wishes, decide what he shall read and argue about, whom he shall befriend and whom avoid. To move from Dean Close to Merton was to enter a more variegated world, a hetereogeneity of belief, race and nationality. True, there were few students from working-class backgrounds, but plenty from the other end of the spectrum, the Anglo-Catholic or agnostic products of Eton and Harrow little known to a boy from a middle-class and Evangelical home. Moreover, with the Rhodes scholarship scheme in place, one in ten students came from overseas; many from the USA and the white dominions, but an increasing number from British India.

Tucked away in a quiet lane behind the busy High Street, Merton is one of the smaller and less visible of Oxford's colleges. Founded in 1264, it is by one reckoning the oldest in the university. It is a proud college and a very pretty one. The historian A. L. Rowse, an exact contemporary of Elwin (at Christ Church), wrote feelingly of 'the beauty of Merton, the high midsummer pomps, honeyed light on stone, the garden within the city walls, the limes and roses, the outlook on Christ Church Meadows.'[2] Merton has a reputation for gaiety that goes back to the Civil War, and a kitchen once deemed to be the best in Oxford, its pleasures recorded in this anonymous ditty:

> Within those walls, where through the glimmering shade,
> Appear the pamphlets in a moulding heap,

> Each in his narrow bed till morning laid,
> The peaceful Fellows of the College sleep.
> No chattering females crowd their social fire,
> No dread of discord have they or of strife;
> Unknown the names of Husband and of sire,
> Unfelt the plagues of matrimonial life.
> Oft have they basked along the sunny walls,
> Oft have the benches bowed beneath their weight.
> How fecund are their looks when dinner calls!
> How smoke the cutlets on their crowded plates!

This was written in the 1870s; by the 1920s the Fellows were married and, if not, more inclined to read books and write them. Merton's reputation for indolence was dealt a decisive blow by the philosopher F. E. Bradley, a Fellow of the college from 1870 to 1924. Bradley's influence was to reach out into the wider world through T. S. Eliot, whom he tutored when the poet was in residence in 1914–15. When Verrier entered Merton a few years later, the Age of Bradley was coming to a close, to be superseded by the equally long-lived Age of Garrod.

H. W. Garrod joined Merton in 1901, as a tutor in Literature and Classics. He was an authority on Keats and Wordsworth, Horace and Charlemagne, and also the author of a famous 'depreciation' of Jane Austen. He was a lifelong bachelor, devoted to his studies and his students. In *Who's Who* he listed his recreations as 'none,' a typical Garrod joke. He wore a battered hat and had at his heels a succession of blue spaniels, always called Chips. Books, dogs and undergraduates took up most of Garrod's time: he loved playing chess and bowls with students.[3] All in all, he set a standard of collegiality that other Fellows strove nobly to fulfil. George Mallaby, who entered Merton the year before Verrier, remembered the bond between teachers and students:

> Between boys and schoolmasters there must always be some reserve, some barrier of disciplined respect, a certain lack of easy candour and relaxed manners. Between dons and undergraduates this need not be so and in the Merton of 1920 it certainly was not so . . . It was not only the weekly tutorial—it was the constant, daily contact with dons, not only your own tutor, but dons of all kinds, theologians, scientists, philosophers, historians who stopped you in the quad for a chat, who spoke at your debates, read papers at your literary societies, watched your games and invited you to meals.[4]

Reading English literature, Verrier had much to do with Garrod and with David Nicol Smith, a Scotsman with an equally versatile mind and range of interests. Nicol Smith's books included studies of Dryden, Hazlitt, and Johnson: he was also a noted Shakespeare scholar. However, the English School's syllabus was rather antiquated; a later student, John Betjeman, described it as 'really Anglo-Saxon, Northumbrian dialect and tedious medieval poems.'[5] Verrier himself most enjoyed the solitary 'modern' paper, on the eighteenth century, the period in which both his teachers were acknowledged specialists. Outside the classroom he assisted Nicol Smith with his *Oxford Anthology of Eighteenth Century English Verse*. He also helped Garrod with an essay on the seventeenth-century dramatist Middleton, learning a lesson about the essential loneliness of the scholar's vocation. When the student's sections were passed by the professor without any alterations, Verrier worried that readers would notice the decline in style. 'There are no two human beings, Mr Elwin,' answered Garrod, 'who will read this article with the same attention which you and I have given it.'[6]

Garrod also presided with indulgent wit over the Bodley Club, a literary discussion group which met in his rooms three or four times a term. Both dons and undergraduates were in attendance: while the former 'dealt each other shrewd blows with Latin quotations,' the latter were encouraged to present papers and speak up in any case.[7] In Verrier's first year, papers were read on Kipling's jingoism, socialism and literature, the Celtic tradition, and the 'Case for Contemporary Poetry.' The Bodley Club partook of its patron's qualities: witty, iconoclastic, inclusive, moving beyond 'the insularity of England into the internationalism of the Kingdom of Letters.'[8]

The Oxford of the twenties has been memorialized by literary historians as the decade of the aesthete, the cultivated, fun-loving upper-class and homoerotic student for whom university was 'a sort of passionate party all the time.' The picture has been drawn and redrawn in a slew of adoring biographies, self-serving memoirs (as in *Memoirs of an Aesthete* by Harold Acton), and novels (pre-eminently Evelyn Waugh's *Brideshead Revisited*). These accounts all centre on the aesthete; when another point of view is allowed, it is that of the 'hearty,' the rugged rugger-playing athlete with whom the dandy was in ideological and occasionally physical combat.[9]

A prominent aesthete at Merton was the Etonian Robert Byron, later to win renown as a travel writer. Byron hung out with sons of prime ministers and with prospective lords and earls, collected paintings and antique furniture, and printed a card which read:

> Mr Robert Byron
>   At Home
> Eight o'clock to midnight
> For the remainder of the Term.

The hearties of Merton, who were more numerous, gathered in the Myrmidon Club. The Myrmidons were wealthy and well connected, but also dissolute and daring, in the habit of breaking college windows and college rules. A leading Myrmidon was the mountaineer A. C. Irvine who, in June 1924 when still an undergraduate, 'most tragically yet most gloriously lost his life in this year's expedition to ascend Mount Everest.' Irvine was last seen with George Mallory a thousand feet below the summit; at Merton (where he had been elected to serve as secretary of the club for the following year) they were sure he had climbed the highest mountain in the world. Affecting a certain style, the Myrmidons smoked Turkish cigarettes in packets stamped with the club's monograms, tipped into silver ashtrays. Once a year the club hosted a seven-course dinner in one of Oxford's most famous restaurants. Guest speakers in Verrier's time (not that he was a member) included the well-known Tory politician Lord Birkenhead.[10]

Evelyn Waugh's biographer Christopher Sykes, writing of the time when both he and his subject were up at Oxford, remarks that it was 'portrayed with popular inaccuracy for years after its cessation as a town populated by aesthetes in flowing hair in perpetual strife with exasperated athletes.'[11] In truth, aesthetes and athletes together made up only a small proportion of undergraduates. A good many others were taken up with studies, scholarship and, perhaps more surprisingly, faith. 'There can surely be no spot in Christendom, with the possible exception of Malta, which is exposed to such a concentration of clerics:' So remarks the *Oxford Magazine* as late as 1946. Then, and for some time previously, the university had been marked by a rich diversity of Christian traditions. Unitarians, Congregationalists and Baptists all ran Oxford colleges. There was also a Roman Catholic chaplaincy whose incumbent in the nineteen-twenties was the formidable Ronald Knox, a man who wrote detective novels in his spare time, the royalties accruing to his church.[12]

The university's official faith, Anglicanism, was a house divided. In the nineteenth century Oxford had spawned the Tractarian movement which split the Church of England into High and Low Church factions. The High Church tradition was carried forward by Keble College, founded in 1872, and in Pusey House, established twelve years later. Anglo-Catholicism was at the peak of its influence in Oxford in the 1920s, attracting converts by its social activities—it sought actively to reclaim working-class communities 'lost' to non-conformism—and through the beauty of its rituals: the 'altar with its candle-sticks and tapers, its censer and its *lavabo* dish, its copes and its wafers and its services so beautiful that "some that had been there desired to end their days in the Bishop's chapel." ' Borrowing the mass and confession from Rome, the Anglo-Catholics provided a grandeur and mystery altogether lacking in the arid pieties of the Evangelical tradition.[13]

The apostle of Anglo-Catholicism at Merton was the college chaplain, F. W. Green. Born in 1884, educated at King Edward VI School, Norwich, and at Brasenose College, Oxford, Green was a High Churchman in politics and a post-Gladstonian Liberal in politics, a radical who deplored the excesses of capitalism and imperialism without going quite so far as to call himself a 'socialist.' A formative influence had been the four years he spent as a curate of St Anne's, Limehouse, in London's East End. Green's chief literary work was a commentary on St Matthew in the Clarendon Bible. Although he published little he read widely; fluent in German, he was also well versed in Continental scholarship (he did not agree with Cardinal Newman that the best defense against rationalist criticism was 'the shield of the Holy Spirit combined with an ignorance of the German language'). Green was devoted to a college in which both his sons studied—so did a nephew, while one of his daughters married a Merton man.[14]

In 1924 Verrier Elwin graduated with a first class, one of only three such in Merton that year. The college gifted him one hundred pounds to support his next degree, which in family tradition was to be in theology.[15] The move from literature to theology implied a shift in allegiance from Garrod to Green. Already, in the latter part of his first degree, Verrier had been noticed absenting himself from meetings of the Bodley Club. One supposes that the discussions in Garrod's rooms were reported back to Warnborough Road, as for instance a talk on the parallels between pagan and Christian myths which concluded: 'So God in great good humour declared himself a rumour.' Through Verrier's erratic attendance—his presence/absence duly noted in the minutes—one senses a *real* tussle, the love of words and dispute set against a fuller immersion in this irreverent and heterodox group, in which priests were habitually referred to as 'Gents with Dog-Collars' and socialism was defended. Eventually caution (or mother) prevailed; elected secretary of the Bodley Club for 1923–4, 'Mr Elwin was unfortunately compelled to refuse the office.' Shortly afterwards he resigned his membership of the club.[16]

Intellectually and otherwise Oxford made Verrier—as he was to remark in very general terms in his autobiography. The frustration for the biographer is that for this period we have no direct self-testimonies: no diaries or letters or printed essays, only a few poems of uncertain quality. When I visited Merton in search of material from the 'twenties that might still be around, the lady librarian, a new arrival, stiffly pointed out that I had come without an appointment—and did I not understand it was getting to the end of term, with Finals approaching? She suggested I go back to Germany (where I was then living) and write afresh to Dr Stephen Gunn, Fellow in History and College Archivist, seeking permission and asking him to suggest a suitable date when I might next come. I walked out in ill temper, followed by a student who had overheard the conversation. In the sunny quad outside he told me he would take me to 'Steve's room.' Contrary to the impression carried in the librarian's voice, Steve turned out to be absurdly young and highly approachable. The student introduced me to his history tutor, I explained my mission, and the three of us then went down into the college vault to fish out some massive and magnificently bound volumes of the *Registrium College Mertonensis*, the Governor's Minutes. The volume I needed, covering the years 1915 to 1936, was duly found and the student instructed to carry it up to the tutor's room.

By now it was time for Steve's next tutorial. He seated me at his desk while he lounged with the students on sofas. They discussed the problem of dearth in Tudor England while I scanned the Governor's Minutes. Verrier Elwin's name popped in and out, as the recipient of this award or that stipend, but of his voice and opinions there was not a sign. I noted, with interest, that the month he entered Merton, June 1921, two women servants were engaged to work in the Fellows' Quadrangle at wages 'not exceeding 27/6 a week.' A little later the Fellows adopted the report of a committee it had appointed, on the 'Sale of Wine to Undergraduates,' which had recommended that the practice not be introduced. All this was helpful as background but it was not what I had hoped to find.

When the tutorial ended and the students left, I told my fellow historian of the poverty of my find. 'Let me ask Dr Highfield's advice,' he answered, and was on the phone to his predecessor as College Archivist. Other sources were identified and instructions as to their location conveyed. We returned to the library whose keeper, noting the company I was now keeping, was an altogether different person. Steve asked her for the keys to the old library, built in the fourteenth century and, according to Benn's *Blue Guide*, 'perhaps the most interesting medieval library in England,' but no longer used on a day-to-day basis. We went up, passing the rows of first editions, towards a cupboard where our quarry lay. When this was opened volumes tumbled out, lots of them, smaller and more modestly bound than the ones I had previously seen. They were the minute-books of the undergraduate societies.

One must be thankful for the British attention to record-keeping, and for cracks in the system which allow interlopers to peep. From the records kept in the old library at Merton we can track Verrier's intellectual and, more hesitantly, his emotional development. We know thus that he did not join the Myrmidons, for he had not the status. We know also that he joined the Bodley Club out of interest, leaving when its deliberations seemed to clash with what he heard at home. And we know too that he both joined and stayed with a third society, run by F. W. Green, to attend whose meetings Mrs Elwin might more readily have assented. This was the Merton College Church Society, founded in 1875, the most animated of its kind in Oxford, celebrating its 600th meeting in October 1924. It met four or five times a term in the chaplain's rooms; starting soon after dinner, meetings broke for Evensong and resumed thereafter. Members were required to be 'communicants of the Church of England, accepting their creeds and formularies,' no such condition obtaining for the other clubs in the college.

The syllabus for the theology degree was in itself dull and conventional: the study of the Old and New Testaments, and of Greek commentaries up to the time of St Augustine. 'While it may no longer be possible to study theology as if the world came into existence in 4004 BC,' remarked one modernist cleric, 'it is still possible in Oxford to do so as if the world went out of existence in AD 461.'[17] The scriptures and very early ecclestiastical history were in, the philosophy and comparative sociology of religion out. The latter omissions were, however, made up by F. W. Green through the speakers he brought in to the Merton College Church Society. Green sought to expose his wards to a wide range of lecturers and topics. The first meeting that Verrier attended, while still an Eng. Lit. student, was addressed by a priest who worked on the road with tramps; the second featured a talk on 'retreats,' another aspect of the religious life that would scarcely have been discussed at home or in Dean Close.

A vocal undergraduate member of the Society was Alston Dix, already moving towards the monastic Catholicism he was to embrace after leaving Merton. (As Dom Gregory, Dix lived in Nashdom Abbey from 1926, later becoming Prior: his published works include *The Image and Likeness of God.*) In March 1923, when another student read a paper on 'Christianity and Communism,' Dix commented that 'capitalism was an evil, and there was no hope of reform so long as Capital monopolized politics. The Church must cut loose from the secular power and work out a social policy based on Christian principles.' Two months later Dix read a paper which argued, with 'a shower of ecclesiastical epigrams,' that the Anglican Church should disestablish itself from the state. For the Church of England had sacrificed its liberty to criticize, sharing in the 'complicity of unjustifiable acts of state-craft;' only through disestablishment would it gain its freedom and a 'real advancement of respect in the heart of the ordinary citizen.' Dix promoted his own brand of catholicism, saying that 'we should be more Catholic in the sense of being inclusive [rather] than in the sense of being orthodox.'[18]

Verrier at first resisted the radicalism of Green and Dix. In June 1922, when a guest speaker urged an 'ultimate reunion' of the Church of England with Rome, Verrier 'defended the Evangelical position against its detractors;' he also spoke enthusiastically of the fruits of missionary work in Sierra Leone. The family heritage he was not prepared to disavow, at least not yet. But the Anglo-Catholics were at work led by Dix, and by Max Petitpierre, a chemistry student who was also to be a future monk of Nashdom Abbey. They used outrageous flattery—Verrier was 'far too good to waste his time on these unintelligent evangelicals'—and an abundance of affection. While Dix was arguing with Verrier in his rooms, Petitpierre would be on his knees, praying that his heart be touched.[19]

The conversion was slow but steady. Appointed President of the Oxford University Bible Union, a fundamentalist stronghold, Verrier made it into a wing of the ecumenical Students Christian Movement, from whose 'liberal wiles' it had hitherto been preserved.[20] By now he was acquiring a reputation as an orator. Bryan Beady, who was two years junior to Verrier at Merton, remembered him as being of 'medium height, with a crop of unruly hair, two searching blue eyes, and the pink and white complexion and bubbling enthusiasm of the schoolboy.' His personality 'combined to an amazing degree the abounding energy of an intensely practical Christian with the profound learning and strange, compelling power of the born mystic.' The conflict within him, between a persisting Evangelical allegiance and an emerging Anglo-Catholic one, only helped make his speeches more effective. 'It was worthwhile,' writes Beady,

> foregoing a dance to hear one of his addresses as president of the Oxford University Bible Union, for Elwin had a gift of speech which Demosthenes might have envied. Metaphors tumbled over each other as he passed in a breath—without the trace of a note—from fervent exhortation to simple

pathos, or clinched a passage of inspired rhetoric with some humorous anecdote which brought a smile to the lips of his most solemn hearer.

Keen Evangelical as he then was . . . he had already soared into realms beyond the ken of his simple-minded colleagues. He took a naive delight in startling them by casually remarking that he had just seen the ghost of Duns Scotus stalking through Mob Quad, or had fallen into a trance after gazing fixedly at an electric light bulb.[21]

In May 1923 Verrier proposed to the College Church Society that coffee and cigarettes no longer be provided at its meetings, and the money saved be sent to slums in London. He was in fact preparing to sacrifice more than these casual stimulants. 'Elwin likes mysticism,' minuted the secretary of the society in November, explaining some months later that he liked mystics even more. In a paper presented on 3 March 1924 Verrier celebrated the mystic as one who 'had a knowledge of the hidden unity of the Universe.' Although the twentieth century despised 'saints as being dreamy and impractical,' his study of medieval mystics showed that they 'combined a passion for God and for [the] Church with a very practical outlook on life.' The discussion that followed was animated and for the most part hostile. The distinguished theologian Gilbert Shaw reminded Verrier that 'all the widespread occult movements of today were the result of a desire for self-expression' akin to mysticism. A student attacked Richard Rolle, one of Verrier's exemplars, as 'immoral.' Even F. W. Green, in the chair, worried that mysticism might mean 'unbalanced practices in prayer,' an unfortunate 'surrendering to the Unknown.' Verrier stoutly stood his ground. The mystic, he said, must be admired for his capacity to suffer and come through times of spiritual darkness.[22]

In June 1924 Verrier was elected president of the College Church Society. Later that year the annual Church Congress was held at Oxford. At a session on 'What the Youth asks of the Church' Verrier was chosen to represent Oxford, Stephen Neill, Cambridge. The crafty Neill obtained a copy of Verrier's speech beforehand, allowing him to make some carefully prepared cracks at his expense.[23] The press reports, however, generously praised both men. In his talk Verrier challenged his elders to recognize the faith of his generation: it was not true, he said, that the young were only interested nowadays in 'Food, Football, and Felix' (the last a reference to a feline forerunner of Mickey Mouse). The *Church Times* wrote of Verrier that 'he was probably the most youthful-looking speaker who has ever addressed a Church Congress. He spoke vigorously and movingly of what the best youth of the day were looking to the Church for, and he pleaded eloquently for all that the Church should be offering them.' Both Neill and Elwin were 'on a high level, and their sincerity and earnestness shone through them with a poignancy almost wistful in its appeal.'[24]

The debate was chaired by a bishop; other bishops were in the audience, as were Verrier's mother and sister. His first public appearance was a triumph: noticed in the newspapers, the subject of an admiring comment by the Dean of St Paul's.[25] Mrs Elwin is likely to have seen the performance as a happy prelude to a successful career in the Church of England—at home rather than abroad, for she was not about to risk another life extinguished early in the tropics. But Verrier was not much attracted by the status of an establishment priest, and certainly not by the money. He was already showing signs of a lifelong disregard for money: he was never to have much of it. Bryan Beady writes of one sunny morning in 1924 or 1925, when he was punting with some friends on the river. They bought a basket of strawberries beforehand but later realized that this did not leave them enough money to pay for the punt. Spotting Verrier standing on Magdalen Bridge, Beady shouted out: 'Lend me seven-and-six.' 'Coming,' replied Verrier, and soon three half-crowns landed on the cushions of the punt as it passed below the bridge. When Beady later repaid the loan, Verrier wrote him a postcard likening the remittance to 'an unexpected gift from a rich uncle.'[26]

Verrier had taken from F. W. Green and Alston Dix the belief that God was, or at any rate should be, on the side of the poor. In October 1925 he read a paper to the Church Society which rehearsed his move away from the 'genteel inanities of conventional religion,' that 'set of dead, schematic rules,' that 'series of many formal syllogisms.' What he termed Public School religion implied a reduction of faith to 'a mere authority, compulsion and regulation,' with 'rebellion an expensive item on the budget.' Four years in Oxford had taught him, however, to

> measure life by loss, not gain . . . Christ speaks to us of the triumphant glories of Resurrection, but no less of the stumbling agonies of the Way of Sorrows. To follow Him literally—and logically—may mean poverty, ill-health, loss of friends, position, fame; it may mean misunderstanding; it is

costly all the way along. And it means these things not only in the dim ideal future, when we become missionaries, or slum-parish priests, or monks, it must mean them here and now in Oxford.[27]

For Verrier, as for his mentors, Christ was not historical but contemporary. A poem written around this time, which reads now like an amalgam of Philip Larkin and Handel's *Messiah*, speaks of how

> In a motor garage the Christ is born,
>   To-day! To-day!
> To the whirr of the wheels and the toot of the horn,
>   To-day! To-day!
> Spanner and plug and bolt and tyre,
> Rolls and Ford and Taxi 'For Hire,'
> They hail in passionate desire
> The baby Christ, the God of the Road, the King,
> the King of Glory.[28]

'What a lot of time I wasted during my undergraduate years on religion,' recalled Verrier in his memoirs, adding: 'but religion was very exciting then and it also, I suppose, provided an alternative interest, taking the place of bridge or racing.' We know that he gave up all pretence of being an athlete after a brief tenure as captain of the soccer second eleven, in a season which was 'a disastrous one for the College, for my team lost every single match, usually by about fifteen goals to nil.'[29] We suspect also that his friendships were confined to his own sex. Dean Close was a boy's school; Merton had no girl students either, and though there were a few elsewhere in Oxford it seems the women Verrier got closest to were the two women servants who joined the college when he did. Nor, for reasons of finance and faith, did he follow other undergraduates into London and return by the last train from Paddington—known as 'The Fornicator.'[30]

His studies, his friends, his inner life and his social life all revolved around religion. This wholehearted if narrow-minded engagement had its rewards, for in the summer of 1926 he was awarded a First in his Theology Finals. It now appeared, as one of his friends was to write, that Verrier had 'the world at his feet. Behind him was a brilliant career, before him golden opportunities of service and preferment.'[31] A fellowship in an Oxford college was there for the taking but his family pressed him to join the Church of England. When he was offered the vice-principal's job at his father's old seminary, Wycliffe Hall, there was strong pressure on him to accept. He joined, playing for time, further pleasing Mother when he was ordained in Christ Church Cathedral by the Bishop of Oxford. But unknown to her and his principal he was secretly attending mass at that bastion of Anglo-Catholicism, Pusey Hall. F. W. Green at Merton advised him to throw over Wycliffe Hall for a parish in the slums of London or Manchester. There was also the example of his friend Dix, who had withdrawn into a monastery.[32]

In August another option presented itself. With some friends Verrier attended a conference at Swanwick of the Students Christian Movement, where they met a visitor from India, looking for young men to take back with him. J. C. Winslow was a product of Eton and Balliol who had gone out to India in 1905 as a missionary of the Society for the Propagation of the Gospel (SPG). Disgusted by the barriers between British and Indian Christians, and deeply impressed by Mahatma Gandhi's movement of national renewal, Winslow decided to leave the SPG and strike out on his own. One of his models was the radical priest Charles Freer Andrews, intimate of Gandhi and a theologian notably sympathetic to eastern religions: Christ, said Andrews, had come to India not to destroy but to fulfil. Winslow himself would not believe that 'Hinduism, with its astonishing richness of spiritual and cultural heritage, is meant simply to be swept away by the religion of Christ.' Rather, Jesus would 'take all those elements in it which are of permanent value, and bring them to a richer completion than they could have attained without Him.'[33]

In 1920 Winslow founded the Christa Seva Sangh (CSS), which drew inspiration from the traditional ashram ideal of Hindus, as well as from its more recent reinterpretation by Gandhi, whose ashram at Sabarmati was at once a centre of the religious life and of service to the poor. The members of the CSS wore the homespun cotton (khadi) promoted by Gandhi, ate vegetarian food, Indian-style (with their fingers, while squatting on the floor), and used Indian motifs in their chapel and in their homes.

The CSS was at first based near Ahmednagar, in the Deccan countryside. Working in low-caste neighbourhoods, Winslow and his men presented the story of Christ in Marathi and through the traditional verse forms, the *bhajan* and *kirtan*. Conversions were few, so in 1925 they moved—on the advice of the Bishop of Bombay, E. J. Palmer, another Balliol man—to the great Maratha city of Poona, as yet 'almost untouched by Christian influence.' Winslow hoped here to expose the brilliant young students of the city's colleges to the richness and power of the Christian tradition.[34]

Winslow was a man of great charm and charisma, with the appearance and style of a man who might yet bring India to Christ where all before him had failed. Tall and bearded, he wore a cassock made of white khadi but with a girdle in saffron, the Hindu colour of renunciation. He was an able speaker and singer, in English as well as Marathi. Prefacing and ending his speech with Marathi hymns, he made a powerful impression on the students at Swanwick. Two of these, Algy Robertson from Cambridge and Oliver Fielding-Clarke from Oxford, promised to join his ashram the next year. A third, Verrier Elwin, was keenly impressed but would not commit himself.[35]

At the time he met Winslow, Verrier had already begun to look eastwards. There was of course a family connection with the Raj, but elements of another India were being made known to him by an undergraduate at Jesus College, Bernard Aluwihare. A fervent anti-colonialist and later Law Minister of independent Ceylon, Aluwihare guided Verrier to the writings of Tagore and the work of Gandhi. He also effected a personal introduction to Sarvepalli Radhakrishnan, soon to be appointed Spalding Professor of Eastern Religions at Oxford. In the summer of 1926 the philosopher took Verrier and Bernard on a leisurely punt down the river, the three discussing comparative religion.[36] Radhakrishnan seems also to have handed out a reading list, for later that year Verrier published a poem, inspired by an Eastern text, on the solitariness of the spiritual life:

The Lantern
(After the Bhagavad Gita)
The silent soul is as a sheltered flame
    That in a windless spot unwavering
Offers its light to God. Its hidden name
    Fire-vested angels sing.

Around it blow the trade-winds of desire;
    Breezes of passion, gusts of sudden dread,
But not a breath intruding stirs the fire,
    By heaven's silence fed.

O Heart that stirreth with our loss,
    Temple of silence built in pain
We light our lanterns at Thy Cross
    A purer flame to gain.[37]

The subject of India and its faiths, meanwhile, had also featured in the meetings of the college Church Society. The Master of University College, Sir Michael Salter—who not long before had visited Rabindranath Tagore at his university in Santiniketan—read a paper on 'The Ancient Hindu Tradition and the Christian Faith.' This advocated an 'intellectual compromise' between the Hindu ideal of Rest and the Christian ideal of active and willing Service. The compromise was in fact being worked out by the Christa Seva Sangh in Poona, as explained by Winslow when he spoke in Merton, on Verrier's invitation, in October 1926. Winslow remarked that many Hindus admired Christ but loathed a church that clothed itself in English rites and English customs. The CSS, on the other hand, took heed of the warning of the Sikh-Christian mystic, Sadhu Sundar Singh, that if the water of life was offered in a Western cup, India would not drink it.

Other wise men came to Merton from the east. One such was Reverend W. E. S. Holland of the YMCA in Allahabad, a cleric sympathetic to Gandhi and his struggle. Speaking in May 1927 on 'Indian nationalism in relation to Christianity,' Holland suggested that the problems of the Church were chiefly of its own making. 'Whenever an Englishman went to India,' he remarked, 'the Indians always asked themselves one question, "Is this man out here for our interests or his own?" and if, as had so often been the case, they found it was his own, they then took no interest in him or what he said.' The message resonated with Winslow's and then, the next month, Green's wards were addressed by the first Indian Bishop of the Anglican Church, Azariah of Dornakal. Azariah talked of the new mood of humility in his church, of attempts to make it more relevant to Indian customs and methods of worship.[38]

Algy Robertson and Oliver Fielding-Clarke had booked their passage to Poona for September but Verrier was, it seems, not quite ready to take the plunge. Wycliffe Hall he knew he had to leave, but he was inclined at first towards a parish at home which might satisfy his theological inclinations without offending Mother. 'My mind anchored me to Oxford,' he remembered later, 'my spirit told me to go and throw my life into an unknown sea which might easily turn out to be a morass.'[39] Robertson and Fielding-Clarke took him on a tour of the lakes, and won him over. The 'call from India' came, if his sister is to be believed, in the grounds of the Royal Hotel, Capel Curig, looking over the waters at Snowdon peak beyond.[40] Why did he choose Winslow's experiment, an unknown quantity, over the tried and honourable paths laid before him by Green and Dix? In his memoirs Verrier wrote that he decided on India as an

> act of reparation, that from my family somebody should go to give instead of to get, to serve with the poorest people instead of ruling them, to become one with the country that we had helped to dominate and subdue. This idea became sufficiently important to break up my Oxford career and was the driving force that carried me through many difficult years in India.[41]

Such was the interpretation offered thirty-five years after the event: let us set against it a letter written to Green in July 1927, which suggested he was going out to India

For these reasons:

(i) It would greatly ease the situation at home. Mother has been wonderful, but we have had a few dreadful scenes, and I can see how deeply she feels it all.
(ii) It will enable me to test both the missionary and religious vocation, not committing me for more than two years.
(iii) It will enable me to settle down in a Liberal Catholic atmosphere. My mind is by no means settled; and I so dislike externals etc. that, if I stayed in England, I should fear one of two things—either a reaction away from organized religion altogether, or the acceptance of all these things on authority, and I doubt if the authority of the C. of E. would be sufficient.
(iv) In Poona, we shall live under discipline: we shall have for 'directors' the neighbouring Cowley Fathers; we shall have a rule.
(v) The Community is to be run on Indian lines, and its policy is precisely that which we have always applauded—great sympathy, the spirit of identification, the presentation of a Christian Consummator, not of an iconoclast.

(vi) We shall do practical and manual work by the side of study, against a great background of prayer.

(vii) The Bishop [of Oxford] approves. He was very much against a London parish. The doctor has passed me. My mother has acquiesced. And the witness of a great peace in my heart gives me hope that I have chosen rightly. . . .

. . . You have always told me to do the unacceptable thing, and now I do hope you will be able to approve of the Indian plan.[42]

It seems that it was more than the idea of reparation which took Verrier to Poona. He was attracted by the personality and liberal catholic beliefs of Winslow, certainly, and by his experiment, its novel synthesis of the vocations of missionary, slum-parish priest, and monk. Most of all, though, India beckoned because of its distance from Oxford, the escape it offered from the scenes at home, the prospect it held for him to work out his faith without having continually to fight for it.

CHAPTER THREE

Between Christ and the Congress

But in the last event I must speak of the English rule in India apart from whence it comes and whither it goes. It stands by itself in history, proud and incomparable, a work of art, a treasure to be put against a velvet cloth in the world's gallery of politics. I am pleased that it is English; I can easily apply the molluscous objectivity of a Huxley or a Toynbee to India as to Shakespeare's sonnets or a well-known lawn. But it needs no patriotism to appreciate such a monument... To see a great race given scope for the exercise of its greatest strength, to see it conduct the art of government on a scale and with a perfection accomplished by no other race, is to achieve that sublime pleasure in the works of man which, ordinarily, is conferred only on the great artists.

Robert Byron, An Essay on India (1931)

Of all the western nations the English are the least capable of appreciating the qualities of Indian civilization, and the most capable of appreciating its defects.... Add to this that whereas all the other conquerors of India had migrated to the country, settled down and lived there, and become assimilated to Indian conditions, the English are, of all races, the least assimilable. They carried to India all their own habits and ways of life; squatted, as it were, in armed camps; spent as in exile twenty or twenty-five years; and returned home, sending out new men to take their place, equally imbued with English ideals and habits, equally unassimilable.

Goldsworthy Lowes Dickinson,
An Essay on India, China and Japan (1913)

On 18 October 1927, five Englishmen bound for India were given a splendid send-off in London. A dismissal service was held at St Matthew's in Westminster: attended by family and friends, and presided over by the legendary Bishop Gore 'mitred and vested in a cape of cloth of gold, to give his advice, his blessing and God-speed.' The Christa Seva Sangh had been described to the bishop as a 'sort of experiment.' 'Experiment!,' remarked Gore in his address, 'I would call it a whole complex of experiments.' Indeed, the occasion reminded him of a 'similar one fifty years ago, when four young priests like you set out for the Oxford Mission to Calcutta. But within a year one had joined the Church of Rome, one had gone out of his mind, and one was in his grave.'[1]

The levity was typical of the man: at a private audience beforehand Gore had wished the wayfarers good luck, adding, 'but you will all be out of the CSS in five years.' The church establishment showed a considerable interest in the volunteers; apart from Gore, the bishops of Salisbury and Kensington also chaired farewell meetings for them. Through two centuries of British rule most Indians had stubbornly stuck to their own faiths, but this new enterprise, which carried the Gospel in an eastern dress, might yet succeed where countless others had failed, more so as the messengers had half-a-dozen Oxbridge degrees between them. The *Church Times* wrote hopefully of the service in Westminster: 'Five young men, four of them priests, knelt before the golden altar of St Matthew's in the gathering gloom of an October afternoon, their last in England. Now they are on their way to India, their mission to reveal how akin the Christ is to the wise, meditative man of the East, far closer to him perhaps than to his bustling, thoughtless brother of the West, with his passion to do rather than to know.'[2]

The next morning Elwin and company took a boat to Paris, calling briefly at a Russian Orthodox academy before boarding the train to Rome. They toured the Vatican and St Peter's but were moved most at the principal Jesuit church, the Sesu, where one morning they saw streams of ordinary people receiving communion before going to work. Verrier was deeply impressed by an altar over which was inscribed, in Italian: 'From the tram-way men of Rome to the Sacred Heart.' That will be the day, he thought, when one can go to St Paul's and see an altar subscribed to by the 'London County Council's tram-drivers and conductors.'[3]

At Assissi, where they went next, the five men celebrated the Eucharist on the roof of their hotel, viewing with wonder 'the whole country over which St Francis roamed.' Travelling overland via Naples they boarded the *S. S. Oronsay* at Genoa on 23 October. They shared the third-class decks with 1100 others and made themselves at home in the way they knew best. Fielding-Clarke was elected superintendent of social activities, summoning people with a bell to chess and sing-song. Algy Robertson, the longest in holy orders, held confirmation classes for the young boys on ship. For Verrier the voyage was made happy and memorable by the 'thrill of landing at Port Said, the serenity of the Suez Canal, the lovely scenery of the Gulf of Suez, the exquisite off-shore breezes as we neared Ceylon.'[4]

The group reached Colombo on 5 November, their hosts the Bishop of Ceylon and the Principal of St Thomas' College, Kandy. Verrier spoke to students of the college while Algy and Bernard preached at churches nearby. Later, they were taken to the rock-temple of Derubulla and the Temple of the Tooth at Kandy. On the 10th they departed for southern India, the last lap of their ecclesiastical orienting journey. Verrier had not previously been out of England; exposed these past weeks to a dazzlingly varied fare of landscapes and faiths, he made his acquaintance now with the oldest of them all, the 'Syrian' Christians of Malabar, converted according to legend by the apostle St Thomas in the first century of the Christian era. They met several of their leaders and a day was taken up with a trek to the Wynaad hills, to see a monastery run by the Syrians on Franciscan lines. Malabar after the rains was glorious and green, its people well fed and well housed, with 'thousands of boys and girls pouring into the schools.' Verrier's first taste of the subcontinent was notably free of poverty, squalor and disease. There was to be plenty of all that later.[5]

From Malabar the party took an overnight bus to Bangalore, to stay there at Bishop Cotton School and learn about the problems of the Anglo-Indian community. They then travelled by train across the Deccan, arriving finally at Poona on 20 November, five weeks after they had started. They were met at the station by Winslow and three of his Indian Brothers, who immediately garlanded them with flowers. The group drove on to the ashram in an open horse-carriage, to receive, as Verrier wrote to his mother, 'the most amazing welcome from the Indian contractors working on our land. Garland after garland was hung around our necks, six or seven in all; bouquets were put into our hands; cuffs of flowers round our wrists; one Indian made a long speech; another sang a poem specially composed for the occasion. The flowers were simply wonderful, masses and masses of them—we were so laden we could hardly move.'[6]

The ashram of the Christa Seva Sangh was being built adjacent to the agricultural college in Shivaji Peth, on the outskirts of Poona. Through the eighteenth century Poona had been the capital of the Peshwas, the post-Mughal dynasty which once controlled huge chunks of central and western India. A home of traditional scholarship, it was more recently the centre of social reform movements against caste and for the emancipation of women. It was also a centre of nationalist propaganda; Bal Gangadhar Tilak and Gopalkrishna Gokhale, Gandhi's great predecessors in the Congress, had both lived and worked there. When Winslow's recruits reached Poona the city was sullenly contemplating the arrival of the Simon Commission, just appointed to enquire into India's future. The nationalists opposed the Commission because it was all-white and because its terms ruled out the granting of independence. Through all this it remained a solidly Hindu, even Brahmanical, city. As 'a strategic point Poona is of almost greater importance than Bombay,' remarked a 1918 report of the Free Church of Scotland; from the missionary point of view there was the hope that its 'quick, intelligent, restless desire for reform or even for change' might yet be 'a desire that should be brought to recognize the leadership and inspiration of Christ.'[7]

There was work to be done, but first an ashram to be built. In November 1927 the CSS was still housed in tents, its members working side by side with coolies, carrying baskets of earth to the building site. Winslow thought the failure of the Indian church had been as much of appearance as ideology. White missionaries mimicked the lifestyle of officials and planters, but the Hindus were to be won 'only by lives of penitential renunciation.' The Quaker and friend of Gandhi, Muriel Lester, wrote that the ideal of the Christian ashram rejected the 'ultra-European architecture and stiff pews' of the older churches in favour of chapels suited to squatting rather than sitting on raised seats, with wide verandahs where 'inquirers, passers-by and self-conscious people might stand, hearing and seeing all, while still preserving their aloofness.' The aim was to make the lives of missionaries as transparent as Gandhi's, such that 'distinctions of race and caste would be blotted out in the joy of serving Christ.'[8]

The priests of the Poona ashram lived in modest rooms shared with their brown brethren, eating, sleeping and praying on the floor. Aspects of

Indian tradition were incorporated in the building of their chapel, in its representations of Christ and its forms of worship. Life was truly Franciscan. The brothers' individual cells were tiny—eight feet by four feet—partitioned by gunny cloth slung across on a wire. A cotton mattress and an open bookshelf were the only items of 'furniture.' Once, when Winslow was away, the Archdeacon of Bombay introduced beds, but these were removed by the founder when he returned.[9]

The sincerity and simplicity of the CSS won ready admiration. Winslow and his men, recalled the distinguished socialist Kamaladevi Chattopadhyay, 'had something of the flavour of the ancient hermits of the early Christian Church.'[10] Another visitor, Jawaharlal Nehru, also marked the CSS as an exception to a 'conservative and reactionary' church whose members were 'usually wholly ignorant of India's past history and culture' and in any case 'more interested in pointing out the sins and failings of the heathen.' On the other hand, noted Nehru, 'the Christa Seva Sangh of Poona contains some fine Englishmen, whose religion has led them to understand and serve and not to patronise . . .'.[11]

The ashram of the Christa Seva Sangh still stands in Shivaji Peth, enclosed on all sides by the city that has grown to surround it. Its inmates are now elderly Englishwomen rather than young Englishmen. They courteously escort the outsider in search of old documents to the library. That room, as also the others, are much the same as they were in 1927. So is the food, the standard and humble ashram fare of saltless *daal* and spiceless curry. But the profile of those who live here has certainly changed. While I looked into old issues of the *Ashram Review*, on the table next to mine a young girl was studying for her law exams. She was a Christian from Kerala whose mother lived in the ashram—two young companions for three European ladies who were the wrong side of seventy.

To visit the Christa Seva Sangh today is to be powerfully reminded of the iron law of Indian institutional decay. The average life of a reasonably well-functioning institution is twenty years; none, it seems, remain in good health after the death or disappearance of the founder. Gandhi's own ashrams, Sabarmati and Sevagram, still function in a desultory and decrepit way, but for all the influence they now command they might as well be dead. Why should Winslow's ashram be any different? It requires an effort of the will to think of it as it once was, a centre of active and radical theological work, a bridge between the worlds of Anglican Christianity and an increasingly assertive Indian nationalism.

Whatever its present state, when the party of Englishmen reached Poona in November 1927 they found the Christa Seva Sangh brimming over with energy and inspiration. As Winslow had hoped, it threw down a gauntlet to the clergymen who ministered to the sahibs and lived like them in walled-in bungalows. To Verrier, out of Oxford, it offered a contrast to past experience that was sharp but not unwelcome. Three weeks after arriving in Poona he wrote to F. W. Green with relief and exultation:

> For once in my life not to be treated as a successful examinee! To have no flattery or attention from one week's end to another! To eat always the same food, largely Indian, and none of it very pleasant! To wear sandals, to be clothed in white, to sleep on hard ground! To eat with one's fingers! To dig and to cart mud about! To be bitten all over by mosquitos! To try and learn a language that looks like this [a line in the Marathi script followed]. It is very odd, and very wonderful. I am learning things about Yoga; and shall be visiting Hindu monasteries and ascetics from time to time. I am shortly to meet Mahatma Gandhi. I had a wonderful time with the Jacobite monks in Travancore, and some interesting talks with two Carmelites. And Rome—on the way—completed my conversion.[12]

In January 1928 Verrier was deputed by the CSS to attend a meeting of an International Fellowship of Religions, held at Gandhi's ashram on the banks of the Sabarmati river in Ahmedabad, a night's train journey from Poona. Addressing the delegates, the Mahatma said that 'all religions were true and also that all had some error in them.' From this it followed that 'we can only pray, if we are Hindus, or if we are Mussalmans, not that a Hindu or a Christian should become a Mussalman, nor should we even secretly pray that anyone should be converted, but our innermost prayer should be that a Hindu should be a better Hindu, a Muslim a better Muslim and a Christian a better Christian. That is the fundamental truth of fellowship.'[13]

That all religions were equally true or equally false: this was an argument that Verrier had not heard before, and at first he did not know what to make of it. One evening the Mahatma took the visiting priest aside for a chat, questioning him keenly about his brotherhood. He was pleased that the CSS men wore khadi—the insignia of national renewal—and also that they had observed a day's silence ('spiritual *hartal*,' as Verrier colourfully called it) on the day the Simon Commission arrived in India. Verrier seemed to recognize in Sabarmati a likely model for their own work, 'a simple arduous life of devoted service rooted in the supernatural world.' If this is 'the Heart of Aryavarta,' he remarked, 'never has a nation's heart beat with a purer passion or a more catholic love.'[14] But the priest also made something of an impression on his hosts. In a report he wrote on the fellowship, Gandhi's secretary Mahadev Desai singled out 'Mr Elwin,' a man 'just out of his teens and fresh from Oxford, come to India, as he said, to do some atonement for the sins of his countrymen in keeping India in chains.'[15]

Many years later Verrier was to write that the week in Sabarmati turned him from a fellow-traveller to an 'ardent disciple' of the Indian national movement: 'It was as if I had suddenly been reborn as an Indian on Indian soil.'[16] At the time, he seemed willing to follow Gandhi's politics, but measured his theological position more critically. On returning to Poona he plunged into Gandhi's writings, reading with fascination and not a little dismay the account of his disputes with Christians in South Africa. When an English friend wrote asking for an 'opinion,' Verrier could not quite make up his mind. Gandhi, he said, had certainly impressed him as a saint,

> with a saint's heroism, a saintly joy, and a saint's love; but [he is] something of the faddist, and *intellectually* singularly unsound. He is a born leader of conduct, but not of thought. His religious position struck me as deeply unsatisfactory (and you know how *very* liberal I am to Hinduism in general; I admire it immensely). But Gandhiji's outlook (as for instance that all religions are true) strikes me as neither genuinely Eastern or Hindu, nor genuinely modern in the best sense of the word. Its an amalgam of Ruskin, Tolstoi, Emerson and that gang—a type which I have never understood or liked. But when I think of Bapu, as we call him, the light of his life, his courtesy, his joy, his charm, his prayerfulness, his self-control, his peace, his sway over his noble splendid followers, I can only bow in reverence. Cut off his head, and I would mark him Xt. But his mind is far behind his life . . .

Follow the man, not his mind; in the beginning Verrier could afford to take Gandhi piecemeal. But his immediate mentor demanded unqualified loyalty, which had its own burdens. On the one side, Winslow followed F. W. Green in conveying Verrier into a realm of thought that was 'immensely deeper, richer, more fruitful' than his native Evangelicalism. 'How woefully inadequate Protestantism seems,' observed Verrier, 'specially here in India; a . . . rationalized faith over a deeply supernatural one; a prayer life haphazard and unorganized over against the grand and stately mechanism of the Yoga, . . . a mushroom growth over a venerable religion that makes even Rome look young.'

The problems lay not with Winslow's catholicism but the demands it made on the body. The Rule of the Ashram enjoined Poverty—through a 'hard, stern, inconvenient, exasperating discipline, a thing to be willed, accepted, loved and given to Him, but no light thing'—and Celibacy, which in Winslow's credo was not based 'on any anti-feminism, any homosexual absorption in our own sex,' but grounded rather 'on a tender reverent recognition of the glory and joy of married life,' a life 'deliberately set aside and offered up for the sake of souls.'

To be poor and celibate in Poona was always intended as a struggle. Indeed, in the first months of 1928 two great temptations crossed Verrier's path. The first was an offer to return to his beloved Oxford as Chaplainfellow of Merton to succeed Green (who had been appointed Canon of Norwich). The second, indubitably more threatening, was the attraction of a lady described as 'a beautiful, holy, spiritual woman-soul who shows to one constantly all that must be left if by God's power I am able to persevere.'[17]

Race unknown, name unmentioned; this one fleeting reference is all we have of Verrier's first proper engagement with the other sex. But against the attractions of the woman-soul stood the Rule of the Sangha: for the moment, the latter triumphed. 'I have felt the brunt of these temptations through the whole territory of my being,' wrote Verrier to a friend, 'they have been hard, unbelievably hard to meet, deeply painful and humbling to feel at all; but they have been necessary to re-adjust and strengthen my outlook on these great, holy, and all-too-lightly-undertaken states of life.'[18]

To re-dedicate himself to Winslow's ideals Verrier indulged, as a colleague remembered, in 'rather exaggerated and unwise mortification.'[19] In his memoirs Verrier was more specific without mentioning the temptation these mortifications were designed to cast out. 'All through 1928,' he recalled, 'I was undoubtedly playing with my health. I not only sat and slept on the floor. I went a little further and sat and slept on a cement floor with nothing to protect me but a thin piece of sacking. I gave up my mattress and even my pillows in an ardour for self-discipline. I went barefoot, ate anything I was given.'[20]

Winslow had placed Verrier in charge of the library, whose growing collection was targeted by the resident rat. The creature's tastes were, in a word, catholic. 'After starting on the *Hibbert Journal*, he devoured several volumes of Copec, and then in mystical mood ate the Koran and the Folly of the Cross in a single night. We fancy the creature might be a Theosophist.'[21] While one Indian bug threatened his books, another less solitary bug made for his intestines. When his diet and sleeping habits, always injudicious, were carried through the hot weather into the monsoon, he suffered a violent attack of dysentery. He was admitted to the Sassoon Hospital and for some weeks hovered between life and death. Winslow cut short a tour of south India to be beside his most brilliant disciple, visiting him daily, a 'most wonderfully soothing and understanding soul.'[22] Bishop Palmer arrived from Bombay, some thought to adminster the last rites. Instead, displaying 'to the full the Oxford blend of idealism and commonsense,' he presented the patient with three bottles of champagne.[23]

The champagne helped but in the end his life was saved by the devoted labours of the doctor, Major Plumptree, and the nurse, Sister Hillsom (who had once ministered to Gandhi).[24] After a month in bed he recovered sufficiently to walk but remained much too weak to return to the ashram. The doctor advised him to go home to Oxford for a year, thence to examine afresh his fittedness, physical and otherwise, for India and the monastic vocation.

In October 1928 Verrier returned to his mother's home in Oxford. Rest did not rule out research and his days were spent for the most part in the Bodleian. As a student Verrier had been constrained by an antiquated syllabus, but now his theological horizons were wider. His reading focused on what might connect his native land with the adopted one: specifically, the parallels between the mystical traditions of medieval Christianity and Hinduism.

In six months Verrier produced two slim books, fine illustrations of what would now perhaps be called the dialogue of faiths. The first study, of a book by an unknown mystic of the fourteenth century, sought to make Christian mysticism intelligible to the Indian. The author of 'The Cloud of Unknowing,' wrote Verrier, interpreted the *sastras* or holy books in the vernacular, in the manner of the great Marathi Bhakti poets Tukaram and Ramdas. Religion was thus made more democratic, available to those who understood neither Latin or Sanskrit. Verrier thought 'The Cloud' provided a commentary on an old Indian debate, between the rival claims of *bhakti* (love) and *jnana* (knowledge). The latter was the way of the yogi, and 'The Cloud' was indeed the nearest thing there was to a Christian yoga, with the difference that it claimed to be the work of the supernatural, bringing the soul closer to God.[25]

The book was read and admired by Indian Christians searching themselves for points of convergence between a foreign faith and spiritual traditions native to Indian soil.[26] Its arguments are pursued further in Verrier's study of the theologian Richard Rolle, whom he called, in an inspired comparison, the leader of 'the bhakti movement in fifteenth century England.' For Rolle, as for the Bhakti poets, music and song were the perfect means to express communion with God. In his love of song, this Englishman is 'already an Oriental: he feels with Chaitanya and Kabir the rhythm of the Universe; with N. V. Tilak he would sing, not merely tell, the praise of Christ.' For Rolle and his fellow mystics religion was a 'natural, unsophisticated thing, a song of joy in the heart, the name of the Beloved on the lips, the spontaneous movement of the soul heavenway.' Their joyousness matched the spirit of Bhakti; indeed, these mystics 'would have been perfectly at home in India. How well Rolle would have understood Tukaram! How entirely Mirabai would have appreciated Mother Julian!'[27]

These books point to a now complete disenchantment with Evangelicalism, with its denial of mysticism and its refusal to listen to other faiths. In a bitter commentary on the Church of England as he knew it, Verrier wrote that for Rolle and company the Church was 'no tyrant forcing their originality into a single mould but a courteous and homely mother in whose arms they [found] security and strength.'[28] In writing these books Verrier had before him the example of Jack Winslow, whose intent was the softening of Christianity with doses of Hindu thought, and of Mahatma Gandhi, who sought to invigorate Hinduism with elements of the Christian tradition. By March he was ready to return to India, to test his ideas in practice, but the doctors would not clear him yet. Marking time, he chaired the third annual meeting of Anglican and Russian Orthodox priests. He saw this as carrying forward the CSS model of 'peace-making,' the open-ness to 'all creeds, sects, even religions.' He also spoke to Indian students of London University, finding to his disappointment that many were 'full of a secularist spirit.'[29]

In June 1929 the doctors passed him as fit for travel in a further three months, leaving him 'counting the days till I can return to my beloved country.'[30] He left finally on 29 September, accompanied by Leonard Schiff, another Oxford man bound for the Christa Seva Sangh. En route they spent a couple of days with the Orthodox outpost in Paris. Their hosts had been forced into exile by the godless Bolsheviks, but Verrier took heart in their deep love of Russia. It held a message for him; committed *to* India but in a religious and racial sense never to be *of* it. From Paris they carried on to Umbria, to spend some time with the nuns of the Eremo Franciscano, who were penfriends of Verrier's and fellow admirers of Mahatma Gandhi. 'I am sure,' he wrote to the Umbria nuns before boarding ship at Naples, 'that it is possible for a Christian and a priest to be a disciple of India, just as French or Russian religious [people are] passionately patriotic and truly wedded to their own culture.' Emboldened by his recent researches, he saw Christianity as the fulfilment of the religious history of India, taking the best of all the faiths it found there. God spoke

> through countless voices in the east, heralds of the Incarnation cry out to us through India's mystics and poets, The Eternal Word is uttered silently in her glorious art and sounds in her songs, the Creator is seen in the grand beauty of her woods and rivers and mountains. India is a land alive with thoughts of God, and as though dazzled by the profusion of His Witness, she has become the mother of religions. For here the path truly is from multiplicity to unity, from the diverse to the single, to the one Utterance and

Truth of God in the Face of Jesus Christ. And yet that One is somehow not only the negation but the crown of all that multiplicity. You reach it not only by subtraction, but by *addition*.

The passage to India lay this time through the Holy Land. Verrier and Leonard did the rounds of Bethlehem and Jerusalem before going off to monasteries in the mountains. One was situated on the High Mountain of Temptation, overlooking the valley of the Jordan, its members working with their hands and worshipping in a cave chapel. Not far away was the fifteen-hundred-year-old monastery of Mar Saba, in the vale of Cedron, whose monks lived in rooms cut into the rock. Verrier was impressed. 'Such is the desert,' he remarked,

> the place where men are homeless and God alone at home. That such asceticism, such heroic pilgrimage, such simplicity and solitude of life and such valour of prayer, should still endure in our world which so hates extremes may well make us admire God for the courage of His saints and wonder at our own half-heartedness.[31]

When he reached Poona in November, Verrier found that in the ashram 'half-heartedness' was being measured in strictly political terms. The city and country were in ferment. Already during his first stint with the CSS the peasants of western India had begun a long struggle against land revenue. While he was away working in the Oxford libraries, the Congress met for its annual meeting, passing on 26 January 1929 a resolution demanding that *purna swaraj* (complete independence) be granted within the year. Meanwhile, the Simon Commission was met everywhere by black-flag demonstrations. The police came out in force, and in one clash in Lucknow the Lion of Punjab, Lala Lajpat Rai, suffered mortal injury. The Viceroy, Lord Irwin, rushed to London for consultations and returned with a promise of a conference to discuss 'Dominion Status,' in itself some way short of what was being demanded by Congress. The younger radicals in the Congress, such as Jawaharlal Nehru and Subhas Chandra Bose, were pressing Mahatma Gandhi to come out of his ashram and start civil disobedience once again.

The stage was set for the most dramatic chapter in India's independence struggle. On 2 March 1930 Gandhi gave notice to Irwin that he planned to march to the sea and break British laws prohibiting the making of salt by individuals. Irwin said nothing, so on the 12th the Mahatma took some eighty followers on a procession towards the sea. The 200 miles from Sabarmati to Dandi, the eventual destination, were covered in a leisurely twenty-four days, almost every step covered by the international press. Gandhi reached Dandi village on the evening of 5 April. The next morning he walked to the sea, picking up a fistful of salt with the words, 'With this I am shaking the foundations of the British Empire.' He was arrested soon afterwards but within weeks civil disobedience became an all-India affair. The salt laws, the forest laws, the liquor laws, all aspects of government policy that were seen as life-limiting or unjust, were violated in a thousand locations. The state bore down swiftly, filling the jails with Congress leaders and volunteers.[32]

By early 1930 the country was completely polarized. Some Indians sided with the Raj, many others stood with the Congress and courted arrest. Most unhappily placed was the Christa Seva Sangh, no doubt an extraordinary experiment but one whose inherent frailties were being daily exposed by the Salt Satyagraha and its aftermath. It now had squarely to face questions it preferred to keep buried under the mud. Was it an Indian ashram or a Western-style monastic order? Was it to be run autocratically by Winslow or democratically as a collective? Should it actively preach or merely set an example through exemplary conduct? Was its message addressed to high castes or to outcastes? When the crunch came would it side with the church establishment or with Indian nationalists?

When the crunch came the founder of the ashram left on furlough. In March Jack Winslow departed for England, apparently to raise money and look for new recruits. It is hard not to escape the conclusion that he did not want to decide one way or the other. That burden now fell on Verrier, appointed acting *acharya* (head) of the Sangh. One member, Algy Robertson, advised him to keep the ashram out of politics and work to make it a pure monastic order. On the other side were those who wanted to align straightaway with the Congress, such as Leonard Schiff, and especially an Indian member from Sholapur: this was Shamrao Hivale, who had joined the Sangh late in 1928, after graduating from Rajaram College in Kolhapur. Shamrao came from a family with a record of public service. His brother, B. P. Hivale, was a well-known educationist based first at Bombay's Wilson College and then at Ahmednagar College in the Deccan. Shamrao himself was a passionate nationalist, devoted equally to the politics of Gandhi and the songs of Tukaram. Short, dark, with wavy hair and sparkling black eyes, he was also a most personable character, with more friends, Christian and non-Christian, than any other member of the Sangh.

Leonard and Shamrao both impressed on Verrier the need to take a stand quickly: but he was inclined their way in any case. The rebel in him was drawn to the Congress (in its fight with the Raj very much the underdog), the follower in him to Gandhi, who was a far more substantial figure than Winslow or Green—the two men whose leadership he had previously acknowledged. True, there was the Mahatma's theological indeterminacy to consider; but at the time it seemed trifling when compared with the political indecisiveness of Father Jack.

For all his sincerity and desire for 'reconciliation,' Winslow always took care to stay on his side of the religious and racial divide. Verrier, by contrast, was already speaking and thinking of India as 'my motherland.' As the head of the Ashram he now put into practice a neat syllogism: the Christa Seva Sangh works for India and Indians, the Congress represents India and Indians, therefore the CSS must stand by Congress and Gandhi.

Verrier's decision to throw the ashram into the rebel camp was influenced by a incident in Bombay shortly after Gandhi's arrest. He was visiting some friends who lived in the Girgaum Back Road, close to Mani Bhavan, the city headquarters of the Congress. The Bhavan had been sealed by the authorities, and a group of Congress sympathizers were trying to work their way closer to the building. From a window high above he watched, feeling like 'one of the most miserable men in the world,' his

> fellow-countrymen delivering lathi charges on innocent and harmless passers-by. There was no demonstration; no shouting of slogans; no breaking of the law; not even such a crowd as would interfere with the traffic; only a number of people [who] wanted to look at their loved Congress House now in the

hands of the police. A charming-looking student went up to one of the British sergeants and asked a question: the latter raised his club and struck him in the face. Four stories up I heard the crack of the blow. The sergeant hurled an old man to the ground. He chased and mercilessly beat a boy who was going along the road. He hustled a respectable businessman, knocking his morning paper out of his hand and contemptuously kicking it across the road. I lost all count of the number of people who were assaulted . . .

No one who has ever watched a lathi charge, especially on innocent people, will ever forget it—those huge sticks whirling in the air, the thud and thwack of the blow falling on head or shoulder, the studied arrogance of those who strike, the amazing Christ-like patience of the sufferers.[33]

Jack Winslow in London had hoped that Verrier would steer 'the good barge "Christa Seva Sangh" clear of the fatal rock of unsympathetic aloofness without involving it in the vortex of political strife.'[34] Post-Dandi such neutrality was impossible, certainly in Poona, home to many Indian nationalists and home too to the jail in which some of them were housed. The good barge now had a Roll of Honour up in its chapel, prayers being offered daily for Gandhi, Nehru, Patel, Bajaj and others behind bars. Verrier himself had no doubt on which side justice and the Christian virtues lay. 'How infinitely pathetic it is' he remarked, 'to see Christianity armed and dominant against Hinduism seeking the Cross with Christ.'[35]

To show solidarity with Congress the ashram members resolved to spin daily, propagate khadi and join in the picketing of liquor shops. They also went about collecting instances of violence on the part of the police. Two Brothers even joined an 'illegal' procession to Yeravada, the jail just outside Poona where Gandhi was incarcerated. One was Leonard Schiff, feelingly described by the district magistrate of Poona as 'obviously a fanatical sympathizer with Gandhi and the present Congress movement.'[36] The Archdeacon of Bombay wrote to Verrier, as the head of the ashram, complaining that Leonard had been spotted in public wearing a Gandhi cap. The Brothers, in response, passed a vote of congratulation on [Leonard] for having worn a Gandhi cap.'[37]

In June the ashram was visited by Reginald Reynolds, a young Quaker deputed by the Society of Friends to visit Gandhi in Yeravada prison. Reynolds came to Poona from Ahmedabad, noticing the difference between an ashram solidly behind its leader and a Sabarmati mourning its absent Mahatma. He was charmed by Verrier, whom he had not previously met. 'He was very good-looking,' he remembered twenty years later, 'and in his white khaddar cassock gave an impression of having stepped straight off the streets of gold through one of those gates of pearl.' Reynolds was sure 'that no Hindu institution ever enjoyed so much laughter'. The visitor also recorded one characteristic Elwinism. A London writer had been pouring out figures on the 'benefits' of British rule in India; when Reynolds commented on his inaccuracies Verrier remarked: 'I thought he was no statistician when I found he had dismissed the Trinity in a footnote.'[38]

The CSS in the summer of 1930 was a happy and united band of brothers. When the Bishop of Bombay questioned Verrier's ability to guide the Sangh in Winslow's absence, the rebel's answer was to seek and get a unanimous vote of confidence 'in his dealing with the present political situation above all criticism.' The same meeting, held on 7 July, also 'most willingly' granted Verrier permission to address the Nationalist Christian Association of Bombay.[39] He was to speak on 'Christ and Satyagraha,' a choice of topic testifying to his growing willingness to assume a role outside the Ashram. The priest was becoming the publicist, 'Verrier' giving way to the more formal and more authoritative 'Father Elwin.'

Verrier's Bombay lecture, delivered before a packed audience at the Blavatsky Hall on 9 July, boldly attempted to reconcile Western Christianity with Indian nationalism. He said he spoke not as a member of the CSS, nor as an Englishman, but 'as one who would like to call himself an Indian and who tries to look at things from the Indian standpoint and to identify himself in every way with the country of his adoption.' But he spoke also as a priest, providing theological comfort to those Indians who wished to defy their bishops by following Gandhi.

Verrier began by acknowledging the traditions of civic obedience in Christianity, the injunctions to maintain the status quo and support the state, to render unto Caesar what is Caesar's. But he gave more weight to alternative traditions which justified resistance to the state: for instance, when authority is not just but usurped—as Indians regarded British rule; when the state brings into force unjust laws—such as forest laws and the salt tax in British India; or when rulers impoverish the spirit of fellowship—as the Raj had done by setting up barriers of race and class.

The Christian dissenter also had before him the figure of Jesus, who 'was certainly regarded by his contemporaries as a dangerous revolutionary in every sphere of life.'

As indeed was Gandhi, a man who took the principle of non-violence into politics, who suffused his struggle with prayer, who insisted on Truth, Discipline, Restraint, Patience and Love. No longer did Verrier think Gandhi to be theologically backward; on the contrary he seemed to him to be the unacknowledged Christ of Hinduism. 'On the whole,' said Father Elwin to his flock in Blavatsky Lodge, 'the campaign initiated by Mahatma Gandhi, both in its method and spirit, is more in accordance with the mind of Christ than any other similar campaign that the world has ever seen.'[40]

To an Indian friend who was likewise devoted to Christ and Gandhi, Verrier described his Bombay lecture as 'completely definite, but restrained.' In fact it was terribly provocative, with the printed pamphlet dedicated to 'All my friends in jail.' *Christ and Satyagraha* was reprinted within the month; when Verrier followed it with a devotional series on the Mahatma, published in the nationalist newspaper *Bombay Chronicle*, it was clear that he was 'perfectly willing, indeed anxious, for imprisonment in the cause of India.'[41] Meanwhile, back in the United Kingdom, Jack Winslow was summoned to a meeting at the India Office. The home secretary of the Government of India had posted to London a copy of *Christ and Satyagraha*, its offending passages marked, asking that the CSS's founder be shown the text 'with a view to impressing upon him the undesirability of members of the mission encouraging the Civil Disobedience movement in any way, either by speech or conduct.' On 29 September Winslow was interviewed by the under-secretary of state who told him sternly that his society was 'under the cloak of religion, lending its support to the avowed enemies of Government.' Father Jack 'fully realized the difficulty of the position and prejudice for the Brotherhood [from] tracts such as *Christ and Satyagraha*:' he thought his disciple had the license to speak on the subject, yet 'definitely disagreed' with his conclusions. Winslow then agreed to 'stiffen' up the CSS rule to limit the freedom of Brothers to give voice to their opinions in public.[42]

Winslow returned to Poona on 23 November, and immediately put out an appeal for reconciliation, the bringing in of 'our Lord's own spirit of loving and understanding sympathy to bear upon the issue in dispute, in place of the spirit of mutual recrimination and slander.'[43] But by now the disciple was out of control, going off in early December to join a fact-finding mission to report on allegations of police brutality in Gujarat. The mission was headed by the respected social worker A. V. Thakkar, like Verrier a man sympathetic to the Congress without actually being part of it.

The team spent two weeks in Gujarat, visiting some sixty villages in all. They stayed some nights at Hindu temples, other nights in peasant homes. Verrier went off one day on a side trip to Dandi, where Gandhi had been arrested in April. He saw there a tiny hut made of bamboo and thatch; this was the 'Palace of the real ruler of India,' a stunning contrast to 'the magnificence of the Viceregal Lodge in Delhi, built on the money of millions who hardly get enough to eat.'[44] He also called with the team on refugee camps in the chiefdom of Baroda, meant for peasants facing repression in British territory. In his report Verrier provided vivid illustrations of the beatings of men and women, the confiscation of property, the burning of homes, and the forcible closure of Gandhian ashrams. As he looked into the faces of greybeards insulted and beaten by the police, Verrier 'seemed to see the thorn crowned face of Jesus suffering in all the sorrows of His children.' As he spoke to widows who had been harassed, he thought of his 'own mother, and I wondered how I should feel if my quiet Oxford home were broken open and my mother and sister assaulted and insulted by the police.' This might all be the work of Indian subordinates, but Verrier believed 'the British officials cannot be exempted from responsibility as a word from higher authority could stop most of the abuses.' Would they not have acted if this tale of beating and insult had come from villages in the Cotswolds?[45]

His countrymen had let him down; so too had his church. At least in

India, he noted mournfully, the Church of England 'bears the appearance so largely of being allied to imperialist Britain.'[46] This 'Christian Priest whose duty is to humanity' (as he now spoke of himself) would take the side of free India in politics, and of Gandhi in person. The C of E had betrayed him; happily, he was wanted by all kinds of people outside it. In April alone he addressed the birthday celebrations of the saint Ramakrishna Paramhansa, spoke on Christianity to the Prarthana Samaj of Poona, and presided over a meeting of the Christian Nationalist Party which welcomed its leaders on their release from jail. Everywhere he went Verrier was shadowed by an intelligence agent whose job was to transcribe and transmit his speeches to the home department of the Government of India. The deputy inspector general of police, forwarding these reports to New Delhi, wrote disgustedly of 'Father Elwin's sickly adulation of Mr Gandhi whom he described as a kind of Messiah, the greatest socialist living who was endeavouring to establish a kingdom of the poor for the poor by the poor . . .' The agent's reports were faithful to the spirit if not always to the letter, as witness an account of a speech in Poona which had Verrier saying: 'I first became acquainted with the teachings of Mahatmaji when I was a student at Cambridge and in those days I used to get a portrait of Mahatmaji in my room in order that I may daily enjoy his sight.'[47]

Against those years of worship Verrier could boast of but one brief meeting with his idol, back in Sabarmati in the early weeks of 1928. In April 1931 Gandhi was out of jail and resting in Bombay; finding himself in the same city, Verrier requested Mahadev Desai to arrange an interview. Mahadev asked him to come at four o'clock the next morning. Arriving at the appointed hour, Verrier found his man brushing his teeth with a stick of *neem*. What was he to do? The occasion, he felt,

> demanded ceremony, obeisance; I longed to kiss his feet. But I have not yet quenched my wretched Western sense of humour. You can't touch the feet even of the greatest man in the world if he has a twig in his mouth and is holding a spittoon. So I made a deep but rather stupid bow, and Bapu, removing his twig, gave me one of those perfect radiant smiles which make a man his friend and follower for ever. He made a few remarks and then continued his ablutions. Presently he took his place for Prayers, and asked me to sit by him. Mirabehn sat on the other side, so that this 'Enemy of the British Empire' sat for his prayer between two Britishers!

Later in the day Verrier accompanied Gandhi to a meeting with mill-hands. A group of young communists heckled the Mahatma unmercifully, calling him a traitor for having signed a pact with the viceroy, as well as a tool of the capitalists who helped fund him. Unperturbed by the 'hissing, shouting and mocking laughter,' Gandhi reminded the young men that he had made the worker's cause his own from his South African days, living with them and sharing their sorrows. But he would not countenance the use of violence; rather, by means of his suffering he would awaken the mill-owners to their sense of duty. This approach to the worker–capitalist relation, thought Verrier, would do nicely for the India–British one, that other conflict subject to Gandhi's 'all-sided weapon of love, which will not overthrow and embitter the opponent, but change his heart.'[48]

In Bombay Verrier also met Vallabhbhai Patel, the Congress strongman and chief organizer of the peasant movements in Gujarat. Patel, who must have been greatly pleased by the priest's report on police atrocities, warmly embraced him. He also bumped into Jawaharlal Nehru but did not get a chance to talk to him. Nehru was forty-two and balding, but withal the hero of young India, and the most likely successor to Gandhi. He was also a very handsome man, Verrier writing home of his 'most beautiful face, the face of a dreamer and idealist, keenly intellectual, indomitable and courageous.'

There was in Verrier a great yearning to *belong*; now the Congress took possession of him, as the Anglo-Catholics and the Christian ashramites had previously. As ever, once he took sides he saw things starkly in black and white. In between meetings with Gandhi and Patel he called on the Bishop of Bombay. E. J. Palmer had been replaced by R. D. Acland, an orthodox priest not bound by ties of personal affection to the Brothers in Poona. In a circular letter which was in itself a massive act of insubordination, Verrier wrote sarcastically of the bishop and his position. Acland's bungalow was on Malabar Hill: the windows looked out over the bay, but down on the other side lay the real India, with its crowded bazaars and hot and stuffy third-class railway carriages. The bishop had made of his home on the hill a little piece of England: when Verrier visited him he was digesting lunch in the cushioned depths of his armchair. 'You are very young,' he told Verrier, flicking the ash off his cigar, 'you are inexperienced, you are very very foolish. You have greatly annoyed Government with your report on Gujerat. Personally I don't believe a word of it. I do not know of a single example where the authorities exceeded their duties. Even if they were brutal, they had to be . . . Where would we be if we did not rule by force?' Verrier did not answer back but thought as he went away, 'Yes my Lord, where will *you* be in a free India.'[49]

Back in Poona, Verrier spent the whole of Good Friday spinning. This, he wrote to Gandhi, was a real 'experience of purification;' the *charkha* itself he knew now to be a 'dual symbol of our union with the poor and with God.' He sent the yarn to Mirabehn (Madelene Slade), apologizing for its poor quality. Mira passed it on to Gandhi for inspection. The Master pronounced it 'quite weavable,' with 'the count somewhere near 20.' Nonetheless, he agreed that 'it is poor for the spirit of love and dedication that lay behind the sacrifical act.'[50] Verrier now longed to follow his yarn to Sabarmati. 'Is there any possibility of my spending a week with your party,' he wrote to Mira, the only English woman or man permitted into the Mahatma's inner circle: 'I do so want just to be able to watch Bapu and learn from him.'[51] Gandhi was then touring rural Gujarat, taking stock of the ashrams and schools set up in the wake of the peasant movement. Verrier caught up with him at the Swaraj Ashram in Bardoli and stayed a week. Bardoli was serving as the 'temporary court of one whom millions enshrine in their hearts as their uncrowned king,' yet Verrier found Gandhi extraordinarily accessible. 'You go to him,' wrote the newest of his followers, 'and for those few minutes he is yours—completely. He is thinking about you, and about nothing else. This great mind, which holds in its grasp the vexed problem of a continent, is for the time entirely directed to your little problem.'

It was most likely on this visit that Gandhi told Verrier that just as he regarded Mirabehn as his daughter, he, Verrier, would be his son.[52] But of course Verrier had already adopted the Mahatma as his stand-in father, successor to the chaplain of Merton and the acharya of the Christa Seva Sangh. Verrier's devotion was unconditional, in line with an Indian interpretation of the father–son relationship. While in Bardoli he washed Gandhi's famous loincloth, cleaned his vessels, and prepared his meal of fruits and nuts. In between the Mahatma found time for some 'heavenly conversations' with him.[53]

Bardoli was the hometown of Vallabhbhai Patel, who knew of Verrier's skills as writer and speaker and knew also the value to the Congress cause of this former Oxford don and still-serving priest. Verrier was thus whisked away from the Swaraj Ashram into the villages to speak on Congress' behalf. On 4 June he spoke at Rayan, in honor of forty-two volunteers released from jail, and two days later spoke at a similar meeting in Varad. In both places he deplored the police *zulum* (terror), praising the *satyagrahis* for meeting the state's weapons of violence and untruth with non-violence and truth. Verrier saw the 'spirit of Gandhi Raj' replacing 'Gunda Raj' (rule by hooligans) in Gujarat. Wherever he went he asked forgiveness for the crimes of his countrymen, not all of whom were, as he reminded his audience and himself, opposed to Indian freedom. Gandhi he saw as 'the friend of [the] good element and [the] enemy of the bad element in England.'[54]

By May 1931, still a good eighteen months short of the five years given him by Bishop Gore, Verrier knew that he must leave the Christa Seva Sangh. He was, and had been for some time now, a deep embarrassment to the CSS in the work it hoped to do within the Indian church. Equally, the CSS was an embarrassment to him in such work as he might do outside. He wanted to exchange the contemplative life—which in India seemed 'not only impossible, but a crime'—for an active one. Was he to go back to England and live the 'life of a second-rate scholar,' or was he to 'have another complete "conversion?" ' In the Poona ashram he saw interesting things and met interesting people, but remained 'entirely apart from the suppressed and down-trodden.' So long as he was in the Sangh he would always be seen as a 'Padre-Sahib.' He had to cut himself from the foreign connection, to work more closely with Indians, perhaps even *under* them.[55]

Verrier felt a 'great inner urge away, to more complete poverty, more complete union with India, greater toil, fuller suffering.' He could not, he sensed, truly help the poor save by becoming one of them. This, in India, could mean only that he should 'find a little hut in the "untouchable" quarter of some village and live there as a poor man.' To his friends in Umbria, to whom he felt most akin theologically, Verrier described this as a step of faith at midnight. I have no material or financial resources of any kind. I do not know whether I shall have anyone with me. I have no idea what the future holds. But the vividly-present love of our most sweet Lord tells me that there is a tiny piece of work to do and I shall live to do it.[56]

Leaving the Christa Seva Sangh was unquestionably the most difficult step in a life already marked by departures. It would be a little easier, perhaps, if another inmate were to flee the Winslowian coop with him. Verrier wrote to the most likely volunteer, Shamrao Hivale, asking whether he would come too. Sham was at the time at Muirfield, training at its Benedictine seminary. While he awaited Sham's reply Verrier's education was 'beginning all over again.' He was now learning to cook, to wash, to spin faster and better, to do all the things that would allow him to live with the poor as they did.

By mutual consent Verrier and the CSS decided to part in November, leaving him five months to search for a home and prepare to live in it. In June he was invited by A. V. Thakkar to come on a tour of the ashrams he ran. Thakkar, who had befriended him in the Gujarat enquiry the previous December, was a sure and experienced guide to the poor of India. Born in 1869, two months after Mahatma Gandhi and in the same state of Gujarat, he had first been trained as an engineer. In 1914 he left his job in the Bombay Municipality to join the Servants of India Society, the social welfare organization founded by Gopalkrishna Gokhale. In 1921 he was sent to organize famine relief in the coastal districts of Maharashtra. This brought him face to face with the poverty of Bhil tribals: two years later he founded the Bhil Seva Mandal at Dahod, the first tribal welfare organization run and staffed by Indians. It ran schools and dispensaries for the Bhils, interceded on their behalf with moneylenders and officials, and promoted khadi and temperance.[57]

Mahatma Gandhi was once asked why he paid little attention to the tribes. He replied: 'I have entrusted that part of our work to A. V. Thakkar.'[58] Universally known as 'Bapa' (Father), Thakkar was undoubtedly a man of great integrity, courage and commitment. Thakkar Bapa, wrote an admirer in 1928, was

> a friend of the poor, the untouchable and the aborigine. The cry of torment, anguish and torture attracts him from one remote corner to the other. Whether it be a famine calamity or a flood devastation, official persecution

or temperance work, khaddar organization or opening wells and tanks for untouchables, you cannot miss the mark and the guiding and unerring hand of Amritlal. The theatre of his activities is among the depressed and the oppressed in out-of-the-way places or among forest tribes in the hills.[59]

Before they left for Dahod and the Bhils, Thakkar took Verrier on a tour of the *bhangi* colonies of Bombay. The priest was shaken by the terrible conditions in which the scavengers lived. He described the typical bhangi quarter as 'no more a collection of tiny kennels, the houses built out of the sides of kerosene tins nailed together, without windows, on ground which, when the rain pours down, becomes a swamp exhaling poisonous vapours. Here live brothers and sisters of our own, condemned by a vile social custom to a life of degrading toil.' The sight of Indian poverty was not a pleasant experience, especially in the cities. 'The worst slums in London,' remarked Verrier, 'are nothing to these tenements, laden with humanity, dripping with filth.'

The Bhils, whom he visited next, were also desperately poor, but lived in altogether more attractive surroundings. Thakkar's ashrams he thought models of their kind: small, familial (not more than fifty Bhil boys and girls in each), teaching the three R's alongside vocational skills. He was delighted by the Bhils; unlike the bhangis not degraded and bowed-down, but with a rich culture still intact. They were, he wrote,

> an attractive people, very dark in colour, men with long hair and almost naked, the women covered with heavy brass bangles. They are primitive in their superstitions, offering clay horses, jars and beehive-shaped vessels to the spirits. They live in fear of ghosts and demons. They specially reverence the moon and the horse. They will eat almost any animal, but not the fowl, which is used by witches. They all carry bows and arrows which they use with great precision. They are strong and brave and you may see old men who have killed leopards and tigers with their hands.[60]

The Bhils would fascinate this student of religions; more so as their beliefs were not to be found in the bound volumes on Eastern religions that he had so assiduously studied in the Bodleian. The trip with Thakkar stimulated Verrier but also confused him. The tribes were as neglected as the untouchables—might not he work with them instead? Whatever he decided, he had first to learn to staff and run his own show. From Dahod he proceeded straight to the mother of all modern ashrams, the one in Ahmedabad. Verrier spent almost a month at Sabarmati, staying with Gandhi in his hut, accompanying him on his morning walks, less willingly submitting to the extraordinarily harsh regimen of a seventeen-hour day taken up with prayer, study, spinning, cooking, washing, language class and more prayer. He certainly enjoyed his conversations with Gandhi and learnt a great deal from them. When he asked the Mahatma why he didn't write a commentary on the Gospel, Gandhi replied: 'Hindus do not all accept my interpretation of my own religion, and I would not care to force on Christians my views on Christianity.' One could best serve one's religion, he was told, not by proselytizing but by merely being a better Christian, or better Hindu, or Mussalman or Buddhist. Verrier had heard this before, in January 1928, but he was now more prepared to accept an idea of theological tolerance that went much beyond even the most liberal of Christian traditions, all of which somewhere deep down still stuck to the idea that their superior Gospel must be made available to those who did not follow it.

At Sabarmati Verrier made some new friendships and renewed some old ones. He talked more to Mahadev Desai, Mirabehn, and Vallabhbhai Patel, and was freshly introduced to Acharya J. B. Kripalani, whom he immediately loved, this 'artist, philosopher, poet-turned-spinner.' Kripalani, like the others, had thrown away 'money, position, prospects' to join Gandhi and his movement. Verrier was struck by the idealism and sacrifice but couldn't help noticing that life in Sabarmati was somewhat one-sided. He noted with interest and possibly some nervousness that the strictest chastity was enjoined both within and outside marriage. The Mahatma himself, for the most part so sweet and reasonable, could be 'very stern in his dealings with those [followers] who have moral lapses, and his normal remedy is immediate expulsion from his ashram, always however with the possibility of a return after real penitence has been shown.' Verrier also complained of the lack of culture: the library was open only once a week, there was little interest in art (Kripalani excepted), and music was loved not for its own sake but rather for what it could give to the morning prayers. Then there was the food, which could only be described as 'ashramatic.' Verrier tried to imagine how that lovable epicurean idiot Bertie Wooster would have reacted on being given for lunch a 'steaming hell-brew served up in a great bucket.' Verrier himself offered, for private consumption, these

> THOUGHTS OF A GOURMET ON BEING CONFRONTED
> WITH AN ASHRAM MEAL
>
> (after Francis Thompson)
>
> O food inedible, we eat thee
> O drink incredible, we greet thee.
> Meal indigestible, we bless thee.
> O naughty swear-word, we suppress thee.[61]

Verrier left Sabarmati undecided as to his future. One part of him wanted to go with Gandhi all the way; the other part wondered whether he was up to it, or even if it was worth it. Would he want to follow and enforce at his own ashram a timetable which went:

4.0.	Rising Bell
4.20	Prayer
6.0	Light Breakfast (cup of milk and piece of bread)
6.10–7.0	Study
7.0.–9.0	Spinning and Carding Class
9.15	Hindi Class
10.0	Bath, washing clothes, etc.
10.45	Mid-day meal of chapattis, boiled vegetables and curds
11.15–12.30	Rest
12.30	Lecture on Technique of Weaving
1.30–3.30	Weaving Shed
4.0–5.0	Spinning
5.0	Bathe in river
5.30	Evening meal of chapattis, boiled vegetables, a little rice, and milk. Some fruit.
6.15	Walk
7.30	Prayer
8.0–9.0	Recreation
9.0	Bed

On returning to Poona Verrier fell ill, the fever brought on one thinks by the uncertainty and the self-doubt. He spent a week in hospital, delirious and in strange company: 'other patients gambling till midnight, goats wandering through the wards, buffaloes walking unconcerned through the corridors.'[62] But by the time he was discharged he had made up his mind. He knew for certain that the Christians did not want him. He had not preached in a church for fourteen months and even the liberal-minded YMCA withdrew an invitation to speak because the secretary and his committee felt 'Father Elwin was undesirable,' because he was both too catholic and too Indian.[63] On the other side he was wanted by the Gandhians, including the youngest and most eccentric among them.

He took as symbolic the manner of his departure from Sabarmati. As he prepared to board the *tonga* that would take him to the station, he was surrounded by Mahadev Desai's little boy, Narayan, and three other children, with the secretary of the All India Cow Protection League. The boys hung on to his thin legs and arms, shouting 'Father Elwin, don't go away, Father Elwin don't go away.'[64]

CHAPTER FOUR

Breaking Ranks

Verrier's whole concern was, in one sense, a series of unconscious ways of rebelling against a dominant mother, a powerful Evangelical ... Each stage of his life was one step further away from his mother. His greatest and most dangerous gift was his enchanting character. This was quite uncultivated and he was equally attractive to men and women. There was a light about him. He had humour, gentleness, depth and a great impressive intellect. If only he had a first-class spiritual director, which he never did, things might have been very different!

Leonard Schiff, once of the Christa Seva Sangh

As a missionary Elwin is probably excellent, but as a friend of India he is too credulous and sentimental to be anything but a dangerous nuisance.

Director, Intelligence Department, Government of India

In August 1931 Mahatma Gandhi sailed for London and the Round Table Conference to discuss India's political future. Meanwhile Verrier in Poona finished a book that stated the Congress case before the British public. Remarkably, he had persuaded his acharya to collaborate, Father Jack perhaps thinking that the conference represented a triumph of reconciliation over recrimination. The celebratory chapters, on 'The half-naked fakir' and 'The meaning of satyagraha,' appeared under Verrier's name, with Winslow appending his own signature to a high-sounding but politically innocuous essay on 'The Place of the Christian Church in a New India.' But the book appeared under both their names, Winslow's first, Verrier remarking maliciously that this was sure 'to get poor old Fr. Jack into great trouble.'[1]

The final parting with the Christa Seva Sangh, pushed forward to

September, was welcomed by both sides. Winslow was glad to be rid of his troublesome subordinate, Verrier relieved to be a 'free unfettered worker.' He was more relieved still when Shamrao Hivale wrote from England that he would come with him wherever they went. Shamrao had temporized for a while, for the principal of the Muirfield seminary assured him he would soon be a minister of the Church of England, with a British parish if he so wished. He had now to judge the prospects of a priesthood against an unlicensed life outside the church. As young Indians of the time would, he took his case before the court of Mahatma Gandhi. Boarding the night train from Leeds, Sham arrived at London early in the morning and made straight to Gandhi's temporary home in the East End. He met the Mahatma on his morning walk; Gandhi heard him out and advised him to join his party and return with them to India.[2]

Verrier was most pleased to know that Sham was coming home, that with him would be an Indian bridge to the poor. They would collect Hindu brothers, Muslim brothers, Christian brothers, in a truly inter-faith fellowship. 'I don't want a lot of theology about it,' wrote the leader, 'but I want so much love, divine, supernatural, holy, Christ-like love, that the [religious] differences will be submerged.'[3]

One senses in this freewheeling ecumenism the influence of those heavenly conversations in Bardoli and Sabarmati. Indeed Gandhi in London offered to old-style Christian imperialists the example of his disciple. Addressing a group of missionaries on 8 October he told them that, were he an English priest, he would 'go into [the poor] as Elwin has gone . . . He will establish Christian ashrams among the untouchables, with a church in a mud-hut for his own and his colleagues' use. He wants simply to live with them as God may guide his life.'[4]

Back in India, however, Verrier had started moving away from the untouchables. Vallabhbhai Patel told him the outcastes were not his problem; the Hindus, who had thrown them out of society, must themselves make 'reparation' for them. The argument made sense to Verrier, but Patel, a canny politician, must also not have wanted Hindus shown up by a Christian radical directing attention to the iniquities of the caste system. In any case, the priest himself began favouring the tribes. For one thing, they lived amidst woods and hills, not in festering city slums or beyond the boundaries of villages. For another, his Bhil experience showed that they had a rich and still-vigorous culture. With the tribes one had a real chance of doing *something*, helping them through schools and hospitals to make an honourable truce with the modern world.

It was another Congressman, Jamnalal Bajaj, who suggested that he work with the great Gond tribe of central India. Bajaj was a prosperous merchant and treasurer of the Congress, based in Wardha, in the Central Provinces. Wardha is close to being the exact geographical centre of India; this, and the proximity of Bajaj and the availability of his funds, was to make Gandhi move there from Sabarmati in 1936. 'Why don't you do something for a tribe,' Jamnalal now asked Verrier, 'which is almost entirely neglected both by national workers and by missionaries?'[5]

In the first week of November Verrier took a train from Bombay to the little market town of Betul, up on the Satpura plateau. From Betul two Congressmen accompanied him into the forest. They called at Banjaridhal where, that previous summer, the tribals had revolted against the forest restrictions. 'No lectures were given,' according to the intelligence report, but the Gonds were asked if they had any complaints to make. The party moved on to the adjoining district of Chhindwara, where Verrier's search took him to the village of Tamia, on the road to Pachmarhi. Tamia was pretty but its attractions had already been noted. Finding it the headquarters of a Swedish mission-centre and hospital, Verrier retreated in haste.

The Central Provinces tour of 'Father Elwin, a European dressed in khadi' was well covered by his faithful CID agent. We know thus that his final port of call was Wardha, where on 15 November he at last made a speech, its contents fancifully embroidered by his shadow. In this account the priest had learnt to make bombs and fire guns in the Great War. Then he read in the trenches a collection of Gandhi's speeches and decided to come to India 'to fight a different battle.' He apologized in person to the Mahatma, taking thereafter to khadi and the charkha, as a disciplined soldier of Indian freedom, or swaraj.[6]

The making of bombs might have not figured in Verrier's c.v., but his first commitment was undoubtedly to Gandhi and swaraj. A mark of this commitment is the fact that it was only after he decided to live with the Gonds that he made contact with Alex Wood, Bishop of Nagpur, in whose diocese the Central Provinces fell and who in the hierarchy of the church was his superior. Verrier finally wrote to the bishop on 12 December of their plans to buy land in Betul with the help of Jamnalal Bajaj, asking for his blessing and license. To write to Wood last, he said, was 'part of my whole scheme—of beginning at the opposite end, and working from the Indian standpoint.' The ashram he planned would be 'open to all religions; it would serve the people, but not be "Missionary" in the ordinary sense. The Christian members would try to express the spirit of Christ in love and service; that would be their sermon. Another thing in my mind was that I should only go where I was invited by the people of India themselves.'[7]

The bishop was not pleased with the timing of the letter, still less with its contents. To his superior, the Metropolitan of India, he communicated his anger at Verrier going to the Gonds at the invitation of Jamnalal Bajaj. Bajaj, he complained, 'has as much right to invite a Christian Mission to the Gonds as I would have to invite a Hindu Mission to start work in Italy.' He was also worried that Verrier was not going to 'cure souls.' He knew of his great gifts as writer and speaker, and doubtless hoped that with his spiritual direction the young man would come to proselytize among the Gonds. To that end he craftily suggested an alternative location. 'I am perfectly certain,' wrote the Bishop to Verrier, 'that you would be welcomed by the Gonds themselves in a certain portion of the Mandla District called Karanjia. This place has acquired more or less a sacred character from the fact that a band of German missionaries opened up work there in 1841 and four of the party died and are buried there. They have had no successors . . .' Karanjia, he said, was a first-class location because it was surrounded by Gond villages, yet was not far from a reservation of the Baigas, 'another people who have been practically untouched by Missions.' The village was also on the pilgrim route to the temple in Amarkantak, the source of the river Narmada, to which came devout Hindus from all over northern India.[8]

Betul, Chhindwara, or Mandla—the final decision would have to await his friend's return. Shamrao had booked himself on the same ship, the *S. S. Pilsna*, as the party coming home from the abortive Round Table Conference. When the *Pilsna* docked in Bombay, on 28 December, Verrier was in the huge crowd that assembled to greet Gandhi. First in line were members of the Congress Working Committee who took the great man away for an emergency meeting. Verrier saw Gandhi but was too shy to greet him. He felt bad about it afterwards, but 'it had to be,' he consoled himself, for the Mahatma 'was facing issues too momentous for any individual to claim him.'[9]

Shamrao Hivale met Verrier straight off the boat, the issues he faced being momentous only for the two of them. The friends left immediately for Matheran, a quiet town perched on top of the Western Ghats, sixty miles south of Bombay. Here they discussed Bajaj's proposal and Wood's, on occasion it seems in the presence of a woman-soul. Once more, all we have is a single reference in a letter written to the Italian sisters. On 2nd January he wrote to them that

> Next week we go out 'not knowing whither.' Government is preventing our getting land; we may remain homeless; we may be arrested . . . And just at this moment a crushing pain has come to me, the greatest trial of years I think—I cannot share it—I can only offer it to the Heart of Sorrow and of Love.[10]

Matheran, with its hills, lakes and long lonely walks along wooded paths, was the perfect setting for romance. At just this point of time, two other eccentrically gifted Englishmen were falling in love in Indian hill-stations. In Simla Malcolm Muggeridge was in the throes of a passionate affair with the Indo-Hungarian artist Amrita Sher-Gil; while in nearby Kulu the journalist Ian Stephens was worshipfully following Penelope Chetwode, daughter of the commander-in-chief of the Indian army, on horseback. One alliance across the racial barrier, the other across a social one, both abetted by the air of the mountains, neither designed to last.

Verrier's flame was not of this eminence. She was, judging from a later confession, a Parsi doctor named Ala Pocha, originally from Poona but now also a member of the Mahatma's outer circle. They met, they talked, they held hands and walked, but in the end it was Verrier who drew away in favour of the Gonds and the vow of celibacy by which he still felt bound.

At Matheran Verrier and Shamrao decided on Karanjia, but they were not to go there just yet. On the morning of the 3rd January a telegram arrived from Mahadev Desai in Bombay, asking them to come at once. The London conference not having yielded what he wanted, Gandhi announced a fresh round of civil disobedience. When Sham and Verrier reached Mani Bhavan that evening, they found a huge but peaceful crowd assembled outside. Inside, Gandhi was sitting on the floor, spinning. As it was his weekly day of silence he scribbled a note saying that Mahadev would give them 'instructions.' These were duly conveyed: a request to travel on behalf of the Congress to report on the political situation in the North-West Frontier Province.

Sham and Verrier slept that night with Gandhi's party, their beds laid out under a tent on the roof of Mani Bhavan. At the crack of dawn they were woken up by a whispered message: 'The police have come.' They got up to see a uniformed commissioner of police touching the Mahatma on his shoulder and saying, 'Mr Gandhi, it is my duty to arrest you.' The prisoner had half-an-hour to get himself ready. Five minutes is what it took to brush his teeth and put on a clean dhoti. Gandhi then led the singing of a Vaishnava hymn, and wrote a few last letters. One was a set of instructions to his partymen, another a message to Verrier which read

> My dear Elwyn [sic],
> I am so glad you have come. I would like you yourself to tell your countrymen that I love them even as I love my own countrymen. I have never done anything towards them in hatred or malice and God willing I shall never do anything in that manner in future. I am acting no differently towards them now from what I have done under similar circumstances towards my own kith and kin.
> with love
yours
M. K. Gandhi[11]

Also arrested in different parts of India were Nehru, Patel, Rajagopalachari, Bajaj and others. The lesser Congressmen, still at large, immediately got to work. Devadas Gandhi, the Mahatma's youngest son, called on some Congress-minded merchants who put up the money for the Frontier trip. Meanwhile Bernard Aluwihare, who was also sleeping on the Mani Bhavan terrace that night, lent his old Oxford friend his suit.

Verrier resorted to being a sahib, travelling under false pretences, else he would not have been allowed into the Frontier. In that province one of Gandhi's most remarkable followers, Khan Abdul Ghaffar Khan, had led a peaceful satyagraha among the gun-toting Pathans. This was known as the movement of Khudai Khitmatgars (Servants of God); at its height it commanded 100,000 volunteers. But in December there had been a massive crackdown which put the leaders and countless Khitmatgars into jail. The Congress leadership had little news from this distant province, and no journalists were allowed in either. Hence the dispatch of a sympathetic Englishman posing as a commercial traveller, the faithful Sham as his Indian 'assistant.'

Verrier and Sham left Bombay on the 6th by the Frontier Mail, stopping in Delhi en route. Here they met one of Mrs Elwin's friends, the wife of Sir Lancelot Graham, secretary to the legislature. When Verrier asked Lady Graham what the attitude of the CP government might be to their projected work with the Gonds, she arranged for him to meet the home secretary, H. W. Emerson. Verrier liked Emerson, a 'hard hitting straight man,' but was dismayed by his advice, which was that he was not likely to be allowed into the Gond country unless he gave an undertaking not to support the Congress in speech or in writing.[12]

Of course neither the Grahams nor Emerson knew why Verrier was in Delhi in the first place. The traveller and his assistant continued their northbound journey, reaching Peshawar on the 9th. In the Frontier, where the Raj was at its most reactionary, where white only talked down to brown, Sham was made to sleep in the verandah outside his friend's room. When they got their bill there were two items, marked 'Food for the Sahib' and 'Food for the Fellow,' the latter at half-price.

Peshawar itself was under curfew and the police were out in force. During the day Verrier stayed indoors while his servant went out into the bazaar to make contacts with Congress sympathizers—merchants, lawyers, students and others. Under cover of darkness some rebels crept into the hotel to pass on eyewitness accounts of the movement and its suppression. One day the visitors hired a car and went out into the hills, calling on the Afridi tribesmen. Then Verrier made the mistake of trying to obtain the other side of the story. He wrote to the deputy commissioner, revealing his mission and requesting an interview. He received in reply an order externing him from the province. The police came round to search their room and luggage; what they failed to find were their notes on the trip, hidden inside a packet of breakfast cereal placed boldy on the table. They left Peshawar by the next available train.[13]

Verrier's Frontier report put together the evidence they collected on state repression: the column marches, the aerial sorties, the massive arrests and beatings of Khudai Khitmatgars. He admitted that the Pathans had occasionally deviated from the path of non-violence, but in his view this did not justify the terror. The 'ordinary Englishman in the Frontier,' he noted, 'is callous and without imagination,' illustrating 'the old India at its worst.' But he was sure his side would win in the end. The spirit of peaceful revolution, among the Pathans and elsewhere, would not 'be crushed, and soon through truth, patience, love and suffering, it will lead the people to victory.'[14]

Verrier and Sham were removed from the Frontier on the 15 January; within a fortnight they were on their way to make their home in a village they had not previously set sight on. Not yet thirty, Verrier had already forsaken a comfortable career in England for an uncertain life overseas; cast his lot with a small, struggling sect rather than rest securely within the folds of the Anglican church; and gone on to become a camp follower and occasional cheerleader of a popular movement aimed at the overthrow of the British empire. But the move to Karanjia was more noteworthy still. There were at this time in India a few Englishmen, such as Jack Winslow, sincerely interested in intercultural dialogue; fewer still, like C. F. Andrews, willing to harness their Christian belief to the antiimperialist struggle; but none who had actually identified with poor Indians to the extent of living with them.

The district of Mandla, in whose northern corner lay the village of Karanjia, was called, by a British civilian who had once served there, the 'Ultima Thule of civilization, the dreaded home of the tiger, the Gond, and the devil.'[15] Rugged and utterly beautiful, dominated by magnificent sal forests, the district is now crisscrossed by an all-weather road which touches Karanjia en route to Amarkantak. But in 1932 one had first to take a train to Pendra Road, thirty-five miles away, and then travel over jungle and ghat by foot, which took three days, or by bullock-cart, which took five. Laden with books, medicine and food, Verrier and Sham took the slower route. Karanjia, which they reached at noon on the 30th, they found to be a scattered collection of hamlets set in a wooded valley. The smallest of the hamlets, with the lovely name of Tikeri Tola, was situated on a hill at the edge of the forest with wonderful views all around.

The visitors had come unannounced and the villagers were at first downright hostile. Verrier later recalled, with some feeling, the moment of their arrival in Karanjia: 'We had been travelling with a buffalo cart for three days; we were very tired; none of the villagers would come near us; ... the D.C. had ordered us out of the district—and I remember sitting down on a big stone, and its coolness reminded me of a stone seat in Merton Chapel where I used to sit on Sunday evenings and look at that glorious place lit dimly by candles and hear the organ—and I wished I was there.'[16]

Sham and Verrier were finally allowed to rent a room by a Mussalman, Hyder Ali, who was outside the caste system anyhow. At first no one was willing to sell milk and vegetables except an old woman out of caste 'on account of an irregular maidenhood.' It was when they were visited by the police that the Gonds decided they were men of standing and began coming round. It helped that Shamrao was able to treat men beaten up by other men or merely bitten by scorpions.[17] By late February Verrier was writing that Sham was already 'the adored of the village going on errands of love to the sick'—he was also his friend's 'delight and comrade and helper.'[18]

The police had come on the advice of the district magistrate of Mandla, alerted by his superiors in the Central Provinces administration, in turn put wise by Emerson in New Delhi. The home secretary thought 'Elwin's presence among the Gonds in present circumstances could hardly fail to be a disturbing influence and probably the cause of trouble.' The priest, he remarked, was 'a highly strung neurotic young man who believes he has a mission in India.' (Political disagreement, in the Raj's understanding, could stem only from an excess of nervous energy.) Unlike Emerson the chief secretary of the Central Provinces had not yet met Elwin, but after a close study of the Bombay Secret Proceedings decided he did not want him in his territory. He warned the commissioner of the Jabalpur division that 'Elwin is a young man with plenty of brains and is also capable of great self-denial and means well apparently, but is neurotic and imbued with that form of charity which sees good only in himself and those who play upon his vanity.'[19]

Like their colleagues in Peshawar the policemen who visited Karanjia failed to find the evidence to clinch their case. This was the manuscript of Verrier's book *Truth about India*, written in his first few weeks in the village and published in London later in the year. Here he drew attention once again to the chasm separating British precept from colonial practice. The 'champions of liberty,' he remarked, had turned the subcontinent 'into a vast prison-house.' Instead of forcing 'our alien, unwarranted, extravagant, irresponsible rule upon India by the sword,' the British should take heed of Gandhi's 'message of friendliness and hope' and depart before they were thrown out. A reviewer wrote of the book that 'though the author does not belong to the Congress, the case for the Congress could hardly be put with more convincing advocacy.'[20]

While Verrier wrote away, Shamrao organized the construction of their ashram. The site was atop Tikeri Tola; the labour, local men and women; the materials they worked with, bamboo, mud, and grass. By early March the building had come up, a little house with five little rooms in front, a chapel at the back, the two enclosed by a mud wall leaving an open courtyard in the centre. The wall was decorated Gond-style, with motifs of tigers, elephants and other animals; Verrier overriding Sham's objections that this would lend support to 'animist superstitions'—he answered that it was really a new zoo for St Francis, after whom the ashram was named. The ashram flew a saffron flag with the cross high above it and was approached by a long flight of steps, much like a temple. All told it had cost one hundred rupees, or seven pounds sterling.[21]

To better know the neighbourhood the two friends visited the source of the Narmada at Amarkantak. Walking round the river with Hindu pilgrims, Shamrao had a 'wonderful interior awakening, a kind of mystic conversion.' He had dreamt that something like this would happen if he were to visit the Holy Land, but God's ways were 'so strange' that, when his soul was touched, it was where thousands down the centuries had searched for other gods. He was now thinking of taking the saffron robe, of being a 'real brother' to everyone.[22]

Shamrao had, in any case, seen their move to the forest as a 'deliberate attempt to find reality away from the bustle and confusion of politics.'[23] But Verrier, poor fellow, remained confused, torn between social work and political work, quiet service or heroic martyrdom. On the one side he agreed with Shamrao that 'the turmoil of the political world made a cold and alien home for the spirit.' On the other side, as he wrote to Mirabehn, he would always 'be ready to go on an enquiry' for the Congress, hoping no doubt he would finally be arrested. One detects a tinge of envy—if Madelene Slade, the admiral's daughter, could be imprisoned several times in Gandhi's cause, why not this son of a bishop? 'How I long to go to jail,' he wrote, 'to show really that I love India.' This love shone through his dreams, too; one of these placed Queen Victoria in Purgatory, to remain there till the last Indian child gained its freedom.

The weekly visits from the police, a letter from the district magistrate stating that 'in view of your political record we do not want you in this district,' all seemed to point to an eventual arrest. As it happened it was not the political but the clerical establishment which took him on. The Bishop of Nagpur wrote saying that he would license him only if he took an oath of allegiance to the king-emperor and a further oath of canonical obedience to himself. Only this, the bishop felt, would separate Verrier 'absolutely from the Congress Party which has been declared an illegal association on account of its unconstitutional and unlawful methods of working.' A lively correspondence followed, with Verrier defending Congress as the 'mouthpiece and representative' of the Indian people and calling Gandhi the 'most sublime and Christ-like figure now living on the planet.' He handed his superior a lesson in theology, quoting St Augustine to the effect that the church would be a city which summons citizens from all tribes; which meant, in the present context, that it 'must enfold within its arms of love everyone in India, from the member of the European Association to the most extreme follower of Pandit Jawaharlal Nehru.' 'No one nowadays,' he loftily concluded, 'makes the unphilosophical and unCatholic separation of politics and religion, and it would be contrary to my whole thinking to do so.'[24]

Bishop Wood replied to the lesson more in sorrow than in anger. Gandhi, he said, far from being Christ-like, wanted 'the re-establishment of some form of the Vedic Religion and culture in India, when his party has the power.' But Verrier, in contrast, appeared to him to 'have gifts which might be of great value if used in the service of our Lord and for extending his Kingdom.' He could not believe that Verrier meant all that he said, and would come to Karanjia to interview him personally. 'I always believe in giving a man a fair chance,' said the bishop.[25]

Wood came to Karanjia on 8th April, accompanied by two of his priests, one of these an Ulsterman and fanatic imperialist. The next day the bishop penned a long account, for the Metropolitan, of what was 'on the whole a most interesting [but] unsatisfactory interview.'[26] He described Verrier as 'very fit and as charming as ever,' Shamrao merely as his 'protege.' The last time he saw them they wore khaddar cassocks in the CSS style, but now they were clad in kurta and dhoti. Verrier had a bare head and bare feet and a black umbrella, 'all signs of the priesthood gone. He looked like Bearse, our Indore Professor, who thinks he has become a Hindu.' The bishop was not much more impressed by the ashram. True, it was perched on a 'delightful little hill,' but it looked decidedly temporary. The roof was thatched; he thought 'the whole thing will go to pieces in the first heavy Monsoon shower.' The room had no furniture of any kind. There were blankets on the floor, though, to sit on. The chapel had an altar with a cross and candles. On its left was displayed a list of prisoners to be prayed for, headed by the Mahatma's name. On the right hung another and more palatable list which included the souls of the German missionaries buried in Karanjia.

A narrative of the interview followed. In response to Verrier's statement that the ashram would 'not be missionary in the ordinary sense,' and no one's religion would be interfered with, the bishop asked the question: 'Our Lord says go, teach and baptise. Gandhi says, go, teach but don't baptise. Whom would he follow?' Verrier became distressed and said their work would be their sermon, but no one would be definitely moved to become Christian. Wood dismissed this as the 'YMCA platform,' with 'all the privileges of Christianity but no urge to baptism.'

The talk then turned to politics. Verrier, in his own account, written three years later, remembers reminding Wood that the bishop served as a chaplain in the Great War, thus giving moral support to those whose job was to kill others. He had acted as a sort of chaplain too, but to a non-violent army using the weapons of non-violence and truth.[27] The bishop recalled it differently, with himself scoring the debating points. Verrier, he said, got 'very impassioned and said the best way to serve the King Emperor was to be the bitter enemy of the Government of India.' Wood rejoined that 'had it not been for the organization of the Government and the self-sacrifice of many of its officers and others during the famines of 1895–6–7 and 1899–1900 most of the Congress supporters would not now be alive to curse the Satanic Government that gave them life.' Even Shamrao, he said meaningfully, was a 'famine-child.'

The bishop finally asked Verrier what link he desired with the church. Did he want to follow C. F. Andrews in rejecting his orders and becoming a 'perjured priest?' The younger man said he didn't want to resign his orders but gave the example of the Bishop of London who had licensed a Bolshevik priest who flew the hammer-and-sickle with the cross atop his church (the priest was probably his old CSS mate, Oliver Fielding-Clarke). He then told Wood that his own clergy flew the Union Jack over their churches. The bishop said this was not with his approval; he only allowed the Red Cross of St George. At this point Shamrao, who had stayed silent, interjected with 'A Bloody Red Cross.' The bishop's seconds also entered the fray. The Ulsterman was boiling over, enraged that Verrier had 'blasphemed' the empire and the Union Jack. He called him a traitor, a renegade and a few other things besides. That ended the interview, the visitors going off without even drinking their tea.

Wood confessed that he couldn't help liking Verrier, 'though his opinions are utterly poisonous gall to me.' He would not license him in his present state of mind but hoped that he would come round to dedicating his prodigious powers to the extension of Christ's kingdom. 'If he would only put Christ before Congress and Khaddar,' he remarked wistfully, 'he would be a perfect missionary—perfectly wonderful.' 'I like the lad,' said Wood, 'but I don't like Shamrao. I think he is there to keep Elwin up to the mark. He is a hard rather stupid Maratha. The most persistent of Indian races.'

This was unfair to Sham who, for the most part, followed Verrier rather than led him. Actually both were quite shaken by the interview and the attitude of the bishop. If Wood did not license him, wrote Verrier to the Metropolitan, 'we shall not grumble. We have youth on our side, and we can afford to wait a decade or two for the recognition of our work. But whatever happens, you may be assured that nothing will shake my allegiance to the Church of my baptism and ordination.'[28] His resolve was strengthened by a moving and most understanding letter from Mahatma Gandhi. 'I wish you would not take to heart what the Bishop has been saying,' urged this veteran of many battles with the bishops of his own religion: 'Your pulpit is the whole earth. The blue sky is the roof of your own church.' The message of Jesus, declared Gandhi, 'is in the main denied in the churches, whether Roman or English, High or Low.' Gandhi thought that excommunication by the bishop was itself 'the surest sign that the truth is in you and with you.'[29] To underline that Christ did not belong only to his highly-salaried defenders, he took up an old suggestion of Verrier that they sing a Christian hymn in Sabarmati. They now sang 'Lead, Kindly, Light' in a Gujarati version every Friday evening at 7.40, wrote the Mahatma; maybe they could join them, at the same time, wherever they were.[30]

Verrier also took heart from the life of St Francis. He had been reading numerous biographies of the saint in preparation for a study commissioned by the Christian Literature Society of India. He found that Francis was much like Gandhi in his love of the poor and love of love, although he 'would not have cared for the Mahatma's food-rules nor had he any real interest in political affairs.' The life of the saint also recalled the life of the Marathi Bhakti poet Tukaram—born likewise into well-to-do stock but who, falling in love with poverty, 'wandered, God-intoxicated, from place to place, singing his songs of love.' Both Tukaram and Francis 'had the same tender love of animals; both were marked by an astonishing humility and a joy that triumphed over every obstacle; both were utterly unconventional and utterly lovable.' Writing the book in May 1932 the author unsurprisingly also found parallels between Francis and himself. The saint of Assissi, wrote this priest who would not be licensed by his own bishop, 'was a churchman who was also a free man. His churchmanship never impeded the onward-rushing splendour of his liberty.' Francis established his order without any reference to a Bishop, and freely preached while a layman. 'The fact that these irregularities were tolerated' was 'an indication that the medieval Church was not the steel-frame organisation of modern rationalist fancy.'[31]

Fighting with his Bishop, writing on St Francis, Verrier made little progress with the work of the ashram. Meanwhile Mrs Elwin, who had not seen her son in three years, wrote asking him to come home for the summer. He was at first worried that if he left India he would not be allowed to return. His passport was due to expire in July: as a precautionary move he visited the passport officer in Bombay. The official told him that due to a technicality it could not be renewed in India, but once he reached London he would have no difficulty in having it endorsed there. Reassured, Verrier made plans to spend four months in England, seeing mother, raising funds for their ashram and, not least, trying to 'stir the conscience of friends about what is happening in India.' There was also the 'prospect of some spiritual fellowship' in Europe, of finding Christians who were willing to talk to and be seen with him. While Verrier was away Shamrao would be learning the ashram trade at Thakkar's Bhil Seva Mandal and at a Christian ashram at Tirupattur in south India.[32]

The day before Verrier left for London he issued a statement denying rumours that by going to the Gonds he had lost faith in the Congress. It remained for him 'the only political organization that represents the masses of India,' while the 'advent of the political idealism of Mr Gandhi [was] the most important event of the twentieth century.' Out of the jungle, temporarily, Verrier plunged with relish into the maelstrom of politics. He stopped in Europe, calling on pro-Indian groups in Italy, France and Switzerland. He spent a day with the Mahatma's most famous biographer, Romain Rolland, at his home in Villeneuve. When he reached London, on 15th July, he was met by his family, but also by Agatha Harrison and Professor Horace Alexander, well-known Quaker admirers of Gandhi. His first public meeting, that same evening, was at the East End: he thought 'Bapu would like that.' In the chair was George Lansbury, leader of the Labour opposition in the House of Commons. The next morning he spoke at the Quaker headquarters, Friends House in Euston, the meeting convened by the India Conciliation Group, the India League and The Friends of India.[33]

In between 'rushing here and there, seeing people and addressing meetings,' Verrier spent time at his home in Oxford. His mother he found on the edge of a nervous breakdown because of his religious views: 'Mother is all with us over India, but religiously she talks a different language.' (She had been converted to his political views by Gandhi and Mahadev Desai when they called on her the previous year). He asked his friends to pray for her: 'her protestantism is such a barrier,' he complained, 'it is fanatical.' When his old director F. W. Green told him that the bishop's refusal to license him did not mean that he couldn't celebrate, he rushed off to the chapel of the APR house in London. But his mother then refused to take the sacraments from him because he had celebrated like a Catholic, in vestments.[34]

In the last week of July Verrier sent in his application for a new passport; it was countersigned by George Lansbury, a final provocation to add to all the others. It now came out that the passport officer in Bombay had lied; he had full authority to extend the document but was advised not to. British consuls in Rome, Paris, Naples, Lyons—wherever Verrier might call en route—had been telegraphed warning them not to give him what he wanted. The Government of India also communicated to the secretary of state in London their wish to see this trouble-maker safely out of India. But he was of that opinion anyhow. The week Verrier landed in England a journal brought out by British sympathizers of Gandhi published an essay by him where he characterized British rule in India as that 'of some hulking bully stamping on a lovely and defenceless bird.' The imagery deeply angered the secretary of state and his underlings: this was the kind of writing, they said, 'that set young Indians out to murder Englishmen.'[35]

On 29th July 1932 Verrier was informed he would be issued a fresh passport but it would be stamped 'invalid for India.' He could go anywhere in the world or the British empire (pretty much the same thing), except where he most wished to be. Verrier was devastated. The next day he wrote a long letter to the secretary of state, Sir Samuel Hoare, explaining that his work with the Gonds was purely non-political. In any event, he did not 'see how the presence of a follower of St Francis working for Christ in the remote jungles of the Central Provinces is going to disturb Law and Order in India.' He complained of the chicanery of the Bombay official; he would have cancelled his passage had he known the truth. For he

> could never have risked—even at serious cost to my health—the possibility of exile from India. My home is in India; my work, my books, my papers, are in India . . . There is a group of devoted Indian Christians who have left everything to join me in working for the poor for whom I am responsible. I have nothing to live on in England, and I have nothing to do in England.[36]

Verrier knew enough of the Raj to think this direct approach might not work. He thus contacted William Paton, secretary of the International Missionary Council, a liberal churchman with wide experience of India. Paton had several times visited the CSS ashram in Poona; indeed, in 1931 he was asked by the India Office to report on the Brothers' activities. He had then described Verrier as 'a very charming person and a considerable scholar' whom he would try and persuade to 'rein in his horns.' Paton was pained by the racial divide erected by British clergymen working in India. He remarked of Verrier and Leonard Schiff that 'foolish though they may be in certain of their words and actions, they have, at great cost to themselves, tried to cross that [racial] barrier and to identify themselves with Indians. In so far as they succeed, they are real instruments of goodwill.'[37]

This time around it was the rebel rather than the authorities who called upon Paton's services. Verrier told him that if only he was allowed to go back to the Gonds, he would give an undertaking to stay away from politics altogether. Conveying this to the India Office, Paton said he could not himself believe 'that so unselfish and manifestly Christian a person can in the long run do other than good by being in India, for his influence tends to make Indians better men and to demolish racial feeling.'[38]

Verrier, spreading his bets, had also approached another of his influential friends. On 31st July he wrote to Lady Graham, briefly in England, but preparing to return with her husband to Sind, of which province he had just been appointed governor. Verrier repeated the offer of an undertaking, for he only wanted to return to their work in Karanjia, which 'is just starting beautifully.' But were he made to remain in England he would be 'forced into all sorts of political activities!'

When Lady Graham wrote stating the government's case that he had been a 'very unfair and very uncharitable opponent,' Verrier answered that

'I see things from underneath and you see them from above, and they look completely different.' In any case all that was behind them, for God had now called him to the Gonds. Would not her husband ask the government to offer a 'honourable' undertaking? The threat he now unveiled was a more telling one. If he couldn't return, said Verrier, his co-workers would 'be miles away from any Church and cut off from the Sacraments which mean so much for them. For their sake so that they may have their communions—I am ready to agree to any conditions.'[39]

The euphemisms, the exaggerations, the threats subtly held out, all bear the mark of a writer who knew his audience and how best to move it. Sir Lancelot Graham sent the letters on to the India Office, adding his opinion that Verrier would honour any undertaking he signed. London consulted the Government of India, who were in no mood to relent. 'Whatever his assurances,' commented the chief secretary of the Central Provinces, 'his harmlessness cannot be taken for granted.' For his record showed 'him to be of so unbalanced a mind that it would be an undoubted relief to Government if he left India and did not return here.' 'It is clear,' added an official of the home department, that 'Mr Elwin was out in India for little more than fishing in troubled waters.' In any case 'he was not a dependable character, and it seems unlikely that any great reliance could be placed on any undertaking to be given by him.'[40]

These opinions were all forwarded to the home secretary, M. G. Hallett. On 23rd August Hallett wrote to the viceroy advising him not to allow Elwin to come back, this 'in his own interests as well as the interests of Government.' On the evidence put on his table, he thought it doubtful that the priest would 'really cut himself adrift' from the Congress. The next day he was visited by Sir Lancelot Graham, carrying copies of his wife's correspondence with Verrier, supported by his own recommendation. Placing this personal approach from a colleague against file notings by his inferiors, Hallett changed his mind. Graham had persuaded him that 'in the jungles of the Gond country [Elwin] will be fairly safe, and it certainly seems hard to keep a man from his mission in life.' Hallett now thought the Government could take the risk of allowing him back in; he would himself draft a foolproof undertaking to bind the priest should he stray back into politics.[41] The undertaking, as finally approved by the India Office, asked Verrier to

(i) confine himself entirely to missionary work among the Gonds;
(ii) take no part in civil disobedience or any other political movement;
(iii) refrain, as far as possible, from associating with any persons engaged in political agitation;
(iv) refrain from writing articles against the government.

Curiously, on the very day, 26th August, that Hallett changed his mind, Verrier was having misgivings about his offer of political abstinence. News came from India that Mirabehn had been arrested once more. 'How brave she is,' he thought,' 'how cowardly I am.'[42] But a month later, when the draft undertaking reached him, he was willing to sign. Ever the scholar, he would however improve and edit the text. Could the India Office please change 'missionary' to 'religious and social' in the first clause? This made no difference to its intent, being rather 'a technical theological point. I do not care to to use the word "missionary" in connection with my work because the word has come to imply an attitude to the problems of comparative religion that I do not myself hold.'[43]

The correction was allowed, Verrier signing the undertaking on 4th October and being issued a passport soon after. But he took it that he was not bound by the undertaking while still in England and worked hard in the days that remained. He first spoke on 'The Religious Philosophy of Mahatma Gandhi' at a crowded meeting at SCM House, applauded by most but heckled by 'some Leninist Negroes, a pietistic Swede, and two Communist Indians.' He repeated the lecture at Friends House, attacked this time by a drunken ex-deputy commissioner from the Central Provinces. While he could, Verrier advanced the Congress case in public and in private. He had tea with the Archbishop of York and urged on him the need for the church to play its part in bringing Indians and Englishmen together. He dined with the News Editor of Reuters and asked for proper and balanced coverage of Indian events. The man replied: 'We estimate things solely by their news-value. Mr Gandhi always has news-value. In USA, however, his news-value has declined since he came to London and parleyed with the British Government.'

Verrier also had a twenty-minute meeting with Lord Irwin in his mansion in Eaton Square, with Irwin's 'opulent-looking' dachshund in attendance. The former Viceroy told Verrier that 'the Government of India has the lowest possible opinion of you.' He also refused to criticize his successor, Lord Willingdon, who had made clear his desire to scotch Gandhi and direct action 'once and for all.'[44]

Back in New Delhi the Government of India was having third thoughts. The Bombay government, which had suffered most at Verrier's hands, passed on two letters it had intercepted: written to friends in the Sabarmati Ashram, and whose contents left one in no doubt of his continuing support for civil disobedience. It also forwarded a copy of *Truth about India*, seized by the Customs, as 'further evidence of the pro-Congress and subversive activities indulged in by this individual.' M. G. Hallett, once more in the hot spot, agreed that the book be banned in India, but felt that the man himself could be allowed back in. In his judgement Elwin seemed 'quite prepared to devote himself to the Gonds.' But his boss, the home member, definitely disagreed, noting that 'if at a moment when Father Elwin is profuse with his promises to us of good behaviour he is actively engaged in the Congress movement in England, I take leave to doubt his sincerity and at any rate his consistency.'

The home member prevailed; on 11th October 1932 the Government of India wired London expressing its 'serious misgivings about [Elwin's] good faith,' and requesting that the undertaking not be offered him. The secretary of state had to wire back saying it was unfortunately 'too late.' For the priest had claimed his passport, and booked his return journey aboard the *S. S. Victoria*.[45]

If a file had been put up earlier, or a few telegrams sent more promptly, Elwin might never have returned to India. It is a little disconcerting to discover that this is something he does not ever seem to have known.

CHAPTER FIVE

An Ashram of One's Own

To you this little village is dear as the moon,
And from the great city you have dragged me away
Here if you want paper you must tear up your clothes,
For ink you must use the kazal from your eyes,
Yet to you this little village is dear as the moon.

Gond folk song

Our company of workers [in the ashram] is now really representative. There are Christians, Hindus, a Brahmin, a Mussalman, Gonds; polygamists, henogamists, monogamists, celibates; polytheists, henotheists, monotheists, theists, animists, pantheists, monists; vegetarians, egg-eaters, rat-eaters, beef-eaters and those to whom even the dung of the cow is sacred; bacon-eaters and those to whom even the smell of the pig is anathema, all united. How nice it is!

Verrier Elwin, diary entry of 20 October 1934

'Father Elwin back in India' screamed a front page story in the *Bombay Chronicle* on the 4th of November 1932. The newspaper's reporter, down to meet Elwin by the quayside, found him carrying a stuffed mongoose and a statue of St Francis, his political beliefs firmly intact. Pressed for a statement on Civil Disobedience, Elwin would only say that Mahatma Gandhi's fast of September, in protest against communal electorates, had 'made a very deep impression on the minds of the English people.' Then he quickly added: 'I am not at liberty to make a statement regarding political matters.'[1] He had said enough; the journalist departed, reassured that the priest's heart still lay with the Congress. Others hoped his pen would be freed to push the nationalist case once more. Welcoming Verrier back, his friend Jamnalal Bajaj wrote: 'No one can doubt your great love for the cause which you have had to abjure—for a short while let us hope.'[2]

This was Verrier's hope too. Forbidden by the terms of his undertaking to follow the Mahatma in politics, he could yet follow him in the principles by which he ran his ashram. Two months after his return, with the buildings in place and a Montessori school opened for ten Gond children, Verrier wrote to his mentor that he and Shamrao felt 'entirely one with Sabarmati and Wardha [Gandhi's two ashrams] though a thousand miles behind.'[3]

This statement was put immediately to the test when, the next week, the Ashram of St Francis had its first visitor, Mary Gillet of the Christa Seva Sangh. A teacher trained in Roehampton, Mary was 'very keen on everything Indian, particularly the freedom struggle.' Through Verrier, whom she first met in England in 1929, she came out to Poona to join the CSS. A socialist of strong convictions, Mary thought the concern of most Christians with the personal application of religion 'has been responsible for the gradual but ever-quickening landslide of Western civilization towards catastrophe.' She wished in India to reaffirm and reinvigorate the social side of the Gospel, taking the side of subject nations against empires and slaves against masters. Soon after coming to Poona she started a play centre for low-caste children, inspired by Gandhi's movement against untouchability. 'Young, modern and brash,' she was apt to do things that others in the CSS disapproved of, such as riding a bicycle in a saree, her dress and brown hair flying in the wind.[4]

When Verrier and Shamrao left the CSS towards the end of 1931, Mary was much troubled. After they departed the Englishmen in charge of the Poona ashram turned it into a monastic order run on rather strict lines. Mary now faced the future with 'some trepidation.' She wasn't sure if 'what I ought to do is the same thing as what I want so much to do,' which was to join Verrier. Visiting Karanjia in January 1933 Mary found at once that

> This ashram of all places I have stayed in most nearly comes up to the Franciscan ideal. The whole countryside is rather like Italy—hills and valleys and blue skies and peasants singing. The ashram stands on the top of a little hill and the village is below. In the morning it is a great delight to sit for

prayers on the hill-top, the sky growing bright with sunrise as the moon goes down and the Southern Cross standing over the hills in front of us.

The chapel is the tiniest imaginable. It is full when four of us are in but I love its smallness and its mud walls. To be in it is to be part of the lovely earth all round. What I like very much about the ashram is that the villagers and anybody just walk in when they like as though it belongs to them—as it does, of course. The wild beast brothers, though rather less welcome, are not less familiar with the place.[5]

The evocation left unsaid the ashram's main attraction: its founder. Mary was in love, but Verrier, at least in the beginning, resisted. She wanted to defy all convention and join them, a lone Englishwoman living with men in the depths of the forest: she wished, as the *CSS Review* not so delicately put it, 'to give her many talents and gifts to Father Elwin and the Gonds.' But Verrier had been warned that admitting women members would take from them the 'heroic note.' She was persistent, perhaps remarkably so, for subsequent developments were swift. On the 25th of January, two weeks after she had arrived on a visit, Mary joined the ashram as 'Brother Mary,' to live with Shamrao and Verrier much as 'Mirabehn lives with Bapu and his brothers'—that is, in the purest platonic friendship.[6] Another fortnight and Verrier and Mary had written to friends that they would be married after Easter in their mud chapel of St Francis, this to be followed by a honeymoon tour by bullock cart through the jungle villages of the district. The marriage would unite them

> in love of Christ and of India, of ashram life and St Francis, of the life of poverty and of the poor. Our marriage therefore will mean little change in our way of life. We want to give our lives to India, to her poor and for her freedom. We shall continue to live as Tertiaries in the ashram, for we have always visualized the possibility of having here married as well as unmarried members. This is a quite normal thing in Indian ashrams.[7]

The last sentence was disingenuous. With the letter was enclosed a photograph of Mary sitting on a string-bed under a mango tree in the courtyard of the ashram. She is wearing a white cotton saree, a mode of dress to which she seems quite accustomed, and has a spinning wheel in front of her. Her head is turned towards Verrier's camera, showing her wavy hair and strong features: a woman of character, of pleasant if not striking appearance. Without question, Verrier and Mary were brought together by more than a devotion to Christ and the poor. They were much attracted to each other, determined to live a married life that was in fact not quite the normal thing in Indian ashrams, where even husband and wife were expected to live together in the purest chastity, in the state of *brahmacharya*.

The first person to react adversely was Shamrao. He thought he would lose his friend, but Verrier assured him he would always 'be the little brother of us and my own companion and dearest friend.' Shamrao soon got over his jealousy, but the couple knew that the opposition outside was likely to be more fierce. As Mary remarked, their decision would make 'a number of people whom I love, very disappointed and unhappy for a time.' 'Will the enclosed news [announcing the marriage] be too great a disappointment to you,' wrote Verrier to the Italian sisters: 'You will stand by us? We shall have much criticism and we shall lose many supporters. We are facing a future of real poverty but we have both wanted that always . . . But I am not sorry for what I am doing! I have found a friend who is the perfect companion in this lovely and difficult task.'[8]

A letter that passed through many drafts was posted to the final court of appeal in Sabarmati. Here Verrier anticipated Gandhi's objections by claiming that Mary and he, though chaste thus far, had not actually taken a pledge of celibacy. We have 'carefully considered our position,' he wrote, 'India is our home: our marriage will be the marriage of two poor people; our children would be the children of poor people.' Then he continued:

> You will be disappointed that we do not feel able at the moment to practice celibacy after marriage. I think I can truly say that the reason for this is not animal passion, but the fact that we have not sufficient intellectual conviction of its immediate necessity or of its wisdom in our own case to enable us to carry it out. I had hoped to be an ascetic, but you yourself have warned me that I must recognise my physical limitations.[9]

Gandhi might in fact have more easily understood a yielding to animal passion, but not, in one of his followers, a disagreement on the principle of brahmacharya. In his credo the conquest of desire was on par with the abolition of untouchability and the promotion of spinning. His own struggles in this respect, as recounted in *The Story of My Experiments with Truth*, had been long and arduous; in his ashram he was continually challenging himself and his followers to lead lives of exemplary purity in thought and action, mind and body. Husband and wife lived together as brother and sister, and sexual 'irregularities' were treated with the utmost severity. This attitude could be carried to excess. Verrier was once staying with some Gandhians in a house by the sea in Bombay, when Mirabehn shut the windows as soon as lunch was served. He protested, for it was a hot day, but Mira said severely: 'No, Verrier, the sea breeze will bring in particles of salt with it. This will fall on the food and make it more difficult for you to control your passions.'[10]

Gandhi's reply to Verrier's letter conveyed an unmistakable sense of being let down. He was not so much disappointed as saddened by their decision. He wrote: 'If you have humbly to acknowledge defeat [in leading the ascetic life] you should do so. Your defeat will be victory for the God of Truth. There is no waste in God's laboratory.'[11]

Gandhi's hand was strengthened when Ala Pocha, the young doctor in his ashram, told him, 'tears dropping from her eyes,' that some time ago Verrier had promised to marry *her*. 'How can I bear this?' wept Ala, 'It was agreed between us that we were both to remain single, or if we could not, we were to marry each other.' Gandhi asked Verrier to clarify what understanding there was between them. If 'your word was never given to Ala as she imagines it was, you and Mary have my blessings.' But 'if there is the slightest possibility of a breach (moral) of word given to Ala, you must both—you and Mary—be prepared to bear what will be the heaviest cross and sacrifice your cherished hope on the altar of Truth which is God. If there is a trace of suspicion of breach, you certainly and Mary and Ala— the latter two if they have the same living faith in Truth as I have credited you with—have to live single lives in spite of yourself.'[12]

Faced with Gandhi's disapproval, Verrier's intellectual conviction collapsed. He confessed to the previous romance with Ala but denied any promise of marriage. In Matheran, back in January 1931, they had 'made love for a few days . . . There was, of course, no carnal intercourse, but we embraced very affectionately. This was wholly wrong, but we were carried away. I have confessed it, and deeply repented. But at that very time it was made absolutely clear between us that there was never to be any thought of marriage, nor any tie or bond whatever between us.' He had seen Ala since, but their later friendship had been—at least on his side—wholly 'free of sex-attraction.' In any case, how could the Mahatma take seriously Ala's claim on him when 'twice in the last year it has been common talk that she herself was going to marry [someone else]?' Nonetheless Verrier expressed his 'sorrow and penitence for any wrong I have done. As you know, I think of my life here as nothing save an offering of penance, and I pray God to accept it.'

On Gandhi's advice this exchange was not shown to Mary. But the marriage itself was abandoned; it seemed the only way the disciple, called to account for a previous lapse, could make up with the master. They had a 'month of the purest happiness' in expectation of the union, wrote Verrier to Gandhi bitterly, but now realized 'to follow this course would be for us a descent from the highest ideal; it would make very difficult the practice of poverty; while it would undoubtedly mean better health for me, the coming of children might cut short our service in India; and it would tend to concentrate our love on one another instead of releasing it for the world. St Francis' message of poverty and your ideal of brahmacharya have made war on our dream of married life and conquered it.'[13]

Verrier consoled himself that he would now 'come closer to Bapu,' but this had been a rebellion thwarted only by the authority of a father figure. He had yielded, but not before a struggle, in the end preferring 'renunciation in all its bareness' to the 'sweetest dreams of marriage.'[14] Mary was not so easily reconciled. 'The pain in leaving the Christa Seva Sangh,' she wrote to a friend, 'has been nothing at all to this—and I have no doubt there are still more perilous mountains ahead.'[15] Gandhi for his part was mightily relieved. 'I was prepared to bless the marriage,' he told C. F. Andrews, 'but I cannot help saying that I blessed the change even more.'[16] In his eyes Verrier and Mary had now forsaken the transience of 'exclusive' marriage for the universal marriage with Truth. Gandhi sensed that Mary was less willing to accept the decision to call it all off. She must recognize, he wrote to Verrier, 'that before God there is no sex or we are all women—His brides married to him in an indissoluble tie. If she has realized the beauty of the immortal marriage, she must dance with joy that she is free from the bondage of the human marriage. The human marriage is good and necessary if the flesh is weak, but if the flesh is strong, it surely is a hindrance for the servant of humanity that Mary has become.'[17]

Verrier and Mary now reverted to living as brother and sister, but Gandhi, nervous that temptation would once again cross their path, advised them 'to separate for the time being and test yourself. [For] if you have shed exclusive love together you should feel happy as well in association as in separation.' He thought Mary should come to one of his ashrams to work among the untouchables, but she seems to have wished only to put distance between herself and the Mahatma. Asked to leave Verrier, she decided to go back to Europe, to visit the Eremo Franciscano in Umbria and then look for work in Austria, where she had friends.

In July, a brief six months after she had arrived (in her mind, at any rate, to stay forever), Mary left Karanjia. She proceeded with Shamrao to Bombay and her ship, having 'come down from the beloved mountains to very drab plains and a lonely road.'[18] Verrier meanwhile made his way to Poona to see Gandhi. The Mahatma had made the old Peshwa city his temporary headquarters; indeed, not long after settling Verrier's matrimonial affairs he began a fast against untouchability in the home of a prosperous Poona industrialist. The fast was over, but when Verrier saw its venue he was appalled. 'Gandhi fasting to death in a marble palace,' he told the Bombay journalist Frank Moraes, 'is like Jesus Christ going to crucifixion in a Rolls-Royce.'[19] As it happened he saw the palace only from the outside, for Gandhi's hostess, a Lady Thackersey, flatly refused to allow a Christian to stay in the house. Verrier made his way to the Servants of India Society, where untouchables like himself were always welcome. Here he ran into the poetess Sarojini Naidu. She told him that low-caste Hindus were not welcome in the marble palace either. 'Even for us,' said Mrs Naidu, 'the hostess is going to smash all the crockery we used and to have special ceremonies of purification after we have gone.'[20]

'I will remain loyal to Bapu to the end of my days,' remarked Verrier of this incident, 'but some of his followers make loyalty very difficult.' The protestation lacked conviction, and in fact Verrier found in Poona a more general disenchantment with Gandhi's leadership. When the new viceroy, Lord Willingdon, refused to meet him, Gandhi began preparations for another round of struggle. His colleagues looked upon the prospect of another term in jail with dread. They knew it to be a 'most stupid and futile business, a sheer waste of man power,' but were so dominated by the Mahatma that they could not but follow his lead. There was an air of sullen resentment all around, Verrier noting that 'the only really happy people were Devadas and his lovely bride Lakshmi, who were bubbling over with joy and quite determined not to go to prison.'[21]

Devadas was Gandhi's youngest son, whose recent marriage had not been subjected to brahmacharya. Verrier does not comment on the apparent hypocrisy—one rule for the adopted son, quite another for the real one—for it seems he had by now prepared himself to resume the ascetic life. From Poona he went to Bombay, said good-bye to Mary, and promptly fell ill with malaria. Then Gandhi sent a message asking him to come to his ashram; he wished to 'make up for the Poona episode.' Verrier dragged himself out of bed and took the night train to Ahmedabad with Shamrao. The Mahatma was 'wonderfully charming:' he had them stay in his cottage and gave them the bed next to his at night. But he took little interest in their ashram, making it clear that he would like Verrier to go back on his undertaking and return to England and promote the Congress cause there. Verrier was disappointed, but in this Gandhi was 'one with all the Congressmen I have met recently—they all think [my ashram] is a waste of time, and that it would be better for me to go about making speeches on their behalf.'[22]

From Ahmedabad Verrier returned to the K. E. M. hospital in Bombay. A relapse of malaria was followed by jaundice, on top of which he was visited daily by police officials checking on what he was reading, whom he was seeing. Weak and depressed, on a diet of milk, juice and glucose alongside two enemas and three doses of castor oil a day, he received a letter from his friends in Umbria asking whether they should admit Mary as a nun. Verrier's answer betrayed the terrific strain he had been under the past few months. Mary was 'too independent,' he wrote angrily,

> too much attached to 'causes' and 'movements,' to believe that the offering of the soul in its entirety to God is more important than anything else in the world.
>
> I think she should go back to her educational work, fight for the causes dear to her, and (I hope) get married. She should finally put out of her mind any idea that she has a vocation to a life in 'religion.' She has tested that vocation in three different places, and it is probable that she has not got it, although she loves Poverty and the poor. She loves Poverty but not obedience.[23]

In November 1933, his health restored, Verrier returned to Karanjia. There had been a slight emendation to their Rule, the addition of a clause enjoining members to 'curb animal passion,' to practice 'purity in personal life.'[24] Recent experience and the wishes of Gandhi thus taken into account, Verrier and Shamrao turned their attention to the programme of the Gond Seva Mandal.

The Ashram of St Francis now consisted of a chapel, a guest house, a dispensary, a retreat room for prayer, and a home for children. Shamrao and Verrier each had their little cell. The chapel, decorated with a painting by an Indian artist, had in front of it the saffron flag of renunciation and the sacred *tulsi* tree. Not that anyone except the founders prayed there, for the Gond Seva Mandal was resolutely opposed to proselytization. His refusal to take the Gospel to the Gonds brought Verrier a reprimand from C. F. Andrews. He should not idealize the tribals and their faiths, wrote Andrews on 12th November, 'as I tended to over-idealize Hinduism at one time.' 'Life in this primitive form,' he continued, 'often becomes a ghastly terror impossible to describe. It would be difficult to overestimate the freedom from these primitive terrors wherewith Christ has set us free . . . I am writing this because I myself have gone to the utmost limits of toleration, bordering on weakness, and I can see the same danger in your case.'[25]

The Bishop of Nagpur had chastised him likewise, but though Verrier vastly respected Andrews he would not budge. An essay published shortly afterwards confirmed that members of the Gond Seva Mandal would be encouraged, Gandhi-style, to deepen their faith by respecting the faith of others. 'In India today,' wrote Verrier, 'every religion can best express itself, not by a mad rush for converts or by erecting walls of self-defense against its rivals, but by the humble spirit of service . . . and through loving co-operation with others.'[26]

From Karanjia Verrier and Shamrao hoped to reach outwards, constructing a series of little branch ashrams in the Gond country. Verrier chose the sites for their beauty: the first at Bondar, on the banks of the river Kanwa, red cliffs on one side, on the other forest climbing up the hills; a second near the village of Harra Tola where the Narmada curved round, enclosing a hill in its embrace before descending to a waterfall; a third at Birbaspur, looking down on the fields of yellow mustard and an expanse of forest and meadow beyond.

The children in their schools were mostly Gond, the teachers moderately educated Hindus or Muslims. The curriculum was based on the Montessori method but flavoured with Indian nationalism. Students were taught the laws of health, simple science based on Jawaharlal Nehru's letters to his daughter from jail, and the teachings of Gandhi. Wearing clothes of khadi provided by the Mandal, the children sang songs composed by Rabindranath Tagore and the medieval Bhakti poets. No rewards or punishments were permitted, the 'ideal of all the teaching [being] the liberation of spirit through self-expression.'[27]

Medical relief, the other main plank of their work, was the province of Shamrao. To his dispensary in Karanjia flocked villagers from a thirty-mile radius, to be treated for gonorrhea, syphilis, leprosy, and an assortment of bites and bruises. A wonderful natural doctor, Shamrao quickly inspired trust among the tribals. When cholera broke out in the village the Gonds were convinced it was the work of witches. Shamrao went and got a stock of vaccines from Dindori town, inoculated the village, and the epidemic disappeared.

Shamrao also helped heal wounds other than the purely physical. In Karanjia he functioned as an unofficial arbiter of disputes, conflicts over land and over women. He sometimes had over fifty cases a month where his decisions, though unsupported by law, were respected. To Verrier, troubled by loneliness and ill health, Shamrao was 'the perfect friend in loyalty, steadfastness, and never failing humour and happiness.'[28]

But Verrier was the ideologue: his mission defined by one British newspaper as the wish 'to teach a primitive people the best things about our civilization,' by a second in the pithy headline, 'BISHOP'S SON ERECTS TEMPLE TO GANDHI IN HEART OF INDIA.'[29] Verrier might have put it less dramatically, but these assessments were on balance correct. A Puritan and Improver, at first he found little to commend in tribal values. The 'Gonds are so unenterprising,' he complained: 'They could easily better their condition by having gardens, but they don't bother.' The 'nomad habits of the aboriginal' made house planning very difficult. He hoped for the formation of a 'sort of Villagers' Association of all those who send their children to school, and are ready to pledge themselves to be temperate in drink, fervent for vaccination, zealous for manure-pits and sanitation, shunning the futility of "Expensive" weddings, jewellry and so on.'[30]

In November 1934 Verrier and Sham were visited by A. V. Thakkar, whose own work among the Bhils had been their early inspiration. Thakkar was shown around the schools and hospitals and later issued a sterling testimonial through the pages of Mahatma Gandhi's weekly, *Harijan*:

> Father Elwin, though a Christian in the truest sense of the term, is not out for proselytization. He does not convert Gonds, but merely serves them. He has no other aim than that of pure unadulterated service from a humanitarian point of view. For this type of service, he is neither thanked by Christians nor by Hindus. The former dislike him for the departure from the orthodox way of work, and the latter distrust him as they cannot imagine any Christian tabooing conversion . . .[31]

For this type of disinterested service Verrier was not thanked by the Christian and the Hindu; nor it seems by the Gond, to whom his Agenda of Improvement—abstinence, hard work, and so forth—did not appeal. When Verrier ordered a bundle of posters on the virtues of Thrift, Vaccination, Stud Bulls, etc., the Gonds could not be bothered to put them up. The chasm between the improving social worker and the conservative tribal was always conducive to disagreement. When the Mandal started sewing classes in their school, the girls were hurriedly withdrawn for their parents thought 'that by stitching they would sew up their wombs and have difficulty at their first deliveries.' A railway station-master, a fervent Hindu, toured the villages proclaiming that the Englishman was here 'not for their sake, but for his Empire.' When they planned to take the children to a picnic to the highest hill in the district, one landlord went round warning parents against this 'Christian innovation.' Their opponents derisively labelled Karanjia 'Isaitola,' the hamlet of Jesus.[32]

The police officials of the district were also most energetic in their opposition. Verrier and Sham were visited every other week by the sub-inspector, who would snoop around the house and demand they reveal their stock of revolutionary pamphlets. When none were forthcoming he would casually help himself, as Indian policemen are wont to do, to flowers and vegetables in the garden. Verrier irritatedly thought the police were working off their suppressed nationalist venom on him, a solitary and defenceless Englishman. More likely they knew of his pro-Congress sympathies and hoped that by harassing him they would please their superiors. On one occasion Shamrao was assaulted and beaten up by a policeman, unprovoked, in the bazaar. This incident at least rallied the Gonds around them for they had to be restrained from storming the police station.³³

In *Leaves from the Jungle*—Verrier's record of life at Karanjia—irritation at Gond indifference to their work alternates with a more sympathetic understanding of the tribal way of life. Why would the Gond take to spinning, he asks, when no cotton is grown anywhere in his country? And why should the aboriginal practice temperance when his jungles were rich in *mahua*, the tree from which he distilled a most potent and liberating spirit? Asked his definition of Hell, one Gond replied; 'Miles and miles of forest without any mahua trees.' Another wished to be buried under the tree so that even in death he might 'suck some pleasure from its roots.' And why should Shamrao and he wear saffron and pray four times a day when the Gonds believed they were doing this only to bribe God into making them rich?

Handspinning, austerity and abstinence thus knocked out, that left only celibacy in the Gandhian credo. But this the Gonds didn't much prize either. Their view, as expressed time and again in their songs, was that 'You may eat, you may drink, but life without a wife is wasted.' Gond girls practised the art of coquetry to perfection; unlike the protected and prissy Hindu they openly encouraged their admirers in the field and forest. As for the men, nothing worried them more than impotence: they were dismayed when Sham's dispensary had no remedies for *that* ailment. Premarital liaisons were frequent, adultery even more so. Verrier counted nineteen elopements in one year in their village alone. Gond divorce was 'so wonderfully simple a ceremony' that it could with profit be adopted in Hollywood. The two parties appeared before their elders, broke a pot and then a piece of straw in half, and were freed of one another.³⁴

Verrier had not come to Mandla to convert the tribes, but it was not long before they had converted him. Encouraged by the Gonds he began shedding his puritan persona piece by piece. In the monsoon of 1933, sick once again with malaria, he confessed to his diary a passion for beer which a 'possibly mistaken' adherence to Gandhian principles had prevented them from stocking. But it could not have been long before he was joining the Gonds in drinking, at marriages and festivals, their rather more intoxicating brews. When the villagers would not take to the spinning wheel Verrier stopped spinning too, though Gandhi wrote at regular intervals urging him to. The Mahatma reminded him that spinning was a form of *tapasya*, or asectic discipline: Verrier answered that it still wasn't the thing for the Gonds, but he and they could try a spell of rice-pounding instead. Then in September 1934 he went so far as to pull out his English clothes in preparation for a trip to Bombay. In Karanjia he wore the shirt and dhoti to be nearer the poor but saw little point in wearing a loincloth in the city. 'Ever since I saw the amazing company of crank disciples of the Mahatma gathered at Sabarmati last year with dhotis exposing more than they ought to and saris flopping about on white bodies I have been shy of wearing Indian dress.' In any case appearances were irrelevant, for 'it is the heart and not the clothes that Indians look at.'[35] He was also having second thoughts about celibacy, these sparked by a reading on the Calcutta Mail of *Virgin and the Gypsy*, D. H. Lawrence's suggestive tale of the seduction by a nomad of the daughter of a country vicar. Brahmacharya he now saw as the hypocritical and hopeless attempt to suppress human desires. When Winslow wrote telling him of a new order of celibates in the CSS, he commented sarcastically on

> The Degrees of Holy Chastity
> Loose Chastity
> Temporary Chastity
> The White Knight Chastity
> Virginal Chastity
>
> and so on. And of course Guided Chastity, which means being chaste till you're guided not to.[36]

Verrier was put off by Gandhism but found little solace in Christianity. The church continued to shun him, the Bishop of Nasik even forbidding his priests from visiting the ashram. On a visit to Poona he sensed that members of the National Christian Council treated him 'like a Bishop's wife greeting a curate whom she suspects of having advanced views on Genesis'—which, in a kind of way, he had. After his mother complained that he was not seeing enough of his 'own people' he replied testily: 'I see as many as are willing to see me.' The Eremo Franciscano run by their friends in Umbria was, he remarked, the one little tributary of the great

Christian river from which Shamrao and he were allowed to drink. 'All other streams and rivers seem to have notices—verboten—written up above them.' Sham and he sometimes felt 'as if the whole world were against us.' In any case he found little to admire in a church that after all these years resolutely kept its distance from Indians, emerging from time to time from bungalows to initiate misdirected schemes of 'village uplift.' When his sister Eldyth contemplated coming out to a mission in the Nilgiris he told her to stay at home, for in India she 'would be forced to live the kind of existence against which my whole life is a protest.'[37]

The protest had already gone public in a review of a book by his schoolfellow Stephen Neill, now a rising missionary in southern India. This book, on the mission of the Indian church, was written 'in the awkward and borrowed phraseology of another age;' Neill was 'still preaching in a black gown.' Elwin singled out the phrases that most disturbed him, his italics marking the distance between him and even the most enlightened of Christian missions. 'We do not expect,' he remarked

> an ex-Fellow of Trinity, Cambridge, and a former leader of the Student Christian Movement, which is supposed to teach its members better things, to refer to the non-Christian in India as a *heathen*, or to fill his pages with such trite missionary cliches as 'work in *virgin soil* usually has to be carried on for a generation *without harvest,* 'On an average a convert is baptised *every five minutes throughout the year,* 'Every city staked out in the name of Christ, '*the front line of advance,*' 'Women have in the Civil Disobedience Movement undergone imprisonment *for what they believe to be the cause of their country,* 'The spread of the Good News.' While of village children he can write, 'These unkempt, shy creatures must be *caught* and *tamed.*'[38]

A 'Christian for the Congress' is how Verrier might have described himself when he first arrived in Karanjia. That label would not now stick on either side: indeed, Verrier was to report with malice and with glee a Gond boy's description of Gandhi (from a photograph) as a 'grumpy old bear with the ears of an elephant,' as well as an abusive exchange in the village in which, after cursing the opponent's mother and sister and casting doubts on his morals and intelligence, 'you cap it all by calling him a Christian.'[39]

In January 1936 Verrier penned a circular letter that captured his double disappointment in more serious terms. On a visit to Wardha the previous November he had found the Mahatma 'bored into a breakdown by his disciples. Some of the most tiresome of these are his Western followers, from whom he ought to be protected by law. Why one of the most acute minds in the country should be wasted settling the matrimonial difficulties of Western adventuresses is a mystery.'

The disgust here is with the mileu as much as the man; Verrier was not a 'crank disciple,' perhaps by now no kind of disciple at all. Gandhi would not be allowed any more to settle *his* matrimonial difficulties. The letter then turned to his troubled relations with the Church of England, of how and why he had at last been compelled 'by the irresistible logic of circumstances' to leave it altogether. He could not forget the 'extraordinary blessedness and happiness' of his early years as a priest, but now the distance between him and the church establishment was too great. One bishop (of Nagpur) said they were doing the work of the devil; a second bishop (of Bombay) called their outlook 'satanic' simply because he lived with poor Indians and had begun to see the world through their eyes. And Indians saw the Church, Protestant, Catholic or Orthodox, as being inescapably tied to racial domination: 'they look at us and remember King Leopold and the Congo, Mussolini in Abysinnia, General Dyer at Amritsar, the Allied Armies in China, the lynching of negroes in America:' acts and actors ignored or even supported by the Church. What right, asked this recreant priest, 'What right have we to preach to this profound, pacific India, while the guns thunder at our back and there lurk in the memory of our hearers a hundred cruelties and oppressions?' He thought the Church should dissociate itself from riches and power, and

> do penance for a hundred years. If we did, before two-thirds of that time were passed, India would be at the feet of Christ. If every Christian in India, led by the Bishops, were to throw off their privileges, forsake their wealth, give up chasing after the educated and well-to-do, in deep humility seek forgiveness and cleansing for themselves instead of preaching to others, and to go to the poorest of the poor, the most forsaken of the outcastes, to tend them and love them and protect them in the love of Christ, not trying to missionize them . . . but simply to wash their feet with the tears of their penitence and anoint them with the spikenard of their love, then they would have done, not any great thing, but their plain duty.

Verrier had come to India and in time to Karanjia to make reparation, but the thought animated few other priests. Unlicensed since 1932, he reckoned it would no longer be honest to remain within the Church at all. On 2nd November 1935 he wrote to the Metropolitan in Calcutta 'formally to announce to you my decision to be no longer a member of the Church of England either as a priest or as a communicant.'[40]

Verrier Elwin walked out of his church without much more than a backward glance, but without his knowing it his letter of resignation caused a great stir in England. High church figures, remembering the expectation with which they had dispatched Verrier and his colleagues back in 1927, wrote asking the Metropolitan to try and bring him back into the fold. One such was William Temple, Archbishop of York, who admired Verrier and had written forewords to his books. Bishop Wood of Nagpur, asked to reply to Temple, sent a long account of his relations with the dissident priest. While he was 'strongly attracted to Elwin and admired his splendid gifts, both literary and devotional,' it was clear that 'his attitude to the Faith was one with which I could not compromise.' The Metropolitan also heard from Bishop William Carey in Eastbourne, who had news that Verrier was very ill and might die soon. Carey was told by several of his friends, including W. E. S. Holland, that Elwin was the 'greatest saint' they had met. Before he died was it not possible 'that someone with love and authority should induce him to resume his priesthood?' He appealed to the Metropolitan in the name of Christ to approach Elwin, in his view fit to rank with the greatest of men thrown out by the Church. 'If he dies,' ended Carey poignantly, 'I shall feel almost an agony of shame that the C of E couldn't keep Wesley, Newman, Elwin.'[41]

Mrs Elwin knew her son would not die yet, but she was no less upset by his decision. With a mother's love and a believer's blindness, she too held the bishops responsible. 'Had my son compromised in the usual fashion of being all things to all men in this age of compromise,' she wrote angrily to the Metropolitan, 'he would now be a most popular preacher receiving a large salary and living in great comfort.' Instead he had followed Christ as he understood him, living in poverty 'among the neglected and suffering Gonds a life of complete devotion—ministering with his own hands to his leprous and repulsively sick folk such as possibly His Lordship of Bombay has never ever seen.' She appended, as a despairing postscript, a letter written her by an Indian which said 'it is men like your son, straight and sincere, the very embodiment of selfless love and truth that bring us to love and revere Jesus Christ . . . we feel more than ever religion has to be *lived* and not merely preached . . . etc. etc.' The letter was a sample of many but, asked this widow of a bishop, 'Is it such men for which the Diocese of Bombay have no use? Or Nagpur?'[42]

Mrs Elwin had got hold of the wrong end of the stick. She believed the Church had no use for Verrier. In fact it was Verrier who had no use for the Church.

Many years later Elwin claimed that the act of leaving the Church brought him 'a hitherto undreamt of intellectual freedom; it adjusted many complexes and inhibitions; it was a kind of conversion in reverse, integrating me and filling me with new life.'[43] The freedoms it brought him were as much sexual as intellectual. Verrier had once written of the celibate vocation that it was 'the offering to God of the most precious thing a man possesses for a special end. The celibate finds his sole joy in Christ: he is free from every tie in order that he might devote himself to the august and urgent needs of his Kingdom.'[44] For this Christian mystic Christ himself had been the lover: all his suppressed passion had been focused on him. In the past when temptation crossed his path—Mary, Ala, the unidentified woman-soul—he submerged himself anew in Christ. But when his faith finally collapsed, sex was the natural corollary.

Information on Verrier's sexual efflorescence, *c.* 1935–6, is meagre, and derives from notes made by an English friend and from the investigations of an Indian official who worked in Mandla in the nineteen sixties.[45] Both are agreed that it was as much an embracing of the tribal ethos as a rejection of Gandhi or St. Francis; a seduction of the virgin priest by Gond gypsies. The Indian investigator framed it in the apologetic if mildly censorious tones of the Hindu middle class. Verrier and Shamrao, he explained, 'did not create [in Mandla] any sort of a licentious society.' For 'a licentious society was already there and these gentlemen unable to raise an iron curtain around themselves were to some extent caught up in the same.'

Verrier put it differently. For the Gonds sex was a 'gesture between friends—neither was over-involved, neither completely in love.' It was most often a basis for liking rather than love. Relationships began in the most casual way. In one early encounter Shamrao met two Gond girls in the market who insisted on coming home with him. The tribal women came to Verrier and Sham not because of money, which they never took, but because they liked them. Monogamy, serial or otherwise, was not necessarily a virtue. Shamrao recalled this laconically: 'women used to change husbands as we change socks and forget about it.'

Verrier's first grand passion was Singharo, a Gond from the village of Sarwachappar. An English visitor described Singharo as having a 'long face, rather coarse features and a sweet expression.' She makes a fleeting appearance in *Leaves from the Jungle*, in a celebration of the Phag festival of May 1935, when she made a beeline for Verrier to douse him in coloured water.[46] Singharo soon went off to the Assam tea gardens, had affairs with the clerks there, and returned with syphilis. Verrier later regretted not marrying her but at the time he did not think himself prepared for it.

Verrier's sexual adventures were known and acknowledged by the Gonds, perhaps even encouraged by them. But they were kept hidden from the outside world: from his family in England, from the friends and patrons of the Gond Seva Mandal, and from Gandhi in his sexless ashram at Wardha. When Shamrao mischievously suggested that he should go to the Mahatma and make a confession in the interests of Truth, Verrier answered: 'How can I go and tell *him* about my girls?'

Some people might wish to change or uplift the tribals; the point, however, was to know them. Verrier's understanding was initiated by Panda Baba, a Gond magician who was both his native informant and his first truly tribal friend. He lived in Bondar, a village two miles from Karanjia, in a house adorned with the symbols of his calling: horse-hair and pointed rods, marigolds and peacock feathers. He was first recruited to teach Verrier and Sham the local dialect, Chattisgarhi. Soon they were accompanying him on his professional calls: to perform the *Bida* ceremony before sowing crops, to sacrifice a chicken and thus cast the evil spirit of disease out of the village. The magician had a phenomenal knowledge of Gond myths. On easy terms with the local ghosts, he alone among the villagers was not 'afraid of the demi-Atlas of our little world, the Sub-Inspector of Police.'[47]

In the first week of February 1934 Panda Baba took Verrier on a field trip to a remote part of the district, the forests of the Baiga tribe. They made their way leisurely, by bullock cart: day after day, wrote the traveller,

> we plunged deeper into the vast loneliness: at first we were in the living forest—there were birds, we could hear the chatter of a monkey teasing a tiger, we could meet people on the road. But later we reached the forests of Baiga Land where hardly a bird rustles the leaves in that uncanny silence and where you may go ten miles without meeting a soul. How thrilling the forest is, with its endless trees which now close in upon you and now open wide to a bare burnt glade, the trees sometimes tall as the mast of some high Ammiral, sometimes short with all their leaves withered by the frost.

The Baigas, when they got to them, were scarcely less thrilling. The men, covered in little less than a loincloth, were strikingly handsome, with slim, shapely bodies and magnificent wavy hair; the women stouter and less attractive, but with their hands and legs tattooed in intricate patterns. Encouraged by Panda Baba the Baiga put on a show of their dances and then, sitting around a fire under a cold moon, related a sad tale of decline in what was for them the darkest of ages, a Kaliyug. For the Baiga were once kings of the forest, free to hunt and fish, and to practice *bewar*, their characteristic form of swidden cultivation. But the forest department had confiscated their bows and arrows and forced them to take to settled agriculture. Their revered ancestor Nanga Baiga had instructed them never to lacerate the breasts of Mother Earth, but now because of hunger and the laws in Kaliyug, they had to dishonour her with the plough. In the old days their diet was rich in game, nuts and fruit, the bounty of the forest, but with the coming of the forest guards all they had, said the Baiga, was a 'little millet, disease and death.'[48]

Verrier was both enchanted by the Baiga and deeply moved by their predicament. Two years with the Gonds persuaded him that the tribals had to be protected from the corrosive influences of the outside world: from the 'exploitation of petty traders, the tyranny of petty officials and the enervating influence of the degenerate civilization of the small towns.' The Gonds were swiftly succumbing to these influences but the Baiga, more remote in their mountain fastness, might yet be saved.

Through letters and talks Verrier tried to interest his Congress friends, but to his dismay the politicians who were most vociferous in claiming swaraj would pay little attention to 'the necessities of the original inhabitants of their country.' 'No Congressman in our part of the country has ever lifted a finger to help us,' he wrote in April 1934, 'no member of the local Indian public has ever contributed a pie to our work.'[49] Ironically, the only outsider to show any interest at all was the odd ICS official. It was to one of these, the deputy commissioner of Mandla, that Verrier addressed the first of what were to be dozens of appeals on behalf of the Baiga. He urged the official to convince the forest department to restore the practice of bewar, for

> although it is obvious that the forest must be protected, I am afraid that the effect of depriving the Baigas of the right to bewar will be gradually to drive them into the Hindu fold. For bewar was the rallying point, the standard, the differentia of their tribe, from which most of what was distinctive about them derived. Now without bewar, without the right to hunt, they are becoming a little ordinary, and will be an easy prey to the Hindu propagandist.[50]

Verrier resolved to 'prepare a small monograph' on the Baiga, to document their customs and draw wider attention to the loss of their forests. He recruited two bright young tribals, Sunderlal and Gulabdas, to make regular forays to the Baiga and collect and transcribe their myths. The defender of the underdog had found a new subject, the most disadvantaged and least visible of India's poor—communities neglected even by a national movement that claimed to be wholly representative. Writing in the *Modern Review*, a Calcutta journal run for and by nationalists, Verrier complained that the hill and forest tribes were a 'despised and callously ignored' group. Their problem was as urgent as that of the untouchables: society had sinned against them as grievously, and yet the one has become a problem of all-India importance: the other remains buried in oblivion. Indian national workers and reformers—with the exception of the heroic little band associated with the Bhil Seva Mandal—have neglected the tribes shamefully. The Congress has neglected them. The Liberals have neglected them. The Khadi workers have neglected them.[51]

The colonial state and the nationalist intelligentsia both seemed to think of the 'forest people as mere cyphers in the population of India.' Determined to redress this, Verrier first sought to collect and publish the vivid folk-poetry of the Mandla tribals. Associated with the great Gond dances, the *karma* and the *dadaria*, were songs of romance which reminded the Oxford scholar of 'Elizabethan love-poetry, perhaps the finest and most direct love-poetry ever written.' Some of these were published by Sham and Verrier in *Songs of the Forest*, a book that brought together love poems with poems about work and nature. There were songs about grasping landlords and about unattainable women, on the poetry and the poverty of tribal life. Here are two examples, the first sung by Pardhan women, the second by Gond men:

> I am looking out of my house;
> The sun is but a bamboo's length above the hills.
> Where can you go now it is grown so late?
> Leaf of the Plantain, lover in whom my heart is bound,
> Like a dry leaf in the wind,
> You are ever blown to and fro away from me.
> Where can you go now it has grown so late?

> The palace is fashioned of chosen stone,
> The doors are also made of stone.
> In every corner burn the shining lights.
> But without a girl all is dark inside.
> On the new road the wheels run swiftly,
> So will I drag you to my heart.
> Inside, without a girl, the house is dark.[52]

Verrier hoped that when printed these songs would make city readers think of the tribals as 'real people, real as themselves,' as the subjects of fellow feeling rather than objects of condescension or pity. Writing was for him a more natural medium than giving injections or running schools. In addition to transcribing and translating the poems and stories of tribals he was working on a novel called 'No Mortal Business,' a detective story with a Christian gloss, a 'sort of combination' of C. F. Andrews and Edgar Wallace.[53]

The source for this teasingly brief description is one of Verrier's circular letters. The manuscript of the novel is lost or perhaps destroyed. The letters themselves were sent out to a range of people, 'from Evangelical pietists to Jewish psychoanalysts, from a German communist to Indian administrators, from a agnostic poet in Hongkong to an Anglo Catholic chaplain in the Leeward Islands, from an Archbishop to Ethel Manin.' One interested reader was the playwright Laurence Housman, whom Verrier befriended while campaigning for Indian independence in England in 1932. Sent the manuscript of 'No Mortal Business,' Housman thought it 'lacked technique as a novel, being far more a study of life and character in a series of incidents.' He asked Verrier to work instead on polishing his letters—that was his 'true literary line,' and from a publisher's point of view 'Letters from the Jungle' would have better prospects than a first novel.[54]

Leaves from the Jungle was published, with the help of a kindly shove from Housman, by John Murray in 1936. A preface sketches three tribal characters: Panda Baba, the repository of Gond myth and magic; Tutta, an epileptic and symbol of poverty who needs but a packet of cheroots, some cheap drink and a consort to be content; and Phulmat, a beauty with the grace and dignity of a princess, an accomplished dancer who represents the romance of the forest. The three faces of Gond life thus introduced, the book covers in diary form the first four years of their life in the village.

Leaves from the Jungle is author-centred but by no means self-absorbed. The Gond Seva Mandal is portrayed as a process of self-discovery, the narrator finding out more about himself as he finds out more about the Gonds. The book provides revelations, through flashes of irony and wit, of Elwin's growing rejection of Gandhi and Christ: as in a description of a khadi mosquito net which 'though utterly patriotic and highly mosquito proof, appears to admit no air whatsoever,' or a confession that he spent a day of rest reading Agatha Christie 'though aware it would be more suitable for me to employ my leisure reciting the Penitential Psalms.' The protective instincts of the anthropologist had replaced the improving agenda of the social worker. 'There are many elements in the Gond ethos which should be conserved,' writes Elwin, 'their simplicity and freedom, their love of children, the position of their women, their independence of spirit, . . . their freedom from many of the usual oriental inhibitions.' Indeed, the tribal 'has a real message for our sophisticated modern world which is threatened with disintegration as a result of its passion for possessions and its lack of love.'[55]

This comes from the only preachy passage in the book; otherwise, the defense of tribal life is conducted with an easy wit and lightness of touch. *Leaves from the Jungle* is the most readable of all Elwin's works, an illustration of 'rollicking anthropology' which celebrates the irreverent and irrepressible gaiety of the Gonds and their chronicler. It received a wonderful reception: the author, said the *Times Literary Supplement*, wrote with 'a Rabelaisian plainness of speech and a Pickwickian zest for the creature comforts of life, even though these pleasures are now enjoyable by him only in imagination;' the *Morning Post* called it a 'remarkable book,' written in a way that excited 'interest, sympathy and smiles;' the *New Statesman* remarked that through the diary 'we know the Gonds more intimately and more thoroughly than any primitive people that have been shown to us in books;' no European since R. L. Stevenson, commented *The Times*, 'has written so well of a life among browns and chocolates.'[56]

The success of *Leaves from the Jungle* confirmed a shift in vocation that was already well under way. Providing education and medical relief were not his line—these were best left to Shamrao. But Verrier could write on the tribals; indeed, he could help the tribals by writing about them. By the time *Leaves* was published the Gond Seva Mandal had shifted its headquarters from Karanjia to the village of Sarwachappar, twenty miles further inland. Their landlord had been giving trouble—he thought the Mandal would make his tenants too independent—and in any case Verrier wanted to move closer to the edge of the great forest and the Baigas. Their new centre had a leper home, a dispensary and a school, but no chapel.

In his first letter from Sarwachappar, written in June 1936, Verrier announced that he had converted to a new creed. 'For however dark and obscure may be my ecclestiastical position,' he remarked, 'in ethnography I am a quite definite and almost bigoted adherent of the Functional School of which [Bronislaw] Malinowski is the proponent.' But this follower of the great Polish anthropologist had more than a strictly scientific interest in the subject, for he believed that

> ethnography is itself a powerful instrument for the succour of the tribesmen. The more you can make people known, the more you will make them loved. If we can inspire officials, traders, contractors with a genuine interest in the life and culture of the villagers with whom they have to deal, they will treat them far better and try to further their interests.[57]

An early visitor to their new home was the sculptress Marguerite Milward, in the middle of a tour of India in search of exotic and interesting subjects. She arrived in Sarwachappar to a grand reception: fifty Gonds threw garlands of marigolds around her neck, until she felt like a temple goddess. The next day she commenced her search for models. The Gond men she found undistinguished but she was enchanted with the women. With Verrier's help she found two 'Gondins,' attractive, much-married, each in the throes of a divorce, and, unlike the Hindu women she knew, confident and eager to pose for the chisel.

Miss Milward was also taken by her hosts to the land of the Baiga. The Gond Seva Mandal had acquired a motor car, gifted by Oliver Fielding-Clarke, formerly of the Christa Seva Sangh. Loaded with people and provisions, the car made slow progress through the jungle, on dirt tracks badly damaged by the rains. The vehicle was abandoned at the foot of the Baiga uplands, whereupon Miss Milward was put onto a *dandi*, a stretcher carried by two Gond bearers.

The Baiga, forewarned and primed by the anthropologist, put up a great show for the visitor. Four villages came together for a gala dance that went on late into the night. Liquor was passed around in tiny leaf cups, and Sham and Verrier danced to merriment and wide approval. The Baiga reminded the sculptress of Italian wandering minstrels—feathers in their hair, colourful beads around their necks and rings in their ears. All in all, the 'fun waxed fast and furious;' everyone was a little drunk and very happy.

But tribal life was not all song and dance, and Miss Milward was also exposed to its other side, poverty and disease. She spent time in Sham's Leper Home, moved by the sight of men and women who accepted 'their awful fate with patience and seemed happy and content.' One night the dancing was stopped when they learnt of the death of a young Gond girl, fifteen and newly married, struck by a disease no one could fathom. Verrier and Sham led a sad little procession to the middle of the forest where a grave was dug with a crow-bar, the evil spirits wished away, and the little corpse lowered to the ground.[58]

Miss Milward left Sarwachappar with a vivid memory of the home of her hosts: 'a typical Gond hut backed up against the wild jungle and facing the sunset and distant plain; a wide verandah, a long room with all the front open to the elements, and in the centre a great desk covered with the Baiga manuscript piled high' (to this had the 'small monograph' grown). When in the village Verrier worked inside the hut, Shamrao for the most part outside it. The sculptress found that the two friends of the Gonds were known as Badabhai and Chhotabhai, little brother and big brother. This nicely expressed their physical contrast—Verrier, tall, fair and broad-shouldered, Sham short, sturdy and dark—as well as their respective vocations. Sham was the little brother in the tribal family, always in close attendance, ready to run errands or provide assistance; Verrier the big brother, affectionate but a little distant, whose help the tribal sought to keep off their backs the unlovely trinity of landlord, moneylender and grasping official.

CHAPTER SIX

Defending the Aboriginal

The noble savage of North America is a very different character from the poor squalid Gond of central India: and not even the genius of a Longfellow or a Fenimore Cooper could throw a halo of sentiment over the latter and his surroundings.

James Forsyth, *The Highlands of Central India* (1871)

The pen is the chief weapon with which I fight for my poor.

Verrier Elwin, in a letter of July 1938

In October 1936 Verrier Elwin went to England for a two-month vacation. The bank balance of the Gond Seva Mandal was running low, down to twenty pounds by the time he bought his ticket. When their patrons frowned on this act of apparent frivolity, he answered that missionaries had their furlough once every few years and he didn't see why, just because he was now freelance, he should be denied privileges granted to the 'regular troops.'

While in England Verrier collected money for the Mandal, spent time with his mother, and made three trips that he had planned. The first was to the Albermarle Street office of John Murray, publishers of the recently printed and hugely acclaimed *Leaves from the Jungle*. He went back several times, to feel himself part of literary history in front of the fireplace where Byron's letters were burnt, to meet and mingle with other Murray authors, and to further a growing friendship and discuss future books with the youngest member of the firm, John Gray Murray.

A second pilgrimage, looked forward to as eagerly, was to the famous

Thursday seminar run by Bronislaw Malinowski at the London School of Economics. Verrier first wrote to the anthropologist asking for a date when he could come. 'You have been a guide and inspiration to me for a long while,' he told him, adding, 'One day a pet monkey ate my copy of your *Sex and Repression in Savage Society*, and although apparently sweet to the taste it was bitter in the belly and it attacked me with great violence. The story has no moral, but I feel it gives me a link with you.'

The great man thought otherwise. When Verrier attended the Thursday seminar, he went up afterwards and repeated the tale of Malinowski's book and his monkey. It was quite the wrong thing to do, for the Pole, working overtime to establish his discipline on a solid scientific footing, had little time for levity. His story told, Verrier looked around hopefully at the master and his disciples, but there was no reaction—all he saw was 'a ring of solemn sociological faces' and he made a quick getaway.[1]

The third visit, even more difficult, was to the office of the secretary of state for India. Verrier had decided it was time to mend fences with the Raj. Most officials of the Central Provinces, high and (especially) low, still treated him as an undesirable alien; they thought he was on the side of Congress, knowing little of his break with Gandhi and the Gandhi-men. The local landlords, meanwhile, continued their propaganda against this 'Christian' social worker, not knowing he no longer considered himself one. Isolated and abandoned, without the anchorage once provided by the Christian faith and the Gandhian church, Verrier wished only to be allowed to continue writing, and for Shamrao to run their hospital and schools without interference.

Seeking a rapprochement with the rulers of India, Verrier once again sought the help of the missionary William Paton.[2] At Paton's request he put down on paper a withdrawal of his philo-Congress views, explaining how he had come to differ with a movement he had once uncritically and completely championed. Since he had begun working with the Gonds, he noted,

> it has been evident that sooner or later I should find myself in opposition to the Indian nationalists, and in the last three years there has been a steadily increasing difference between me and the Congress Party, for which at one time I had considerable sympathy.

For example, it seems to be the aim of the Congress politicians to bring the aboriginals within the Hindu fold and then to treat them as though they had no special claims; they resent the establishment of Excluded and Partially Excluded Areas [established by the British government to protect the aboriginals]; they dread the claims of Anthropology to guide these areas. This company of vegetarians and tetotallers would like to force their own bourgeois and Puritan doctrines on the free wild people of the forests.

On the other hand I myself consider the aboriginals to be pre-Hindu and that the adoption of Hinduism will be a major disaster for them; I welcome the Excluded Areas, and only wish that there were very many more of them; I consider that scientific anthropology should guide and regulate the administration of all primitive peoples and that they should not be handed over to elected politicians who have no knowledge of their special problems; and I think that the social and moral outlook of the Congress would cut the tap-root of vitality of aboriginal India. . . .

I want therefore to make it clear that although I have still a few personal friends within its ranks, I am no longer a supporter of the Indian National Congress, and I want rather to carry on my work for the aboriginals in the closest co-operation with the local officers of the British Government . . .

In view of all this, I think it would be a good thing if my position could be cleared. I do not see any reason why I should now be regarded as a politically suspicious character: on the contrary, I think that there is every reason why my humanitarian and ethnographical work should be supported. Certainly, some steps should, I think, be taken to ensure that I am not needlessly humiliated and that my work is no more wantonly obstructed by local officials . . .

It has not been easy to write this, for it is never very pleasant to admit that one has been wrong. But for the sake of my villagers, for whom I would do anything in the world, it is essential that I should make my peace with Government.

This was an extraordinary recantation, more so for being voluntary, unlike the undertaking to stay away from politics that the government had extracted in 1932. Forwarding the statement to the India Office, William Paton described Elwin as 'a man whose spiritual sensitiveness has led him astray, [but] he is wholly unselfish, and is, I think, now concerned wholly with the well-being of these Gond people.' It was 'difficult sometimes to realize how great is the change that has been wrought in him by some years of continuous labour in the jungle, but I have no doubt of the fact.' 'I can assure you,' wrote Paton, that 'Elwin is one of the most interesting and attractive people anywhere to be found: a first-class mind, a real scholar, and altogether a rather outstanding person. He will, I think, kill himself in India with overwork, and I wish I could find some way whereby he could be more effectively guided and helped.' The India Office was persuaded this was a genuine change of heart, that Elwin was now 'purely a philanthropologist, who was most anxious to make his position right with the authorities.' But they wondered how minor officials could be stopped from harassing him, 'short of furnishing a placard to put on his back labelled, "This man is now *persona grata* with Government!" '

Elwin knew a better way. On the 25th of November he met R. T. Peel of the India Office and told him his difficulties would at once be solved if he was appointed to an official position and made an honorary magistrate. This would keep the police at bay and might also be a real help to the tribesmen, at present forced to place their cases in the hands of lawyers and their touts in distant Mandla.

'This is as complete a retraction of his former views as one could wish for' gloated Peel, and his colleagues by and large agreed. R. A. Butler, an ambitious M.P. marking time in the India Office, summed up the case in magisterial fashion: 'Father Elwin was a nuisance in my father's day but the report of Mr Peel is conclusive. Father Elwin will always be better at humanitarian work than politics. His note in the volume presented to Paret on the aborigines was interesting rather than practical.'

The man Butler called Paret was actually the Oxford anthropologist R. R. Marett—a volume was indeed presented to him in 1936 but Butler, a future Master of Trinity, had not read it, for Elwin was not among its contributors. Butler's note did not of course reach Verrier, but he was able to check another of its errors. As in 1932, he would correct the India Office on a technical theological point. 'I am "Father" Elwin no longer,' he told them, 'as I am no longer in the Church. Perhaps that is symbolical. Father Elwin is dead in more ways than one.'

When the file reached India the governor of the Central Provinces initiated steps to appoint Elwin honorary magistrate, with powers to hear and dispose of tribal litigation. His office did not 'bear any grudge for his previous errors;' this 'repentant sinner' was now doing 'really good and self-sacrificing work.' Less impressed was R. M. Maxwell, home secretary to the Government of India who, between 1930 and 1932, had been assigned by the Bombay government to monitor Elwin's work for the Congress. This was 'not a very well-balanced person,' warned Maxwell: 'I should not be surprised to see him carried away by his sympathies if Government once more came into conflict with his former friends.'

Just before he left England Verrier was interviewed by *The Observer* on his work among the Gonds. 'The aboriginal tribes are now in a minority,' he told the paper, 'and they have neither writers or politicians of their own. I am trying to establish myself as an authority, to get myself into a position where I can fight for their interests, otherwise they will be swamped by a very corrupt form of civilisation, not the finer side of Hinduism and Islam, but the exploiting greed which comes from the towns.' He hoped to see the Gonds 'develop a new kind of tribal life based on the old, but free from some of its inhibitions such as witchcraft and magic—a revivified tribal life.'[3]

The interview set out Verrier's new mission for the Gonds; to renew from within rather than civilize from without. But when he returned to Sarwachappar in the last fortnight of 1936, he found that their landlord had evicted them from one of their buildings. The grouse was apparently that the Gond Seva Mandal was making trouble by teaching tribal tenants to read and write and keep accounts.[4] It was not a happy omen. Soon, Sarwachappar and its surroundings were engulfed by a movement to bring tribals into the Hindu fold. Local reformers wanted the Gond to wear the sacred thread, abstain from liquor, give up music and dance, not keep pigs and chicken, not plough their land with cows, and put their women in purdah. And so

> Song and dance, the only distinctive elements of Gond culture, have been driven from our district. Chickens and pigs are the only tax-free animals. The Gonds have been compelled in the name of religion and government to kill them off—a very serious economic loss.
>
> The poor Gond has often to yoke his cows (who are past giving milk) to the plough. Now he is not allowed to do so . . .
>
> Liquor is the only tonic available to the malaria-ridden Gond. It is the

one warming and cheering thing in his nakedness. Now this is taken from him and nothing put in its place.

One of the most attractive features of the Gond was the decent way he treated his women, and his refusal to regard any human being as untouchable. He has now been forced to adopt the Hindu attitude in these matters.[5]

Verrier found the Gonds had gone flat, like stale beer; there was no more kick in them. He warned his tribal friends that if 'they went in for this sort of thing, the anger of heaven would be upon them, taxation would increase and rain would fall all through the hot weather.' Shamrao, more to the point, told the men that since eating eggs was vital to good sexual performance, killing chickens would bring on an epidemic of impotence. Defying the reformers, the Gond Seva Mandal organized a series of dance competitions, each with a first prize of fifty rupees. In the first of these, in February 1937, only five villages participated; two months later, when the frenzy had subsided, as many as fifty came forward to dance.

The 'Raj Gond' movement, as it was called, coincided with the coming to power of Congress in the elections of 1937. In Verrier's mind the two were not unconnected. In August he visited Gandhi at his new ashram at Wardha to acquaint him of the aboriginals' plight. But he found that for 'all his desire for Home Rule Mahatma Gandhi did not appear to think that the original inhabitants of India deserved any special consideration.' The Congress, he concluded cynically, wished on the one hand to use the tribals as cannon-fodder in their political campaigns and on the other to convert them all to vegetarianism, abstinence and settled cultivation—the plough was 'everywhere the symbol of the Congress-Hindu culture that is sweeping tribal areas.'[6] He now had a personal grouse to add, for one of the first acts of the Congress ministry had been to abolish all honorary magistrateships, his included, this when 'there were other reforms of greater urgency to which they might have turned their attention.' Verrier was so fed up with their 'caste and humbug and prohibition' that at times he felt like fleeing India for 'one of the Buddhist countries like Burma or Ceylon.'[7] There was the odd politician he still liked—such as Jawaharlal Nehru, liberal and cosmopolitan, 'all breed and backbone.' After having lunch with Nehru in Bombay in September, Verrier wrote to his mother: 'What a prince he is! Such a gentleman. And so utterly civilized.'[8] But Congressmen in general were a 'lot of Puritanical Nosey-Parkers.' Verrier reported a conversation on religion between two ministers, one a typical 'Evangelical Hindu,' the other a rare Modernist. The Evangelical remarked solemnly that he could never begin his day without spending an hour in prayer and meditation. The Modernist replied: 'It would be much better if you spent it attending to your files.'[9]

In his Poona days Verrier had seen Congress as little less than the liberator of all Indians, especially the poor: but now, in Mandla, he set against its indifference the 'kindness and sympathy which I have found from the higher officials of the Central Provinces Government, and the keen interest and concern with which they view the primitive areas.'[10] The governor of the Central Provinces, Sir Francis Wylie, lent a sympathetic ear to Verrier's diagnosis of the tribal problem—so much so that this former enemy of the British empire found himself a frequent visitor to, and the occasional guest of, Government House, Nagpur. Verrier wrote to his friend Sarat Chandra Roy, the Ranchi lawyer and doyen of Indian anthropology, that Wylie was 'keenly interested in the things that interest us,' that is, the condition of the aboriginals. The governor was even to visit their village in due course.[11]

In 1938 the Gond Seva Mandal changed its name to the Bhumijan Seva Mandal, to acknowledge its work for other tribes and castes ('Bhumijan' simply means 'people of the soil'). That, at any rate, was the official explanation, although irritation at the Raj Gond movement might have had something to do with it. The reformers had also forced Verrier and Sham to change their headquarters. In June they moved from Sarwachappar to Patangarh, a village nine miles to the north, situated on a promontory just off the Amarkantak–Dindori road. On the edge of the hill stands a shrine to Thakur Deo, a stone idol resting under a pipal tree. Village folklore has it that Verrier and Sham first wished to build their home around the shrine. While work was in progress Verrier had a dream in which the deity conveyed his anger at their trespass. Fence and walls were dismantled forthwith and a new building begun on a spot a hundred yards further east.[12]

The new ashram consisted of low thatched mud buildings around a courtyard gay with flowers, a neem tree with a monkey in the middle. There were two old pipal trees in their property: a platform was constructed around one as a meeting-place, the second served as graceful backdrop to Sham's informal court. From Patan there were magnificent views in all directions, views of the shining waters of the Narmada half-a-mile away, and of the great hills of the Maikal Range 'piled up on one another.' A visitor found 'the colours in the ever-changing landscape a perpetual delight.'[13] The villagers were warm, amusing, friendly; there was a fair sprinkling of Pardhans, the rather improper and fun-loving tribe of minstrels who lived with the Gonds and gave life to them. 'The Gond Puritan movement has made no headway *here*,' crowed Verrier. Coming to Patangarh from Sarwachappar was like abandoning a conventicle of the Plymouth Brethren for a cocktail party.[14]

In the last weeks of 1938 Eldyth Elwin came out for a three-month visit.[15] She found her brother looking 'very sweet—pink and blue-eyed,' spending his days writing, directing the garden, playing with children, the 'little girls and boys clasping him as he anthropologizes.' He worked most mornings in the library, its bookshelfs built into the wall. In the middle of the room lay a vast table made of planks supported on mud legs, covered over with books and notes. On the floor below lay copies of the *TLS*, the *New Statesman, Time and Tide*, and *Punch*. While Verrier read or wrote Eldyth helped Sham with the injections and tried to teach English in the school. Both the friends were much loved: 'If they are not vocal about religion at the moment,' wrote Eldyth to Mrs Elwin consolingly, 'they certainly live it in that respect.'

To impress his sister Verrier took her to Nagpur. They stayed at Government House, meeting and mingling with the chief justice, the home member, and sundry secretaries and brigadiers. Eldyth accompanied Sir Francis Wylie to a cricket match: 'sentries, flags flying on car, greetings by Vice-Chancellor, special seats, all just like Royalty.' Sir Francis rather preferred his outings with her brother, the long walks in which they got 'such visible pleasure from talking to each other. Verrier being an unofficial intellectual H. E. can let go on him.'

For all the pomp, Eldyth was decidedly ambivalent about the official British in India. In her breathless letters from Government House, full of parties and bigwigs, she paused to remark: 'Sometimes I like it, at others I don't at all!' Her brother's feelings were more mixed still, for he had to keep both the governor and the government (a Congress one) in good humour. Eldyth was also taken by him to a nationalist *tamasha*, the annual session of the Congress held that year outside Jabalpur. To this show the

Gond Seva Mandal brought a troupe of tribal boys who put on a great display of their dances to a crowd of five thousand. Verrier and Sham hoped that this would lead to a warmer appreciation of tribal culture, perhaps even an incorporation of Gond dances in the curriculum of all schools within the province.

The tribal dance was very much a sideshow to the main business of Congress, which that year was a famous fight for control of the organization between Mahatma Gandhi and the young tiger from Bengal, Subhas Chandra Bose. Eldyth found 'great speculation as to whether Gandhi or Bose will die first.' But a large fat woman doctor, a member of the reception committee, would talk only of Verrier, for she was 'steeped in his works.' In the Central Provinces of 1938 British imperialist would not speak to Indian nationalist, but for the sake of his tribals Verrier Elwin would speak to and write for both.

While still in Sarwachappar, battling the Puritans, Verrier found time to finish two novels. The first, *Phulmat of the Hills*, published by John Murray in 1937, tells the story of a Pardhan girl of extraordinary sweetness, a gifted dancer much admired in her village. Struck by leprosy, Phulmat is abandoned by her lover. In grief she takes to the road, and after a long, difficult journey opens a shop in a distant village where her antecedents are not known. Here she lives out her days, selling cigarettes and betel nut and thinking of her lost lover.

The narrative of *Phulmat* is replete with poems, riddles and stories put in the mouths of its characters, interspersed with straight dialogue. The tribals set great store by the artful telling of stories, good music and fine dancing, all activities at which the tragic Phulmat excels. Yet if Elwin's aboriginals are not savage, they are not always noble either, being subject to the everyday human emotions of greed and envy: thus the possessiveness of lovers, the jealousy of those spurned in love, the casting of spells upon enemies. Panda Baba, the Gond *gunia* of *Leaves from the Jungle*, makes a cameo appearance in the novel, aroused by a Baiga magician who steals his clients.[16]

Phulmat is a tale of some ethnographic interest, held together by the focus on the fate of its central character. One reviewer, H. E. Bates, thought the book 'a piece of the best kind of romance, rich in emotion but unsentimental, rich in colour but firmly rooted in fact, . . . realistic and as frank, in its portrayal of love, as Maupassant.'

A Cloud That's Dragonish, published by Murray in the following year, has a less convincing plot. *Cloud* is a tribal whodunnit about witchcraft, each of its chapters carrying an epigram on the persecution of witches in medieval Europe to remind its readers that their superstitions were once just as absurd. The book describes a mysterious series of deaths in the village of Sitalpani, deaths of livestock, pets and human beings. The villagers believe this to be the handiwork of a witch and suspicion shifts from one woman to another. They are finally convinced that the culprit is Motiari, a beautiful Gond girl. But the Gond *gunia* Panda Baba magically appears from his own village fifty miles away and through a series of deductive inferences uncovers the real murderer. This is a Pardhan youth, Lamu. Lamu's mother had been persecuted as a witch and killed in another village by Motiari's father. Vowing revenge, when he grows up Lamu kills the murderer and is determined to kill the daughter as well. On being exposed by Panda Baba he commits suicide.[17]

In a circular letter announcing the publication of *Phulmat*, Verrier warned his friends they might find the book 'coarse and realistic. So it is. But it is no good trying to describe a primitive village as though it were a Brompton drawing room.' The Gonds and the Baigas, he said, 'are more or less absorbed in two things—food and sex—and their conversation is like the prose parts of Shakespeare. So I want you to believe that "Phulmat of the Hills" is not pornographic, but simply photographic.'[18]

Although the tribals in these novels change partners as they would socks, the author's treatment of sex is in fact highly coded and discreet. Love-making is mentioned but never described, the beauty of the female form alluded to but never anatomized. Far more explicit in both respects was his long-awaited ethnography of the Baiga. In late 1937 he posted the manuscript to the publisher. John Murray were worried by its frank discussion of sex: marking out in an early draft the passages and sections deemed 'unsuitable for the feminine lay-reader.' This kind of stuff, they said, was foreign to their tradition. Elwin revised the manuscript, '"restrained" and "censored" to the utmost limit that I find compatible with the demands of science.' If Murray still found the discussion troublesome, he advised them to hire someone who would 'turn all the dubious stuff into Latin.'[19] The compromise finally agreed was to place the main chapter on sex in the middle of the book, with the author stating most clearly in the preface that he did not hold up the Baiga's 'sexual philosophy or practice to imitation.'

Richly suggestive, massively documented, written with verve and passion, *The Baiga* ran to 550 closely printed pages, the most complete account of an Indian tribe yet published. In the tradition of functionalist anthropology, the book presented a full account of tribal social organization, treating in some detail the rules of marriage, the rituals of birth and death, the production and consumption of food, the principles of jurispudence, the forms of magic and dance. In all this pride of place was given to two elements of Baiga life: the practice of sex and the history of *bewar* (shifting cultivation).

When Elwin came to publish his ethnography of the Baiga, he had before him the example of Malinowski, the author of *Sex and Repression in Savage Society* (1927) and *The Sexual Life of Savages* (1929). Where Malinowski's work had given Elwin scientific sanction and a honourable precedent, the Pole was a dry-as-dust technician analysing the sexual consciousness in terms of incest taboos and mother-right, the totemic organization of clans and the economy of wife-exchange. In his books the discussion of sex is generalized rather than particular, with individuals subsumed for the most part in the grid of social structure. In contrast Elwin's account is animated and vigorous, illuminating through character and example what was for the tribe, as for him, 'the most important and enthralling thing in life.'

An early chapter presents life histories of fifteen typical Baigas. This is a rich portrait gallery where individual memories cluster around common themes—wives and lovers, disease and death, official penetration and official exploitation. Making sense of these lives, the anthropologist contrasts the apparent poverty of material circumstance with the richness of remembered sexual experience. Lahakat, an elderly man wrapped in a torn blanket, has conquered fifty girls before turning twenty-five; Baihar, a haggard old woman, was once a famous beauty, wept over by many men, successively and successfully seduced by a forest guard, a magician, and her own brother; Rawan, a celebrated hunter, would track down girls to the river, break their water pots with a well-directed arrow, and make love to them on the spot. And there is Yogi Dewar, a sprightly centenarian who remembers the 1857 Mutiny in astonishing detail and who has twenty-five children by six wives, the last of whom is his granddaughter.

Ancient India was 'rich in sexological literature,' remarks Elwin, but recent writers 'have generally been too much under the influence of the prevailing Puritan conventions to treat the subject freely.' Science called him to break the taboo, for the Baiga he found were ruled not so much by the forest guard and the police constable as by the raging fires of sexual desire. In their lives 'celibacy is unheard of, continence is never practised.' Their children were apparently born with a 'complete equipment of phallic knowledge.' Baiga knowledge of each other's bodies was extraordinarily attentive to detail: the men, for instance, could distinguish between twelve kinds of breasts, ranking them in almost precise order of attractiveness. Even Baiga *gali* (abuse) was rich in sexual suggestiveness.[20]

Baiga sex was free, warm and spontaneous, a necessary background to the material concerns of the tribe. These centred around bewar, the system of axe-cultivation to which they were passionately attached. God himself had established the Baiga in the practise of bewar, with the admonition: 'You must not tear down the breasts of your Mother Earth with the plough like the Gond or Hindu.' These sentiments were given short shrift by the British who, from the beginnings of their rule, tried systematically to destroy bewar. Colonial objections to *bewar* were rooted in an ideology of Improvement (settled cultivation would 'civilize' the tribes by curing them of their wayward habits) as well as driven by commercial forestry and its need to exclude the Baiga from areas where timber was being felled. Bewar was quickly banned in almost all districts of the Central Provinces, being confined ultimately to a small patch of forest, about 24,000 acres in all, in the Ramgarh *tehsil* of Mandla district. This was known as the Baiga Chak (reserve).

When the Chak was formed, the government received a good many petitions from Baiga who lived outside the reserve. Dholi Baiga of Udhor, writing in 1892, said that after bewar was stopped,

We daily starve, having had no food grain in our possession. The only wealth we possess is our axe. We have no clothes to cover our bodies with, but we pass cold nights by the fireside. We are now dying for want of food. We cannot go elsewhere, as the British government is everywhere. What fault have we done that the government does not take care of us? Prisoners are supplied with ample food in jail. A cultivator of [the soil] is not deprived of his holding, but the Government does not give us our right who have lived here for generations past.

Forty years later, when Elwin first arrived in the Baiga country, he found the aboriginals still not fully reconciled to the ban on bewar. 'Every Baiga who has yielded to the plough,' he remarked, 'knows himself to be standing on *papi-dharti*, sinful earth.' 'When the bewar was stopped and we first touched the plough,' remembered one Baiga, 'a man died in every house.' Another claimed that before the forest department made them ordinary serfs, the penis of the Baiga had been five times as large as anybody else's. Elwin was convinced that restrictions on bewar, coupled with the ban on hunting in the forest, had crippled the tribe. By depriving them of their livelihood, by tearing a page out of their mythology, by bulldozing them into a way of life foreign to their tradition and inclinations, the state had done colossal harm to their spirit.[21]

What could be done? The Baiga dreamt of a new Baiga Raj, with a king of their own, the restoration of bewar, and unlimited opportunities to hunt and fish. 'The English are giving everyone swaraj,' said one, 'why can't they give us *bewar-swaraj*?' Elwin thought the solution lay in the formation of a national park covering the wilder and inaccessible parts of Mandla, where the Baiga would be sovereign. Non-aboriginals would be excluded, as would missionaries of all stripes, Christian as well as Hindu. The Indian Penal Code would be withdrawn and the Baiga governed by their own laws. Above all, they would be given the freedom of the forest so that their 'once proud-quivered loins' need not tremble any more 'at the lash of every little whipper-snapper of a forest guard.' Thus might the Baiga be saved from the fate 'which an over-hasty and unregulated process of "uplift" and "civilization" has brought upon aboriginal peoples in other parts of India.'[22]

The Baiga was the work of a novelist who had strayed into anthropology. In the prefaces to their books, professional anthropologists like to thank Professor X and Dr Y, the director of this archive and the keeper of that museum. But Elwin gave pride of place to

> my Baiga friends [to whom] I owe the real making of this book and, in passing, some of the happiest hours of my life spent in their company. I cannot name them all, but at least I must not forget my *mahaprasad* Mahatu (my 'family magician,' a great adept, though his love-charms are faulty) and his sons, Mithu and Jantri; Jethu, the lame gunia of Bohi, and those entrancing boys Panku and Charka; Hothu, who was my generous host in Taliyapani, and Bahadur who entertained me at Hirapur; Dhan Singh and Thaggur who have often brought the mysterious benefits of their magic to my own village; Pachlu, the 'professional savage' of Jholar; Rawan, the great hunter of Bilaspur; Lahakat, the Don Juan of Amadob; Daseru, dreamer of strange dreams; the mild and gentle Ketu; Yogi Dewar, the Mutiny veteran, whom I have not seen sober; the many-husbanded Mahi, a perfect 'Cockney' type, coarse and irresistible; the old and knowledgeable Baisakin and her co-wife Malho, just a little jealous; and the children, Phagni and Gondin, Mangli and Bhairi, Goru and Jhingra.[23]

It was the novelist J. C. Squire who first drew attention, delightedly, to this decidedly unscientific preface.[24] The book's uncertain location between literature and science was also pinpointed by the philosopher Alan Watts. In a report to the publisher Watts called it

> a curious mixture—on the one hand a piece of very valuable, thorough and apparently reliable research, and on the other a collection of weird, amusing and bawdy stories. The author frequently changes his style to suit the subject; at one time he writes in the cold and technical jargon of science, and at another in plain (and almost cheerful English), and in the latter instance the book is always entertaining, though often unsavoury, reading.

Presented as an anthropological monograph, 'this was beneath the surface ... [a] most human and delightful book. The author does not regard the Baiga tribes as laboratory specimens; it is quite evident that he loves and respects them, and often succeeds in making the reader share his feelings.' Thus the work's 'scientific thoroughness is enhanced, as it were, mellowed by a thoroughly human and sympathetic approach to the subject.'[25]

Early reviews of *The Baiga* were heartening. The author, remarked the *TLS*, was an 'anthropologist by grace' rather than by profession, 'doing his best to think as black as his firsts in the Oxford schools will let him.'[26]

J. H. Hutton, Professor of Social Anthropology at Cambridge, thought the book 'the greatest thing of its kind that has been done,' showing 'Elwin's complete entry into the primitive point of view.' Beryl de Zoete spoke in the *New Statesman* of 'a vast and entirely fascinating encyclopaedia' deserving of 'extraordinary praise.' W. V. Grigson of the Indian Civil Service commended the book's ethnographic merits and its practical value in 'pointing out to the Hindu majority the conditions of their less advanced fellow-countrymen and, of even greater importance, those elements of tribal culture which are of permanent survival value: they are many.'[27]

The views of the Hindu majority are unrecorded, as are those of the Gandhians, although what they might have thought of the book had they cared to read it can be inferred from the remarks of a Christian in the *International Review of Missions*. The sections on sex, wrote this angry reviewer, 'are characterized by a gusto strangely out of place in a professedly scientific treatise.' This critic closed the book with an uneasy conscience, for 'in the name of science the ragged "purdah" of the Baiga has been violated and the world at large invited to take a good look. In circuses and zoos the cages of anthropoid apes are screened from curious eyes, at certain intimate moments of their occupants' lives. Mr Elwin's humble friends and confidantes have been less fortunate in this respect than captive chimpanzees.'[28]

The Baiga was published in September 1939, days before the outbreak of war in Europe. 'Poor book!' remarked Verrier when the first copy arrived in Patangarh: 'Who is going to buy it in war-time?' There were other reasons why his support for the European 'struggle of democracy over totalitarianism' was less than enthusiastic. When his mother wrote of the difficulties of life in war-torn England, Verrier seized on the note of patriotic hysteria that her letters seemed to betray. 'We are amused at you calling this a safe and peaceful place!' he wrote in early November; 'I suppose there is not one of our people who could not with advantage change places with a Tommy in the trenches. The expectation of life here is lower than in the Maginot Line, and leprosy, malaria, syphilis and other diseases are more frequent and more deadly than bombs.' Three weeks later, having submitted an essay on aboriginal policy for the Wellcome Medal of the Royal Anthropological Institute, he noted: 'I don't see why, when everyone is getting medals for killing people, I shouldn't try to get one for suggesting methods of keeping them alive.'[29]

The exchanges with his mother, of which only his side has survived, lay behind a combative circular letter that he sent out in January 1940. England's war aims, he insisted, 'must include a square deal for the aboriginals as well as for India. And the "war aims" of the Indian Nationalist should equally include normal human rights for the original inhabitants of India.' Appealing to subscribers not to abandon the Gond Seva Mandal, Verrier said the tribals of Mandla were not really 'out of the war,' for they lived

> permanently under war conditions. There is a black-out in the village every night. Every evening, far more deadly than the Messerschmidt, comes a flight of mosquitoes with a load of parasites that kill three million annually. We always have a rationing system, for the villagers never have enough to eat. For four months in the year the rains set up a great blockade of mud between these villages and the outside world. The Gond is just as down-trodden and oppressed as the Pole or the German Jew. Many years ago, his kingdoms and great estates were taken from him by conquest or deceit. The Baigas, lords of the jungle, have been robbed of their ancestral home, deprived of their human rights, taxed and suppressed and regimented into decay by the very people who now profess to stand up for the integrity of small nations. Nearly every wrong that the Nazi has inflicted on the Czech and Pole has been suffered by our aboriginals.[30]

The war lost the Gond Seva Mandal some old supporters, but *The Baiga* had meanwhile enlisted some new ones. One of these was W. G. (Bill) Archer, an unorthodox and most untypical member of the ICS based in Bihar. A historian of sparkling intelligence from Cambridge, Archer and his Oxonian wife Mildred had opted out of the stuffy social circle of the civilian elite. They made friends easily with Indians and especially with tribals. Posted in Ranchi, at the edge of the forest, Archer began collecting the tribal folk songs of Chotanagpur. *The Baiga* appeared as he was finishing a book of his own, on the folk poetry of the Uraon. He at once wrote Verrier a fan-letter inviting him to Bihar.

The Archers had 'long known Verrier by reputation, admired his writings and been attracted by his unconventional way of life.' When he arrived at their doorstep in January 1940 they were not disappointed. He was a world removed from the company of the PWD engineer and the superintendent of police, the dreary circuit of district town and hill station that comprised much of their life. When they took him to Patna, the seat of government, Verrier insisted on going around to Government House to sign the book, dressed in shorts, sandals and a bright blue shirt. The ADC on duty fidgeted nervously but his hosts were delighted. The attraction was mutual, for the Archers were in their own way as unconventional as he—Bill a poet and aesthete, at odds with the stiff and arrogant image of the ICS man, Mildred a writer and left-leaning Labourite, no memsahib at all.[31]

The two Englishmen paid a courtesy call on S. C. Roy, the lawyer-ethnographer who lived in Ranchi. Verrier was tremendously impressed by Roy who, as a native, had a clear advantage over white men when it came to doing field-work with the tribes. 'I do wish we were both small and black,' joked Verrier, 'and could go and live in a [village] without attracting any notice. That is my one constant prayer that in my next incarnation I may be small and black and very very clever, so that I can do something worthwhile.'[32]

Verrier returned from Ranchi to find a vast pile of letters waiting at Patangarh. One was from Mahadev Desai, a second from Sir Francis Wylie—both wanted to visit. What if they arrived at the same time? That would be a 'real Trimmer's cross-roads,' he thought. In the event neither came, so he was able to get back to work. The tour with the Archers inspired him to return to a subject he had temporarily set aside. While living in Karanjia he had woken each morning to the sound of bellows from a furnace run by the Agaria tribe of iron-smelters. In Bihar he had been taken to the territory of the Asur, metal workers who lived high up on the Chotanagpur plateau and who were distantly connected to the Agaria of Mandla. Verrier now went back to his notes on the tribe. His book on them was completed in April 1940 but published, when Hitler's war allowed it, only two years later.

The Agaria tells a melancholy tale of the decline of an ancient craft at the hands of state hostility and market competition. Each furnace was taxed at eight rupees a year, more than a quarter of an Agaria's total earnings, which were a measly thirty rupees. The new forest laws forbade the collection of wood and its conversion to charcoal. The Agaria went into the state forests anyway, by stealth, but with a guilty conscience—many of their dreams were about being surprised by forest guards. That other great innovation of British rule, the railway, had flooded the market with factory-made iron. Breaking forest laws, migrating to districts where taxes were lower, persuading peasants that their softer ores made better ploughshares, the Agaria survived with a 'heroic persistence.' All the same, the number of operating furnaces fell from 510 to 336 between 1909 and 1938. The decline of material culture everywhere brought 'idleness, dulness, immorality and hunger.' Where the furnaces had closed down, 'all the romance, mythology and religion that centred around Lohasur,' the god of iron, had disappeared too.[33]

The Agaria was the first of Elwin's books to be published by the Indian branch of Oxford University Press. John Murray were not willing to take it on in wartime; the OUP were, but even they wanted a subsidy. This was procured from the great steel-making firm of the Tatas, whose head, J. R. D. Tata, had a well-deserved reputation as a patron of science and scholarship. I doubt that he or anyone else in the firm really read the book—its defense of an indigenous craft was at the same time an indictment of their factory-made product. The method and subject were of course more to the liking of Gandhians—as close to their professed interests, we might say, as the author's previous book, *The Baiga*, was distant. It is a mark of the absoluteness of Verrier's transition from the attractions of monastic asceticism to those of tribal hedonism that he asked OUP to approach potential Gandhian customers on their own. 'How far would any of the Gandhi-people be inclined to buy the book,' wrote the author to his editor: 'It is after all an account of an indigenous village industry with whose preservation the Congress is supposed to be vitally concerned. I am so out of touch that I do not know who are the proper people to approach in this matter, but I expect you could find out.'[34]

A most revealing review of *The Agaria* was published in the *American Anthropologist* by the French-Hungarian scholar George Devereux. He allowed that the data was 'rich, detailed, authoritative;' what was lacking was systematic conceptual analysis. With Elwin flitting back and forth between 'the card-index pattern, Frazerian comparisons, functionalism [and] psychiatry,' the book had 'neither internal or external order.' But behind these symptoms lay a deeper cause: quite evidently Elwin had spent 'too much time in the field.' What he needed 'most at this juncture is a refresher, a plunge in the Pieran spring of the London School of Economics, or one of the progressive departments of anthropology in the United States.' Devereux hoped that 'in the interests of science some foundation [would] stake this most distinguished field-worker and scholar to such a venture.'[35]

This last comment recalls M. N. Srinivas' later formulation of the three births of an anthropologist. For Srinivas, an anthropologist is 'once-born' when he goes to the field for the first time, thrust abruptly into an unfamiliar world. He is 'twice-born' when, after living for some time among the community, he is able to see things from their perspective: a second birth akin to a Buddhist surge of consciousness for which years of study or mere linguistic facility do not prepare you. An anthropologist is truly 'thrice-born' only when he moves back to the university, his fieldwork completed. Here he reflects on his material and situates it in a theoretical context, while being alerted to competing subjectivities by colleagues returning from their field-sites and communities. The anthropologist's special allegiance to his own tribe can never be entirely abandoned, but his third incarnation allows him the hope of achieving at least a partial objectivity, which is the mark of a scholar as distinct from a propagandist.[36]

In his own way Elwin anticipated this formulation, for in one of his books he beautifully describes the anthropologist's second birth. 'In every investigation of a civilization not one's own,' he writes, 'there comes—usually only after months or years of routine investigation, tedious checking and the patient accumulation of facts—a moment of sudden glory when one sees everything fall into place, when the colours of the pattern are revealed, and one finds oneself no longer an alien and an outsider, but within.'[37]

The charge that he was not anthropologist or scientist enough was one with which Elwin was to become tiresomely familiar. To the professional who prides himself on his detachment Elwin would remain forever in the stage of twice-bornness, always and invariably seeing things from the perspective of the community he studied and identified with. A third birth required a move to the academic founts of the LSE, and this was not a move he was willing to make. It was not so much that no foundation was willing to fund this venture, but rather that, unlike the university anthropologist, he had come to the field with no intention of going back to the Senior Common Room.

But on the other hand being in the field for so long gave Elwin an insider's view of the kind denied to scientific anthropologists, for whom the tribe or village is rather frequently a fact to be placed in a theory or, if one were inclined to be cynical, simply the vehicle for professional advancement. Elwin placed no such burdens on his field-site—actually his home— which is why *The Agaria* and *The Baiga* are marked by this unusual ability to see tribal life from within. These are studies in salvage ethnography, sympathetic portrayals of ways of life before the drowning wave of progress finally rolled them over. Writing in the middle of the most savage war in history, Elwin contrasted the 'millions of tonnes of death-dealing steel employed in modern battle' to the 'few thousand tonnes smelted annually in the clay furnaces of central India,' these being used for making the ploughs and harrows that raised rich crops in the Maikal Hills. 'This aboriginal iron has brought the law of plenty to the jungle,' he remarked, while 'that civilized iron is bringing the law of the jungle to the lands of plenty.'[38] The fate of the Agaria was thus a 'implicit condemnation of industrialism,' the plight of the Baiga an indictment of the 'scientific' and narrowly commercial forestry that had displaced them.

The Baiga, remarked Elwin in his great book on that tribe, 'know little of civilization and think little of it.' He himself knew a great deal about civilization and yet thought little of it. In this sense he might be said to exemplify the ideology of 'cultural primitivism,' defined by A. O. Lovejoy and George Boas as the 'discontent of the civilized with civilization, or with some conspicuous and characteristic feature of it.'[39] Primitivism has of course been one of the most enduring strands in European thought; in the words of a more recent commentator, Tzvetan Todorov, it is 'less the description of a reality than the formulation of an ideal.'[40]

Elwin's own espousal of cultural primitivism was not wholly an invention. For one thing the Gond, the Baiga and the Agaria all believed that the past had been better than the present, that there had truly once been a Golden Age when their kings ruled, when their powers of magic and healing were unimpaired, when their beloved bewar and iron-smelting were freely pursued. Elwin's attack on civilization was also splendidly timed, for, with the long shadow of Nazism cast across the warring nations of Europe, the primitivist could effectively challenge a view of human progress in which savages of the forest were placed at the bottom of the hierarchy and modern European society at its apex.

Most of all Verrier Elwin must be distinguished from other primitivists in that he actually lived with the communities whose culture he so vigorously celebrated. The narrator of primitivist reveries has the choice, which he generally exercises, 'to return, at the end of his sojourn, to the highly civilized countries he came from.' From Vespucci to Chateaubriand down to the anthropologists of the twentieth century, the European traveller in search of the exotic invariably goes back to where he came from.[41] In an unpublished fragment of autobiography, Elwin wrote of what marked him out from others who extolled the primitive life: 'Not many of those who wrote so eloquently of the return to nature,' he remarked, 'were prepared, however, to take the journey themselves, *at least not without a return ticket.*'[42]

Verrier Elwin lived with the primitive, he loved with them, he defended them. There is a poignant and heroic logic to this which distinguishes Elwin's brand of activist anthropology from academic anthropology. The Baiga, he wrote, 'have for the last seventy years consistently and bitterly criticized the inequity in their treatment. But they have no champion to fight for them, no spokesman to voice their grievances.' Likewise, iron-smelting was one of a score of village industries being destroyed by the Industrial Revolution, but thus far 'no mahatma has arisen to revive it.' Champion, spokesman, even mahatma perhaps, that is how Verrier Elwin saw himself. By trumping Gandhi with sex and the bishops with anthropology, this Christian for the Congress had now become a defender of the aboriginal.

CHAPTER SEVEN

Going Gond

I am rather anxious about his future, which seems to me to be very obscure and uncertain. He is a man of very great possibilities, but I begin to doubt somewhat gravely whether they will be realized.

William Paton on Verrier Elwin, September 1933

Mr Verrier Elwin
Deserves and may well win
Renown in the world of letters
For recording the life of our
moral betters.

Bombay journalist, *c.* 1940

Elwin—you mean the anthropologist who married his fieldwork?

Professor of Sociology, Delhi University, *c.* 1990

The villages of the upper Narmada valley were remote and inaccessible when Verrier Elwin lived there, and so they are today. When I visited them with a friend in the first weeks of 1998, we began our journey by boarding the Utkal Express at New Delhi. This is a sad and grimy train, twenty-two coaches pulled along by the sheer will power of a dying diesel engine. Its condition suggests the countryside it shall pass through: eastern Uttar Pradesh, Rajasthan, Madhya Pradesh, Bihar and Orissa, the poorest parts of India, millions of acres of farmland occasionally fertilized by rain and worked tirelessly by underfed and unschooled peasants.

A long day and a night later we get off at Anuppur, in the Shahdol district of Madhya Pradesh on the edge of the Maikal Hills. We take a jeep to Amarkantak, a two-hour ride up the ghat. We climb through open canopy forests, native sal trees interspersed with exotic pine and eucalyptus. We pass a truck parked astride the road, in front of it a group of Gond girls, dancing. They are dressed in vivid polyester sarees and are demanding *chanda* (tribute) from the driver, for it is the day of Makar Sankranti, the harvest festival. We are now in recognizably tribal country, the forests thicker and with the sal having successfully stood its ground against interlopers. At Kirar Ghat the driver halts to allow us a view of the Sone valley below.

We stop again at Amarkantak, briefly, to confirm our reservations at the Kabir Chabutra rest-house. This lies a further six miles into the forest, in a lovely isolated spot overlooking a deep gorge. The bungalow was built by the Public Works Department in 1913; twenty-five years later it was where the governor of the Central Provinces stayed when he came to visit Elwin. My companion is himself a high official of the Government of India, here travelling more-or-less incognito. He is, I tell him, the most distinguished civil servant to stay at Kabir Chabutra since Sir Francis Wylie.

Kabir Chabutra is within striking distance of the villages once patronized by the Gond Seva Mandal. Wylie must have walked down to see Elwin—or was carried there by *dandy*—but we can go more conveniently, by jeep. The road winds through old-growth forest well stocked with Hanuman langur, black-faced creatures who go swinging on trees or sit by the road-side watching trucks go by. The forest has other residents too, as some posters by the side of the road inform us. One, a spectacular sketch of a forest fire with tigers and elephants fleeing, soberly tells the reader that it is his duty to protect the woods from burning (*vano ko aag se bachaiye/ vano ki suraksha aapka daayitva hai*). The illustrators and copywriters of the Madhya Pradesh government have chosen the eight miles from Kabir Chabutra to Karanjia as a prime target for their art. The posters are plentiful and varied, seeking to bond the tribals to a government they might not so willingly heed. *Kisano ki sarkar, aapki sarkar*, your government is of and by the peasants, says one signboard, and then on the reverse, *savdhaan!*—be cautious. This is addressed to the rash driver but could perhaps be read as a warning to the Gond not to take the first slogan too seriously. One poster seems calculated to displease the feminist: *Chauka, baasan aur putai, phir bhi mahila kare padhai:* The woman may cook, wash and clean, yet in school she must still be seen. Another would have offended Elwin: a moralistic Gandhian attack on drink, the tribal's sustenance, it read: *Nasha nischit maut hai, aaj svayam ki, kal parivar ki, parso rashtra ki* (Drunkenness is certain death, yours today, the family's tomorrow, the nation's day-after.)

Karanjia is a large, sprawling village spread across both sides of the road. It boasts a quiet police *thana* and a busy high school, with portraits of Bose, Gandhi and other nationalists on the walls and lots of chattering children within. There is also a timber yard, filled with logs of sal trees once attacked by the borer beetle and since cheerfully felled by contractors. It is, as in Elwin's day, a mixed village, dominated by Gonds but with more than a handful of Pankas, Baigas, Banias and Ahirs. His name is known by all but his face is remembered only by two ancient Gonds of the Baghel clan who studied in one of his schools. But it is an Ahir cowherd who takes us to where *Badabhai* and *Chhotabhai* lived, on the hill above Tikeri Tola. Elwin had an eye for views and the ashram of St Francis would have looked out across fields to the Amarkantak hills beyond. The sight is glorious, and Mary Gillet's words ring in my ears: 'Hills and valleys and blue skies and peasants singing.' Sadly, of the buildings where she briefly lived there is not a sign. The walls of the ashram have returned to mud, washed away in the many monsoons that have hit the hill since Verrier and Shamrao moved down the valley to Sarwachappar. There is a nice pipal tree, planted by them apparently, and a sturdy stone well at the foot of the hill built for their convenience. That is all.

In the oral history of Karanjia, we discover, Elwin is mentioned only in dispatches. Next on our tourist route is the village of Ryatwar, three miles away, where we have reason to believe his memory is rather more enduring. The road to Ryatwar is a dirt track, mustard fields on both sides, the terrain gently sloping down to the Narmada beyond. We ford a little stream flowing into the great river and approach the hamlet. The jeep stops next to a group of Gond men, squatting and smoking under a *harra* tree. Heart in mouth I approach them and ask: '*Aap batayinge Elwin ka makaan kahan hain.*' Could you tell me where the house of the Elwins is? They direct me back a hundred yards, to a pink washed school building.

Adjacent to this is a low Gond house with mud walls plastered white and a tiled roof, its small garden ringed, English style, by a thorned hedge. In the courtyard stands an old lady wearing a white sari with a discreet striped border, her head covered. It is late afternoon, the most written-about hour of the Indian day, the time the cows come home and the sun starts to set. '*Aap Kosi behn hain*,' we ask. '*Ji haan*,' she answers, '*wo hi hoon*.' Yes, I am Kosi. The moment will not return, so I ask her at once whether I can take a picture. She nods in assent, adjusts her sari, smoothens her hair, and pulls her *palloo* more closely around her head. The ease and grace, the sheer naturalness with which she composes herself, takes my breath away, for she has not, I think, stood before a camera in half a century.

But there was a time when plenty of people took plenty of pictures of her. For this was, indeed is, Kosi Elwin, once the wife of Verrier Elwin.

The lady in the courtyard that magical afternoon in Ryatwar was born Kosi Armu but took the name Elwin before a magistrate in Jabalpur almost sixty years earlier. Verrier and Kosi were married on 4th April 1940: a decade later the union ended in divorce. The memory was so wounding that Elwin could not bring himself to write about his first wife in his autobiography, where Kosi and the years of their marriage are disposed off in two paragraphs. 'I cannot even now look back on this period of my life without a deep sense of pain and failure,' he remarks—'indeed I can hardly bear to write about it.'[1]

Written in the nineteen-sixties seemingly for an audience of home-loving, petty-bourgeois Indians, *The Tribal World of Verrier Elwin* is not an autobiography in the confessional mode. Kosi gets two paras, while other, more fleeting loves—Mary Gillet, Ala Pocha, Singharo—go unmentioned. Elwin's reticence is an open invitation to the biographer. But the keepers of his flame have kept the tracks well covered. His literary executor denied me access to Elwin's diaries for the period because of what they contained about Kosi. Elwin's English family, in making their generous donation of his letters to the India Office Library in London, took care to efface traces of the marriage. Verrier's weekly letters home, from his arrival in India in September 1927 to his death thirty-six years later, can all be consulted except those letters in which he might have talked of Kosi. No evidence can be found here of where he met his first wife, or of when and how he told his family of his wish to marry her. About the only letter on the subject is one to Mrs M. O. Elwin from Sir Francis Wylie, governor of the Central Provinces, conveying his failure in persuading her son to call off the marriage. The fact that Wylie's letter is preserved is symbolic, perhaps; the warning of a Big Man ignored at one's peril.

The story of Kosi Elwin has been subject to a mildly Stalinist obliteration in which Verrier, his family and his executors all seem to have collaborated. The biographer has to make do with letters written to friends who preserved them, and whose families had no reason not to place them in the public domain. We are lucky, too, that by 1940 Verrier was something of a public figure, his marriage to a tribal girl attracting the attention of journals and journalists. The evidence from both private letters and public prints suggests that at the time of their marriage, and for several years after, Verrier was deeply in love with Kosi. Their relationship seems also to have placed a part, perhaps even a central part, in the making of some of his best (and best-known) books. Love and work, the personal and the public, were joined in Verrier Elwin's evocative portrayals of tribal culture in works like *The Aboriginals* (1943) and *The Muria and their Ghotul* (1946).

The influence of Kosi on Verrier's subsequent career can more easily be understood by asking the kind of question the professional historian is taught to scorn. *What if* Verrier had defied Mahatma Gandhi and married Mary Gillet in 1933? The union would have confirmed them in a life of social work, working for but not with the Gonds. Their children, like the children of other expatriates, would have been sent to school in England. More than a lone Englishman, a white couple would have stood apart from the Gonds—racially, culturally and imaginatively. Married to Mary Gillet, Verrier would have doubtless led a life of service and sacrifice but not, one thinks, of colour and controversy.

'I do wish Verrier would get married,' wrote Shamrao Hivale to Mrs Elwin in August, 1939, adding, 'If we go to Bombay in November he might find a good girl there.' His mother was being gently set up, for Verrier was in search rather of a woman to take with him to the city, not a 'city wife.' He now wanted a permanent relationship but, as he told Bill Archer, at the same time 'shrank from holing with a mistress.' That was 'too surreptitious' and would 'complicate ordinary social relations' (outside the village, that is). He had his eye on Kosi, one of the more attractive and certainly the most intelligent of the girls around Patangarh. They must have first met when Verrier was still in Karanjia, for Kosi remembers briefly attending the Gond Seva Mandal school. This would have been in 1934 or 1935. A little later, the girl having become a woman, the acquaintance was renewed and deepened. At this distance in time Kosi's powers of recall are understandably attenuated; nor would she easily talk of her former husband. But she did remember, quite clearly, Eldyth Elwin's visit of 1938–9. This means Kosi would already have been a habitué of Patangarh, the village a good four-hour walk from her native Ryatwar. She and Verrier were very likely lovers living under the same roof when Elydth was around, although whether the sister approved one can't tell. At any rate, Verrier seems to have waited a year or so before deciding to take the next step. Shamrao's letter of August 1939 was an early testing of the waters. Once mother had assented in principle to Verrier marrying, they would ease her by stages into the real situation. A hint was dropped that the daughter-in-law would be Indian, though of the less unpalatable, i.e. city-dwelling and English-speaking, kind. The revelation that she was a tribal would come after the deed was done.

Mrs Minnie Elwin would certainly have regarded her daughter-in-law as a savage. But Kosi would tell you herself that she was a *Raj* Gond, a member of the tribal aristocracy who claimed kinship with the Gond monarchs of medieval Chattisgarh. Kosi's family were poor, but 'devilish dignified' in view of their lineage—in Verrier's description much like 'decayed baronets in a P. G. Wodehouse story.' They would not approve of their daughter marrying out of caste, so Verrier resorted to what he termed 'Love-Marriage-by-Capture.' He took Kosi off to Jabalpur, where they were married under the Special Marriages Act, designed for such inter-religious and inter-racial unions. The deed done, the bride's family were brought round by a feast and a promise that the legal bond would be confirmed by a ceremony according to Gond rites.[2]

The tribal wedding was carried over four full days, as described by the groom in his scholarly essay 'I Married a Gond.' The first day was taken up with the construction of a wedding booth made of wood and bamboo, and with the customary preparation of Verrier and Kosi. On the second morning the bride and the groom were separately anointed, with oil and turmeric, then bathed and dressed—in his case in a yellow *dhoti*, a long cassock-like upper garment, and a crown of coloured paper. The two then watched as their respective parties fought a mock battle with sticks and spears. The battle's result was foretold in favour of the groom who 'at a Gond wedding is a hero not subject to casualties.' Finally, in the evening Verrier and Kosi were taken three times around the wedding pole in the ceremony that confirmed their union.

On the third day Verrier carried Kosi off in triumph to his home village. This, as both lived in Patangarh, was deemed to be Sarwachappar, the hamlet ten miles distant where the Bhumijan Seva Mandal still maintained a home for lepers. At Sarwachappar they went thrice more around a pole and then settled down to hear the marriage sermon. The Gond *pujari* tailored his talk to the extraordinary circumstance of a tribal girl marrying an Englishman. As bullocks are yoked to a plough, began the priest,

> so too have you been yoked together today. Listen, brother, when she is foolish, do not despise her thinking her a mere daughter of the forest. Never find fault with her, or grumble at her. And you girl, never say he is bad, he forgets me, he does not love me, and so leave him. He is English. He has come from another land to love us. From how great a distance have you and he come together, over land and sea, over mountain and forest, drawn together by fate. To you he is *Raja;* to him you are *Rani,* and because of you two we are all of royal blood. And listen again, brother! Today you eat her tender flesh; tomorrow do not despise her bones. Never leave this girl, nor leave this country; for she is yours and this land is yours. All things taste sweeter as they ripen, but with a woman it is not so. But you must consider her always, and in your mouth she must taste sweet even in her old age. And brother, for love of this girl do not forget us. For love of woman makes a man forget all things and turns his mind aside.
>
> And now take this girl. We are giving you a winnowing-fan full of gold. Use it well. Eat and live in joy. Live for age after age. Of one may there be twenty-one by the grace of God.

Verrier's account of the marriage pays close attention to the rituals and to the eating, dancing and singing that accompanied them. Scientific accuracy is leavened with irony and self-mockery, and the essay drops its veil of objectivity altogether when it comes to the ceremony's concluding ritual. This was the shooting, early on the fourth day, by the groom of a model of a deer made of leaves. Performed in front of a large crowd, the act was redolent with sexual symbolism and Verrier was to describe it privately as a 'frightful ordeal.' For if he had missed altogether he would have been thought to be impotent and Kosi was not the 'sort of girl with whom that affliction could be regarded as a matter of indifference.'[3] There are echoes here of George Orwell's essay 'Shooting an Elephant,' with marksmanship in this case proof of marital fitness rather than the authority to rule. Verrier failed to knock down the deer in six tries but on the seventh attempt sent 'a perfect shot right through the deer where its heart would have been, and the [tribal] boys with shouts of triumph picked it up and carried it home. . . . It was a great relief—*Oxford* was not decadent after all.'[4]

Verrier's rich and extended description of his marriage gave a novel twist to the anthropologist's credo of 'participant' observation. Some thought then and later that he had married Kosi in the spirit of science. Eldyth and her mother consoled themselves that it was all a 'whisky-inspired whim,' although an elderly uncle, pious and suspicious, declared Verrier married Kosi because 'he had to.'[5] In any case the first reaction of both family and friends was chilly disapproval. The couple received only three wedding presents from outside (one came from Bill and Mildred Archer), while a number of donors, among them the American Women's Club of Bombay, withdrew support to their Leper Home and schools on account of Verrier having married a 'savage.'[6]

At the time of the marriage Verrier was thirty-seven and had been twelve years in India. He lived and ate much like the Gonds he had come to serve, yet his education and orientation radically marked him out from his milieu. He spoke Chattisgarhi, the local dialect, but knew no other Indian language, and was always most comfortable speaking English. In some ways indeed he still thought of himself as an Oxford man. By 1940 his inclinations were increasingly towards literary and scientific rather than humanitarian work. This was nicely captured by a Bombay journalist who, on meeting Verrier a year before his marriage, described him thus : 'He drifted in looking very healthy, blue-eyed and happy, with that scholarly stoop of his, a roll of proofs in his hand and a cheery smile that, I thought, must light up the forest glades wonderfully.'[7]

Verrier was tall and fair, his bride dark and diminutive. A contemporary photograph shows a very pretty young woman, perhaps twenty to her husband's thirty-seven, with an alert and amused expression, beautiful even teeth and hair worn short, Western-style. There is no trace of selfconsciousness. Kosi's poise was in contrast to the diffidence, even fear, which her husband reported other tribals showing when confronted by his camera—they feared his box was 'a sort of anthropometric instrument by which I could measure the stature of likely recruits for the Army.'[8] Born and raised in a village near Patangarh, Kosi did not know a word of English ('except "Get Out" which she could hardly fail to pick up'), had never been in a train or seen a film or listened to the wireless. Effervescent, a gifted singer and dancer, 'a mine of poetry and ideas,' Kosi was, to quote Bill Archer, 'a raging, roaring girl' not in the least in awe of her husband.[9]

His friends' reservations appear on the face of it to be not without foundation. His family too had made it plain that they'd much rather he'd married someone of his class and colour. These criticisms wounded Verrier and seem to have penetrated deep into the subconscious: a diary entry reports a dream where he'd 'bigamously married Margaret Moore [an English acquaintance] and spent many distracted hours wondering how on earth to get out of it.' The announcement of the marriage was Verrier's first *public* avowal of his flight from celibacy, and he now had a good deal to explain and answer for. Characteristically, he answered his critics with defiance. To those who supposed that Shamrao and he had taken a lifelong vow of brahmacharya, he replied that the Gonds themselves viewed the unmarried life as 'something abnormal, almost as a perversion.' In their folktales the celibate Hindu sadhus were represented as greedy and lustful villains. But where village life made it impossible for Verrier to marry an Englishwoman, it seemed both 'logical and intelligible to take a tribal wife.' His marriage to a talented and witty Gond girl would in fact anchor him to the people he worked with and identify him more fully with their cause.[10] Indeed, in Kosi Verrier loved 'not only a beautiful and accomplished individual but a whole tribe.'[11] Some of his friends might disapprove because they looked down on aboriginals but, as Verrier wryly noted, 'Kosi's family, though very nice about it, consider that she has married very much beneath her.' A circular letter written on Christmas Eve took on the opposition. 'My wife's people,' wrote Verrier, '*my people*, have more of the secret of living—love, truth and non-attachment—which is the secret of Christmas than the warring nations of Europe.'[12]

Verrier was to take heart in the reception that Bombay, itself a city of mixed marriages, accorded Kosi. When he took Kosi there in the last week of July they spent a marvellous fortnight being feted everywhere. 'All the gloomy prophecies that my marriage would mean social death were falsified,' wrote Verrier to Bill Archer: 'Kosi was absolutely lionised: reporters hovering around, the guest of honour at the Taj Hotel, a reception for us at the smart Willingdon Club, dinner with the Tatas, the iron king of India, the Wadias, the Khataus.'[13] At the Willingdon Club Kosi sat next to Krishna Hutheesingh, Jawaharlal Nehru's younger sister. Kosi was dressed in a cotton sari patterned with flowers, 'with picturesque silver *dhars* ornamenting her ears, silver amulets on her arms and a belt hanging loosely from her slim waist.' She attracted 'some curious looks cast in her direction now and then'—when spoken to she 'replied with a charming smile which changed her whole expression.'[14] Verrier was giving one of his fund-raising talks at the Willingdon, but Kosi had her chance to perform too. When her husband spoke over All India Radio on 'The Folk Poetry of the Maikal Hills' the lecture was illustrated by snatches of Gond forest songs, *dadarias*, rendered by Kosi in 'a clear, natural voice that was very charming.' The programme, said one reviewer, was 'easily the most attractive feature of the week.'[15]

Kosi's own impressions of Bombay are not entirely unrecorded. She visited the cinema several times; what amused her most was a movie with the title 'Too Many Husbands.'[16] Interviewed by a reporter of the *Illustrated Weekly of India*, Kosi described the city in vivid metaphors. The long line of cars on the Marine Drive 'raised in her mind a picture of lines and lines of crows in a vast forest expanse,' the roar of the sea 'reminded her of the shrill winds whistling through their forest trees on a dark night.' The journalist marvelled at the 'calm dignity with which Kosibai, whose life hitherto had been spent in a tiny mud hut in a remote village, rose to her new experiences' in the city, showing 'no signs of embarrassment before the complicated etiquette' of the banquets in their honour. Kosi told the reporter of the 'very privileged position' enjoyed by women among the Gonds and Baigas, for which feminists might well envy them. Women had the right of revenge, most spectacularly in the festival known as 'Stiria Raj,' when wives cast spells and intimidated their husbands, singing, 'We have now taken control of the kingdom.' Tribal women, remarked this Gond wife of an Oxford man, 'have a very happy family life, there being a tolerant understanding between the sexes which is lacking in other "civilized parts of the country." '[17]

These words might have come out of one of Verrier's essays. I suspect they were his, made up as he translated his wife's Chattisgarhi into the reporter's English. But Kosi Elwin was very much her own woman: independent, intelligent and self-willed, and in some matters vastly more experienced than her husband. Her view was that sex was her right: she'd 'shout and rage, get tight, brag of her lovers, scorn V's skill and then expect a night of passionate love.' Verrier found her elusive and fascinating. To Bill Archer, who was married to a proper Englishwoman, he bragged often of Kosi's skills. 'I very much wonder if your Uraons do not sing to each other in bed,' he wrote: 'It is such a delightful and—for them—natural way of love-making. Kosi is very good at it.'[18]

This was a tease, for Archer, despite writing a book on the Uraons, never got close enough to study them in bed. Through Kosi Verrier could triumphantly underline a greater intimacy with *his* tribe. In October 1941 Kosi gave birth to a son whom they named Jawahar, both for the Gond Raja of Sarangarh, a friend of Verrier, and for Jawaharlal Nehru (but the boy was usually called Kumar). Fatherhood appears only to have confirmed Verrier's love for his tribal wife. He was delighted when a friend said the boy bore something of a resemblance to the British prime minister. How perfect, he answered, that a Jawaharlal should look like a Churchill.[19] When Kumar turned one, his father hailed him as a 'great character and brilliantly clear;' like Jeeves, 'his head sticks out at the back and his head sparkles with the purest intelligence.'[20]

Now that Verrier was married, his friend had to follow suit. 'I am anxious for Shamrao to get married as soon as possible,' wrote Verrier to Bill Archer, 'for—of course—as my younger brother he is a menace' (as a potential lover of Kosi).[21] Sham was at first interested in a Pardhan girl but unlike Verrier he preferred to wed a virgin. These were not easy to locate in Patangarh. The problem was alleviated by the fact that his family's wishes on the matter were paramount. In early 1941 he married their choice, Kusum, an Indian Christian from Poona. In Patangarh the two couples lived under one roof, the wives being socially guided by the husbands. Kusum and Kosi took English lessons together so as to partake of the dinner conversation.

The great ecologist G. Evelyn Hutchinson, himself thrice married, believed that sex is 'a part of living behaviour which at least in man, and no doubt in some other vertebrates, is largely on the side of love.'[22] This sentiment Verrier would have endorsed, although in his years as a follower of St Francis and Mahatma Gandhi he had tried hard to believe otherwise. His marriage to Kosi was a final repudiation of both those traditions and for the rest of his life he joyfully celebrated sex, identifying it largely with love. With the Gond and the Baiga he had come to believe that 'the physical must express and interpret the desires of the mind and the heart.'[23]

But as it turned out, Kosi also helped the anthropologist win wider acceptance amongst the communities he was studying. Verrier's old Warden at Merton College once claimed that the marriage to Kosi 'was made in the interests of science. It was the only way in which he could get initiated into the mysteries of her people.' This claim was made when the Warden's successor, alarmed at the prospect of having to entertain Elwin and his aboriginal wife at High Table, wished to terminate Merton's research grant to the anthropologist.[24] Verrier's marriage to Kosi had some beneficial consequences for science which were not anticipated. He married Kosi because he loved her.

Kosi's contributions to Elwin's scientific research were made in Bastar, a large and isolated chiefdom adjoining the Central Provinces which had an overwhelmingly tribal population. Densely forested, Bastar was rich in timber and minerals, coveted by British merchants and entrepreneurs. In 1910 a major rebellion broke out against the state's attempts to curb tribal rights in forests in favour of timber companies. A British battalion was called in to quell the uprising. Thereafter the administration were more circumspect. A key figure in the new policy of letting the tribals be was W. V. Grigson of the Indian Civil Service, who was Diwan (Administrator) of Bastar in the 1920s and 1930s.[25]

Grigson was an officer of exceptional intelligence and foresight with a deep commitment to the tribals. His book *The Maria Gonds of Bastar*, published in 1938, first alerted Verrier to the rich possibilities of ethnographic research in the state. Restless, in search of new tribes to write about, Bastar seemed to him the perfect escape from the 'foul and rotten company of lawyers and landlords' in the over-administered and over-civilized district of Mandla. Grigson put Verrier in touch with his successor as Diwan, E. S. Hyde, who helped make the arrangements for his research. He was appointed Honorary Ethnographer and Census Officer of Bastar State, which gave him the freedom to move around in the territory. The Maharani of Bastar further smoothed his path by providing an elephant, the only effective all-year means of transport in the forest.[26]

In the autumn of 1940 Verrier and Kosi moved to their new home in Bastar, in a village close to the capital Jagdalpur, within easy range of the hills. For the sum of three hundred rupees Verrier built a house with high walls and long low windows looking out to the best of Bastar's many splendid views, the Chitrakot falls on the Indravati river. This began what Shamrao Hivale called 'probably the happiest years in Verrier's life.'[27] One reason for the happiness was the love and companionship of Kosi, and in time of Kumar; another, the dignity and freedom of the state's aboriginals. The chiefdom, Verrier told his mother, was 'unbelievably peaceful;' its people 'gentle, friendly, with no desire for property or power.' He contrasted Bastar's tribals to warring Europeans. The tribals were a 'great lesson to the world at this time. So long as men cling to the desire of empire and wealth such catastrophes as the present one are certain to occur.'[28]

Bastar also appealed to Elwin on account of its apparent success, under Grigson and subsequent diwans, in guaranteeing tribal autonomy and independence. The tribals appeared happy and content. Their religious and cultural institutions were thriving, their indigenous industry had not been destroyed, their sense of beauty remained keen, their standard of human enjoyment was exceptionally high. They were in sum a 'dignified and noble people,' supported by a sympathetic administration whose 'prophylactic and remedial measures' had done much to protect aboriginal rights in land and preserve village institutions. Bastar was unquestionably 'the brightest spot in the aboriginal situation,' an example worthy of study by both the 'Congress people and the Administration of British India,'[29] especially the former, who were waiting in the wings to take power once the war got over. Verrier knew from experience that Congressmen were likely to be indifferent to the tribes. 'My only hope,' he remarked, 'is the little group of intellectuals round Jawaharlal Nehru: his National Planning Committee is prepared to consider the anthropological point of view with regard to the aboriginals.'[30]

In private letters and published essays Elwin drew a pointed comparison between the aboriginal situation in his own Central Provinces and in Bastar. In the C. P., he noted, 'hunting has been forbidden for decades, adventure has been wiped out by Law and Order, achievement has been dented by disease and hunger.' There the tribesmen were oppressed by landlords and moneylenders, and subject to extortion by state officials. But the Bastar aboriginal retained control over his lands and forests, while an administration specially adapted to his needs had protected him from scheming politicians and corrupt officials. The 'vigorous and healthy' life of tribal society in Bastar contrasted with the 'decay and inertia' elsewhere in aboriginal India. He found it 'most refreshing to go to Bastar from the reform-stricken and barren districts of the Central Provinces.' Every time he entered the state from British territory he seemed to hear the whole countryside bursting into song around him.[31]

While touring in Bastar Verrier heard of the death of his old headmaster Dr Flecker, the man who 'caused me a great deal of trouble when I was a child.' Christianity in all its forms he had long since rejected, but he now found to his surprise that he had to revise his opinion on another of the great faiths. Since he came to Mandla he had developed a strong dislike of Hinduism, for it was Hindus who—as moneylenders, landlords and officials—were the chief tormentors of his Baiga and Gonds. But in Bastar he discovered that Hinduism as a theological system was not that far removed from aboriginal thought. For the social life of the chiefdom revolved around the Dassera festival, when thousands of tribals from the hills descended on Jagdalpur to pay tribute to their king, whom they worshipped as the messenger on earth of Durga.[32] The anthropologist concluded that the faith of the Bastar tribal 'was really closely related to Shaivite Hinduism. It is true that the feeling-tones are different but so are those of Protestantism and Catholicism. Yet we call both those totally different faiths Christianity.' Like Buddhism and Jainism, tribal religions were part of the Hindu family, although 'the members of the family are undoubtedly more attractive than the parent.' Despite its undeniable connection to the greater Hindu tradition there was a freedom and flexibility to tribal faith—in Bastar 'religion is always on the move. Even the legends change from village to village.' And, what mattered most to this former priest, there was 'no sacred book, no canon, no deposit of faith committed to a central authorized guardian, no regular liturgy.'[33]

Verrier Elwin's research in Bastar at first focused on one tribe and one institution—the *ghotul* of the Muria. The ghotul, a dormitory for initiating the young into the mysteries and wonders of sex, fascinated the anthropologist, himself finding his own way, rather late in life, through these wonders and mysteries. Within a few months of moving to Bastar he resolved to write 'a fairly long book on the subject, which might well be a best seller.'[34]

He spent over a hundred nights in different ghotuls while a battery of research assistants gathered information on other dormitories. His field research was enormously helped by the presence of his wife who, as a member of the greater Gond family, could claim kinship with the Muria. Her beauty attracted young men who clustered around her in village after village. This irritated Verrier who for more reasons than one wished her to be with the women. A stenographer accompanying the couple recalled that Kosi was 'instrumental in winning over the Muria women-folk,' allowing Elwin a glimpse of aspects of their lives which were otherwise a closely guarded secret.[35] Among the tasks assigned to Kosi were the playing of a gramophone to break the ice in a new field site, and the learning and performing of their dances with Muria girls. The dreams of these girls and women were also recorded by her. The anthropologist taught Kosi the use of a camera, which she then used to furtively photograph distinctive features of Muria apparel—such as the *mudang* or decorated waist-band—which no one except other women and husbands were allowed to see. It helped that Kosi was a common name among the Muria and Elwin happily expended film shooting his Kosi with one of theirs. The ethnographer's acceptance was further aided by their child, a great draw passed adoringly from hand to hand by the Bastar villagers.[36]

The ghotul is described by the anthropologist as something of a night club coming to life at dusk, after the day's work in the fields. It was an arena of encounter and friendship, of play, music and dance where *chelik* (boy) and *motiari* (girl) formed deep and loving relationships. But life in the dormitory was also regulated. Chelik and motiari were expected to come every day, to keep the dormitory clean, to share in the common labour, and to not quarrel or fight. Sexual transgression—sleeping with someone else's chosen partner, for instance—was also punished. Discipline was maintained by senior boys and girls and, as the Muria said, 'We obey our ghotul laws more faithfully than the laws of government, for we ourselves made [them].' The anthropologist noted with interest that though dormitories had doors, these could not be shut from the outside: 'The ghotul is never locked up. It is a shrine and no one would steal from it.'

Training the young in the arts of sex and the conventions of social life, the ghotul was also a stimulus to artistic expression. Its walls were painted with models of motiaris and tigers, its pillars carved with animals fighting or tribals dancing. Within, girls decorated themselves with colourful head-bands and a profusion of necklaces and bead-collars, all hand-crafted. The art of combing and comb-making was highly developed. Combs came in many shapes and sizes, carved by the chelik for his motiari. They were used for the hair and to titillate the skin on arms and back. If a girl possessed a large number of combs it implied that 'she has a very devoted lover.'

Elwin's research bore fruit in a detailed, candid, evocative account of pre-marital sex, of the role of touch and smell in arousing a partner, the use of love-charms in winning a reluctant lover. Sex was fun: the 'best of *ghotul* games . . . the dance of the genitals . . . an ecstatic swinging in the arms of the beloved.' But it was not, at least among the Muria, disfigured by lust or degraded by possessiveness or defiled by jealousy. Nor was it a bed of primitive promiscuity. Indeed, in the classical, *jotidar* type of ghotul, individual chelik and motiari paired off in a relationship that might last as long as five or six years, till both left the dormitory. In a diary entry of 12th December 1941, quite early in his fieldwork, Elwin noted: 'It is amazing how little jealousy and permissiveness there seems to be generally in these ghotuls.'

In defending the ghotul from the obvious criticisms of the civilized world, Elwin pointed out that that there were virtually no cases of venereal disease among the Muria. Prostitution, rape and child marriage, so visibly present in more 'advanced' societies, were all too absent here. More strikingly, the sexual freedom of the ghotul was followed by a stable, secure, serenely happy married life. In the process of growing up the 'life of prenuptial freedom' ended in a 'longing [for] security and permanence.' In any married couple, neither was virgin absolutely: but *both were virgins to each other.* Husband and wife had each been carefully trained in the arts of sex. Statistics provided proof of the strength of the Muria marriage bond. By Elwin's calculations, among the Muria of Bastar the divorce rate was less than three per cent, whereas among the Gonds of the Patangarh area the percentage was in excess of forty. Before and after marriage, he concluded, 'Muria domestic life might well be a model and example for the whole world.'[37]

The Muria and their Ghotul was described by its author as a 'pocket battleship' of a book. It ran to seven hundred and thirty printed pages, almost two hundred more than *The Baiga*, featuring one hundred and fifty photographs and almost as many line drawings. But beyond its rich description of a tribe at work and at play the book can be read as a statement of Elwin's own attitudes to love, sex and marriage. He reports, for instance, the tribal view of celibacy that men and women who practise it are restless and frustrated, and, after they die, a perpetual nuisance to those left behind on earth—on whom they cast spells. 'The state of *sannyas* (renunciation),' remarks Elwin, is 'everywhere associated in the aboriginals' mind with idleness and beggary rather than with chastity.' Against that Hindu and Gandhian ideal, the Muria and Elwin insisted 'sex is a good thing, healthy, beautiful, interesting, the crown and climax of love.'[38]

In the last pages of his book Elwin bravely connects the Muria ghotul to a pre-Puritan India, to a time when Hindus had cultivated and lovingly memorialized the pleasures of the body. The message of the ghotul, he claims,

> that youth must be served, that freedom and happiness are more to be treasured than any material gain, that friendliness and sympathy, hospitality and unity are of the first importance, and above all that human love—and its physical expression—is beautiful, clean and precious, is typically Indian. The ghotul is no Austro-asiatic alien in the Indian scene. Here is the atmosphere of the best old India; here is something of the life (though on a humble scale) portrayed [in the paintings] at Ajanta; here is something (though now altogether human) of the Krishna legend and its ultimate significance.

In reaching out to a hostile public Elwin hoped to enlist the aid of Jawaharlal Nehru, the modern Hindu most likely to sympathize with the culture of the Murias. Preparing his book for the press, he wrote to his editor wishing he'd get Nehru to write a Foreword 'intelligently from the point of view of education,' and adding, 'I doubt if it were possible.'[39] The doubt concerned not Nehru's intelligence but his availability. Locked up in Ahmednagar jail at the time, Nehru could not be reached by author or publisher and the book finally went out into the world without his stamp.

The Muria and their Ghotul was completed in 1943 but only published four years later, its production held up by wartime shortages of paper and film. It took a grant of two hundred pounds from Merton and eight thousand rupees raised by Verrier's Bombay friends—the Parsi industrialists J. R. D. Tata and Jehangir Patel—before Oxford University Press felt able to send the manuscript to a printer. Well before its publication the book's contents were a source of much speculation. One interested party was Henry Luce's *Life* magazine which, in June 1944, bid for exclusive excerpt and photo rights to go with an interview with the author. The story was to be written by Bill Fisher, a *Life* contributor who had visited Elwin in the field.

The attentions of a popular illustrated magazine are not to be scorned, but Elwin's authorial vanity was tempered by more practical considerations: to wit, the likely fall-out among nationalist and puritan circles in India. As it was, a series of illustrated essays he was publishing on the Bastar tribes and which were appearing in the *Illustrated Weekly of India* had attracted a torrent of letters from readers worried that portraits of half-naked and bejewelled tribals would 'degrade India in the eyes of the foreigner.'[40] Now it was being proposed that more revealing pictures be published under his name, and this in an American magazine. 'I think it would be most unwise,' wrote Elwin to his publisher, R. E. Hawkins of OUP,

> to hang a *Life* story about me on a lot of stuff about girls and boys poking each other. The reaction in India might be most unfortunate. It is one thing to write a large, heavy and complete work on pre-nuptial freedom in the ghotul. It is quite another to have bits of it splashed in a popular magazine as a means of introducing me to the American public. You might increase sales in America, but it will not increase sales in India if I begin to be regarded as a second Miss Mayo.
>
> I also think that the photographs used must be chosen with discretion. There must be no busts or bosoms, which Bill Fisher was anxious to have. We mustn't give 'savage' pictures . . . This is an excellent chance for advertisement, but I feel very strongly that we must not do anything in America that will have bad reactions in India.[41]

'No busts or bosoms' was not a condition *Life* were prepared to meet. They did not run the story, but the Muria ghotul eventually found its way into American consciousness through the Kinsey report, where Elwin is cited more often than the great Sanskrit treatise on love-making, the Kama Sutra.[42] *The Muria and their Ghotul* is not, I think, Elwin's best work of anthropology, but it is indisputably the best-known. It has been translated into several languages and appeared in an abridged edition with an alluring title, *The Kingdom of the Young*. The ghotul itself has been restudied by several later anthropologists,[43] and the BBC even made a film on it.

The Muria and their Ghotul, wrote W. G. Archer in *The Listener*, was an encyclopaedic work written 'with incisiveness and charm,' an 'unforgettable picture of an Indian tribe at work and in love.' A more dispassionate reviewer in a more weighty journal, *Man*, was Edmund Leach, one of the rising stars of British social anthropology. Leach thought likewise that 'this lavishly produced work worthily upholds its author's reputation both as a conscientious ethnographer and as a writer of exceptional aesthetic sensibility.' True, the professional would complain that 'on the theoretical side generally, the analysis is crude and old-fashioned,' yet it remained 'Elwin's remarkable achievement to describe [ghotul] behaviour with sympathy, intimacy and detachment. If this part of the book were to appear as a supplementary volume to Havelock Ellis's *Studies in the Psychology of Sex* it would be in proper company. In its own way it is masterly.'[44]

By the early forties sexual behaviour was well established as one of Elwin's chief scholarly interests. The author, a decade earlier, of tracts on *The Supremacy of the Spiritual* and *Mahatma Gandhi's Philosophy of Truth* was now publishing essays in learned journals on 'The Theory and Practice of Sexual Intercourse among the Aboriginals of the Maikal Hills' and 'The Attitude of Indian Aboriginals Towards Sexual Impotence.' *The Muria and their Ghotul* deepened and consolidated this interest, prompting a Bombay friend, Evelyn Wood (in whose house the final draft was composed), to write a 'Triolet on the Union of Anthropology with Psychotherapy:'

> Ellis to Elwin! Shades of Sex:
> Waves in one human spectogram
> In whose green heart may love annex
> Ellis to Elwin.
>   Shades of sex,
> Long may your bonds and lusts perplex
> Those who hate fact—love holy sham
> Waves in one human spectogram.[45]

The Muria and their Ghotul might be viewed as the last act in a long-drawn-out Oedipal conflict with 'Bapu,' Gandhi the father. Oddly enough, while he was working on the book he had been asked to contribute to a *festschrift* for the Mahatma's seventy-fifth birthday. He could scarcely draw upon his latest researches but was not up to writing on Gandhi either. He finally settled on a tribute to his friend Mahadev Desai who had just died in jail. The Mahatma's secretary was one of the few 'Gandhi-people' with whom he had remained in touch. In the preface to his new translation of *The Story of my Experiments with Truth* (1940), Mahadev wrote that 'from the point of view of language [the translation] has had the benefit of careful revision by a revered friend, who, among many other things, has the reputation of being an eminent English scholar. Before undertaking this task, he made it a condition that his name should on no account be given out. I accept the condition. It is needless to say that it heightens my sense of gratitude to him.'[46]

The abbreviated c.v. provided by Mahadev Desai points to Verrier and no one else. But why would he not want his name 'given out?' Because he thought it would violate the terms of the October 1932 agreement between him and the India Office, clause (iii) of which specified that he would 'refrain, as far as possible, from associating with any persons engaged in political agitation'—and Gandhi was then planning a fresh satyagraha? Or because he did not want to sail under false colours and be seen as the servant and intimate of the Mahatma when he no longer was?

The essay on Mahadev is a minor gem, a homage to the human being and the *litterateur*. Mahadev was a man of wide culture with a catholic taste in art and literature. He was 'too big to be mean.' Verrier asks us to see Mahadev as Gandhi's Boswell, perhaps also as Plato to his Socrates, the interpreter who most conscientiously and definitively put his message out to the world.[47]

The intention might have been to take the Mahatma down a peg or two, for the other contributors to the book, who included Nehru and Albert Einstein, wrote on Gandhi himself. Yet even the tolerant Mahadev is unlikely to have approved of Verrier's book on the ghotul. When that work was in press the author recieved a letter from the Archers, who were reading with interest Ethel Manin's book *Privileged Spectator* (1936) in which the British writer and traveller had written of Verrier as 'a remarkable follower of Mahatma Gandhi.' Verrier, in reply, imagined Bill and Mildred 'reading those bloody paragraphs [on Gandhi and himself] shitting with laughter and making dirty cracks between each one. The only thing that gives me satisfaction is the thought of the intense annoyance those pages must have given the divine Mahatma if ever he saw them and found himself bracketed with a drunken ping-pong and you know what, like me.'[48]

Neither *Privileged Spectator* nor *The Muria and their Ghotul* were likely to be high on Gandhi's reading list. But some of his followers had read about Verrier and his book and formed their own opinions. One who was part of the Mahatma's circle at this time, when asked about Elwin, angrily replied—'That man a follower of Mahatma Gandhi! He was, waist-downwards, totally immoral!'[49]

The attention surrounding *The Muria and their Ghotul* has obscured a second book that Elwin wrote in Bastar. This was a study of murder and suicide among the 'Bison-Horn' Maria who were, on the face of it, a particularly violent tribe. Their annual incidence of homicide well exceeded the average for Bastar as a whole and they were also more prone to taking their own life.

In his book Elwin sought to understand the origins of violence and set it in context. He worked with a sample of one hundred murders and fifty suicides, in each case using the court record of the crime as a basis for further, first-hand investigation in the village where it had occurred.

The anthropologist found that murders among the Maria were not, as commonly supposed, strongly linked to the consumption of alcohol. Crimes were rarely committed during festivals or marriages, when drink was most freely consumed. Nor were murders committed for gain. One cause of Maria crime was witchcraft, the tribals believing it right and proper to kill a witch or sorcerer who through magic and spells disturbed the social order. But in killing witches the Maria were a victim of 'intellectual error' rather than of 'murderous passion.' As Elwin pointed out, two hundred years earlier the 'best brains' in Europe believed and acted likewise.

Adultery was also a common motive for murder. Maria men were 'suspicious and exacting' husbands, 'jealous and possessive' by temperament. Some men considered themselves quite justified in killing a disloyal wife. This contrasted with the extraordinary lack of sexual possessiveness among the Muria. There the ghotul—absent here—alerted the young early to the 'impropriety of jealousy.'

In this slim and concisely argued book Elwin sought to explain tribal crime, perhaps even explain it away. Despite the record of the Maria,

Indian aboriginals had on the whole 'a high reputation for their pacific and kindly character.' In any case, compared to the 'dark and complicated wickedness of so many European murders,' Maria crime was most often committed in a fit of passion or rage: rarely premeditated, it was borne out of an 'astonishing innocence.' These tribesmen, wrote Elwin,

> do not cheat and exploit the poor and the weak. They are mostly ignorant of caste and race prejudice. They do not prostitute their women or degrade them by foolish laws and customs. They do not form themselves into armies and destroy one another by foul chemical means. They do not tell pompous lies over the radio. Many of their darkest sins are simply the result of ignorance. A few of them are cruel and savage, but the majority are kind and loving, admirable in their home, steadfast in their tribal loyalties, manly, independent, honourable.

Elwin hoped that magistrates who read *Maria Murder and Suicide* would show more understanding in their judgements. The book ends with an account of the sufferings of Maria prisoners, their loneliness and deprivation in Jagdalpur jail. The anthropologist urged that murderers condemned to death be allowed, on the eve of their execution, to visit the temple of Danteshwari, the tutelary goddess of Bastar. More daringly, he hoped for the creation of a special prison for aboriginals where jail life might be enlivened by dance and song, and where the prisoners would be taught crafts useful to them after their release. This would be a camp rather than a jail, where the aboriginal spirit would be 're-created, not broken.'[50]

'I don't think we will do any "social" work, except perhaps a little medicine to help the people.' Thus wrote Elwin to the administrator of Bastar while planning his move to the state.[51] By the end of his stint, three years later, the one-time social worker's preferred self-description was 'anthropologist.' Elwin had by this time consolidated his professional status by taking over, with his friend Bill Archer, the running of the quarterly journal *Man in India*. This periodical was started in 1921 by Sarat Chandra Roy, the Ranchi lawyer commonly acknowledged as the founder of Indian anthropology. Elwin himself had great affection for Roy, a 'kindly amiable spirit' without whose efforts he believed 'Indian anthropology might never have come to birth at all . . .' When Roy died in 1941 Archer and he moved quickly to take over the journal from the family, the coup helped both by Verrier's friendship with the old man and Bill's status as a high official in the Government of Bihar.[52]

Elwin's area of research had now shifted to the eastern province of Orissa, a shift well marked by the essays he was to publish in *Man in India*. With its numerous tribes 'unknown' to science, Orissa was territory even more virgin than Bastar. Verrier first visited the province towards the end of 1942 on an assignment arranged by Norval Mitchell, a former administrator of Bastar who had taken over as political agent to the princely states of Orissa. Almost the first group he met in the uplands of the Keonjhar district were the swidden-cultivating, leaf-clad Juang, 'quite the wildest and strangest' of all the tribes he had encountered anywhere. The Juang were shy, reclusive and distinctly unhelpful. Verrier complained that they 'do not want visitors and they do not mind saying so. They refuse to show the traveller the right road or point out to him a wrong one. They give fantastically incorrect directions to prevent him from proceeding on his tour . . . The distances are great and the paths difficult even with elephants. There is no tradition, as in Bastar, of village hospitality.'

The Juang's suspicion of outsiders went back to an incident in 1871, when a fanatic English official began a campaign to rid them of their leaf-dress, well suited to the climate and terrain, in exchange for more civilized attire. This campaign culminated in a public meeting in which two thousand pieces of cloth were handed out to the women, after which the leaves that had previously clad them were silently burnt.

Elwin found that the Juang looked back to that episode much as a conquered nation recalls the day of defeat in battle. Although some interior villages clung defiantly to the leaf-dress, the tribe as a whole had 'suffered a psychological and spiritual shock from which it has never recovered.' 'Civilization,' he commented bitterly, 'which in the course of a hundred years has done nothing whatever for the Juang, which has given them no hospitals or schools, which has taught them neither agriculture nor any industry, has paid its debt to the tribe by a forcible attempt to stop the leaf-attire.'[53]

As with the Baiga, Elwin was both enchanted by the tribe and depressed by their fate. 'A really beautiful girl in leaves is a sight for the gods,' he wrote to Archer, 'and I have recklessly expended colour-film.' The Juang were now threatened with the expansion of the forest department, but the anthropologist hoped 'a book might save them. I am now mewing my far-from-mighty middle-age for a great battle with the Forest Adviser.'[54]

The debate with the forest department was carried out in two reports the government had asked him to write. One report pertained to three small chiefdoms, the other to areas administered directly by the British. Elwin's brief in both cases was to recommend ways of containing shifting cultivation without causing popular discontent. This was a theme close to his heart and here he carried forward the arguments presented with such eloquence in *The Baiga*.

The Government of Orissa, persuaded by its forestry officials that swidden was a pernicious practice that destroyed the forest and caused floods, assigned Elwin the limited task of showing how the aboriginal could be 'led away from shifting-cultivation into the settled life of the permanent cultivator . . .' His own reports subtly but persistently undermined the premise that swidden should be done away with altogether. He demonstrated that axe-cultivation proper, following long rotations and where the earth was broken up only with a stick, allowed for vigorous regrowth of forests on fallow fields. Only in areas where the plough had been introduced were erosion and deforestation serious problems. And like the Baiga, the Orissa tribes were unwilling to abandon a form of livelihood that had sustained them for centuries, and which no previous ruler sought to contain.

Just as he distinguished between kinds of swidden, Elwin distinguished between different tribes practising it. Some communities were in close contact with the wider economy and society, and thus more likely to adapt to change. Here settled cultivation could well be encouraged, taking care that the aboriginals were properly protected from moneylenders and landlords and provided schools and hospitals to help them hold their own in the modern world. Rather different were the 'real primitives' living in isolated valleys, who had a strong mystical attachment to the territory inhabited by them and a clear sense of collective ownership over hill and

1. Baby Verrier with Bishop and Mrs Elwin (OUP)

2. Verrier, aged five (British Library)

3. Dean Close's prize student, 1919 (OUP)

4. A gent with a dog collar—the Vice Principal of Wycliffe Hall seminary, Oxford, 1926 (Wycliffe Hall)

5. Elwin with Gandhi, Sabarmati Ashram, 1931, the dutiful Miraben following (OUP)

6. Elwin with his fellow followers Jamnalal Bajaj and Pyarelal (in spectacles), Dhulia Jail, 1932 (OUP)

7. Mary Gillet, in the courtyard of the Ashram of St. Francis, Tikeri Tola, 1933 (Verrier Elwin/British Library)

8. Shamrao Hivale, sometime in the mid 1930s (Verrier Elwin/British Library)

9. Kosi Elwin, c. 1940 (Verrier Elwin/British Library)

10. A Baiga veteran (Verrier Elwin/OUP)

11. Muria chelik and motiari outside the ghotul (Sunil Janah/OUP)

forest. It was here that the prohibition of swidden was 'likely to cause psychological damage and thus in the long-run deep-rooted hostility to Government.' Alert as ever to the telling parallel, Elwin wrote that at a time when the conscience of the world was 'vigorously condemning the Nazis for depriving the minorities of Europe of their freedom and their lands,' the expropriation of aboriginal lands and forests would not be judged kindly by history.[55] He thought the Government of Orissa should restore to these communities the rights over the forest, himself marking out three potential sanctuaries where tribals could cut swidden freely, each family being allotted the exclusive use of twenty acres of forest. All outsiders—landlords, moneylenders, and missionaries—ought to be removed from these reserves.[56]

Wherever he roamed in Bastar, the Central Provinces or Orissa, Verrier Elwin discovered deep differences between tribal communities relatively untouched by the outside world and those that had been radically affected by it. In the Orissa districts of Ganjam and Koraput he found one class of aboriginals who were 'poor, miserable and diseased . . . They have lost their standards; they no longer have the beauty and dignity of an ordered coherent culture to support them; they are adrift in a modern world that so far has done little to afford them anchorage.' But travelling in the interior hills he found 'a very different picture. Here we find living in almost unfettered freedom and in the enjoyment of ancient and characteristic institutions some of the most ancient people of India . . . These people have maintained their morale and their will to happiness. Geographical factors have protected them and still contribute much to their well-being.'[57]

The tribal protected in his mountain fastness was distinguished for his love of nature, his community spirit, his open and unrepressed attitude towards sex, and not least the position of his women. The Baiga woman 'generally chooses her husband and changes him at will; she may dance in public; she may take her wares to the bazaar and open her own shop there . . .; she may drink and smoke in her husband's presence'—freedoms all denied to the caste-Hindu woman.[58] The Baiga were no exception, for in most tribal societies

> the woman holds a high and honourable place. She goes proudly free about the countryside. In field and forest she labours in happy companionship with her husband. She is not subjected to early child-bearing; she is married when she is mature, and if her marriage is a failure (which it seldom is) she has the right of divorce. The lamentable restrictions of widowhood do not await her: should her husband die, she is allowed, even enjoined, to remarry: and in many tribes she may inherit property. Her free and open life fills her mind with poetry and sharpens her tongue with wit. As a companion she is humorous and interesting; as a wife devoted; as a mother, heroic in the service of her children.[59]

But it was only the tribal isolated in the highlands who really *lived*; his religion characteristic and alive, his social organization unimpaired, his traditions of art and dance unbroken, his mythology still vital. 'It has been said,' wrote Elwin in his 1943 pamphlet *The Aboriginals*, 'that the hoot of the motor-horn would sound the knell of the aboriginal tribes as such; but now petrol rationing has stepped in to delay the funeral.' In the 'old days when there were neither roads nor motor-cars,' he was told by a Bastar tribal, 'the Muria were honest, truthful and virtuous.'[60]

Even where their souls were not soiled with the grime of passing motor-buses, the aboriginals were assaulted by civilization in numerous ways. British economic policies, favouring individual titles to property and creating a market for land, dispossessed thousands of tribal families and placed many others in a position of bondage to moneylenders. Forest and game laws reduced the access of aboriginal to the fruits of nature, and in some instances, as for example where shifting cultivation was banned, deprived them of their livelihood altogether. The suppression of the home distillery, forcing the tribal to buy liquor only from outlets licensed by the state, had brought him into contact with a most 'degraded type of alien,' the liquor contractor. The Indian Penal Code and the Indian Forest Act formed two pillars of a massive, alien system of jurisprudence which ran counter to tribal custom, subjecting them to endless harassment at the hands of lawyers, lawyer's touts, and ill-informed judges.[61]

Colonial policies worked to impoverish the aboriginals but Hindu society, where it did penetrate tribal areas, attacked their culture with equal ruthlessness. Extended contact with Hindus crushed the aboriginals' love of art, music and dance; taught them to worship alien gods and develop a contempt for their own; introduced child-marriage; constricted their 'generous hearts' with the practice of untouchability; and encouraged them to put their free and happy women in purdah.[62]

This collective deprivation had resulted in a psychological trauma, a 'loss of nerve.' Facing economic decline and the hostility of the state, the Agaria dreamt that when he dug for iron he came up with stones. The Baiga attributed the decline of his powers of magic to the plough. Most cynical of all, the Mandla Gond believed that when the railway came 'Annadeo, the God of food, ran away from the jungle. He sat in the train and went to Bombay, and there he makes the [city] people fat.' It was a world in which the livelihood of aboriginals had been taken away, their culture crushed, a world where even the gods had turned against them. *Abika raj kalau, larka larki malau* (The world today is black, our boys and girls are like monkeys, degraded) remarked a Muria of Narayanpur, a comment that sums up Elwin's own view of the clash of cultures in aboriginal India.

Starting out in one village in Mandla, Verrier Elwin had become by the early forties a spokesman for all twenty million tribals in India. 'The pen is the chief weapon with which I fight for my poor,' he had written to an Italian friend in July 1938 while completing *The Baiga*.[63] That book was the first in a series of rich ethnographies and essays through which Elwin fought for his poor, the voiceless aboriginal. His mission is best explained in the preface to *The Muria and their Ghotul*. It was A. E. Housman's ambition, wrote Elwin

> that one day a copy of *The Shropshire Lad* taken into battle should stop a bullet aimed at a soldier's heart. I have a similar desire for this, as for all my other books, that in the battle for existence which the Indian aboriginal now has to wage, it may protect him from some of the deadly shafts of exploitation, interference and repression that civilization so constantly launches at his heart. If this book does anything to help the Muria to continue as they are today, free and innocent, I shall be content.[64]

CHAPTER EIGHT

Anthropologist at Large

FOR VERRIER ELWIN

Beyond the white fantastic mountains
The war is fracturing the foreign cities
The Western style makes toys of the dead
And in the little brittle churches
The girls are praying with long hair
For the hours of the future and the sexless houses.

Among your burning hills, the lonely jungle
Roars in the summer. The sterile land
Rests; and news comes up like clouds
While you are active in the needs of peace
Saving the gestures of the happy lovers
The poems vivid as the tiger
Faced with destruction from the septic plains
And with your love and art delay
The crawling agony and the death of the tribes.

W. G. Archer

The only fear that haunts me day and night is, 'Will they separate Verrier and me?' No, they won't, for I shall go wherever Verrier goes.

Shamrao Hivale, on hearing the news of the fall of Burma

For Verrier Elwin the 1940s were a time of intense activity, at home and in the world, yet he was to draw a veil over them in his memoirs. His reticence with regard to Kosi has been noted; likewise, the attention generated by his work for and with the tribes is summed up in this solitary sentence: 'A lot of people were down on me in those days and, for an ordinary person, I had a rather disproportionate volume of notice in the press, some of it extravagantly kind, some bitterly hostile.'[1]

Of course Elwin was not an ordinary person at all. 'Verrier Elwin and Tribal India,' recalled one senior Indian scholar, 'were terms of instantaneous association: one could not be thought of without the other.'[2] He was especially well regarded in Bombay, a city with a dense concentration of intellectuals and policymakers which was at this time the commercial and in many respects political capital of India. His circle of admirers included Parsi millionaires who financed his research and his books, expatriate Englishmen who published them, Hindu and Muslim writers who looked to him for guidance and inspiration.

Elwin basked happily in the adoration. He loved the company, the food, the attention, the luxuries of Bombay. He would return to the forest from the 'contagion of the troublous city' knowing always that he would be back next year. When he visited Bombay in the monsoon, newspapers gave handsome coverage to his talks and lectures to the Rotary Club, the Asiatic Society, the Progressive Group, on subjects as varied as 'The Poetry of T. S. Eliot' and 'Aboriginals and the Census.' As an admiring journalist said in 1941, Elwin had been adopted by Bombay society as its 'pet anthropologist.'[3]

The journalist was D. F. Karaka, biographer of Gandhi and Nehru. With the exception only of his fellow Oxonian Frank Moraes, Karaka was the most eminent newspaperman of his generation. In his columns in the *Bombay Chronicle*, as well as in his books, he captured the influence and singular appeal of the Merton scholar who had made his home with the tribes. 'Brilliant in conversation, cultured and polished in speech, a man of letters whose prose was of the best of our generation,' he wrote, 'Elwin's work in anthropology ranks among the great modern contributions on the subject of Man.' There are other people who have attested to the quality of Elwin's prose and scholarship, but for the power of his presence and speech we are obliged to a transcript kept by Karaka. 'We are so used to poverty in India,' Elwin told the Rotary Club, that

> we forget what it is. I remember one day a family coming to us in tears, for their hut and all they possessed had been destroyed by fire. When I asked how much they wanted to put them on their feet again they said, 'Four rupees'—the price of a single copy of *Brave New World*.

That is poverty.

In Bastar State once, a Maria was condemned to death and on the eve of execution they asked him if there was any luxury he would like. He asked for some chapatti and fish curry, made after the city style. They gave it to him and he ate half of it with great enjoyment, then wrapped the remainder up in the leafplate and gave it to the jailor, telling him that his little son was waiting outside the prison door. The boy had never tasted such a delicacy, but he should have it now.

That is poverty.

Poverty is to see little children taken from you at the height of their beauty. It is to see your wife age quickly and your mother's back bend below the load of life. It is to be defenceless against the arrogant official, to stand unarmed before the exploiters and the cheats.

Poverty is to stand for hours before the gate of the court of justice and to be refused admission. It is to find officialdom deaf and the great and wealthy blind.

I have seen children fighting over a scanty meal of roasted rat. I have seen old women pounding wearily at the pith of the sago palm to make a kind of flour. I have watched men climb trees to get red ants to serve instead of chillies.

Poverty is hunger, frustration, bereavement, futility. There is nothing beautiful about it.[4]

Elwin's speech, wrote Karaka, was the finest he had heard since 'the day George Lansbury [the Labour politician] spoke at the Oxford Union.' The anthropologist was himself

> of the Oxford that has done and will do something in the world as distinct from the Oxford of the layman's conception—the Oxford that produced two Masters of the Fox Hounds, one drunk and one platonically patriotic. Elwin is the genuine article. I can almost see him walking out of the Gothic entrance of Merton, across the cobbled street, his shoulder raised in his characteristic style, hands in his pockets, books under his arms. Is it Schopenhauer or Huxley or the symphony of Beethoven he is thinking about?[5]

The journalist marvelled, as Indians will, at the element of heroic self-sacrifice, at the distance between the Gonds of Mandla and the dons of Merton. Like Karaka, thousands of urban Indians were first told the meaning of poverty by an Englishman whom tradition and history should have marked for an Oxford college or Anglican cathedral. Consider now the testimony of Krishna Hutheesingh, a member of political India's first family. Hearing Elwin speak at Bombay's smartest and most select club, she

> went absolutely numb as he unfolded tale after tale of poverty and woe... I looked around at all the wealth, beauty and power present in that room, and I wondered how this story of a forgotten people was affecting them. Some faces looked quite unconcerned, others seemed to be smiling. Was it such an incredible story, I wondered, that they could not really believe it and hence the slightly sarcastic smile? Perhaps they thought that even if it were true, was it not after all ordained by the Almighty that some people should be poor and others rich?
>
> But there were other faces, too, listening to every word Elwin uttered... I chanced to glance down and my eyes fell on my hands and clothes—hands that had known no hard work and clothes that might easily have cost enough to feed ten Gonds or even more! Clothes on which I had spent time and money with never a thought what that money could be used for. I felt terribly ashamed of myself and felt I could not in my fine clothes face Verrier after his talk. I wanted to hide somewhere away from prying eyes, so upset did I feel.[6]

There was notice that was 'extravagantly kind' and notice which was 'bitterly hostile.' Elwin's diagnosis of the tribal predicament was always contentious. Congress-minded Hindus like his old friend A. V. Thakkar complained he was an 'isolationist' who wished to keep the aboriginals away from the national movement and all it offered. Elwin replied that he was a 'protectionist' who wished to protect the aboriginal from aggressive and insensitive outsiders. But the charge stuck. An associate of Thakkar then wrote that he was 'more than a descriptive anthropologist; he is a politician with a policy to propound and propagate.' He accused Elwin of wishing, like the Muslim League, to divide Mother India on communal lines, their 'Pakistan' to be matched by his 'Aboriginalisthan,' a special protectorate to be ruled by ethnographers like himself.[7]

Elwin's antagonists seized on a proposal made in the closing pages of *The Baiga* where he argued for the creation of a National Park. Here the tribe would have freedom to hunt, fish and practice bewar and non-aboriginals would be prohibited entry. The term 'national park' was unfortunate for it led critics to immediately accuse him of wanting to put the tribe into a zoo wherein the anthropologist, alone among outsiders, would have privileged access. As this criticism has dogged appreciation of Elwin's work down to the present,[8] his own answer is worth recalling. 'One of the more foolish things that has been said about us recently,' wrote Elwin in March 1942 on behalf of the Bhumijan Seva Mandal,

> is that we want to keep the aboriginal in a zoo. This is particularly ungenerous in our case. For what is the meaning of putting an animal in the Zoo? You take it away from its home, you deprive it of its freedom, and you rob it of its natural diet and normal existence. But my whole life has been devoted to fighting for the freedom of the aboriginals, to restore to them their ancestral jungle and mountain country which is their home and to enable them to live their own lives, to have their own diet, and to refresh themselves with their traditional recreations.[9]

This lover of the aboriginal had his own ideas of what was bizarre and what normal. 'If I wanted to have an Anthropological Zoo'

> I would not fill it with Marias and Baigas; I would have a very different company. I would put in one enclosure the whole of the Sevagram Ashram; in a pleasantly-furnished cage within speaking distance of the Mahatma I would confine the President of the Muslim League. Some way off the office-bearers of the Bombay Purity League would draw crowds of sight-seers eager to watch them sip their lemonade. Elsewhere, carefully segregated, I would include a selection of Hindu Sanatanists as well as a sprinkling of the more diehard officials of the Indian Civil Service. Such types, which will soon be as extinct as the dodo, are of the highest sociological interest and certainly ought to be preserved. The mentality of [the viceroy] Lord Linlithgow will surely be a matter of far greater interest and astonishment to the scientists of another age than that of some poor Santal. I would like to put [the secretary of state for India] Mr Amery too in my collection, but such specimens are expensive and the cost of transporting him from England in wartime would be too great.[10]

This spendidly witty spoof on the fanatical and feuding factions that were messing up Indian politics was simultaneously and implicitly a clarification of his own position on the absurdity of an aboriginal zoo. Yet the charge that Elwin wished to put away aboriginals into a reserve and thus keep them from the mainstream of Indian life would not go away. It was made most effectively perhaps by G. S. Ghurye, professor of sociology at the University of Bombay. In character and style of scholarship Ghurye was worlds removed from Elwin. He was a careful textual scholar who never left his desk, a library worm who had all of three days' field research to his credit. He was also a Brahmin steeped in Sanskrit and a puritan who did not allow his wife to put spices into their food or his college-going daughter watch movies. Conventional and fastidious in matters of dress and deportment, Ghurye demanded and received deference from students, colleagues and family alike.[11]

In September 1943 Ghurye published *The Aborigines—So Called—and their Future*. Elwin is the often named and sometimes unnamed antagonist of this book. Basing himself in the main on *The Baiga*, Ghurye attacked Elwin as a 'no-changer' and 'revivalist,' as one who wished to see 'the aborigines reinstated in their old tribal ways, irrespective of any other consideration.' While 'everything savouring of the Hindu upsets Mr Elwin,' the Bombay professor demonstrated through a wealth of examples the parallels between tribal and Hindu beliefs. Tribals, he pointed out, had long been involved in Hindu religious movements and structures of authority. The 'only proper description of these people,' argued Ghurye, was that they are 'the imperfectly integrated classes of Hindu society.' Anthropological accuracy demanded that they be called 'backward Hindus' rather than 'aborigines.'

Ghurye accepted that tribal encounters with Hindus sometimes led to distress but disputed the claim that economic loss was followed by psychic despair, the alleged 'loss of nerve.' Indeed contact with Hindus might benefit the tribals—by exposing them to better methods of cultivation or curing them of drunkenness. Nor would he agree that assimilation would make tribals serfs and destroy their culture and suppress their women. He saw in nationalist India a mood of equality: popular movements among Hindus themselves against untouchability and for the emancipation of women would countenance neither tribal entry at the bottom of the caste hierarchy nor the exploitation of their women. Likewise, the growing interest in folk culture and folk dance would work to protect some aspects of tribal song and dance; these would form part of 'the total complex which is arising called Indian culture.' And where Elwin detested the practice of child marriage Ghurye thought its introduction would temper tribal sexual license, check the spread of venereal disease, and contribute to marital stability.

In Ghurye's eyes British imperial rule was the larger cause of tribal discontent. It was the inroads of the British system of law and revenue that had in the first place created conditions for the erosion of tribal solidarity. The establishment of individual property rights in land, the creation of a land market, stringent forest laws, and an exploitative excise policy had all worked to impoverish tribals, pushing them into the clutches of landlords, moneylenders, and liquor contractors. As the economist D. R. Gadgil noted in a perceptive foreword to the book, Hindu exploitation of tribals was a secondary phenomenon enabled precisely by the primary phenomenon of British dominion. It was the establishment and consolidation of British rule that had 'brought about a revolution in the nature and extent of the contact with the aborigine.' The problem of tribal poverty was thus inseparable from the history of colonial exploitation, a connection which had escaped isolationists like Elwin.[12]

The professor's own values emerge at various points in his book. He had a strong aversion to drink, which he saw as a curse on tribal life—leading to unsteadiness, dissipation of energy, and indolence—as well as a distaste for pre-marital sex. Ghurye was both a Puritan and an Improver whose interpretation of tribe-Hindu relations flowed logically into an enthusiasm for reform.

While *The Aborigines—So-Called—and their Future* was in press the OUP put out Elwin's *The Aboriginals*, which presented to a wider public the policy of the protectionist. This appeared as number 14 in a prestigious and widely circulating series called 'Oxford Pamphlets on Indian Affairs.' Other contributors included leading economists and future ministers writing on finance, land, language, the position of women, and other subjects facing the Congress government-in-waiting. The pamphlets were much read and much discussed, Elwin's more than most others. Professor Ghurye was furious: *The Aboriginals* had appeared too late for him to take account of it in his book. The job of demolishing this latest heresy was assigned to his most able student M. N. Srinivas. Reviewing the pamphlet in the *Journal of the University of Bombay*, this young scholar dismissed Elwin's invocation of 'loss of nerve' as a 'conveniently vague expression,' a misleading application in the Indian context of the idea of a loss of interest in life which the anthropologist W. H. R. Rivers had developed in Melanesia and where it had a solid and verifiable basis in depopulation, disease and starvation. Srinivas also challenged the claim that the policy of protection was based on the authority of science. To the argument that an importation of plough-cultivation would prove fatal to the bewar-loving Baiga, Srinivas responded:

> Mr Elwin here forgets a fact which every tyro in Anthropology knows: cultures are never static, but dynamic. Old traits are thrown off or modified and new ones adopted. And that is life. Of course a certain immigrant trait may be disastrous to the group. But that has to be proved in every case. There is nothing to prove that the Baigas are incapable of taking to [plough] agriculture. We may have to do it with special caution and slowness, but that is quite different from maintaining that it can't be done at all.[13]

In an interview with me, M. N. Srinivas recalled that he was specifically asked by his teacher to take on *The Aboriginals*. There is little question that Ghurye had a deep animus against Elwin. He was jealous of Elwin's popularity and disapproved of his personal life (or what he imagined it to be). Ghurye never forgave one of his students, Durga Bhagwat, for taking Elwin's advice before doing fieldwork with the Gonds. When he found himself in the same room as Elwin in a seminar at the Asiatic Society of Bombay, he turned to a friend and whispered: 'Do you see his face? He has the mouth of a sexual pervert.'[14]

As it was, Elwin most keenly felt the force of Ghurye's attack. Two comments in Shamrao Hivale's book *Scholar Gypsy* are revealing. One refers to a 'very unfair book' by a 'Bombay scholar:' the other, identifying the scholar by name, talks of Elwin's admiration for Ghurye's intellect and power of stimulating research in his pupils, but continues: 'unhappily he lacks the social gifts.'[15] As ever, it was in a letter to Bill Archer that Elwin most fully revealed his feelings. Ghurye's book, he told his friend, was an 'odious book written by [an] anthropological Quisling . . . [which] may do incalculable harm to the aboriginals and to our whole cause, if it is not well and thoroughly refuted. I do beg you to take this very seriously indeed. The fact that Ghurye has chosen me for his chief attack is quite unimportant. My reputation will not suffer because of the criticism of

Ghurye, but I am deeply concerned about the effect that such a book by a Hindu may have on the minds of politicians and administrators dealing with the aboriginals.'

I believe Elwin protested too much, that he knew Ghurye's book might harm his reputation as well as the tribal cause. He now wanted to set aside an issue of *Man in India* to 'putting Ghurye in his place,' with reviews of the *The Aborigines—So Called—and their Future* commissioned from W. V. Grigson of the ICS, the Austrian expert on Indian tribes C. von Fürer Haimendorf, and the Indian anthropologist B.S. Guha—all men likely to come down on Elwin's side. On Archer's advice, though, *Man in India* took the more prudent and politic course of ignoring the book.[16]

Ghurye's book was to deeply scar Elwin, its influence manifest in what he was to write and do in the months and years that followed. In January 1944 he delivered the presidential address to the anthropology section of the Indian Science Congress, speaking on 'Truth in Anthropology.' The subject was inspired, he said, by Mahatma Gandhi, who 'has set us all thinking again in terms of Truth.' His talk was for the most part an exercise in self-justification. He separated himself from the anthropologists (unnamed, but obviously British) who 'interested themselves in the complicated business of deciding the exact way in which aboriginal religion should be distinguished from the Hindu religion.' He also drew the line at 'Indian writers, whom I will not name, [who] have produced articles and monographs after a week or a fortnight's stay in tribal villages. My own book on the Baiga was published seven years after I had settled down in the Baiga country . . .' He complained of the poor quality of illustrations and book production in Indian anthropology, saying that 'art and poetry are the sisters of science in the great family of Truth.' He ended his address on a mystical note, offering science as his secular path to salvation:

> And the scholar's quest is one that cannot fail. Truth is the one thing that cannot be sought in vain. He may not find the truth he expects, or even the truth he wants, but he will one day, if he has been loyal to the spirit that drives him onwards, see the veils of ignorance and delusion torn away and the

shadows of partial understanding banished by the pure radiance of Eternal Truth in its beauty. Then the scholar will himself be transformed into Truth, and one with Truth that is eternal, he will find his immortality, perhaps the only immortality there is.[17]

In May of that year Elwin was awarded a Doctor of Science degree from Oxford University. He had submitted *The Baiga* and a few essays in lieu of a dissertation, asking Merton to forward and follow up the case. It was an award he energetically lobbied for, with a sharp awareness of the legitimacy it would confer on his work. 'This will do us a lot of good in India,' he told his mother—she received the degree on his behalf—'because my critics had always been saying, "Why, if he poses as a scholar, isn't he a doctor?"'[18]

In the late summer of 1944 Oxford University Press issued two books by Verrier Elwin, each identifying the author on the title page as 'D.Sc. (OXON).' In theme and substance the works nicely complemented one another. *Folk-Tales of Mahakoshal* presented 150 folk tales collected from all over the Central Provinces, stories laboriously transcribed in those pre-tape recorder days by Verrier, Shamrao, and especially their two assistants Gulabdas and Sunderlal. These were wonderfully complicated stories of love and adventure, the chase for a beloved conducted on earth and through the underworld, the man in pursuit of his princess thwarted by ogres and demons but aided by kindly animals. Other stories spoke of sibling rivalry, the jealousy of older brothers against a cossetted younger one, or of the rivalry between the several queens of a single raja—again with the youngest the object of envy and hatred by the older occupants of the king's bed. The tales showed a 'strong sympathy for the underdog,' for the little brother and the newest queen generally triumphed over the hurdles placed before them.

The quarrels in the royal harem pointed to the 'dangers and distresses of polygamy:' otherwise, as the collector happily noted, the tales had no 'moral.' Some of the best ones were collected from his two villages, Patangarh and Karanjia. All were tribal in origin but their structure and idiom borrowed heavily from the epics. As Elwin delicately put it, 'even the remotest and shyest aboriginals have been affected by the wide diffusion during the centuries of the chief motifs of Hindu fiction.'[19]

Folk-Songs of the Maikal Hills drew even more directly on Elwin's home turf, presenting in verse form the poetry of the Gond and his neighbours. He was helped once more by local assistants, while 'to Kosi Elwin a special debt is due for the singing of many beautiful songs.' The book was co-authored with Shamrao Hivale and was in essence a careful elaboration of their modest early effort of a decade before, *Songs of the Forest*. Many of the songs were meant to accompany Gond dances—the karma, the saila, and the dadaria. The book helpfully provided musical notations as well as discussed the techniques of the dances.

A large chunk of the 600 songs in *Folk-Songs of the Maikal Hills* dealt with romance, often with the parrot as a go-between and carrier of messages between lovers. There were songs of the seasons and poems about the tortured relationship of mother-in-law to daughter-in-law. Other songs were less traditional, being commentaries on the artefacts of modernity entering tribal life. One poem poignantly captured the oppressions of civilization:

> In this kingdom of the English how hard it is to live
> To pay the cattle-tax we have to sell a cow
> To pay the forest-tax we have to sell a bullock
> To pay the land-tax we have to sell a buffalo
> How are we to get our food?
> In this kingdom of the English how hard it is to live
> In the village sits the Landlord
> In the gate sits the Kotwar
> In the garden sits the Patwari
> In the field sits the Government
> In the kingdom of the English how hard it is to live.

The Gond was thwarted at every turn. But, as a poem placed by the translator on the facing page explained, there was at least one remaining source of solace:

> Liquor, you turn us into kings
> What matter if the world ignores us?
> The Brahmin lives by his books
> The Panka boys run off with Panka girls
> The Dhulia is happy with his basket
> The Ahir with his cows
> But one bottle makes a Gond a Governor
> What matter if the Congress ignores us?[20]

Also finished in the summer of 1944, but its printing held up by a publisher anxious to stagger the productions of his most prolific author, was a collection of the folk-poetry of Chattisgarh. This took as its theatre the territory to the south and east of Mandla, the districts of Durg, Raipur and Bilaspur, where tribals lived cheek-by-jowl with Hindu artisans and peasants. The presentation of verses was linked through a narrative commentary which drew parallels between Chattisgarhi images and English ones. Some motifs reminded Elwin of a poem by an English modern—Huxley, Dylan Thomas or Lawrence; an image here and there reminded him of a great romantic—Wordsworth or Blake; and the odd idea recalled even older works by Chaucer or Shakespeare. For good measure comparisons with the Spanish of Garcia Lorca and the Chinese-to-English renditions of Arthur Waley were thrown in. Some of this was pure showing-off but it was also, I think, an attempt to elevate the 'primitive' to the level of European poetry, to show him as part of some Jungian collective subconscious or of the greater human family, using similar symbols and images for the same basic feelings and emotions.

As for the songs themselves, they dealt with love and marriage in the main, or with the financial privations of village life. Elwin liked these short, sharp disquisitions on impotence, a subject 'discreetly veiled in sophisticated society' but 'discussed with the utmost frankness in the Indian village:'

> There is a lock
> On the new door
> My key is broken
> What shall I do?

> There is a charred shaft
> For the new axe
> I was not thinking
> That is how I spoilt it.

> The golden ring
> Looks lovely in your ears
> Your husband is impotent
> So you take delight with others.

My own favourite is a satirical poem about 'The Soldier on Leave' which reveals the continuing innovation in folk poetry:

This year he is enjoying his Holi
A topi on his head, a pair of boots, gaiters
Coat, waist-coat, pantaloons
A five-coloured muffler around his neck
Cigarettes in a packet and a box of matches
He cleans himself with a brush
He has done his hair 'English style'
No oil for him—he puts attar
He looks like a Bengali
His dhoti goes down to his ankles
At home he talks English, the house-folk do not understand
He calls for 'Water' and when they bring bread
He abuses them for their ignorance
'Commere, commere' he says to his friend, 'let's go to the istation'
Babu has shown 'Singal down,' the train will soon be coming
He talks English *gitpit gitpit* and no one understands
No more 'Salaam' or 'Ram-ram' for him, he bids you 'Guda moraning.'[21]

Elwin's collections of folk poetry and myth did for the tribes what his Oxford mentors Garrod and Nicol Smith had done for English poetry: that is, produce consolidated, critical editions of the classic literature of a place and a people. But as ever, there was a polemical purpose. The publication of the poems and tales would he hoped help banish the 'dark and gloomy shadow over a great part of aboriginal India of the Puritan "reformer" and the missionary of whatever faith,' and challenge the leaders of the 'abominable movement' to stop tribal recreations on the grounds that they were 'indecent.' To 'steal a song,' wrote Elwin, 'is far worse than to steal gold.' The American Baptists in Assam and the Gandhian nationalists in Orissa were both working overtime to abolish the village dormitory and the great feasts, and to introduce prohibition among the tribes. But as Elwin pointed out, 'the romance and gaiety of tribal life is necessary for its preservation.' The new taboos would destroy the dancing and religious life of the tribals and fall most heavily on one section among them. For 'so long as song and dance is free, village women get a square deal. With the coming of a taboo on their dancing, comes also a restriction of their freedom, the decay of their morals, the loss of rights.' He quoted, strategically, the Indian poet and collector Devendra Satyarthi: 'India's national movement does not seem to have recognized the importance of folk-songs as yet. A nation reborn must be inspired by its folk-songs . . . [by] the colour, fire and sparkle of the peasants' poetry . . .'[22]

No sooner had he sent off his collections to the printer than Elwin commenced a battle against the puritans. While he had been away in Bastar Catholics missionaries were making steady progress among the Gonds of Mandla. By the middle of 1944 there were thirty-five Dutch priests in the district, working with a large body of clerks and teachers brought from Ranchi in Bihar, an old centre of missionary work among tribals. Their activities expanded enormously in the war years, helped by massive covert government funding. To his horror Elwin counted more than a hundred schools run by the Catholics, schools that bore 'little resemblance to educational institutions' but were 'simply centres of proselytization.'[23]

In a polemic circulated for support in June 1944 Elwin criticized missionary work as an anachronism: no one believed any longer that salvation was to be found in the Catholic church, an institution that had fathered the Inquisition and had a long history of supporting dictators. Free countries did not permit their populations to be proselytized and India, on the verge of its own independence, was not a 'savage' or 'heathen' country but had religious traditions far older than Catholic Europe. The aboriginals of India themselves had 'their own life, their own art and culture [and] their own religion, to which they are deeply attached and which is by no means to be despised.' All over the world the conversion of tribals by missionaries had undermined traditional political institutions, intensified personal rivalries, and implanted a false sense of prudery and sin. The change of religion, in India as in Africa or Melanesia, 'destroys tribal unity, strips the people of age-old moral sanctions, separates them from the mass of their fellow-countrymen and in many cases leads to a decadence that is as pathetic as it is deplorable.'[24]

Elwin was also appalled by the Dutchmen's attack on Gond culture. The priests wanted the government to pass a law providing 'quick punishment of the man a married woman runs away to.' They claimed the love of the Gond for the karma dance was instrumental in the break-up of tribal marriages: the 'first reason' why women deserted their husbands was 'the excessive sexual excitement caused by frequent singing and dancing of karma with its obscene songs and drink throughout the night.'[25] Married to an accomplished Gond dancer himself, Elwin reacted sharply to these judgements. Forbidding the dance might lead to more adultery than less for it would make life intolerably dull for the woman. Karma was 'the sole surviving instrument of Gond culture; it is a symbol of the freedom and independence of the Gond woman; it is a source of a living art and poetry, in Mandla especially its tunes and rhythms are some of the most beautiful in India.'[26]

Elwin's most effective attack on the Catholics was an essay which appeared in *The Hindustan Times* on 14th June 1944. Both the timing—just months after Ghurye had mauled him—and the place of publication—the foremost nationalist newspaper—are significant. So too is the imagery, an unmistakably Hindu one. The priests in Mandla, claimed Elwin

> are the Chindits of the Christian Army. Compared to them, most other missionaries get to work like Italian infantrymen. These Fathers are from Holland. Fortified by the philosophia perennis, inspired not only by a divine love of souls but by the remarkable Dutch instinct for colonial expansion, they are busy turning Mandla into a Dutch colony... Within ten years Mandla—the ancient home of the Rishis, former kingdom of the Gonds, whose fields are blessed by the sacred Narmada—will be virtually a Dutch colony with a hundred thousand Catholic converts.[27]

Three weeks later Elwin sent in an update on the situation in 'the occupied territory of Mandla,' with more evidence of conversion through coercion and bribery. His comparisons were characteristically focused and most carefully chosen. The priests, he reported, had given the tribals medals to kiss morning and evening. On one side of each medal was embossed the image of the Queen of Heaven, on the other 'the unprepossessing features of the Italian potentate who blessed Badoglio's armies on their way to the rape of Abysinnia. It was not indeed, a bad symbol for the conquest of Mandla—for the aboriginals and Hindus of the district are as simple and as defenceless against foreign aggression as were the ill-armed Abysinnians.'[28]

Elwin's attack brought forth a wide-ranging response from his adversaries. In three separate replies in the *Hindustan Times* the priests acknowledged their intention of making converts, but denied coercion.[29]

A well-attended meeting held at the Catholic Institute in Nagpur recorded the protest of the Christians of the Central Provinces at Elwin's challenge to 'the inherent and fundamental Christian right of absolute freedom to propagate the Gospel of Christ in any part of India.' One speaker warned 'Hindu friends that any move to restrict freedom to propagate religion would come back on them like a boomerang.'[30]

Echoes of the debate reached distant Ranchi where an Oraon convert published a pamphlet in defense of missions and missionaries. Unlike Elwin and like Ghurye, this tribal thought his people needed more, not less, civilization. 'Mr Elwin may deride our schools, but we prefer ignorance to knowledge,' wrote Simon Bara. Let 'the death of ancient dialects and the disappearance of venerable customs be a loss to science; we are the gainers by becoming partners in the common cultural heritage of mankind.' Christian priests, he claimed, had saved the Bihar tribals from 'degrading superstition and excessive indulgence in drink . . . out of dying and dwindling tribes' they had 'made virile and vigorous races which face the future full of hope and courage.'[31]

The Dutch Catholics even made contact with Leo Amery, secretary of state for India, a devout Christian and fanatic imperialist. The attitude of British officials towards Elwin had swung from open antagonism (c. 1929–32) to cautious suspicion (after 1933). Practising Christians all, they could not abide this latest manifestation. 'Father [sic] Elwin is not a highly responsible individual,' said one London bureaucrat. 'As regards Verrier Elwin,' remarked the Governor of the Central Provinces, 'for an objective account of his career please see "Who's Who." Elwin is in short an eccentric who has gone "all tribal," especially since he married a tribal.' The government's policy, said this official, should be 'to let Elwin butt his head against the stone wall of the Christian missionary spirit throughout the world.' The under-secretary of state for India saw 'nothing but disaster from excluding Christian missionaries from work among primitive people. The anthropologists would seem to me far more guilty of exploiting people unable to look after themselves if they were to succeed in getting them pickled as an exhibit instead of being helped to develop to the full stature of the human race [as Christians, that is].'[32] Amery himself wrote scornfully of the 'gospel preached by Verrier Elwin, which is, I gather, that the backward tribes should be isolated in reservations, shut off by ring fences, from the rest of India. [This] is already becoming impracticable and may prove dangerous: to say nothing of the political morality of maintaining those people as "museum pieces." ' Amery's own hope was that the tribal areas in India would be constituted as a Crown Colony, directly ruled from London, 'until such time as His Majesty's Government, after the inhabitants have been consulted, feel justified in transferring them to an Indian Government . . . [These areas] might remain under the Crown Representative for a generation or more.'[33]

Some MPs in Britain even asked the secretary of state to deport Elwin from India. Amery wrote hopefully to Lord Wavell, the viceroy, but Wavell, a sensible and fair-minded man, answered that to interfere in the 'unedifying dispute' between Elwin and the priests would only 'arouse suspicion both between the various communities and against the British.'[34] But Elwin had also been seeking help, writing to the industrialist Purshottamdas Thakurdas, the veteran Congress leader Bhulabhai Desai, and his old mentor and more recently adversary A. V. Thakkar. After visiting Mandla Thakkar deputed his associate P. G. Vannikar to organize a Gond Sevak Mandal in cooperation with Shamrao. They were soon joined by a Hindu service organization, the Arya Dharma Seva Sangh. In a short while the three groups were able to close down twenty-five mission schools. By the end of 1946 Elwin could report with satisfaction that the stone wall of the missionary spirit was in fact made of sand, that the advance of the Dutch priests 'had been halted and their work greatly constricted.'[35]

The struggle with the missionaries allowed Elwin to reaffirm his Indian identity, to make a tenuous peace with nationalist social workers and sociologists. Elwin was in principle opposed to both Christian priests and 'Congress minded Hindus,' but, asked (or forced) to choose, there was little doubt which side he would come down on. For one thing he saw the Congress as a less intrusive force: he acknowledged aboriginal religion had some affinity with Hinduism, none at all with Christianity. For another, he was keenly aware of Congress's rising influence with the coming of Indian independence.

Elwin's moves were tactical and opportunistic, but not in a narrowly personal sense. By allying with the nationalists he thought he might more effectively protect his tribals. 'The aim of the movement against the missionaries,' he wrote, 'is to awaken the Hindu community to its duty towards the aboriginal.' We would 'ensure greater permanent good for these people by frankly admitting that they are members of the Hindu family and by saying to the Hindu, "This is essentially your job; get on with it." '36 He urged 'all Hindu organizations interested in this problem to pass resolutions accepting the major aboriginal communities as Kshatriyas which is what they are and what they claim to be, to stop talking of them as "backward" and "depressed" [and] to drop the horrible word "uplift" from their vocabulary.'37

Elwin had a great liking for debate and polemic—'How I do love controversy,' he once remarked, 'it is one of the keenest choices of the mind and I can well understand the feelings of Poets like Milton and A. E. Housman in their love of fighting German scholars.'38 But he also understood the value and purpose of the strategic retreat. In an India on the verge of independence, with Hindu politicians and modernizing technologists set to assume power, he knew how and when to moderate his criticisms of civilization. The first (July 1943) edition of his pamphlet *The Aboriginals* had seen Elwin at his most combative:

> Let us finally face an unpleasant fact. There is no possibility in India and the world as things are today of substituting civilisation for primitiveness: the only alternative to primitiveness is decadence.
>
> Until modern life is itself reformed, until civilization is itself civilized, until war is banished from Europe and untouchability from India, there is no point in trying to change the aboriginals.
>
> Far better let them be for the time being—not for ever, of course; that would be absurd. Perhaps in twenty, fifty, or a hundred years a race of men may arise who are qualified to assimilate these fine people into their society without doing them harm. Such men do not exist today.
>
> I advocate, therefore, for the aboriginals a policy of temporary isolation and protection, and for their civilized neighbours a policy of immediate reform.
>
> If you want to help the aboriginal, do not try to reform him: reform the lawyer, the doctor, the schoolmaster, the official, the merchant, with whom he has to deal. Until that is done, it is far better to leave the aboriginal alone . . .39

These paragraphs were all dropped from the revised edition of the pamphlet printed in November 1944. In the meantime Elwin had been attacked by Ghurye and others and done some rethinking of his own. The corresponding section on policy now more clearly distinguished between two classes of aboriginals: the twenty million who already had some contact with civilization and the five million 'real primitives' who had thus far stayed away from it. The first class would have 'to take their chance with the rest of the population;' their problem was that of poor peasants everywhere. It would be 'deplorable if yet another minority community, which would clamour for special representation, weightage and a percentage of Government jobs, were to be created. The twenty million aboriginals need what all village India needs—freedom, prosperity, peace, good education, medicine, a new system of agriculture and a fair deal under industrialization'—to be achieved by plans and schemes devised by 'wiser heads than mine.'

It was the remaining five million tribals who 'should be left alone and should be given the strictest protection that our Governments can afford.' Elwin admitted that this was 'a desperate measure and one that is easily misunderstood and still more easily misrepresented.' It was 'based on no philosophic principle. Least of all does it suggest that the aboriginals are to be kept for ever primitive. I only urge that unless we can civilise them properly it is better not to intereferewith the small minority of the most primitive hillmen at all. Casual benefits only destroy and degrade; it needs a lifetime of love and toil to achieve permanent advance.' 'I do not suggest,' wrote Elwin, 'that the primitive hillman is better than the finest flower of modern culture, but my experience, which is now extensive, is that these tribes in the freedom and glory of their mountains are infinitely better and better off than the semi-civilised and decadent clerks and coolies which is all that we seem to produce by our present methods of uplift and reform.'[40]

Verrier's one-time guru Mahatma Gandhi liked to speak of the 'beauty of compromise.' In tone and content the revised edition of *The Aboriginals* makes many concessions to the dominant mood. But, again like Gandhi Elwin would not bargain on the essentials. Reform the reformers, respect the tribes: such was the message conveyed by the stirring paragraphs that ended both editions of the controversial pamphlet:

> We may fight for three freedoms—freedom from fear, freedom from want, freedom from interference. We may see that the aboriginals get a square deal economically. We may see that they are freed from cheats and impostors, from oppressive landlords and moneylenders, from corrupt and rapacious

officials. We may see that they get medicinal aid from doctors with some sense of professional integrity. If there must be schools, we may see that these teach useful crafts like carpentry and agriculture, and not a useless literacy. We may work to raise the prestige and the honour of the aboriginals in the eyes of their neighbours. We may guard them against adventurers who would rob them of their songs, their dances, their festivals, their laughter.

The essential thing is not to 'uplift' them into a social and economic sphere to which they cannot adapt themselves, but to restore to them the liberties of their own countryside.

And finally, the pointed reminder to 'freedom-fighters' who spoke self-righteously of themselves as Indian and others as foreign:

> But whatever is done, and I would be the last to lay down a general programme, it must be done with caution and above all with love and reverence. The aboriginals are the real swadeshi products of India, in whose presence everything is foreign. These are the ancient people with moral claims and rights thousands of years old. They were here first: they should come first in our regard.

While writing ferociously for the popular and not-so-popular press, Elwin also found time for extended spells of fieldwork. At the urging of Sir Francis Wylie (by now political adviser to the viceroy), he had been appointed honorary ethnographer to the Government of Orissa. In wartime, when transport and supplies were difficult to come by, official status made fieldwork that much easier. Between 1943 and 1946 he toured Orissa each year, renewing contacts with known tribes and meeting, for the first time, unknown ones.

In the winter of 1943–4 Elwin travelled among the Kuttia Kondhs of the Baliguda hills. The country was wild but not especially beautiful: occasionally one got fine views but otherwise 'a sense of extraordinary isolation.' The girls were attractive, their hair most appealingly fluffed out to the sides. 'Boys and girls rampage up and down in each other's arms,' he noted in his diary: 'best girl dancers wriggle bodies in singularly seductive manner.' But the anthropologist was also drawn willy-nilly into the tormented past of the Kondhs. The catalysmic event in their recent history had been suppression, in the late nineteenth century, of the practice of human sacrifice. Elwin sympathized rather more with this manifestation of the civilizing mission, yet drew attention to some of the consequences. Although the Kondhs explained away the origins of human sacrifice in terms of divine intervention, he thought their stories about the suppression distinctly regretful. Their priests still possessed the old instruments of sacrifice—the knifes, chains and bowls to catch the blood of the victim. These were now used to sacrifice buffaloes but the priests said that on full moon nights they sometimes heard these tools weep for the human blood now denied them. As a Kondh song went, 'Long ago there came sahibs and we gave them elephants and horses / And all they did was destroy our customs.' The sahibs of the nineteen forties would not leave them alone either. The forest department had started a campaign to enclose forests, stop swidden, and bring Kondhs down to the plains and make honest rice-cultivators of them. 'We took a goat to a Sahib,' recounted one tribal, 'and told him our woes, saying we must cut swidden in the forest reserve, or we'll die. He said don't cut or the conservator will tie you up and take you to jail. We said that will be better than this jail.' 'Who made the forest?' asked the Kondh: 'For whom did He make them? For the Government or for the people?'[41]

A tribe that Elwin came to know well were the Bondo, who lived on a remote and elevated plateau in the district of Koraput, 'their life characterized by great independence, liberty and equality—and the highest homicide rate in India.' On his first two visits, in December 1943 and March 1945, the villagers were most unhelpful—the men would come round begging for tobacco but would not, in return, sell food or help them shift camp. When he tried to take photographs the Bondos stopped him; they thought the camera would extract a vital essence from their bodies. Rumours were abroad that the sahib had come to take recruits for the army, or send all the children to America to become Christians, or worst of all to introduce prohibition. But by the time of his third trip, in January 1946, Elwin found that suspicion had eased: 'no depredations from tigers had followed my earlier visits, there had been no fresh taxation, no policy of prohibition had been introduced, no girls had been carried off to the war, we had begun to fit into the picture'—to the extent that some of his best friends were convicted murderers.[42]

On this last trip Verrier was accompanied by two English friends, a timber contractor H. V. Blackburn, and an aircraftsman Harry Milham. Milham has left an account of the field methods of an anthropologist who could not stay sober. Their visit was timed to coincide with the 'pao parab,' the Bondo's annual festival of the full moon which had never been described before. From the rail-head at Raipur the three Englishmen drove eight hours to Jeypore in the heart of the Koraput hills and the seat of its ruling prince. Over a bottle of rum in a dak bungalow Elwin told his colleagues about the tribe they were soon to stay with. The 'temper of the people,' he said, ' was quite unpredictable and it was quite possible they would "bump us off." '

The trio set off next morning for the Bondo country. They were preceded by Elwin's faithful research assistant Sunderlal Narmada, who prepared the ground for their arrival. From the road-head it was a steep climb to the Bondo villages. En route Elwin badly bruised his toe. He was climbing barefoot as was his custom, and had what 'appeared to be his usual argument with a projecting rock.' They finally reached the village of Bodopalle where the first person they met was Muliya, a double murderer released from prison after a life sentence and apparently a 'great pal' of Elwin.

After pitching camp the anthropologist played his gramophone and handed out cigarettes. Even the womenfolk came out to listen to the music, but then, to his fury, Elwin heard that the villagers had postponed the festival. The 'official' explanation was that the first crop of millet had not yet been gathered, but the visitors had an uncomfortable suspicion that the real reason was their own presence as outsiders. When 'all the blandishments and bribery' they could muster 'were met with smiles and inaction,' Elwin tried to stir things up with a bow-and-arrow competition. He put up a cigarette packet at a distance of fifty feet and invited shots. Two men hit the target three times in succession. Then the timber contractor, Blackburn, took out his .22 rifle and gave an exhibition of marksmanship. He shot a dove and a jungle fowl, retrieved by a 'retinue of delighted boys.'

The Bondos still wouldn't put on their show, so the party moved on to the next village, Bodopada. The setting was gorgeous: 'the green of the trees among the thatched roofs, the plaster and bamboo walls of the huts, the dark green of tobacco plots, all against a background of gently sloping hills with their patches of cultivation and the light green of sago palms and shrubbery.' Here too the English trio played the gramophone, then chased and fought each other to amuse the villagers. Elwin showed photographs taken on his last visit and the Bondos excitedly identified themselves. Milham had by now downed his inhibitions in plenty of Gordon's Dry and was taking a long look at the women:

> Their dress is very little, a bark fibre strip about 9 inches in depth and held around the waist by a string. The cloth, which has regular vertical patterns of colour, drops alarmingly at the back, leaving most of the behind bare. The left thigh is completely bare and the cloth looks very insecure but it normally does the job for which it was intended . . .
> The upper body is bare except for a most amazing collection of beads which give quite a well clothed appearance from a distance. Their arms carry many metal bracelets. Their shaven heads with their bands of yellow bamboo strips, make them appear ugly at first sight but one realises that some of them are very beautiful and all have really lovely eyes . . .

Elwin, who had seen all this before, remained depressed. He thought the village was deliberately holding up the moon festival. They had not yet made the special food known as Kirimtor, a kind of vegetarian sausage made of rice flour and boiled pulses. Then at nightfall came the welcome news that the Bondo were at last making Kirimtor. The festival itself commenced the next morning, around noon. A space was cleared out in the middle of the village ground and the drummers assembled. To their music two boys of eight started fighting with sticks. The drumming got faster and the hitting fiercer, till the headman judged the contestants had had enough. The boys hugged one another and then went over to the priest to accept their leaf plate of Kirimtor, which they passed on to their proud parents.

The battles continued with other boys, successively older and more violent in their hitting. The spectators meanwhile were steadily drinking mahua. The anthropologist made up a theory on the spot: 'The origin of the ceremony,' he claimed, 'lay in the attempt to prove that hitting a man can result in a friendly solution rather than a murder.' By now it was dark, and although it was a full moon night a fire was lit to illuminate the arena. Village girls sang to the music while men danced in bamboo head-dresses with peacock feathers popping out. Elwin was dragged into the ring and swung around in a tight circle, straining to keep time. He danced till midnight, drinking very quickly between dances. Sunderlal, who had seen all *this* before, did his best to get him to go to bed. But he wouldn't listen and as soon as the music started would stagger up to join the dance.

Milham and Blackburn were watching from the sidelines. There came a time when their friend disappeared from view. Sunderlal was alerted and he walked into the crowd to find Elwin lying in the middle, flat on his back and dead to the world. He was carried to his tent and dumped into bed, fully dressed. But he woke up later, said 'Good Heavens,' got up and rejoined the dance. He got a great ovation, as it was now 4 a.m.

The next day the party started back for Jeypore. On the climb down Elwin cut his toe again. To the pain in the foot was added a pain in the head. He was in no mood for conversation, remembered Milham, and 'as he sat down on a rock, holding the top of his head with both hands, he would have made a perfect subject for one of the teetotal pictures of the 1890s. The evil effects of Demon drink were shown in every line of his drooping body.'[43]

Another tribe that charmed the anthropologist were the Saoras, who were less prone to violence but equally wary of the outsider. They worshipped a god called Sahibosum who helped keep away touring officials. Located strategically, at the boundary of the village, Sahibosum was made of wood in the image of a sahib, complete with trousers and sola topee. If the sahib came anyway, the Saoras would mark his departure with a purificatory sacrifice. For this they had a standard tariff: a goat for a forest guard, a fowl for a constable, a big black pig for the anthropologist.

The Saora villages were situated on stone terraces built up one above the other. The fields were walled in and well cared for, irrigated with skill and producing rice of high quality. Their theology was as advanced as their agriculture. It centred on sacrifice and was run by shamans. The Saora were adept artists, their paintings crowded over with whimsical deities and dangerous animals and officials. The pictographs were made by the householders, under the close direction of the shaman, who identified the gods to be portrayed or appeased.[44] Collecting material on Saora religion, Elwin wrote to Archer that it was 'so restful to work on something which has nothing to do with sex.'[45] The novelty of the subject was also communicated to his old publishers. He had not published with John Murray for some time. The war had something to do with this, but perhaps also the nature of the books he offered them. He now wrote to Murray asking whether they would consider publishing a book on Saora religion, a book with 'not a word about sex from cover to cover.'[46]

Elwin was now planning a series on Orissa tribes, each book focusing on a different theme: 'Bondo—megalithic culture, crime and character; Saora—religion; Gadaba—weaving; Kond—agriculture; Juang—functional character of myth.'[47] The writer and polemicist had completely supplanted the social worker. Patangarh was for him merely home base, the place he returned to from his travels to unpack and transcribe his notes, thus to better write his books. When he returned from one of his trips and began immediately to draft a new chapter, Kosi commented that 'I married a man not a typewriter.' Anxious to get on with his work Verrier then ran away to Sarwachappar, saying he could not write his book with everyone screaming at the top of their voices. This was an act of self-centredness that even Shamrao would not condone. He hoped that Kumar 'does not become like Verrier who seems to do nothing in life but work.' Kosi was more scathing. She took to calling his books his *chutki*, or younger wife, implying Verrier was more in love with his books than with her.[48]

Verrier once confessed to Bill Archer that both he and Kosi were polygamous by nature. 'Each infidelity made her more fascinating—without it he might have tired of her after two or three years—with this common background casual encounters with other girls were both necessary and possible. [He] would take it whenever he could;' once with a Panka ayah in Patangarh, at another time with a beautiful Jewish girl in Bombay. Kosi also would take it whenever she could. Verrier told Archer, not without pride, of her seduction by an English friend in Bombay. After Kosi had retired to her room the men talked and drank and Verrier, true to form, seems to have passed out first. To get to the lavatory the other fellow had to go through Kosi's room. He went 'four times in one hour and first time smiled, the second touched her hair—the third stroked her—the fourth time took her.'[49]

By 1944 Verrier was utterly absorbed in his books and the marriage came under some strain. To his mother he presented an encouraging picture of Kosi as a bourgeois wife: 'she is doing very good knitting; she is making woollen scarves for the lepers.'[50] One doesn't know about the lepers, but Kosi was not pleased with her work-obsessed husband. While he was away in Orissa she began an affair that was anything but casual. Late in 1945 she became pregnant; we cannot be certain by whom, although we know it was not by Verrier (it was probably a Muslim shopkeeper named Sahid). After the excitement of Kumar's arrival he was most laconic about the appearance of this child. He was touring in Orissa when Kosi went off to Bombay to 'produce her second edition.' From Gunupur in the uplands of Koraput he wrote to Archer: 'I must go and see Kosi and the baby on 20 May: *I can't put it off any longer.*'[51]

In July 1946 a conclave was held in Bombay. Jehangir Patel, the textile magnate who was now the Bhumijan Seva Mandal's most reliable patron, thought Verrier should file for divorce. Even Shamrao, the arch reconciler, insisted that Kosi could not be forgiven. He took her and the baby off to Patan while Verrier talked with a firm of solicitors. But after he returned to the village Verrier decided he would give his wife another chance. He had just been offered a job in the Anthropological Survey of India; the Survey was based in Banaras but was soon to move to Calcutta. Might he and Kosi not forget the mess in Patan and move to the city? 'I am going to start what I hope will be a new life with Kosi,' he wrote to Patel. To his solicitor he sent a remarkable letter explaining why he did not wish to proceed with the divorce. He listed the reasons for his change of mind:

1. My affection for my wife has remained unaltered by anything that has happened. She has done her best to kill that love, but since it has proved tough enough to survive even this, there must be something in it.
2. From the very beginning I have told my friends that I regarded the blame

for the crisis that arose to be as much mine as Kosi's. The few faults in my wife's life are more than matched by far graver faults in mine...

3. There is another reason why I cannot bring myself to blame Kosi. She is a victim of what we anthropologists call acculturation. That is to say she is an aboriginal, whom I took out of her moral surroundings and religo-cultural sanctions and taboos. It is generally found that when this happens, the aboriginal suffers an extreme disturbance and often behaves in a way that we would not call normal. It may be that I too am a victim of acculturation—for I have suffered almost as complete a transplantation from the life of the ordinary barra sahib as she has from the life of her village.

4. There is to me something almost intolerable in saying things even privately, still more in open court, against the woman who has honoured me by becoming my wife. I wanted to arrange matters so that she should divorce me, not the other way, but I feared that such a course might injure my scientific work...

5. I am now probably going to live in Calcutta and I want to make one last attempt to turn my married life from failure to success. Kosi may be happier there; she will have the children with her, and we have many friends in the city. For the first time I will be in a position to give her the comfort she deserves. We will, on both sides, forgive and forget. If this new attempt is a failure, we will then have to revise the situation.[52]

Kosi for her part had agreed to tell her 'Mussalman shopkeeper off.'[53] Both Jehangir Patel and J. R. D. Tata, Verrier's friends and sponsors, were not happy with the reconciliation. 'I don't know whether to be sorry or glad about his decision,' wrote Tata to Patel, 'but I suppose it is up to him in the end and to shape his own life and his friends can only advise'[54]— as well as keep the secret, he might have added, for these two Parsi captains and the Parsi solicitor were apparently the only people outside Patan who knew of the affair.

Verrier had to suppress the infidelity and illegitimacy for various reasons—mother, their patrons, and not least the puritan nationalists who were at once the main audience for his work and the likely future rulers of the tribes. Kosi's second son he named Vijay after the cricketer Vijay Merchant, then playing with great success on the All India Tour of England, but referred to him in private as his 'interim baby.' Reading between the lines of a letter to his mother, it is possible to distinguish his feelings for one Elwin boy from the other: 'Kumar and Vijay are well. Kumar in particular is a supreme darling, the dearest, tenderest little boy you ever saw, most understanding and intelligent, though at present backward academically.'[55]

Through the nineteen forties, while Verrier was travelling on government commission and in search of new tribes to study or protect, Shamrao Hivale was rooted in Mandla, carrying on the work of the Bhumijan Seva Mandal. Under his friend's influence, and with his assistance, Shamrao also completed a study of the Pardhans, the community of ministrels who lived alongside the Gonds.[56]

Shamrao was an unlikely and even unwilling author, yet the year 1946 saw two works published in his name: *The Pardhans of the Upper Narmada Valley* and *Scholar Gypsy: A Study of Verrier Elwin*. *Scholar Gypsy* reproduces massive chunks of Verrier's circular letters, reviews of his books, and admiring comments from Indian and European visitors, linked by the odd paragraph of connecting commentary written by Shamrao himself. It is a very scarce book, almost impossible to find even in the best Indian libraries. Nor was it much noticed when it appeared. The idea behind it seems to have been to provide Verrier a reliable curriculum vitae to live and work in independent India. Not unexpectedly, the book highlights the years of service to the Congress and the bitter battles with the Church. The controversies with sociologists are mentioned obliquely, but the reservations with regard to the Mahatma not at all. To the charge that Verrier was obsessed with sex Sham offered a statistical refutation: only 280 out of 2750 pages of his major monographs dealt with the subject, which 'hardly suggests that he is absorbed in sex.' Other criticisms, such as that the anthropologist wished to pickle tribals as museum-pieces, are answered with words—Verrier's words.

Scholar Gypsy is very much a commissioned work, with Sham the scribe, narrator and propagandist for Verrier's achievements. I suspect the subject chose the illustrations as well. There are several of him in his Gandhian years, with Mirabehn, with J. B. Kripalani, and by the Mahatma's bedside when the old man was ill. There are two photographs of

Kumar—here called Jawaharlal—but none of Vijay. The rare comments that Sham allows himself are in character. On Verrier's personality: 'I have watched him in various capacities—as a most loving, loyal and gentle friend and husband and father. But I have also seen him as a hard and determined enemy of those who have tried to meddle or interfere wantonly in the lives of his people.' On his faith, or rather lack of it: 'The greatest change has been in Verrier's attitude to religion. When I first knew him he was almost a religious maniac. Today he has no religion at all, believing neither in a Supreme Being nor in the future life. But his scientific interest in religion remains, and he is at present engaged on what may be the most important of his books, a study of primitive religion among the Lanjhia Saoras.' And most evocatively, on what he threw away:

> There can be no doubt that if he had continued as he began, he would today have been a Prince of the Church, living in his Palace at Durham or Winchester, in dignity and honour. And now when I look at him, sitting at his desk, bare-foot, in patched and tattered clothes, perhaps struggling against the onset of malaria, I wonder if his sacrifice was worthwhile or whether, when he turned his back on Oxford, he did not make a terrible mistake.[57]

For Shamrao the production of books was merely a diversion. While Verrier was on the move he worked devotedly among the poor and diseased. He supervised ten primary schools, ran the dispensary, and paid a weekly visit to the lepers in their home in Sarwachappar; an eight-mile walk each way from their village of Patangarh: in the rains, 'a most exhausting tramp through mud.' A government official visiting the Leper Home said of it that 'whatever can be done by human love has been done.'[58] In 1943 Shamrao was at last appointed an honorary magistrate in belated recognition of a dozen years of service among the Gonds. This appointment saved villagers the long journey to the court in Dindori town, where they had previously to contend with sharp lawyers and canny officials. Shamrao had more cases in a month than Verrier had in the year (1937–8) he was a magistrate; almost all disputes he handled were settled by mutual agreement.[59]

Verrier once wrote that Shamrao was his 'constant companion, supporter and consoler.'[60] It seemed sometimes that all of Patangarh regarded him in this light. Perhaps the strangest of all his cases was the affair between a fifty-year-old Pardhan woman, married with three children, and a Gond boy of seventeen working as her field servant. When the news reached their house Verrier took out his copy of Freud, for this was 'a clear case of mother-substitute fixation.' But Shamrao at once summoned the concerned parties and commenced to reconcile them. The woman declared her passion for her lover in a loud voice: it was reciprocated. The husband sat in a corner, abashed, while the crowd of assembled villagers could not contain their mirth. The counsellor persuaded the woman to return to her family and sent the Gond boy off to work in one of their hostels in Sunpur, a better job and in a different village. He succeeded in doing for free 'what a Harley Street psychologist would probably have charged a heavy fee for.'[61]

Shamrao and his mate were to be separated when Verrier moved to Banaras to join the Anthropological Survey of India as deputy to the director, B. S. Guha. A Harvard-trained scientist with a fascination for blood groups, Guha visited Verrier in the field in Bastar and endeared himself as a 'caustic and entertaining old thing, with the lowest possible opinion of all anthropologists except himself and me.' The Survey was a new department of the Government of India, charged with studying and prescribing policies for rural communities. Verrier was attracted to the job partly for economic reasons: he had a growing family to support, while donations to the Bhumijan Seva Mandal had dried up during the war. Moreover, with an interim Nationalist Government headed by Jawaharlal Nehru in office, this was a chance to influence aboriginal policy in free India. When Elwin joined the Survey, Nehru had just made an 'admirable statement on aboriginal policy:' the task was to convince 'his less intelligent colleagues that the primitive presents any problem at all to the modern world and that to open cheap little primary schools and make people teetotal does not necessarily cure all their ills.' Elwin now saw a 'great and urgent danger that Nationalist India, which is naturally anxious to get on after a century of stagnation, will be in too great a hurry to reform and change her aboriginals and, by forcing the pace, will bring social and cultural disintegration upon them.'[62]

The Survey seems to have had its genesis in a note Elwin wrote to Francis Wylie in November 1944, suggesting that a full-time adviser be appointed to advise the Government of India on aboriginal problems. 'The appointment of an Indian scientist of distinction,' he wrote, 'would convince people that Government means business. It would be a token (long overdue) that we did not believe that the only people capable of handling aboriginals were foreigners. It would, I think, inspire Indians themselves to work for the aboriginals and to take them seriously.' Wylie passed on the note to the viceroy, and in time the Anthropological Survey was formed with Guha as director.[63] In September 1946 Verrier left Patangarh to take up the first job he'd had in twenty years (since Wycliffe Hall). 'I am now the hell of a chap,' he wrote to Bill Archer: 'Deputy Director of the Anthropological Survey of India.' At last he had 'emulated his revered male parent' by becoming a 'D.D.'[64]

Bill Archer himself was at the time deputy commissioner for the Naga Hills. In May–June 1947 the DD went to see the DC, taking the uninitialled Shamrao with him. For the past few months Verrier had been sitting on a mountain of files, and he looked forward to getting out of his office. Archer took them to the *morungs* or dormitories of the Konyaks, with the decorated boys dancing, 'delicious creatures,' to the girls singing in their deep voices. They were less impressed by the Naga religion, the fervent Christianity of the new convert carried out in 'hideous tin Baptist chapels.' But Verrier was charmed by the capital of Assam, Shillong, a town set among hill and pine. 'What a lovely place, what superb people!' he wrote to his mother, ' I feel we have wasted twenty years messing about in central India instead of coming here.' Both he and Sham felt depressed when they got into the Assam Mail and crossed the Brahmaputra back into the plains.[65]

The DD now had the funds and status to explore new tribes and new areas. His larger hope for the Anthropological Survey was that it would play its part in integrating the elements of a culturally diverse nation. For the acquistion of knowledge was 'not only of scientific importance, but of the utmost practical value in administration, as well as for ensuring fellowship and understanding among the population.'[66] His own experiences tended to confirm the practical value of anthropological research. His book on the Baiga helped free the tribe from forced labour, diluted the state's drive to abolish shifting cultivation, and induced a sympathetic attitude among officials. As a result of his Agaria study the tax on their furnaces was reduced by half. He was greatly encouraged by the interest taken in his work by administrators in Bastar and Orissa, a concern he thought likely to translate into steps for the alleviation of aboriginal discontent.[67]

In Elwin's view the craft of anthropology aided cultural understanding and provided a scientific basis to policies aimed at the poor and vulnerable. As for the anthropologists themselves, they were natural allies of the oppressed. As he put it in a broadcast over All India Radio in 1947,

> The fact today that the world has a conscience about its primitive populations is to no little extent due to the anthropologists and the new attitude on which they have insisted. I do not know of any body of men . . . who are more devoted to the poor than these scientists. The anthropologist is the true Dinabandhu [friend of the poor] for he lives among the poor; he learns to love them as people, he does not think of them as 'masses' to be uplifted with a vague and too-often sterile enthusiasm.

'All over the world,' he continued,

> the anthropologists have fought for the rights of primitive folk; they have transformed the situation in parts of Central Africa; they have tempered the destructive impact of civilization in Indonesia and Australia; the great American and Russian Bureaus of Ethnology have not only helped to weld those vast continents into unity but they have gained for their ancient populations a square deal.[68]

What Elwin did not, could not, add was that he had done as much as anyone else to awaken the conscience of society to the plight of 'primitive' peoples, to temper the often destructive impact of civilization and to try and gain for the aboriginals a square deal in a country on the verge of political independence.

CHAPTER NINE

Staying On

God has already heavily punished any Englishman who tries to bring East and West together, instead of throwing in his lot entirely with either belligerent. His life is one long penance: he gets the stones from both parties—the Indian regards him as a lukewarm, if not false, friend, the British Imperialist says 'he is the most dangerous man of all, for he sometimes seems to talk sense'—that is, of course, sense from a British point of view. At the Last Day both Indian Nationalist and British Imperialist will find at least one point of agreement—in voting that such men be sent to Jehannum, Narak, Hell.

E. J. Thompson[1]

On 15th August 1947 India became independent. In New Delhi Jawaharlal Nehru delivered a famous speech on his country's 'tryst with destiny,' while at a more modest ceremony in Banaras the deputy director of the Anthropological Survey helped hoist the national tricolour. Reporting the latter event Shamrao Hivale recalled a day, nearly twenty years earlier, when his friend had unfurled the Indian flag above the ashram of the Christa Seva Sangh, an act as 'dangerous then as it is now respectable.' Verrier's dearest ambition, commented Shamrao, was 'to take the nationality of our free India so that he may be able to do legally what he has always done in fact, belong to our nation.'[2]

Some other Indians were not so sure about Verrier Elwin's *bona fides*. Two days before Independence he found himself testifying before a sub-committee of the Constitutent Assembly of India. One of its members sharply asked Elwin about his 'policy of isolation.' Now a government servant, Elwin explained his position (as he was to tell Bill Archer) in phrases 'nicely trimmed to the spirit of the age.' Isolation, he told the committee, had once been advocated by him as a strictly temporary measure to protect the weaker tribes from the economic exploitation and psychic degradation that might result from uncontrolled contact. He had not recommended it for the vast majority of tribals whom he called, in a very heavily trimmed phrase indeed, 'Hindus in the kindergarten class.' These had to be 'educated, developed and brought into the mainstream of modern Indian life as soon as possible.' Moreover, with a national and socialist government in place Elwin saw that there was no place any more for isolation or exclusion. This government would protect the aboriginal by eliminating landlords, checking moneylenders, and keeping out missionaries: all of which the colonial rulers had conspicuously failed to do. True, carefully trained officials were needed for the 'wilder and weaker tribes,' to monitor and guide their welfare, to make sure they received the best and not the worst that civilization had to offer. However, a policy of isolation *qua* isolation had no place when 'the imperative need of the country is for unity. We do not want any new minorities. We want one people, advancing together towards a common goal. Separate areas will promote the habit of disunity. Separate electorates, separate representation, separate areas should all disappear with the passing of the old regime.'

The India of 1947–8 was a country determined to make the most of an overdue independence, to put behind it the divisive conflicts of class and community that had so painfully marked the last phase of the struggle for freedom. The Pakistan movement had been successful, taking with it a huge chunk of the territory of Mother India: in what remained, the talk was only of 'national unity' and 'solidarity,' or, in the economic sphere, of 'building socialism,' inclusive, catch-all categories that pre-empted critics of the mainstream advocating their own distinctive and partial interests. Like representatives of the Muslims and the Untouchables, this defender of tribals had to adopt the language and phrases of the nationalist, to swallow hard and swallow them. But even at his most conciliatory Elwin would enter a note of defiance. When other people discuss the aboriginals, he remarked, they almost always

> stress the bad things in their habits and customs. I do not know that their society is disfigured by worse evils than those that affect general civilization, whether Asiatic or European. But may I remind you that they have many beautiful and noble qualities also—their manly virtue, their freedom and

independence, the very high place they generally give to their women, their truthfulness, their freedom from mean and petty vices, their capacity for artistic creation, their instinct for recreation expressed in dance and song, their capacity for laughter, their simple natural attitude to life and its pleasures, the courage with which they overcome poverty and disease. These are precious things. In Britain we are proud of our hillmen, the highlanders of Scotland. We too should not be ashamed of our aboriginals, we should be proud of them and look forward to the fine things they will give us. And so, in pleading for caution and care in dealing with them, I plead also for sincere reverence for them; they must not be despised as savages; they have gifts we need and they will in time contribute to the national life.[3]

Ask not what civilization can give the aboriginal, remember only what he can give it.

In this testimony of 13th August 1947 Elwin uses 'we,' in relation to *both* Britain and India. This unselfconscious invocation might be proof only of his identification with both cultures; or, despite what Shamrao Hivale had to say, of his unwillingness, at the moment of the transfer of power, to completely abandon one national allegiance for the other.

The patriotic fervour released at Indian independence made Verrier's position a uniquely vulnerable one. Forgotten by now was his work for Gandhi and civil disobedience in the early thirties. Fresh in nationalist memory was his more recent defence of the tribes. To the unthinking patriot this seemed another ploy to 'divide' India. His unhappiness and insecurity find poignant expression in a letter mourning the departure for England of Bill Archer, who was returning home with other members of the ICS. Archer was himself very depressed. He had wanted to stay on in the Naga Hills, where he was, in December 1947, serving as deputy commissioner. But that post was not meant for an Englishman in free India. Abruptly transferred and offered a choice between a posting in the plains and early retirement, he chose to go home. 'You may console yourself,' Verrier told him, 'that I am if anything being tortured more; for I have hell within as well as without. We poets in our youth begin in gladness but thereof in the end comes despondency and madness.' He continued:

Your friendship has been precious to me beyond words, and I dread your going from India. Soon there will be nothing to drink, no one to talk to, and no one to copulate—and I shall sink down to being a poor white, brooding over unpublishable manuscripts and thinking up unprintable jokes.'[4]

The Anthropological Survey was then based in Banaras. Verrier thought the city 'intolerably dull' and looked forward to the Survey's impending move to Calcutta. Meanwhile at home trouble was brewing again. A series of one-line entries in his diary says it all: 'Frightful quarrel between Sham and Kosi (who had taken bhang) [10th July 1947].' 'Kosi fights all day on the best whisky and vermouth [25th July].' 'Kosi tight and quarrelling for the first time in a month [20th November].' 'K. broke Sham's box and got tight again [21st November].' 'K. again tight. I felt very exhausted' (25th November). In between bouts Kosi still had the capacity to charm. An entry of 4th August reveals some of what had first attracted the scholar to the Gond: 'Kosi says, "How I love the wind and the smell of the green green grasses," and one day, speaking of dead leaves whirled about by the wind, "The leaves are flying like butterflies." '

On 31st December 1947 Verrier marked in his diary books sent to press and in progress, adding: 'This was the first year I've had money of my own and travelled everywhere first class. But this was more than offset by the annoyance of being a subordinate.' In the last week of the first month of the next year Mahatma Gandhi was assassinated. How did the disciple-turned-rebel take this? His letters do not speak of the happening. His diary is only marginally more revealing. On the day of the shooting, 30th January, he wrote: 'News of Bapu's assassination in evening about 10 minutes after event. Listened to radio all evening.' And the next day: 'All day preoccupied with Bapu's funeral. Listened to broadcast, off and on, from 11 am to 5 pm.'[5]

Verrier had not spoken to Gandhi after 1940 or 1941, and there is no record of his reactions to the events of the last years of the Mahatma's life—the Quit India movement, the fasts and walks for communal harmony, the Partition of India. Emotions now swirled around in his mind, some negative, others more positive. It is striking that he calls Gandhi 'Bapu,' Father, for it had been a long time since he had thought or spoken of him as such. Were his feelings akin then to those of the Delhi newspaper which the day after the event substituted sombre commentary with the eloquently simple banner headline, 'FATHER, FORGIVE US'?

In early February the Survey finally moved its office and officers to Calcutta. Boarding the train at Mughalsarai on the 5th, Verrier dared to 'hope, but probably fruitlessly, never to see this damned Ganges again.' His companions on the journey were a Sikh CID man and two Bihari merchants. They 'discussed, at the top of their voices, Gandhiji's assassination, but I did not think that their hearts really bled for him.'[6] There is strength of feeling here, the quasi-proprietorial claim of the disciple who had worshipped Gandhi in the flesh, as against the fainter bleeding hearts of those who knew the saint only through story and picture.

Calcutta meant friends, interesting ones, but the atmosphere in the Survey was the same, 'phoney and futile.' The work in the office bored Verrier; he was drafting reports rather than writing books. He decided to resign with effect from the 1st of February 1948, and go back to Patangarh. 'I am planning to sit on my arse and write,' he informed Archer, 'so long as I don't develop boils. I have my "Saora Religion" and "Orissa Legends" to finish, which will keep me busy and happy for a long time. It is a big jump back in the dark, and into a dark rather darker than before, but I expect we will be all right.' Within a month he had been made to change his mind: 'Tremendous pressure has been put on me from everybody, especially Sham and the family, to stay on and so I am staying on, for a little longer. I doubt it will be much longer.'[7]

He stayed on in the Survey, only to find relations with his boss steadily deteriorating. Guha was resentful of his greater renown and cussedly interfered with his research. The director warned him not to be in contact with Grigson, Archer and other 'imperialists.' Those associations, he said, would bring the Survey into 'disrepute.' Verrier took a 'certain cynical amusement in reflecting that it was not so long ago that the Government of India made me give an undertaking not to associate with any of my Congress friends.' Then he was denied permission, due solely to the colour of his skin, to do research in the border regions of Assam. 'We are surrounded by treachery,' he wrote bitterly to Archer, 'it is hard to say who is one's friend.' Guha, his boss, claimed the ban came from the Governor of Assam, Sir Akbar Hydari, but Hydari told Verrier 'it was "your pal" Guha who had warned him against me.'[8]

Verrier sought solace outside work. His flat on Pollock Street was the centre of a circle of highly talented friends, their company in the evening compensating for the dullness of the job during the day. They included the painter Jamini Roy, the poet Sudhin Datta, the editor Lindsay Emmerson, the dancer Ragini Devi, the photographer Sunil Janah, the geologist John Auden (brother of the poet), and the communist P. C. Joshi. There were lots of parties in their houses and his, and hangovers every other morning.

At these parties Kosi drank, but who could she talk to? Sunil Janah recalls her at a gathering of poets and intellectuals, painfully shy and totally out of place.[9] Her husband's diary entries tell of heroic but ultimately vain attempts to keep the marriage going. 'Took Kosi to a bad dinner at Firpos [10th May 1948].' 'Went with Kosi to Peiping Restaurant and then to "The White Unicorn," which we much enjoyed.' This seems to have been the last of the happy days. The entries turn progressively more serious. 'All the morning Kosi still tight and nearly drove me crazy, specially as I was trying to read Hill's excellent "My own Murderer" [6th July].' 'Still fighting against ill-health. Anderson put me on a curious diet of enormous meals. These were days of great strain, for we were working up to the parting with Kosi [1st to 8th August].'

The 'we' refers pre-eminently to Shamrao, who had come from Patan to preside over the ruins of a marriage that could no longer be saved. A young man from Patangarh, recruited by Verrier for the Anthropological Survey, remembers how ferociously Mrs Elwin attacked the bottle in Banaras and Calcutta: '*din raat tun thi*,' he said, she was smashed day and night.[10] Kosi's second son seems also to have been a complicating factor. Verrier maintained that he was prepared to love Vijay as a creation of Kosi's. It was 'not the illegitimacy he minded,' he said, 'it was K's bragging attitude.'[11] Sham took Kosi back to Patangarh, where she moved in with her old lover Sahid. Although he found it 'unpleasant and hypocritical,' Verrier had to start divorce proceedings in the Calcutta High Court to obtain custody of his son, Kumar. The case was handled by the firm of Fowler and Sons with Sahid named as co-respondent.[12]

When I met Kosi, forty-some years later, it was remarkable how little bitterness there was, overtly, towards Verrier. True, she referred to him only as 'Elwin,' the impersonal form perhaps denoting that from this distance in time he could be viewed as part of the history of her self and her tribe. Our conversations were slow-moving, in deference to her age and our strangeness, stretches of silence interspersed with the odd question from me and the odd, mostly single-sentence, comment from her. Two of these reflected sharply on Sham. '*Saas ne mujhe England bulaya,*' she said sudddenly, Mother-in-law asked Verrier to bring me to see her in England, and then: '*lekhin Shamrao bola ki main bhi teri seva karta hoon, aur agar Kosi jayegi to Kusum ko bhi jaana hai.*' Sham apparently insisted that if Kosi went Kusum must go as well, and of course there wasn't enough money for both. Kosi even claimed that Mahatma Gandhi called them to Wardha, but again the cussed Sham said Verrier could not take her unless Kusum and he accompanied them.[13]

Kosi also spoke of a visit successfully made to the bungalow of J. R. D. Tata high on Altamount Road in Bombay. In her eyes it was Shamrao who came in the way of her more fully participating in the spacious social world of her husband. '*Koi bade ghar jaana ho to Sham bol padta tha, ham ko bhi aana hai,*' she said: if we were invited to a big man's house, Shamrao would say they had to come too. Sham was possessive about his friend, certainly—'*main bhi teri seva karta hoon,*'—the remark he is supposed to have made to Verrier, would translate literally as 'I also serve you.' He saw himself as having prior claim on Verrier, as one who had shared his life long before this Gond girl came into it. But in Kosi's recollections there seems also to be some kind of displacement, a retrospective refusal to recognize the serious incompatibility between wife and husband, the all-too-natural and characteristically Indian tendency to blame it on someone else.

In March 1949 Verrier was granted a Decree Nisi granting the divorce and custody of the elder child, with the Decree Absolute due in another six months.[14] All that now kept him in the Anthropological Survey was the money, and in the end it was not enough. He left the Survey in April, concluding what he called the 'most wasted and uncreative' period of his life.[15] Back in Patangarh, without job or wife, Verrier was now 'rather oppressed by many anxieties.' If he had the money, he told Archer, he would go 'to live in Micronesia or Tahiti or somewhere.' In another letter he listed the places he wished to visit or stay in—'Paris, the South Seas and Oubangui-Chari, in that order.' After twenty years in the hamlets and forests of India Verrier was, with reason, tired of it, fantasizing of a move to a glamorous, disease-free environment.[16]

His reservations about life in India were as much political as personal. The Congress, having moved from being a party of protest to the party in power, was now enforcing its command on a not entirely willing populace. Verrier dared not openly criticize the new rulers of free India; but more discreet methods were available. From this period date two murder mysteries that he wrote under the pseudonym of Adrian Brent. In plot and portrayal of character these novels are undistinguished and were not to find a publisher. Each makes playful reference to the 'anthropologist Verrier Elwin', author of *The Muria and their Ghotul*, 'a book which discusses primitive sex in an amiable and reticent manner' and which had attracted German anthropologists to the study of Indian tribes. However, the novelist's comments on the state of Indian politics are penetrating and deadly serious. The first novel is set in Bombay, a colourful, cosmopolitan city, much loved by the author, but at this time ruled over by a pious and interfering Congress. The provincial government is headed by Morarji Desai, the most ascetic and humourless of Gandhians. This government 'with Puritan enthusiasm was banning more and more of the legitimate human pleasures [drink and sex], with the natural result that people turned to those that were not so legitimate.' One of its ministers, in a cameo appearance, is caught 'hurrying from a meeting of the Anti-Vivisection Society, where he had had tea, to preside at a conference of the Bombay Anti-Contraceptive League, where he would be given lemonade.' The cloth of these politicians, the handspun khadi, once the 'symbol of insurgence against British rule,' is now 'an almost official uniform, the sign of authority and power.'[17]

The second novel, set in Calcutta, more directly addresses the status of Europeans who stayed on. Here an unidentified white woman carries out a series of murders. After this story breaks in *The Statesman*, the newspaper's sales that day 'broke all records. Marwaris, who had never read anything but the financial news, Congressmen whose literature was confined to the *Harijan* and the *Amrita Bazaar Patrika*, sent their servants to Chowringhee Square to obtain copies.' But by the morrow, titillation gives way to xenophobia. In the afternoon

> a public meeting was held on the Maidan to demand a round up of all the white women between the ages of 18 and 35 in India ... Students of the Intermediate Classes in the Calcutta University, prompted thereto by agitated paterfamiliases, took out a procession protesting against this latest attempt by the white races to dominate India. An officer of the Tourism Promotion Department flew from New Delhi to remonstrate; such agitation would ruin the tourist trade, already badly hit by Prohibition.[18]

This white man had committed no murders himself, but his past had been contentious and controversial, and he felt deeply vulnerable in the India of 1948 and 1949. For the first time since landing on the Malabar coast twenty-two years earlier, Verrier seriously contemplated leaving India. In the summer of 1949, more or less immediately after quitting the Anthropological Survey, he visited England for the first time in a decade. This was a trip he much looked forward to, not least to visit his beloved Oxford, where he was to talk at the Institute of Social Anthropology. He hoped also to persuade Merton to renew their research grant to him, which the College had let lapse at the end of the war.

Verrier expected Oxford to mean friends and allies. But it had been a long time since he was last there; few remembered him, fewer still wanted him. Meyer Fortes, a coming name in British anthropology, was warm and helpful, but the doyen of the Oxford school, Edward Evans-Pritchard, was cold and distant. So too was Evans-Pritchard's (and formerly G. S. Ghurye's) acolyte, 'the unpleasant little [M. N.] Srinivas.'[19] All in all the visit was a crushing disappointment personally, and what hurt Verrier more, intellectually. He had chosen to screen and explain a film he had shot on the Muria ghotul. It was a choice of subject inappropriate to the place and audience, and was frostily received by the Oxford anthropologists.[20] Evans-Pritchard was particularly scandalized and wont in later years to refer to Verrier as 'that sex maniac.'[21] A more material blow was Merton's refusal to revive their grant. His old Warden, Sir John Miles, had retired, and his successor disapproved strongly of the anthropologist's 'strange conjugal relationships.' It did little good when Verrier told him they had ended; the difficulty was that they were contracted in the first place. If he wanted money, he should look for it in India or America. In any case, the college felt he should have left India when others of his class and colour did. 'The time was ripe,' remarked the Warden, 'for you to leave your work in the field for a time and put in for a chair in England.'[22]

Verrier was also put out by the outlook of the British upper classes, struggling to come to terms with the loss of empire. The mother of the anthropologist and ex-ICS man J. P. Mills remembered how 'it was so nice in Simla in '15 and '16. The babus were not allowed on the Mall. I hear it is different now.' His own mother complained bitterly about the Labour government; she resented the working classes getting medical relief and living for the first time in halfway decent houses. She even told Verrier he should not share things with Shamrao. Other friends avoided talking about India 'as a man avoids talking about his wife whom he loved but had to divorce.'[23]

This last comment was made without any self-consciousness. We are left to supply the gloss: the British elite would forget India as he was forgetting Kosi. The British upper classes had been served up a socialist government instead; Verrier's own substitute was altogether more palatable. Before his trip to England he had begun an affair with Kachari, a Pardhan girl of Patangarh. Kachari was staggeringly beautiful. A photograph of the time shows her sitting on a stone bench beneath a ficus tree, a white sari setting off her dark and glowing skin, her long hair beguilingly left untied, a radiant smile on her face, altogether uncommonly appealing.

Kachari moved in with Verrier sometime in late 1949. He was enchanted with her, giving her the name 'Lila,' which may be *very* crudely translated as play or playful love. His inspiration was the most sensually evocative of Indian love stories, the Krishna Lila. This Lila was no Kosi. She did not drink and was a fine home-maker and cook, her Pardhan repertoire generously accommodating the humdrum English preparation of liver-and-onions which was a particular favourite with her lover. For all her beauty and competence Verrier was most reluctant to formalize the relationship. City friends who had predicted the failure of his first marriage were still at hand. One of them told him that if he loved another tribal, better to keep her as a mistress than a wife. True, Verrier would write in his diary of his 'Pardhan in-laws,' and in the code of the village they were probably treated as such. But there was no thought in his mind of a legal marriage, even though Lila was soon expecting a child by him.

The child, a boy named Wasant, was born in October 1950, when the father was not in Patangarh but in Colombo, where he had gone at the invitation of his old Oxford friend Bernard Aluwihare. While in Ceylon Verrier showed his photographs and spoke out on the condition of the island's aboriginals, the Veddas. The countryside was beautiful beyond words: 'the flowering trees along the roads, the fine rest-houses, the rivers, the mountains, the handsome youths, the lovely girls . . .' 'How charming it is,' he wrote to his mother, 'one long enchantment.' The Singhalese he found 'so sensible—the people of the Middle Way. What India might be like without the Congress . . . Everything I do goes into the papers—shopkeepers ask for my autograph! I shall be thoroughly spoiled for dear old India with its mess and dust and muddle.' But with independence had also come race-feeling. Some Sinhalese he spoke to were clear that the planters and other whites would have to go. In any case, he concluded, 'India is *deep*—Ceylon perhaps a little superficial.'[24]

Verrier returned to Patangarh and left almost immediately for a field trip to the Saoras. He spent seven weeks on tour, in villages so remote that not even a constable had visited them. He went seven weeks without a drop of either fresh milk or alcohol. He had put himself on this wagon despite the knowledge 'that aboriginals like their anthropologists a bit high.' It was a time of linguistic temperance as well—not a word of English, which was 'quite a record even for me.' On this trip he had one of the most moving encounters in all his years with the tribes. In the hamlet of Serango a little boy who was dying of malnutrition attached himself to the anthropologist. Raisinda would climb on Verrier's lap, put his head on his shoulder and try to sleep. He couldn't lie down for he choked terribly when he did. Sitting on Verrier's lap he exclaimed, 'Mother!' Sunderlal, Verrier's assistant and Man Friday, gently corrected him: 'That is Bodo babu (big brother).' 'No,' replied the boy, 'he is my mother.' Verrier dreamt at night that he was in a great cave in utter darkness and the Jamuasum (the Saora god of death) was coming for the boy in the form of a vast shape rolling irresistibly across the ground. I tried desperately to strike a match to bring some light, but every match failed and I woke sweating with horror, but the words on my lips—'Love is the true weapon; love is the dress; love is my gold.'

Love the true weapon, because just before going to bed I got the news of the UNO defeat in Korea; love the dress, because I had realized that bitterly cold night that I was warmer because I had less bedding, some of it having gone to Raisinda; love is my gold had reference to our financial situation which is very serious.

One day Verrier found Raisinda 'fumbling with one of my pockets. I wondered what he was looking for—but he was putting a half smoked very precious cheroot into my pocket for safe keeping.' Soon afterwards he died. Verrier's attentions and medicines came too late to save the boy, who 'epitomized all the hunger and loneliness of the world in his frail body.'[25]

Raisinda died in late December; on the last day of the month, and year, Verrier summed up the situation in his diary:

1950. Not really a successful year. Applications for grants and fellowships all failed, except for the Leverhulme Grant—which was really a damned insult. My attempt to be a detective novelist, on which I wasted a great deal of time (though I enjoyed it), was also a failure. The implications of life in free India slowly become more and more depressingly apparent. It also gradually becomes evident that TWARU was not likely to function as a effective unit. The year was overshadowed by constant quarrels and tensions—most of them emanating from one source—most of which were quite unnecessary. I myself was too often worried by financial and other worries. Kumar can hardly be said to have made progress.

On the other hand, my own visits to Bombay in February and to Ceylon in October were successful, and my Saora tour in November-December was one of the best I have had. In the field of research, most of my work was tedious but very necessary . . .

Financially, the year has ended with us in a worse position than we have been for many years.

In health, I had one bad attack of dysentery and three sharp attacks of malaria in the last three months. I felt a good deal older, less resilient and it is increasingly hard to endure hardship.

My attempts to give up alcohol have been to some extent frustrated by the efforts of friends, but I managed it for considerable periods, especially during the last four months—Ceylon was almost, and the Saora trip entirely dry. It has not had a good effect, but I do not see that, financially, there is any alternative.

Above all, the present has been continually shadowed by the future. How long can this go on? Shall I be forced to adopt some new profession? Is it going to be possible even to do research, let alone do anything to help the aboriginals, in India today?[26]

Elwin intended his diaries to be seen by a future biographer, but in those left behind there remain huge gaps: months and years at a stretch. It is not clear who did the weeding—the writer, his executor, his family, or unaffiliated termites. In what remains there are also silences and references left unexplained, for an Englishman will have his reticences, even with his diary. Who, for instance, was the 'one source' of the year's quarrels? Various candidates present themselves. Was it mother, asking him to return home for good? Or the puritan-Gandhian capitalist Jehangir Patel asking for accounts of money spent and work accomplished? Or Shamrao's wife Kusum, known to be frustrated in the village, with little money and four or five children to rear and educate? Or the gentle Lila, hoping he would formalize the relationship by way of marriage?

The speculations will stay. We must move back to empirically firmer ground. Over the last weeks of fieldwork in Orissa during January 1951, Verrier was joined by Shamrao and their friend Victor Sassoon, a photographer from a prosperous Calcutta family. Victor quickly substituted Bill Archer in Verrier's affections: it helped that he was a good ten years younger, an admiring younger colleague rather than an equal and contemporary. Victor was rich and daring, a man who would fund Verrier's research and go into the forest with him. The Orissa trip was the first of several they made together. From the Saora hills they came down to the holiday resort of Gopalpur-on-Sea. Their hotel was full of Jesuits who glared at Verrier, and he back at them. After two months of rice and *daal*, he was pigging it: 'for breakfast, porridge, whiting, eggs and bacon, and all the bread, butter and marmalade you can put away; for lunch—oyster, soup, mackerel, meat curry and rice, an excellent pudding, fruit and cheese.'

But he still didn't know what to do with his life. Victor offered to take him to Africa.[27]

On his way back from England in 1949 Verrier had spent a couple of weeks in West Africa, travelling through the Ivory Coast and Nigeria. For some reason he stayed clear of Freetown, his father's old bishopric. The 1951 trip with Sassoon was to the other side of the continent, the British-ruled territories of Kenya and Tanganyika. Its highlight was a meeting with Louis Leakey, a self-confessed 'White African' whose career in so many ways paralleled his. Leakey showed him around his museum and his Maasai. Verrier was impressed by the legend, 'a real charmer and quite brilliant,' but less so by his second wife, the paleontologist Mary, whom he found 'very learned but rather dreary.'[28]

About Africa Elwin had mixed feelings. Both Sasoon and Bill Archer, knowing his depressed state of mind, urged him to move there. 'We would plead with you,' wrote Archer, 'to consider the world of African poetry which is still almost completely unexplored and to which you could make a uniquely exciting contribution. But I expect you will prefer to go your own rather wilful way—only don't kill yourself, just yet!' Although Verrier had enjoyed his visits to the continent and even contemplated writing a narrative of his travels, any thoughts of permanent residence were dispelled by the mounting antagonism he noticed between whites and blacks. 'There is something so fundamentally wrong,' he wrote to his mother, 'in the white settlers grabbing all the best land from the Africans [and] in the real hatred of the English for the Indians here.' In this atmosphere of hatred the figure of the Botswana chief Seretse Khama stood out. He had married an Englishwoman, for which he was hated by the whites and thrown out by his own clan. The marriage, and the social location betwixt and betweeen, reminded Verrier of his own. He wrote a sonnet on Khama and for a while even thought of writing a biography.[29]

Almost the first news Verrier got on his return to India in June was a report of a speech by Jawaharlal Nehru in Bangalore. The prime minister had expressed the view that prohibition should not be introduced in tribal areas, saying, 'you will break up their lives if you suddenly introduce it.' Verrier was temporarily pleased. Of course the killjoys had not been vanquished by Nehru's words: when he read of Nehru' speech he was in fact staying with one, Jehangir Patel. The magnate would wake him up at six a.m. and make him do yoga. One evening, when Verrier wasted his food at dinner, Patel coolly reminded him of the history of famine in India. 'What humiliation and misery it is,' thought Verrier, 'to be poor and so dependent on such creatures.'[30]

Verrier returned to Patangarh, where a letter from Mother awaited him. 'You can't go on as a cave man,' she had written, 'when God has given you brains and powers for larger use. My darling boy, I am sure you should be finished with Patan and such life.' He was not finished with Patan yet, nor was Sham, but Kusum Hivale was. She moved to Jabalpur with her kids and Kumar, who all went to school there. Back in the village Sham began an affair with a Gond called Bilsi, somewhat disturbing the domestic arrangements. Lila did not like the new entrant, which meant that Verrier had occasionally to cook for the love birds and take the food to their nest, that being Sham's room, now usually bolted from the inside. He worked when he could on his Saora book. The house was ideal for writing, he wrote to Victor Sassoon, but one grew old too quickly in Patangarh:

> The days are not full enough
> And the nights are not full enough
> And life slips by like a field mouse
> Not shaking the grass.[31]

Restless, uncertain, confused, Verrier took up an old invitation to visit Thailand. He went there in December 1951, accompanied by Sham, their host an old Oxford mate, the poet and professor A. C. Braine-Hartnell. A week in Bangkok was all they could take. But then another Englishman, Gerald Sparrow, offered to take them north. A former president of the Cambridge Union, now a flamboyant Bangkok lawyer, race-horse owner and night-club proprietor, Sparrow had left his English wife for a Siamese sweetheart. He booked four seats on the plane that linked the Thai capital with the northern temple city of Chiengmai. When they reached their destination Chaluey, Sparrow's companion, thought it a shame that Verrier had no girl with him. The 'iced-up' English gentleman, she said, needed someone presentable to make him come out. So they were joined by Rada, a lively and well-travelled dancer. Shamrao either did not want a partner or did not get one. Anyway, the party then spent a glorious week eating, drinking and visiting the old Buddhist temples all around. On their last night they dined on roast suckling-pig washed down by Black Label whisky and Thai beer. Afterwards Rada was persuaded to dance. She started with a spoof on the American idiom, 'the primitive and idiotic characteristics of the dance exaggerated and guyed,' followed appropriately by a classical Siamese dance, with its 'measured dignified rhythms, her face retaining the mask-like passivity that the performance demanded.' When Chaluey followed with a plaintive Malay love song Shamrao was heard to mutter, 'If only India was like this!'

Next morning they had to take the plane back to Bangkok. Reluctantly, most reluctantly, they 'waved farewell to our lovely and gifted Rada. As we became air-borne, we saw her waving a little lace handkerchief until we were out of sight.'[32]

When Sparrow published his account of the visit some years later, Verrier denied the existence of the enchanting Rada. His friend had made her up, he said, to make him more interesting.[33] It is possible that Sparrow embroidered more than the handkerchief, but by the time the tale appeared in print Verrier had good reason to deny any liaison in Chiengmai. It remains Sparrow's word against Elwin's. The definitive evidence may lie in the guest book of the Doi Sutep temple, which the lawyer claimed was signed by 'Verrier Elwin, Shamrao, Rada, Chaluey, Gerald Sparrow.'

A pleasing consequence of the Thailand trip was a series of poems written about Verrier. Shaun Mandy of the *Illustrated Weekly of India* thought he had first claim on anything that came out of his friend's travels, but this time Lindsay Emmerson of *The Statesman* had obtained a commission beforehand. When Mandy heard that he was not going to get an account of Thailand he wrote

A PLEA FOR DR ELWIN

I'm most terribly afraid
You've already been waylaid
By that genius of The Statesman, Lindsay E
Who'll purloin your Thailand pix
With his lucre and his trix
Till there's nothing left at all for me to see.

If it isn't too late
You could lurk around and wait
Till Lindsay E's absorbed in prolix edits.
And snatch some prints away
For The Weekly to display
With the loveliest banner lines for you as credits.

> Please, Dr Elwin, don't let Lindsay E
> Run wild about the garden and
> Eat every gooseberry
> Don't let him rape the trees, until there's nothing left
> And the garden's all bereft.
> Please, Dr Elwin, keep a bush for me.

Lindsay Emmerson offered, in response, this untitled poem on

> An Editor in Bombay
> Once wrote to Calcutta to say—
> >   Though with compliments kind—
> >   A piece of his mind
> About luring V. Elwin away.
>
> The recipient has, in Calcutta,
> An unlimited stomach for butter;
> >   Yet discovers in it,
> >   And its flashes of wit,
> The mild reprobatory matter.
>
> The learned man living in Patan,
> In conditions remarkably Spartan,
> >   Is well known to be,
> >   For photography,
> What the Weekly has got a good start on.
>
> Yet when he returned from Bangkok—
> Not to give other journals a knock,
> >   But because he is Verrier,
> >   And the more of him the merrier—
> We naturally collared his stock.

Then from camp Ukai on the Tapi River in Gujarat came this learnedly allusive commentary from the geologist John Auden, a man with poetry in his blood:

> What strange flirtation can this be,
> Two begging for what but one did see,
> And having seen, did then imprison
> Without any aberration
> In a box where light
> Defeats the darkest night?
>
> No vision here of Aunt Emily,
> Eldest sister of unwedded three,

Archly smiling as the man did bid,
Corsetted of all that must be hid;
Unlovely bosom;
Too sterile womb.

Nor is there exposed our uncle when,
Mayor of Margate, he had risen
To the summit of his smug cancer,
Chain on navel, verbal diarrhoea;
Striped were the pants
of his sycophants:
Bad too the breath
Of coming death.

No, our Guru from the Patan heights
Had other things in mind, quite other flights
Of mental fancy, as on air he ran
To the loveliness of Siam.
Unbroken hearts
Where no fear starts.

Uncolonised, no dignity to span,
No color bar across the face of man,
No sooty fumes from dismal terraces;
Ecology of those old heresies
Which bred in Marx
His parallax.

Pantheistic and free to be
One with the apple on its tree,
All nature there in paradise,
Not heeding overmuch advice,
Nor what Newton saw
In universal law.

Could it be that Emmerson,
And his friendly rival Sean,
Could exahaust the great Guru's stock
Before it blossoms in a book?
Not yet indeed,
Even in their need.

Lava quod est Emmerson
Riga quod est Shawn-Sean.

And now, briefest and best, Mandy's final reply:

> Did you hear anything? Hark, listen, hist!
> Why, that's the MUSE of a geologist.
> The Muse, you say, she surely shows a bit.
> —The Saucy, florit chit!
> But just the type, perhaps, that neatly vamps,
> Geologists when lonely in their jungle camps.[34]

Not to forget editors in their dark cubicles. These pedestrian verses are of interest principally to the biographer. As illustration of how Englishmen in exile, drunk and bored, amused themselves, they are fairly typical and regrettably undistinguished.

Once more, Verrier's return to India is marked in his diary by a reference to Nehru. In England, on his first official trip there, Nehru had spoken in the House of Commons for a 'new type of association with a touch of healing' between the United Kingdom and India. Verrier commented, justly, that these words 'in their context are a miracle.'[35]

Nehru's words were also eminently Gandhian, as Verrier well knew. He was now deep into a reappraisal of Gandhi and thus of the land from whence he came. In his memoirs Verrier was to write of what made him move away from the Mahatma: his 'emphatic views on Prohibition (which I considered damaging to the tribes), his philosophy of sex-relations (which I considered damaging to everybody), and what seemed to be a certain distortion of values—the excessive emphasis on diet, for example, . . . separated me from him.' Then he added: 'Today I feel very sorry about this, for it was in his last years that Gandhi reached his highest stature and I deprived myself of the warmth of his affection and the strength he would have given me during a difficult period. But it was a feeling of Truth that kept me away from going to see him and from this point of view my instinct was right.'[36]

As we have seen, Gandhi's assassination provoked a fresh assessment, a striving towards balance in Verrier's feelings for the man. Travelling in

Africa in 1949 he had been disturbed by the rise of a 'national movement without a Gandhi:' that is, without goodwill towards its opponents. The next year he helped Valji Govind Desai, an old friend from the Sabarmati days, with his translation of Gandhi's *Satyagraha in South Africa*. In contrast with his coyness when Mahadev Desai wanted to thank him with regard to the *Autobiography*, this time he allowed his assistance to be placed on record.[37] There is also a telling exchange in one of his unpublished novels. When an Eurasian says that all Indian policemen and officials are corrupt and can be bribed, it is significantly a Muslim named Masood who replies: 'Well yes, Mr Gore, most of them are. But you must not forget Mahatma Gandhi. He was a very great man. I don't think that you European gentlemen have ever quite understood his influence. Some of his followers can never be bribed, not by anything. They will give up their lives to defeat us.'[38]

This partial, posthumous reconciliation with Gandhi was contemporaneous with and possibly a source of influence on Verrier's reconciliation with India. Various alternatives had been tried and found wanting. Ceylon and Thailand were superficial, England inhospitable, Paris and the South Seas unreachable. Africa seemed the most likely but he had not the willingness, approaching fifty, to begin life afresh in a continent seething with racial tension. When Sassoon wrote saying he and Archer were working on a Colonial Office fellowship for him to do research in Africa, Verrier asked them to stop proceedings. 'I wouldn't take a job from the Colonial Office,' he wrote, 'I have spent my life in opposition to them and all they stand for, and it is too late to change now.'[39]

Reading these pages, with their tough account of a tormented decision, at least two kinds of critics shall sharpen their knives: the hidebound patriot who doubted Elwin's commitment to India in the first place, and the theorist of multiculturalism, always ready to judge and criticize. To the former I would say that this Englishman did more than anyone to make visible the plight of a deeply disadvantaged and numerically substantial section of the Indian nation. As for the second kind of critic, who speaks of the happy mixing of cultures through processes of 'hybridity' and 'translation,' this sort has almost without exception made the voyage *in*, from the colonized culture to the colonizer. They have moved from East to West, from disease-ridden and poor countries to aseptic and rich ones. Since the transition has been easy for them, they will see in Elwin's hesitation and uncertainty a negative attitude to the culture in which he had made his home.

The patriots and the multiculturalists both need to be reminded of a remark of the Cambridge historian F. W. Maitland: 'That which is now in the past was once in the future.' A passport is now almost a matter of convenience; in Elwin's time a change of nationality was a real struggle. And how can one forget that he had moved the other and indisputably more difficult way, from the life of the privileged among the privileged to a life among the Gonds? After twenty-five years of this, if he occasionally tired of the illness and poverty, are we in any position to cast stones?

Once Verrier decided to stay on in India, Shamrao and he reverted to their familiar division of labour: social work for the one, writing and advocacy for the other. The Bhumijan Seva Mandal changed its name twice after independence. In 1949 it became the Tribal Art and Research Unit (TARU) and then, a year later, the Tribal Welfare, Art and Research Unit (TWARU)—this to recall its original aims and also to acknowledge Shamrao's continuing welfare work. By any name, the organization was starved of money. After independence some businessmen who had supported their work withdrew in the belief that the national government would now take care of tribal welfare. They came to depend more and more on the largesse of Jehangir Patel. Verrier also suspected that Congress propaganda against him had contributed to their financial crisis. His letters of the time speak repeatedly of TWARU being 'right out of funds.' Their difficulties were compounded when in May 1951 a typhoon destroyed their home in Patangarh. It was of course uninsured and had to be rebuilt from scratch.[40]

Shamrao carried on regardless: healing physical wounds in the dispensary and leper home, healing emotional wounds everywhere else. Verrier thus described a typical day in his friend's life, the variety of people and problems he attended to:

> someone's precious buffalo is sick; there is trouble over land; a wife has run away and must be reconciled to her husband; an old woman has no food in the house; a simple Gond has got entangled in the law-courts; a barren woman is accused of being a witch; there is a scare that kidnappers have come

for children (on behalf of the Public Works Department!) to sacrifice in the foundation of shaky bridges and the people have to be reassured; a dying child calls for comfort.[41]

Verrier liked to compare his comrade to a Hindu widow, old style, at everybody's beck and call, but Shamrao more wryly believed the social worker's lot to be like that of a peon (*chaprasi*) in a government office, for 'he never knows what he will have to do next.' Hindu widow or chaprasi, he was deeply devoted to his wards. Here is Shamrao's description of their home for lepers:

> It is a very beautiful home, built in the simple style they appreciate, with a large garden that in the rains at least is quite lovely, and views of mountains in all directions. The home is indeed the creation of a poet. Verrier once said that when he felt really depressed he went to the lepers to get cheered up! Often when I have been by myself at Patangarh and feeling lonely I go and sit among these brave and simple people and look at their flowers and the surrounding hills which make one forget the ugliness and the wounds; their great disaster puts one's little troubles in their right proportion. It is astonishing how humorous and witty the lepers are and how interested in the outside world; they always ask first about Verrier and the children, and then about the war, the Congress and India's freedom.[42]

If the lepers asked about Verrier it was because he was not much in Patangarh: his province was the entire tribal population of the peninsula, his task bringing their situation to wider notice. His own work with the pen was justified, as he saw it, by the fact that the

> real protector of the aboriginals is knowledge. Only Knowledge can give the general public the right angle on these people. Only Knowledge can convince administrator and reformer alike that they are not mere savages to be uplifted, but human beings like themselves with a logical and often admirable way of life well adapted to the physical and economic conditions under which they live. Only Knowledge can escort them safely through the perilous passage of acculturation. Only Knowledge which goes on to Love, can inspire men and women with the desire to go and serve them in lonely and malaria-ridden places.[43]

It was typical of Verrier that he would think of aboriginals and their predicament in the plural. It was left to Shamrao, silently but no less effectively, to express *his* love in a more intimate, immediate, personal sense, to one-tribal-at-a-time.

CHAPTER TEN

An Englishman in India

ADIBASI 1952

by Verrier Elwin

How tired they are, and what a sombre grace
  Time has drawn on the wise old faces, grey
With the death of children, and no release
  From want that rules day after anxious day.

There was life there once, and joy in recreation,
  Dancing and laughter, love among the trees,
But little now save sullen speculation
  Of what the future has and where it leads.

Old rules are broken, boys go to the town;
  Children are married in a loveless tie;
The ancient forest is no more their own;
  The women lose their treasured liberty.

New customs which are little understood
  Drive out the old, leave nothing in their place.
The old men suck their wooden pipes and brood,
  And tremble for the future of their race.

'Verrier Elwin is only really happy when he can think of himself as a misunderstood and persecuted man.' So said the Bishop of Bombay back in 1936.[1] In some senses Elwin was really happy only as a *writer*, for the break with the Church and Gandhi had then released a surge of creativity. Now here he was, in the nineteen fifties, once again a misunderstood and persecuted man, confused about his nationality, without a job, his marriage in tatters, a son to look after and educate. Characteristically, he found happiness anew in his work and a stream of books and articles poured forth from his pen.

Of these the longest in preparation was a personal record of tribal art. A draft was assembled as early as August 1947, with Verrier keen to have it published soon, to pre-empt his friend and fellow collector. 'Archer is straining every nerve to forestall me,' he wrote to R. E. Hawkins, 'and we should get out our book before he gets out his, if for no other reason.'[2] The OUP wanted a subsidy to pay for the 230 illustrations. The book was finally published in 1951 with the aid of ten thousand rupees provided by Jehangir Patel, the Bombay cotton magnate who had long and generously supported their work. When the book appeared Verrier wrote in triumph to his mother: 'Bill Archer is very jealous of it; he wanted his name to be on the title-page, but when I refused he began saying it was no good, poor fish.'[3]

Elwin remarked to an Indian friend that the book wished to show in 'the most emphatic way the cultural and aesthetic traditions of the *adibasis*.'[4] With rich detail, but a minimum of interpretation, he documented the varied forms of decoration in tribal life—of the body, of houses, of objects of worship—as well as the materials from which these were made. But the book is also pervaded by a sense of wistfulness, a note of loss almost; for the opening up of tribal areas had taken a huge toll of their creativity. In matters of art the 'great days of the Indian tribesman are gone; all we can do now is search in the debris for traces of inspiration and scraps of beauty.'[5]

While they collected money to print *The Tribal Art of Middle India* the OUP put out *Myths of Middle India*, the fourth volume in his series on the contributions of Indian tribals to the literature of the world. The collection, said Elwin modestly, 'attempts nothing more than to present samples and specimens of an oral literature whose variety and extent is still largely unsuspected by scholars.' An American reviewer more accurately termed the book 'a landmark in the exploration of the intellectual history of mankind.'[6] It was an aboriginal Purana, a compendium of tribal stories about natural and human creation, rich in expressive imagery, with stars flashing and gods appearing and disappearing, tales of magic and wonder impossible to summarize or condense.

Let me try, nevertheless, with a Baiga tale about the origin of drink. Bhimsen, the Pandava of legendary appetite, asked Bhagavan for food—having demolished twenty-five sacks of rice and twelve of *daal*, he then asked for a drink. God had none, so Bhim went into the forest and searched. After a long time he came to a mahua tree, with birds of all kinds pecking into its hollow and nodding their heads. The mighty Pandava leaned into the hollow, had a gulp, and decided he must introduce Bhagavan to the holy spirit. The subsequent developments underlined a basic truth of tribal, indeed human, life—that some can take it and some can't. 'Then Bhimsen filled twelve gourds full of the mahua liquor and brought it back for Bhagavan to drink. They sat down, Bhagavan and the wind and the crow, and they drank the liquor out of leaf-cups. Then when their heads were nodding, Bhimsen got up and walked round the earth.'[7]

In 1950 appeared Elwin's study of the Bondo, the tiny tribe living in the uplands of the Koraput district in Orissa. *Bondo Highlander* is in some respects the most disappointing of all his books. It is a conventional, gazetteer-like ethnography, a synoptic survey of the chief elements in Bondo social organization: the rules of marriage, individual affiliation by clan and moiety, the tribal pantheon and the rituals for cementing village solidarity, the role of weaving in the life of their women. Absent from this book is the polemical edge of his other studies, for it is not about a great tribal institution (bewar, the ghotul, whatever) under threat. There is a weariness to the narrative, perhaps because the anthropologist himself was not much attracted to the tribe. One reason was that Bondo dancing was 'wretched stuff,' with 'little rhythm, no variety, no dignity.' But there are withal some characteristic touches, as for instance a swipe at the 'puerile reformist evangelism of self-conscious Hindu propagandists,' and a singling out, among the Bondo of the Jeypore chiefdom, of the 'absence of obsequiousness and the sense of being in a historic tradition [that] is one of the most pleasing characteristics of state subjects everywhere in India.'[8]

Elwin predicted that *Bondo Highlander*, being a comparatively light book, was 'not likely to please the anthropological pundits, but it might go all the better with the public for that very reason.'[9] A particularly vicious piece of punditry was a review by D. N. Majumdar, Professor of Anthropology at Lucknow University. Majumdar had reason to dislike Elwin. He had studied tribals, even tribals in Bastar, long before the Englishman. But Elwin's reputation quickly eclipsed his; worse, he thought Elwin's barbs at anthropologists who hurried in and out of the field were aimed especially at him. When S. C. Dube published his first book, on the Kamar, Elwin gave it a generous review in the *Illustrated Weekly of India* but wondered why the bright young scholar was keeping such dubious company. The reference was to the Ethnographic and Folk Culture Society of Lucknow, a society floated by none other than D. N. Majumdar, which had published Dube's book.[10] Now, as he prepared to review *Bondo Highlander*, Majumdar's attention was drawn to one of Elwin's recent articles which said emphatically that 'there has been more shoddy and second-rate work done in this subject here in India than in any other country in the world. "Tip and run" anthropologists visit an area for two or three weeks, take hundreds of hurried and inaccurate measurements, ask a lot of leading questions, and retire to their Universities to write pompous articles about what they have failed to observe.'[11]

Majumdar's review, when it appeared, answered all the slights accumulated over the years. It started by referring to 'Verrier Elwin, formerly Rev. Father Elwin.' Anthropology, said the Professor, 'is Elwin's latest hobby,' which he was helped to indulge in by wealthy friends and patrons:

> The Tatas and Sarabhais find money for his books, his researches are paid for by the Warden and Fellows of Merton College, Oxford, by the Government of India, for the five [*sic*] years he was working as the Deputy Director of Anthropology Department, and by the various State Governments who subsidise his work or his welfare activities. He has created a class of readers who eagerly await his book, and they sell. All handicaps that stifle anthropological research and create frustration among anthropologists are inoperative in his case.

Elwin was was thus blessed, and according to Majumdar dishonest too. It was Christoph von Fürer-Haimendorf who had 'opened up the Bondos' and written a number of papers on them, preparatory to the production of an authoritative monograph: 'professional etiquette should have restrained Elwin' from writing a book on a subject which the Austrian had clearly marked out as his own. The book itself was what one could expect of an ethnographer who 'does not even require to know the language or the dialect of the tribe.' There was also Elwin's sentimentalism, which 'appears to have compromised with science, and the reader is often left to guess how far his vivid pictures of tribal life are real and how far they are tinged by his imagination and flair for description.' Of course the book would find its buyers for, said Majumdar in conclusion, 'the nude pictures make the book eminently saleable.'[12]

Majumdar's review suggests malice tinged with envy rather than scholarly disagreement, but the truth is that Elwin himself ranked the book very low in his list of creations. It was priced at thirty rupees, or one pound and two shillings, which, as Verrier admitted, was 'too much, even in these inflated days, for there is not really very much in the book.'[13] *Bondo Highlander* is the work of a man tired with his craft. In the years since he began, the craft of anthropology had become a science, moving away from its origins in folklore and literature towards the structural analysis of kinship, power, agrarian relations and other impersonal phenomena. The professionals had little time any more for the gifted amateur, but nor had he for them. Professionalization had brought with it a soulless dissecting precision far removed from the literary liveliness he so valued in anthropological writing. It bored and exasperated him. While finishing his book on the Bondo Verrier wrote with disgust of the scientific ethnographies reaching him from England which, like the works of Tommy Tupper, were 'distinguished mainly for their rectitude, exactitude and appalling dullness.' The days when an anthropologist such as James Frazer could inspire a poem like *The Waste Land* were far behind them. For 'the thrill of Tylor, Frazer and Jane Harrison has departed: there was life there, poetry, drama, loveliness, turns of phrase like a flashing of a sword, chapters with stars at elbow and foot.' The field had now passed into the hands of the 'serologist, genealogist, the utterly dreary folk,' men (and one woman) for whom Elwin proposed this anthropo-Dunciad, naming the most famous British anthropologists of his generation:

> Where Evans-Pritchard, Fortes and the rest
> Suck social facts from Audrey Richards' breast,
> And should you ever see me really bored
> I'm trying to read a book by Daryll Forde
> Though, I confess, of thousands who get me down,
> There's no one to compare with Radcliffe-Brown,

There's only one good thing to say for Marret
And that is, he's as dead as Browning (Barrett)
If from pre-history you'd me deter
Just show me moribund Professor Fleure.[14]

Bondo Highlander was supposed to be the first in a series of books on the Orissa tribes, but Verrier had energy and time for only two more. The first was a collection of tribal myths in the province. The stories were presented with little comment or analysis; the author, it seems, was written out, for he referred the reader to the critical essays in his *Myths of Middle India*. The topics covered were much the same: the origin of the world, of different plants and animals, of man and his institutions. A nice tale featuring Bhim illustrated the absorbing interest of tribals in the forest. When Mahaprabhu made a Raja for men and appointed chiefs and headmen too, the trees complained that he had not made a government for them. So God sent Bhim to the forest, where the Pandava engaged in friendly combat with a specimen of every species. The tamarind resisted most strongly, so Mahaprabhu, on Bhim's advice, appointed it king of the trees. But he also chose the *banyan* as the *mantri*, or minister, and the *pipal* as the watchman, saying to the latter: ' "Whenever any wind comes, warn the other trees." That is why the pipal shakes its leaves to let the other trees know when even a little wind is in the air.'[15]

Unquestionably Elwin's best book on Orissa was his ethnography of the Saora, finished in 1952 and published three years later. Elwin first visited the Saora in 1943, and over the years went back to them whenever he could. He enjoyed working with the tribe, not least because the Saora countryside was 'so beautiful that it takes one's breath away.' Through the hills and valleys of the Ganjam district he tramped barefoot, a ragged shirt on his back, a hat of leaves on his head—and while he rested a chair under his bottom and a pen in his hand. The Saora themselves were spendidly truculent, refusing to allow schools be opened in their villages and resisting puritan pressures to give up tobacco and drink.[16]

The anthropologist chose to focus on religion, a theme which took him back to his days at Oxford, when faith had absorbed him just as much as it absorbed the Saora now. As the book was about rather an Oxford subject, he joked to his publisher that it should be subsidized by the vast resources of the University Chest.[17] The intensity of spiritual experience among the tribe also recalled the high drama of the Catholic faith to which he had once been so powerfully drawn. To get from the Saora villages to the neighbouring Gadaba country, he remarked, was 'like passing from Catholic Spain to Protestant England. To the Saora, religion is art, drama, life itself; to the Gadabas it is "something for Sunday morning," something for the main crises of life, like birth or death but not for every day.'[18]

Elwin's study of the Saora has been called 'the most detailed account of an Indian tribal religion that ever flowed from an anthropologist's pen.'[19] It covers an impressive range of topics: the apparatus and techniques of ritual, the causes and cure of disease, the rites of fertility and the rites for the dead, the varied forms of invocation and prayer. The book also pays careful attention to the artefacts of Saora religion: the different types of altar, the instruments and objects of sacrifice, the ikons or pictographs through which religious sensibilities found artistic expression.

The centrepiece of *The Religion of an Indian Tribe* is its account of Saora shamanism. Shamans, who could be both men and women (for the latter Elwin coined the term 'shamanins') led a peculiar kind of double life. Each shaman had a tutelary, a spiritual spouse so to speak, who lived in the Underworld. Union with a tutelary did not rule out marriage in Saora society, so that the shaman had two spouses and sometimes two sets of children as well. It was the tutelary who, by possessing the shaman, acted as an intermediary between the village and the nether world.

The divine world of this Orissa tribe was a malevolent one. Both gods and ancestors brought danger to the Saora: by breaking up marriages, attacking crops, or bearing disease. Here the shaman came into play, to cajole, flatter and placate ancestors, to keep them away from mischief in the living world.

The book is on a scrupulously non-political subject. But submerged in the dense thicket of ethnographic reportage and theological discussion are occasional flashes of Elwin the Protectionist, the defender of the integrity of tribal culture. There are cracks against the tyranny of caste and the 'visiting Congress busybody,' against the rigorous puritan ethic 'of self denial and ascetic renunciation, the dismal code of condemnation of free happiness'—a code thankfully alien to the Saora. And there is a celebration of the 'united and democratic character' of the tribe, their loyalty to one another, and the high and honoured place of their women.

Saora women, indeed, had 'an important role alike in festivity and funeral;' their 'voice is not unheard in tribal affairs: they can more than hold their own with their men.' To 'this happy state of affairs the institution of the shamanin had made its contribution. For here is a body of women dedicated to the public service and fulfilling that dedication with grace and energy. Here are women, believed to be vitally in touch with supernatural affairs, on whom one can rely, women who respond to the sick and anxious with professional thoroughness and affectionate concern.' The tribal woman had already won the status the city-based feminist was fighting for.[20]

When the Saora book went to press Elwin was just short of his fiftieth birthday. He saw it at the time as his last major work for his health was indifferent and he was not in the mood for fresh fieldwork. He told Archer he found it 'difficult to start again the whole weary business of writing another monograph.' 'The poetry field is very fully exploited,' he added, 'and I am dubious now how far any more treasures are to be found. Tribal art is virtually dead.'[21] 'Now that I have finished off my big books,' he wrote to his mother, 'I am writing articles mostly . . . It is odd how much more fame and how much more money one can get from an article in a newspaper, which may take two hours to write, than from a book which may take five years.'[22]

The comment recalls Arthur Koestler's remark that he would gladly exchange a hundred readers of his work today for ten readers ten years later, or for a single reader a hundred years later. The fame of a newspaper or magazine article is fleeting, forgotten tomorrow or in a week. Only books, good books, endure. Elwin's 'big books' are still read and admired and reprinted. His articles, virtually unknown, lie buried in old, yellowing periodicals in decaying Indian libraries.

Out of work, and with research money drying up, Elwin found that book reviews and newspaper articles were a quick and painless way of sustaining his and Shamrao's families. His output in these years was prodigious. Between 1949 and 1953 he wrote hundreds of reviews for the

Times of India of Bombay and *The Statesman* of Calcutta, all of which were, in the custom of the day, unsigned. The books piled up in Patangarh while he was on tour: he attacked them ferociously on his return, sometimes writing as many as five reviews a day.[23]

One must suppose Elwin took more care of his signed articles, of which too there were not a few. A stray page in his papers, undated but probably from the early fifties, contains these jottings of articles to write and journals to place them in:[24]

Possible Articles:

Tribal Poetry for 'The March of India'
Twenty Years [in Tribal India] for Christmas Statesman
The Weapon of Poetry for Christmas Statesman
East Africa, for Thought
Ideas of Beauty, for Statesman

Humour:

Thurber	Saki
Crispin	Wilde
P. G. Wodehouse	Dickens

Biography of the Gods:

Nanga Banga
Lingo
Kittung
Kariya Kuar
Nirantali
Hirakhan Kshattri

Tribal Folklore:

Rainbow
Bees
Death
The Land of Women
Eclipses
Birds
Trees

Picture Features:
> General of Tribal India for National Geographic
> Page for Statesman
> Africa dance
> Fishing
> Gopalpur
> Priestesses
> Sahebosum

This listing draws upon forty years of wide reading and twenty of deep research, but its diversity and range of themes is astonishing all the same—from English literature through African poety and Indian folklore to autobiography. Some of these essays were obviously written for fun, others for effect, and all for money. There was one set of essays not mentioned in this list that he was deadly serious about. These were published between 1950 and 1955 in the *Illustrated Weekly of India*, the magazine edited from Bombay by Shaun Mandy, and most popular among the Indian intelligentsia.

Elwin's essays in the *Illustrated Weekly* aimed above all at alerting the Indian elite to the rich culture and present dilemmas of tribals. The Bombay magazine was then patronized by the educated upper class, from whose ranks were drawn the businessmen, bureaucrats and journalists who constituted the core of India's ruling class. This was a class separated by a huge cultural gulf from tribals, yet possessed substantial power to influence their lives.

Some of Elwin's essays introduce individual communities to his readers; others highlight the forms of recreation in tribal India; yet others focus on material culture, for instance on weaving and carving. The depiction of tribal life is introduced and sustained by a rhetorical strategy which helps ease the reader into an unfamiliar world. A fine example is an essay on the scroll paintings of the Jadupatua, a sister community of the great Santhal tribe of eastern India. These paintings are compared by Elwin to the comic strips of the modern world: they comprise stories with a strongly moral tone, where justice and truth always triumph in the end, though not without a struggle. Through their renditions of folk legends the Jadupatua scrolls purveyed 'some kind of elementary moral teaching, that pride and meanness and theft, and refusal to fulfil one's moral duty, are bad things.'[25]

The celebration of tribal life and values is inevitably a key motif in these essays. A series on forest tribes singled out the Baiga for 'their wit and poetry and character;' the Sacra for their industry, manifest in their carefully terraced fields, 'rightly praised as works of great engineering skill;' the Gadabas for their 'happiness . . . [their] jolly, carefree children' and the dignity, charm and independence of their women.[26] And with regard to the Muria love for dance, Elwin notes that the tribe 'can put on an evening's programme which is perhaps more varied and expert than anywhere else in India.'[27]

This celebration is as ever interwoven with a critique of civilized society. Sometimes the tribal ethos is claimed to be years ahead of the civilized: 'tribal women are as free today as all India's women were yesterday and will be tomorrow . . . There is no purdah, no ban on widow-remarriage; men and women work together as comrades in field and forest.' Much 'of what the women's reform leaders demand so sonorously from public platforms has been the Gadaba woman's right for generations.'[28] Or else, the presence of virtues in one society is highlighted to pinpoint their absence in another. A beautiful essay on games played by children of the forest ends with these words:

> . . . nearly all the games are just—games. There is singularly little competition. Even when villages dance against each other, or children go in for guessing games or Hunt the Slipper, there is no prize—or rather, as in "Alice," everybody wins and all have prizes. If a visitor offers a prize for any games the winning child immediately divides it with everybody else.
>
> . . . The tribal games do not divide people, do not excite jealousy or make a weak child despondent. The ugly, the poor, even the deformed have their full share in the fun, and no one is left out, no one loses, no one is ever a failure.
>
> There is much wisdom in these things.[29]

Cumulatively, Elwin's essays in the *Illustrated Weekly of India* hoped to persuade the Indian elite of the beauty, dignity and variety of tribal life. Tribals were not just an 'interesting and picturesque "extra," ' but worthy and hardworking citizens with much to contribute to national life. He asked his readers 'to use their influence wherever possible' in protecting tribal art and culture from the forces that threatened to destroy it.[30] As always, he hoped to foster an attitude of love and understanding towards the tribes. At the heart of all work for aboriginal India, he wrote, is

> the need for a change of attitude. Modern man must treat these people with respect. Words like 'backward,' 'uplift,' and all that savours of scorn or patronage must go from our vocabulary. Knowledge must come first and then the love that is the only thing strong and untainted enough to make work lasting. We have tried to work for this new attitude. By books, articles, films, pictures, lectures—extending now over a long period—we have tried to show the beauty and dignity of tribal life, that it is not something 'savage' of which we are to be ashamed and which we must eliminate, but that it is something with fine and durable values to give to modern India and the world.[31]

The modern man whose attention Elwin most eagerly sought was the Indian prime minister, Jawaharlal Nehru. The run-of-the-mill Congressman he despised, but Nehru was a different matter: fun-loving rather than puritanical, catholic rather than insular, liberal, humane, a writer and scholar, out of Harrow and Cambridge, in his own words the 'last Englishman to rule India.' Elwin's *Weekly* essays were meant for the intellectuals and civil servants who, at one or more remove, clustered around Nehru. Elwin must have hoped that they would be read by the prime minister too. On one occasion he was able to address the great man himself. Asked to write for a volume marking Nehru's sixtieth birthday, he commented on the 'strange link, which has often been noticed by travellers and scientists, between the most highly cultured and the most primitive of mankind.' Elwin had 'no doubt whatever that this instinctive rapport and sense of kinship is invariably felt by Jawaharlal Nehru whenever he meets an aboriginal.' The thirty million tribals of India, he went on, 'have cause to rejoice that in this time of rapid culture-change there is at the head of affairs a man who combines a scientific intelligence with a broad humanity.'[32]

In public Elwin urged a fair deal for the tribals. In private he continued to be deeply pessimistic about their future. Six months after independence he saw only 'one Protector of Aborigines in India, and that is the mosquito. May it infest every pietist and reformer with cerebral malaria.' There was no hope even for his beloved Bastar, which had been merged with the Central Provinces, 'and that means the end of the ghotul and the bison-horn dance within five (three, two?) years.' All that one could do, he remarked, 'was to assist at the funeral of delight and laughter in the tribal hills.'[33] Two years later, in July 1950, he had added one more Protector of the Aborigines, which were now 'the Mosquito and Corruption.' Where the mosquito might deter outsiders (unlike the tribals, not genetically protected against malaria), corruption made sure that 'the attempts to open up tribal territory by road fail because the Public Works Department officers pinch the money. Schools don't do much harm because the Inspector and teachers pinch the money. Even the reformers have caught the prevailing urge.'[34]

This was a depression reinforced by his circumstance: the loss of the Anthropological Survey job and Kosi, TWARU in constant need of his efforts to raise money, and not least a child to care for. Since Shamrao had several, the friends had invested in a house in Jabalpur. Kusum Hivale lived in the town with the children, who went erratically to school. Sham's wife wanted him with them, but he preferred to commute between Patangarh and Jabalpur. Sham was torn between family and friend: he was, as he wrote to Mrs Minnie Elwin, sometimes 'in a pathetic state, for I daren't leave Verrier alone in Patangarh during the rains [when he came down unfailingly with malaria], and at the same time I have frantic letters from Kusum and Suresh begging me to come to Jubbulpore. I am going tomorrow for a few days, but I have made all arrangements and I am sending [Verrier] plenty of vegetables, fruit, bread and even sardines from there.'[35]

Kumar lived with Shamrao's family, going to school with his mate Suresh Hivale and coming over to Patangarh during holidays. At this time (1951–2) he was, with Verrier's encouragement, playing with Meccano sets and collecting stamps, very English pastimes for a tropical boy with a tribal parent. The father thought the boy 'a beautiful and affectionate child:' to Verrier's delight he revealed a distinct talent for painting and drawing. Might he not, when he grew up, go to Tagore's school at Santiniketan? But the Gond in him would also come out, for there was little he liked better than climbing trees and imitating bird-calls. He was once thrown out of class for mewing like a cat, and a minor scandal erupted when he sold a New Testament (a present from his English grandmother) to a Parsi boy, buying himself sweets with the proceeds. The principal summoned the father, who was secretly pleased. His son, he thought, 'might do worse than become an anti-clerical gourmet.'[36]

The real trouble was that Kumar was hopelessly laggard at his studies. His father, alas, had little time to take care of *that*. At last, and reluctantly, Verrier decided to put Kumar in boarding school, choosing St Mary's, Bombay, where his progress would be watched over by priests and the family of the journalist Frank Moraes, whose son, the boy-poet Dom, was two classes ahead of him.[37]

Verrier went to Bombay when he could, taking his son to the beach and the zoo. In between visits he would be sent reports by Dom Moraes. 'Kumar is thriving, or so I think,' wrote the precocious guardian, 'but I don't think his exam results were very good. Does it matter?'[38] With the reports would be enclosed Dom's latest poems. The failed old poet and the aspiring younger one forged a deep friendship, helped no doubt by the absence of Dom's father—a famous and continually travelling editor— and the lack of learning of Verrier's son. The man criticized the boy's verses and introduced him to his own favourite poets: Dylan Thomas, Sidney Keyes and Wordsworth. From the jungle Verrier's 'long badly-typed letters crossed the thousands of miles to Bombay. They spoke of arduous trips and of fever, but only briefly: otherwise, as though he was writing them from rooms in All Souls, they discussed poetry, and on occasion, life.' Years later Moraes remembered the man himself as 'very tall, with a scholarly stoop. He had vividly blue eyes set in a kestrel face and longish, white raggedly out hair. He smoked terrible black cigars and chuckled constantly to himself . . . He loved poetry and in a way lived it.'[39]

Kumar had been placed, he hoped, in safe hands, but how to spend the rest of his own life remained a problem. The present headman of Patangarh, then a boy, remembers the daily routine, *c.* 1951–2, of the village's most distinguished resident. First, in the morning, Verrier would have his bed-tea (*palang chai*), at least three kettles of it, followed by a bath and breakfast. He would then retreat to his room, saying no one should disturb him, and work non-stop till lunch. A siesta, more work, a walk through the village, and it was time for dinner and bed. The little Pardhan boys would say of Verrier banging away on the typewriter: '*bade bhaiyya notaa chaap rahe hain*' (our older brother is printing [currency] notes).[40]

What he was doing was writing the essays that would bring him and Sham a few of those notes. But life in Patangarh was dreary, lacking variety and challenge, and newspaper articles bored him. Putting the last touches to *The Religion of an Indian Tribe*, Verrier felt 'so homesick for the Saora country I could almost cry, and I kick myself daily for not going and settling there while there was still time.' His 'real trouble,' he confessed to Bill Archer, was that he had

> an insatiable desire to experience and create—and neither seems within the bounds of possibility. Sex doesn't bother me very much now, at least not the sex that demands satisfaction. But I do want sexual stimulus. That is to say, whatever new research I do must be among a sexually attractive people—nudes or half-nudes. I don't want to have them, but I do like having them about.[41]

The tragedy was that the tribes of middle India, even the most isolated ones, were clothing themselves in the soiled garb of civilization. In January 1952 Verrier was on a field trip in South Bihar, scouting around without much enthusiasm for fresh tribes and fresh themes. He had with him a cook, a driver, and the indispensable Sunderlal but felt lonely, 'with no one to talk to in English. Shamrao, like an owl, is sitting in Jubbulpore.' Verrier wrote to Sham that either he must tour with him, or that he must himself marry Lila, or marry someone else, or get a 'new beautiful and intelligent male disciple. But there is no fun in touring by oneself like this.'[42]

He called on Bill Archer's old tribe, the Uraons, to find they had 'sadly deteriorated in the ten years since I was here last.' Fearful of puritans, they now referred to their dormitory, the *dhumkuria*, as the 'meeting-place.' The way Uraon women covered their heads at his approach made him feel as if he had entered a ladies' lavatory by mistake.[43] Sitting in a dreary rest house in the town of Hazaribagh he wrote to Archer:

> At fifty a man's chief temptation is to ask whether Pound the poet or the pound sterling is more important. I haven't any real doubts, but occasionally, especially when sitting on my arse all by myself in this conspicuously depressing dak bungalow, I wonder if I had . . . or if I had . . .
>
> What I really want, my Bill, is a woman and an assignment. How happy I was in Bastar with something to *do*, that called out something in me, and

when I could afford to do it. How happy too in Orissa. But now I have no more excuse to travel still that loved hillside . . .

When I say a woman, I mean a legal woman, a registered woman, a woman I can tell the world of, in brief a wife.[44]

The break-up with Kosi behind him, Verrier looked eagerly for a 'stable, happy marriage.' He was now willing to renounce the casual encounter for the right wife. Some clues to the kind of woman he was in search of might be found in his book on the Bondo, which was sent to press soon after his divorce. Among the Orissa tribe sexual practices were discreet, controlled and carefully guided; both boys and girls appeared to be 'remarkably abstinent during the pre-betrothal, if not the pre-marital period.' The Bondo were unique among the tribes he knew in their attitude to sex and marriage, seeking permanence and attachment rather than passion. In this respect at least the anthropologist had once more found a tribe to match his predilection and circumstance. In the nineteen thirties, when Elwin was unmarried and in the process of freeing himself from an ascetic past, he had gloried in the Baiga's open and joyful delight in sex. A little later, working with the Muria of Bastar while his own marriage was doing supremely well, he contrasted the tribe's premarital freedom with their post-marriage fidelity. Now with the Bondo, a failed marriage behind him, he marvelled at their steadiness and steadfastness, their search for a legal, lifelong, yet romantic attachment with a partner of their choosing.[45]

Despite his love for Lila, Verrier was worried that a second marriage to a tribal might end as badly as the first. Sometimes he felt that the right wife this time could only be an educated Indian. To Bill Archer he specified an awesome list of features. She must not be too soft, but something hard to strike on; musn't be too acquiescent or yielding; must have a mind and personality of her own like the poetess Sarojini Naidu but with sexual charm. Another model he had in mind was Shiela Auden, a great beauty from the Bengali aristocracy, herself a painter, married to John Auden of the Geological Survey of India.[46]

By the middle of 1952 Lila and he had been living together for almost three years. Some friends knew of her but the time had not come to make their relationship public or formal. She was pregnant once more, but this made him even more hesitant to make her his wife. It was decided now that India would be his country, but his partner and profession were yet unclear. In May he received a letter from Jehangir Patel asking him to look for a job, the implication being that the patronage was finite. Verrier wrote a pathetic letter to Victor expressing his mixed-up feelings for J. P.—

> So easy it is for a little Bombay cotton broker to write off the work and ideals of over twenty years. I have replied that I propose to carry on and do what I can. As a matter of fact, I wish I could get JP out of my hair; I think many people, with whom he is most unpopular, might give us more assistance and he is becoming more and more of an irritant rather than a help. But of course, I am very fond of him in one way and he has been a great help to us in the past.[47]

In the last week of May Lila gave birth to their second son, Nakul. The birth is merely noted, not commented upon, more space being given in his diary to a letter from the editor of the *Illustrated Weekly of India*, Shaun Mandy, passing on a communication he had received from Harold Acton. At Oxford the two had inhabited very different worlds, but Acton had now written to Mandy of his admiration for Elwin's writings and 'envy [of] his achievements, which makes me seem a sad materialist by contrast.' More cheering still was the news of an address delivered by Nehru to a conference of social workers in New Delhi. The prime minister had condemned those who wished to make tribals 'second-rate copies of ourselves.' Nehru said the civilized had much to learn from the tribals, for 'they are an extremely disciplined people, often a great deal more democratic than most others in India. Above all they are a people who sing and dance and try to enjoy life, not people who sit in stock exchanges, shout at one another and think themselves civilised.'[48] Verrier was buoyed by the report of a speech which was 'the Elwin message almost word for word on those illustrious lips. It must have driven the reformers to fury.' Although he acknowledged that Nehru's talk was 'as far from reality as I am,' he was now a 'little more hopeful about the future of the tribes.'[49]

In August 1952 Verrier was due for his customary visit to Bombay. This time the trip was a special one, to commemorate his fiftieth birthday and the completion of twenty years with the tribes. To get to Bombay from Patangarh was quite a task for two travellers who had neither the official support commanded by sahibs nor the comforts and conveniences of modern travel. Verrier and Sham, two middle-aged men, first walked five miles in the monsoon mud to the main road, then hitched a ride on a lorry to the nearest dak bungalow. Up early the next morning they took another lorry to Dindori town, then a bus to Jabalpur (this a seven-and-a-half hour ride, and bumpy), where they caught the train to Bombay.

Having got to the city, Verrier was a good deal more hopeful about his own future. Ebrahim Alkazi and Alyque Padamsee, young lions of the Bombay stage, had put up a production of Ibsen's *Ghosts* sponsored by the 'Verrier Elwin Committee.' The industrialist Sir Homi Mody presided over a Neptune Ball in aid of 'Verrier Elwin's Tribal Welfare and Art Research Unit.' Jehangir Patel, knowing little of his protege's mixed feelings, invited a hundred guests to the Taj Hotel for a lobster lunch in his honour, followed by a champagne dinner. This was the first of a round of parties in tribute:

> a great reception at the Rotary, flowers and flags, a dinner presided over by the Chief Justice who called me a 'great scholar and a great gentleman;' a grand other dinner by the Chairman of Indian Airways to which the American Consul and British High Commissioner and a score of others were called to meet me; and a tea party with the Indian Chancellor of the Exchequer; and drinks with India's most famous novelist [Mulk Raj Anand], and a gathering yesterday of an Art Society which made a chocolate cake in the shape and titling of *The Tribal Art of Middle India*.[50]

This account was penned for his mother, the bishop's wife, who was always impressed by big names. But Verrier was terrifically proud too. The affection and enthusiasm with which Shamrao and he were met and the coverage in the press (which had been particulary tickled by his remark that 'in the matter of puritanism, the people of Bombay and the aboriginals seem to be in the same boat') confirmed for him that their cause was prospering once more. From Bombay they proceeded to Delhi, where Verrier's talk at the Rotary Club was chaired by Jaipal Singh, also an Oxford man and a rising tribal politician from Bihar. When Verrier finished Jaipal offered a splendid vote of thanks in which 'he was so rude to the Hindus that my delicately put cracks were quite forgotten!' 'Our ceaseless propaganda is having a little effect,' wrote Verrier to his sister, 'even these wretched Congressmen are coming round a bit.' He was now feeling more secure: when Eldyth reported that a friend had told her 'India had finished with Verrier,' he replied angrily, ' I fear not.'[51]

In Delhi Verrier had hoped to meet Nehru, but the great man was on tour. He left a letter for him nonetheless: 'Dear Jawaharlalji,' he began,

> it is a long time since the days when I used to have the happiness of meeting you when I was working with Gandhiji, but I venture to write to you now. Partly I want to thank you for the magnificent speech you made on the tribal problem last June, which so exactly expressed my own feelings and which gave me personally enormous encouragement and support. It is now just 21 years since I first went to live among the tribal people, but nothing has cheered me so much and promised greater happiness for the people whose own I have become.

He told Nehru of his wish to study the beautiful objects of Assam in order to write a sequel to his *Tribal Art of Middle India*. He did not need the state's support—the money was being raised, as ever, from the Bombay millionaires—but sought its seal of approval. 'It would help me greatly,' he wrote, 'if I knew I had your approval of this and perhaps commendation from you to the Assam Government.'[52]

Nehru then wrote, in the manner of one wretched Congressman to another, to the governor of Assam, Jairamdas Daulatram. The governor was a practical fellow, a no-nonsense Gandhian: why should he allow the anthropologist to collect art when he could be of much better use to him and his government? Daulatram invited Elwin to Assam for three months. He could do his research on the side, but he might also write a report on the prospects for the region's tribes who were untouched by Hindu influence and prone to rebellion against the state.

To Verrier, looking for a way out of the mess in Mandla, this was an offer he could scarcely refuse. The Assam trip was pregnant with promise but also fraught with danger. Indications that Verrier thought it might be another turning point in his life, the last perhaps, lie in a will he drafted the week before he was due to go. This left five thousand rupees, the bulk of his savings, to Lila, the rest to Sham. He was not leaving any money separately to his son, he said, for Kumar already had shares and certificates in his name and would inherit money from his aunt Eldyth. However, Verrier directed 'Mr and Mrs Hivale to care for him as if he was their own child.' As for his other possessions, the library went to Shamrao, 'except that I direct that my copy of Temple's "Legends of the Punjab" which is one of the few perfect copies in existence, shall be presented to the National

Library, Calcutta, and that my copy of Dalton's "Descriptive Ethnology of Bengal" shall be presented to Mr J. P. Patel.' Finally, his 'collection of ethnographic negatives should be presented by Mr Hivale to any person or institution which in his opinion is likely to make good use of it. The five reels of cine-film now with my sister Eldyth should be presented to the Royal Anthropological Institute.'[53]

Verrier set out with Shamrao for Assam on 15th November, driving from Patangarh across the breadth of the subcontinent. Calling at Jabalpur, Maihar, Banaras and Gaya, they arrived after a week at a dak bungalow on the banks of the Brahmaputra, their first stop in Assam. They had driven through shifting landscapes—flat plains, sal forests, tea gardens—and their accommodation had been as varied—'one night in a comfortable hotel, one night in a Punjabi hotel crawling with bugs, sometimes on the ground, sometimes in the car.' And now at last they were in Assam; looking out across the water to the Himalaya the state presented 'a lovely first view to the visitor.'

On 3rd December Verrier met the governor in Shillong. From 'this enchanting place, with its pines, lakes and perfect scenery and friendly people, both great and small,' he moved on to an extended tour of the Nagas of Manipur. He was fifty and overweight and the marches were hard—rough paths straight over the crest of eight-thousand-foot mountains—but the Nagas hospitable and the views magnificent. Verrier revelled in 'the natural scenery and the charm of the people,' gathering for his collection specimens of cloth and ornaments. In a village high up in the Thangkhul Naga hills, with an Assamese deputy commissioner who also adored P. G. Wodehouse, he felt 'on top of the world.'[54] They had climbed all day, arriving at their destination to find before them a

> scene of fantastic and unearthly beauty. In a great grove of orange trees some thirty splendid youths, their limbs glowing golden in the setting sun, clad in rich red cloth and having on their heads great white crowns like wings, were marching up and down with spears, and chanting ancient melodies that recalled a long-forgotten world. It was a death chant, and it was one that I should be proud to have sung over my own body when it goes to the dust.[55]

Here were people who really lived: their control over land and forest complete, their traditions of weaving and dance splendidly intact. Singing, dancing, eating in common out of a great big wooden platter, these were tribes that had not decayed. Verrier later recalled feeling 'violently excited' by the tribes he saw on this trip.[56] He was now convinced that his future, or what was left of it, lay in the north-east. Stopping at enchanting Shillong on his way home he submitted his report to the governor with a personal note asking him to 'look on me as someone who would count it a great happiness to be at any time of service to you in the Adibasi cause.'[57]

On his way back from Assam Verrier tarried awhile in Calcutta. Walking down Chowringhee one day he was stopped by two American girls. 'Was he Dr Elwin,' they asked. They had seen a photograph of him in *The Statesman*—then, as now, with his trademark cigar. The girls, or ladies rather, were Jean Merrill and Ronnie Silbert, Fulbright scholars in their late twenties, one studying folk-tales, the other folk-lore. They were pleased to meet the established scholar and he was delighted with Jean in particular. She was pretty and witty, a former journalist who was 'very sound on Ezra Pound.' For two weeks they saw Calcutta through his eyes and then Verrier invited them to Patangarh. His friend John Auden believed the American girls were lovers but Verrier thought (or hoped) not. Sham and he had convinced themselves that in Jean lay the 'perfect solution to our problems.' After the girls came to Patan Verrier took Jean for a walk up the hill and proposed to her. Alas, she turned him down like a 'bloody bedspread,' although she was very sweet about it.

Verrier was disconsolate—'I have given civilisation its last chance and it doesn't want me,' he wrote to Victor. His feelings were expressed in language that came out of Jane Austen via P. G. Wodehouse:

> If the Creator had sat down to think out how to make a perfect wife for that poor fish Verrier, and had made her to my ideal specifications, with a few improvements of his own, he would have produced something like Jean, not quite so good perhaps but near it. We had built up a whole world of dreams; we had made our arrangements with Lila; I had a bottle of champagne ready, and now . . .[58]

One doesn't know how seriously to take all this. I suspect Verrier fell in love with the idea of Jean, the idea of a girl who was well read, urbane, civilized, up on poetry and literature and the cinema, in sum everything a tribal girl was not. There was the feeling in him that if at fifty he let go of this apparition of beauty and beatitude, nothing like it would come his way again. He also seems to have mistaken the typical American openness and frankness for amorous interest, even love. In relation to Lila, even if he had made no commitment of formal matrimony, his behaviour seems less easy to excuse: she was already the mother of his children. On Jean's part one supposes she was not uninterested in a fling with a widely travelled and experienced Englishman—though it appears the affair was not consummated—but marriage was a different kettle of fish altogether. Why would a Fulbright scholar chuck up country, career, prospects, for an isolated life in village India of the fifties?

In his diary Verrier marked the last day of February with a line by Sidney Keyes: 'There was a month and two people walked in it'—and continued:

> What a month! I shall never write the word 'February' without a slight tremor. It has been dominated by the Impossible She, who should have been the ideal, the perfect solution. It has been a month of paralysis, of bittersweet lessons learnt about myself, of great goodness and unselfishness on the part of Sham [who was prepared both to accept Jean and to supervise an amicable parting with Lila], of love from Wasant, of passionate affection from Lila, of divided aims, of conflicting duties. I thought I might grow young again, that life would become a new thing. But evidently it was not to be that way, so we must find another way. The essential thing is that failure in one thing should never mean failure in everything. The essential thing is that we should not let disappointment make me old. The greatest problem of all is to remain young. Our real enemy is not scandal, nor poverty, nor hardship, nor even our vices—but Time. Jean would have halted Time— she would have, as Rabelais might have said, touched its arse with a thistle.[59]

That Verrier was more in love with the idea than the person is made to seem more likely by the verve with which he bounced back. For close at hand was the Other Way, the Possible She. She would keep him young, was in fact keeping him young. Soon after Jean left Patan he decided he would make a honest man of himself by marrying Lila. He introduced his future wife to his mother in the most roundabout way. 'I forgot if I told you,' he wrote, 'I had adopted a lovely little Pardhan boy called Wasant, who is now about two-and-a-half years old and is completely fascinating.' It took another three months for Wasant to be identified as Lila's child. On 19th June Verrier wrote home of his decision to marry again:

> Dr Johnson said of a friend who married a second time that it was the 'triumph of hope over experience,' and let us hope that Hope, that blessed thing, will be rewarded this time. I did not write about it before because I was not quite certain, and I never like to start a hare until it is necessary!
>
> Her name is Lila, and she is a Pardhan, a member of the tribe about whom Shamrao has written. The Pardhans are the witty, charming, music-and-poetry-loving tribe who live with the Gonds and give life to them. Lila is 30 years old and has two exquisite little boys, from a previous husband whom she has divorced. One of them is Wasant, whom I have already adopted, and who is the joy of my life, the most perfect child I have ever seen. I will send you photos of them by the next mail. She is a very sweet girl, beautiful to look at, good-tempered, doesn't drink, and will be a great help to us in our work, for she is extremely competent. When our grass was burnt this year, she immediately set to (when Sham and I were away) and got 20,000 bundles of new grass—had she not done so we would never have been able to build the house. She is very tender-hearted towards the poor . . . She can read and write in Hindi, and I am teaching her English. I think she will be a very good wife, especially as she is very fond of me.[60]

The fib about the children from a previous husband was necessary under the circumstances. Otherwise, Verrier was stressing what made Lila different from Kosi—the domesticity, the stability, the abstinence—but his mother and Eldyth were 'terribly disturbed' by the news. Mrs Elwin wrote to Kusum Hivale of her wish that Verrier could marry again,

> *suitably*, but to again marry a girl from a tribe, however dear and fine she may be, involves too many risks—too much of what she may inherit and pass on to his children, if he has any more. He is now a man of position and influence and as such should travel widely and have contact with many men and women. I pray much about it and for my darling first born—but I dare not interfere and in any case, he takes his own way—and his poor old mother hasn't much influence.[61]

The devoted Shamrao, pressed by Verrier to comfort Mother, insisted that 'there was no fear of it turning out the way his first marriage did.' Lila 'understands Verrier and his ways almost as well as I do;' she would make a great difference to the eleven months of the year that her son spent in village India.[62]

Mrs Elwin remained unconvinced, as did Verrier's friends. Bill Archer, who had welcomed Kosi straightaway, this time warned that 'trouble' would start if Lila accompanied her husband to Bombay or Calcutta, for she might have 'her head turned by her status.'[63] Jehangir Patel assured Verrier of his 'full co-operation if you do marry Lila,' but felt nevertheless that the advantages

> are more than counter-balanced to my way of thinking (and I may be wrong) by the blunt fact that Lila will not be able to become your companion as far as your 'head' is concerned. A wife should be a pal for 'the head and the heart' and now around the age of 50 the 'head' is more than the heart to be reckoned with. If you are not able to satisfy Lila the same thing will happen as with Kosi. Of one thing I am quite sure and confident and that is on no account should you have any more children. It's selfish and most unfair to the child. Perhaps and naturally Lila will want a child. The fact that she has already experienced motherhood—as you informed me—is also against your union being happy.[64]

The words of caution were well meant, but Verrier had made up his mind to trust in Hope over Experience. Within all this dilly-dallying over Lila, it seems always implicit that Lila herself would want nothing other than marriage to Elwin; which, given the times and the context in which she was placed, was almost certainly true. Elwin asked the registrar of marriages in Jabalpur for a date but was told they would have to wait two months. In anticipation he set about remodelling their house. The best Gond artists were called in to decorate the living room: one wall painted over with animals, tiger, crabs and cows, the other with warriors fighting and magicians 'divining all sorts of things.' The bathroom had a scene of Gond girls at a well, trees growing exuberantly above. The carpenters meanwhile had put his books in a glass-fronted case, his radio-set in a recess tastefully tucked away in the wall.

The house having now become a home, Lila and he were married before a magistrate in Jabalpur on 20th September 1953. That morning he felt a last twinge of panic, but with an effort of will it disappeared: 'Felt apprehensive at dawn that this was perhaps the most foolish thing I had ever done. Social death, the end of my career, a finis to sexual adventure, a lifetime of low-voltage contentment—are these ahead of me now? Later, cheered up a bit. This is a good thing to do. I have loved Lila for a long time and still love her and she loves me. The way of attainment is through endless pity, forgiveness, love—and I need these things fully as much as she does.'⁶⁵

His town friends threw a party after the registration, the scene finely described by the bridegroom-novelist-anthropologist: 'The Nags provided Indian sweets and the traditional sprinkling with rose-water. Ishwar Singh, the old fat ex-Director of Public Instruction; the Deputy Inspector-General of Police; Romesh Misra, the family doctor; Narad, the chief journalist in his Gandhi cap; the Director of Railway Traffic and his pretty wife; the Conservator of Forests and some others.'⁶⁶ In the last category fell an old student of Deccan College in Poona, who in the thirties had been lectured to by the *upacharya* of the Christa Seva Sangh. 'To hear Father Elwin read Shakespeare was an unforgettable experience,' as indeed twenty years later was the first sight of his second wife. Lila on the day of the wedding, wrote this former student, was 'young, dark and healthy in appearance, her masses of hair extravagantly oiled falling about her shoulders, like a mantle.'⁶⁷

Unlike the first time, registration at Jabalpur was not followed by a formal village wedding (and the groom prudently refrained from writing an essay titled 'I Married a Pardhan'), but the celebrations in Patangarh were anything but muted. A huge feast was thrown on the 30th for 312 invited guests and a number of gatecrashers. The party began with drums and music at eight in the morning. The goats were killed at ten and drinks served at noon. By early afternoon the crowd had begun to warm up, and Lila and Verrier were whirled round an improvised marriage pole. The company only sat down for lunch at six-thirty and stragglers were still being served food at midnight.

Verrier had his wife. All that remained now was the assignment. In May the education minister of the Government of India had written offering him the directorship of the Anthropological Survey, in succession to B. S. Guha, but the pay was not enough to 'reconcile one to living in a city like

Calcutta.' He also had word that he might be asked to advise the governor of Assam, a job he 'would like to do even if they paid nothing.'[68] He suspected that Guha, his friend turned rival, had suggested Verrier's name for this, if only to clear the decks for his getting another term at the survey.

Anyway, once the balloon was floated it was kept aloft by some officials at the ministry of external affairs who admired Elwin, and by their boss who admired him too. Nehru had recommended Elwin to the governor of Assam in November 1952; later, when sent his tour report, he forwarded it to all chief ministers of states with tribal populations, asking them to take heed of its warning that if 'we try to impose our ways on [tribals], imagining that we are doing them good . . . , we merely alienate them and, at the same time, probably injure them in many ways. They lose their artistic way of life and become drab imitations of something else.'[69] Now, as minister for external affairs (a portfolio he held all through his prime ministership), he quickly acquiesced to the suggestion that the anthropologist be drafted into the administration. With his approval Verrier was appointed, in November 1953, as Tribal Adviser to the administration of the North East Frontier Agency (NEFA), based in Shillong. The appointment took effect from the 1st of January 1954, in the first instance for a period of three years.[70]

In the second week of December Verrier visited Delhi to be briefed. Lila came with him and acquitted herself splendidly in their meetings with ministers, members of parliament, writers and journalists. His wife, he told his mother, met 'all these VIP's with such poise and charm—a week turned her into a new girl.' In Delhi he 'fell in love with her all over again.' She even accompanied him to Teen Murti House, where they had breakfast with its occupant. Lila's impressions of the prime minister are not known but her husband was carried away: 'What a charmer he is! And what style he keeps!' They saw his Giant Panda, and when the two men went for a walk in the garden, Nehru told Elwin he hoped he would advise them not only on the frontier but 'on the whole tribal problem in India.'[71]

Lesser Indians whom Verrier met in Delhi included the health minister Rajkumari Amrit Kaur (another ex-inmate of Sabarmati), the writer Khushwant Singh and assorted MPs from the north-east. He also met Gandhi's son Devadas (now the editor of the *Hindustan Times*), who asked after mother and Eldyth, and the Mahatma's secretary, 'dear old Pyarelal, now married to a sweet ugly little woman, who also enquired tenderly for you both.'[72] Calling on Gandhians, being briefed by Congress ministers, Verrier had made an honourable peace with Indian nationalism.

The Elwins returned to Patangarh only to pack and leave in a hurry. Verrier knew already that this was a job with real possibilities: for in isolated NEFA, tucked away in a corner of the Himalaya between India, Burma and Tibet, there was still hope the 'tribesmen would escape the cultural and moral degradation that is rapidly overtaking their fellows in some other parts of India.'[73] He was much pleased by a letter from J. R. D. Tata who was 'happy that the Government of India have at last awakened to your existence and immense value to the country, in your life-time.'[74] Tata wrote this as one whose own value to India was never really recognized by the powerful, within whose blinkered socialism even the most patriotic and productive industrialists were suspected of avarice.

Verrier felt like someone who 'asked for a sandwich and has been handed a eight-course banquet.' His contract was for three years but the ministry told him they would like him to go on till he was dead. 'This is a stupendous business,' he told his friend and editor R. E. Hawkins, 'and I don't know how far I will be able to fulfil it. But the field is so exciting and so virginal that I will do my best to penetrate it.' Sham would stay on in Mandla for the time being, but if 'all goes well we might hand over the Patan show to another organization and shift everything to Assam for a final effort before departing this life.'[75]

Verrier confided to his diary that his emotions on leaving Patangarh were 'less acute than I feared. I hate leaving the house, every corner of which was built with such loving care; but the garden is rather a flop and the people whom we have loved for so long, have become rather boozed and dreary. I have a feeling that we have done our stuff here and perhaps the new Assam assignment will prove a much bigger and more exciting thing, a door to a new life, to being useful for once.'[76]

To his new boss, the governor of Assam, Verrier wrote of his wish to start, on the side, an independent research institute with 'associated welfare activities' to be run by his companion of the past quarter-century. He hoped thus to 'gradually close down our work in Mandla and bring everything over here. Shamrao Hivale, who has been with me for 27 years and from I do not like to be separated, might well be used by us . . .' While Sham awaited the call, Verrier would move to Shillong, a change of residence that also involved a final and irrevocable change in nationality. He had already asked for the forms through which to apply for Indian citizenship, writing to the governor that he was now 'spending his last few days on earth as a formal Englishman.'[77]

CHAPTER ELEVEN

A Sahib (Sometimes) in the Secretariat

Grigson has pulled over his creative activity the very efficient condom of official promotion.
Verrier Elwin to W. G. Archer, August 1942

I don't think we can live without each other—at least I can't. You have your work and books, but I seem to have nothing. But I do have you that I know.
Shamrao Hivale to Verrier Elwin, November 1953

In December 1953 Verrier Elwin flew from Calcutta to Guwahati and took a taxi to Shillong. Following him forty-four years later I found the road out of the airport lined with policemen, a man with a rifle at every fifty yards. The driver explained that the prime minister had been in Guwahati the previous day, inaugurating his party's campaign for the forthcoming general election. Such politicians, coming and going, were now potential targets for the insurgents of the United Liberation Front of Assam.

Just before the bridge over the Brahmaputra river we turned right, bypassing Guwahati town. We crossed the border into the state of Meghalaya, carved out of Assam in 1972. Flatlands gave way very quickly to hills and the policemen disappeared. I tried to match the landscape to others I knew. The shape and height of the hills were reminscent of my native Garhwal, but the hills themselves were greener and not disfigured by limestone mines or steeply cut terraces or eucalyptus plantations. Bananas like Bengal, areca nut palms like the Western Ghats of Karnataka, sal trees like Madhya Pradesh—out here *everything* seems to grow. The predatory capitalism of the rich and the over-population of the poor have not reached this part of the world.

We climbed higher, along a surprisingly gentle gradient. The hills were still richly covered with trees, plants, creepers, bushes; now and then an odd pine, and a lovely tree with lilac blossoms. Also a sign, every two hundred yards, asking us to KEEP MEGHALAYA GREEN—which it is. We rounded a bend and saw water. It was a lake, getting bigger and bigger, curving round two hills, enveloping them. Some foreigners were nearby filming the water. I asked the Bengali driver what the lake was called. 'Barapani,' he replied, 'Big Water.' So it appears to the plainsman, but the local Khasi, as I was to discover, call it 'Umiam,' or tear-drop.

After Barapani the pines dominate: pines, peasants, lakes, hills. They had once beckoned the Wordsworth-worshipping Elwin. Even the village houses were pretty, built on stilts and with quaint little windows.

We approached the city on the hill. On its outskirts is a settlement called Mawlai, peopled by Khasis originally converted by Welsh Presbyterians. In three minutes, and looking all to one side of the road, a church advertised 'Bible Study Classes,' a house was called Amazing Grace; there was a theological college, a graveyard, a Mary Magdalene Convent. It seemed an old settlement. Elwin would have passed it on his way up. But was Shillong so expressively Christian then? Perhaps not. In 1954 this was not the state of Meghalaya, but the state of Assam, whose capital city was run by Hindus. Only after they departed down to Guwahati did the Khasis come into their own.

By the time I reached my lodgings it was five o'clock, too late and dark to visit the Elwins. I walked down to the bazaar and bought the day's newspapers. Two reports dominated the front page: Prime Minister Inder Kumar Gujral's speech in Guwahati and a series of bomb blasts on certain trains. The previous day, I suddenly realized, had been 6th December, the fifth anniversary of the demolition by a Hindu mob of the Babri Masjid in Ayodhya. Gujral marked the occasion with a homily on the traditions of Indian secularism, on the need to make minorities safe and secure in the land. The bombs were the handiwork of Muslim extremists, an act of vengeance for the work, five years earlier, of their Hindu counterparts.

I. K. Gujral was the poor man's Jawaharlal Nehru, a politician schooled in the old school of Indian nationalism. He lacked Nehru's charm, charisma, intellect, and moral authority, but stood nonetheless for the same idea of India: an India that is inclusive, tolerant, accommodating different faiths and traditions: the idea of India that Elwin came to Shillong to help Nehru build, the India now threatened by corrosive corruption from within and religious fundamentalism from without. As I walked down to dinner I recalled, with a chill not owing to the winter wind, a remark by Elwin: 'If, after the passing of the present leadership in India, there was a strong reaction towards a more orthodox Hinduism, as many leading Christians and Muslims, rightly or wrongly, fear, then the Christian tribals would be likely to react against India.'[1]

Verrier Elwin approached his new job with much excitement and just a little trepidation. 'If I am to succeed in this Frontier assignment,' he noted in his diary,

    certain things will be vitally necessary:

1. Physical fitness, for which
   I must be careful not to exceed in food or drinks
   I must not over-tire myself unnecessarily
   I must have a better and fuller sex-life with Lila

2. Mental fitness, involving
   elimination of irritated thoughts
   elimination of petty grievances
   elimination of worry about small things
   elimination of jealousy

3. Financial stability, for which
   I must save all I can
   Avoid expenditure on alcohol
   I must spend more on essentials.

This was written on Christmas Eve 1953, in Patangarh. The next week Verrier set off for Calcutta, where he picked up his friend Victor Sassoon.

They flew to Guwahati on New Year's Eve and drove on to Shillong. Victor helped find a decent house, a lovely isolated bungalow on a hill, shaded by pines and with a garden full of marigolds. Restoring the water supply, which had been cut off by the neighbour after a fight with the previous occupant, was Verrier's first priority; the purchase of a second-hand car, which was also chosen by Victor, was the next. There was no telephone, but 'after twenty years of Mandla anything seems comfortable.' Shillong itself, with its bracing climate and pine forests, reminded him of the Alps. 'I wished we had always lived here,' he wrote to his mother; 'the air is delicious, like Swiss air, and it will probably add ten years to my life.' Lila and the boys had also arrived. He was pleased, she much more so, telling him: 'How happy I am when I am with you.'[2]

Elwin's appointment was for three years in the first instance, at a salary of Rs 1500 per month, the rent paid for. But as he told the governor, 'I now want to settle down in Assam for good, whether or not my official services are required later.' There was here a 'whole new world of exploration and research;' with luck he might independently open a small institute for research and welfare. If that took off they would close down their work in Mandla and Shamrao would come and join him. His old mate, Elwin told the governor, was 'uniquely gifted in dealing with tribal people. I hope that in the end he will come here and work with me, either officially or unofficially.'[3]

In his first fortnight at Shillong Verrier bumped into Devadas Gandhi. Devadas was in town, showing a film of the Old Man. To Elwin, his half-brother in a manner of speaking, he was 'most friendly.' The meeting with the younger Gandhi was symbolic, for Verrier was an employee of the Government of India, hoping also to become a citizen of India. In his citizenship application he provided a crisp summary of all that he had done in and for his adopted land: his association with Gandhi during the Civil Disobedience movement, his reports on behalf of the Congress in Gujarat and the North-West Frontier, his twenty years' work for the tribals of central India. 'I mention these things,' he told the official processing his request, 'to show that my desire for Indian citizenship is not a new or merely sentimental thing, but has been tested by circumstances over a long period. And further India is my home and my love; I am deeply attached to her thought, her culture and her people; half my life has been spent within her borders; and I have the happiness to be married to an Indian lady.'[4]

In an appendix to his application Elwin listed the places where he had been resident since September 1927: as a Christian for the Congress with the Christa Seva Sangh in Poona; as a social worker with Shamrao and the Gond Seva Mandal in Mandla; as a roving ethnographer on his own in Bastar and Orissa; as a research administrator with the Anthropological Survey in Banaras and Calcutta; as an adviser to government in Shillong. Many different homes and assignments: but there was one entry I have left out. Against the years 1929–30 was inserted: 'Sabarmati Ashram, Ahmedabad, Bombay Presidency.'

While a frequent visitor to Sabarmati, Elwin was never strictly speaking resident there. To call Gandhi's ashram one of his Indian homes was not of course a patent untruth, more an embellishment. But that he sought to place it alongside his more authentic homes reveals the continuing insecurity of an Englishman in hyper-nationalist India. For if any claim could certify his patriotism, it was this.

* * *

The North East Frontier Agency (NEFA) is now Arunachal Pradesh, a full-fledged state of the Indian Republic, with its own legislature and council of ministers. In January 1954, however, it was directly under the Foreign Ministry at New Delhi. The governor of Assam, based in Shillong, was in effect the Government of India's man on the spot, with additional charge of NEFA. A key figure was the adviser to the governor, in Verrier Elwin's time usually a member of the Indian Civil Service. Elwin's own designation was 'Adviser on Tribal Affairs.'

Placed where the Himalaya move into monsoon South East Asia, Arunachal Pradesh is a land of extraordinary beauty, dominated by steep mountains, thick forests and fast-flowing rivers. The hills climb up to Tibet on one side, Bhutan on another, Burma on a third. More than half the size of England, the territory was in 1954 home to a mere half million people, most of them swidden cultivators. The pastoralists of the high valleys near Tibet practised Buddhism; otherwise the tribes were marked by a heterogeneity of belief and custom, worrisome to the administrator but, one supposes, attractive to the anthropologist.

British rule had exercised a shadowy suzerainty over NEFA. Three political officers had controlled the territory, their main job being to prevent tribals raiding the Assam tea estates. About once a year they undertook a long march through their domain, accompanied by a couple of hundred coolies and bodyguards carrying salt and tea and tobacco for the chiefs. The main nationalist party, the Congress, had no presence here. In parts of Nagaland, which bordered NEFA to the south-east and where American missionaries were active, there had arisen a separatist movement led by A. Z. Phizo.

The Government of India, coming in when the British left, knew it must move slowly among a potentially hostile populace divided into numerous tribes, previously unknown to science and to Hindu civilization. An elected assembly on the principle of universal adult franchise was deemed premature; advocated instead were village and district councils through which the 'most educated and progressive' tribals might be associated with the administration. To make them and their fellows feel 'one with India,' officers were chosen and trained with care. As a foreign ministry official wrote in 1953, NEFA required 'special types of officials and workers who will go and mix with [the tribals] socially, live and eat with them and endear themselves to them by serving their real interests.'[5]

The new Adviser on Tribal Affairs had much practice in living and eating with the tribes. Now there were new ones to know and the family had barely settled in when Verrier was off on his first tour. He chose for this the Tuensang Frontier Division bordering the Naga Hills, the scene of a bloody encounter with the army just the previous October. The governor offered him an escort; this he refused, saying that as a disciple of Gandhi he would go to the Nagas non-violently.

Verrier deposited his citizenship forms on 27th February; the next morning he left on a two-month-long trip. From Shillong he went by car to Jorhat, the Assam town surrounded by tea plantations; from there by jeep to Mokokchung, a distance of forty-seven miles which he had walked in 1947 to visit Bill Archer. The next morning the jeep took him to Tuensang town, where the road ended.

Over the next seven weeks Verrier walked more than two hundred miles amidst superb scenery, fine weather and new tribes. These last he knew would fall on his route, and so he took along only one book, Boswell's *Life of Johnson*.

The first tribe he met depressed him. They were the Tagins of the Sipi valley, horribly affected by dermatitis, their white skin peeling off in flakes. The Tagins 'make one want to weep, poor creatures; they are half-starved, have no dances, no arts (except cane-work) and not even any stories.' He moved on to the Konyaks, a tribe more to his liking. They had wonderful glowing bodies and fine skills in woodcraft, brassware and weaving; indeed the boys and girls were 'in the ornamentation of their own persona, themselves works of art.' Verrier stayed in a *morung*, the village dormitory or guard-house, with its lavatory above a pig-sty outside. The idea was to squat and shit from a raised platform while the animals below cleaned up the bounties they received from above. The arrangements appealed to Verrier; he felt so fit all week that on only one occasion 'did the pigs turn away from their breakfast, rightly revolted.'[6]

Two poems written in quick succession nicely capture Verrier's conflicting emotions, the romance of being with new tribes tempered with the responsibility towards what he had waiting for him in Shillong. The first one is

ON A KONYAK GIRL SEEN AT NIGHT
Delicate light of a torch
On bare delicate limbs
In a dark street.

Golden-brown the porch
Of the house of desire.
Swift were her feet.

Where were you going? To steal
The heart of a lover waiting
Behind the door?

At least he could touch you, feel
And enter the luminous house.
I only saw.

This reads like one of his better, more heartfelt efforts, yet it made him feel guilty, for on the next page of his diary we find a tribute

A SAHIB (SOMETIMES) IN THE SECRETARIAT 241

TO LILA, ON BEING BORED AT MON

Great hills lie lonely broadening down
To desolate valleys cut by angry streams
And the shadows of the clouds pass over them,
But there is no one, no one but in my dreams.

No one at all to whom I can open my heart.
Yet there is everyone, a world of beauty around
Beauty delicate, stirring, abiding yet quickly passing,
As lovely, as elusive as I have ever found.

The laughter, excitement, wonder passes me by,
For without you to share it, what is the gain?
The lonely heart turns only in on itself,
And joy in solitude is three parts pain.

When will you come to me, breaking out of my dream?
Tangibly come with your quiet and tender heart?
Or, must I hasten to you, forgetting adventure,
Crossing the cruel hills, all that hold us apart?

The Konyaks and their neighbours, the Phoms, had been headhunters, and headhunting had been recently forbidden by the Government of India. As the first outsider to move in these villages without an escort, Elwin found the people friendly but not pleased with the ban. 'If you talk to a Phom or Konyak on such tedious topics as theology, economics or social organization he quickly slips away to have a refreshing drink of rice-beer. Open the question of head-hunting and his eyes light up, his whole body comes to life and a torrent of exciting and highly improper information pours from his lips.'[7]

In the village of Shiangha Chingnyu, where 400 skulls were displayed in the morung, the headman told Verrier their one desire was to go to war again. 'Our young men have become women,' he said, 'our soil is no longer fertile.' Across the valley was Chokayu village which had lost 700 heads on a tragic morning in 1947: *they* were quite happy with the ban. Elwin allowed that the stop to head-hunting without a shot being fired had been a 'marvellous achievement.' But as it happened the dance among the Konyak had since become 'deplorably dull,' and the once splendid morungs had fallen into disrepair. A real need was 'to find a moral substitute for head-hunting'—dance, art, weaving, games—'something that will preserve the qualities of courage and daring, of discipline and organization, of artistic effort and colour that characterise head-hunting and war.'

An alternative moral code of a kind had begun seeping into Tuensang. This was the Baptist faith, brought in by Ao pastors from Nagaland. Verrier found fifty schools in the division run via 'remote control' by American priests themselves forbidden to enter NEFA. But the native evangelists trained by them were, alas, 'more fanatical, more irresponsible, and more effective than any foreigners could be,' teaching 'undiluted communalism' in the form of religion, promoting a 'scurrilous villification' of Hinduism, promising material advance through conversion, sowing the seeds of separatism. The teaching of the pastors, he thought, led 'straight to a xenophobic and separatist mentality in which there can be no love for "heathen" India.' But his worries were as much aesthetic as political. The Baptists he termed, in an inspired comparison, 'the R.S.S. of Christianity,' like that Hindu sect reducing a great religion to a set of narrow-minded prejudices. It would rob the tribesmen of their art, their dance, their colour, and give nothing in return. He quoted R. S. Thomas on the work of the Baptists in the Welsh valleys:

> The adroit castrator
> Of art: the bitter negation
> of song and dance and the heart's innocent joy.
> You have botched our flesh and left us only the soul's
> Terrible impotence in a warm world.

Wandering in Tuensang, among naked or near-naked people—'the more naked a tribe is the more fuss it makes about its clothes, when it wears them'—caught up in the excitement of the chase, identifying and parrying the shafts of civilization, Verrier was defending aboriginals once more, and with an official mandate to boot. His Tuensang report—thirty closely typed foolscap pages—was a harbinger of dozens to come that likewise mixed reportage with poetry, philosophy and practical action. The principle he held out to the locust-army of officials coming into NEFA was that 'it is better to let change come from within rather than be imposed from outside.' He was especially angered by the mockery of tribal customs. One schoolmaster instructed Phom women not to shave their heads; an official dressed the boys in hideous and ill-fitting black suits; another warned that the government would be displeased if they did not abandon the custom of placing their dead in the high branches of banyan trees. This last interference brought forth a passage of vintage Elwinism:

> Now although in the cosmopolitan city of Bombay, one of India's most advanced communities [the Parsis] expose their dead to the beaks and claws of vultures, although in Benares the corpses of those [Hindus] dying of cholera are flung upon the bosom of Mother Ganges and allowed to drift down the stream, I agree that it would be a good thing if the Phoms and Konyaks buried, or better still, cremated their dead. On the other hand, the evils of their usual custom have been exaggerated. I went very carefully into this, visiting the disposal-places in every village, and I found that generally the dead were treated with reverence and dignity. The bodies were wrapped in cloth and leaves, often placed in wooden coffins, and with very few exceptions, placed well outside the village. Great care is taken to decorate the tomb, grave-effigies are carved, and some of the Konyaks make remarkable stone amphoras in which the skulls are ultimately interred.
>
> Now we have already disturbed tribal sentiment to the depths by stopping head-hunting. The people are saying that their crops are less fertile, their young men less virile. This is inevitable. But I wonder if it is wise to inflict a still further blow to tribal sentiment by interfering with their death-customs. Anyone who has read Frazer's 'The Fear of the Dead in Primitive Religion' will know how extraordinarily sensitive tribal people are to everything connected with the disposal of a corpse. Should there now be an epidemic, or a crop-failure, it might well be attributed to the fact that corpses are being buried instead of being disposed of in the classic manner.... A Gaonbura who was showing me the new graves said rather bitterly, 'You see we are all Christians now.'

In mid-April Verrier returned to Shillong, establishing a pattern followed unvaryingly for the next few years: summers in the secretariat, winters on tour. Shillong itself was a charming little town, a smaller, less stuffy version of the great imperial summer capital, Simla. And Verrier was now a sahib. The casual attire of shirt and shorts or kurta pyjama, which had carried him through twenty years in central India, had been exchanged for a suit and tie—in office, at any rate. At home he liked to wear an Adi coat over his shirt. He had also become a member of the Shillong Club, an institution he simply had to join even though he was often bored by its members. At home he entertained his colleagues and their wives, for which purpose he sometimes borrowed the cook of his neighbour, the Maharaja of Mayurbhanj. Verrier's collection of tribal artefacts quickly became one of the sights of Shillong, a port of call for all visiting dignitaries, whether 'Income Tax people, Admirals, hotelliers, club secretaries, tea-planters [or] All India Radio Types.'[8] Lila, meanwhile, had become a memsahib, a hostess uncannily matching drinks with social types—there she was 'swimming among all the guests like a queen, so self-possessed and gracious, now pressing a large whisky on a Brigadier, now handing a tomato juice to a Hindu financier.'[9] Dressed in vivid colours, her glorious head of hair left untied, she attracted the admiration of the men and of a good many women too. He was of middling rank, she of lowly origin, but the Elwins were nonetheless the first family of Shillong, an invitation to their home more prized than an entreé to Government House.[10] K. L. Mehta, as Adviser to the Governor who was technically Elwin's boss, told him that 'your house is like a eighteenth-century salon where everyone comes to get inspiration and ideas.'[11]

But let me dispel the note of cynicism that has crept in here. The NEFA job was for Elwin a 'sort of crown to all those years of struggle' in which he had tried desperately but with little success to protect communities in Bastar, Balaghat, Mandla, Koraput, Ganjam and god-knows-where. Now, in these disease-free highlands, backed by the Indian state and its benign head, he thought he and his tribals had something more of a chance. Certainly he worked ferociously hard, recruiting officials, training them, sending a steady stream of cautionary notes to his superiors. He liked putting a 'Secret' stamp on his letters. It made him feel like a character in a thriller. But the recipients were not always pleased with the contents. Their complaints reached the governor, who suggested that if Elwin 'wished to be rude the telephone did not commit one so finally.'[12]

A final printed commitment of sorts was called for when Elwin was asked in May 1954 to write a book introducing Gandhi to the north-east. It was a short study, fifty pages in all, yet he found it 'extremely difficult' to write.[13] He had now to settle accounts with a man to whom he had successively been student, interpreter, disciple, son, rebel and stranger. He offered a chastened version of his old Second Coming interpretation of

Gandhi the Mahatma. The carrier of a new civilization had become the sympathetic outsider with a message for the tribes. For the adivasis, wrote Elwin, Gandhi's

> life and teaching has vitally important lessons. There is first the lesson of peace. Disputes between villages and individuals can never be really solved by violence... Love is the only way of progress, forgiveness is the true discipline and bond of social life.
>
> Then there is the lesson of self-reliance. We are to be ourselves, not imitations of other people. We are not to be ashamed of our own culture, our own religion, our art, our dress; however simple it may be, it is ours and we may be proud of it. That is the meaning of *swadeshi*...
>
> And then there is the lesson of tolerance, which is also the lesson of unity. Bapu loved India as a whole. He saw it, in all its diversity of hills and plains, as a single unity. He saw its people, with their different languages, their varied dress, their distinct religions, blended into one great nation, a family united in the love of Truth and Peace, moving forward to a time when all men could live together in friendliness and equality.[14]

In September, as Verrier was finishing the book on Gandhi, he was visited by Shamrao, who could not but compare his friend's circumstances with his own. Sham stayed two weeks and then returned most reluctantly to Patangarh. Writing to Eldyth about her brother's happy new life, he wished he 'could say the same about my life—but I cannot be happy unless I am with him [while] he can be [happy without me] because he *has* his *work* and now even Kumar' (who had moved from his boarding school in Bombay to St Edmund's in Shillong). 'I wish I could fly back to Shillong right now,' remarked Shamrao, but in his loneliness he was also dreaming of more distant and pleasurable locations. 'England will always live in my memory as the dream-land,' he said, 'and if a rich friend gave me a few thousand pounds, I would leave Mother India for England, as if a man-eater was chasing me! If only one of my children could go to Oxford. But I am afraid none of them are clever enough to get a chance of that kind.' Life would not be the same for Shamrao after his companion left Mandla, but even in his grief this saint would think of others. It was only now, he told Eldyth, that he understood how she and her mother felt, separated from Verrier for so long.[15]

The separation from Shamrao was not to Verrier's liking either. Otherwise life was much less of a struggle than it ever had been: a happy home, a steady job, support for his work from high quarters, indeed from the highest quarters. 'I am very well,' he wrote to Archer in the last week of September 1954,

> and happier than I have been at any time for the past 20 years, happier, I think, than when I first went to Karanjia. But of course painfully respectable now, a fact which, say what you will, takes a little of the adventure out of life. Yet there is nothing like being legally married to a girl you are in love with, and I am extremely happy with Lila and grow fonder of her every day. Kumar is growing up as a very good sweet boy, with no academic interests at all, but a passion for painting and a certain instinct for art . . .
>
> It is refreshing to work with people one can respect, and most of our men are really first-class and I am extremely fond of some of them. The Governor is a pet, though naturally difficult at times . . . But what is satisfying is that I do have a chance to influence things in the right direction—all the training of officers has been put into my hands, for example.
>
> But of course, however sound the P.M. may be on the tribal problem (and he is very sound, as is the Governor), and however carefully we may brief our officers, the mere contact with this miserable outside world is going to destroy a great deal. The thing is to do as little harm as possible and as slowly as possible![16]

A month later his adored wife gave birth to a boy, her third, his fourth. Verrier at first wanted to call him Shamrao Victor but finally decided on Ashok, after the great Mauryan emperor. Ashok's arrival delayed the winter tour, but for only a few weeks. In late November Verrier was with the Wanchos of Tirap, 'many of them stark naked, many girls attired with flowers and ornaments.' The tribe put on a war-dance for the visitor. A party of painted warriors pretended to invade the village and cut off heads, celebrating the triumph with deep-throated singing. The views were spectacular. From the top of one village he looked down upon the rolling plains of the Brahmaputra on one side and up to the snow peaks of Tibet on the other.

On tour in Tirap, Verrier wrote in his diary that he had 'much better control than before and tend to brood less over things. But I must conquer my resentment at not being treated as a person of importance. This is a great defect. And when I get back, I must do more for and with Lila: it is essential to hold and deepen her love by expressing my own deep love for her. I must get more lust into me: I am growing tame.' The introspection is less intense, less anguished than before, and indeed the routine end-of-year retrospect, entered the next day, simply read: 'So ends a great and happy year.'[17]

From Tirap Verrier moved up the Siang river towards Tibet and the homeland of the Abor tribe. The terrain was the most difficult he'd encountered in twenty-five years of touring, but the people were welcoming and friendly. Outside each village they were met by gaily-clad girls bearing gifts of rice-beer and sugarcane. The girls escorted them to the village boundary where Abor men pelted them with bananas, this a 'prophylactic measure designed to drive away any infectious disease you may be bringing with you from civilization.' The women were always at their looms, their weaving almost as fine as the Nagas. Verrier collected twenty different patterns to go with as many folk tales.[18] Only in one 'sleepy dull village' was the reception less than enthusiastic; after the highs of the past few weeks Verrier felt as 'flat as a Congress Minister without a crowd.'[19]

At fifty-two, every tour seemed the most arduous ever, but the compensations were enormous. In March Elwin 'did' four valleys in four weeks: the Sipi, the Simmi, the lower Kamla and the Pein, each with different and distinctive tribes. To meet these he 'walked or rather waddled, scrambled, tumbled and slithered for 150 miles.' In April he visited the Sherdupkens of the Kameng Frontier Division. The Buddhist herders were gentle and warm, their land 'a mixture of Scotland and Austria.' As ever, it was only the sign of civilization that displeased. The Sherdupken chief, Dorje Thong-Dok, an 'exceptionally intelligent and charming' man, looked 'like the prince he claimed to be when he is wearing his national dress, but in a homburg hat and an English suit he looks rather like a tout on a race-course.' The nobility had set the tone for Elwin also saw one commoner clad in blue trousers, green shirt and velvet sweater, a second in shorts, khaki coat and chauffeur's cap. 'Compared to the splendid tokens of prestige which tradition has sanctioned,' he remarked ruefully, 'these sartorial infelicities look clownish and pathetic.'[20]

Back in Shillong Verrier worked away at his files and gave evidence before the States Reorganization Commission. At a party for the commission one of its members, the historian and diplomat K. M. Panikkar, announced in a loud voice that the great translator of Japanese and Chinese poetry Arthur Waley had told him that if he wished to understand the poetry of India he should read Verrier Elwin. This 'naturally inflated me greatly,' wrote the man so honoured, 'because Waley had said so, partly because Panikkar remembered it, and naturally above all because he said me and not Bill Archer.'[21]

Shamrao came calling in May, this time with Kusum and the kids. There were ten children in the house: the host found it 'a distraction, a very happy one, but still a distraction.' An eleventh arrived in June when Kusum gave birth to her seventh child. The work and bills mounted, Verrier giving expression to an early intimation of mortality: 'Expenses here are terrible,' he wrote to mother, 'and I am using up a lot of such savings as I had; I shall have very little to leave Lila and the children when I am gone.' Sham was most keen to move to Assam but it appears that Lila did not think it a good idea. While they lived in Patan they could share and share alike, but in Shillong there were fearful costs associated with a sahib's life: guests to be entertained, clubs to be seen in, wife and children to be clothed up to a certain fashion. Lila knew, and her husband knew too, that if the Hivales came one family would pay most of the bills.

The Hivales left in August, flying out in two batches from Guwahati to Calcutta. Verrier noticed a 'curious difference betwen east and west; he [Shamrao] must go in two planes, so that if one crashes some members of the family will survive. While I—and Lila too—feel that if we are to be killed we would prefer to die together!' Verrier accompanied them to Jabalpur to sort out the TWARU accounts and draft a report that would reasonably satisfy Jehangir Patel to keep his grant going. He then proceeded to Ahmedabad by way of Bombay. The administration had asked him to inspect the Calico Textile Museum as a possible model for one in NEFA. Verrier took an afternoon out to visit the Sabarmati Ashram, to see after a very long time the place where he and Gandhi had once prayed.[22]

For almost a decade, from 1928 to 1936, Gandhi had been the determining influence on Elwin's life. The break with the Mahatma was all the more bitter for the closeness of the bond. Now, as the breach healed within Verrier, he was coming closer to the other great Indian, Jawaharlal Nehru. If Gandhi is acknowledged as Bapu, the Father of the Nation, Nehru was often called 'Chacha,' the father's younger brother. The terms precisely capture what both meant for Elwin: the one an inspiring but occasionally overbearing father-figure, the other a benevolent and helpfully encouraging uncle.

In late August Nehru was in Shillong on work. He insisted on a tour of Elwin's museum despite the open jealousy of the governor—Jairamdas Daulatram had been replaced by an army general obsessed with hierarchy. The visit and its aftermath are described in a letter to Eldyth that can only be set down in full:

30.8.55

My darling Eldyth,
    Let me set down some of the highlights of these two remarkable days.
    About a month ago I wrote to T. N. Kaul, Joint Secretary in the Ministry of External Affairs and suggested that the Prime Minister might care to come and see my small collection of art specimens and photos; I also wrote a personal letter to the P.M. himself. To my great surprise I got a reply saying that the P.M. had written to the Governor suggesting that this visit might be included in the programme.
    Intense passions were immediately aroused. But I must say that the Adviser, Ken Mehta, was most generous about it. He himself suggested it and while ordinarily, if the P.M. had gone anywhere, he should have gone to him, he backed up the proposal for him to come to me. After all, it was the devil of an honour. The Governor, however, who is a small mean man, did all he could to prevent it and after it was arranged had the press informed that the P.M. was not coming to our house but to the NEFA office. I forestalled him, however, for I have many friends among pressmen, though even so a number of papers reported the story as a visit to the NEFA office. The old bastard grudged me even my small hour of glory.
    The P.M. arrived in Shillong on the 27th. That day we were visited by the D.C. and the S.P. and a body of C.I.D. men, who inspected everything. The police thought the visit was a bad show; far too many trees and bushes about—how are we to protect him? They went through the house, peered under beds, peeped under bushes, and departed muttering.
    On the 28th I had to go off to Raj Bhavan at 9.0. I arrived a quarter of an hour too soon, sweating a bit, and was ushered in into what I thought was

a rather inferior room (for a P.M.) at 9.35. [The P.M.] was completely charming, chatted away as if we were a pair of old buddies, and kept me for 40 minutes, though he had a long list of interviews. At the conclusion he asked me to stay on in NEFA after my three year contract was over.

Then I went out, and the Adviser and the Development Commissioner had interviews. At 11.0. we all trooped into a Conference Room—Ken Mehta, Raschid Yusuf Ali, Rathee (Financial Adviser with a heart of gold), the formidable and arrogant L. and the Governor himself, who sat throughout in an obsequious attitude which gave us all pleasure. The P.M. then spoke for little over an hour, one of the most superb impromptu speeches I have ever heard, and all the more gratifying in that he emphasised all the things that I have been advocating since I came here. Dress, customs, excess of staff, attitude to the tribes—it was a great triumph. The Governor sat with a face of doom, as he heard one after another of his plans crumbling into dust. L., who had made a very mean crack at me, got it in the neck, and cut a very sorry figure. I sat between dear Khemlal Rathee and Raschid and it was all we could do to avoid cheering as point after point came out on our side in exquisite language.

But cornered rats can bite and we must be humble.

The party broke up and I hustled into a staff car and we went as fast as we could towards our house. The Governor (who insisted on coming to ensure that we didn't get up to any mischief) and P.M. with his private escort, a charming creature called Handu, followed in another car. The roads were lined with people and they waved to us under the impression that we were persons of importance.

All this time, Lila was in the house, which was surrounded by C.I.D. and security police. She gave tea and sweets etc. to no fewer than 35 of them! Four ladies were invited—Mrs Rathee and her lovely five children, Mrs Mehta, Amina Yusuf Ali and Mrs Luthra. They supported Lila during the long period of waiting, but on such occasions Lila is really wonderful, completely self-possessed and much less nervous than me.

We arrived and the children gathered on the front steps, while photographers and police clustered round, and there was a bit of a wait. Then the pilot car with the D.C. and the S.P. drove up, and then the P.M. and Governor, followed by a number of jeeps containing the usual escort. The P.M. got out and Kumar and Dharamvir Ratthee garlanded the visitors with Tibetan scarves which I had brought back from Kameng. The P.M. selected a spray of orchids from the flowers in the car and gave it to Lila (we are presssing it under the mattress of the big bed).

Introductions were made and the great man closely accompanied by the little man went round the house. He saw the show-cases, then went round

A SAHIB (SOMETIMES) IN THE SECRETARIAT 251

the picture-room of NEFA, then into the picture-room of Orissa and Bastar, and finally into the Santal Room. I offered him a cup of coffee or, I said in my agitation, would you prefer a cup of sherry. As the Governor was present, he said, 'No, I would much prefer coffee,' which I don't believe. After this I showed him the old pictures, 100 years old, by Dalton and some of the 1847 Butler paintings. It went well, but I was paralysed, as always by the presence of the Glaxo Baby (as he used to be known in Congress circles) and was curiously nervous. But the P.M. is so incalculable that you never know what he will do. He asked me about polygamy; he saw a photo of a girl with her breasts covered with a bit of cloth and observed, 'I suppose the dirty-minded photographer made her cover them up;' he asked me what a 'falsie' was. I said it was something to make you bulge a bit and he said he didn't suppose most tribal girls needed that. But though I think I did pretty well during my private interview, I am afraid I was a bit of a flop during the inspection.

But at least he showed no signs of desiring to return to the conventional boredom of Raj Bhavan, and sat down and spread out his legs, though it was now 1.10 and lunch was scheduled for 1.15, at least a quarter of an hour away. He talked about a Dance Academy and a general Museum for Assam, while flash bulbs flashed and people peered through the windows trying to get a peep. At last they decided they must have lunch and said good-bye.

Directly they had gone we got out the rejected sherry—it was the most expensive Shillong could provide and we had borrowed some glasses suitable for such eminent lips—and had quick ones, then we ourselves got into the staff car again and went back to Raj Bhavan for lunch.

Here, as usual, the food was bad, and the conversation uneven. With all the recourses of modern cookery, why should one give the greatest man in the world, who has banqueted from China to Peru, brain cutlets and an unappetising curry-rice followed by an ice-cream which the P.M. tasted and laid aside. He made up, however, on fresh fruit. For the first ten minutes he sat with his head on his chest, brooding, and didn't say a word. Naturally no one else said a word either. I was sitting, for some curious reason on the Governor's right (a good place, however, for all the best tit-bits are set round that august presence), and he did make one or two whispered remarks to me. Then suddenly the P.M. woke up and talked brilliantly . . . He wanted to see Indian music paganised—for how can you sing with your eyes shut and your head sunk in reverence on your chest. The Russian singing was far better, and he described how he had heard 500 Russian girls singing the Indian national anthem magnificently and far better than it was ever done in pious India.

Even the weariest river winds somehow safe to the dessert and in the end we got up and he bade us farewell. By now I was pretty well pooped, but I felt I must talk over things with Khemlal, so I dragged him home with me and we discussed the events of the morning over a cup of tea.

The day was not yet over, however. There was the dinner to attend. I got into my tuxedo and went along. There were all the Ministers and one or two Deputy Ministers, and a few Assam high officials. Never have I seen such a gang of morons. Two of them sat in corners of the room reading magazines. Others sat round in apprehensive silence. I found myself on a sofa with the Minister for This and That (for the life of me, I can't remember either his name or function). I would make a remark, he would reply and then stare straight in front of him again. After a bit I gave up and stared straight in front of me myself. For 20 minutes we didn't even get a tomato juice, and all the world a solemn silence held. Then in came the Governor and [the P.M.], and we at least got the tomato juice and I was able to break away from my Minister and had an entertaining conversation with Handu (I always get along well with high-placed policemen) about Science Fiction; I bet he was the only man in the room, beside the P.M. who had read Forster's *The Machine Stops.*

But all too soon, the dread words 'Dinner is Ready' were uttered and we trooped reluctantly into the palace of gastronomic irrelevancies. I have eaten the same dinner so often that I know it by heart, the off-colour canape, the soup, the made-up fish (this was the best dish and I wish I had the courage to take two portions), the shocking curry-rice, and the cake pudding, dry and tasteless.

Raj Bhavan dinners do have at least a valuable ethical effect, for they are carefully calculated to show you just where you stand in the scheme of things. I of course was at the bottom of the table and my only consolation was to see that Ken Mehta, whose income is exactly double mine, was in a corresponding place, though on the right and not the left, to mine at the other end of the table. I watched the Ministers pretty closely. Sushir Datta, the Chief Secretary, a brilliant Cambridge man and an enthusiastic drinker, was between the Minister for Excise and the Deputy Minister of Cow-Protection (or something of the sort). They didn't speak to him and he . . . didn't speak to them. Five of the Ministers, to my certain knowledge, didn't open their mouths throughout the meal, except of course to eat, which they did heartily and with apparent pleasure. The Governor, our host, sat in embattled silence from soup to nuts. Poor [P.M.] did his best, but he had enough of solo lecturing and after a time he wearied and for minutes at a time, this glittering company sat silent except for the clicking of dentures and the smooth susurration of ingesting vitamins. There was one old Minister near me in a beard and a dhoti tucking in as if he had not had a square meal for weeks.

When at last we got away and returned to the drawing-room; the Governor had given orders that cigars were to be brought for Dr Elwin, but when it was discovered that you had to buy 50 at a time, it was supposed that there might be audit objections, so the project was dropped; and we sat round in embarrassed silence. [The P.M.] lay back in a chair; the Governor and Chief Minister sat near twiddling their fingers but not saying a single word; after 15 minutes of this entertainment the P.M. evidently thought he would be more comfortable in bed and got up and went away.

Even now the day was not over, for on reaching home I found Lila in tears, and Nakula very bad with his whooping-cough. So I sent the car for Dr Dilip Guha and he came and spent about an hour making his examinations, and we eventually got to bed very late and worried about the child . . .

The next day I felt rotten but had to struggle through a heavy day's work. Whooping cough is a distressing disease to watch.

With very much love
Verrier[23]

On Nehru's return to Delhi he sent the NEFA administration a note urging them to go slow and not uproot tribals 'from their way of life with its standards and discipline and give them nothing in its place.' He asked them to listen carefully to their Adviser on Tribal Affairs, for 'Verrier Elwin is a recognized authority on the Indian tribes [who] brings to his task an understanding and sympathy which is unusual and most helpful. His advice is therefore of great value.'[24]

The certificate was pocketed with pleasure. Indeed, in his day-to-day work in NEFA Elwin shrewdly and effectively used the prime minister's name and prestige to advance his own agenda. Writing to his superiors on shops, or architecture, or dancing, he would cite Nehru prefatory to his own suggestions. 'The Prime Minister has spoken so emphatically on the matter . . .;' 'It is, as the Prime Minister has said, grossly presumptuous for us to tell [the tribals] what to do and what not to do . . .;' 'I have simply been trying to implement the very emphatic and explicit notes of the Prime Minister . . .'—phrases such as these are strewn through his notes and memoranda of the time.[25]

The prime minister's appeal for Elwin is easy to understand. As long as he lived, writers, thinkers and scientists flocked to Nehru, the world's philosopher-king in a democratic age. Nehru's absence of racial feeling, his complete lack of bitterness towards the men who had once ruled India, was very apparent and endearing. In 1955 Nehru met Churchill in London, a meeting of two prime ministers but also a meeting between the most fanatical opponent of the Indian freedom movement and the man who had spent fourteen years in British jails. A newspaper reported Nehru greeting his fellow Harrovian with the remark, 'And how are you, sir?' Elwin was moved to circulate the report within the NEFA administration, with the comment: 'What in slavery would be obsequious, in freedom is an act of courtesy.'[26]

Equally, Nehru was much attracted to Elwin: to the brilliant Oxford scholar (Nehru himself had an indifferent Second from Cambridge); to the lover of good books and the writer of several; to the gypsy who in the thirties and forties had roamed the wilds while he had been in prison. Soon after Elwin had joined the government, Nehru told Jehangir Patel that 'I hear such mixed reports about Verrier. He womanizes, etc.' Patel replied, 'What does it matter to you?' The prime minister, roaring with laughter agreed: 'Yes, it is quite true. What does it matter?' Patel then launched an eloquent defense: 'Why do you measure Verrier with the yardstick that you would use for Bapu and the other saints? I will trust Verrier all my life. Nobody knows his job as he does. Look at the great books he has written. You have written books yourself and you know how much it takes. He couldn't have written them without great work, could he? We have had great quarrels but I never had a chance to quarrel about his work.'[27]

Nehru had reason to admire Elwin's work and, surrounded by files and file-pushers, relish his company too. When the anthropologist visited Delhi in October 1955 he called on the prime minister, who gave him nearly an hour of his busy morning. Nehru was 'most affable and delightful,' but Elwin was too awed to speak. As he put it: 'afterwards I thought of so many things I might have said and got across that I felt as depressed as I used to preach and felt that the Spirit had not been on me.' However, it seemed to have gone all right for in the afternoon he received a cheque from the prime minister's special fund, to be spent at his discretion 'on art and dancing in NEFA and other places.'[28] Soon afterwards Nehru wrote of being 'overwhelmed by bankers and financiers' whose company he must have disliked as much as he enjoyed Elwin's. On a later visit to the capital Elwin went round to the prime minister's house to discuss NEFA affairs, but Nehru seized on the opportunity to talk instead of Vladimir Nabokov's *Lolita*.[29]

An early victory of the Adviser on Tribal Affairs was to retain the term 'political officer.' When word reached him that the governor wished to replace it with the more orthodox 'deputy commissioner' he was outraged. The term 'P.O.,' he noted, 'does give a certain sense of romance and adventure to what is an extremely difficult task; it also stresses the unique character of the work; and is in many ways appropriate to an enterprise which is both political and humane.' To call POs DCs would 'conventionalize' NEFA, bring it closer to the districts of the plains, 'subject to the same corruptions, the same lawyers and merchants and the same unwieldy apparatus of a Deputy Commissioner's office.'[30]

Every winter on tour Elwin experienced afresh the unconventionality of NEFA, the absence of lawyers, merchants and other corruptions of civilization. In November 1955 he set out for the Mishmi Hills, taking Lila. This was her first journey outside Shillong since she had arrived there almost two years previously. The Mishmis lived in long low houses, each branch of the family making itself a new set of rooms off the main corridor. They were not head-hunters but hair-and-thumb hunters, traditionally marking their conquests with tufts of hair hung up in their house, burying the thumbs of their victims with the skulls of wild animals taken in the chase. The Idi Mishmis reminded him of the Baigas, 'very wild and shaggy, real jungle folk,' with their poisoned arrows and bows fired like a gun. Halfway through the tour he suffered a 'real disaster' when Sunderlal—whom he had come to depend upon so heavily for twenty years—fell ill and had to return.[31] Lila returned too, while Verrier struck deeper into the interior. From an Idu village in Dibang he wrote to an English friend on 'a table the size of a postage stamp.' The Mishmis were completely enchanting, he said: once he had done with them he would move on to the Wanchos in Tirap before proceeding to Delhi for a round of selection interviews. He hoped then to return for a long trip to the Tibetan border in northern Siang, to conclude the winter's touring with a visit to the Kalyo-Keagnyus in Tuensang. Counting the tribes and the valleys on his list he remarked: 'When I put this all down I wish I was twenty years younger!'[32] Otherwise he was content enough, his year-end summary speaking of good tours and reports, happy relations with Lila and the children, and new friendships. The only black spot was an increased worry about Shamrao. He listed thirteen new year resolutions for 1956: to be a better father, husband, to drink less, etc., the most elaborate being to 'follow Truth fearlessly, to speak my mind without fear of consequences, to fight harder for the tribes and their real benefit and happiness—but to be tactful about it if possible.'[33]

On some of the more difficult tours Verrier was accompanied by his eldest son Kumar. In the last week of 1955 they reached Nisa, a village in Tirap last visited by a white man sixty years earlier. Their entry was hailed by the cry 'The Jai Hind has come.' The nationalist salutation had been turned into a noun. Verrier found it 'a rather pleasant variation on the usual Sahib.' Any suspicion that it might instead be a sarcastic comment on Indian hegemony was dispelled when the chief presented the son of the Jai Hind a monkey which slept, ate and played with the teenager. Another chief in another village gave Kumar a wild cat. Kosi's son had a wonderful way with animals; the cat sat purring in his lap though no one else would go near it. But as the cat ate a chicken a day, computed by Elwin as double the boy's school fees, they reluctantly left it behind. Father and son moved on to the Bori tribe, to get to whom they had to 'struggle over great rocks, edge our way along cliff-faces, creep along precipices and landslides.' Most exciting of all were the bridges: long tunnels of cane swinging over the river—one had 'to be an acrobat for NEFA.' The next winter they crossed the Siang river in a bamboo raft, then climbed a cliff by a rickety bamboo ladder. They also crossed illegally into Tibet, where Kumar carved his name on a tree. On this tour they covered 180 miles on foot, climbing up an aggregate of 40,000 feet and climbing down as much. The fifty-four-year-old sahib took 'a certain satisfaction in the sheer physical achievement.'[34]

To the junior officers Elwin successfully conveyed the romance and adventure of work in NEFA. There was his personality, the learning carried with ease and conveyed with wit, its manifestations gleefully passed around the NEFA secretariat, such as this answer to a letter addressed to 'Rev. Elwin:' 'Who has addressed this envelope? The abbreviation "Rev" may, of course, stand for Reverend, Revered or Revolutionary. If the first is intended, it is insulting; if the second, it is undeserved; if the third, it is flattering, but indiscreet.'[35] Then there were the associations with the Father of the Nation and its present ruler, and yet the absence of any feeling of colour or status or rank. There was the example set by his long and difficult tours at his age; and most of all there were his reports, evocative accounts of new and colourful tribes he met each winter. Who would not be attracted to life among the Taraons, hailed for 'the quite wonderful coiffure of the women which would not disgrace a Parisian lady of fashion;' or among the Monpa, a Buddhist tribe 'distinguished for its terraced cultivation, its carpet making and its love of horses' and for being 'quiet, gentle, friendly, courteous, industrious, good to animals, good to children;' or among the Kama Mishmi, whose 'weaving is among the finest in NEFA and is of extraordinary variety,' the designs attributed in legend to butterflies, fish, and snakes.[36]

Elwin was deeply affected by what an educated Mishmi had once told him: 'Remember that we are not by culture or even by race Indian. If you continue to send among us officers who look down on our culture and religion, and above all look down on us as human beings, then within a few years we will be against you.'[37] Under his guidance the Indian Frontier Administrative Service developed a cadre of capable and massively committed young men, almost unique in Indian political history for their readiness to live with and think like the people they had been sent to govern. The officers of the IFAS dwelt in thatched huts, bathed in streams, toured on foot and subsisted on daal and rice for months on end—these were dropped by helicopter, for Elwin insisted that officers not take food from villagers unless it was surplus produce voluntarily sold. Men like Bob Khathing, Rashid Yusuf Ali, Nalini Jayal, Murkot Ramunny, R. N. Haldipur, and Har Mander Singh—to mention just six names, of people belonging to four religions and hailing from diverse parts of India—were taught to practice the intellectual and emotional as well as purely law-and-order side of governance. 'I don't want you to ever give tribals a feeling of inferiority,' Elwin told them, 'Integration can only take place on the basis of equality: moral and political equality.' They must know the people, he said, know what stirred them, moved them, energized them. When on tour they must drink with the tribals . . . drink, he added significantly, from the same *collective* bowl. He asked the POs to write reports on the flora and fauna of the district, the habits, customs, rites, ornaments, and crafts of the people. They sent him drafts which were returned with queries written over in green ink.[38]

There were of course officers who complained of missing the amenities of the 'civilized' plains, others who feared the ritual pollution that came from such close contact with out-of-caste men. Elwin acknowledged that NEFA had 'no railway trains, no limousines, no cinemas, no electricity, no plumbing, no refrigerators, no television,' but then it had 'no Stock Exchange, no colour bar, no caste, no atom bombs, no slums' either. Nor were its people altogether lacking in high culture. In the summer of 1956 Elwin visited the great monastery at Tawang, the epicentre of NEFA Buddhism, which with its narrow streets and great library and 'gentle casual atmosphere which concealed so much formality and protocol' reminded him irresistibly of Oxford. To the monastery came students from the villages around, attached in groups to senior lamas. They worked in the library in an atmosphere of art and learning, books and manuscripts on the tables, paintings and scrolls on the walls. And a 'monastic book is a real book, about the size of half a dozen books of this careless modern world.' The great treasure of the Tawang library was the Getompa, three volumes of which were lettered in gold. This was brought out to the visitor 'in much the same way that an Oxford College librarian would produce a copy of the First Folio of Shakespeare; scarves were offered to it, and it was opened with rather reluctant devotion.'

Another Oxonian trait in Tawang was its reverence for the theatre. The monastery had cupboards full of costumes, masks and other props. The lamas acted in dance-dramas, one of which, the Thutotdam, had the players dressed as skeletons, portraying the journey of the soul after death. All told, the atmosphere was 'almost that of one of the elder European Universities.' The Khempu or Abbot, Gelong Kesang Phuntsog, with his unpretentiousness and 'luminous beauty of character,' reminded

Elwin of a dean of Christ Church he had known long ago. The Khempu was one of the 'few real saints one may meet in a lifetime; ... he is a completely charming personality and every time I met him I felt the better for it.'[39]

In September 1956, not long after he returned from Tawang, came news from England of his mother's death. His reaction is unrecorded and I wonder what Mrs Minnie Elwin would have made of this latest defection towards Buddhism. Verrier once told Bill Archer of his experience that 'the finest moments in life have been the very reverse of Christian religion and morality.'[40] The rejection of Christianity had been followed by a long period of agnosticism, with him out of sync with all forms of established religion despite a continuing professional interest in them. But after he visited Tawang this former priest, this twice-lapsed Christian, this renegade Gandhian came to pin his faith on 'some form of liberal Buddhism.' In December he was in Delhi, his visit coinciding with that of the Dalai and Panchen Lamas. Elwin spent the best part of a day with them, received their blessings and went along to a great banquet in their honour. This was held at the Rashtrapati Bhavan. The company were fed while seated on the floor, Indian and Christa-Seva-Sangh style. Afterwards Nehru took the Dalai Lama—already a spiritual guide even though a mere lad—for an elephant ride.[41]

Buddhism, and especially its idea of *karuna* or compassion, helped tame and reconcile the conflicts of allegiance that had hitherto dominated Verrier's life. He was no longer concerned, he told a friend, 'whether there was a life after death or whether there was a god or not.' But he knew 'there was a meaning to life, which one can experience in love, in recognition of goodness and in the true appreciation of beauty ... Heaven and Hell are within ourselves. The key to self-realization is to find peace within us.'[42]

In November 1957 Elwin stayed with the Khamptis, finding to his dismay that Buddhism was losing its sway over the young. The temple at Chowkham resembled an Anglican church in England: 'There were present plenty of old ladies and a few devoted old gentlemen and there were the boys who live in the hostel attached to the Temple who would correspond to the choir-boys in a cathedral school, but except for a few girls in their teens the younger generation was notably absent.' The Indian government was constitutionally wedded to banishing religion from public life, yet

Elwin suggested that it should, at least in the high valleys, 'encourage people in the practice of their traditional faith.' The administration, he thought, should encourage the formation of Temple Committees to repair and maintain shrines; plant trees and plan gardens around them ('so that all who see them may remember the Eternal Beauty'); organize pilgrimages to Tawang; and harmonize in schools the spiritual and secular aspects of education.

The Buddhist area, wrote Elwin, 'presents us with a problem unlike that offered in any other part of NEFA. Elsewhere we have the difficult, indeed vexatious, puzzle of the impact of the atomic age on a Stone Age people. But here we have the conflict between two civilizations, one of which is immensely superior in technological achievement while the other is equally distinguished by spiritual faith, by simple dignity, by compassionate manners.'[43]

Elwin himself carried to the civilization of power a token from this other. The token was a brass figurine of the Buddha, a present from the Khempu of Tawang. From now it was to be found always in his pocket, at home and on tour.

CHAPTER TWELVE

Nehru's Missionary

Far too much has been written on the aboriginal problem. If the measures taken were in any way commensurate with the enquiries, reports, monographs and correspondence about them, the aboriginals would be the happiest people in India.

Verrier Elwin, in a note of November 1944

Convinced that humanity and variety are synonymous, Elwin has always condemned the busybodies who, be it in the name of religion or at the behest of politics, would impose on primitive innocence the standardized sophistications of modern civilization, and just as in the old days he aroused the active hostility of many a British official by his open association with the movement for Indian independence, so now his disapproval of cumulative encroachments on the integrity of primitive culture may seem suspect to champions of militant nationalism.

Sudhindranath Dutta, writing in 1952

If we can develop a NEFA of the Prime Minister's dreams what a marvellous place it would be!

Verrier Elwin, in a note of November 1955

'Whether I shall ever write another book I don't know,' remarked Elwin to Bill Archer nine months after moving to NEFA, 'but perhaps I have written enough.'[1] 'You go on producing lovely books and enriching the world with beauty,' he wrote four years later—this a reference to Archer's growing corpus of works on Indian art—'I continue to distract my little world with controversy.

However, both of us are aiming at the preservation of something good and beautiful.'²

As it happened Elwin was to write another half dozen books, one of them greatly influential in its time. This was *A Philosophy for NEFA*, first published in 1957 followed by a much expanded edition two years later. *A Philosophy for NEFA* is the book of an anthropologist for the administration, but also of an Englishman for India. The author calls himself a 'missionary of Mr Nehru's gospel,' and a 'very bad "Gandhi man" ' who learnt from the Mahatma to approach the poor through the mind of the poor. In the text Gandhi is quoted no less than fifteen times and Nehru on more than twenty-five occasions. The chapter epigraphs are attributed to other Indian patriots, including G. B. Pant, then home minister of the Government of India, and C. Rajagopalachari, who had been the first Indian governor-general. The most telling quote comes from A. V. Thakkar: 'Separation and Isolation are dangerous theories and strike at the root of national solidarity. Safety lies in union not in isolation.'

No man ever entirely forgets his past, but located as he was between England and India, and between tribe and state, Elwin perhaps forgot less than most. The Thakkar quote stands at the head of a chapter called 'The Fundamental Problem' where the author carefully distances himself from his own prior, 'primitivist' persona of the nineteen-thirties and 'forties. Writing of the policy of Isolation, for instance, he suggests it was a strictly temporary measure for some small tribes under colonial conditions: 'neither I nor any other anthropologist would dream of suggesting such a policy since Independence.' But this assertion of Indian patriotism is also, and intriguingly, a disavowal of his poetic self. It is 'the literary men, the artists, the poets [and] the philosophers,' he now claims, 'who have wanted to keep the tribal people as they were: the artist Gauguin has probably had more influence on the modern attitude to the "primitive" than all the anthropologists put together. In any case, the scientists [among whom he numbers himself] are just not interested in that sort of thing. They are more concerned with developing rather than static societies, with culture-change rather than with culture "as it is" . . .'³

Elwin's language in *A Philosophy for NEFA* had to take account of an India restless and on the move, eager to grow, progress, modernize, develop. However, the retreat from protection by no means implied an endorsement of its opposite, that is, the wholesale detribalization of the communities of NEFA and their absorption into the fabric of (Hindu) India. The extremes of Isolation and Assimilation are now both rejected in favour of a Middle Way, the way of Integration. This would foster 'a spirit of love and loyalty for India, without a trace of suspicion that Government has come into tribal areas to colonize or exploit, a full integration of mind and heart with the great society of which the tribal people form a part, and to whose infinite variety they may make a unique contribution.' Phrased in the language of economic development rather than national unity, the great problem is 'how to bring the blessings and advantages of modern medicine, agriculture and education to them, without destroying the rare and precious values of tribal life.'[4]

In a note for official circulation Elwin explained the purpose of the book thus:

> The world is now convinced that India can rule itself; it is less certain that she can do the right thing by her tribal population. All sorts of fantastic misconceptions of our policy in the tribal areas are current abroad: we are supposed to be going in for wholesale Hinduization, we are making them vegetarians and teetotallers, we are allowing merchants and money-lenders to exploit them. I am confident that this book will do a great deal to remove these wrong ideas if we can get it across to the right people. Even in India, it will, as now rewritten, remove many wrong ideas about the NEFA Administration.[5]

The audience of *A Philosophy for NEFA* was, in the first instance, government officials serving in tribal areas. These officials and their wives are urged to rid themselves of any feelings of cultural superiority, to be guided in all their actions by humility—rather than by 'that hard professional inquisitive interference in other people's lives so characteristic of the social worker'—and not to use those awful words 'backward' and 'uplift.' For officers to claim that 'they are "modern" and "advanced" [while] their tribal brethren are lagging behind,' continues Elwin, implies 'a value-judgement, which the conscience of the world may yet reverse. For who is really backward—the honest peasant working in simplicity and truth among the hills, or the representative of modern progress embroiled in the mad race for power and wealth, the symbol of whose achievement is the hydrogen bomb.'[6]

Evidently, allegiance to the Indian government did not imply an endorsement of civilization.

'Make haste slowly' was the leitmotif of *A Philosophy for NEFA* as well as the torrent of reports and memoranda that flowed from Elwin's pen. In 1955, when the Government of India was set to adopt the ambitious Second Five Year Plan, with its charter of rapid industrialization and economic growth, Elwin wished that NEFA had a 'Fifty-Year Plan rather than a Five-Year Plan.' For 'if tribals move too fast,' he explained with his experience in central India in mind, 'they tend to move downwards.'[7]

The NEFA tribals were to be protected; *that* term was also no longer permissible. Thus, in a canny and not altogether insincere manner, Elwin spoke more often of the importance of 'self-reliance.' On tour in the Abor country in March 1957 he came across a bazaar of shops run by Marwari traders from western India, a community noted for cunning and sharp practice. He called the bazaar a 'poisoned arrow aimed at the heart of Abor culture.' The Marwari shops seduced tribals away from self-reliance; moreover, with pictures of gods and goddesses prominently displayed on their walls, they served as centres of Hindu propaganda. He wanted a strict watch on the expansion of shops in NEFA, even supplying a list of commodities they could and could not stock. The import and sale of hurricane lamps, torches, cigarettes, fountain pens and agricultural implements were allowed, but not of 'singlets, sola topis, chauffeur's caps, cosmetics, brassieres, plastic ornaments and belts, expensive and unsuitable shoes.' Shops had to be controlled, he noted, 'to save the tribals from having their taste debased and their money wasted by the import of unnecessary, unsuitable and unartistic goods.'[8]

Here Elwin invoked both Nehru the aesthete's distaste for traders and trading—'we must not encourage the tribal people to get into bad artistic habits which normally follow in the wake of what is called civilization' wrote the prime minister to the NEFA administration—as well as Gandhi, whose swadeshi campaign (the burning and boycott of foreign goods), provided a fine justification. In any case hand-weaving was perhaps 'the chief artistic achievement of the people of NEFA;' were the state to help renew this 'indigenous khadi enterprise,' money that went into the pockets of traders might stay within the community. Unhappily, government weaving centres imposed colours and designs inferior to those that existed already. 'It is absolutely useless,' wrote Elwin after visiting one such centre, 'to bring girls from the villages and spend a lot of money teaching them to weave worse than they weave at home.'[9]

Elwin spoke often of his wish 'to make of the whole of NEFA a work of art.' In 1956 he suggested the creation of a Tagore Memorial Fellowship, for the study of dance and music and the promotion of these in areas where they were absent; and of a Gandhi Memorial Fellowship for the study and guided spread of indigenous traditions of weaving.[10] Two years later, in between the first and second editions of *A Philosophy for NEFA*, he published a volume on the art of the territory. This showcased examples of pottery, mask-making, basketry, jewelry and, above all, weaving. The book was an extended and well illustrated argument on behalf of the artistic traditions of NEFA, traditions now under threat. Here, as elsewhere, folk-artists had increasingly to contend with

> the competition of the cheap oleograph, the commercial calendar, the gaudy mythological reproduction, the political leader in bad print. These are not only easy to obtain but they have the false prestige of modernity, and the village artist becomes haunted by a sense of inferiority and ceases to create. Indeed it is this inferiority complex that is the castrator of the artistic impulse in every field, and unless we can encourage the villager to believe in himself, the folk arts, which cannot be kept alive merely by artificial stimuli, will perish.

These forces could be fought by keeping out the puritans who would abolish much of what was best in tribal expressive traditions, and, more positively, by thoughtful state intervention. His book was written in the belief that 'by encouraging the arts of the tribal people, creating in them a pride in their own products, keeping before them their own finest patterns and designs, and by providing them with raw materials, it will be possible to inspire a renaissance of creative activity throughout the hill areas of India . . .

Elwin believed that the state must nurture the 'natural good taste' of the tribals and itself blend into the social life of NEFA, growing into the landscape rather than standing in stark contrast to it. As it happened, tribals tended to do things in circles, but the newly built offices and schools followed straight lines. For a people who liked to sit around a fire or gather in a circle around a teacher, he remarked, 'our benches in tidy rows, our dreary rooms with never a fire in them, the regimentation of lines and rectangles is unfamiliar.' He carried this complaint to Nehru, who chastised the chief minister of Assam: 'If a school or dispensary is built in a tribal village in a manner which is completely different from the village style, this is a foreign element which sticks out from the rest of the village . . . If we have to make the tribal people at home with our officers, then our officers should not live in a building which is completely out of keeping with the surroundings.'[12]

The most remarkable of Elwin's proposals was to set up a Sudhaar Kendra, a social rehabilitation centre, for the humane treatment of convicted tribals. Reading the All India Prisons Act he was appalled by its sanction of whipping, fettering and solitary confinement. 'Does anybody know what the prisons of India are really like today?' he asked in June 1956:

> Ten or fifteen years ago, with the flower of the nation in jail, we had every opportunity to discover and men who had themselves languished in prison cells emerged from them with the sincere determination to set things rights when they had the power. But what actually has been achieved? Are our prisons today running on really modern, humane and scientific lines, or are they merely the same prisons with a few reforms and amenities? Has the public attitude to prisons changed, or do we still sheer away from the subject in distaste?[13]

NEFA itself had no jail, so when a group of Tagins were convicted of murder they were sent to a prison in Banaras. Elwin knew the city from his days with the Anthropological Survey—hot, damp and not likely to suit the tribal mind or body. He recommended the Tagins be transferred to Lucknow, and be allowed to spend summers in Almora jail up in the Kumaun Himalaya. Meanwhile he set to work on a plan for a new NEFA prison which was to be as much of a work of art as a prison could.

Elwin viewed the jail as an aspect of 'psychiatric imperialism,' imposing Western ideas of guilt and punishment on a people more worried about shame and status. For the tribal, preoccupied with self-esteem, a fine might work better than incarceration. He thought also that 'the best way of reforming prisons is to put fewer people in prison.' To be sure, some tribals had to be confined, but if Elwin had his way this would be only in a Sudhaar Kendra that would provide the 'healing touch' to individuals momentarily led astray. He identified a site for such a Centre in Lohitpur, among the hills and woods the tribals loved so well. The establishment of the Centre, he told his NEFA colleagues, 'gives us the opportunity of producing something which might be a model to all parts of tribal India and I hope very much that everything connected with it—architecture, food, prison industries, discipline and so on—will be devised on the most up to date and liberal penological principles.'

In Elwin's design the Centre would have high walls for security but would otherwise closely approximate the spirit of tribal life. Inmates would be housed in long dormitories with platforms for sitting out, Abor-style. A community recreation hall, modelled on the morung, would allow people to meet and sing around a fire. A Naga log-drum would summon men to work and meals. The food would be cooked by the tribals themselves. It would have plenty of meat, and the administration would 'be generous with regard to tobacco and the tribal version of betel, and *on special occasion permit even a moderate quantity of rice-beer to be brewed.*'[14]

In Bastar in the nineteen-forties Elwin had been deeply affected by the condition of tribals in Jagdalpur jail.[15] That experience influenced this visionary scheme which, like many others, remained buried in the files.

Both editions of *A Philosophy for NEFA* carried commendatory forewords by Jawaharlal Nehru. The first time around, Nehru directed the reader to a correct understanding of which way the chain of influence ran. 'Verrier Elwin,' he wrote in a foreword dated 16th February 1957,

> has done me the honour of saying that he is a missionary of my views on tribal affairs. As a matter of fact, I have learnt much from him, for he is both an expert on this subject with great experience and a friend of the tribal folk.

I have little experience of tribal life and my own views, vague as they were, have developed under the impact of certain circumstances and of Verrier Elwin's own writings. It would, therefore, be more correct to say that I have learnt from him rather than that I have influenced him in any way.

Nehru went on to ask officers in NEFA to 'read carefully what Dr Elwin has written and absorb this philosophy so that they may act in accordance with it.' Then he added (and this was Elwin's real triumph): 'Indeed, I hope that this broad approach will be applied outside the NEFA also to other tribals in India.'

Each man's exaggerated deference to the other is in keeping with the north Indian tradition of *taqqaluf* where one must never claim anything for oneself but always hand it to the other fellow. On 25th August 1958 we find Elwin writing to a colleague in Delhi thus:

As far as *I can understand the Prime Minister's direction* on work in the tribal areas, the four fundamental points are these:

(a) That we should not send too many outsiders into the tribal areas;
(b) that we should not over-adminster the tribal areas;
(c) that we should not overwhelm the people by a multiplicity of schemes but aim at doing a few fundamental things really well;
(d) that we should impose nothing on the people but help them to develop according to their own tradition and genius.[16]

And now move on very quickly to 9th October 1958, the date of Nehru's foreword to the second edition of *A Philosophy for NEFA*. He outlines here 'five fundamental principles' of development in tribal areas:

1. People should develop along the lines of their own genius and we should avoid imposing anything on them. We should try to encourage in every way their own traditional arts and culture.
2. Tribal rights in land and forests should be protected.
3. We should try to train and build up a team of their own people to do the work of administration and development. Some technical personnel from outside will, no doubt, be needed, especially in the beginning. But we should avoid introducing too many outsiders into tribal territory.
4. We should not over-adminster these areas or overwhelm them with a multiplicity of schemes. We should rather work through, and not in rivalry to, their own social and cultural institutions.
5. We should judge results, not by statistics or the amount of money spent, but by the quality of human character that is evolved.

This foreword was publicized by Elwin as the 'Prime Minister's Panchsheel for tribal development,' the word carrying, he hoped, resonance of the other Panchsheel, the famous five principles for international co-operation offered by Nehru at the Bandung conference of 1955. But did the great man write the foreword himself? Or was this the Elwin gospel being carried, for strategic purposes, through the prime minister's persuasively powerful pen? Jawaharlal Nehru is almost unique among postwar statesmen in writing his own stuff—letters, notes, speeches, books, what-have-you, but an exception seems to have been made here. For the spill-over of words and phrases from the letter of 25th August indicates that the anthropologist must have supplied the first draft. But then that letter was itself advertised as the work of a scribe interpreting the master thinker! Perhaps what matters, in the end, is not proof of authorship but concordance of views between Oxford scholar and Cambridge scientist, the way in which the work of a relatively minor official of a great state was given credence and influence by the support and signature of its head.

That *A Philosophy of NEFA* was both approved and 'forwarded' by the prime minister was calculated to reassure many and enrage some. The Elwin connection, remarked a commentator in the respected *Economic Weekly* of Bombay, was

> further evidence of the schizophrenia of the Nehru mind, the Indian mind. The Prime Minister has not really made up his mind whether he wants the [tribals] to be like himself or remain themselves. He is a great one for civilization, meaning hospitals and refrigerators and automobiles; he is also a romantic of the upper class coloniser type. The quaintness of the [tribal] fascinates him as much as it fascinates Verrier Elwyn [*sic*]; he too is 'gone on' what is so utterly different from him. There is the pathetic Wellsian faith in the march of civilisation, and there is the T. E. Lawrencian fascination for the tribal, the primitive, the elemental. As a personal attitude it is certainly a tenable one. Less so, perhaps, as the begetter of a governmental policy.[17]

In the late fifties the prime minister's bitterest political foe was the brilliant maverick socialist Ram Manohar Lohia, whose numerous interventions in the Indian Parliament had as their main and sometimes sole purpose the discomfiture of Nehru and the ruling Congress party. A political scientist with a Ph.D. from Germany, Lohia was also an extreme

Anglophobe, a trait whose relevance to our story will soon be apparent. For, on 12th November 1958, Lohia arrived at the outpost of Jairampur, on the borders of NEFA. He had come to challenge the policy whereby all outsiders, whether citizens of India or not, had to obtain 'Inner Line' permits to enter the territory. Lohia held that all Indians had the right to wander freely anywhere in their country. But the NEFA guards did not agree: he did not have a pass so he was not allowed to enter. Lohia was enraged. The governor of Assam told him he could get a permit whenever he wished but would first have to come to Shillong and apply for one. Lohia was not prepared to accept this and a year later once again attempted to enter NEFA without a permit. This time he was arrested and brought down to the town of Dibrugarh in Assam, where he was set free. In a press statement he condemned the policy of the NEFA administration as a relic of British colonialism. Lohia insisted that he wished to visit the area only out of a desire to see his land 'in all its various beautiful shapes.' This 'foolish' policy of not allowing other Indians into the territory, he claimed,

> might be partly owing to the fact that a very peculiar type of an erstwhile clergyman, Sri Verrier Elwin, is the adviser of the Governor of Assam in respect of the matters concerning the Adivasis (tribals) of Assam. This former clergyman has carved out a principle of a 'reserved forest' in the same manner as the lions of Gir. But the detachment of these Adivasis with the outer world is all the more greater . . . Until the month of October last year, the photographs of Shiv, Durga, Gandhiji or even Nehru were not permitted to be displayed in the shops, because in the opinion of this former clergyman, there were possibilities of the people of [NEFA] being offended or getting corrupt.[18]

Where some national politicians accused Elwin of separating NEFA from India, the Assamese, the dominant linguistic group in the north-east, suspected him of suppressing the territory's historic links with them. The press in Assam consistently charged NEFA officers with isolating the tribals from their closest neighbours with whom, it was claimed, they had affinities of language, lifestyle and religious belief, as well as associations going back hundreds of years. Months after Elwin moved to Shillong, Assamese journalists sharpened their attacks on NEFA officials, who smelt a mythical 'Assamese imperialism in the tribal areas of the north-east, leading them to weed out Assamese officials from the NEFA Administration.'[19]

The journalists were only taking a cue from their politicians. In November 1955, discussing the report of the States Reorganization Committee, the Assam legislature complained that it failed to recognize their claims to include NEFA in their state. 'We took it for granted,' said one member, 'that [the] North-East Frontier areas are already part of Assam and that their ultimate integration is only a question of time.' A second member clarified what this 'integration' was all about when he called for the free mixing of the tribes of NEFA and the Assamese, which would 'in process of time, leave no difference between Hill people and Plains people.' It seems integration meant many things to many people, for the levelling of difference was precisely what Elwin and his colleagues were working against. The NEFA administration was further condemned in the Assam legislature for demolishing the 'healthy process of gradual integration of all the people of North-East Frontier Agency and the rest [sic] of Assam which was developing slowly but surely over centuries...' As one politician put it, in a rare flash of wit, a feeling was growing that NEFA now meant 'No Entry For the Assamese.'[20]

The politicians of Assam worked long and hard to absorb NEFA into their state. They sent forth two study teams to the territory; both found what they wished to find, to wit, that the 'people of NEFA desire closer contact with the people of Assam and they consider the people of Assam to be friends and kinsmen.' The legislators asked for the speedy adminstrative integration of NEFA with Assam, the creation of a common secretariat, the formulation of a common plan of economic development for the region as a whole, and the propagation of Assamese in preference to Hindi: all measures stoutly opposed by Elwin and his colleagues.[21]

The first of these delegations remarked that the people of NEFA did 'not want to be kept aloof as specimens of [an] anthropological museum;' the second that 'the Philosophy of NEFA should be reoriented in the light of developing circumstances of the time.' This was perhaps as far as they could go in their criticisms of Elwin; for these were Congress politicians who knew of the anthropologist's closeness to the Supreme Leader, of whom they were in such mortal dread. But the Assamese press was bound by no such inhibitions and often singled out the peculiar type of erstwhile clergyman by name. In a speech in Shillong Nehru had proclaimed, 'I like variety. I like diversity.' The same evening Elwin and Lila were among the guests at a reception for the prime minister. A bitchy journalist, also present, commented on seeing Elwin enter 'with his wife from Bihar [*sic*]:' 'Here comes Nehru's variety.'[22]

Such remarks, in print and otherwise, finally moved Elwin to complain to the governor of Assam. He wrote that he counted himself among those who 'strongly oppose and criticise any idea of isolating the tribal people from their neighbours,' adding that he was himself 'very fond of the Assamese' and an admirer of their culture. He also mentioned in this connection two NEFA calendars designed by him, which had pictorially emphasised 'the importance of the integration of the tribal people with the rest of India and with Assam.'[23]

In that order, of course, for as one of his disciples remembered it, Elwin would not abide in his beloved NEFA any move towards 'Assam-ilation.'[24] Most contentious here was the question of the medium of instruction in NEFA schools. In addition to the tribal dialects, Elwin wanted the national language, Hindi, to be taught, rather than Assamese. Genuflections to Assamese culture in a NEFA calendar were one thing, the language of instruction (and perhaps in time indoctrination) quite another. On this question, at any rate, Elwin and the NEFA administration were unyielding.

A third group which viewed Elwin's work in NEFA with suspicion consisted of his old adversaries, the professional anthropologists. The Anthropological Survey of India wished to assert its own authority over NEFA, claiming a countrywide mandate to commission and supervise research. This was resisted by Elwin, who regarded NEFA as his own bailiwick, a field not open to independent research by other anthropologists, even if they were also in the employ of the Indian state. When the Survey proposed to send a research group into the territory, Elwin advised the governor to forbid them, saying that 'the invasion of NEFA by parties of anthropologists, who may not be trained in our policies, is not desirable. We may remember the P. M.'s directive that we should not allow too many outside bodies into NEFA and finally, the articles produced by the Calcutta anthropologists are sometimes misleading and tend to give a wrong impression of the Administration and its work.'[25]

The territorial imperative aside, Indian anthropologists had other reservations regarding NEFA, as expressed in an April 1957 talk to a conference of social workers by the distinguished Calcutta anthropologist Nirmal Kumar Bose. Like Elwin, Bose was a writer and scholar with a wide range of interests, not a narrow specialist at all; and like Elwin he had for a time been close to Gandhi, whose secretary and interpreter he had been when the Mahatma toured the villages of rural Bengal in 1946–7, dousing the flames of communal passion. Anyhow, for some reason the two men disliked one another, as witness their printed references to the other person's work. Bose, who had also studied the Juangs of Orissa, accused Elwin of photographing the tribe in leaves simply to show a 'vicarious pleasure in the existence of such "natural" savages in midst of India's fast changing economic life;' Elwin, who had also known the Mahatma, accused Bose of totally misunderstanding the man in his 'rather bad book,' *My Days with Gandhi*.[26]

Behind the personal animosity lay two different approaches to the tribal predicament.[27] In his 1957 lecture Bose criticized anthropologists who went 'curio-hunting' and then expresssed an 'unbalanced' romantic concern for tribals. These scholars highlighted aspects of tribal culture which marked them off from their Hindu neighbours, but Bose would rather stress their affinities with other poor Indians. 'Let us not by a special concern for tribal people, as distinguished from other sections of the masses who suffer from very nearly the same disabilities,' he remarked, encourage a 'force endangering social solidarity of the Indian people. Let us unite, not in freeing the tribal people from all bondage, but in devising means which will free all disinherited people from bondage of any kind, whether they are tribal or non tribal in origin.'[28]

Elwin was not mentioned by name in Bose's address, but he and his work were the chief target. Where the Calcutta man spoke for the unity of the poor, other anthropologists attacked Elwin in the name of political unity, or the oneness of India. One such was D. N. Majumdar of Lucknow University, the butcher back in 1952 of the Bondo book. He now took on *A Philosophy of NEFA*, but under a pseudonym. Writing as 'E.T.,' the initials of one of his submissive students, Majumdar charged Elwin with once more trying to pass off his own 'segregation' approach as the so-called anthropological solution to the tribal question. But in the earlier debates too, wrote the Lucknow professor, 'no Indian, no *Indian* anthropologist, toed the line with Elwin.' Indeed, the 'Indian Constitution gave an adequate reply. It was an "intervention therapy" that was recommended and the colossal efforts being made by the Government to rehabilitate the tribes and level them up indicate the dynamic upsurge leading to acculturation and assimilation.' But 'now it is Dr Elwin again [with regard to NEFA] who has reverted to the position of exclusiveness and segregation. If the tribals have a way of life, so they have, and if we have no right to force our way of life on them, are we to suppose that we should concede what the tribals want? We know what they want; the echo of Jharkhand [the movement for a separate tribal province in central India] has reached NEFA—should we follow the philosophy of inaction and intervention? Our stakes are too great . . .'[29]

Preserving the tribes as museum pieces for the sake of science, isolating them from their nearest Hindu neighbours, undermining through his work the prospects for national unity—these criticisms of Elwin's work in NEFA recall for us, as indeed they must have for him, the disputes of the nineteen-forties. The controversialist in him would not keep quiet, but his official status called for a more measured response. References to his critics are scattered through his file notings, but the most public defense was published in the Delhi monthly, *Seminar*. This took up the attacks by Dr Ram Manohar Lohia and that old anthropological Quisling, G. S. Ghurye of Bombay University. In early 1959 Professor Ghurye brought out a revised edition of his book of 1943, *The Aborigines—So Called—and their Future*. The study had a new title, and in several respects had been brought up-to-date, but it retained almost all its original and derisive references to Elwin and his work, without taking account of his writings in the interim.

Elwin took the intellectual more seriously than the politician, for Lohia (who 'seems to have developed a positive complex about me') is disposed off in a couple of paragraphs. He then turned to Ghurye's claim that he remained 'an isolationist, a no-changer and a revivalist,' based on views expressed twenty years previously, and even so, distorted by the Bombay scholar. He quoted from his old studies, *The Baiga* and *The Aboriginals*, to suggest that he had only advocated a temporary policy of isolation for a few vulnerable communities—this too in conditions of colonial rule where social work among the tribes was in its infancy. In any case, with Independence and the 'great awakening throughout the country,' tribal people had found their voice and a place of dignity in free India. No one now, wrote Elwin, 'would advocate a policy of isolation, although it is as important as ever to give some protection to the tribal people in the transition period during which they must learn to stand on their own feet and become strong enough to resist those who would exploit them.' Like everyone else, he was for change and development, with only this caveat: 'what I and those who think with me desire is change for the better and not degradation and decay.'

The tone of the essay, the careful clarification of his own views and his gestures to the dominant mood of 'change' and 'progress,' suggest that Ghurye had once more forced Elwin on to the back foot. And yet, when compared with his sharp interventions of the nineteen forties this is an altogether more assured, less polemical Elwin. Then he stood isolated, with Indian politicians, social workers and scholars all ranged against him. The only men on his side in those controversies were the odd British civil servant and amateur anthropologist: friends who were, in political and strategic terms, distinctly an embarassment.

In his battles in independent India, however, Elwin could call upon a wide array of supporters. Thus praise for *A Philosophy for NEFA* came from all over and from bigwigs of all kinds: from the vice-president of India (Sir Sarvepalli Radhakrishnan), the governor of Bihar (Dr Zakir Hussain), the home minister and the education minister, the high commissioner to the United Kingdom (Vijayalakshmi Pandit, Nehru's sister), the industrialist J. R. D. Tata. Some of these letters, generally from the not-so-mighty, were deeply felt. An Australian scholar, while complimenting the author, noted mournfully that the aboriginals in his country had already been beaten up beyond repair. A British anthropologist wanted him to write a more general work on tribal policy in the underdeveloped world: 'It would be absolutely invaluable in our Colonies and ex-Colonies, especially in Africa, and Pandit Nehru's name would carry enormous weight.

As far as I know nothing of the kind has been written and the fate of African tribals as things are at present is too horrible to contemplate.' The Austrian ethnographer C. von Fürer Haimendorf, who had lived with the Konyaks in the thirties, wrote of reading *A Philosophy* 'with mounting interest and a good deal of nostalgia. I really envy you the opportunity of working among the people of the N. E. Frontier.' Apa Pant, a maharajah-turned-Gandhian-turned diplomat, then serving as Indian ambassador to Bhutan, prayed that Elwin and his philosophy—the 'human, spiritual approach so well expressed in your book'—be granted 'enough time' to succeed. But he wondered 'whether isolated pockets of contented people with vast areas of habitable land would be allowed to exist in this mad world of ours.'[30]

A file in Elwin's papers preserves these letters and others of its kind; they nourished him, but more welcome than private encouragement was the public defense of him and his work. Many of the reviews of *A Philosophy for NEFA* were warmly appreciative, of the book and of the man. 'Great men are rare anywhere,' wrote *The Statesman*, 'in the right place rarer still. It is a question whether India is not exploiting Dr Elwin . . ., but at any rate she is giving both herself and him one of the most magnificent opportunities of recent times.' Tribal policy in NEFA, remarked the newspaper, was 'perhaps the most intelligent and enlightened approach to a terribly complicated problem yet devised.'[31] Another journalist, writing in the *Economic Weekly* after a tour through Elwin's domain, claimed that 'in some ways, NEFA might be considered a paradise. There are no taxes, no money-lenders, no middle men to exploit the people. Most of the officials recruited for service in NEFA have high qualifications and treat the tribesmen with consideration and sympathy . . . One would have to reach far and wide in history to find any comparable parallel to the liberality of the NEFA administration.'[32]

The men who ruled India also went out to bat for Elwin. Nehru's generous praise in print has been noted; nor was he shy of stating, to the press or in Parliament, that he 'broadly agreed with the approach of Dr Verrier Elwin.'[33] The home minister, Govind Ballabh Pant, was another admirer, telling a public meeting in Shillong that 'the great achievement of Dr Elwin in the last twenty years has been to make people all over India regard the tribals with respect. Previously we had looked on

12. The Deputy Director of the Anthropological Survey of India, on the balcony of his Calcutta home, 1949 (Sunil Janah)

13. Lila Elwin, c. 1963 (Sunil Janah/OUP)

14. Kumar Elwin, somewhere on the Frontier, c. 1960 (OUP)

15. The sahib and the scholar—Elwin with Professor C. von Fürer Haimendorf, Shillong, 1954 (OUP)

16. A Konyak Naga girl (Verrier Elwin/OUP)

17. Jawaharlal Nehru visiting Elwin's house and museum, Shillong, 1955, with Jairamdas Daulatram in the background (OUP)

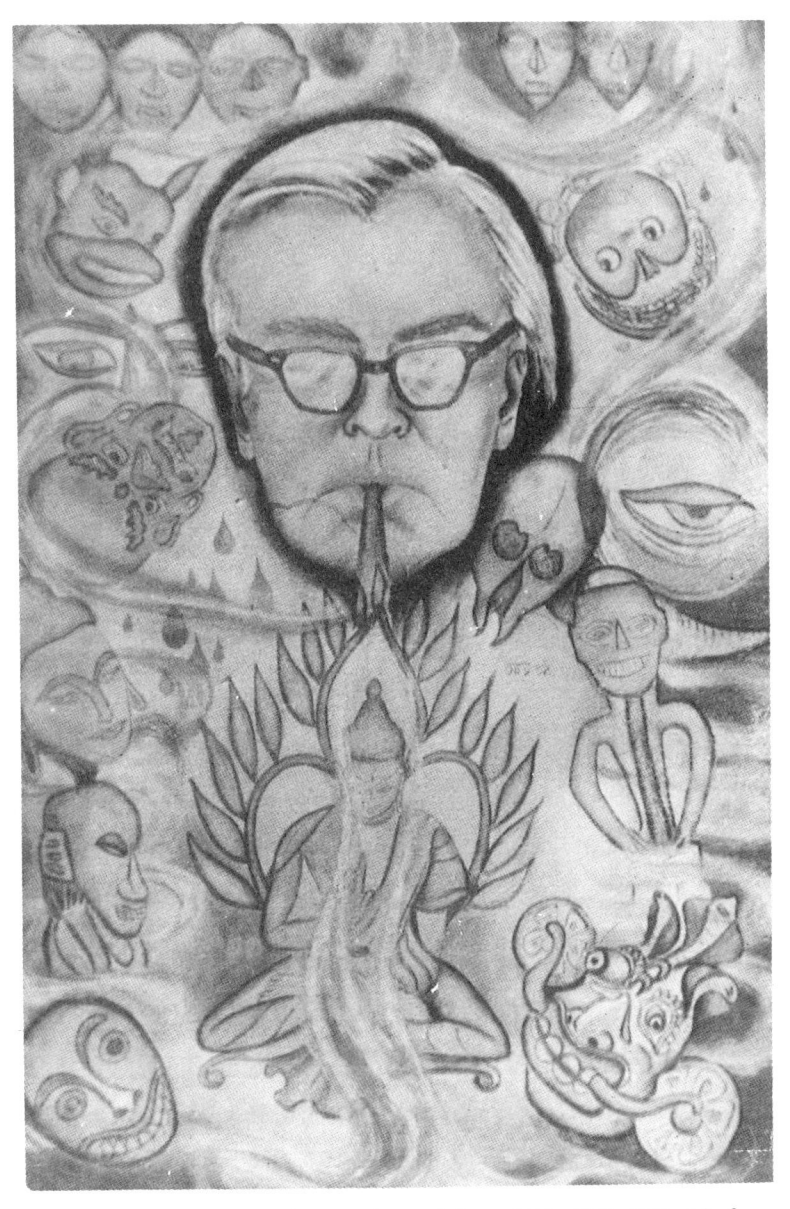

18. Cover portrait of the Indian edition of *The Tribal World of Verrier Elwin* (OUP)

19. Elwin receiving the Padma Bhushan from the President of India, New Delhi, 1961 (Nehru Memorial Museum and Library)

them as savages. But he has shown us that they have a culture and arts of their own.'[34]

The critics would not go away. In a Lok Sabha debate a Member of Parliament from Assam took a swipe at the policies recommended in *A Philosophy for NEFA*. 'Should we cut a frontier into piecemeal entities like this,' asked Hem Barua, or 'should we not have a consolidated entity in the frontier for the sake of our defense?' This was in effect a plea for the creation of a greater Assam, to include, as in colonial times, all the tribal tracts of the north-east. Barua then made a reference to the 'British philosopher-anthropologist' who seemed so influential in the north-east. He was at once contradicted by Jaipal Singh, leader of the Jharkhand movement for a separate tribal state, and also an Oxford contemporary of Elwin. 'Dr Verrier Elwin,' he reminded his colleague, 'is more Indian now than Shri Hem Barua. He is more tribal now than Jaipal Singh.'[35]

CHAPTER THIRTEEN

An Englishman for India

And thus this gentle rebel became the last in the line of Oxford scholar administrators in India, with an office in the secretariat.
    Ronald Symons on Verrier Elwin, in *Oxford and Empire* (1986)

Sri Madhava Ashish, a venerable Hindu monk of English extraction, once told me that his mentor Sri Krishna Prem and he were the second and third foreigners to be granted Indian citizenship. He believed Verrier Elwin was the first. If true, this was a considerable honour. The evidence to confirm or dispute this claim must exist somewhere in the ministry of home affairs, whose files are not available for public scrutiny.

Verrier himself was now comfortable with his new nationality, the confusions and uncertainties of the early fifties behind him. The job in NEFA had much to do with this, the support in the secretariat and the thrills of the chase besides. After his mother died England became more distant still. He had not been there for years and had no plans to go either.

Almost for the first time Verrier was content at work and at home, free of the torments that had chased him since Oxford. Lila he adored. He was too busy and too old to have as complete a relationship with their sons but he tried as best he could—fortnightly dinners out, alternately at the Pinewood Hotel, Shillong's best, and at a Chinese restaurant, as well as trips to the cinema with blankets and thermos of coffee in tow. What struck the boys most forcibly about their father was his cigar. A drawing by

Wasant, pasted in Verrier's diary, is called 'Daddy with Cigar;' another by Ashok, more inventive, has the little boy smoking the dreadful thing himself, with Mummy ticking off Daddy for allowing him to have one.

On 10th January 1959 Verrier drafted a new will which superseded the old one. This bequeathed 10 per cent of his estate to Kumar, the rest to Lila. If Lila died before him the estate was to be shared equally by Kumar, Wasant, Nakul and Ashok. The lack of any mention of Shamrao also suggests the way in which Verrier closed an earlier chapter of his life. 'I declare,' the will said,

> that in or about the year 1940 I was married to one Kausilya commonly known as Kosi. I have only one child by the said Kosi, namely a son by name Jawaharlal (commonly called Kumar) who was born in or about the year 1941. The said Kosi in or about the year 1947 [*sic*] gave birth to a boy who is named Bijay. The said Bijay is not my child and I have never accepted him as such. Because of the misconduct of the said Kosi, I have divorced her in or about the year 1949 . . . My wife and I have three children, all boys, named Wasant, Nakul and Ashok respectively. Besides [these] there is no living person who has any claim on my estate.[1]

Verrier Elwin was very likely the first Englishman to become an Indian, and most certainly the best known. His official position and proximity to Nehru seemed to many to be just reward for dogged and devoted work for the tribes. Even those who dissented from his views conceded he had stayed the course: twenty-five years in tribal India, twenty-five fine books about them.

An elegantly bound Visitors Book in the possession of Elwin's family in Shillong marks the names of those who came calling. His visitors included maharajahs, generals, and ministers; young Gandhians (Natwar Thakkar, running an ashram for the Nagas at Mokokchung), old Gandhians (Asha Devi Arayanayakam, running a school started by the Mahatma at Sevagram), suspicious Gandhians (D. J. Naik of A. V. Thakkar's Bhil Seva Mandal at Dahod, who allowed that this was 'a wonderful collection, which indicates the love of Dr Elwin for the tribes'), friendly

Gandhians (Kamaladevi Chattopadhyay, Jayaprakash Narayan, and Narayan Desai, son of Mahadev). An old friend who came was Christoph von Fürer Haimendorf, the London professor who rather wished he had Elwin's job. A new friend was Catherine Galbraith, wife of the American Ambassador (her entry: 'A fascinating morning, and I hope we meet again').

Like all of us, Elwin hoarded praise,[2] more so if it came from his ancient enemies—the middle-class Hindus who, now and then, had cavilled at his portraits of their culture; and the professional anthropologists who, over the years, had allowed him in only to throw him out again. But now that he was old and wise and big, the letters came pouring in. Some offered honest praise, others asked for jobs for their kin or forewords for their books. R. N. Gurtu, a Merton man who had not seen Verrier since Oxford, was stirred to write after seeing a collection of his books on display in Allahabad: 'I have led an arid life, though I ended up as a judge of the High Court, arid when I see the works of Elwin which lie before me.' A more recent acquaintance, an officer of the Indian Frontier Administrative Service, wrote of his 'singular luck' in being trained by Elwin, of the 'fatherly affection' he had received from him. 'I have always looked at your life with curiosity and affection,' wrote M. D. Tyagi: 'There are very few persons in this world who have staked their all to live their ideals. You are one of them.'

A young Indian studying in Illinois told Elwin that 'anthropologists in this country refer to you as one of the few great field-workers in anthropology.' Another asked Nehru's confidant to use his 'influence over the power-elite of our country' to help appoint his father (who was teaching in Calcutta University) to the first national professorship in anthropology. One eminent Western scholar, Rodney Needham, begged to be allowed into NEFA—and if that were not possible, for Elwin to send one of his best assistants to be trained in Oxford. A second, Claude Lévi-Strauss, recommended a student for a job and then asked with hopeful interest: 'Are you planning to write any ethnography on the peoples of north-eastern India?' The American Museum of Natural History invited him to spend three months in the United States, introducing and displaying his great collection of tribal artefacts. They would pack and transport his stuff and pay for him, but negotiations broke down when he insisted that they pay for Lila too.

A letter that gave much satisfaction arrived from George Devereux who, long ago, had reviewed *The Agaria* in tones of lofty condescension. The Frenchman then urged Elwin to leave the forest for the graduate seminar; now he completely withdrew his earlier remarks. 'I think you are a very enviable person,' wrote Devereux,

> who has laid out for himself a much wiser and much more gratifying course in life than most of us. Perhaps you do not have a grand piano in your sitting room, nor a Cadillac or a Rolls Royce in your garage—instead, you have chosen to live with people and to work among and with them. I rather think that your human horizons are wider than those of most of us.
>
> I speak of this with some feeling since, in 1935, when I could choose between staying forever among the mountain people of Indochina—who, as you know, are very much like your Gonds and your Nagas—and going back to the hurly-burly of so-called civilization, I underwent a very real inner struggle—and probably chose the wrong solution.

A letter of open admiration also came from Wayland Young, the pacifist, author, and liberal peer. Young, an editor with Jonathan Cape, wrote of having been a 'tremendous admirer' of Elwin's work since reading *The Muria and their Ghotul*, a book which made tribals 'come alive enough for a lot of their sayings and views of the world to pass into the ordinary fabric of life for my wife and me and friends.' 'Will you allow me,' he asked, 'to enter the field of those who are pursuing you for a book? Or are you tied up with the Oxford University Press? Any old thing whether tribal erotics or general observations on the life and lot of those who seek to advise Governments on tribal affairs, or the nature of God and man, or anything else?'

From literary London too came a man whose range of interests and experience matched his. Arthur Koestler had been told of Verrier by Shaun Mandy, and saw in him a likely informant for a book he planned on the religions of the east. He arrived in Shillong in February 1959 and stayed a fortnight with the Elwins. The visitor, wrote Verrier, 'had an electric effect on us all, even the children who loved him. He radiated peace and strength and seemed to like us as much as we liked him.' Koestler was indeed entranced by them all, especially Lila, whom he kissed good-bye in continental fashion. The day before, she had pushed him into a bath he had not entered all week; and when he came out dressed she forcibly cleaned his shoes.

In the evenings the Hungarian-born Englishman and the British-born Indian had 'long enchanting talks.' These fed into *The Lotus and the Robot*, where Koestler's cold-eyed scepticism judged both Gandhism and Zen Buddhism to be unworthy of the modern world. The book, to Verrier's great pride but also some embarrassment, was dedicated to him.[3]

Arthur Koestler, somewhat surpisingly, was to become the recipient by letter of Verrier's confidences, taking the place in this respect of Shamrao—who lived in Madhya Pradesh and never replied in any case—as well as of Bill Archer, whom he had not seen for years, and of Victor Sassoon, who had migrated to Bangkok and disappeared into its fleshpots. After Koestler left Verrier toured the Buddhist uplands, conversing with peasants and visiting their temples. He meditated for hours alone, in front of their exquisite little images of the Buddha. He wrote about his visit to Koestler, the lapsed Zionist-Communist: 'Whether it was the beauty or the love and kindness of the people, I recaptured some of the ecstasy and peace of the days long ago when I found it at the feet of another deity, a god that in my own case later failed.'[4]

Verrier returned with some reluctance to Shillong. Later that month the Dalai Lama himself was seen where Verrier had just been. The monarch of Tibetan Buddhism had dramatically entered NEFA following the failure of a popular uprising against the Chinese. He was first given refuge at the monastery in Tawang, before coming down to Assam.

Elwin was in the plains at the time of the Dalai Lama's entry into India and was disappointed at not being able to go to Tawang to greet him. But he offered *Holiday Magazine* of London an exclusive story, with photographs, of the god-prince's escape from communism. His account was finally published not in *Holiday* but in the more established *Geographical Magazine*. He wrote here of the Tibetan leader feeling immediately at home among the 'simple Buddhist tribesmen' of NEFA, followers of the same faith and devoted to him and his ideals. Here was proof that while great empires such as Communist China will rise and fall, the 'spiritual kingdom endures through exile, hardship and danger.' Elwin smartly gave himself and his government a puff: the Dalai Lama, he noted, had thanked the Indian officers who 'spared no effort in making his stay and journey through this extremely well-administered part of India as comfortable as possible.' The reader, the Western reader, was asked to choose between totalitarianism and democracy, between China's persecution of Tibetans and India's treatments of its minorities who lived, at any rate in NEFA, in 'peaceful, happy villages.'[5]

By now Elwin was being increasingly called to wider duties. In May the home ministry invited him to chair a committee to study the progress of economic development in tribal areas. The assignment was 'rather a triumph,' he told a friend, 'for the home ministry is the centre of Indian puritanism: I shall probably start some furious controversies.'[6] Through its work Elwin renewed contact with the tribes of central India, visiting remote areas of Andhra Pradesh, Orissa and Bihar, 'charging about the country in jeeps like a school inspector.' But for some reason he scrupulously avoided Bastar, despite the warm and repeated invitations of a member of his committee who worked there. I suspect that with his own happy memories of the place he could not bear to find out what civilization had done to Bastar's tribals in the twenty years since he had last seen them.

Elwin saw his report, submitted in March 1960, as a sequel to *A Philosophy for NEFA*, applying its ideas throughout India.[7] Thus shifting cultivation, regarded by foresters as 'almost the essential tribal vice,' was once more defended as a necessary adaptation to a difficult terrain. The state and its officials are asked to acquire the 'tribal touch,' to look at things 'through tribal eyes and from the tribal point of view.' A tribal bias, explained Elwin, 'means that we recognize and honour their way of doing things, *not because it is old and picturesque, but because it is theirs*, and they have as much right to their culture as anyone else in India.' The tribal touch in practice implied a respect for herbal medicine, traditional tribal housing and ways of educating the young, as in the ghotul. Development programmes, it was suggested, might work with and through these institutions rather than in opposition to them.

There is however a sombre and sometimes bitter tone that runs through the home ministry report. For Indian independence, 'which has brought the glories and inspiration of freedom to millions, has given little to these poor people.' The committee, noted its chairman, had 'been deeply shocked by the poverty of the tribal people, the exploitation that they still suffer, the lack of consideration with which they are all too often treated, the burden of fear and anxiety under which they live, the pressure on them of unfamiliar regulations, and the loss of many good elements in their own tradition and culture.' This appears in a prologue: the report's epilogue, meanwhile, explains that much of tribal suffering and deprivation is

> the fault of us, the 'civilized' people. We have driven them into the hills because we wanted their land and now we blame them for cultivating it in the only way we left for them. We have robbed them of their arts by sending them the cheap and tawdry products of a commercial economy. We have even taken away their food by stopping their hunting, or by introducing new taboos which deprive them of the valuable protein elements in meat and fish. We sell them spirits which are far more injurious than the homemade beer and wines which are nourishing and familiar to them, and use the proceeds to uplift them with ideals. We look down on them and rob them of their self-confidence, and take away their freedom by laws which they do not understand.

There is a note of anger here that is by and large missing from Elwin's writings on NEFA, where of course civilization in its many exploitative guises had not yet properly penetrated. Back briefly in central India he challenged head on the commonly accepted meanings of 'primitive' and 'civilized.' 'Primitiveness,' in his view, should be taken to mean 'self-reliance, community work and a spirit of co-operation, artistic creativeness, honesty, truthfulness, hospitality, a highly organized society.' 'Who is backward,' asks Elwin, 'the creative artist at her tribal loom, the gentle mother with her child among the hills, or the inventor of the atom bomb which may destroy her and all the world? Are these self-reliant, co-operative tribes the really backward as against the self-seeking, individualistic, crafty products of our industrial civilization?'[8]

Elwin was next asked to prepare a book on the Nagas, that truculent minority in free India. From 1947 the Indian government had tried with mixed success to control or co-opt an armed struggle for an independent Naga homeland. When in 1960 New Delhi began negotiating with such rebels as were willing to talk, the Western press, and in particular *The Observer* of London, carried a series of reports on 'atrocities' by the Indian army. The government turned to the most fluent and the most credible writer in its ranks, asking him to write a book presenting India's case abroad. Elwin agreed, but most unwillingly. 'I feel that I am entirely the wrong person to do it,' he told a colleague, 'but as it has been allotted to me I must do what I can.' To R. E. Hawkins he described it as 'the most difficult job I have yet done.' The assignment must surely have recalled for him the time of Gandhi's civil disobedience movement, when he had so passionately upheld the right to self-determination of a subject people. Curiously, a British Anglican priest, Michael Scott, was most active in the Naga cause; he was very nearly to the arms-carrying rebels what Elwin had once been to the non-violent Congress.

Jawaharlal Nehru, while certainly affected by the criticisms in the British press, did not count the Nagas among his favourite people. Back in 1953 he was visiting Kohima with the Burmese prime minister U Nu when a Naga delegation wished to present him with a petition asking for a just consideration of their demands. They hoped to hand this over to the prime minister at his public meeting, but some arrogant underlings would not allow them to do this. Nehru was a little late coming to the meeting, by which time the crowd, told of the rebuff, had started dispersing. His daughter Indira Gandhi, speaking unwittingly into the live microphone, said agitatedly, '*Papa, wo jaa rahe hain*' (father, they are all going). Nehru replied, gravely, '*Haan beti, main dekh raha hoon*' (yes, daughter, I can see them go.)[9] Never before had the people's prince been treated so, and Nehru did not forget the slight. He never returned to Nagaland and could not bring himself to trust Naga leaders like Phizo or Naga sympathizers like Scott. Meeting Elwin in July 1960 he professed not to be worried about accusations of rape made against armymen. 'I have gone into the matter very carefully,' he said, 'and I can only find five authenticated accusations of rape by such a large body of troops during the last five years. I do not think that this is really very much.'[10]

Elwin privately described his Nagaland book as attempting 'in as subtle and dispassionate a way as possible to put India's case on all matters about which there has been controversy'—matters such as the treatment of minorities in India as a whole, the legitimacy of India's claims over Naga territory, the representativeness, or lack of it, of the Naga insurgents, and the truth of the allegations regarding army brutality. All the same in presenting India's case Elwin was unwilling to go as far as the foreign ministry wanted him to. He refused to exonerate the Indian army of all the charges brought against it. Critical remarks were necessary not only because they were true but because their absence would raise suspicion: 'from the point of view of readers, especially in England, I believe that if we admit a certain [number of] mistakes we are more likely to convince them of the strength of our case.' He would mention the deaths of tribals as a consequence of their being forced into grouped villages, he said, because he could not 'go against my conscience in these matters.'

Through successive drafts of the book Elwin battled with Indian officials about the use of the word 'rebel.' His superiors prefered 'hostiles' as a characterization of the insurgents; they also complained of his 'tendency to stress the strength of the Naga independence movement.' Elwin held his ground, noting that the best known usage of 'hostiles' was to 'describe a Red Indian who opposed the white settlers in America—hardly a desirable association.' To use 'hostile' as a noun, as he was asked to do, seemed to suggest 'some extra-terrestrial monsters coming from outside space.' His own alternative, 'rebel,' also indicated that the Nagas were 'Indians rebelling against their own legally constituted authority.' 'Rebel' he was finally allowed to retain, but he had however to drop 'rebellion.'[11]

When the Naga struggle began in 1947 his friend Bill Archer had just given up charge of his post at Mokokchung. On the train out of the hills Archer wondered what the future held for the Nagas. 'Would India confuse nationalism with uniformity,' he asked, 'and slowly reduce them to a depressed, unhappy caste? Or would the Indian government swiftly reach some sensible settlement which would allow them to remain Nagas and preserve their vivid way of life?'[12]

What in December 1947 was posed as very much an open question was answered resoundingly in the affirmative by Elwin in 1960. His book on Nagaland is a combination of many things: a breezy survey of the different Naga tribes, a celebration of their artistic traditions, a potted history of the rebellion—but it is above all a claim that the Nagas shall be integrated (as he was) with honour in the Indian nation. The anthropologist most subtly portrays the Nagas as an 'important branch of the great and varied Indian family:' with their production systems like those of other Indian tribes, their religious ceremonials and patterns of sacrifice not dissimilar to Hinduism in its older Vedic forms. If traditional India had something in common with the Nagas, the new India had much to offer them too. The story of India, wrote Elwin,

> has been, in Dr S. K. Chatterjee's words, "a synthesis of races and cultures leading to the creation and characterization of a composite Indian civilization, diverse in its origins but united in its ideals and aspirations—ideals and aspirations which are acceptable to all mankind; while India looks forward to a still greater unification of all mankind, both within her shores and outside."
>
> As Nagaland realizes its position in this great country, of which it is so precious a part, it will share in the fulfilment of this ideal.[13]

All his life Elwin had to work his way between competing allegiances—moral, religious, scientific, sexual, political—yet the Nagaland assignment presented a dilemma of almost unsurpassed painfulness. Long ago, when his publisher had asked him to write a book he did not feel up to writing, he quoted Herbert Paul: 'Seek the prizes of your own calling and be resolutely *hors de combat* to all others.'[14] So long as he was a freelancer he could stand by this, but as an employee of the Government of India he had to bend, slightly. But one thinks that as he wrote his book he espied, watching him, the judgmental shadows of his friends W. G. Archer and J. H. Hutton, men who had known and served the Nagas and were, if anything, prone to overlook the excesses of their side. When Hutton posted him a statement in the London press that was critical of the Indian army, Elwin replied angrily: 'These enthusiastic clergymen, who really know nothing about the subject and whose knowledge of the Nagas is based on a few gentlemen dressed up like members of the YMCA in London, have been talking through their hats and there is little doubt that they have done a lot of harm and have led to a greater loss of life.'[15]

Perhaps the happiest moment in the whole assignment came when Elwin visited a new Gandhian ashram in Mokokchung. To his delight and surprise they served him pork and rice-beer.[16] These Gandhians would accommodate the Naga way of life, but would the government? The conviction carried in his book turns less certain in an anonymous comment he published in *The Statesman*. Reviewing a book on 'Clemency' Canning, the viceroy appointed after the rebellion of 1857, Elwin noted his opposition to the burning of villages and his disregard of the criticisms of the Anglo-Indian press. 'Those who have to deal with the rebel Nagas in the eastern Hills,' he remarked, 'could read this book with profit.'[17]

The unease persisted much after the Nagaland book was printed and published. When R. E. Hawkins passed on a reader's complaint that there seemed some discrepancy between the Elwin of 1930 and the Elwin of 1960, he answered that he had

> consistently behind the scenes, urged the policy of tolerance and compassion; and that I have always pressed for that emancipation from Delhi which has now been achieved for the Nagas by the establishment of Nagaland. I don't myself see much inconsistency between my youth and age, for there is not really any comparison between the Satyagrahis fighting for Freedom and the Nagas and, by and large, I feel that India has given the Nagas a very square deal. But the whole business of any idealist belonging to an official set-up is extremely complicated. On the very day before India marched into Goa [to free it from Portuguese rule] I gave a lecture in Delhi on the importance of non-violence![18]

Since coming to Shillong Verrier had not had a day's holiday. The Government of India had more than its money's worth and knew it. It fell to his friend K. L. Mehta, a former adviser to the governor in NEFA who was now a joint secretary in New Delhi, to convey the 'sanction of the President to the continued appointment of Dr Verrier Elwin as Adviser on Tribal Affairs for a further period of five years from 1/1/1960.' Mehta received in reply a letter asking, 'But who will sanction the continued existence of Dr Verrier Elwin for this period?' It then quoted the Dhammapada:

> Here shall I dwell in the rain, here in winter and summer—thus the fool thinks and does not think of death. Death comes and carries off that man

boastful of his children and flocks, his mind distracted, as a flood carries off a sleeping village.[19]

Death would call anyway, but there was still work to be done, tours to be made and reports to be written or rewritten. In a profile he wrote as a broadcast to the NEFA outback sometime in June 1960, Elwin remarked of being 'surrounded by floods of galley proofs and reams of paper.' Later that year he was invited to join a high-powered Commission on Scheduled Areas and Scheduled Tribes, eight of whose members were 'teetotal and vegetarian Congress Members of Parliament,' one of these the chairman, U. N. Dhebar, a former chief minister of Gujarat. The opposition consisted of himself and his friend Jaipal Singh, the Jharkhand leader.[20]

Elwin's work with the Dhebar Commission began with a week's tour of Rajasthan in December. This desert state he scarcely knew, and what he saw of its administration he did not much like. A four-page crisply argued report to the governor characteristically combined philosophy with fine detail. Why were Bhil girls, who traditionally wore embroidered skirts, put into white saris, in the manner of Hindu widows, when they entered government schools? Why was the vegetarianism of the rest of the state being imported into Bhil territory? Boys and girls in school hostels from homes where fish and meat were prized foods would be undernourished; moreover, the moralizing bluster of the improving teacher would develop in them a 'sense of guilt so that when they go home they will feel they ought not to eat nonvegetarian food.' Why did school textbooks not speak of Bhil heroes and Bhil myths? 'History lessons bringing in the Bhils would help to preserve their pride in themselves (which seems to be going down). Even in mixed schools it would not do the non-tribal boys any harm to learn something of the history and tradition of their tribal fellow-students and might do something to make them respect them more.' Why couldn't archery be encouraged instead of soccer, wood-carving and mask-making (old Bhil crafts) rather than weaving?[21]

Verrier returned to Shillong in early January; on the 26th (Republic Day) he heard over the radio that he had been awarded the Padma Bhushan. This he described to Eldyth as roughly equivalent to a 'knighthood, but a good knighthood, a GCSI or a GCB.' For the investiture, in April, he took Lila with him. The award was given by the president, Rajendra Prasad; like that old Gandhian Verrier also wore a buttoned-up khadi suit, the first time he'd worn the stuff in years. The next day he had a private lunch with Nehru, where he 'managed to get in a good many points about which I was concerned across to him.''

There were however things he could not speak to the great man about. He had no pension and worried about Lila and the children. 'I am finding it extremely difficult to make ends meet,' he told Eldyth, 'taxation is terrible and the price of things is going up almost every month—what will happen when my appointment here comes to an end or I myself go to heaven I really do not know, for the rupee is really losing its value.'[22]

The financial worries apart, Lila and Verrier seemed to have a good thing going, she providing the stability and sustenance, the base from which he would reach out to the outside world and to which he would always return. Shamrao Hivale once wrote of the Pardhan wife that she was 'at once a source of supreme delight and intense anxiety to her husband.'[23] The description, both parts, better fits Kosi, who was of course a Gond. The fires of that union had been swamped by a gush of cold water, but the flame of this one was steady and serene, to be put out only by his death or hers. That at any rate is what the evidence I collected—in letters, in print, and through interviews—would point to. It was therefore a surprise, a shock even, to find in absolutely the last archival collection I laid my hands upon—that of Arthur Koestler—a letter from Verrier of 7th June 1961 that spoke of how

> in the last three months I have fallen into the worst emotional tangle of my life, all the more devastating as it can't come to anything, for I will never do anything to hurt Lila—I am very much in love with her and she is the rock which will go on. But the other person, who is brilliant and has the erotic impact of a dozen atom bombs has introduced me to quite a different kind of love, for all my varied experiences have been tribal, uncomplicated, delicious but non-frustrating. I will adjust myself in time and meanwhile it has done me good, I think, in increasing compassion and understanding of something new to me, and has certainly made me very humble. You are the only person in the world I've told about this.

Her name was Margot, she was married to someone called Bob, and they had children of their own. More details are hard to come by, but they seem to have been British, with Bob probably a planter in the estates around Shillong. She was in love with Verrier too, but her situation made it equally unlikely that they could go further. Letters were exchanged, assignations made, but beyond that it seemed futile. It is no accident that, some weeks after he unburdened himself to Koestler, Verrier had a heart attack. The doctor's report identified a 'ventricle infracted by a coronary thrombosis.' But the patient would make a characteristic joke: it sounded, he said, 'like a young woman describing how she lost her virginity.' He was prescribed eight weeks' rest, but the papers kept coming. U. N. Dhebar brought some of them when he came to Shillong to ask his member to rewrite a draft of their report.

Whatever his reservations about the other teetotaller-vegetarians, Elwin got on well with Dhebar. Their chief disagreement was on the question of prohibition, which Dhebar recommended and Elwin of course opposed. He told his chairman that 'to the tribal people the necessity of liquor in religious and other ceremonies is as real as wine for use in the Mass is to a Catholic.' The analogy was lost to one more familiar with ashrams than cathedrals, but otherwise Dhebar allowed the scribe his way. With the Gandhian looking on, they translated into plain English '600 pages of admirable suggestions but atrocious writing.' It was hard going, but Elwin welcomed the chance of leaving out a good many things he did not like and putting in other things which required more emphasis. The draft quoted a forest botanist as saying, in 1942, that 'of all practices initiated by man, shifting cultivation is the most noxious,' to which the printed report responded, in Elwin's voice: 'The atom bomb had not, of course, been invented at that time.' By the end he had also made sure that this was the first such report which did not have to use those abominable terms, 'backward,' 'uplift' and 'superstition.'[24]

Dhebar finally flew away in September, but the effort had left Elwin tired and irritable. When a young scholar from Nagpur sent him an essay on the old isolation/assimilation debate he replied in somewhat intemperate tones. 'I think,' he wrote, that 'you give rather too much attention to Dr Ghurye who is so prejudiced against his rivals that his work is generally remarkably inaccurate.' The Nagpur scholar had also suggested that Elwin's two marriages 'indicated his appreciation of the tribal people.' The anthropologist did not see this as a compliment. 'I do not quite see what my private affairs have to do with your argument,' he answered, 'the fact that I could marry two or twenty tribal girls would not necessarily give any indication of my appreciation of the tribal people in general but would merely suggest that in erotic matters I was not limited by racial considerations. Moreover the way it is put does not seem to be in very good taste.'[25]

In the last week of 1961 Elwin was due to give the Sardar Patel lectures on All India Radio—India's Reith Lectures, to stretch the analogy a little. Previous lecturers included the writer-statesman C. Rajagopalachari and the great scientists K. S. Krishnan and J. B. S. Haldane. The sponsors hoped he would speak on tribals, but he answered that the subject was by now 'hackneyed and over-written.' This was true in a way, but perhaps he had no wish to become once again the centre of controversy. He finally chose to speak on the theme of love.[26]

The Patel lectures, entitled *A Philosophy of Love*, are a summing-up of the experiences of a scholar-activist, a conspectus of all the men and ideas that came to influence him. The title is from John Donne, to whom he had been introduced by H. W. Flecker at Dean Close. The lectures draw richly on the work of all those Verrier had loved, and what they had to say about love. He revisits here the Christian mystics—Richard Rolle, Catherine of Genoa, John of the Cross—and their Indian counterparts, Kabir and Mirabai. He comes then to Mahatma Gandhi, who brought down the ideal of love 'almost with a bump, to earth, away from abstractions to [the] realities' of human and national friendships; and ends with a bow to compassion, forgiveness and humility, identified by him as the three virtues cherished by all religions.

Only six pages of *A Philosophy of Love* are devoted to love among the tribes. But the lecturer's lifelong engagement manifests itself in other ways. He insists that erotic love does 'not appear as the enemy of what we call the higher love but part of it'—this in contrast to the 'violent reactions of Christian ascetics' and the 'hypocritical outlook of many Puritans.' As both the tribal and classical Indian traditions recognize, sexual love is a 'good beautiful thing,' an art almost. Modern Indians would do well to study ancient techniques of love-making, not 'to extend their lusts outside the marriage-bond but in order to make a greater success of love within it.'

While drafting the lectures Verrier read a news report of the wedding of one of Mahatma Gandhi's grandsons, with a photograph of the couple being blessed by Morarji Desai. He pasted the report in his diary, writing underneath: ' "We must not let our lusts enter into marriage"—Gandhi.' In fact, when Elwin told All India Radio he would speak not on tribals but on love, they asked him to focus on Gandhi. He answered that 'to take the Gandhian philosophy of love as a subject [would] commit me too much to one point of view.'[27] *A Philosophy of Love* can be read as the last of his arguments with Gandhi, albeit an argument conducted with the greatest courtesy. Inspired perhaps by his Buddhism, there is a mellowness to the book as a whole, an uncharacteristic but welcome respect for faiths that he had once held and since rejected.

Psychologists, notes Elwin, have remarked of the frustrated life of the ascetic that 'the mystics or devotees give to their divine lovers what they have been unable to find on earth:' an interpretation that actually well fits his own early intensely personal love for Christ. He now enters into a disagreement with the Christian ascetic and the Gandhian who regard the married life as 'somehow inferior to celibacy.' In 1933, that belief had persuaded Verrier and Mary Gillet to abandon their partnership. Thirty years and two marriages later, Elwin was convinced that the 'danger in marriage is not that we love too much but that we should love too little.'[28]

By a happy coincidence, immediately following the Patel lectures, Elwin presided over a marriage born of love. Amina Yusuf Ali, a Muslim friend who was also the illustrator of his NEFA books, was to marry a Hindu disciple, Nalini Jayal, of the Indian Frontier Administrative Service. The union was opposed by both families, for Amina came from the high Hyderabad aristocracy, Jayal from the equally conservative Brahmin stock of upper Garhwal. The former Christian and priest took it upon himself to arrange this wedding of Hindu and Muslim. He did it with gusto, offering his house, arranging the decorations, even acting as the bride's father.[29]

For some years now Verrier had been as much out of NEFA as within it, so in February 1962 he turned with pleasure to the design of the next year's official calendar. Previous calendars had always illustrated a theme of his choosing—cottage industry, tribal dances, wildlife preservation—and for 1963 he chose 'Integration.' He planned six portraits of how NEFA might be linked with the rest of India. Each picture would capture a group of tribals in a frame of leafy branches—'to give the idea of the forest setting'—looking at, respectively, the Taj Mahal, a hydroelectric project, a statue of Gandhi, a picture of the president with the vice-president and prime minister, one of Sanchi or Bodh Gaya with the Kamengs (themselves Buddhists) doing the viewing, and last of all 'some scene typifying Assam's history and culture.'[30]

There were parts of NEFA he had not seen; the question was whether he would ever get to them. Files in the secretariat took up his days, the writing of his memoirs the evenings. Despite interested letters from Cape and Hutchinson he had decided to publish his autobiography with Oxford University Press. Home to work and back again; that was the routine he now followed, and in June even this was abbreviated. When he complained of breathlessness the doctor confined him to the house for a month. In July he wrote grumpily to his OUP editor, R. E. Hawkins: 'I am getting better slowly but I am still being bullied by my doctor. Yesterday I got the concession that I might go to the cinema once a week and visit an agreeable friend for half an hour once a week. Otherwise I remain under house-arrest.' In time he was allowed to go back to work, but he could not tour that winter.[31] 'The ban on clambering about over the frontier mountains and losing myself in the wilds,' he wrote to Arthur Koestler, 'has been a very severe blow, for I love the remote, the lonely and the obscure. But these are things that happen, I suppose, if one is presumptuous enough to live to the age of sixty.' Koestler's reply was cheerily reassuring: 'I am not unduly worried about your heart attacks. All my medical friends tell me that a few light attacks at the right age are the best life insurance, though nobody can quite explain why. I know of several paradigmatic octogenarian examples.'[32]

In November 1962 the Chinese marched into NEFA and overran the Indian army, an ill-fed, poorly-clothed and completely unprepared soldiery that had been hitherto drilled to think of their northern neighbours as their 'Asian brothers.' Some officials, fearing the worst, fled Shillong for the plains, but Verrier and Lila refused to 'join the pathetic rank of evacuees.' However, Verrier's blood pressure went up twenty points after the fall of Tawang and a further five points after the fall of Bomdi La. He found it 'agonising to hear of places like Tawang or dear little Jang where Lila and I picked wild strawberries long ago, or Wallong where I did an adventurous air-flight with Khemlal Rathee, falling into the hands of the Chinese.' Luckily Kumar, then a trainee with the Assam Rifles, was not close to the fighting.[33]

The Chinese invasion drew fresh criticism of the philosophy for NEFA. A few months before the war a Major Sitaram Johri published a book critical of the NEFA administration. The book and its arguments were now revived. Elwin and his colleagues were accused of isolating their territory from Assam and India, to deadly effect. The 'NEFA official class,' wrote Major Johri, 'is so drugged with adulation that it would never advocate the "open door" policy in the territory lest their privileges might be curtailed. The NEFA . . . must remain an inaccessible Shangrila for the public.' If NEFA had not been kept separate and distinct, it was implied, the Chinese would not have dared come in. The need now was to 'multiply the area of association and contact with the outside world and not keep [the tribals] within their own narrow circle.'[34] It was even suggested by Opposition politicians in Delhi that 100,000 farmers from Punjab be settled in NEFA, both to further the assimilation of tribals and to dissuade the Chinese from coming again.[35]

Elwin was worried by this last proposal. At another time he would have written to Nehru, but the prime minister was deeply disturbed himself, his authority and political standing eroded by the fiasco on the frontier. So he sent in his protest to Indira Gandhi. Her reply is an early indication of how far she was to depart from her father's politics, a presaging perhaps of the state of Emergency she was to impose on India some thirteen years later. 'Thank you for sending me your notes on NEFA,' she wrote: 'I do agree with much that you say but now that the doors have opened, it will be increasingly difficult to keep out undesirable elements or ideas. This is the price we pay for democracy, [which] not only throws up the mediocre person but gives strength to the most vocal howsoever they may lack knowledge and understanding.'[36]

The India-China war also brought a letter from one who had been out of Verrier's life for thirty years—Mary Gillet. She was working at a teacher's training college in Berkshire, still single, still helping and serving. Mary wrote that the news of the Chinese invasion had placed 'India and you and your family and Shamrao in particular in my thoughts... The world doesn't seem to have grown much happier since you and I were young in it! I should love to know India now that the barriers between Indians and English are down.'[37]

The Chinese had gone but Verrier's gloom deepened. When R. E. Hawkins suggested that he name his memoirs 'Pilgrim's Way to NEFA,' he replied that 'there is the difficulty that if you are not likely to publish till 1964, by then I will either be dead or turned out or perhaps NEFA itself may have come to an end.'[38] Meanwhile news came from Mandla that Shamrao was desperately short of money and that his wife had fallen in love with a younger man. Verrier was not in a position to help much, for his health continued to decline. 'I am being filled up with antibiotics which make me feel rather miserable,' he wrote to Hawkins in March of 1963. The next bulletin, three weeks later, complained of 'a rather shattering attack when whatever infection was moving around inflamed both my liver and my gall bladder.'[39]

In April Eldyth arrived for a month's holiday. She had not been in India for twenty-five years and had not seen her brother for fourteen. Reading his autobiography in manuscript she complained about the first chapter. The family's faith, she said, was not as dreary as he made out: could he not show mother and Evangelicalism 'real respect'? As for the rest of the book, though, it was a 'wonderful tale,' an 'unfolding of scientific compassion leading to so much. How pitiful it would be if I tried to write my life!' The day she left Shillong Verrier had another attack. He could not sleep night after night, and was finally admitted to the military hospital and put on oxygen. He corrected the proofs of his memoirs amidst mounting depression. 'Everything is very uncertain,' he told Eldyth, 'China and where we will be ourselves and what is going to happen in India itself.' A big blow was Kumar's failure in the matriculation, for had he passed the exam his father's friends had arranged everything to make him an officer.[40]

Through 1963 Verrier was in and out of hospital. His blood pressure remained high and he complained of breathlessness and heaviness in the chest. From May he had been totally sedentary and worked, when not in hospital, out of home. Writing on 12th June, the governor of Assam conveyed his worries and those of his boss: 'I hope you will be careful and not exert yourself for some time. The Prime Minister whom I met the other day was much concerned about your health.'[41]

The same week there arrived a letter from the great man himself. The cares of a defeated state had diminished his interest in the tribals but not it seems in their defender. Nehru came to Assam to open a new bridge over the Brahmaputra but had not time to go up the hill to Shillong. 'My dear Elwin,' he wrote, 'For many years, whenever I have come to Assam I have looked forward to meeting you. If I had gone to Shillong on this occasion, I would certainly have tried to see you.' He went on: 'I have been much concerned to learn of your ill-health and that you have been in hospital for some time. I hope you are getting well there and the rest is doing you good. I hope to meet you when I next come to this part of the world.'[42]

Also in June came Shamrao Hivale. He was broke and unhappy and must have communicated this to his friend, though no record remains. But Lila's son, then a boy of nine, recalls the visit being shot through with tension, for Sham, always proprietorial about Verrier, 'was very arrogant towards my mother.'[43] Quick on Sham's heels arrived his chief tormentor, Jehangir Patel. Before coming he had written to Verrier that he was considering withdrawing support to the school still run by TWARU in Patangarh; Sham, he said, 'is good for another 15 years work but he is one of the laziest human beings in India.'[44] The judgement was deeply unfair and it is difficult to escape the conclusion that the Bombay millionaires would much rather fund a flamboyantly articulate Englishman than a quietly serving Indian. When Elwin left Patan and TWARU the glamour went out of their sponsorship. Even J. R. D. Tata, requested by Verrier to support Sham, granted him a measly one hundred rupees a month.

The summer, and the month of June most particularly, was the time for Verrier's most loved and longstanding friends to call or send word, to bring to him in his bed the memories and associations that had made and unmade his life. On the 19th a lovely letter arrived from W. G. Archer. He thought back

> to those glorious years from 1940 to 1946 when we were running neck and neck and there seemed no end to the tribal poetry which one or other of us would suddenly reveal. . . . I sometimes wonder despite your work for NEFA your own best time was not in Middle India. I still think that the Baiga

is your finest book and after that, Folk Songs of the Maikal Hills. How proud I am that you dedicated it to me!'

Archer was hoping now to get back to his work on the Santals, which he had set aside in 1949 when he joined the Victoria and Albert Museum: 'The Santal book will get done and you must muster all your breath and rally that stupid old heart so that I can dedicate it to you and we can enjoy together my Santal days. . . . Dear Verrier, you should have died so many times in the past. Don't die now.'[45]

In the autumn came two visitors who have left us cameo impressions of Shillong's greatest man. Armand Denis was writing a Baedeker's guide to quaint tribes and quainter customs and wanted to speak to the author of *The Muria and their Ghotul*. He first heard of Elwin from an old Franciscan in England who remembered Brother Verrier as a 'young man of great beauty and sanctity.' The monk also filled him in on the renegade's friendship with Gandhi and his work with the tribes. Denis arrived in Shillong without an appointment and was told that Elwin was not seeing people: indeed, the previous day he had turned away a lady sociologist from America. But when he rang the house Elwin picked up the phone and, in a 'collector's piece among voices—those high pitched, carefully modulated tones you sometimes hear from elderly high church clergymen', invited him over.

Elwin met the visitor in his dressing-gown, puffing one of those smelly Trichnopoly cigars that so infuriated his doctor. (The patient insisted that the damage had already been done, long ago.) They talked of the Muria and other tribes in a

> remarkable room, crammed with pictures, books and objects of folk art. An iron brazier of charcoal glowed in the centre of the floor. Devil masks from Nepal glared across at a regiment of small gilt buddhas on the table opposite, and above Elwin's own battered armchair hung a painting from Tibet in which an azure-bodied Krishna was gently copulating with a female supplicant.[46]

Tara Ali Baig arrived not long after Armand Denis. This diplomat's-wife-turned-social worker had known Elwin years ago in Bombay when they attended the same parties. Now she had come to talk of her work among village children. She asked a man who knew something of poverty and suffering whether he ever regretted leaving the life of an Oxford don. Elwin answered characteristically with a poem:

> Love had he found in huts where poor men lie;
> His daily teachers were the woods and rills,
> The silence that is in the starry sky
> The sleep that is among the lonely hills.[47]

A third caller was the scholar-wanderer Nirmal Kumar Bose, the other Indian anthropologist of towering moral stature. He and Elwin had disagreed on the tribals in print; in conversation they seem to have argued about Gandhi, whom both had followed and then fought with. Elwin wrote dismissively in his autobiography, then in proofs, of Bose's book on the Mahatma, but it seems he had not read it carefully enough, or at all. 'Dear Dr Elwin,' wrote Bose on his return to Calcutta, 'I am sending you a copy of my book "My Days with Gandhi" and I hope to hear from you when you have finished reading it. May I thank you once again for the fine evening I spent in your home?'[48]

Verrier had now turned his guestroom into a sort of Buddhist shrine. To Koestler, who had stayed in that room and who had written dismissively of his religion, he wrote that he got 'a good deal of consolation' from praying there. Buddhism, he said, 'does not seem to be much good as a social gospel but certainly as a psychological cure for anxiety, desire and anger I find it very effective.'[49]

The visitors stimulated the mind, the meditation calmed the spirit, the body continued to decline. Verrier's doctor and some of his friends thought it would do him good if he moved out of Shillong to a lower altitude. But where could he go? In December he was asked by C. D. Deshmukh, vice-chancellor of the University of Delhi, whether he would spend two months teaching there. The implication was that something more promising and permanent might follow.[50]

On the last day of 1963 Verrier completed an abridgement of *The Muria and their Ghotul*, asked for by the OUP. He returned with a certain melancholy to his days in Bastar and Central India. The original book, he wrote in the new preface, was 'a contemporary record,' this version but 'an aspect of India's tribal history.' 'I believe the ghotul survives,' he remarked, although 'it must have known many changes.' The changes are enumerated without their consequences being stated outright: one thousand schools where there had once been half-a-dozen, the 'great schemes of Community Development' spread out over the district, thousands of refugees from East Pakistan in a forest previously reserved for the Murias. He had been fortunate to be able to record, in 1941–2, 'a unique phase of human development about to disappear.' Many friends had helped him in that endeavour; they were fully acknowledged, he said, in the original edition. But in this shortened version he was 'dominated by the necessity to keep within the spatial limits laid on me by my publishers, and that is the only reason why I do not repeat my obligations here.'[51] The *only* reason? Could there be a second, I wonder, the presence in that book and preface, as indeed in the author's life and love, of his first wife, Kosi?

In January Verrier again experienced heartache, a 'mild cerebro-vascular spasm' according to the doctor's report. For a fortnight he could not lift his right arm. On the 26th, Republic Day, he dictated a preface for a source-book on the judicial and political institutions of NEFA. The volume was composed of notes on tribal councils compiled by his colleagues in the NEFA Research Department. In publishing them he hoped that in time 'more and more responsibility for development will be transferred from officialdom to the tribal bodies. There can be no doubt that this will do a great deal to give the people self-confidence, to make them feel that they are masters of their own destiny and that nothing is being imposed on them, and to forward true progress throughout the hills.'[52]

All his life Elwin had urged on the powerful the claims of the powerless and presented to the centre the perspective of the periphery. It was his privilege to move with ease from one sphere to another, to feel equally at home with prime ministers and peasants. The book on political decentralization sent to press, he now prepared to visit the citadel of political power in Delhi. He was due there on the 20th of February to attend a meeting of the Frontier Services Selection Board. On the 8th he wrote to Eldyth that he was not very keen on going, 'but I think as they are now considering the question of my extension in service, it will be a good thing for me to put in an appearance and show myself looking fit and well.' He always liked to help pick young officers for NEFA and hoped also to meet Deshmukh about the Delhi professorship.

Between the 11th and 15th Verrier was not at all well. He was breathing with difficulty and hardly sleeping at night. The heart-specialist examined him and advised against the trip, which was to be in a pressurized aircraft. Verrier argued with him for more than half-an-hour. If he had to go, said the doctor, he must take periodic rest and avoid foods that caused flatulence; he also prescribed five different pills.[53] His personal assistant, S. Lahiri, also asked Verrier not to go. He agreed, but next day sent the P.A. a note saying, 'I think I will defy the doctors after all and go.' He drove down to Guwahati on the 19th to board a plane for Calcutta and thence on to Delhi. When he reached the capital he sent Lila a telegram saying he was fine.

In Delhi Verrier stayed with K. L. Rathee, a former financial adviser to the NEFA administration. On the 20th he spent the whole day with the selection committee. The next morning he called on Jawaharlal Nehru, one supposes to keep him up-to-date on NEFA. Verrier had not met him for more than two years, but it was of books and tribals they must have talked that day. In the afternoon Verrier visited the home ministry. His young colleague Rashid Yusuf Ali now worked there; when Verrier walked into his office he had on his desk a fresh proposal to send sturdy Punjabi farmers to settle in NEFA. It came from a senior politician, a Hindu who complained bitterly that the north-east was run by a Muslim chief secretary of Assam (Kidwai), a Parsi adviser to the governor (N. K. Rustomji), and a Christian (Elwin), who apparently commanded the most influence of all.[54]

The critic was out-of-date, his criticisms unfair and certain to wound. Elwin was back in the home ministry the next morning, the 22nd, it seems to find ways of keeping the intruders out. He returned to the Rathees for lunch. That evening he complained of heartache, and was rushed to Willingdon Hospital. Here he was put on oxygen but his condition deteriorated and within two hours he was dead. As William Paton had predicted many years earlier, Verrier Elwin killed himself in India with overwork.

On the 23rd Nehru was the first to offer a wreath. The next day the body was flown to Shillong. Elwin was cremated here on the afternoon of the 24th, amidst the chanting of Buddhist hymns. The ashes were then taken to a lonely, glorious spot on the Siang river, where they were immersed by his eldest son, Kumar. His P.A. conveyed an apology to his sister Eldyth. 'You may be hurt to hear about his funeral,' wrote S. Lahiri, 'but it was his desire that he should be cremated. He expressed this desire to many people.'[55] The son of the bishop had rebelled to the end.

CHAPTER FOURTEEN

Outsider Within: The Worlds of Verrier Elwin

I understand more clearly today what I read long ago about the inadequacy of all autobiography as history. I know that I do not set down in this story all that I remember. Who can say how much I must give and how much omit in the interests of truth? And what would be the value in a court of law of the inadequate ex parte evidence being tendered by me of certain events in my life? If some busybody were to cross-examine me on the chapters already written, he could probably shed much more light on them, and if it were a hostile critic's cross-examination, he might even flatter himself for having shown up the 'hollowness of many of my pretensions.'

M. K. Gandhi, *The Story of My Experiments with Truth*

How can the autobiographer tell the real truth. . . .? Since he has chosen to write, he is an artist, he is a man who feels, like every artist, the need of escape; and if his narrative is to be a real escape, there must be for the author the pretext of a life more in keeping with his desires than his own life has actually been. To endow himself with this life, he will do what the novelist does; he will create it. The only difference between him and the novelist is that, as he creates it, he will say, and perhaps even believe, that it is his own, whilst the novelist is conscious of his creative act.

André Maurois

How perfect that he wrote this [auto]biography himself, and with such obvious pleasure, before it was too late and when some other hand would have had to write it.

Maeve Scott, friend of Elwin, writing to R. E. Hawkins

The historian David Cannadine once remarked that biography is the only certain form of life after death. He had apparently forgotten about autobiography. For every autobiography is a pre-emptive strike against the future biographer, a formidable and frequently unbeatable challenge to the authenticity of his work. Fortunate the biographer whose subject has not left his own memoirs; he has no carefully crafted record to contend with, to clarify or contest. But here we have to reckon with Verrier Elwin's own remarkable memoirs, finished in his lifetime and published three months after his death.

'What shall I find in your biography that I won't in Elwin's autobiography?' This is a question often asked of me, and with good reason. For *The Tribal World of Verrier Elwin: An Autobiography* is a smooth, coherent, and most readable narrative of a man's life and times. Its plot is exquisite in its simplicity. A young priest out of Oxford meets Mahatma Gandhi and is instantly transformed, reborn as an Indian on Indian soil. His life given over to Gandhi and India, his subsequent missions in central and north-eastern India then follow as exemplifications of this devotion to his adopted land. Elwin's autobiography thus emphasizes the part played by the Mahatma's great lieutenants, Vallabhbhai Patel and Jamnalal Bajaj, in his move to Mandla; so also the significance of the personality and ideas of Nehru in the making of the philosophy for NEFA. So also the urgent desperation with which Elwin scoured the sources for a picture of himself with Gandhi in Sabarmati: and when the original was untraceable, he included nonetheless a 'reprint of a reprint of a reprint of a one-time photograph.'[1] Thus too the scrupulous omission of his controversies with other Indians, whether politicians, social workers, or anthropologists.

The preface to *Tribal World* freely acknowledges that 'much of it is written from the Indian point of view;' indeed, Elwin almost called it the 'Autobiography of a British-born Indian.'[2] Within this organizing principle, the book contains evocative descriptions of Oxford and of his early years in India, crisp accounts of the tribes he worked with in the thirties and forties, and finally an extended treatment of his 'philanthropological' work in the North East Frontier Agency. While the first part of the book makes for marvellous reading, the narrative grows more bland with the autobiographer's rise to prominence. With Elwin determined to name and acknowledge every official he knew, high or low, the NEFA chapters read like a long thank you letter to his Indian friends.

Elwin had in fact first thought of writing his memoirs well before he went to NEFA. In 1949 his friend R. E. Hawkins, who ran the Indian branch of Oxford University Press, received a letter from his counterpart in New York, wondering whether Elwin, clearly a 'remarkable character,' could be persuaded to write his autobiography, which when published 'could be something of a sensation in the good sense.' Knowing his friend to be in dire straits—this was roughly the time Elwin was 'a poor white thinking up unprintable jokes' in Patangarh—Hawkins passed on the suggestion, noting that Jim Corbett had made eight thousand dollars in the first year out of the American edition of his *Man Eaters of Kumaon*, a book that was in its own way the autobiography of a remarkable character.[3]

Then recovering from a bruising divorce, Elwin was not interested. When he did begin his autobiography thirteen years later, the prospect of earning some money for a growing family was one motive; the desire to record his life before anybody else did was a second. The long periods of rest prescribed by the doctor after his heart attack, alongside the ban on touring, enabled him to work almost uninterruptedly on the book, which was sent to Hawkins in March 1962.

Memoirs are made of memories, but as André Maurois once noted the autobiographer's memory 'not only fails, whether by the simple process of time or by deliberate censorship, but, above all, it rationalizes; it creates, after the event, the feelings or the ideas which might have been the cause of the event, but which in fact are invented by us after it has occurred.'[4] Here the correspondence between Elwin and Hawkins provides glimpses of the many pitfalls in the writing of Elwin's memoirs, and of how the writer attempted to negotiate them. Recognizing that it would be 'extremely difficult to be quite sure what to say when writing one's own life,' he asked his editor and friend of twenty years to point out anything that struck the wrong note, 'anything pretentious or pompous or dull.' Hawkins commented that the book revealed very little about Elwin the writer. 'You are chiefly known by your books,' he remarked, 'and I should have expected a much larger part of your autobiography to be concerned with the writing of them—the gathering of material, difficulties of working far from libraries, methods, contacts with other anthropologists, etc.'

Hawkins also complained that the book revealed little of Elwin the man. He could understand Verrier's reluctance to give his *vie amourese*, but not his reticence on the background to the dramatic shifts in his life: the struggle with Christianity, the rejection of civilization, the marriage to a tribal girl, the final adoption of Indian citizenship. The reader, especially the Western reader, wrote Hawkins, 'would like to know far more than you tell him here about the reasons which led you to take these steps, and the mental anguish that must have accompanied many of them.' But as it stood this was a serenely happy book. 'My grouse, indeed,' remarked the publisher who understood Elwin's life better than almost anybody else, 'is that you have omitted nearly all the shadows.'[5]

Elwin knew this too. He wrote to Arthur Koestler saying he had been re-reading his own draft autobiography alongside Koestler's published one: 'What an astonishing different kind of life we each have had! I very much liked your chapter on "Pitfalls for an Autobiographer" but looking at it again yesterday I came to the conclusion that I have fallen into almost all of them.'[6] For all this, he was to disregard R. E. Hawkins' advice. 'My path,' wrote Elwin in the preface to the printed book, 'has sometimes been shadowed by clouds and I have hinted at them in the following pages, but I have not enlarged on them, for I don't think they are very interesting.' A tame apologia perhaps, but whatever it was, the *Tribal World of Verrier Elwin* sidesteps or moves quickly past the major turning points in his life, with the one exception being his break with the Church.

The writing of Elwin's autobiography was shaped by his vulnerability as a British-born Indian, and by his own desire not to rake up or revive controversy. On 9th August 1963, by which time the page proofs were being processed, he sent in what was 'one final—and this is really final—alteration.' In view of the 'rather strained relations between Assam and NEFA at present,' he had added a paragraph 'mentioning my Assam friends.' 'It will not make any difference to the value of the book,' he said, 'but it may make a good deal of difference to me here.'[7] Hawkins accepted the paragraph but then wrote the next week of his wish to sell pre-publication excerpts to the *Illustrated Weekly of India*. Elwin answered to say that the OUP must on no account draw on the NEFA chapters: these were all right when read in the book, but 'if they appear in bits in a periodical they would be bound to cause trouble and I do not want to enter into controversy at this juncture.'[8]

Till the last moment Elwin was editing his text for personal and political rather than literary reasons or the interests of accuracy and greater self-revelation. In the archives of the OUP is a copy of the manuscript almost as it appeared in print, with only a few paragraphs scored out. Excised is a passage describing how he differs from other primitivists in going to the forest without a 'return ticket'—perhaps he thought this did not sit well with the British tradition of self-deprecation. Removed is an innocent joke—'Since I came to India I have never used toilet-paper at home but made do with newspaper—the savings mount up over the years:' he may have thought this would be taken by humourless *lota*-using nationalists as proof that he was never really Indian. Another witty remark taken out at the proof stage pokes fun at Gandhians and *babu* English: 'the Puritan attack is essentially on sex and perhaps the journalist who wrote that the followers of Gandhi are "joy-kills who do not understand the rupture [*sic*] of love" was not far off the mark.'

Most revealing of all is the removal of two comments on his friend Arthur Koestler's book *The Lotus and the Robot*. There had been much hostility to its representation of Indian spiritual traditions and the Government of India had taken typically the stupid and not unprecedented step of banning the book. Elwin, to whom Koestler's book was dedicated, had remarked that the ban was 'an unfortunate and mistaken act.' To 'someone trained in the Oxford tradition of criticism,' it seemed 'almost incredible that a great country should ban a book on religious grounds.'[9]

Elwin's autobiography, in a word, smoothly suppresses the complexity and ambiguities of his life in presenting to the world a mostly happy tale of an Englishman becoming Indian and an Oxford scholar going native. Almost the only indication of the shadows lies in the cover portrait, drawn by the Polish emigré artist Otto Kadlescovics. The artist's interpretation of the man was altogether more complex than the self-portrait in the book itself. Kadlescovics thus explained his drawing:

> The nightmarish masks represent the temptations of the soul. The Naga ones suggest the urge to violence and hatred and among the others are masks of envy and pride. The Eyes represent, in one case the eyes of desire

lusting for the world and its pleasures, and the large single one is the sardonic, critical eye. [Verrier] looks on the world in three different ways—with spiritual idealistic eyes, slightly masked by tobacco-smoke; with eyes that love beauty; and a last eye that was critical and perhaps slightly sinister.[10]

For all that it leaves out, Elwin's autobiography remains a charming and sometimes moving book. Published so soon after his death, with his memory and work fresh in the mind, it received a wonderful reception. In May 1963, as the book went to press, Hawkins wrote to Eldyth Elwin of his hope that 'Verrier will be alive to see the reviews.'[11] In the event it was left to Elwin's sister, editor and friends to glory in the praise which followed the book's publication.

In India the book was read as an account of an exemplary Indian; in the United Kingdom, where it overcame the disadvantage of being released on Election Day, it was the story of an eccentrically gifted and risk-loving Englishman; in the United States people saw it as the testimony of the brilliant scholar who turned his back on civilization. His sister was to complain that the blurb of the American edition 'twice refers to "natives!" What would Verrier say!'[12] But the word was being used strategically by the publisher even if it was not, by Eldyth's norms and ours, politically correct. In all three countries *The Tribal World of Verrier Elwin* was widely and generously reviewed. To be sure, there were critical remarks. But these tended to be on points of detail. An Indian anthropologist of the younger generation noted that Elwin's policies for the tribes had the logic of 'poetry and romance,' though not always the 'logic of economics and politics.' The British writer Naomi Mitchison, whose brother J. B. S. Haldane became an Indian citizen not long after Elwin, felt the author sometimes saw things 'almost too much from the best Indian point of view.' One reviewer wished the book had more of Shamrao, the lifelong companion whose calm support allowed Elwin to produce 'stupendous work' despite an 'unsteadiness of temperament.' A critic in the *New York*

Times wondered at the absence of a proper account of either of his two marriages. And the smouldering resentments of the Assamese intelligentsia surfaced for one last time in a review which complained that Elwin till the end

> seemed to be very meticulous against the non-tribals coming to NEFA for fear that the latter might exploit [the tribals]. But while this view was appreciated as having some value, it was also pointed out by his critics that if the tribes were allowed to grow and develop [isolated] from the people of the plains [i.e. the Assamese], the task of forging an assimilation at a later stage might have to face formidable difficulties.[13]

All these criticisms, however, only qualified the most extravagant praise of the book as a 'fascinating and remarkable' document; and of the man as one who lived in an 'astonishing and admirable state of near-Christian grace.' Writing of the scholar, the Indian anthropologist S. C. Dube noted that Elwin 'was not a dry-as-dust technician; he was a poet, an artist and a philosopher' who by his 'individual effort produced more and better work than many of the expensively staffed and large research organizations in the country.' Writing of the man, Naomi Mitchison said Elwin 'was one of the small handful of people whom I, in my spiritual arrogance, genuinely respected . . . If there were a few thousand Verrier Elwins about, one would really begin to feel quite hopeful about the world.' An anonymous reviewer in *The Statesman* summed up the loss to literature and to humanity. When news came of Elwin's sudden death, he wrote, 'from secretariat to little mud huts, from NEFA to Madhya Pradesh, in urban artistic, literary and journalistic circles as in remote villages, many thousands who had met or read of him knew that greatness had departed.'[14] A compliment the author would have liked came in the form of the Sahitya Akademi award, only the third time the Indian Academy of Letters had honoured a book written in English. The citation said that *The Tribal World* was 'written with sincerity, courage and charm;' it 'reveals a mind in which Western and Indian idealism were uniquely blended.'

The most remarkable tribute of all was from the pen of the Bombay poet Nissim Ezekiel. Elwin's autobiography was written with 'great charm and persuasion;' one of its great merits, wrote Ezekiel, was that 'his final position on all matters is made absolutely clear. There is not a single ambiguous sentence in [the book] and yet [no] dogmatic pronouncement in it.'[15] That so sensitive a poet was taken in by the smoothness of the narrative is testimony to Elwin's success in banishing from the book the shadows that so relentlessly followed him through his thirty-seven years in India.

It was the pioneer of modern biographical studies, Leslie Stephen, who noted that an autobiography is interesting not so much for what it contains as for what it leaves out. A more contemporary, hence more cynical, critic puts it this way:

> Not all but a fair part of the pleasure of reading autobiography is in catching the autobiographer out in suspicious reticences, self-serving misconceptions, cover-ups, and of course, delightfully clever deceptions. What is he hiding, what's he withholding, why doesn't he talk about his first wife, who's he kidding leaving out his children, odd he never mentions money— such are the questions that roam randomly through your normally licentious reader of autobiography. The intelligent person reads autobiography for two things: the facts and the lies, knowing that the lies are far more interesting than the facts.[16]

One man who appears to have read Verrier Elwin's autobiography in this light was R. E. Hawkins, before it was published; another who certainly did but after it appeared in print was Bill Archer. Asked to review the book by a London newspaper, Archer wrote a handsome tribute, highlighting those aspects of Elwin's work that most appealed to him: the dazzling revelations of the role of love and sex in tribal life, and the marvellous renditions of tribal songs which were quite 'the best translations of Eastern poetry since Arthur Waley.' Elwin, wrote Archer in a claim no one can possibly dispute, had through his thirty-year involvement 'got to know more about India's tribes than any Englishman or Indian before or since.'[17]

Sometimes reviews conceal as much as autobiographies. In a series of scribbled notes he wrote for himself, Archer raised powerful and disturbing questions that he kept out of his printed appreciation of *The*

Tribal World of Verrier Elwin. These notes are a strange mixture of insight and invective. They reveal intimate knowledge as well as unrestrained envy. Bill Archer had wanted to stay on in India. Abruptly posted out of the Naga hills in 1947, he returned to England with some reluctance. Here he carved out a new and successful career as a historian of Indian art, while watching from afar his friend emerge as a figure of high esteem in independent India.

Archer's private comments on Elwin's autobiography first take up some methodological questions: the relationship between 'the writer and his material—the methods and ethics of the freelance do-gooder—but perhaps above all the problem of *whether an Englishman can ever become truly Indian*. Elwin took Indian nationality and his book reveals all the shifts, evasions, compromises that he had to resort to in order to reside as an Indian public figure in the land.' Archer concludes that the book was 'not a declaration of genuine belief' but 'just a bit of propaganda for his continued support by the [Indian] Government.'

Turning from the book's intent to its tone, Archer found it to be 'so effusive that everyone including himself disappears in a haze.' There were

> no personal reactions to anyone or anything
> . . . what made him tick?
> how did he see himself?
> did he believe in anything?
> what made him write?
> what made him become boringly scientific?
> why did he cover up?
> the utter mess and muddle at Patangarh—
> . . . what were his field methods?
> how did he write?
> why did he lose all touch with England?
> on none of these does he say a thing.

Alongside these criticisms Archer's notes contain sharp observations on the man himself. His comments have a peculiar hit-and-miss quality to them, occasionally right on target, at other times wide off the mark. In the first category falls the observation that Elwin 'did not like Hindus and was awkward in their company,' the only Indians he identified with being 'tribals and Westernized ones;' in the second class comes the astonishing charge that Elwin was himself the 'great destroyer' of tribal life who, by publicizing it, 'blew it up on the screen,' attracting the anti-tribal outsider and reformer.

There is a sharpness to Archer's remarks that sometimes borders on the brutal. He claims that Elwin 'never really shed the clergyman's approach—he was always announcing virtues and ideals:' the remark has some truth to it but its manner of expression betrays bitter hostility and prejudice. In the midst of his fusillade Archer pauses briefly to acknowledge what was original about Elwin—this was the 'clear vivid style—the gift for the passionate rhetoric—the neat story—the poet-translator:' his great achievement being 'the discovery of Indian sex and tribal poetry.' All this pertains to Elwin the writer, the pioneering ethnographer of the tribes of central India. Archer disregards or dismisses Elwin's work as an Englishman for India, as well as his claims for applied anthropology advanced in his influential *A Philosophy for NEFA* and in the autobiography itself.[18]

In reading Verrier Elwin's autobiography for its silences and evasions, Bill Archer provided an indirect justification for the present work. Ten years before Archer, the ground had been cleared by Shamrao Hivale, albeit in his own characteristically loving way. While conveying Verrier's decision to wed a second tribal girl to a family traumatized by the fact and failure of the first marriage, he wrote:

> Anyway all these geniuses, poets, prophets and reformers are queer and often quite mad and so why worry? Now that they are telling us truths about these great men like Ruskin, Wordsworth and others—actually one begins to like them much better than before when we felt they were so terribly "proper" or even saints. I wonder what we shall feel if we live to read in cold print the entire truth about Verrier! So my dear Eldyth, if this marriage has upset you or mother Elwin or the rest of the family and friends, I think we ought not let it make *any difference* in our regard or love for him.[19]

I cannot claim to have provided 'the entire truth about Verrier.' But I have tried to do what no autobiographer can: to situate a life and work in context, providing a perspective of their time and place. I have also dogged the shadows which Elwin chose to keep out of his own book and so reveal that his life was more troubled and altogether more interesting than he made it out to be. The life as I see it was marked by paradox, by twist and turn. The son of a bishop who was trained to follow him fought bitterly with the church; the celibate disciple of Gandhi who dissented and left him became a celebrator and chronicler of sex; the once-fervent Indian nationalist who defended the aboriginals against a homogenizing nationalism; the associate of Nehru who loathed, and was loathed by, other Congressmen in independent India; the anthropologist who would much rather be a novelist; the Englishman who lived and loved with the tribes. Of these juxtapositions Elwin himself wrote only of the first and last, and then in a misleading way, as if to go from Christian to anti-Christian, or from Oxford to Patangarh, were moves that were for the most part painless.

But let me end with one of Bill Archer's questions. Can an Englishman ever become truly Indian? Responding to the same book and the same question, but recalling a life spent in sacrifice and service to the Indian poor, another reviewer answered: 'Elwin showed us how to be an Indian, what it is to be an Indian.'[20] Days after his death an editorial in the *Amrita Bazaar Patrika* spoke likewise of India losing 'not only her most eminent anthropologist but another—and perhaps the last—of those liberal-minded Englishmen who had made this country their home and completely identified themselves with its people.' And there was also, in the same issue of the Calcutta newspaper, a poignant insert placed by the staff and actors of a famous Bengali stage company:

In memory of
Dr Verrier Elwin
the best of Indians.[21]

These emphatic endorsements do not of course invalidate Archer's original question, which might in fact be put in other ways. Can an Oxford scholar ever go truly native? Or a novelist become a scientist? Or a political dissenter a high state official?

That, indeed, is the singular theme of Elwin's life. The man was apparently *always* out of place, always where tradition and history least expected him to be: a clergyman with Gandhi, a scholar in a tribal hamlet, a poet in the science of anthropology, a rebel with an office in the secretariat. Placed on the margins, poised uncertainly between two worlds, he would imaginatively interpret one world to another. In his life and in all his work there is visible a passionate desire to make adversaries see the truth in each other: to show Hindus the mystical side of Christianity, for example, or the British the justice of the Indian demand for freedom, or ethnography what it might learn from literature, or the civilized world what it might learn from the tribes.

In this century it has been Verrier Elwin, more than anyone else, who has shown us that the dialogue of cultures need not always be a dialogue of the deaf.

EPILOGUE

Disputed Legacies

On 20th May 1964 the *Times of India* reported that the Government of India wished to endow a fellowship in Verrier Elwin's memory. The award was conceived in the cross-cultural spirit in which he lived his life, for it was to be given to an anthropologist who wished to work 'in remote and inaccessible corners of the world outside India.' The initiative apparently came from Mrs Indira Gandhi and from the education minister, M. C. Chagla, a Bombay jurist who knew or knew of Elwin.[1]

The newspaper report was the first and last thing one heard of the Elwin Fellowship. Jawaharlal Nehru died the following week, and his daughter and their nation went into deep and prolonged mourning. The Nehruvians forgot about the anthropologist but he had meanwhile been rediscovered by the Gandhians. In July 1964 a South Indian follower of the Mahatma came across a copy of one of Elwin's pamphlets in a used bookstore. Elwin had written *Religious and Cultural Aspects of Khadi* in 1931; shortly thereafter he had repudiated both khadi and its most famous proponent. This rebellion was underplayed in Elwin's lately published autobiography, and it was to be thoroughly tamed when the khadi pamphlet was republished towards the end of 1964. Its discoverer and printer procured an admiring preface from Vinoba Bhave, Gandhi's self-appointed spiritual successor. 'The little brochure of Verrier Elwin is ever green,' wrote Bhave, 'I read it through and through. It is so inspiring.' Elwin himself was introduced by the publisher as a

> British anthropologist devoted to Gandhiji. Immediately after his education, he went to Africa to serve the people there. But he came back to India and devoted his whole life to the service of the aborigines in the Madhya

Pradesh. He identified himself with the aborigines and he married an aboriginal lady and devoted his whole life for their uplift. After India became free, he took the responsibility of a Welfare Officer among the aborigines till he passed away recently.[2]

Thus was the dissident's career refashioned as a life of devoted service to the Mahatma and Mother India, and the opponent of uplift and welfare was thereby turned into its votary. This was a misdescription for which, it must be admitted, *The Tribal World of Verrier Elwin* provided a handy model. Another effective way of dealing with the rebel was found by his old school, Dean Close. Elwin was by any reckoning an outstanding product of a less-than-celebrated institution, but when an Official History was published in 1966 it omitted to mention him, this despite his many contributions to literature and scholarship.[3] The school, unsurprisingly, had long been embarrassed by Elwin's career. Well before the History, an alumni directory had appeared in 1950: this marked the years of Elwin's entry to and exit from Dean Close, listed the academic prizes he won at Oxford, and went on to enumerate the string of acceptable achievements—'Ordained in 1926; Vice Principal, Wycliffe Hall; Chaplain and Lecturer in Theology, Merton College; Examining Chaplain to Bishop of Blackburn,' etc., before abruptly ending, thus: '1928, Poona, India.' Twenty-two years rich in incident and achievement were wiped out.[4] Now, in the nineties, the school continues to regard Elwin as 'something of a black sheep in comparison with his near contemporary Bishop Stephen Neill,' whose career they would rather more willingly memorialize.[5]

What Verrier Elwin did after 1928 could be forgotten by Christians in Cheltenham but not in India. A Naga historian writing in 1974 gently criticized Elwin for his criticism of missionaries, arguing that it was Christianity that pushed the Nagas 'out of the seclusion and isolation from which they were suffering for centuries into [contact with the] open ideas, ideals and civilizations of the peoples of the world.'[6] To be deplored is better than to be ignored: in any case, there are Indian Christians who cheerfully concede that Elwin had a point. A Jesuit theologian of Poona, a spokesman for religious pluralism, wrote in 1984 of the deep-seated intolerance of Christian missionaries working in India, of a history of religious barbarism peppered with 'rare but notable exceptions—a de Nobili, a Rice, a C. F. Andrews, a Verrier Elwin.'[7] The essence of the exception has since been distilled in a fine anthology of Elwin's religious writings published in 1993 by the Indian Society for Promoting Christian Knowledge. This volume's editor suggested, much as Verrier's mother had back in 1936, that the church lost him because it was not tolerant and farsighted enough.[8] Verrier's former colleague in the Christa Seva Sangh, Leonard Schiff, also felt sorry that his great work was done outside and frequently in opposition to the church. 'The then Bishop of Nagpur must answer for a lot here,' Schiff told an interviewer in 1971: 'The Bishop could only think in terms of the law, and his approach to Elwin was pedestrian.'[9]

One thinks that the church would have lost Elwin anyway. Even if a less dogmatic spiritual director had persuaded him to stay on in 1935, the attractions of the tribal ethos would sooner or later have come in conflict with the imperatives of Christian proselytization. However, the Indian church is *now* more catholic and accommodating of other faiths, perhaps in some small measure due to the labours of Elwin and his ilk. It is also more reliably patriotic, as witness an interdenominational gathering at St Columbus' Cathedral in New Delhi on 15th August 1997. Catholics, Syrian Christians, Baptists, Pentecostals, Methodists, even Anglicans, here offered to the fiftieth anniversary of Indian independence a scroll which pledged to help 'keep the integrity of our beloved country and well being of the people above all narrow and divisive considerations.'[10]

Elwin's rebellion against the third of his churches, Science, was always half-hearted and incomplete. But where the Gandhians and Christians have sought, not always convincingly, to reclaim him, the academics continue to view him with distrust. While he lived, professional anthropologists saw Elwin as a diligent fieldworker and a writer of exceptional sensitivity whose theories, alas, were both inadequate and out of date. One review can stand in for a dozen. Reviewing the *The Religion of an Indian Tribe*, the famous Africanist Victor Turner acknowledged the author's 'vivid and elegant prose,' the 'aesthetic fastidiousness of his photography and illustrations,' while regretting the 'omission of a prior analysis of the social and political structure'—that is, of the rules of property and inheritance, as well as the rights and obligations of different segments of Saora society.

This was written in 1957. A decade later, and with Elwin dead, Victor Turner returned to the book in a long essay commissioned for a research primer on *The Craft of Social Anthropology*. He complained here that Elwin 'does not write as a social anthropologist but as an eclectic ethnographer, and where he interprets, he uses the language of a theologian.' In an essay addressed to the aspiring anthropologist, Turner provides pointers to the 'sociological analysis of the structural relationships within and between Saora villages' that could have provided 'an indispensable introduction to Elwin's study of Saora ritual.' For that study had little to say of the modes of succession and inheritance, the magnitude and mobility of villages, the forms of conflict, the social composition of households and hamlets, and the links between kinship, residence and marriage. Instead of 'the systematic collection of this kind of data,' all Elwin had provided were bare 'morsels of sociological information' interpolated in descriptions of religious custom.[11]

And thus the scientific anthropologist made an example of the eclectic ethnographer who had an eye for an interesting problem, but not the nerve or technique to work towards its successful resolution. A Cambridge scholar, inspired by both Turner and Elwin, has since studied the practice of shamanism among the Saora. This is only one of a series of recent re-studies of Elwin's tribes and themes by professional anthropologists. One aspirant has lived in the Muria ghotul, a second in the Baiga Chak, a third with the Bonda in his highlands. In each case the student has been inspired by Elwin to do fieldwork among a tribe he studied, to provide a fuller and more scientific account of the community and its institutions. By revisiting sites studied by Elwin forty years previously, in the hope of proving him wrong or merely half-right, the professionals are (perhaps without knowing it, and certainly without admitting it) paying handsome tribute to the amateur.[12] Would that their books were as readable!

Not all scholars have studied Elwin only to correct or criticize him. A few gathered soon after Elwin's death to bring out a well-rounded *festschrift* in his memory, an unusual honour for a man who did not teach in a university nor who, in a formal sense, ever had students.[13] And a constructive tribute was offered by a group of metallurgists who chanced upon one of Elwin's less-known monographs. They used his evidence and documentation to recreate a functioning Agaria furnace, displayed at the Congress on Traditional Sciences hosted by the Indian Institute of Technology, Bombay, in December 1993.

The people in the places studied by the roving anthropologist have also proposed memorials to remember him by. When Elwin's ashes were sent for immersion to upper Siang, a portion was set aside for safe keeping at the Gompa in Mankhota, it seems for a future memorial asked for by the tribals of the valley.[14] Then in 1979 an official of the Madhya Pradesh government, himself an ethnographer *manqué*, suggested the setting up of an Elwin Memorial Institute in Mandla town—'equipped with an auditorium, a library, and a research unit for social-anthropology'—in tribute to a scholar whose books and essays had made the people of the district known throughout the world.[15] Most recently, a Bastar journalist and social activist, Mohammed Iqbal, has proposed the renovation of Elwin's old house near the Chitrakot falls, and its use as a home and practising exhibition for tribal art and craft.[16] That none of these schemes have thus far borne fruit is because of the Indian culture of memorial-building, in which private initiative must necessarily come to naught in the absence of state sanction and support.

We might remember Elwin as Gandhian, Christian, or anthropologist, but he would want to be remembered most of all as the defender of the aboriginal. What then of the fate of the tribals he lived and loved with? Have the adivasis of central India been wiped out with the malarial mosquito, and the tribes of the north-east succumbed to the blandishments of civilization? Is there any trace *anywhere* of his philosophy and practice?

Travelling through Elwin's home district of Mandla one sees signs of the continuing struggle between isolation and assimilation. The Gonds still dance and drink—I was lucky to go there during festival time—and retain a proud sense of their identity. In Patangarh now are slogans on the walls calling people to vote for the Gondwana Party, a new formation which stands for a separate province for the tribals. 'Jai Bara Deo jai Gondwana,' the slogan runs, an affirmation of the ancient and distinctly non-Hindu deity of the Gonds. But driving down the valley we saw other and possibly more telling signs. In the village of Chandanghat, by the Narmada river on the pilgrim route, we spied a brand new building, plastered an austere white, advertising a 'Saraswati Savarkar Shishu Mandir.' It was a school promoted by the Rashtriya Swayamsevak Sangh, run to reclaim the tribals to the mother religion, and named both for the Hindu goddess of learning and the most fanatical of Hindu nationalists.

The cultural battle is unresolved, but in independent India, as Elwin feared, it is the pressures of economic development that have told most heavily on the tribals. Their forests have been encroached upon by paper mills, their lands inundated by dams or destroyed by mines. Unhappily, the resources most needed by an industrializing society—water, wood, minerals—are found in India only where tribals live. So the tribals have had to make way for factories and mines, but not without a fight. In this imperfect but not unsubstantial democracy, tribals remain uneducated but not necessarily unrepresented. For one thing, they are assured under law of seven-and-a-half per cent of all jobs in government and of all seats in parliament and state legislatures. For another, the relatively open political system allows for, and even encourages, non-violent protest.[17]

The juxtaposition of economic loss and political voice comes out most clearly in the controversy over the Sardar Sarovar Dam. This dam, being built on a river that Elwin knew so well and lived so close to for so long, will displace some 100,000 people, more than half of whom are tribals. A Narmada Bachao Andolan, led by a forty-year-old woman activist, Medha Patkar—someone from civilization who turned her back on it, like our hero—has won much praise and some hostility by organizing strikes, blockades, and fasts to stop the construction. Patkar and her colleagues speak for the 'victims of development,' but development's beneficiaries have spoken loudly too. The anti-dam movement has been met by an equally strong pro-dam movement, made up of the farmers and politicians of Gujarat, the state where will flow the irrigation water from the project. Picked up by a press that is the most articulate in Asia, the Narmada debate brings back, for the historically minded, the Ghurye-Elwin controversy of the 1940s. Consider these comments of an aggressively modernising economist, speaking to an audience of urban upper-class Indians:

> Those opposed to the dams on the Narmada are . . . outraged by the displacement of tribals from their traditional areas and way of life . . . [But] I would like an India where all tribals are made richer and more sophisticated than me within two generations . . . I believe we must give the tribals education, medicine, roads and the comforts we take for granted. The moment we do so, however, they will cease to be tribals, and become like us. That, I believe, is what we must strive for. . . . Instead of trying to preserve tribals in jungles, let us move to a world where all tribals are taken out of jungles and converted into ex-tribals like us.[18]

And with them, or rather against them, view these remarks from a dissenting report submitted to the World Bank, which had been an enthusiastic sponsor of the dam project:

> Many tribal people in the submergence villages . . . spoke to us about their land and way of life: they often referred to a timeless relationship with the earth, the forest, and the animals. They identified themselves with their land and with the river. . . .
>
> Our opinion is that the evidence demonstrates the tribal status of a large proportion of people to be affected by Sardar Sarovar Projects . . . Concern for such groups is an aspect of the world's increased awareness of how isolated cultures have all too often paid an appalling price for development. The mechanisms by which they become separated from their lands and stripped of their own cultural integrity are all too well known.[19]

The ghost of Elwin is also visible in the report of the Bhuria Committee which was submitted to the Indian Parliament in 1995. Tribal societies, suggests this report, 'have been practicing democracies, having been characterized by [an] egalitarian spirit'—this 'communitarian and co-operative spirit visible in many undertakings like shifting cultivation [and] house construction.' And again: 'Tribal life and economy in the not too distant past bore a harmonious relationship with nature and its endowment. It was an example of sustainable development. But with the influx of outside populations it suffered grievous blows.' To reverse this process the Committee recommends that 'tribal communities should be respected as in command of the economic resources,' with Gram Sabhas or village councils placed in charge of land, forests, and minerals, with larger tribal regions given 'sub-state' status, and with 'traditional tribal conventions and laws [to] continue to hold validity.'[20]

One region where these policies had already been followed, to some degree, was the North-east Frontier Agency, now renamed Arunachal Pradesh. There are seven states in India's north-east. All, with the exception of Arunachal, are hotbeds of seccession and insurgency. Nagas, Mizos, Bodos, Kukis and Ahoms wage war on the Indian state, but Monpas and Mishmis do not, or at least not yet. Arunachal Pradesh, notes the journalist George Verghese in a recent book, is an 'island of peace' with a 'degree of political stability not witnessed elsewhere in the Northeast.'[21] In the same vein, Christoph von Fürer Haimendorf writes of Arunachal as the 'best administered and most peaceful tribal area in the whole of India.'[22] Officials in the know ascribe the state of comparative calm in good measure to Verrier Elwin's influence. Because he elevated Hindi over Assamese as the 'second' language, they say, a generation brought up to speak Hindi has been bound more firmly to India, not least because it can better appreciate that great cultural unifier, the Bombay film. Because he insisted on restricting outsiders entering the state or owning property, and instilled in officers an attitude of care and compassion, tribals have been able to move into modern life with more assurance and greater stability.[23] The name of the state itself speaks of integration with India: derived from Sanskrit, a 'Pradesh' like other Indian provinces, it contrasts most tellingly with neighbouring Naga-*land*.

Visiting Arunachal in 1994, one reporter spoke to a woman officer born the year Elwin died who nonetheless 'swore' by him and his works. He also met educated Adi tribesmen who revered the anthropologist, for they knew their tradition and myths from what he had collected and printed about them.[24] Two years later, the traveller and writer Bill Aitken made a long motorcycle journey through the state. Arunachal struck him as 'a haven of lost subcontinental values,' with its village life offering 'democratic solutions to problems that the hierarchy of caste in mainstream India would not easily allow.' But to his sorrow he found some government anthropologists who 'opposed Elwin's enlightened mission to allow the tribals to follow their own faith.' Much will depend, he wrote, 'on the maturity of politicians to maintain Arunachal's unique state of tranquility.'[25]

In his darker moments Elwin would have admitted his work was merely to delay the inevitable, to help the Arunachalis hold out and hold their own for a few decades. Civilization would catch up with them or crush them, as it had done in Bastar and Mandla. There it took the form of Christian and Hindu missionaries; but here it has come chiefly in the shape of a chainsaw, which even his beloved 'Inner-Line Permit' was unable to keep out. Aided by corrupt politicians the plywood industry has deforested large parts of Arunachal in the last decade. The axe has been stopped, one hopes more than temporarily, by a recent decision of the Supreme Court in New Delhi ordering all saw mills to shut down. But social harmony has also been disturbed by the settlement within the state of about 50,000 Chakma refugees, leading to conflict over land and jobs. The Buddhist Chakma are theoretically 'outsiders,' but they have come fleeing religious and economic persecution in their native Bangladesh. Their conflict with the Arunachali 'insiders' is thus, as Elwin would have recognized, a struggle of right against right. All the same, to demand that the Chakmas leave the state, the students of Arunachal have taken to the streets, and they might yet take to arms.

Elwin is remembered for his studies of tribal economics and politics, but also for his work on tribal art and aesthetics. When in the early eighties the Madhya Pradesh government started a museum in the state capital, Bhopal, they were imaginative enough to appoint the painter J. Swaminathan as its curator. Besides his prodigious contributions to modern Indian art, Swaminathan was also known as a poet in Hindi and as being steeped in the works of Thomas Hardy—exactly the kind of man who would have admired Elwin. Reading *The Tribal Art of Middle India*, published thirty years earlier, he was inspired to train and send out thirty art students on a search of what remained. The students fanned out into the forests and uplands while Swaminathan himself headed for Patangarh. Here he found one house decorated with the most vivid portraits of birds in flight and tribal deities in zestful mood. These were the work of Jangarh Shyam, 'a young Pardhan artist with an inborn genius for drawing and painting and modelling.' Through these excursions the Bharat Bhavan in Bhopal built up a very fine collection of tribal art, its centrepiece the paintings of Jangarh, a Pardhan from Elwin's village and a kinsman of his wife Lila.[26]

The legacy of Verrier Elwin peeps in and out of dozens of arguments about or within tribal India. To know his work is to better understand the debates of the thirties and the fifties, but also of the seventies and the nineties. He has at times been the object of reverential praise, at other times the target of sudden and unpremeditated attack. A 1972 volume on tribals issued under the auspices of the Vivekananda Kendra—a voice of reform Hinduism based in Kanyakumari in deepest south India—drew heavily from his books, excerpting chunks from his reports and monographs. Elwin himself was described as a 'noted anthropologist' and a 'veteran son of India who rendered life-long service to the cause of the Indian tribes, perhaps as nobody as done . . .'[27] In 1985 a long essay honouring him was published in *The Pioneer* of Lucknow, a town far from anywhere the anthropologist had lived or worked. Elwin deserved to be remembered, it said, 'as the inspirer of burning love [for tribals] in the hearts of Nehru, Indira and all Indians.' 'No academic professional anthropologist,' it noted, 'ever had such a long period of intimate contact with the tribal people.'[28]

Of detractors there have been more than a few. Some showed up at a conference held in Calcutta in December 1966, two years and a bit after Elwin and Nehru were both dead, and in an India eager to shed some part of their legacy. The journalist Harish Chandola complained here that Elwin 'wanted his work to be the law for NEFA. He did not want the NEFA and the Naga people to come closer to the masses of the Indian people. But he is dead now. Who is now obstructing the process of our coming closer to them politically and economically? Is it the administrative progeny of Dr Elwin?'[29] Those who equate patriotism with assimilation have continued to attack Elwin for allegedly undermining the cultural unity of the Indian nation. In the *Economic and Political Weekly* a sociologist spoke dismissively of 'that voluptuously impetuous anthropologist Verrier Elwin who could successfully integrate himself with the Indian powers that be by alluring them for a long time with his neo-colonialist diversionary thought.'[30] This was in 1981; ten years later the Marathi writer Durga Bhagwat, who had once been a friend of Elwin and a fellow student of Gond myths, wrote in her memoirs that he was chiefly responsible for the turmoil in the north-east. She claimed that the prime minister chose Elwin as an adviser because they both studied at Oxbridge. 'For Nehru's love of Oxford,' remarked Bhagwat, 'the Adivasis of India paid dearly.' When he placed the responsibility for tribal policy in Elwin's hands, she argued, the process of systematically separating the north-east from India began. When the writer visited Assam she was asked, 'Are you from India?' Recalling the incident, Bhagwat wrote bitterly and unfairly that this sense of being 'non-Indian' was fathered by Verrier Elwin.[31]

Another *ad hominem* attack was offered in 1985 by Charan Singh, a man who was once prime minister of India for a few months. As a lifelong opponent of Jawaharlal Nehru and his progeny, Charan Singh used Elwin as a stick to beat Nehru with. Like several others, he picked on the colour of Elwin's skin and the fact that he had once been a priest. He claimed that 'Nehru went to the extent of appointing a foreign Christian missionary known as Dr Elwin as an adviser to the Governor of Assam and NEFA on matters relating to tribal affairs.' This called for a rejoinder from Murkot Ramunny which explained Elwin's religious history, his willing embrace of Indian citizenship, and the essence of his 'integrationist' philosophy of the tribes: 'We owe it to this great Indian who did so much for the poorest of the poor, for whom so little has been done, by so many.'[32] As an officer of the Indian Frontier Administrative Service Ramunny had once been an associate of Elwin, even a *bhakta* perhaps.

Elwin's ideas have also been ably defended by some who never knew him. One such is Dr H. Sudarshan, a doctor who lives with the Soliga tribals of Karnataka, a selfless social worker who might be described as a Shamrao Hivale with a medical degree. 'The concept of isolation as proposed by Verrier Elwin,' remarks Sudarshan,

> has met with bitter objections by men like Dr Lohia. However, Dr Elwin had a number of progressive ideas about tribal development but he preferred isolation to a *wrong* line of development . . . In fact it appears to us that a religion based isolation is a far better idea than submitting the tribals to dogmatic religious conversions—be it Hindu, Christian or Muslim. Nothing hampers the evolution of culture more than the imposition of an alien religion. Had there been no exploitation of the tribals, there would have been no need for voluntary or governmental intervention and the tribals would have determined their own course of evolution. But intervention

becomes inevitable due to exploitation. However, if this intervention causes erosion of tribal culture and values, then the purpose of intervention is defeated.

Elwin could not have said it better, and it comes as no surprise that Sudarshan then quotes Nehru's foreword to *A Philosophy for NEFA* as a 'very apt' credo for its time and ours.[33]

We come in the end to that indefatigable critic Professor G. S. Ghurye, the author of weighty attacks on Elwin published in 1943 and 1959. In 1980, aged eighty-seven, Ghurye published *The Burning Caldron of North-East India*, a slimmer and altogether more eccentric book than its predecessors. Elwin was here charged, as a 'British' isolationist who exercised a malevolent influence on the elite of independent India, with contributing to the 'balkanization of Bharat.' Ghurye claimed that the Adviser on Tribal Affairs had been 'the anthropological dictator of NEFA' for a decade, deciding how crores of rupees from the central treasury were to be spent. Or misspent, since it seems the money went on the 'revivalist perpetuation of the habits, dress and customs of NEFA.' Elwin, said the professor, was 'a revitalizer of almost all the cultural complex of those tribes, a complex which was most inconsistent with the cultural complex of the rest of India (Bharat) . . .' The Hindu anthropologist even accused his long dead adversary of aiding the Chinese invasion of 1962, this by encouraging his officers to dance with tribal girls who wormed secrets out of them before passing them on to Mao's men. It seems that while the officers played with the tribals the Chinese came to occupy 24,000 square miles of Indian territory.[34]

As always with Ghurye on Elwin, intellectual criticism is inseparable from personal jealousy. He was furious that it was the amateur and not he who was 'Bombay's pet anthropologist' in the forties, and furious too when Nehru and company listened to Elwin and not him in the fifties and sixties. Now, in 1998, fewer, far fewer, read Ghurye than Elwin, whose books are regularly reprinted by Oxford University Press.[35] There is however one battle that Ghurye has posthumously won. A Shiv Sena government, recently come to power in Bombay, has spent much energy on obliterating Muslim and British names and replacing them with certifiably Hindu ones. The spirit of the professor seems congenial to the chauvinists, for the intersection outside the freshly named Mumbai University has been renamed 'Govind Sadashiv Ghurye Chowk.' In death, if not in life, G. S. Ghurye has become his city's pet anthropologist.

Elwin's personal and familial legacies have been as fiercely contested as his professional and political ones. After he died in February 1964 his friends J. P. Patel (who had funded much of his central India work) and N. K. Rustomji (who was a close colleague in the NEFA administration) took care of Lila's affairs. Patel provided a living allowance and paid the children's school fees, while Rustomji used his official connections to conclude a sale of Elwin's tribal artefacts, which were acquired by the National Museum in New Delhi for Rs 250,000. Lila, a resourceful and remarkably competent homemaker, bought a two-storeyed bungalow with the proceeds, renting out a portion. She was now moderately well placed to bring up her own sons, but she soon fell out with Verrier's. Kumar was in love with a Shillong girl, Hilda; when Lila expressed a certain disapproval he ran away. She met him accidentally in the bazaar and ordered him home. He obeyed but left in a few days. He was also drinking a lot, to the disapproval this time of his commandant in the Assam Rifles. In November 1966 Lila wrote to his aunt, Eldyth: 'God only knows what will happen to him if he goes on like this.'[36]

Not long afterwards Kumar left Assam, to return to Madhya Pradesh. Somehow he located and made up with a mother he had not seen for something like twenty years. Kosi was at this time living with Vijay, her second son. Vijay had taken Elwin's name although—so far as one can be sure in these matters—he was not Verrier's child. Kumar got a job as a compositor in a printing press in Jabalpur, where he lived in a crowded two-room tenement with his wife, his mother, and his half-brother.

Also in Jabalpur, by this time, was Shamrao Hivale. Although Sham had been separated from Verrier for the last ten years of his life, his death affected him deeply. Some of what he felt comes through in a letter written to R. E. Hawkins:

My dear Hawk,

  Its nearly two weeks since the cruel death has taken away Verrier and yet I can't get used to it and I feel as if he would call me 'Sham' from any side. You are one of the very few people of whom I can't think without thinking of Verrier or even think about Bombay without thinking of your unusually quiet and peaceful house where we lived without any awkwardness or inhibitions that was inevitable in Bombay as a result of his or our life in Patangarh or in the Tribal villages. I can hardly sit when I think of you two talking to each other. The sight was almost perfect. And now I shall never see that sight again.

  ... I am anxiously waiting for JP's letter. I can imagine how miserable you two must feel. I wonder if I will ever have the courage to meet the Bombay friends again.

  Let me thank you again and again for the wonderful time we used to have in your charming home. . . .[37]

When Verrier died a good part of Shamrao died too. It appears that he soon set into a deep depression. Unfortunately (in view of what was to follow) someone in his family discovered the 1952 will by Verrier bequeathing most of his assets to his dearest friend. On Shamrao's behalf, but we may be certain without his consent, a case was filed in 1968 in the Madhya Pradesh High Court against Lila Elwin who, as Verrier's legal heir, had inherited what he had left. Lila's lawyer now submitted the later will (of 1959) that left 10 per cent to Kumar and 90 per cent to her. Then Kumar, Vijay and Kosi entered a caveat, contending that both wills were forgeries, and arguing that Dr Elwin had died without disposing of his property. In November 1970 the judge finally disposed of the case in favour of Lila, saying that the earlier will had not been attested. He however advised Kumar and Kosi to file separately for the recovery of their share of Verrier's property.

  The dispute dragged on. In March 1971 Kosi, Kumar and Vijay filed a fresh suit in the M.P. High Court, naming as respondents Lila as well as Shamrao. Kosi's lawyer argued that at the time of marriage it was agreed that on Verrier's death she and her children would be entitled to his assets: which, in their opinion, included whatever was left in Shillong, the house occupied by Sham's family in Napier Town in Jabalpur (bought in part with Verrier's money), and not least the royalties from his books. Deposing before the court on 21st July 1979, Kosi claimed that by Gond custom a marriage could only be dissolved by customary law, namely, a decision of the village panchayat to whom the person seeking divorce must appeal. But Verrier had instead approached the Calcutta High Court, whose *ex parte* decree of 12 December 1949 Kosi refused to accept since she and her panchayat had no knowledge of it.

The argument by tribal tradition was Elwinesque, but the Jabalpur court would have none of it. For Lila and Kusum Hivale (who was her husband's guardian, Shamrao having been declared of 'unsound mind') maintained that the marriage between Kosi and Verrier had been legally dissolved, that Vijay was not a son of Verrier, and that Kumar had already taken the sum of Rs 5500 in lieu of his share of his father's assets. In his order of 17th April 1980 Justice B. C. Varma found that the Jabalpur house did not belong to Verrier, that Lila and Verrier were lawfully wedded, that Verrier and Kosi had been legally divorced, and that the 1959 will was legitimate.

Kosi, ever the fighter, now filed a special leave petition in the Supreme Court of India. Her lawyer placed emphasis once more on the fact that Verrier and she had been married by tribal custom. He said the Calcutta decree was 'an ex parte proceedings against an illiterate tribal woman who knew nothing about the position of law and was fully dependent for matrimonial obligations as prevalent among the tribals according to their customs.' Kosi also claimed that Lila had been married to a liquor contractor named Bulla, and that *this* marriage too was never dissolved.[38]

Appeal to the Supreme Court was also unsuccessful. Meanwhile in April 1981, in between these various litigations, Dom Moraes arrived in Jabalpur. He had been commissioned by the Madhya Pradesh government to write a book on the state and thought naturally that he would pay tribute to his old hero and reader of his first poems. Moraes came from Patangarh and Amarkantak, where he had met many Gonds who had known Elwin, including a lady who claimed to be his first wife and a man who claimed to be his son. The day after they reached Jabalpur his companion told him that Kumar lived in the town. Moraes arranged to meet him and was devastated by what he saw. He remembered Kumar from their time as fellow-students at St Mary's School in Bombay, as a child full of zest, someone who imitated the monkey in the zoo and jumped up and down on his seat in the cinema. The man was a shadow of the boy. 'His cheeks were sunken, his eyes bloodshot, and there was more grey in his hair than mine. I put my arms round him, and it was like embracing a ghost: there seemed no substance in his body . . . What shocked me most was that a habit of servility seemed to have seized him: at first he refused to sit down in my presence, and after the first few minutes he started to call me sir.'

Kumar told Moraes that the happiest time of his life had been when he went trekking in the NEFA highlands with his father. 'Of course my life has changed terribly since Daddy died,' he said. 'I remember in Shillong, when in the evening Daddy would have his drinks and his cigars and his servants would bring it all to him. Now I can't afford to smoke. I can't afford to drink, and I am a servant myself.' When Moraes asked why he had not written to one of Verrier's friends for help, Kumar replied that he thought 'matters of money are bad between friends. I would never embarass my father's friends by asking them for money.'[39]

Weeks after this meeting Kumar died of a burst ulcer. He was only forty. 'All my thoughts are with your mother,' wrote a friend to Vijay, 'In this life she has moved from tragedy to tragedy.'[40] Dom Moraes used his influence to get Kosi a stipend from the state government. She now lives in the village of Ryatwar, with Vijay, his Gond wife, and their three children. They live off the pension and the earnings from some land they own in the village.

Kosi's break-up with Elwin was as much her doing as his, but her present situation is deeply poignant: a woman once married to a famous scholar and friend of the famous and powerful, herself entertained by them, is spending out her days amidst the poverty and obscurity into which she was born. But in some ways Vijay's situation is more poignant still. He was abandoned by his natural father, disowned with Kosi by his adoptive one, and finally discarded with his mother by the lover (Sahid) who took her up after she left Elwin. And he has lived out his adult life under the fiction, which he must know to be a fiction, that he is the son of Verrier Elwin. He has taken his name, calls him *pitaji* (father), and tells visitors that he only wants his good works to be remembered. He shows some correspondence with the Bodleian Library in Oxford, to whom he had written asking for a list of his 'father's' works. Filed neatly is the Bodleian's reply, with the list it provided Vijay of its holdings under the name of Verrier Elwin.

Lila Elwin stays in Shillong with Ashok, who runs a pharmacy, and with Wasant, who is a teacher. They live in a large, rambling, double-storeyed house, a portion let out, fittingly, to a research centre in Tibetan medicine whose patron is the Dalai Lama. Her third son, Nakul, runs a school in Tura in the Garo Hills. All the boys have married local girls. They have ten children between them. When I met Lila in December 1997 she was accompanying one of her grandchildren to a picnic. The next week, she would be off to visit another in her boarding school in Roorkee. In Shillong she is mostly home-bound, though she dutifully appears for the annual Verrier Elwin Memorial Lecture organized by the North-Eastern Hill University. She remains a lady of great poise, although she would not speak of her husband to the strangers from the plains who keep coming around to ask.

Lila would not talk, but Ashok Elwin did. He is a photographer himself and a careful keeper of Elwin's massive collection of negatives spanning many years and many locations. While we spoke a friend came in to pass on the latest news of a campaign they were involved in. This aimed at protecting the old bridle-path which ran up from the plains to Shillong, which a new and historically insensitive administration wished to demolish: the protection of cultural heritage, an obsession both tribal and English, a struggle that would have met with his father's complete approval.

Back in England Eldyth Elwin remained, till her recent death, devoted to Verrier's memory. To his publishers, John Murray in London and Oxford University Press in Bombay, she wrote a stream of letters asking that this book or that be reissued or reprinted. To a prospective historian of the Christa Seva Sangh, she bravely tried to reconcile her brother's journey of upturned allegiances to her own steady faith. Even after Verrier left the CSS, she told the questioner, his 'life was very arduous and even later he hardly had any possessions and comfort. The tribal people loved him, and I think he lived a life among them that would have delighted

St Francis.'⁴¹ Delighted in some parts, certainly, but one cannot be sure what the saint of Assisi would have made of Kosi and Lila, *The Baiga*, or *The Muria and their Ghotul*.

When I met Eldyth Elwin in 1991, and again in 1992, she lived in a nursing home outside Oxford. She was alone, infirm and blind, but her room was lit up for her by rows of her brother's books and photographs. Underneath her bed was a trunk containing his letters and clippings, the core of what was to become the Verrier Elwin Collection at the India Office Library in London. She complained to me that Verrier's association with Gandhi had been disregarded both in Richard Attenborough's film and a recent biography of the Mahatma by an Oxford historian. She spoke then of 'the poem with which Verrier won the Newdigate;' unfortunately she no longer possessed a copy. The error was wonderfully revealing, for although her brother had won many prizes at Oxford, the Newdigate had not been one of them. As he recalled in his memoirs, he had submitted a long poem on Michelangelo; it came a mere fifth, perhaps because it was, as his teacher H. W. Garrod pointed out, 'too much of a sermon.'⁴²

I shall end this account with a fragment of personal experience. In September 1992 I spoke on Elwin at the Nehru Centre in London, newly set up to promote cultural understanding between England and India. The subject attracted an array of men and women from the various worlds which Elwin had touched. To my great good luck, some of these contributed to the discussion. Archbishop Trevor Huddleston (among the foremost British opponents of apartheid) said that the example of Elwin, the brilliant scholar who gave it all up to go overseas and serve the poor, inspired some Oxford Christians of the thirties, such as himself, to do likewise. Charles Lewis of Oxford University Press remembered his first assignment in India, which was to do the publicity for Elwin's last book. The playwright Ebrahim Alkazi recalled how, as a young man, he would direct plays in Bombay to raise money for the Tribal Welfare and Research Unit of Patangarh. The photographer Sunil Janah, Elwin's companion on many journeys through Bastar and Orissa, told a lovely story of their first trip together. In Raipur, on the edge of the Chattisgarh forest, they were directed one evening to the home of a timber contractor who was knowledgeable about the tribals. This man met them in his garden, where they talked, but at regular intervals he would go back into his house. He offered Elwin and Janah no refreshments. Fortunately, they had in their bags a bottle of rum from which they took swigs while their host went in. They later found that to drink rapidly and on the sly was also the purpose of *his* periodic disappearances, for he had been told only of Elwin's sinless past in ashram and church and knew little of his joyful present.

My own talk at the Nehru Centre was altogether more serious. It ended with a discussion of the Narmada controversy. After Huddleston and company had spoken, wistfully and humorously, an intervention of controlled anger came from Maharani Gayatri Devi of Jaipur, one of the great beauties of this century, and even at seventy the most striking woman I had seen. 'I am a tribal,' she dramatically announced: this a reference to the allegedly aboriginal origins of the Cooch-Behar family into which she was born: 'And speaking as a tribal, I charge the Congress governments which have ruled India with brutally disturbing the cultural ethos of the tribals by taking away their lands, damming their rivers and forcing them into second-rate schools where they are taught to despise their tradition.' Now the Maharani, it needs to be added, had been a political foe of Jawaharlal Nehru and was later jailed by his daughter. I could not answer her charges, but the chairman did. He was C. Subramaniam, at the time the governor of Maharashtra, and in his pomp a senior minister in the cabinets of Nehru and Indira Gandhi. The post-independence Congress, he now rejoined, wished to bring the fruits of modernity to all sections of India, but it respected the culture of the tribals, and designed special and less intrusive policies for them. I listened with attention to the argument between the minister and the maharani, or more accurately perhaps, between Elwin Mark I and Elwin Mark II, between the Protectionist and the Integrationist.

One keeps coming across evidence of Elwin's posthumous influence, instances of his work being attacked or affirmed. The most curious example occurs in a recent biography of P. G. Wodehouse. Seeking to establish the Oxford college which Bertie Wooster graced—if graced is the word—the author cites two essays by Elwin as showing authoritatively that Worster went to Magdalen. Elwin had also established the years Bertie was up, 1918 to 1921, but was stumped as to what he might have read. It could not have been Greats or Classics, for he knew not a word of Latin, and the 'imagination boggled' at the thought of Bertie reading Theology or English, Verrier's own disciplines. The biographer presents Elwin's conclusions approvingly and then refers to *Motley*, the book where the essays appeared, as 'one of the best and scarcest books of literary criticism.'[43] Apparently the Wodehouse scholar, a man of learning and experience (we may assume), knew nothing of Elwin the theologian or novelist, the anthropologist or activist, the Gandhian, Christian, Englishman and Indian. For all this to be forgotten or ignored, and to be remembered only as a student and scholar of English literature! I am certain Elwin would not have been displeased.

APPENDIX ONE

The Social Worker: A Constitution Not Always Honoured

In 1933 or 1934 Verrier Elwin drafted this constitution of the Gond Seva Mandal. The second section, on the Mandal's principles, gives a fascinating insight into his thinking at the time, his delicate juggling of the competing influences of F. W. Green, Mahatma Gandhi, and the Gonds. This version is from a typescript in File R of 1935, Commissioner's Record Room, Jabalpur. I am grateful to Dr Archana Prasad for providing me with a copy.

THE GOND SEVA MANDAL
CONSTITUTION AND RULES

1. The name of this Society shall be the Gond Seva Mandal.
2. The object of the Gond Seva Mandal shall be to serve the Gonds and other forest tribes of the Central Provinces of India.
3. In furtherance of this object, the Mandal shall carry on educational and medical work, and shall undertake any activities—other than missionary and political—which shall contribute to the well-being and enlightenment of the forest-tribes.
4. Membership of the Mandal shall be open to all, men and women, married or unmarried, whatever their nationality or creed, who are ready to devote themselves to the object of the Mandal and observe its rules and principles.
5. There shall be three classes of members:
   (a) Probationary members, who shall work in the Mandal for not less than three months and who may be retained as such for any period not exceeding two years.

(b) Members, who after a probationary period of not less than six months, engage to work in the Mandal for three years, and give a pledge to observe the rules and principles of the Mandal. At the end of the three years period, a member is free either to resign or to offer himself for re-election by the Sabha.

(c) Life-members, who after serving for two periods of three years, profess the intention of serving in the Mandal for life, and are accepted by a unanimous vote of the existing life-members. In the first six years of the life of the Mandal it shall, in exceptional cases, be within the competence of the life-members to accept new life-members before they have completed the full period of their probation.

6. The general direction of the affairs of the Mandal shall be managed by the members and life-members as hereinafter provided.
7. The life members and members shall together compose a Sabha which shall elect one of the life-members as its Mantri or chief servant, to hold office for five years, with the possibility of re-election. It shall elect the same or another life-member as Treasurer on the same terms, and a member to act as secretary of the Sabha to hold office for another year.
8. It shall be competent for the Mandal to acquire and hold moveable and immoveable properties, and such properties shall vest in the Mantri on behalf of the Mandal and he shall deal with them in consultation with the life-members. The funds of the Mandal shall be deposited in a Bank in the name of the Mandal, and the account shall be operated upon by the Treasurer in consultation with the life-members. All the other affairs of the Mandal shall be directed by the members and life-members sitting together in the Sabha.
9. New members will be admitted to the Sabha on obtaining a two-thirds majority vote in their favour. No member can be removed from the Sabha save for grave cause and a two-thirds vote against him.
10. The Sabha shall meet at the headquarters of the Mandal as often as is necessary for the transaction of business, and five members shall form a quorum.
11. The members of the Mandal shall devote themselves entirely to the bona-fide humanitarian service of the poor, and shall not use their

activities as a cloak for religious or political propaganda. They shall neither prepare for, nor ultimately engage in, any campaign of civil disobedience. The Mandal shall not enter into terms of association with any religious, missionary or political body.
12. Not inconsistently with the object of the Mandal, the life-members shall have the power to revise the constitution from time to time by a majority of two-thirds of the members present at a meeting. For the purpose and for the transaction of business relating to property and finance the Mantri may call a meeting of life-members as and when he considers necessary.
13. This constitution shall come into effect as from March 1st 19 . . .

Principles

The Mandal is founded on the following principles.
1. TRUTH. There can be no brotherhood and no service without Truth. Only out of a pure transparent heart can there come acts of love and mercy. It is necessary for the spirit of Truth to direct not only our speech, but every aspect of our lives and every detail of our organisation. Then only can we be worthy to serve God who is Truth.
2. LOVE. The servant of the poor must consciously direct all his actions in the spirit of universal love. He will be courteous, gentle, fearless, non-violent in thought, speech and action. Love implies fearlessness, and the members will try to overcome fear of sickness, wild animals, the secular and religious authorities, and death itself. They will try to overcome by love the critics and opponents of their work.
3. PURITY. Purity of personal life is an essential basis of sincere service. Members will therefore endeavour to curb animal passion and fight against every kind of impurity in thought, word and deed. As an aid to purity, control of the palate is advocated. Those who desire to serve the poor, even if they cannot share the actual food of the poor, will regard eating as necessary chiefly for the sustaining of the body and keeping it a fit instrument for service. They will therefore constantly try to regulate and simplify their diet. But as they accept the discipline of fasting, so they will not despise the joy of feasting at the proper time. No food laws may be passed by the Mandal.

4. PRAYER. Communion with God can alone keep the heart transparent and fill the life with love. Without prayer, service becomes lifeless. All members, therefore, will join in the morning and evening prayer (which is of such a character that adherents of all religions can join in it) and they will try to maintain the attitude of prayerfulness in all that they do.

5. SIMPLICITY OF LIFE. The members will try to set an example for the people by the right use of such money as they have. They will gladly accept such small allowance as the Mandal is able to make them for their needs. They will not contract any debt without the permission of the Sabha. They will not waste money, and they will not encourage others to waste money on expensive weddings, funerals, jewellry or caste dinners.

6. RESPECT. The members regard with respect every manifestation of the religious spirit. While they are not committed to any particular theory of the relations of all religions to one another, they refrain from all proselytising. Each member is encouraged to hold firmly and to practise his own religion. But this loyalty to his own faith must only deepen his respect for that of others. In the same way he will treat with equal respect rich and poor, Indians or foreigners, friends or foes.

7. KNOWLEDGE. Knowledge, art, music, etc are not to be despised by the lover of the poor. Knowledge, by purifying and enlarging the mind, actually equips him with the means of better service. Members will be encouraged to make research in the customs and ancient traditions of the people, and to give some time at least daily to general study.

8. UNITY. The members aim at a sincere unity of spirit. The Mandal desires to embrace in one fellowship Hindu and Christian, Mussalman and Parsi, Gond and Panka, Brahmin and Harijan. It will try to co-operate with all men of good will, whatever their political or religious opinions, who are endeavouring to ameliorate the lot of the poor.

9. DISCIPLINE. No organisation can exist without discipline. The members will aim at exact punctuality, the loyal fulfilment of the tasks alloted to them, and the perfect cleanliness of the land and buildings where they live.

10. BREAD-LABOUR. The ideal of identification with the poor is meaningless unless it finds expression in some form of bread-labour. Moreover the servant of the poor who comes not to be ministered to but to minister must reduce to a minimum the service that he receives from others. Sacrificial spinning is a perfect symbol of love for and identification with the poor. Members will not be ashamed to do their own cleaning, wood-cutting, cooking, grinding and rice-pounding.
11. HINDI. The educational work of the Mandal, which will be in the national language, will aim at fostering a truly national spirit: it will try to recreate the national self-respect of the forest tribes and to foster pride in their ancient heritage. The official language of the Mandal is Hindi, which every member will undertake to learn and use.
12. INTERNATIONALIST. The outlook of the Mandal will never be merely nationalist. As it aims at binding together in one fellowship of service members of different religions, so it desires to unite those of different races. Its members will ever strive to make their love more universal, their sympathies more catholic.

APPENDIX TWO

The Author: An Unwritten Book

In the Verrier Elwin Papers in the Nehru Memorial Museum and Library there are two files (numbers 160 and 161) containing his notes on the Kondhs. These run to some five hundred pages, and were to be used in a book he planned to write on the tribe. His work in NEFA meant that the book was never written, but a chapter scheme left by him tells us how it was to have been structured.

THE ECONOMICS OF THE KUTTIA KOND
INTRODUCTION
The people
The country and climate
Village
House
Dress and ornament

THE ECONOMICS OF RELIGIOUS OBLIGATION
The cost of customary worship
The medicine-man and fees of the gods
Obligations to the dead

THE ECONOMICS OF SOCIAL DUTY
Corporate enterprise
Payments to the State
Payments to the Patro
Payments to tribal priests and headmen
Tribal justice and its cost

APPENDIX TWO

THE ECONOMICS OF FAMILY RELATIONSHIPS

The Family
Reciprocal obligations
Birth
Marriage
Death

THE SUPPLY OF FOOD

Axe-cultivation
Forest products
Hunting and fishing
Domestic animals
Liquor

THE CONSUMPTION OF FOOD

The Store-room
The Kitchen
The Dining Room
The Tavern

PROPERTY AND DEBT

Income
Expenditure
Property
Debt
The Disposal of Surplus Goods

POVERTY AND 'CRIME'

The Kond in revolt
The Kond dacoit
The Kond murderer

Also in the notes on the Kondhs is this checklist of questions to ask on tribal hunting, a fine illustration of the field-methods of this ostensibly 'amateur' anthropologist.

Ceremonial hunt
Any stories of Forest Guards interfering
Guns?
Traps
Slings

How do they beat?
How divide? Carry home?
Where do they deposit it?
How cook?
Rites?

Methods of stringing bow
Pits

Eating of bear, monkey, bison
crow, kite
frogs, snakes, lizard
rats, birds, porcupine

APPENDIX THREE

The Public Official: Policies 'Rejected or Forgotten'

Two-and-a-half years after Verrier Elwin joined the NEFA Administration, he wrote a note asking 'how far the various suggestions [made on the basis of his tours in the interior], many of which have been generally approved, have actually been implemented.' Striking in its comprehensiveness and attention to detail, the note is dated the 10th of April, 1956, and is reproduced here from File 133, Elwin Papers, NMML, New Delhi.

[Abbreviations: G = Governor; AG = Adviser to Governor; DAG = Deputy Adviser to Governor; DC = Development Commissioner; EO = Educational Officer; PO = Political Officer; ATA = Adviser on Tribal Affairs; PM = Prime Minister]

The following points arise for discussion and implementation from suggestions made by the ATA in his various tour notes:

1. The problem of slavery. Can we accelerate the liberation of slaves? Should we pay compensation?
2. The problem of opium in Tirap and Lohit. Should we try to move faster?
3. Dress for school-children. What has been finally decided? Has a directive actually issued? Has any progress been made in the production of suitable clothes?
4. The promotion of weaving. What has been decided? Can we distribute yarn at subsidised rates, and if so how much? What progress has been made about getting 'weaving organisers?' Or starting itinerant weaving schools? Should we or shouldn't we close down some of the weaving sections in places like Teju and Dambuk, where the people

already weave well? What can we do about the bad designs coming in to the Pasighat weaving centre?

5. Political presents. Is our directive being followed with regard to the kind of things being given? Should we not call for a report?
6. Relief. AG some time ago suggested a directive; has one issued? If not, what action can we take? What actually is the present policy?
7. Has any report come in about the political situation in the neighbourhood of Roing (as apart from enquiry into specific allegations)?
8. Has any action been taken about the Supervisor who so offended the Mishmi boys at Pasighat?
9. What action has been taken about the Lohit schools?
10. What can we do to improve the morale and discipline of the Army Supply Corps boys and stop them (a) black-marketing in cloth, cigarettes etc and (b) introducing bad habits like card-playing to the tribal people?
11. The Adviser suggested that there should be a directive about the propaganda used by teachers to persuade children to go to school, e. g., that they would then get Government jobs, and to stress that there must be no forcing of children to attend. Has this been done?
12. School architecture. Has any decision been made about this? Can we improve it and make it more tribal, especially when buildings are put up on a self-help basis and are thus not tied down by the engineering rules?
13. What is the final decision about the rules for [officials'] learning tribal languages and passing the exams?
14. Cottage Industry Training and Production Centres. What are DC's reactions to my suggestion to cut out the 'training' and make them 'production' centres?

Has the suggestion of having small museums been approved and has Finance agreed?

What of the suggestion that instructors and supervisors should make short tours to acquaint themselves with the realities of tribal life? Has it been possible to employ tribal wood-carving instructors in Teju, Mon and Tuensang?

APPENDIX THREE 345

15. Has a directive about the control of shops been issued, and have we any information as to how it is being implemented?
16. What about sweepers? DC and I have both noticed a certain lukewarmness in implementing our directives on this subject. Is there any way whereby we can eliminate sweepers from the hospitals?
17. Has any action been taken to capture for Government the trade (a) in Lama coats and ornaments in Lohit and (b) the trade in Khampti and Tangsa bags etc in Tirap?
18. I suggested for schoolboys in Lohit and Siang the attractive small coat made of the 'Abor rug' material, a specimen of which is in my Museum. Has that commended itself to the EO? If so, has anything been done about it?
19. Variety shows. I am afraid I have myself held up the DC's directive on 'instructional entertainment' until we could discuss the matter fully and issue a comprehensive directive on what I have called the NEFA Theatre. We should take this up now.
20. Venereal disease. I have already suggested that we might have the C[hief] M[edical] O[fficer]'s advice on this. I feel it is a most important matter.
21. Has the PO Tirap been asked to enquire about the alleged visit of Burmese officials across the border, and if so has any reply been received?
22. What are DC's views about a BS [Boys School?] at Laju?
23. What progress has been made towards solving the porter problem? Has anything been done to obtain animal transport?
24. AG has asked for action with regard to getting good portraits of the PM and President. What has been done?
25. What are DC's views about an N[ational] E[ducation] S[cheme] block for the upper Tirap valley, which would have the special aim at eliminating opium by substituting other interests?
26. Orders have already issued regarding hair-cutting of children in Tangsa schools and the wearing of the Tangsa lungi.
27. Are the PO's implementing the instructions, based on the PM's wishes, regarding the singing of Ramdun etc?
28. Has any progress been made in the way of adapting our architecture generally to tribal models?

29. Can we do something about having a Cleanliness Week?
30. DAG has noted that he would correspond with the PO Tirap about the Tangsa girls and what action has been taken to improve the situation. Has this been done and has any reply been sent?
31. I would be very grateful if the EO could let me have a report on the progress made in encouraging tribal games.
32. I would also be grateful for a note on progress made in combating dermatitis in northern Subansiri. I have noticed the same infection in northern Siang: it seems to affect the Tagins and certain groups of Galongs and not other tribes. This is a most urgent human problem and I do hope that real progress has been made.
33. G. made certain suggestions about training Tagin girls in weaving. Have we had any success in this?
34. G. noted on my Subansiri report last year that 'we should take systematic steps to develop the fibre cloth industry in our Divisions. Kameng has a good tradition of it.' What has been done about this?
35. G. further noted that he had issued instructions 'long ago' for the development of the wool and yarn industry in the Monpa area. Has this made progress?
36. I have also raised the question of providing wool for the weavers in northern Siang (for Boris, Pailibos and Bhokars etc). What can we do about this?
37. I suggested last year, and G issued orders approving the suggestion that, in G's words, 'we may correspond with Kalimpong authorities for the supplies of deo-ghantis [bells?] if the rates are reasonable. I think we can easily order 100 for each division.' Was this ever taken up?
38. What progress has been made in developing Sherdukpen agriculture in the area around Rupa and Shergaon, as I suggested last year? AG asked the A(gricultural) O(fficer) to make 'a personal study' of the local plough with a view to its improvement. Has he done this?
39. Have we been able to make progress in the introduction of cash crops such as pepper and cardamom, especially in areas near the plains where the people could market their wares?

40. AG has noted on my Kameng report that it will be 'well worth examining' whether we can utilise temple or monastic buildings for our schools as is done in Siam. Has anyone examined this?
41. Charts and pictures in schools. I have frequently drawn attention to the poor quality of these, and on my first visit to Margherita in 1954 the DC (then PO) and I spoke very strongly about it to the education people. Yet I still see exactly the same pictures and charts which we both condemned so heartily displaying their dreary inappropriateness on the walls of our schools. Why?
42. AG notes that it is a 'good idea' to have a few pictures illustrating the life of Buddha and a simple life of Buddha and his teachings to be used in our schools in the Buddhist-tribal areas. Has anything been done?
43. AG also notes that my suggestion about the repair of prayer-wheels in the Buddhist parts of Kameng 'should be attended to right away.' Has it been?
44. I made suggestions about a special hat for leading men with a badge of the Asoka pillar. Has this been rejected or just forgotten?
45. *ATA's notes on his tour in Siang 1956.* The suggestions in this note have only just been put up, and I have not seen AG's notings. The following points may be considered.
    (a) I would much appreciate a copy of DC's views and DAG's on roman script and use of Assamese.
    (b) Flowers are suggested for the Leprosy Home at Along, and better implements for the smithy tiers.
    (c) Designs for Galong weaving.
    (d) A possible rule that instructresses in Weaving Schools should wear khadi if not local hand-woven cloth.
    (e) The provision of large quantities of yarn at subsidised rates. We also have to discover the right kind of yarn as well as right colours.
    (f) Encouragement of shopkeepers on the positive side to stock the right kind of useful goods.
    (g) The making available of cheap but good books for purchase by our people.
    (h) The substitution of undesirable pictures and calendars in shops by our own NEFA calendars and other pictures.
    (i) This is not included in my original suggestions, but I feel it is

imperative to engage at least two artists, one for the Research Department, when Shri Dholling leaves us, and the other for the Development group of departments on a *much higher* salary than approved at present. How can we guide tribal taste in text-books, charts, pictures etc if we can only engage mediocre artists who will not put their hearts into the job on the miserable pittance which Government seems to think suitable for anyone who works for art, good taste and beauty?

    (j) The production of small books of songs.

    (k) Prizes in NEFA

    (l) The engagement of one or two dance experts, themselves tribals, to encourage and teach dancing in areas where it does not exist.

    (m) Stepping up of provision of wire ropes for bridges in Siang.

46. What is being done about Interpreters?

47. I suggest it is time now that we get reports on the Divisions about the implementation of the directives on Religion. How in fact are the festivals of Durga, Holi and Christmas being celebrated? Is anyone taking seriously the encouragement of tribal religions?

48. We also need a report as to how far directives have actually reached all our officers, especially those in outposts.

49. I had suggested (a) importing a stock of Manipuri shawls, some cheap and some of better quality, but all colourful, into Tirap, and if possible some of the Ao and other Naga shawls; (b) the importation of Mishmi coats into Tirap and the starting of weaving black coats of the Mishmi type but with Wancho or Nocte or Tangsa designs for the usual Mishmi or Abor decoration.

50. Could not the excellent chairs being made at Namsang be made in other carpentry sections also? And the Kampti or Singhpo loom?

Acknowledgements

I first heard of Verrier Elwin in the monsoon of 1978, from a kindly Oriya veterinarian named Das. We were both in the hills of Koraput, he running a government clinic, me studying, on behalf of the Delhi School of Economics, the 'assimilation of tribals into industrial society.' For weeks prior to our meeting I had pored over the productivity records of an aircraft factory situated in that unlikely location, and concluded, at the 1 per cent level of significance, that tribal workers were as efficient as non-tribal ones. The work complete, on my last Sunday I was taken by my host, a Mr Patro, on a courtesy tour of a Gadaba village where I met Dr Das. 'Many years ago,' he remarked, 'a scholar like you came from far away to study the tribals of Koraput. Do you know of Verrier Elwin?' I did not, so the doctor told me a little, enough for it to be clear that the parallels between Elwin and myself ended rather abruptly.

Back in Delhi I picked up *Leaves from the Jungle* from the library. In print six decades after its first publication, *Leaves* has been many things to many people: it was to send me away from economics towards social anthropology and history. Verrier Elwin has since been a visible and occasionally invisible presence in my life. That it has taken so long for this work to come to a close is in part due to other commitments, and in part due to the man's fanatically prodigious output. I can see why Kosi Elwin thought she had married a typewriter, for a reasonably comprehensive bibliography of her husband's works by the Japanese scholar Takeshii Fuji runs to some forty closely printed pages. It lists more than thirty books and almost four hundred articles. There are also the letters sent and received, as well as intelligence reports, newspaper reports, church and college records, school records, Gond Seva Mandal records, government records. . . .

But I protest too much, for the chase has been rich and invigorating and abetted by conscientious record-keepers, tolerant employers, loving friends. In the first category fall the staff of the following libraries and archives, ordered roughly according to the burdens placed upon them: the Oriental and India Office Collections (formerly the India Office and Records), London; the Nehru Memorial Museum and Library, New Delhi; the National Archives of India, New Delhi; the National Library, Calcutta; Oxford University Press, Mumbai; Merton College, Oxford; the Centre for South Asian Studies, Cambridge; Bishop's College, Calcutta; John Murray, London; the Bodleian Library, Oxford; the Christa Seva Sangh, Pune; Hilfield Priory, Dorset; the Society for the Propagation of the Gospel, London; Dean Close Memorial School, Cheltenham; the British Library Newspaper Collection, Collindale; the *Church Times* Record Office, London; the Institute of Social Anthropology, Oxford; Wycliffe Hall, Oxford; the United Theological College, Bangalore; Green Library, Stanford; Friends House, London; and St Stephen's College, Delhi.

Then come the institutions who have paid the bills in my itinerant career. Some of their money has gone unjustifiably, one could say unaccountably, towards understanding Elwin. I thank the Indian Institute of Management, Calcutta; the Centre for Studies in Social Sciences, Calcutta; Yale University, New Haven; the Indian Institute of Science, Bangalore; the Institute of Economic Growth, Delhi; St Antony's College, Oxford; the University of California at Berkeley; and the Ford Foundation, New Delhi. I must acknowledge above all two centres that know about collegiality precisely because they are not colleges in the formal sense. The first is the Nehru Memorial Museum and Library, which gave me a fellowship with a long rope, privileged access to its records, and to cap it an office overlooking the back lawn of Teen Murti House, so that I might write of Elwin as if he were in sight of me, walking and talking with his hero—also one of mine. The second is the Wissenschaftskolleg zu Berlin, where this book was conceived in its present form, and whose Fellows urged me cheerfully and consolingly along.

The last category is the most spacious and is itself subdivisible. First, the true believers in knowledge as common property, those people who generously and selflessly gave me access to original records in their possession. These good souls are Ashok Elwin, Daniel O'Connor, Paul Newton, Benedict Green, Archana Prasad, Nandini Sundar, William Emilsen, Jacques Pouchepadass, Arvind Khare, Michael Young, and Amit Baruah.

ACKNOWLEDGEMENTS

Then there are the colleagues and strangers who passed on tips and sources or subjected themselves to interviews or sermons or chapters or sections. I thank Mildred Archer, Ravi Bhagwat, Richard Bingle, Stanley Brandes, David Brokensha, Shareen Brysac, Mahendra Desai, Vasudha Dhagamwar, F. W. Dillistone, the late Shyama Charan Dube, the late Eldyth Elwin, Anjan Ghosh, Ann Grodzins Gold, Chris Gregory, S. J. Gunn, R. N. and Krishna Haldipur, Zoya Hasan, J. R. F. Highfield (of Merton College), Rivka Israel, Pico Iyer, Sunil Janah, Amina Jayal, Mukul Kesavan, Sunil Khilnani, Elizabeth Krishna, Charles Lewis, Alan Macfarlane, T. N. Madan, Hans Medick, Arvind Krishna Mehrotra, Karl Meyer, Shibani Mitra, Prabhu Mohapatra, O. K. Moorthy, Dom Moraes, Santosh Mookherjee (of Oxford University Press), K. K. S. Murthy (proprietor of the Select Bookshop, Bangalore), Bansi Narmada (son of Elwin's long-time research assistant Sunderlal Narmada), Humphrey Osmond (of Dean Close School), the late G. Parthasarathi, Gyanendra Pandey, Vivek Rae, N. Raghunathan, Satish Saberwal, Savyasachi, Vikram Seth, Har Mander Singh, Khushwant Singh, James Scott, K. Sivaramakrishnan, M. N. Srinivas, Ramaswamy Sudarshan, the late J. Swaminathan, Adil Tyabji, Khalid Tyabji, and C. S. Venkatachar. I have benefited much from comments on the penultimate version by Kirin Narayan, a friend, and from Wendy Doniger and Lee Siegel, two no longer anonymous readers.

I grieve that two friends who encouraged me for many years did not live to see this book in print. One was the journalist P. K. Srinivasan, an admirer of English culture and, with discrimination, of Englishmen; the other the scholar and democrat C. V. Subba Rao, who in a brief life did as much as anyone since Elwin to draw attention to the problems of India's tribes.

A few debts, the most consequential perhaps, remain to be acknowledged. T. David Brent of the University of Chicago Press has been a wonderfully supportive editor. My 'Wiko' colleague Nicholas Boyle taught me aspects of the biographer's craft, gently squeezing out the residues of my sociological training (some remain, alas). Both David and Nicholas prodded me, as a pious agnostic, to more seriously explore the faiths of my subject. Keshav Desiraju and Gopal Gandhi, sahibs sometimes in the secretariat, both steeped in Indian history and world literature, saved me from numerous errors of fact and interpretation. They also brought me back to Elwin whenever I strayed too far from him. And Rukun Advani has read drafts and half-drafts with a novelist's eye and a friend's concern. As with my other books, Rukun directed this one from pen to paper and finally to print.

Savaging the Civilized is dedicated to my wife, Sujata. 'At the bottom of his heart,' wrote Raymond Chandler, 'every decent man knows that his approach to the woman he loves is like an approach to a shrine.' It has been that way for some time now, for I first heard of Sujata the week I first heard of Elwin. Her goodness and tranquillity have sustained me since.

Notes

NOTES TO PROLOGUE

1. Tamara's dispatches are reproduced in Shamrao Hivale, *Scholar Gypsy: A Study of Verrier Elwin* (Bombay 1946), pp. 212–14.
2. Romain Rolland, foreword to Elwin's *Leaves from the Jungle: A Diary of Life in a Gond Village* (London 1936).
3. *TLS*, 20 January 1950.
4. E. P. Thompson, *No Alien Homage: Edward Thompson and Rabindranath Tagore* (New Delhi 1993), p. 10.
5. Cf. correspondence in File E10, Oxford University Press Archives, Mumbai.

NOTES TO CHAPTER ONE

1. Anon., *Wycliffe Hall, Oxford, 1877–1927* (privately printed pamphlet, issued on the occasion of the seminary's Golden Jubilee).
2. F. S. Johnson, *The Story of a Mission: The Sierra Leone Church: First Daughter of the C. M. S.* (London 1953).
3. James Denton, 'An African College: Its Story,' *Church Missionary Review*, August 1905; Christopher Fyfe, 'Royal Charter for Fourah Bay College,' *West African Review*, March 1960.
4. W. Vivian, 'The Missionary in West Africa,' *Journal of the African Society*, vol. 3, 1903–4, pp. 100–3; also H. R. Fox Bourne, 'Sierra Leone Troubles,' *The Fortnightly Review*, August 1898.
5. E. H. Elwin, 'The Temne Mission after the Revolt,' *Church Missionary Intelligencer*, October 1899, pp. 837–40.
6. Verrier Elwin, *The Tribal World of Verrier Elwin: An Autobiography* (Bombay and New York 1964), p. 2 (hereafter *Tribal World*).
7. Quoted in T. J. Thompson, *The Jubilee and Centenary Volume of Fourah Bay College* (Freetown 1930), pp. 106–7.
8. As reported in the *Sierra Leone Weekly News*, 22 February 1902 (based on an earlier report in *The Times* of London).
9. To the distance in years was added an emotional and intellectual distance, such that in later life Verrier had almost nothing to do with Basil. He will not appear again in this biography.

10. The verdicts, respectively, of Reverend F. W. Dillistone in an interview with this writer in June 1991, of Shamrao Hivale in *Scholar Gypsy: A Study of Verrier Elwin* (Bombay 1946), p. 3, and of Frank Moraes in his *Witness to an Era* (Bombay 1973), p. 22.
11. *Tribal World*, pp. 9–12.
12. Many years later, and aided by her granddaughter Eldyth, Flora Holman wrote down these and other tales from the Raj. See 'A true story of Indian life in the days of John Company,' typescript in Mss. Eur. D. 950/27, Elwin Papers, India Office Library, London (hereafter IOL).
13. As reported in *Church Missionary Review*, April 1909.
14. Archer, 'Notes on Verrier Elwin,' Mss. Eur. F. 236/228, IOL.
15. Hivale, *Scholar Gypsy*, p. 2.
16. *Tribal World*, pp. 2–3, 9–10.
17. Close's life and work are described in R. J. W. Evans, 'Town, Gown and Cloth: An Essay on the Foundations of the School,' in M. A. Girling and Sir Leonard Hooper, editors, *Dean Close: The First Hundred Years* (Cheltenham 1986).
18. This sketch of H. W. Flecker draws on books by a student, grandson and friend respectively: *God's Apprentice: The Autobiography of Stephen Neill*, edited by Eleanor M. Jackson (London 1984); John Sherwood, *No Golden Journey: A Biography of James Elroy Flecker* (London 1973); Charles Williams, *Flecker of Dean Close* (London 1946).
19. Geraldine Hodgson, *The Life of James Elroy Flecker, From Letters and Materials Provided by his Mother* (Oxford 1925); also Verrier Elwin, 'The Poetry of J. E. Flecker,' *The Statesman* (Calcutta), 28 June 1953.
20. R. F. McNeile, compiler, *A History of Dean Close School* (privately printed in 1966).
21. Quoted in Archer, 'Notes on Verrier Elwin.'

NOTES TO CHAPTER TWO

1. From a letter of January 1923 written by Robert Byron in Lucy Butler, editor, *Robert Byron: Letters Home* (London 1991), pp. 17–18.
2. Rowse, *Friends and Contemporaries* (London 1989).
3. 'Professor Garrod,' *The Postmaster*, vol. 1, no. 1, 1952; also the entry on Garrod in the *Merton College Register, 1900–1964* (Oxford 1964).
4. George Mallaby, *From my Level: Unwritten Minutes* (London 1965), p. 240.
5. *John Betjeman's Oxford* (reprint, Oxford 1990), p. 27; also D. J. Palmer, *The Rise of English Studies* (London 1965), pp. 115–30.
6. *Tribal World*, p. 22.

NOTES TO CHAPTER TWO 355

7. Letter of 12 March 1914, Kuruvilla Zachariah Papers, Merton College Archives, Oxford.
8. This last a phrase used in an paper presented by Verrier to the Bodley Club, a study of the range of geographical allusions in the plays and poems of Shakespeare. Verrier Elwin, 'Topographical Anachronisms,' manuscript in Mss Eur. D. 950/26, IOL.
9. Cf. Martin Green, *Children of the Sun: A Narrative of 'Decadence' in England after 1918* (London 1977); Cyril Connolly, 'The Twenties,' in his *The Evening Colonnade* (New York 1971); Robert Graves and Alan Hodge, *The Long Week-end: A Social History of Great Britian, 1918–39* (revised editon, New York 1963).
10. *Myrmidon Club Minutes, 1909—*, Merton College Archives.
11. Sykes, *Four Studies in Loyalty* (London 1946), p. 80.
12. F. M. Turner, 'Religion,' in Brian Harrison, editor, *The History of the University of Oxford: Volume VIII: The Twentieth Century* (Oxford 1994).
13. S. C. Ollard, *The Anglo-Catholic Revival: Some Persons and Principles* (London 1925).
14. Obituary in *Church Times*, 23 January 1953; letter from Benedict Green (F. W. Green's son) to the author, 21 June 1995.
15. See *Registrum College Mertonensis, 1915–36*.
16. *Bodley Club Minutes, 1914–23*, Merton College Archives.
17. Quoted in Turner, 'Religion,' p. 307.
18. Minutes of meetings of 16 March and 8 May 1922, in *Church Society Minutes, 1907–22*, Merton College Archives.
19. *Tribal World*, pp. 29–30.
20. Oliver Fielding-Clarke, *Unfinished Conflict: An Autobiography* (London 1970), p. 149f.
21. Bryan Beady, 'A Gandhi Disciple at Oxford,' *The Evening News*, 21 January 1932. Duns Scotus was a famous Franciscan of the fourteenth century, and the subject of Donne's poem "Duns Scotus' Oxford."
22. Church Society minutes of meetings held on 25 May 1923, 3 December 1923 and 3 March 1924, *Church Society Minutes, 1922—*, Merton College Archives.
23. *Tribal World*, pp. 24–5.
24. *Church Times*, 3 October 1924.
25. Cf. *The Decanian*, December 1924, p. 73.
26. Beady, 'A Gandhi Disciple at Oxford.'
27. Verrier Elwin, *Onward Bound* (pamplet printed in 1926 by the Oxford University Church Union), p. 10.
28. Untitled poem in Mss. Eur. 950/26, IOL.
29. *Tribal World*, p. 23.

30. Cf. Brian Harrison, 'College Life, 1918–39,' in Harrison, editor, *The History of the University of Oxford: Volume VIII: The Twentieth Century* (Oxford 1994).
31. Hivale, *Scholar Gypsy*, p. 9.
32. *Tribal World*, pp. 31–4.
33. J. C. Winslow, *The Indian Mystic: Some Thoughts on India's Contribution to Christianity* (London 1926), pp. 7–9.
34. J. C. Winslow, *Christa Seva Sangh* (London 1930).
35. Barbara Noreen, *A Wheat Grain Sown in India* (privately printed by the author, Wantage 1988).
36. *Tribal World*, p. 28.
37. Poem reproduced in Verrier Elwin, *Desiderium* (London 1926).
38. Minutes of meetings of 28 October 1926, 17 May 1927 and 3 June 1927, *Church Society Minutes, 1922—*, Merton College Archives.
39. Quoted in *Scholar Gypsy*, p. 11.
40. Cf. picture postcard with handwritten caption, 'Where Verrier got his call for India,' in Mss. Eur. D. 950/24, IOL.
41. *Tribal World*, p. 36.
42. Elwin to F. W. Green, 31 July 1927 (addressed, significantly, to 'My dear Guru'), letter in the possession of Benedict Green.

NOTES TO CHAPTER THREE

1. Quoted in J. C. Winslow, *The Eyelids of the Dawn: Memories, Reflections and Hopes* (London 1954), pp. 89–90.
2. *The Church Times*, 21 October 1927.
3. Oliver Fielding-Clarke, *Unfinished Conflict: An Autobiography* (London 1970), pp. 153–4.
4. H. V. E(lwin), 'A Passage to India,' in *The Servant of Christ* (newsletter of the Christa Seva Sangh), Feast of the Purification, 1928, copies held in the archives of Hilfield Priory, Dorset.
5. *Tribal World*, pp. 40–1.
6. Elwin to his mother, 22 November 1927, Mss. Eur. D. 950/1, IOL.
7. Quoted in Alexa Grace Cameron, 'Christian Missions and the Social Reform Movement in the City of Poona in Western India (1880–1920),' unpublished D.Phil. dissertation, Department of Education, New York University, 1973, p. 143.
8. Muriel Lester, *My Host the Hindu* (London 1931), pp. 128–9.
9. Father J. Sadananda, 'The aims and aspirations of the CSS,' unpublished typescript in W. Q. Lash Papers, Hilfield Priory, Dorset.
10. Chattopadhyay, *Inner Recesses, Outer Spaces: Memoirs* (New Delhi 1986), pp. 92–3.

NOTES TO CHAPTER THREE

11. Nehru, *An Autobiography* (1936: reprint London 1949), p. 375.
12. Letter of 5 December 1927, F. W. Green Papers, in the possession of Benedict Green.
13. 'Discussion on Fellowship,' in *Collected Works of Mahatma Gandhi*, vol. 35, p. 461.
14. H. V. E(lwin), 'The Friendly Road,' *The Servant of Christ*, Feast of St Barnabas, 1928, Hilfield Priory, Dorset.
15. *Young India*, 19 January 1928.
16. *Tribal World*, p. 42.
17. Elwin to George, 24 May 1928, Green Papers.
18. Ibid.
19. Roderick M. Bell to Brother John Charles, 8 November 1971, in 'File of Interviews and Correspondence with Brother John Charles,' Hilfield Priory, Dorset.
20. *Tribal World*, pp. 43–4.
21. H. V. E(lwin), 'The Library,' *The Servant of Christ*, Feast of St Francis, 1928.
22. Elwin to his mother, 6 September 1928, Mss. Eur. D. 950/1.
23. As recounted in *Tribal World*, p. 44.
24. Elwin to his mother, 31 August 1929, Mss Eur. D. 950/1.
25. Verrier Elwin, *Christian Dhyana, or Prayer of Loving Regard: A Study of 'The Cloud of Unknowing'* (London 1930).
26. Cf. the reference to the book in H. A. Popley, *K. T. Paul: Christian Leader* (Calcutta 1938), p. 189.
27. Verrier Elwin, *Richard Rolle: A Christian Sanyasi* (Madras 1930), preface and pp. 3, 7, 29, 67–73, 75–9, etc.
28. Ibid., p. 5.
29. Elwin to Sorella Amata, 12 March 1929, Mss. Eur. D. 950/7, IOL.
30. Idem., 27 June 1929.
31. Idem., 6 October 1929 (emphasis in original).
32. See Denis Dalton, *Mahatma Gandhi: Non-Violent Power in Action* (New York 1993), chapter IV.
33. Verrier Elwin, *Christ and Satyagraha* (Bombay 1930), pp. 3–4.
34. Circular letter from J. C. Winslow, Feast of St Francis, 1930, in L/P/J/6/2013, IOL.
35. Elwin to Sorella Amata, 30 April 1930, Mss Eur. D. 950/7, IOL.
36. Note of 22 July 1930, File 338 of 1930, Home (Political) department, National Archives of India, New Delhi (hereafter NAI).
37. 'Minutes of the Special Chapter of the CSS held on 18th June, 1930,' Folder 1, CSS/CPSS Record Room, Poona.
38. Reginald Reynolds, *To Live in Mankind: A Quest for Gandhi* (London 1951), pp. 72–7.

39. 'Minutes of the General Sabha held on 7th July 1930,' Folder 1, CSS/CPSS Record Room, Poona.
40. *Christ and Satyagraha*, pp. 5, 17, 18, 23, 47, etc.
41. Elwin to J. C. Kumarappa, letters of 26 June and 7 July 1930, Kumarappa Papers, Nehru Memorial Museum and Library, New Delhi (hereafter NMML). The *Bombay Chronicle* series, published in ten parts under the running title 'Studies in the Teaching of Gandhiji,' appeared between 24th September and 8th November 1930.
42. Notes of 4 September and 29 September 1930, both in L/P/J/6/2013, IOL.
43. *Servant of Christ*, no. 9, copy in File 338 of 1930, Home (Pol.), NAI.
44. Circular Letter (hereafter CL) from Elwin, written from Matheran, Ash Wednesday 1931, in W. Q. Lash Papers, Hilfield Priory, Dorset.
45. Verrier Elwin, 'A Fortnight in Gujerat: What Personal Investigation Revealed,' in three parts, *Bombay Chronicle*, 12, 13 and 14 January 1931.
46. Elwin to Sorella Amata, 30 April 1930, Mss. Eur. D. 950/7, IOL.
47. 'Copy of a speech delivered by Father Elwin at Shivaji Mandir, Poona, on 23 May 1931,' in File 11/II/1931, Home (Pol.), NAI.
48. Verrier Elwin, 'A Darshan of Bapu,' *The CSS Review*, vol. 1, no. 4, June 1931.
49. CL from Elwin, Labour Day 1931, in Lash Papers.
50. *Young India*, 21 May 1931.
51. Elwin to Mirabehn, 7 May 1931, copy in File 11/II/1931, Home (Pol.), NAI.
52. Cf. *Tribal World*, pp. 54–6.
53. Verrier Elwin, 'Ten Days with Mahatma Gandhi,' *The CSS Review*, vol. 1, no. 6, August 1931; also Elwin to Sorella Amata, 31 May 1931, Mss Eur. D. 950/7, IOL.
54. 'Extracts from the confidential weekly diary of the District Superintendent of Police, Surat, for 8 June and 13 June 1931;' 'Translation of a speech delivered by Father Elwin at Rayan, 4 June 1931,' both in File 11/II/1931, Home (Pol.), NAI.
55. Elwin to F. W. Green, 11 May 1931, Green Papers.
56. Elwin to Sorella Amata, 31 May 1931, Mss. Eur. D. 950/7, IOL.
57. Thakkar's life, work and writings are well covered in T. N. Jagadishan and Shyamlal, editors, *Thakkar Bapa Eightieth Birthday Commemoration Volume* (Madras 1949).
58. Quoted by Elwin in a note of 17 November 1961, File 69, Elwin Papers, NMML.
59. H. P. Desai, 'A. V. Thakkar: The Man and his Work,' *The Modern Review*, January 1928.

60. CL dated The Visitation, 1931, in Mss. Eur. 950/12, IOL.
61. Ibid.
62. Elwin to Sorella-Mother, 18 August 1931, Mss. Eur. D. 950/7, IOL.
63. CL from Elwin, Labour Day 1931, in Lash Papers.
64. Source cited in footnote 60 above.

NOTES TO CHAPTER FOUR

1. J. C. Winslow and Verrier Elwin, *The Dawn of Indian Freedom* (London 1931); Elwin to his mother, undated letter (August 1931?), in Mss. Eur. D. 950/1, IOL.
2. As recounted in a profile of Shamrao Hivale published in the *Times of India*, 29 April 1956.
3. Elwin to Sorella Amata, letters of 14 September and 18 September 1931, Mss. Eur. D. 950/7, IOL.
4. *Collected Works of Mahatma Gandhi*, vol. 48, p. 125.
5. *Tribal World*, p. 58f.
6. These paragraphs draw on the letters and notes in file 150/CDM, 1932 ('Correspondence regarding the activities of Father Verrier Elwin in the Central Provinces'), Political and Military Records, Madhya Pradesh Secretariat Record Room, Bhopal (hereafter MPSRR).
7. Elwin to Bishop Wood, 12 December 1931, copy in 'Personal' Box no. 2, Bishop's College Archives, Calcutta.
8. Wood to Bishop Foss Westcott, 15 December 1931; Wood to Elwin, 15 December 1931, both in Personal Box no. 2, Bishop's College Archives, Calcutta.
9. Elwin to 'My dear little Mother,' 2 January 1932, Mss. Eur. D. 950/7, IOL.
10. Elwin to 'My dear little Mother,' 2 January 1932, Mss. Eur. D. 950/7, IOL
11. *Tribal World*, p. 67.
12. Intercepted letter from Elwin to Brijkrishna Chandiwala, 7 January 1932, in File 5/7/1932, Home (Pol.), NAI.
13. *Tribal World*, pp. 70–3; *The Hindustan Times* (New Delhi), 27 January 1932.
14. Verrier Elwin, *What is Happening in the Northwest Province* (January 1932). This pamphlet was banned and confiscated by the government as soon as it was printed; for years even the author did not have a copy. The copy I have consulted, marked 'proscribed pamphlet,' is in File 29/9/1932, Home (Pol.), NAI.
15. Quoted in *District Gazetteer of Mandla* (1929), p. 2.

16. CL dated 28 January 1935, Mss. Eur. D. 950/12, IOL.
17. Verrier Elwin, *Leaves from the Jungle: A Diary of Life in a Gond Village* (1936; reprint New Delhi 1990, hereafter *Leaves*), pp. 31–3.
18. Elwin to Sorella Carisimma, letters of 7 February and 23 February 1932, Mss Eur. D. 950/7, IOL.
19. Letter of 24 February 1932, in file 150/CDM, 1932, Political and Military Records, MPSRR.
20. Verrier Elwin, *Truth about India: Can we Get it?* (London 1932); notice in *The Indian Review*, November 1932, p. 794.
21. *Leaves*, p. 40f; Elwin to Nonna, 30 March 1932, Mss Eur. D. 950/7, IOL.
22. Elwin to Sorella Amata, 30 March 1932; Shamrao to Sorella Amata, 16 April 1932, both in Mss. Eur. D. 950/7, IOL.
23. Shamrao Hivale, *Scholar Gypsy: A Study of Verrier Elwin* (Bombay 1946), p. 40.
24. Elwin to Wood, 1 March 1932, in Personal Box no. 2, Bishop's College Archives, Calcutta.
25. Wood to Elwin, 16 March 1932, in ibid.
26. Wood to Westcott, 9 April 1932, ibid., on which the next few paragraphs are based.
27. *Leaves*, p. 45.
28. Elwin to Westcott, 29 April 1932, in Personal Box no. 2, Bishop's College Archives, Calcutta.
29. Gandhi to Elwin, 25 April 1932, in the *Collected Works of Mahatma Gandhi*, vol. 49, p. 367.
30. Gandhi to Elwin, 27 May 1932, ibid., pp. 485–6.
31. Verrier Elwin, *St Francis of Assissi* (Madras 1933), pp. 3–5, 21, etc.
32. Elwin to 'My dear, dear friend,' 17 May 1932, Mss. Eur. D. 950/7, IOL.
33. Clipping from *The Times of India* and Elwin's letter to Naraindas Gandhi, 20 July 1932, both in File 25/38/1932, Home (Pol.), NAI; also *Tribal World*, pp. 79–80.
34. Elwin to 'My dear, dear friend,' 23 July 1932, Mss. Eur. D. 950/7, IOL.
35. Verrier Elwin, 'India Today,' *The India Review*, 9 July 1932, with attached note by Sir Malcolm Seton, both in L/P/J/6/2013, IOL.
36. Letter from Elwin to Secretary of State, 30 July 1932, in File 25/89/1932, Home (Pol.), NAI.
37. Note on meeting between Lord Snell and William Paton, dated 9 July 1931; Paton to Snell, 20 July 1931, both in L/P/J/6/2013, IOL.
38. Paton to Sir Findlater Stewart, letters of 3 August and 2 September 1932, in ibid.
39. Elwin to Lady Graham, letters of 31 July and 6 August 1932, File 25/89/1932, Home (Pol.), NAI.

40. Note by H. G. Gowan of 18 August 1932; note by C. M. Trivedi of 8 August 1932, both in ibid.
41. Hallett's notes of 23 August and 26 September 1932, in ibid.
42. Elwin to Nonna Amata Carissima, 26 August 1932, Mss Eur. D. 950/7, IOL.
43. Elwin to R. T. Peel, Under Secretary of State, dated 3 October 1932, in L/P/J/6/2013, IOL.
44. CL, dated Folkstone 10 October 1932, Mss. Eur. D. 950/12, IOL.
45. Bombay Government's notes of 13 September and 29 September 1932; Hallett's note of 6 October 1932; Haig's note of 8 October 1932; telegram from Home Department, Simla, to Secretary of State, 11 December 1932; and reply from Secretary of State, 12 November 1932, all in File 25/89/1932, Home (Pol.), NAI.

NOTES TO CHAPTER FIVE

1. *Bombay Chronicle*, 4 November 1932.
2. Bajaj to Elwin, dated Dhulia jail 10 November 1932, in File No. E1, Bajaj Papers, NMML.
3. Elwin to Gandhi, 7 January 1933, in Bhabagrahi Misra, *Verrier Elwin: Pioneer Indian Anthropologist* (London 1973), Appendix II ('Gandhi—Elwin correspondence'), pp. 116–17.
4. Barbara Noreen, *A Wheat Grain Sown in India* (Wantage 1988), pp. 52, 140, 142; Mary Gillet, 'Impressions of CSS and Hopes for the Future,' and 'Christ and Justice,' *The CSS Review* (Poona), issues of February 1932 and February 1933 respectively.
5. Mary Gillet to Sorella Maria, 14 January 1933, in Mss Eur. D. 950/8, IOL.
6. Elwin to Giovania, 25 January 1933, Mss Eur. D. 950/8.
7. Verrier Elwin and Mary Gillet, circular letter to friends, Candlemass 1933, ibid.
8. Elwin to Sorella Amata, Candlemass 1933, in Mss. Eur. D. 950/8.
9. Elwin to Gandhi, 12 February 1933, in Misra, op. cit., pp. 118–19.
10. *Tribal World*, pp. 56–7.
11. Quoted in Elwin to Sorella Amata, Candlemass 1933, Mss Eur. D. 950/8.
12. Gandhi to Elwin, 23 February 1933, *Collected Works of Mahatma Gandhi*, vol. 53, pp. 376–7.
13. Elwin to Gandhi, letters of 27 February 1933 and 18 March 1933, in Misra, op. cit., pp. 120, 123–5.
14. Elwin to Sorella Amata, 4 March 1933, Mss Eur. D. 950/8, IOL.
15. Mary Gillet to Sorella Maria, 4 March 1933, ibid.

16. Gandhi to Andrews, 7 April 1933, *Collected Works of Mahatma Gandhi*, vol. 54, pp. 328–9.
17. Gandhi to Elwin, 11 March 1933, in ibid., pp. 59–60.
18. Mary Gillet to Sorella Maria, 5 August 1933, Mss Eur. D. 950/8, IOL.
19. As quoted in Frank Moraes, *Witness to an Era* (New Delhi 1973), p. 33.
20. Entries for 15 & 16 July 1933, in Verrier Elwin, *Leaves from the Jungle: A Diary of Life in a Gond Village* (London 1936: reprint New Delhi 1990), pp. 67–9.
21. Circular Letter (hereafter CL) from Elwin, 20 July 1933, Mss Eur. D. 950/8, IOL.
22. CL of 28 July 1933, ibid.
23. Elwin to Sorella Maria, 2 September 1933, ibid.
24. 'The Gond Seva Mandal: Constitution and Rules' (1933–4), in File R of 1935, Commissioner's Record Room, Jabalpur.
25. Quoted in Hugh Tinker, *The Ordeal of Love: C. F. Andrews and India* (Delhi 1979), pp. 270–1.
26. Verrier Elwin, 'The Gond Seva Mandal,' *Hindustan Times*, 14 May 1934.
27. CLs by Elwin of Easter 1933, Epiphany 1934 and Easter 1934, Mss Eur. D. 950/12, IOL.
28. Elwin to Sorella Maria, 13 April 1934, Mss Eur. D. 950/9.
29. Clipping from the *News Chronicle* (undated, probably 1933 or 1934), Mss Eur. D. 950/14.
30. Elwin to Sorella Amata, 24 June 1933, Mss Eur. D. 950/8; CLs of 28 January and 12 May 1935, Mss Eur. D. 950/12.
31. A. V. Thakkar, 'My Tour Diary,' *Harijan*, 28 November 1934.
32. CL of 17 March 1935, Mss Eur. D. 950/9; *Leaves from the Jungle*, pp. 53–4, 139.
33. CL of 3 March 1934, Mss Eur. D. 950/9; Shamrao Hivale, *Scholar Gypsy: A Study of Verrier Elwin* (Bombay 1946), p. 153; *Leaves from the Jungle*, p. 103.
34. *Leaves from the Jungle*, pp. 6, 11, 12–13, 38, 41, 62, 65, 83, 114.
35. CL of 8 September 1934, Mss Eur. D. 950/9.
36. Elwin to Bill Lash, 22 May 1934, Lash Papers, Hilfield Priory, Dorset.
37. Elwin to his mother, 26 July 1935, and to his sister, 2 August 1935, Mss Eur. D. 950/1; Elwin to Sorella Maria, 10 April 1935, Mss Eur. D. 950/9; William Emilson, *Violence and Atonement: The Missionary Experiences of Mohandas Gandhi, Samuel Stokes and Verrier Elwin before 1935* (Frankfurt 1994), p. 341.
38. Verrier Elwin, review of Stephen Neill's *Builders of the Indian Church*, in *The Ashram Review*, September 1934, pp. 71–2.
39. CLs of 21 April and 4 August 1934, Mss Eur. D. 950/9.

40. CL dated 24 January 1936, Mss Eur. D. 950/13.
41. Wood to Temple, 4 February 1937; Carey to Foss Westcott, 27 September 1937, both in Personal Box no. 2, Bishop's College Archives, Calcutta.
42. Mrs M. O. Elwin to Foss Westcott, 13 December 1935, in ibid.
43. Foreword to the second edition of *Leaves from the Jungle* (Bombay 1958), pp. xxviii.
44. Verrier Elwin, *Studies in the Gospel* (Madras 1929), p. 56.
45. W. G. Archer, 'Notes on Verrier Elwin' (no date, probably from the 1940s), Mss Eur. F. 236/228, IOL; Dharmendra Prasad, 'Elwin in Mandla,' *India Cultures Quarterly*, vol. 34, nos. 1 and 2, 1979, the two sources on which this account relies.
46. Marguerite Milward, *Artist in Unknown India* (London 1948), pp. 155–6; *Leaves from the Jungle*, p. 146.
47. *Leaves from the Jungle*, pp. 3 to 10.
48. Verrier Elwin, 'In Baiga Land,' *The Modern Review* (Calcutta), April 1934.
49. CLs of Easter 1934 and 12 May 1935, Mss Eur. D. 950/12, IOL; Verrier Elwin, 'The Gond Seva Mandal,' *Hindustan Times*, 14 May 1934; news report in the *Bombay Chronicle*, 26 September 1935.
50. Elwin to the Deputy Commissioner, Mandla District, 14 May 1934, File 33 of 1937, District Record Room, Mandla.
51. Verrier Elwin, 'Gonds,' *Modern Review*, November 1933, pp. 547–8.
52. Shamrao Hivale and Verrier Elwin, *Songs of the Forest: The Folk-Poetry of the Gonds* (London 1935).
53. CLs of 17 March and 13 April 1934, Mss Eur. D. 950/9, IOL.
54. Lawrence Housman to Mrs M. O. Elwin, 21 October 1934, Mss Eur. D. 950/1, IOL.
55. *Leaves from the Jungle*, pp. 31, 118, 27.
56. *TLS*, 19 September 1936; other quotes from publicity material in John Murray Archives, London.
57. CL of 25 June 1936, Mss Eur. D. 950/13, IOL.
58. Marguerite Milward, *Artist in Unknown India*, pp. 152–68.

NOTES TO CHAPTER SIX

1. Elwin to Malinowski, letters of 3 November and 13 November 1936, Malinowski Papers, London School of Economics and Political Science; *Tribal World*, pp. 113–14.
2. The rest of this section is based on the notes and correspondence in L/P & J/2013, IOL.
3. The *Observer* interview was reproduced in *The Bombay Sentinel*, 21 December 1936.

4. Cf. *Bombay Chronicle*, 22 December 1936.
5. Elwin to E. S. Hyde, 17 February 1937, Box III, Hyde Papers, Centre for South Asian Studies, Cambridge.
6. Elwin to H. C. Greenfield, Divisional Commissioner, Jabalpur, 15 November 1937, Jabalpur Collectorate Records.
7. Elwin to Hyde, 20 June 1937, Hyde Papers.
8. Elwin to his mother, 11 September 1937, in Mss Eur. D. 950/1, IOL.
9. Elwin to his mother, 5 October 1937, Mss Eur. D. 950/1; Shamrao Hivale, *Scholar Gypsy: A Study of Verrier Elwin* (Bombay 1946), pp. 142, 153.
10. CL from Elwin dated 8 April 1937, Mss Eur. D. 950/13.
11. Elwin to S. C. Roy, 18 November 1938, in File No. DM 2, John Murray Archives, London.
12. Interview with Sahib Lal, Patangarh, January 1998.
13. Margaret Moore, 'A Visit to the Ashram,' in Temp Mss 4619, Agatha Harrison Papers, Friends House, London.
14. CL of June 1938, in *Scholar Gypsy*, pp. 149–50.
15. Eldyth's letters home, on which the following paragraphs are based, are in Mss. Eur. D. 950/18, IOL.
16. Verrier Elwin, *Phulmat of the Hills: A Tale of the Gonds* (London 1937).
17. Verrier Elwin, *A Cloud That's Dragonish: A Tale of Primitives* (London 1938).
18. CL of 4 January 1937, Mss. Eur. D. 950/13, IOL.
19. Elwin to Lord Gorell, 26 December 1937; John Murray to Elwin, 20 January 1938; Elwin to John Murray, 10 March 1938, all in File DM2, John Murray Archives.
20. Verrier Elwin, *The Baiga* (London 1939), Preface, chapters IV and VIII.
21. *The Baiga*, especially pp. 76–130.
22. *The Baiga*, pp. 511, 515–17.
23. *The Baiga*, p. xxx.
24. Sir John Squire, 'The Charm of the Aboriginal,' *Illustrated London News*, 23 December 1939.
25. Report by Alan Watts, dated 12 May 1938, File DG 40, John Murray Archives, London.
26. *TLS*, 9 December 1939.
27. J. H. Hutton to John Murray, 19 August 1938, File No. DG 40, John Murray Archives; W. V. Grigson, review of *The Baiga* in *Man*, March–April 1941, pp. 38–40; Beryl de Zoete, quoted in *Scholar Gypsy*, p. 186.
28. C. G. Chenevix Trench, review of *The Baiga*, *International Review of Missions*, no. 114, April 1940, pp. 283–6.
29. Elwin to his mother, letters of 13 September, 26 September, 25 November and 12 December 1939, Mss Eur. D. 950/2. Elwin did in due course win the Wellcome medal.

30. CL from Elwin dated 4 January 1940, Mss Eur. D. 950/14.
31. William and Mildred Archer, *India Seen and Observed* (London 1994); *Scholar Gypsy*, pp. 178, 186.
32. Elwin to Archer, 13 March 1940, Mss. Eur. F. 236/259, IOL.
33. Verrier Elwin, *The Agaria* (Bombay 1942).
34. Elwin to Barbara Smith, 19 July 1942, in File E 5, Oxford University Press Archives, Bombay.
35. Review by George Devereux in *The American Anthropologist*, vol. 48, no. 1, 1946, pp. 110–11.
36. M. N. Srinivas, 'The Observer and the Observed in the Study of Cultures,' in his *The Cohesive Role of Sanskritization and Other Essays* (New Delhi 1987).
37. Verrier Elwin, *The Muria and their Ghotul* (Bombay 1947), pp. viii–ix.
38. *The Agaria*, p. xxi.
39. Lovejoy and Boas, *Primitivism and Related Ideas in Antiquity* (Baltimore 1935).
40. Todorov, *On Human Diversity: Nationalism, Racism and Exoticism in French Thought*, translated by Catherine Porter (Cambridge, Mass. 1993).
41. See Lovejoy and Boas, *Primitivism*, pp. 7–8; Todorov, *On Human Diversity*, pp. 312, 316, etc.
42. 'The Tribal World of Verrier Elwin: An Autobiography,' manuscript copy in the archives of the Oxford University Press, Bombay, pp. 68–9, emphasis added.

NOTES TO CHAPTER SEVEN

1. *Tribal World*, p. 138.
2. Elwin to Archer, 12 June 1940; Note entitled 'I Married a Gond,' both in Mss Eur. F. 236/259, IOL.
3. Elwin to Archer, 2 May 1940, Mss Eur. F. 236/259.
4. Verrier Elwin, 'I Married a Gond,' *Man in India*, vol. 20, no. 4, 1940.
5. Elwin to his sister, 20 January 1940, Mss Eur. D. 950/2, IOL; Elwin to Archer, 2 May 1940, Mss Eur. F. 236/259.
6. Elwin to Archer, letters of 21 April and 12 June 1940, Mss Eur. F. 236/259.
7. *The Evening News of India*, 17 March 1939.
8. Verrier Elwin, 'With a Camera in the Indian Jungle,' *Sunday Statesman* (Calcutta), 1 March 1942.
9. Archer, 'Notes on Verrier Elwin,' Mss. Eur. F. 236/228; Elwin to Archer, 3 April 1940, Mss Eur. F. 236/259, IOL.
10. Circular letter (hereafter CL) from Elwin of 1 May 1940, Mss Eur. D. 950/14, IOL.

11. Elwin to E. S. Hyde, 12 April 1940, Box III, Hyde Papers, Centre for South Asian Studies, Cambridge.
12. CL from Elwin of 24 December 1940, Box III, Hyde Papers (emphasis added).
13. Elwin to Archer, 23 August 1940, Mss Eur. F. 236/259.
14. Krishna Hutheesingh, 'Verrier Elwin,' *National Herald* (Lucknow), 13 September 1940.
15. *The Times of India*, 31 July 1940.
16. As reported in the *Bombay Chronicle*, 6 August 1941.
17. Saguna Karnad, 'A Gond Girl Looks at Bombay,' *The Illustrated Weekly of India*, 8 September 1940.
18. Archer, 'Notes on Verrier Elwin;' Elwin to Archer, 23 August 1940, Mss Eur. F. 236/259.
19. quoted in D. F. Karaka, *This India* (Bombay 1944), p. 92.
20. Elwin to Archer, November 1942, Mss Eur. F. 236/259.
21. Elwin to Archer, 2 May 1940, ibid.
22. Quoted in Tim Hilton's obituary of Hutchinson, *The Guardian* (London), 6 June 1991.
23. W. G. Archer, 'Notes on Verrier Elwin.'
24. John Miles (former Warden of Merton College, Oxford) to Warden of Merton, 17 August 1949, File No D-1-46, Merton College Archives, Oxford.
25. Cf. Nandini Sundar, *Subalterns and Sovereigns: An Anthropological History of Bastar, 1840–1995* (New Delhi 1998).
26. Elwin to E. S. Hyde, letters of 9 February 1936, 20 June 1937, 28 October 1937, 31 December 1938, 7 August 1939, 11 February 1940, 12 April 1940 and 15 April 1940, all in Box III, Hyde papers; Elwin to his sister Eldyth, 26 October 1940, Mss Eur. D. 950/2, IOL.
27. Shamrao Hivale, *Scholar Gypsy: A Study of Verrier Elwin* (Bombay 1946), p. 187.
28. Elwin to his mother, 14 December 1940, Mss Eur. D. 950/2.
29. Untitled note by Verrier Elwin on the administration of the Bastar State (written in 1941 or 1942), File A, Box VIII, Hyde Papers.
30. Elwin to E. S. Hyde, 8 February 1941, Box III, Hyde Papers.
31. Verrier Elwin, *Loss of Nerve: A Comparative Study of the Contact of Peoples in the Aboriginal Areas of the Bastar State and the Central Provinces of India* (Bombay 1941); Elwin to R. E. Hawkins, 28 August 1940, File E 5, Oxford University Press (OUP) Archives, Bombay.
32. The Bastar Dassera festival is described in D. N. Majumdar's classic essay, 'Tribal Cultures and Acculturation,' Presidential Address to the Section of Anthropology, printed in *Proceedings of the Twenty-sixth Indian Science Congress, Lahore, 1939* (Calcutta 1940), pp. 179–224.

33. Elwin to Archer, 8 November 1941, Mss. Eur. F. 236/259, IOL; Elwin to E. S. Hyde, 8 November 1941, Box III, Hyde Papers, Cambridge.
34. Elwin to his sister, 9 December 1940, Mss Eur. D. 950/2, IOL.
35. Jerome Menzies, letter to the editor, *Indian Express* (Bombay), 28 December 1978.
36. Entries for 4 December and 5 December 1941, and for 3 January, 6 February, 9 February, 9 March and 10 March 1942 in 'Journal of Tour in South Maria country, November 1941 to March 1942,' Mss Eur. D. 950/15, IOL.
37. Verrier Elwin, *The Muria and their Ghotul* (Bombay 1947), pp. ix, 292, 334, 419, 431, 475, 614–16, 620, 633, 636, 655–6, 659, etc.
38. Ibid., pp. 420, 656.
39. Elwin to Hawkins, 8 February 1943, File E6, OUP Archives.
40. Cf. *Illustrated Weekly of India*, 9 July 1942.
41. Elwin to Hawkins, 18 June 1944, File E 6, OUP Archives. 'Miss Mayo' was the American writer Katherine Mayo, whose book *Mother India* was an attack on caste and the suppression of women in India: although not quite dismissed by Gandhi as a 'drain-inspector's report'—Gandhi thought it deserved attention for pointing out Indian indifference to hygiene—the book nonetheless had called forth nine book-length rejoinders by lesser Indians.
42. Alfred Kinsey, et. al., *Sexual Behavior in the Human Female* (Philadelphia 1953).
43. Cf. Simeran Man Singh Gell, *The Ghotul in Muria Society* (London 1992).
44. *The Listener*, 9 December 1948; *Man*, vol. 49, November 1948.
45. Evelyn Wood, quoted in *Scholar Gypsy*, p. 193.
46. Translator's preface, in M. K. Gandhi, *An Autobiography or the Story of my Experiments with Truth* (second edition: Ahmedabad 1940).
47. Verrier Elwin, 'Mahadev,' in D. G. Tendulkar, M. Chalapathi Rau, Mridula Sarabhai and Vithalbhai K. Jhaveri, editors, *Gandhiji: His Life and Work* (Bombay 1944).
48. Elwin to Archer, 17 September 1946, Mss. Eur. F. 236/264, IOL.
49. Conversation with K. Rangaswami, February 1994.
50. Verrier Elwin, *Maria Murder and Suicide* (Bombay 1943), pp. ix–x, xxv, 3–5, 36–8, 51, 53, 81, 98–9, 207–9, 215, 219–20, etc.
51. Elwin to E. S. Hyde, 26 February 1939, File A, Box VIII, Hyde Papers.
52. Elwin to Archer, 18 July 1942, Mss Eur. F. 236/260, IOL.
53. Elwin to R. E. Hawkins, 6 December 1942, File E6, OUP Archives; Verrier Elwin, 'Notes on the Juang,' *Man in India*, vol. 28, no. 1, 1948.
54. Elwin to Archer, 6 December and 19 December 1942, Mss. Eur. F. 236/260.
55. Verrier Elwin, *Report of a Tour in the Bonai, Keonjhar and Pal Laharia*

States (1943, privately circulated, printed at The British India Press, Bombay).
56. Cf. Elwin's letters to J. H. Hutton quoted in A. C. Sinha, 'Indian Social Anthropology and its Cambridge Connections,' *The Eastern Anthropologist*, vol. 44, no. 4, October–December 1991.
57. 'Dr Verrier Elwin's report on tribals of Ganjam and Koraput,' dated April 1945, in File No. 145, Elwin Papers, Nehru Memorial Museum and Library, New Delhi.
58. *The Baiga*, p. 235.
59. Verrier Elwin, *The Aboriginals* (Bombay 1943), pp. 18–19.
60. *The Aboriginals*, p. 8; *The Muria and their Ghotul*, p. 368.
61. Elwin, *Loss of Nerve*, pp. 9–27; *Maria Murder and Suicide*, pp. 35–6.
62. *Loss of Nerve*, p. 44; Note on education by Elwin reproduced in W. V. Grigson, *The Aboriginal Problem in the Central Provinces* (Nagpur 1943), pp. 399–403.
63. Elwin to Sorella Maria, 15 March 1938, Mss Eur. D. 950/10, IOL.
64. *The Muria and their Ghotul*, p. xii.

NOTES TO CHAPTER EIGHT

1. *Tribal World*, pp. 137–8.
2. S. C. Dube, review of *Tribal World*, in *The Eastern Anthropologist*, vol. 12, no. 2, 1964, pp. 134–6.
3. *Bombay Chronicle*, 17 October 1941.
4. D. F. Karaka, *I've Shed my Tears: A Candid View of Resurgent India* (New York 1947), pp. 100–1.
5. D. F. Karaka, 'Verrier Elwin,' *Bombay Chronicle*, 7 August 1940.
6. Krishna Hutheesingh, 'Verrier Elwin,' *National Herald* (Lucknow), 13 September 1940.
7. Cf. Correspondence between Elwin and Thakkar in P. Kodanda Rao Papers, NMML; P. Kodanda Rao, 'Aboriginalisthan: Anthropologist's Imperium,' *Social Science Quarterly*, vol. 30, no. 2, October 1943.
8. Most recently in Vinay Srivastava, 'The Ethnographer and the People: Reflections on Field Work,' in two parts, *Economic and Political Weekly*, 1–8 and 15 June 1991, an account of a 1987 visit to the Baiga Chak in the tracks of Elwin.
9. Bhumijan Seva Mandal, Bulletin Number 1, 1 March 1942, Mss Eur. D. 950/17, IOL.
10. Verrier Elwin, 'Do We Really Want to Keep Them in a Zoo,' typescript in Subject File no. 7, P. Kodanda Rao Papers, Nehru Memorial Museum and Library, New Delhi, p. 2.
11. Cf. G. S. Ghurye, *I and Other Explorations* (Bombay 1973); Dhirendra

NOTES TO CHAPTER EIGHT

Narain. 'Govind Sadashiv Ghurye: Reminscences,' in A. R. Momin, editor, *The Legacy of G. S. Ghurye: A Centennial Festschrift* (Bombay 1996); 'Prof. G. S. Ghurye: An Introduction,' in K. M. Kapadia, editor, *Professor Ghurye Felicitation Volume* (Bombay 1955).

12. G. S. Ghurye, *The Aborigines—So Called—and their Future* (Poona 1943).
13. M. N. Srinivas, review of *The Aboriginals*, in *Journal of the University of Bombay* (History, Economics and Sociology), New Series, vol. 12, no. 4, January 1944, pp. 91–4.
14. Interview with M. N. Srinivas, Bangalore, August 1994.
15. Hivale, *Scholar Gypsy: A Study of Verrier Elwin* (Bombay 1946), pp.187, 194.
16. Elwin to W. G. Archer, 6 January 1944, Mss Eur. F. 236/262, IOL.
17. Verrier Elwin, 'Truth in Anthropology,' Presidential address to the Section of Anthropology and Archaeology, in *Proceedings of the 31st Session of the Indian Science Congress* (New Delhi 1944), pp. 91–107.
18. Elwin to his mother, 28 May 1944, Mss Eur. D. 950/3, IOL.
19. Verrier Elwin, *Folk-Tales of Mahakoshal* (Bombay 1944).
20. Verrier Elwin and Shamrao Hivale, *Folk-Songs of the Maikal Hills* (Bombay 1944).
21. Verrier Elwin, *Folk-Songs of Chattisgarh* (Bombay 1946).
22. Verrier Elwin, 'Epilogue,' *Man in India*, vol. 23, no. 1, March 1943 (Folk-Song number), p. 88; *Folk-Songs of the Maikal Hills*, pp. xvi, xix–xx, xxviii.
23. Undated typescript entitled 'Bhumijan Seva Mandal,' in Elwin correspondence, Bhulabhai Desai papers, NMML; Elwin to E. S. Hyde, 6 July 1944, Box III, Hyde Papers, Cambridge.
24. Verrier Elwin, 'Missionaries and Aboriginals,' undated typescript (probably written in 1944), in Bhulabhai Desai Papers, NMML.
25. 'Report of Some Catholic Priests of Mandla District in Connection with the Questionnaires Issued by the Aboriginal Tribes Enquiry Officer,' Box II, Hyde Papers.
26. Elwin to W. V. Grigson, 6 December 1940; Elwin, 'Note on the Gond "Karma" ' (undated ts., prob. from early 1940s), both in Box II, Hyde Papers.
27. *The Hindustan Times* (New Delhi), 14 June 1944.
28. *The Hindustan Times*, 8 July 1944.
29. Ibid.
30. As reported in *The Guardian* (Madras), 7 December 1944.
31. Simon Bara, *Aboriginals and Missionaries: A Rejoinder to Verrier Elwin* (Ranchi 1944).
32. See correspondence in L/P & J/6919 of 1944, IOL.
33. Amery to Wavell, notes of 9 August and 28 September 1944, L/P & J/6787, IOL.

34. Wavell to Amery, 3 December 1944, in Nicholas Mansergh, editor, *The Transfer of Power, Volume V* (London 1974), pp. 263–4.
35. Undated circular letter (prob. 1945 or 1946) from Elwin; Elwin to P. Thakurdas, 2 January 1945; circular letter from P. Thakurdas of 15 January 1947, all in File 337, Purshottamdas Thakurdas Papers, NMML.
36. Elwin to Sir Francis Wylie, 8 November 1944, in L/P & J/6787, IOL.
37. Quoted in *The Guardian* (Madras), 23 November 1944.
38. Elwin to Archer, 30 November 1941, Mss Eur. F. 236/259, IOL.
39. *The Aboriginals* (Bombay 1943), pp. 31–2.
40. *The Aboriginals* (second edition: Bombay 1944), pp. 29–31.
41. Verrier Elwin, 'Notes on a Kondh Tour,' *Man in India*, vol. 24, no. 1, March 1944; 'Notes on the Kondhs,' in File 160, Elwin Papers, NMML; Felix Padel, *The Sacrifice of Human Being: British Rule and the Konds of Orissa* (New Delhi 1995).
42. Verrier Elwin, *Bondo Highlander* (Bombay 1950), Preface; 'Tribal Life in Middle India,' *Geographical Magazine*, February 1950; 'My Worst Journey,' *Geographical Magazine*, October 1954.
43. Based on a handwritten, untitled narrative of 34 pages in File 64, Elwin Papers, NMML.
44. Verrier Elwin, 'Saora Pictographs,' *Marg*, vol. 2, no. 3, Summer 1948.
45. Elwin to Archer, 7 July 1945, Mss Eur. F. 236/263, IOL.
46. Elwin to John Murray, 11 July 1945, File DG 40, John Murray Archives, London.
47. Untitled note of 1945, File 160, Elwin Papers, NMML.
48. Entries by Shamrao for 14 May and 15 May 1942, Journal for April–August 1942, Mss. Eur. 950/16, IOL.
49. Archer, 'Notes on Verrier Elwin,' Mss. Eur. F. 236/228, IOL.
50. Elwin to his mother, 7 May 1944, Mss. Eur. D. 950/3, IOL.
51. Elwin to Archer, letters of 9 January 19 April, and 29 April 1946, Mss. Eur. F. 236/264, IOL.
52. Elwin to S. S. Khambata (of Wadia and Ghandy, Solicitors, Bombay), 31 July 1946, Verrier Elwin Papers, Shillong.
53. Diary entry of 30 November 1946, ibid.
54. Tata to Patel, 23 September 1946, ibid.
55. Elwin to his mother, 5 November 1947, Mss. Eur. D. 950/3, IOL.
56. Shamrao Hivale, *The Pardhans of the Upper Nerbudda Valley* (Bombay 1946).
57. Shamrao Hivale, *Scholar Gypsy*, pp. 9, 216, 217, etc.
58. Quoted in the *Bombay Chronicle*, 29 September 1941.
59. Shamrao's work is described in Elwin to E. S. Hyde, 24 July 1943, File A, Box VIII, Hyde papers; Elwin to Hyde, letters of 23 May 1941 and 6 July 1944, Box III, Hyde Papers; CL from Elwin of 1 October 1941, Mss Eur.

D. 950/14; Bhumijan Seva Mandal Bulletins dated March 1942, August 1943 and September 1945, in Mss Eur. D. 950/17.
60. *The Muria and their Ghotul*, p. xiii.
61. Entries of 5 August and 6 August 1942 in Journal for April–August 1942, Mss. Eur. 950/16, IOL.
62. CL of 29 September 1946, Mss Eur. D. 950/17.
63. Cf. correspondence in L/P & J/6787, IOL.
64. Elwin to Archer, 17 September 1946, Mss. Eur. F. 236/264, IOL. His father, of course, was another kind of D.D., a Doctor of Divinity.
65. Elwin to his mother, letters of 12 May and 28 May 1947, Mss. Eur. 950/3, IOL; diary entries of 8 June, 22 June and 30 June 1947, Elwin Papers, Shillong.
66. Verrier Elwin, 'The Anthropological Survey of India: Part I, History and Recent Development: Part II, The Five Year Plan,' *Man*, vol. 68, June and July 1948, pp. 68–9, 80–1.
67. CL from Elwin of 1 October 1941, Mss Eur. D. 950/14, IOL; Bhumijan Seva Mandal Bulletins dated March 1942, July 1942, August 1943 and October 1944, all in Mss Eur. D. 950/17, IOL.
68. 'Anthropology and the Ordinary Man.' Typescript of two talks by Verrier Elwin on All India Radio, in File No. IV, G. E. Mallam Papers, Centre for South Asian Studies, Cambridge.

NOTES TO CHAPTER NINE

1. Letter from Thompson to Gandhi, 2 October 1931, quoted in William W. Emilsen, *Violence and Atonement: The Missionary Experiences of Mohandas Gandhi, Samuel Stokes and Verrier Elwin in India before 1935* (Frankfurt 1994), p. 141.
2. Circular letter (hereafter CL) from Shamrao Hivale, 15 November 1947, Mss Eur. F. 236/265, IOL.
3. 'Extracts from the evidence given by Dr. Verrier Elwin before the Excluded and partially Excluded Areas sub-committee of the Constituent Assembly of India at New Delhi on 13 August 1947,' in Mss Eur. F. 236/265, IOL.
4. Elwin to Archer, 16 December 1947, Mss Eur. F. 236/265, IOL.
5. These two paragraphs are based on Elwin's diary for 1947–8, Verrier Elwin Papers, Shillong.
6. Entry for 5th February, ibid.
7. Elwin to Archer, letters of 16 December 1947 and 12 January 1948, Mss Eur. F. 236/265, IOL.
8. Elwin to Archer, 8 January 1949, Mss Eur. F. 236/266, IOL.
9. Interview with Sunil Janah, London, September 1992.
10. Interview with Jivan Lal, Patangarh, January 1998.

11. W. G. Archer, 'Notes on Verrier Elwin,' Mss. Eur. 236/228, IOL.
12. Elwin to Archer, 8 January 1949, Mss Eur. F. 236/266, IOL.
13. Interview with Kosi Elwin, Ryatwar, January 1998.
14. Cf. letters from George Kennedy (of Fowler and Sons) to Elwin, 11 March and 19 November 1949, Elwin Papers, Shillong.
15. Elwin to Archer, 27 October 1948, Mss Eur. F. 236/265, IOL.
16. Letters from Elwin to Archer of 17 August 1948, 8 January 1949, 25 January 1951 and 29 August 1951, Mss Eur. F. 236/266, IOL.
17. Adrian Brent, *The Snares of Death*, typescript in File 148, Elwin Papers, NMML.
18. Adrian Brent, *The Five Men*, typescript in File 70, Elwin Papers, NMML.
19. Diary entry of 30 May 1949, Elwin Papers, Shillong.
20. Elwin to Mildred Archer, 3 June 1949, Mss. Eur. F. 236/266, IOL.
21. As recalled by a distinguished British anthropologist and former student of Evans-Pritchard, in a conversation with me in June 1991.
22. Cf. correspondence in File D. 1. 46, Merton College Archives.
23. Diary entry of 5 June 1949, Elwin Papers, Shillong.
24. Elwin to his mother, letters of 27 October and 10 December 1950, Mss Eur. D. 950/3, IOL.
25. Elwin to his mother, letters of 5 December, 10 December, and 18 December 1950 and 4 January 1951, Mss Eur. D. 950/2.
26. Diary entry for 31 December 1950, Elwin Papers, Shillong.
27. Elwin to his mother, 30 January 1951, Mss Eur. D. 950/3.
28. Elwin to his mother, 11 June and 30 June 1951, Mss Eur. D. 950/3.
29. Archer to Elwin, 12 November 1951, Mss. Eur. F. 236/266, IOL; Elwin to his mother, 22 October 1949, Mss Eur. D. 950/3, IOL.
30. Diary entries of 14 July and 23 July 1951, Elwin Papers, Shillong.
31. Diary entries for 13 October and 14 October 1951, ibid.
32. Gerald Sparrow, *Land of the Moonflower* (London 1958), pp. 140–51.
33. *Tribal World*, pp. 220–2.
34. These poems are reproduced from the diary for 1951, Elwin Papers, Shillong.
35. Diary entry for 4 January 1952, Elwin Papers, Shillong.
36. *Tribal World*, p. 85.
37. See M. K. Gandhi, *Satyagraha in South Africa* (second English edition: Ahmedabad 1950), Translator's Note.
38. Pp. 62–3 of 'The Snares of Death,' typescript in File 148, Elwin Papers, NMML.
39. Elwin to Victor Sassoon, 26 January 1951, copy in Elwin Papers, Shillong.
40. Cf. Elwin to his mother, 6 May 1951, Mss Eur. D. 950/3, IOL; Elwin to his sister Eldyth, 5 May 1953, Mss Eur. D. 950/4, IOL; Elwin to Barbara

Smith, 15 May 1952, File 434E, OUP Archives, Bombay; Elwin to Archer, letters of 25 January 1949 and 11 February 1950, Mss Eur. F. 236/266, IOL.
41. TWARU Newsletter No. 5, July 1953, in File 337, Purshottamdas Thakurdas Papers, NMML.
42. CL from Shamrao Hivale, 15 November 1947, Mss Eur. F. 236/266, IOL.
43. Printed appeal for TARU, enclosed with VE's letter to Sir Purshottamdas Thakurdas of 8 December 1949, in File 337, Thakurdas Papers, NMML.

NOTES TO CHAPTER TEN

1. R. D. Acland to W. Q. Lash, 30 May 1936, in Lash Papers, Hilfield Priory, Dorset.
2. Elwin to Hawkins, 8 August 1947, File 509, OUP Archives, Mumbai.
3. Letter of 8 April 1951, Mss. Eur. D. 950/3, IOL.
4. Elwin to Devendra Satyarthi, 22 February 1952, File 509R, OUP Archives.
5. Verrier Elwin, *The Tribal Art of Middle India: A Personal Record* (Bombay 1951).
6. Marion W. Smith, review of *Myths of Middle India*, in *American Anthropologist*, vol. 50, no. 3, 1950, pp. 535–6.
7. Verrier Elwin, *Myths of Middle India* (Bombay 1949).
8. Verrier Elwin, *Bondo Highlander* (Bombay 1950), pp. 5, 7, 22, 87, etc.
9. Elwin to P. J. Chester, 25 September 1947, File E7, OUP Archives.
10. Interview with S. C. Dube, New Delhi, January 1994.
11. See *Illustrated Weekly of India*, 25 November 1951.
12. D. N. Majumdar, review of *Bondo Highlander*, *Man in India*, vol. 32, no. 1, 1952, pp. 43–6.
13. Elwin to his mother, 8 January 1951, Mss Eur. D. 950/3, IOL.
14. Elwin to Archer, 29 August 1951, Mss. Eur. F. 236/266, IOL. Elwin's place in the history of anthropology is discussed more fully in my essay, 'Between Anthropology and Literature: The Ethnographies of Verrier Elwin,' *Journal of the Royal Anthropological Institute (incorporating Man)*, vol. 3, no. 2, June 1998.
15. Verrier Elwin, *Tribal Myths of Orissa* (Bombay 1954).
16. Elwin to his mother, 6 May 1948 and 29 November 1950, Mss Eur. D. 950/4, IOL.
17. Elwin to P. J. Chester, dtd 15 October 1951, File 509R, OUP Archives.
18. Verrier Elwin, 'Forest People 4: The Gadabas,' *Illustrated Weekly of India* (hereafter IWI), 30 July 1950.
19. Review of *The Religion of an Indian Tribe* by C. von Fürer-Haimendorf in *Bulletin of the School of Oriental and African Studies*, vol. 19, part 3, 1957, pp. 602–3.

20. Verrier Elwin, *The Religion of an Indian Tribe* (Bombay 1955), pp. 8, 10, 141, 171, 559, 561, 571, etc.
21. Elwin to Archer, 31 July 1952, Mss. Eur. F. 236/266, IOL.
22. Elwin to his mother, 7 July 1952, Mss Eur. D. 950/3, IOL.
23. Cf. Elwin to his mother, letters of 29 November 1950 and 19 October 1952, ibid.
24. From File 64, Elwin Papers, NMML.
25. Verrier Elwin, 'Comic Strips of Rural India,' in three parts, *Illustrated Weekly of India* (hereafter IWI), 15, 22 and 29 June 1952.
26. Verrier Elwin, 'Forest Peoples,' in six parts, IWI, 9 July, 16 July, 23 July, 30 July, 6 August, and 13 August 1950.
27. 'The Dance in Tribal India: Part V,' IWI, 19 June 1955.
28. Verrier Elwin, 'Forest Peoples: Part IV: the Gadabas,' IWI, 30 July 1950; also his 'Aboriginals in Free India,' *The March of India*, May 1952.
29. Verrier Elwin, 'Children of the Forest at Play,' IWI, 26 October 1952.
30. Cf. 'The Dance in Tribal India: Part I,' IWI, 22 May 1955; 'The Carved Totems of the Uraons,' IWI, 5 April 1953.
31. CL of 15 November 1948, Mss Eur. D. 950/17, IOL.
32. Verrier Elwin, 'Ancient and Modern Man,' in *Nehru Abhinandan Granth: A Birthday Book* (New Delhi 1949).
33. Elwin to Archer, 4 January 1948, Mss Eur. F. 236/266, IOL.
34. Elwin to Archer, 10 July 1950, ibid.
35. Shamrao Hivale to Mrs M. O. Elwin, 28 June 1951, Mss. Eur. D. 950/4, IOL.
36. Elwin to Archer, 6 October 1950, Mss. Eur. F. 236/266, IOL.
37. Elwin to his mother, letters of 20 January and 29 January 1952, Mss. Eur. D. 950/3, IOL.
38. Dom Moraes to Elwin, 30 October 1953, Miscellaneous Correspondence, Elwin Papers, NMML.
39. Dom Moraes, *Answered by Flutes: Reflections on Madhya Pradesh* (Bombay 1983), p. 158; idem, *My Son's Father: An Autobiography* (London 1968), pp. 82–3; interview with Dom Moraes, Bombay, December 1990.
40. Interview with Sahib Lal, Patangarh, January 1998.
41. Elwin to Archer, letters of 14 September and 15 November 1951, Mss. Eur. F. 236/266, IOL.
42. Diary entry of 27th January 1952, Elwin Papers, Shillong.
43. Elwin to his mother, letters of 20 January, 29 January and 4 February 1952, Mss. Eur. D. 950/4, IOL.
44. Elwin to Archer, 11 February 1952, Mss. Eur. F. 236/266, IOL.
45. Cf. *Bondo Highlander*, chapter v, 'The Establishment of Love.'
46. quoted in Archer, 'Notes on Verrier Elwin,' in Mss Eur. F. 236/228, IOL.
47. Elwin to Sassoon, 2 May 1952, Elwin Papers, Shillong.

48. 'The Tribal Folk,' in *Jawaharlal Nehru's Speeches, Volume II* (New Delhi 1954), pp. 576–83.
49. Elwin to Archer, 31 July 1952, Mss Eur. F. 236/266, IOL; Elwin to Sassoon, 23 June 1952, Elwin Papers, Shillong.
50. Elwin to his mother, 31 August 1952, Mss Eur. D. 950/3, IOL.
51. Elwin to his sister, 29 September 1952, ibid.
52. Elwin to Nehru, 21 September 1952, copy in Miscellaneous Correspondence, Elwin Papers, NMML.
53. Copy of will dated 10th November 1952, in the possession of Arvind Khare.
54. Elwin to his mother, letters of 27 November, 3 December, 15 December, and 30 December 1952, and 6 January and 12 January 1953, Mss Eur. 950/3 & 4, IOL.
55. Verrier Elwin, 'Impressions of Assam,' in Satis Chandra Kakati, editor, *Discovery of Assam* (Gauhati 1954), p. 177.
56. *Tribal World*, p. 229.
57. Elwin to Jairamdas Daulatram, 24 January 1953, Elwin Papers, NMML.
58. Elwin to Sassoon, 18 February 1953, Elwin Papers, Shillong.
59. Diary entry of 28 February 1953 (Holi), ibid.
60. Elwin to his mother, 19 June 1953, Mss Eur. D. 950/4, IOL.
61. Mrs M. O. Elwin to Mrs K. Hivale, 22 August 1953, Elwin Papers, Shillong.
62. Shamrao to Eldyth, letters of 5 September and 22 October 1953, Mss Eur. D. 950/4.
63. Cf. Elwin to Archer, 23 October 1953, Mss Eur. F. 236/266, IOL.
64. Jehangir Patel to Elwin, 12 July 1953, Elwin Papers, NMML.
65. Diary entry of 20 September 1953, Elwin Papers, Shillong.
66. Elwin to his mother, 21 September 1953, Mss. Eur. D. 950/4, IOL.
67. A. A. Noronha, 'Dr Verrier Elwin: Reminscences,' in W. Q. Lash Papers, Hilfield Priory, Dorset.
68. Elwin to his mother, 6 June 1953, Mss Eur. D. 950/4, IOL.
69. Letter of 1 March 1953, in *Jawaharlal Nehru: Letters to Chief Ministers, Volume III* (New Delhi, n.d.), pp. 247–8.
70. The circumstances of Elwin's NEFA appointment are described in letters to his mother of 6 June and 26 November 1953, Mss. Eur. D. 950/4, IOL; *Tribal World*, pp. 229–33.
71. Elwin to his mother, letters of 12 December and 19 December 1953, Mss. Eur. D. 950/4.
72. Elwin to his mother, 12 December 1953, Mss. Eur. D. 950/4.
73. Elwin to T. N. Kaul, 11 December 1953, File 8, Elwin Papers, NMML.
74. J. R. D. Tata to Verrier Elwin, 4 January 1954, Elwin Papers, Shillong.
75. Elwin to Hawkins, 12 January 1954, File 434E, OUP Archives.
76. Diary entry of 22 December 1953, Elwin Papers, Shillong.
77. Elwin to Jairamdas Daulatram, 12 December 1953, Elwin Papers, NMML.

NOTES TO CHAPTER ELEVEN

1. Elwin to K. L. Mehta, 15 May 1955, File 7, Elwin Papers, NMML.
2. Elwin to his mother, letters of 12 January, 17 January and 25 January 1954, in Mss. Eur. D. 950/5, IOL.
3. Elwin to Jairamdas Daulatram, 2 January 1954, File 151, Elwin Papers, NMML.
4. Elwin to the Deputy Commissioner, United Khasi and Jaintia Hills, 20 February 1954, File 141, Elwin Papers, NMML.
5. T. N. Kaul, 'A brief note on NEFA, Manipur State, Naga Hill District (Kohima) and Lushai Hills' (Secret), dated 21 April 1953, File 8, Elwin Papers, NMML.
6. Elwin to his mother, letters of 10 March and 25 March 1954, Mss. Eur. D. 950/5, IOL.
7. Unless otherwise mentioned, the quotes in the rest of this section are taken from the unpublished 'Tour Notes of Dr Verrier Elwin for the months of March–April, 1954 on the Tuensang Frontier Division,' in File 139, Elwin Papers, NMML.
8. Elwin to his mother, 29 June 1954, Mss. Eur. D. 950/5, IOL.
9. Elwin to his mother, letters of 20 February and 19 June 1955, ibid.
10. Interview with Amina Jayal, New Delhi, April 1994.
11. Diary entry of 9 July 1954, Elwin Papers, Shillong.
12. Page 363 of manuscript version of *Tribal World*, OUP Archives, Bombay.
13. Elwin to his mother, 5 July 1954, Mss. Eur. D. 950/5, IOL.
14. Verrier Elwin, *Gandhiji: Bapu of his People* (Shillong 1956), pp. 44–5. The book was translated into several languages, including Tibetan, Hindi and Assamese.
15. Shamrao to Eldyth, 20 September 1954, Mss Eur. D. 950/5, IOL.
16. Elwin to Archer, 28 September 1954, Mss. Eur. F. 236/266, IOL.
17. Diary entries of 30 December and 31 December 1954, Elwin Papers, Shillong.
18. Elwin to his mother, letters of 22 January, 7 February and 20 February 1955, Mss Eur. D. 950/5, IOL.
19. Diary entry of 17 January 1955, Elwin Papers, Shillong.
20. 'Touring among the Sherdupkens in April 1955,' in File 138, Elwin Papers, NMML.
21. Elwin to his mother, 14 May 1955, Mss. Eur. D. 950/5, IOL.
22. Elwin to his mother, letters of 6 May, 8 May, 9 July, 7 August and 14 August 1955, Mss, Eur. D. 950/5, IOL.
23. Elwin to his sister, 20 August 1955, ibid.
24. Jawaharlal Nehru, confidential note on NEFA of 28 August 1955, File 149, Elwin Papers, NMML.

25. Cf. Elwin's notes of 1 November 1955 and of 19 April 1956, and his report of a tour between 23 October and 3 December 1958, in Files 116, 133 and 139 respectively, Elwin Papers, NMML.
26. Note in File 7, Elwin Papers, NMML.
27. Quoted in Shamrao Hivale's letter to Elwin, 26 February 1954, Elwin Papers, Shillong.
28. Elwin to his sister, 10 October 1955, Mss Eur. D. 950/5, IOL.
29. Elwin to R. E. Hawkins, 8 August 1959, File E (parts 7 and 8), OUP Archives, Bombay. Also *Tribal World*, pp. 249–50.
30. Elwin to K. L. Mehta, 12 December 1955, File 119, Elwin Papers, NMML.
31. 'Report on a Tour of Mishmi Hills, November 1955,' Mss. Eur. D. 950/5, IOL.
32. Elwin to Sir Robert Reid, 30 November 1955, Mss. Eur. E. 278/16, IOL.
33. Diary entries for 31 November 1955 and 1 January 1956, Elwin Papers, Shillong.
34. Elwin to his mother, letters of 29 December 1955, 9 January, and 14 January 1956; Elwin to his sister, letters of 8 December 1956 and 28 January 1958, Mss Eur. D. 950/6, IOL.
35. Quoted in K. L. Mehta, *In Different Worlds* (New Delhi 1985), pp. 159–60.
36. Verrier Elwin, 'The People of NEFA' (in six parts), *The Illustrated Weekly of India*, 30 September to 4 November 1956.
37. Quoted in his 'Report of Tour in Lohit Frontier Division in November 1955,' File 138, Elwin Papers, NMML.
38. This paragraph draws on interviews with Har Mander Singh, New Delhi, February 1994; with R. N. Haldipur, Bangalore, September 1997; and with Rashid Yusuf Ali, Shillong, December 1997.
39. Verrier Elwin, 'The People of NEFA: VI: Tawang', *The Illustrated Weekly of India*, 4 November 1956.
40. Quoted in 'Notes on Verrier Elwin,' Mss. Eur. F. 236/228, IOL.
41. Elwin to his sister, 8 December 1956, Mss. Eur. 950/5, IOL.
42. Interview with O. K. Moorthy, New Delhi, August 1992; Mehta, *In Different Worlds*, pp. 161–2.
43. 'Report of Tour in Lohit Frontier Division in November 1957,' File 139, Elwin Papers, NMML.

NOTES TO CHAPTER TWELVE

1. Elwin to Archer, 28 September 1954, Mss Eur. F. 236/266, IOL.
2. Elwin to Archer, 10 January 1959, ibid.
3. Verrier Elwin, *A Philosophy for NEFA* (second edition: Shillong 1959), p. 46. All quotes are from this edition.

4. *A Philosophy for NEFA*, pp. 53–60.
5. Note dated 23 August 1958, File 23, Elwin Papers, NMML.
6. *A Philosophy for NEFA*, pp. 131, 146–7, 152–3, 246, etc.
7. Elwin to K. L. Mehta (Adviser to Governor), 16 September 1955, File 7, Elwin Papers, NMML; 'Comment on a Memorandum on the Impact of Modern Civilization on the Tribal People of Madhya Pradesh,' in File 8, Elwin Papers, NMML.
8. 'A Critical Survey in 1957,' File 139, Elwin Papers, NMML; note by Elwin of 24 October 1955, File 116, Elwin Papers, NMML.
9. Elwin to Commissioner of NEFA, 4 October 1962, File 46; tour diary, entry for 5 March 1962, in File 139; report of a trip made to Tripura in 1958, File 133; correspondence and notes in file 116 (all files in Elwin Papers, NMML).
10. Elwin to Adviser to Governor, 2 March 1956, File 130, Elwin Papers, NMML.
11. Verrier Elwin, *The Art of the North East Frontier of India* (Shillong 1958); also Elwin, 'Introduction,' in Anon., *Folk Paintings of India* (New Delhi 1961).
12. Undated note by Elwin on architecture in Tirap; Nehru to B. P. Chaliha, 1 August 1958, both in File 47, Elwin Papers, NMML ('Architectural Designs, 1955–61').
13. Verrier Elwin, review of John Bartlow Martin, *Break Down the Walls* (a book on Australian prisons), *Illustrated Weekly of India*, 3 June 1956.
14. Cf. notes and correspondence in File 69, Elwin Papers, NMML.
15. Verrier Elwin, *Maria Murder and Suicide* (Bombay 1943), esp. chapter XVIII.
16. Elwin to M. C. Nanavatty, 25 August 1958, File 91, Elwin Papers, NMML, emphasis supplied.
17. 'Flibbertigibbet', 'Going Gaga over the Nagas,' *The Economic Weekly*, 7 September 1957.
18. Onkar Sharad, *Lohia: A Biography* (Delhi 1972), pp. 269–71.
19. Translation of news report in *Natun Assamiya*, 15 May 1954, Elwin Papers, NMML.
20. *Discussion on the Motion to consider the recommendations of the States Reorganization Commission relating to Assam (extracts from the proceedings of the Assam Legislative Assembly at its meeting held on the 17th November, 1955)* (Shillong 1955).
21. *A Report on the Visit to North-East Frontier Agency by the Delegation of the Assam Legislative Assembly in the Month of December, 1962* (Shillong 1963); *A Report on the Visit of North-East Frontier Agency by the Second*

Delegation of the Assam Legislative Assembly in the Month of April, 1963 (Shillong 1963)
22. Press cutting in Elwin Papers, Shillong.
23. Elwin to Vishnu Sahay (Governor of Assam), 13 June 1963, quoted in K. S. Singh, *Ethnicity, Identity and Development* (Verrier Elwin Memorial Lectures of 1985, published in 1990 by Manohar, New Delhi), pp. 13–14.
24. Interview with Rashid Yusuf Ali, Shillong, December 1997.
25. Note by Elwin of 19 February 1957, File 18, Elwin Papers, NMML; Elwin to K. L. Mehta, 15 October 1957, File 113, Elwin Papers, NMML.
26. Cf. N. K. Bose, 'Tribal Economy' (first published in 1955), reprinted in his *Culture and Society in India* (Bombay 1967), p. 174; *Tribal World*, p. 317.
27. Cf, in this connection, Bose's important essay, 'The Hindu Method of Tribal Absorption,' first published in *Science and Culture*, 1941, and reprinted in his *Culture and Society in India*, pp. 203–15.
28. N. K. Bose, 'Anthropology and Tribal Welfare,' *Man in India*, vol. 37, no. 3, 1957 (based on the address to the Fourth Tribal Welfare Conference, Koraput, 30 April 1957). In a later essay Bose criticized Elwin for his 'sentimental approach to a rather serious problem.' N. K. Bose, 'Change in Tribal Cultures before and after Independence,' *Man in India*, vol. 44, no. 1, 1964.
29. Review of *A Philosophy of NEFA* by 'E.T.' (pseudonym used by D. N. Majumdar), in *The Eastern Anthropologist*, vol. 12, no. 3, 1959 (emphasis added).
30. Letters in File 49, Elwin Papers, NMML.
31. *The Sunday Statesman*, 10 May 1959.
32. Gertrude Emerson Sen, 'Sortie over NEFA,' *Economic Weekly*, Annual Number, January 1960.
33. Cf. *The Statesman*, 9 October 1959.
34. Diary entry of 1 November 1955, Elwin Papers, Shillong.
35. *Lok Sabha Debates*, 18 August 1960.

NOTES TO CHAPTER THIRTEEN

1. Will dated 10 January 1959, copy in the possession of Arvind Khare. Bijay was, of course, born in 1946, not 1947.
2. In four files in his papers (Files 19, 23, 39 and 62, Elwin Papers, NMML), on which the following paragraphs draw.
3. Elwin to his sister, letters of 5 February, 17 February and 3 March 1959, Mss. Eur. D. 950/6, IOL.
4. Elwin to Koestler, 3 March 1959, Koestler Papers, University of Edinburgh.

5. Verrier Elwin, 'The Dalai Lama comes to India,' *The Geographical Magazine*, July 1959.
6. Elwin to Koestler, 14 May 1959, Koestler Papers.
7. Elwin to Nehru, 27 August 1960, File 89, Elwin Papers, NMML; Elwin to Major General A. S. Guraya, Inspector General of the Assam Rifles, undated, File 74, Elwin Papers, NMML.
8. *Report of the Committee on Special Multipurpose Tribal Blocks* (New Delhi 1960), pp. i, 14–17, 21, 25, 29, 31, 45–6, 48–9, 178, etc.
9. As recalled in P. D. Strachey, *Nagaland Nightmare* (Bombay 1968), pp. 58–60.
10. Diary entry of 18 July 1960, Elwin Papers, Shillong.
11. These paragraphs are based on the letters and notings in Files 20, 59 and 120, Elwin Papers, NMML.
12. W. G. Archer, 'In the Assam Mail,' typescript dated 4 December 1947, Mss Eur. F. 236/275, IOL.
13. Verrier Elwin, *Nagaland* (Shillong 1960), p. 104.
14. Elwin to R. E. Hawkins, 28 August 1940, File E5, OUP Archives, Mumbai.
15. Elwin to Hutton, 20 October 1962, Elwin Papers (personal correspondence files), NMML.
16. Elwin to Murkot Ramunny, 3 September 1960, File 59, Elwin Papers, NMML.
17. Unsigned, undated typescript in File 4, Elwin Papers, NMML.
18. Elwin to Hawkins, 20 September 1962, File E10, OUP Archives, Mumbai.
19. As recounted by K. L. Mehta in a letter to *The Statesman*, 9 April 1964.
20. Elwin to J. H. Hutton, 5 November 1960, Elwin Papers (personal correspondence files), NMML.
21. Undated 'Aide Memoire' in File 28, Elwin Papers, NMML.
22. Elwin to his sister, letters of 1 February, 20 April and 27 April 1961, Mss. Eur. D. 950/6.
23. *The Pardhans of the Upper Nerbudda Valley* (Bombay 1946), p. 149.
24. Elwin to his sister, 3 August 1961, Mss Eur. D. 950/6, IOL; *Report of the Scheduled Areas and Scheduled Tribes Commission* (New Delhi 1962).
25. Elwin to T. S. Wilkinson, 22 September 1961, Elwin Papers, Shillong. The essay was published, without the references to Elwin's marriages, as T. S. Wilkinson, 'Isolation, Assimilation and Integration in their Historical Perspective,' *Tribal Research Institute Bulletin*, vol. 2, no. 1, June 1962—it is a little-known but remarkably fair account of the Elwin-Ghurye controversy.
26. Cf. correspondence in File 41, Elwin Papers, NMML.
27. Elwin to P. C. Chatterjee, 30 May 1961, File 41, Elwin Papers, NMML.
28. Verrier Elwin, *A Philosophy of Love* (Delhi 1961).

29. Interview with Amina Jayal, New Delhi, April 1994.
30. Cf. File 68, Elwin Papers, NMML.
31. Elwin to Hawkins, 25 July 1962; Elwin to Hutton, 20 October 1962, personal correspondence files, Elwin Papers, NMML.
32. Elwin to Koestler, 17 October 1962; Koestler to Elwin, 24 October 1962, Koestler Papers, Edinburgh.
33. Elwin to his sister, letters of 29 November and 11 December 1962, Mss. Eur. D. 950/6, IOL.
34. Major Sitaram Johri, *Where India, China and Burma Meet* (Calcutta 1962), pp. 16, 78–9, 106, 110, 277, etc.
35. Elwin to R. N. Haldipur, 26 December 1962, File 104, Elwin Papers, NMML.
36. Indira Gandhi to Elwin, 14 January 1963, Elwin Papers, Shillong.
37. Mary Gillett to Elwin, 19 November 1962, Elwin Papers, Shillong.
38. Elwin to Hawkins, 21 December 1962, File E10, OUP Archives, Mumbai.
39. Elwin to Hawkins, letters of 13 March and 14 April 1963, Elwin Papers (personal correspondence files), NMML.
40. Elwin to his sister, letters of 15 May, 27 May and 10 July 1963, Mss. Eur. D. 950/6, IOL.
41. Vishnu Sahay to Elwin, 12 June 1963, File 6, Elwin Papers, NMML.
42. Nehru to Elwin, 8 June 1963, Elwin Papers, Shillong.
43. Interview with Ashok Elwin, Shillong, December 1997.
44. Patel to Elwin, 29 June 1963, Elwin Papers (personal correspondence files), NMML.
45. Archer to Elwin, 12 June 1963, Mss. Eur. F. 236/266, IOL.
46. Armand Denis, *Taboo* (London 1966), chapter XI.
47. Tara Ali Baig, *Portraits of an Era* (New Delhi 1988), p. 45f. The lines are from Wordsworth's 'Song at the Feast of Brougham Castle;' the next stanza, also a favourite of Elwin's, runs thus:

'In him the savage virtue of the Race,
Revenge, and all ferocious thoughts were dead;
Nor did he change; but kept in lofty place
The wisdom which adversity had bred.'

The two stanzas had been prophetically invoked by Elwin in his early essay, 'Mahatma Gandhi and William Wordsworth,' *The Modern Review*, February 1931.

48. Bose to Elwin, 28 November 1963, in File 39, Elwin Papers, NMML.
49. Elwin to Koestler, 28 December 1963, Koestler Papers, Edinburgh.
50. Cf. Sourin Roy to Elwin, 17 February 1964, Elwin Papers, NMML.
51. Preface dated 31 November 1963, in Verrier Elwin, *The Kingdom of the Young* (Bombay 1968).

52. Verrier Elwin, editor, *Democracy in NEFA* (Shillong 1965), Preface and p. 23.
53. Medical report of Lt. Col. (Dr) C. R. Gopinath, Military Hospital, Shillong, 14 February 1964, in File 140, Elwin Papers, NMML.
54. Interview with Rashid Yusuf Ali, Shillong, December 1997.
55. Lahiri to Eldyth, 28 February 1964, Mss. Eur. D. 950/21, IOL.

NOTES TO CHAPTER FOURTEEN

1. As characterized by Sunil Janah, the friend who finally touched up the photograph for publication. Cf. Elwin–Janah correspondence, Elwin Papers, NMML.
2. *Tribal World*, p. viii. In a letter to an editor at the OUP, Elwin wrote that 'it was only when I came to write this book that I realized how Indianized I have grown.' Elwin to Toyne, 12 (?) 1961, File E10, OUP Archives, Bombay.
3. Philip Vaudin to R. E. Hawkins, 13 October 1949; Hawkins to Elwin, 25 November 1949, both in File E10, OUP Archives.
4. Andre Maurois, 'Autobiography,' in his *Aspects of Biography* (Cambridge 1929), p. 145.
5. Hawkins to Elwin, 9 April 1962; also Elwin to Hawkins, letters of 15 March and 17 March 1962, all in File E10, OUP Archives.
6. Elwin to Koestler, 11 April 1962, Koestler Papers, Edinburgh.
7. Elwin to Hawkins, 9 August 1963, File E10, OUP Archives, Mumbai.
8. Elwin to Hawkins, 16 August 1963, File 62, Elwin Papers, NMML.
9. Manuscript copy of *Tribal World*, OUP Archives, Mumbai, pp.161, 165–6, 492–3, 521.
10. As described in Elwin to Hawkins, 24 June 1963, File E10, OUP Archives.
11. Letter of 28 May 1963, in ibid.
12. Eldyth Elwin to R. E. Hawkins, 9 August 1964, ibid.
13. Cf. reviews by K. S. Mathur in the *International Journal of Comparative Sociology*, vol. 8, 1965, pp.127–8; by Naomi Mitchison in the *Glasgow Herald*, 31 October 1964; by Bool Chand in *Kurukshetra*, July 1964; and by Robin White in the *New York Times Book Review*, 21 June 1964; unsigned review in *The Assam Tribune*, (Gauhati), 30 May 1964.
14. S. C. Dube, review in *The Eastern Anthropologist*, vol. 17, no. 2, 1964; Mitchison, op. cit.; *The Sunday Statesman*, 5 April 1964.
15. Review in *Imprint*, March 1965.
16. Joseph Epstein, 'First Person Singular,' *The Hudson Review*, 45 (3), Autumn 1992, p. 370.

17. W. G. Archer, 'Converted by India,' *The Daily Telegraph* (London), 10 October 1964.
18. Untitled, undated notes by W. G. Archer in Mss. Eur. F. 236/266, IOL.
19. Shamrao Hivale to Eldyth Elwin, 5 September 1953, Mss Eur. D. 950/4, IOL.
20. SVV, 'Marginalia,' *The Illustrated Weekly of India*, 3 May 1964.
21. Inserted by the Little Theatre Group and the Minerva Theatre in the *Amrita Bazaar Patrika*, 25 February 1964.

NOTES TO THE EPILOGUE

1. *The Times of India*, 20 May 1964.
2. Verrier Elwin, *Religious and Cultural Aspects of Khadi* (1931: reprinted by Sarvodaya Prachuralaya, Thanjavur, 1964).
3. R. F. McNeile, compiler, *A History of Dean Close School* (printed by the School in 1966). A reviewer in *The Decanian*, Summer 1966, was sensibly 'puzzled by the absence from chapter XIII of the name of Verrier Elwin, for instance, the only O.D. to take a double first from Oxford and who became one of the world's foremost anthropologists.'
4. *Dean Close School Alumni, 1886 to 1948* (Winchester 1950).
5. Cf. Humphrey Osmond to Paul Newton, 19 April 1991.
6. Asoso Yonuo, *The Rising Nagas: A Historical and Political Study* (Delhi 1974), p. 120.
7. George M. Soares-Prabhu, *Incultural Liberation Dialogue: Challenges to Christian Theology in Asia Today* (Pune 1984).
8. Daniel O'Connor, editor, *Din-Sevak: Verrier Elwin's Life of Service in Tribal India* (Delhi 1993).
9. Leonard Schiff, interview with John Charles, 2 July 1971, in Archives of the Hilfield Priory, Dorset.
10. Reported in *The Times of India*, New Delhi, 16 August 1997.
11. Victor Turner, Review of *The Religion of an Indian Tribe*, in *Man*, article 50, May 1957; Turner, 'Aspects of Saora Ritual and Shamanism: An Approach to the Data of Ritual,' in A. L. Epstein, edited, *The Craft of Social Anthropology* (London 1967). See also Ramachandra Guha, 'Between Anthropology and Literature: The Ethnographies of Verrier Elwin,' *Journal of the Royal Anthropological Institute (incorporating Man)*, vol. 3, no. 2, June 1998.
12. Piers Vitebsky, *Dialogues with the Dead: Intimations of Mortality among the Sora of Eastern India* (Cambridge 1993); Simeran Man Singh Gell, *The Ghotul in Muria Society* (London 1993); Bikram Narayan Nanda, *Contours of Continuity and Change among the Bonda of Koraput* (New Delhi 1994);

Vinay Srivastava, 'The Ethnographer and the People: Reflections on Fieldwork,' in 2 parts, *Economic and Political Weekly*, 1–8, 15 June 1991.
13. M. C. Pradhan, R. D. Singh, P. K. Misra and D. B. Sastry, editors, *Anthropology and Archaeology: Essays in Commemoration of Verrier Elwin* (Bombay 1969). The essays ranged from a study of tribal assertion in modern Bihar to party conflict in a Kerala village: the publishers were Elwin's own, the Indian Branch of Oxford University Press.
14. Note by B. Das Shastri, 12 March 1964, File 158, Elwin Papers, NMML.
15. Dharmendra Prasad, 'Elwin in Mandla,' *India Cultures Quarterly*, volume 34, nos 1 and 2, 1979, pp. 19–21.
16. Personal communication from Nandini Sundar.
17. This paragraph brutally summarizes a history told in more detail in Madhav Gadgil and Ramachandra Guha, *Ecology and Equity: The Use and Abuse of Nature in Contemporary India* (London 1995). Also see Amita Baviskar, *In the Belly of the River: Tribal Conflicts Over Development in the Narmada Valley* (New Delhi 1996).
18. Swaminathan S. Anklesaria Aiyar, 'We are all Tribals,' *The Sunday Times of India*, 11 October 1992.
19. Bradford Morse, et al., *Sardar Sarovar: Report of the Independent Review* (Ottawa 1992), pp. 68–9, 78.
20. Quotes from *Report of the High Level Committee to Make Recommendations on the Salient Features of the Law for Extending Provisions of the Constitutional (73rd) Amendment Act 1992, to Scheduled Areas* (New Delhi 1995).
21. B. G. Verghese, *India's Northeast Resurgent: Ethnicity, Insurgency, Governance, Development* (New Delhi 1997), chapter XI.
22. Haimendorf, 'The Example of Verrier Elwin,' *Anthropology Today*, vol. 11, no. 4, August 1985.
23. Interviews with Vivek Rae, New Delhi, January 1991, and with R. N. Haldipur, Bangalore, August 1997.
24. Reports by Parsa Venkateshwar Rao Jr. in *The Indian Express*, 18 and 20 April 1994.
25. Cf. the three-part series by Bill Aitken in *The Telegraph* (Calcutta), 25 May and 1 and 8 June 1996.
26. Cf. introduction and paintings reproduced in J. Swaminathan, ed., *The Perceiving Fingers* (Bhopal 1987); interview with J. Swaminathan, New Delhi, March 1992. An anecdotal and affectionate account of the Swaminathan–Patangarh–Jangarh–Elwin connection can be found in Mark Tully's *No Full Stops in India* (London 1991).
27. *Vivekananda Kendra Patrika*, vol. 1, no. 2, 1972, special issue on Hill India.
28. Uma Shanker Misra, 'Remembering the Scholar Gypsy,' *The Pioneer*, 21 April 1985.

29. *A Common Perspective for North-East India: Speeches and Papers of National Seminar on Hill People of North-Eastern India, held in Calcutta from December 3 to 6, 1966* (Calcutta 1967), pp. 158–9.
30. A. R. Kamath, 'Rural Sociology in the Fifties,' *Economic and Political Weekly*, 4 April 1981.
31. Durga Bhagwat, *Athavale Tase* (As I Remember It) (Bombay 1991), pp. 160–5.
32. *The Hindu*, 29 October 1985.
33. *Soliga: The Tribe and Its Stride* (published by Vivekananda Girijana Kalyana Kendra, B. R. Hills, Mysore 1991), p. 18.
34. G. S. Ghurye, *The Burning Caldron of North-East India* (Bombay 1980), pp. 6–7, 17, 22, 26–7, 53, 100, etc.
35. Books republished in the last decade include *Leaves from the Jungle, The Agaria, Maria Murder and Suicide, The Muria and their Ghotul, Myths of Middle India,* and *The Tribal World of Verrier Elwin.*
36. Lila to Eldyth, 18 November 1966, Mss. Eur. D. 950/21, IOL.
37. Shamrao to Hawkins, 12 March 1964, File E10, OUP Archives, Mumbai.
38. This account is based on papers held by Arvind Khare, who assisted Kosi and Kumar in the cases.
39. Dom Moraes, *Answered by Flutes: Reflections from Madhya Pradesh* (Bombay 1983), pp. 158–165; also interview with Dom Moraes, Mumbai, December 1990.
40. Dharmendra Prasad to Vijay Elwin, dated 22 June 1981, letter in the possession of Arvind Khare.
41. Eldyth Elwin to John Charles, 23 April 1971, Archives of the Hilfield Priory, Dorset.
42. *Tribal World*, p. 20.
43. Barry Phelps, *P. G. Wodehouse: Man and Myth* (London 1992), p. 201. Also Verrier Elwin, *Motley* (Calcutta 1954), and Elwin, 'The College Life of Bertie Wooster,' *The Sunday Statesman*, (?) November 1953.

Index

Except for the entry under his own name, Verrier Elwin has been abbreviated to VE throughout. Entries marked with an asterisk denote tribal communities visited or studied by Verrier Elwin.

*Abors 247, 264, 348
Acland, R. D. (Bishop of Bombay) 50–1; on VE 51, 92, 206
Acton, Harold 17; on VE 222
*Adis 322
*Agarias 151, 182–3, 318; VE on 119–20, 122–3
Aitken, Bill, on VE 322
Alexander, Horace 72
Alkazi, Ebrahim 223, 332
Aluwihare, Bernard 27, 63, 194
American Museum of Natural History 280–1
Amery, L. S., on VE 167–8; VE on 156
Amrit Kaur, Rajkumari 231
Amrita Bazaar Patrika, on VE 313
Anand, Mulk Raj 223
Andrews, C. F. vi, 26, 65, 70, 83, 86, 99, 316
Anthropological Survey of India 177, 184, 187, 188, 189, 230–1, 238; VE joins 181–2; VE leaves 190–1, 218; VE on 183, 272
Arayanayakam, Asha Devi 279
Archer, Mildred 118–19, 131, 144

Archer, W. G. 118–19, 131, 182, 184, 203, 229, 234, 239, 282, 286; as VE's collaborator and confidant 119, 129, 144, 146–7, 148, 159–60, 176, 186–7, 188, 191, 196, 197, 213, 220–1, 246, 259, 261–2; as VE's competitor 134, 207, 248, 297; praises VE 119, 142, 297–8; writes poem on VE 152; criticizes VE 310–12
Arunachal Pradesh—*see* North East Frontier Agency
Arya Dharma Seva Sangh 168
Ashram of St Francis 67, 79, 86
Assamese intelligentsia, on VE 271–2, 309
Attenborough, Sir Richard 332
Auden, John 189, 221, 226; writes poem on VE 200–1
Auden, Shiela 221
Azariah, E. S. (Bishop of Dornakal) 28

Baig, Tara Ali 288–9
*Baigas v, 61, 100, 101, 137, 148, 156, 182, 208, 255, 318; attitudes to celibacy and sex 112–14, 221; position of

women 149–50; love of *bewar* (swidden) cultivation 96–7, 114–15, 148, 159; VE on 97, 113–16, 160, 216
Bajaj, Jamnalal 45, 60, 61, 62, 63, 79, 304
Bara, Simon, on VE 167
Barua, Hem 277
Bates, H. E., on VE 112
Beady, Bryan, on VE 22–3, 24
Besant, Annie, compared to VE vi–vii
Betjeman, John 16
Bhagavad Gita 27; VE on 27–8
Bhagwat, Durga 159; on VE 324–5
Bhave, Vinoba 315
Bhil Seva Mandal 53, 54, 72, 279; VE on 98
*Bhils 53–4, 59–60, 88; VE on 54, 289
Bhumijan Seva Mandal 130, 156, 177, 179, 181, 204
Bhuria Committee 321–2
Bilsi 198
Blackburn, H. V. 173–5
Boas, George 122
*Bondos 173–5, 176, 209–10, 318; VE on 208, 221
*Boris 256, 346
Bose, N. K. 273, 299
Bose, Subhas Chandra 42, 111, 126
Braine-Hartnell, A. C. 198
Butler, R. A., on VE 106
Byron, Robert 14, 17, 31

Cannadine, David 303
Carey, Bishop William, on VE 93
Chagla, M. C. 315
Chakmas 323
Chaluey 198–9

Chandola, Harish, on VE 324
Chatterjee, Suniti Kumar 287
Chattopadhyay, Kamaladevi 35, 280
Chetwode, Penelope 62
Christa Seva Sangh 32, 50, 51, 74, 79; life in 33, 34–6, 46; religious orientation 26–7, 28, 30; political orientation 37, 43–6, 47–8; VE as leader of 43–6; VE's disagreements with 52–3, 58–9, 90
Christian missionaries 2–5, 9–10, 26–7, 61, 172, 235, 323; on VE 69–70, 86, 117, 167–8, 316; VE on 68, 91, 92, 149, 164, 165–6, 182, 242
Church Missionary Society 2–3
Church of England 4, 7–8, 18, 21–2, 26, 28, 32, 49, 65, 69–71; VE on 23–4, 29, 40–1, 71, 90–1, 92–3, 94
Church Times, The, on VE 23–4, 32
Churchill, Winston 254
Close, Francis 7–8
Congress Party vi, vii, 42–3, 70, 78, 110–11, 158, 168, 179, 191, 205, 237, 238, 239; VE on 44–5, 58, 67, 68, 72, 76, 104–5, 108, 120, 192, 212
Congressmen 60, 63–4, 104–5, 192, 224, 232, 313; on VE 271; VE on 85, 97, 108–9, 137, 188, 223, 289
Corbett, Jim 305

Dalai Lama 259, 282–3, 331
Datta, Sudhin 189; on VE 261
Daulatram, Jairamdas 224, 232, 249

de Zoete, Beryl, on VE 117
Dean Close Memorial School (VE's school) 7–8, 14, 25, 292; religious orientation 9–12, 316; political orientation 9–10
Denis, Armand, on VE 298
Desai, Bhulabhai 168
Desai, Mahadev 49, 55, 57, 63, 73, 119; on VE 37, 143–4; VE on 144
Desai, Morarji 191, 293
Desai, Narayan 57, 280
Desai, Valji Govind 203
Deshmukh, C. D. 299, 300
Devereux, George, on VE 120–1, 281
Dewey, Clive 1
Dhebar, U. N. 289, 291
Dickinson, Goldsworthy Lowes 31
Dix, Alston (Dom Gregory) 21–2, 24, 26, 29
Dube, S. C. 209; on VE 153, 309

Economic Weekly (later *Economic and Political Weekly*), on VE 269, 276, 324
Elwin, Ashok (VE's fourth son) 246, 279, 297, 331
Elwin, Basil (VE's brother) 5
Elwin, Bishop E. H. (VE's father) 1–2, 27, 182, 197; religious views 3–4; as Bishop of Sierra Leone 4–6; early death 6
Elwin, Eldyth (VE's sister) 5, 224–5, 231, 245, 289, 290, 327; VE's relationship with 5–6, 91, 223, 228, 296, 302, 312, 331–2; visits to India 110–11, 129, 296
Elwin, Kosi (VE's first wife) 218, 229, 256, 327, 328–9, 332; beauty 129, 132, 133, 138;

independence of mind 133–4; love of alcohol 135, 187, 189; meets VE 129; VE's enchantment with 132, 134–5, 187; marries VE 129–30, 132–3; extra-marital affairs 176–9, 189; break-up of marriage 127, 189–91, 290; influence on VE's scientific work 128, 135, 138–9, 166; VE's attempts to forget 127–8, 152, 193, 279, 300; present situation 126–7, 330
Elwin, Kumar (VE's first son) 136, 180, 190, 198, 224, 250, 279, 295, 302, 327, 328; VE's love for 134, 178–9, 189, 245, 246; lack of interest in studies 195, 219, 246; love of nature 218–19, 256; death 329–30
Elwin, Lila (VE's second wife) 198, 224, 253, 255, 272, 281, 294–5, 297, 323, 328–9, 332; beauty 193, 230, 231, 244; as homemaker 193, 228, 244, 250, 282; VE begins affair with 193–4, 220, 221–2; marries VE 227–30; love for VE 196, 227, 229–30, 237, 290; VE's love for 229–30, 231, 236, 241, 246, 248, 256, 278, 279; present situation 327, 331
Elwin, Mrs M. O. (VE's mother) 4–5, 6, 9, 33, 39, 128, 129, 161, 177, 218, 231; religious views 5, 7, 19, 24, 26, 73, 93–4, 296; VE's relationship with 7, 13, 19, 24, 29, 72, 93–4, 117, 190, 198, 228–9, 312; death 259
Elwin, Nakul (VE's third son) 222, 279, 331

ELWIN, VERRIER, life and career:
early years: birth 1; family 1–7, 13, 19; school 7–12; college 13–19
homes in India: Poona (1927–32) 33–6, 38–9, 42–6, 51; Karanjia village, Mandla district (1932–5) 65–72, 79–84, 86–91, 119; Sarwachappar village, Mandla district (1935–7) 100–2, 107; Patangarh village, Mandla district (1937–40, 1942–6, 1949–54) 110, 117–18, 129, 130, 134–5, 176–9, 191, 193–4, 198, 204–5, 219–20, 222, 229–30, 232; Chitrakot, Bastar State (1940–2) 135–8; Banaras (1946–8) 181, 182, 187–8; Calcutta (1948–9) 188–91; Shillong (1954–64) 237, 243–4, 246, 247–8, 249–53, 270, 281–2, 288, 294–301
jobs and assignments: Vice Principal, Wycliffe Hall (1926–7) 26, 29; Deputy Director, Anthropological Survey of India (1946–9) 181–3, 184, 187–9, 190–1; Adviser on Tribal Affairs, North East Frontier Agency (1954–64) 231, 237–9, 242–4, 253, 255–8, 283, 293–4, 300–1; commissions of enquiry, service on 48–9, 63–5, 283–4, 289, 291; others 136, 148–9, 171
tours and travels in: Bombay 44, 46, 49–51, 54, 61–2, 133–4, 153, 219, 222–3, 248; Gujarat 36–7, 48–9, 51–2, 54–7, 248; North West Frontier Province 63–5; Central Provinces 60–1, 96–7, 101, 110–11; Bastar State 137–9, 145; Orissa 147–9, 171–6, 194–6, 211; Bihar 119, 220–1; North East Frontier Agency 239–43, 246–7, 255–6; Nagaland 182, 225–6; Europe 32–3, 41, 72; Palestine 42; England 39–41, 72–7, 102–7, 192–3; Africa 196–7; Ceylon 33, 194; Thailand 198–9
honours and awards 10, 12, 118 (364n.29), 161, 289–90, 292–3
personality and character: physical appearance 5, 22, 24, 46, 119, 132, 219, 225, 226, 243, 279, 297; food and drink habits 55–6, 89, 175, 195, 197–8, 251, 252, 278; oratorical skills 22–3, 23–4, 37, 46, 52, 153–5, 223; financial situation 24, 102, 191, 195, 204, 213, 218, 219–20, 220–1, 224–5, 237, 248, 290, 305; health and ill-health 39, 56–7, 85, 93, 195, 291, 294, 296–301
sexual orientations: celibate 25, 34–5, 38, 62, 83, 85, 86, 94; celebratory 112–14, 132, 134, 135, 139–43, 202, 220, 221, 254, 291–2, 292–3; affairs 62, 79–85, 94–5, 193–4, 198–9, 221, 226–7, 290–1; marriages v, **127–31, 176–7, 189,** 228–30, 236, 246, 290
religious orientations: evangelical 5, 7, 8–9, 22; Anglo-Catholic 22–5, 26, 29–30, 32, 36, 38, 41–2, 68, 71–2, 73; philo-Hindu 36, 37, 40–1, 137–8, 166, 168–9, 185; anti-clerical 40–1, 45, 49, 50–1, 71–2, 76, 86, 90–3;

anti-Christian 99, 165–6, 168, 242, 259; anti-Hindu 105, 107–8, 157; philo-Buddhist 194, 258–60, 282–3, 288–9, 299
identities: priest 24–5, 41, 46, 49, 70; Gandhian 46–7, 49, 51, 52, 60, 67, 68, 79, 188–9, 224; Englishman 49, 88, 105, 186, 187, 192, 203–4, 232, 277, 278, 286, 304, 306, 307, 308, 309, 311, 313; Indian 41, 44, 46, 52, 57, 68, 184, 186, 203–4, 232, 237–8, 239, 262, 277, 285, 286–7, 304, 306, 308, 309, 311, 313; anthropologist 101, 105, 106, 115–17, 121, 146–7, 160–1, 183; defender of the aboriginal 98, 123, 151, 155, 156, 170–1, 180, 205, 212, 242
views and opinions: criticisms of imperialism 44–5, 46–7, 48–9, 65, 67, 70, 73, 203; criticisms of civilization 122–3, 136, 147, 169, 243, 258, 263–4, 265, 284, 289, 291; celebration of tribal life 54, 100, 137, 148, 149–50, 164–6, 185–6, 207, 215–17, 225, 240, 283; on tribal exploitation 97–8, 107, 114–15, 117–18, 137, 148–9, 150–1, 153–5, 170–1, 218, 232, 284
death 301–2

ELWIN, VERRIER, works by
Books
Agaria, The (1942) 119–21, 122, 281, 318–19
Art of the North East Frontier of India, The (1958) 265
Baiga, The (1939) 113–18, 122, 140, 155, 161, 297–8, 332
Bondo Highlander (1950) 208–11
Cloud That's Dragonish, A (1938) 112
Christian Dhyana, or Prayer of Loving Regard: A Study of 'The Cloud of Unknowing' (1930) 40
Dawn of Indian Freedom, The (1931: with J. C. Winslow) 58
Democracy in NEFA (1965) 300
Folk-Songs of Chattisgarh (1946) 163–4
Folk-Songs of the Maikal Hills (1944: with Shamrao Hivale) 161–2, 298
Folk-Tales of Mahakoshal (1944) 161
Gandhiji: Bapu of his People (1956) 244–5
Kingdom of the Young, The (1968) 299–300
Leaves from the Jungle: A Diary of Life in a Gond Village (1936: second edition, 1958) 89, 95, 99–100, 103, 111, 349
Maria Murder and Suicide (1943) 145–6
Muria and their Ghotul, The (1947) 128, 140–5, 191, 281, 298, 299–300, 332
Myths of Middle India (1949) 207–8, 211
Nagaland (1960) 284–7
Phulmat of the Hills: A Tale of the Gonds (1937) 111–12
Philosophy for NEFA, A (1957: second edition, 1959) 262–5, 267, 268, 269, 273, 275, 276, 277, 312, 326
Philosophy of Love, A (1962) 292–3
Religion of an Indian Tribe, The (1955) 211–13, 220, 317–18

Richard Rolle: A Christian Sanyasi (1930) 40
St Francis of Assissi (1933) 71–2
Songs of the Forest: The Folk Poetry of the Gonds (1935: with Shamrao Hivale) 98
Tribal Art of Middle India: A Personal Record (1951) 207, 224, 323
Tribal Myths of Orissa (1954) 211
Tribal World of Verrier Elwin: An Autobiography, The (1964) 127, 294, 296, 303–12
Truth about India: Can we Get it? (1932) 67, 77

Pamphlets
Aboriginals, The (1943: second edition, 1944) 128, 158–9, 169–70
Christ and Satyagraha (1930) 46–8
Loss of Nerve: A Comparative Study of the Contact of Peoples in the Aboriginal Areas of the Bastar State and the Central Provinces of India (1941) 136, 366n.31
Mahatma Gandhi's Philosophy of Truth (1933) 143
Onward Bound (1926) 24–5, 355n.27
Religious and Cultural Aspects of Khadi (1931) 315
Studies in the Gospel (1929) 363n.44
Supremacy of the Spiritual (1933) 143
What's Happening in the Northwest Province (1932) 65

Other Writings
newspaper and magazine articles 47, 48 (355n.45), 97–8, 130–1, 213–17, 220, 257, 266, 274–5, 288, 334
poems 25, 27–8, 206, 210–11, 332
unpublished essays and reports 10–11, 23, 148 (368n.57), 165–6, 242–3, 264, 266–7
unpublished novels 98–9, 191–2, 203

Elwin, Vijay 178, 180, 189, 327, 328–31
Elwin, Wasant (VE's second son) 194, 227–8, 279, 331
Emerson, H. W. 64; on VE 66
Emmerson, Lindsay 189; writes poem on VE 200
Eremo Franciscano 41, 52–3, 62, 81, 84, 85, 90–1
Evans-Pritchard, E. E., on VE 192; VE on 210
Ezekiel, Nissim, on VE 309–10

Fielding-Clarke, Oliver 27, 28, 29, 33, 70, 101
Fisher, Bill 141–2
Flecker, H. W. (VE's headmaster) 8–9, 10, 137, 292
Flecker, James Elroy 9
Fleure, H. J. 211
Forde, Daryll 210
Forster, E. M. 252
Forsyth, James 103
Fortes, Meyer 192, 210
Francis (St), of Assissi 32, 67, 78, 79–80, 135, 332; VE on 71–2, 73–4, 83, 94
Friends House 73

*Gadabas 176, 212, 216
Gadgil, D. R. 158
Galbraith, Catherine 280
Gandhi, Devadas 63, 84–5, 231, 237–8

INDEX

Gandhi, Indira 285, 295, 315, 324, 333
Gandhi, Lakshmi Devadas 84
Gandhi, Mohandas Karamchand (Mahatma) vi, viii, 26, 27, 28, 34, 39, 45, 53, 73, 79, 87, 111, 123, 126, 128, 135, 153, 160, 170, 206, 248, 254, 270, 273, 285, 294, 298, 299, 303, 332; religious views 36–7, 41, 44, 55, 68, 69; political views/campaigns 10, 43, 47, 50, 58, 61–2, 63, 67, 73, 264–5; VE's meetings with 37, 49–50, 51, 55–7, 63, 85, 108; VE's devotion to 47, 49, 51–2, 60, 61–2, 72, 76, 78, 86, 304, 315–16; VE's disagreements with 37–8, 81, 85, 89–90, 91–2, 94–5, 99, 104, 108, 140, 143–5, 179, 292–3, 313; encourages VE 59, 63, 71; chastises VE 82–4; VE's reconciliation with 187–8, 202–3, 237–8, 244–5, 248–9, 262
Gandhians 117, 120, 126, 140, 164, 224, 232, 279–80, 287–8, 289–90, 317; on VE 37, 57, 144–5, 279, 315–16; VE on 89, 90, 92, 191, 307
Garrod, H. W. (VE's tutor) 15–16, 19, 164, 332
Gayatri Devi, Maharani, of Jaipur 333
Ghurye, G. S. 157, 159, 166, 167, 169, 192, 320; attacks VE 157–8, 326–7; VE responds to 159–60, 274–5, 291
Gillet, Mary 79, 80, 126, 127, 128, 295–6; VE's relationship with 80–5, 293
Gokhale, Gopalkrishna 34, 53

Gond Seva Mandal 86, 95, 99, 100, 101, 118, 125, 238; Constitution 334–9; activities 88, 102, 107, 108, 110–11, 129; changes of name 109, 221
Gonds v, 78, 97, 101–2, 111–12, 125–6, 128, 137, 140, 159, 180–1, 229, 281, 290; myths and customs 96, 98, 107–8, 109, 130–1, 161–2, 319–20; attitudes to celibacy and sex 89, 94–5, 112, 132, 163; position of women 89, 108, 134, 165–6; poverty of 93, 117–18, 151, 153–4, 162; and VE 60, 61, 66, 73, 74, 75, 86–90, 93, 94–5, 107; and Shamrao Hivale 66, 68, 87–9, 94–5; VE on 98, 100, 107–8
Gore, Bishop Charles 31–2, 52
Graham, Lady 64, 74–5
Graham, Sir Lancelot 64, 74, 75
Green, F. W. (VE's tutor) 28, 38; religious views 18–19, 23; VE's relationship with 196, 197–8, 222, 225, 229, 254
Grigson, W. V. 117, 136, 160, 188, 234
Guha, B. S. 160, 181, 182, 188–9, 230–1
Gulabdas (VE's research assistant) 97, 161
Gurtu, R. N. 280

Haimendorf, C. von Fürer 160, 209, 280, 322; on VE 212, 276
Haldane, J. B. S. 292, 308
Haldipur, R. N. 257–8
Hallett, M. G. 76; on VE 75, 77
Harrison, Agatha 72
Hawkins, R. E. (VE's editor and publisher) 142, 207, 232, 285,

287, 288, 294, 303, 308, 327–8; criticism of VE's autobiography 296, 305–6, 310
Hindu missionaries 157–8, 320, 323; VE on 107–8, 168–9, 242
Hivale, Kusum 135, 190, 196, 198, 218, 224, 228, 248, 296, 329
Hivale, Shamrao 79, 84, 85, 88, 96, 181, 182, 186, 187, 188, 196, 213, 220, 296, 325, 328–9; physical appearance 44, 102; political orientation 44, 68, 88–9; religious orientation 59, 67–8, 70, 91; sexual orientation 81, 89, 94–5, 108, 132, 198; as social worker and healer 66–8, 72, 87, 89, 100, 102, 104, 110, 180–1, 204–5, 297; as VE's companion and helper 53, 61–5, 69, 70–1, 79, 80–1, 86–7, 94–5, 101–2, 109–10, 129, 177, 179–81, 189–90, 198–9, 218, 222–3, 224–5, 226–8, 232–3, 234, 245–6, 256, 282, 308; on VE 1, 25–6, 136, 176, 184, 205, 312, 327–8; VE on 67–8, 81, 134, 180, 204–5, 237; books by 98, 159, 161–2, 179–80; marriage and family 134–5, 218, 248
Hivale, Suresh 218
Hoare, Sir Samuel 73
Holland, W. E. S. 28, 93
Holman, Flora (VE's grandmother) 5–6
Housman, A. E. 151
Housman, Lawrence 99
Huddleston, Archbishop Trevor 332, 333
Hussain, Zakir 275
Hutchinson, G. Evelyn 135
Hutheesingh, Krishna 133; on VE 155

Hutton, J. H. 287; on VE 117
Hydari, Sir Akbar 188–9
Hyde, E. S. 136

Indian Civil Service 1, 97, 118–19, 156, 186, 238
Indian Frontier Administrative Service 257–8, 280, 300, 325
Indian National Congress—*see* Congress Party
Irvine, A. C. 17
Irwin, Lord 43, 76–7

*Jadupatuas 215–16
Janah, Sunil 189, 332–3
Jayal, N. D. 257–8, 293
John Murray (VE's publishers) 99, 101, 103, 111–13, 120, 176, 331
Johri, Sitaram 295
Joshi, P. C. 189
*Juangs 178, 273; VE on 147–8

Kadlescovics, Otto, on VE 307–8
*Kalyo Kegnyus 256
Karaka, D. F., on VE 153, 154
Kaul, T. N. 249
Khama, Seretse 197
*Khamptis 259
Khan, Khan Abdul Ghaffar 64
Khathing, Bob 257–8
Khudai Khitmatgars 64–5
Knox, Ronald 18
Koestler, Arthur 213, 281–2, 290–1, 294, 299, 306, 307
*Kondhs 176; VE on 171–2, 340–2
*Konyaks 182, 240, 241, 243
Kripalani, J. B. 179; VE on 55
Krishnan, K. S. 292

Lahiri, S. 301, 302

INDEX

Lansbury, George 72, 73, 154
Leach, Edmund, on VE 142–3
Leakey, Louis 197
Leakey, Mary 197
Lester, Muriel 34
Levi-Strauss, Claude 280
Lewis, Charles 332
Lohia, Ram Manohar 325; on VE 269–70; VE on 274
Lovejoy, A. O. 122

Maitland, F. W. 204
Majumdar, D. N. 208–9, 366n.32; on VE 209–10, 273–4
Malinowski, Bronislaw 113; VE on 101; VE meets 104
Mallaby, George 17
Manin, Ethel, on VE 144
*Marias 156; VE on 145–6, 154
Marrett, R. R. 211
Matthew, Herbert v
Maundy, C. R. 215, 222; writes poems on VE 199–200, 202
Maurois, André 303, 305
Maxwell, R. N., on VE 106–7
Mayo, Katherine 142, 367n.41
Mehta, K. L. 244, 249, 250, 252, 288
Merchant, Vijay 178
Merrill, Jean 226–7
Merton College (VE's college) 1–2, 153, 154, 316; social/intellectual life 13–16, 17, 19–21; religious life 18–19, 21–3, 28; VE's identification with 38, 66, 161; funds VE's research 135, 192–3, 209
Miles, Sir John 192
Milham, Harry 173–5
Mills, J. P. 193
Milward, Marguerite 101–2; on VE 102

Mira Behn (alias Madeleine Slade) vii, 49, 51, 55, 68, 76, 82, 179
*Mishmis 255, 257, 348
Mitchell, A. N. 147
Mitchison, Naomi, on VE 308, 309
Modi, Sir Homi 223
Mohammed Iqbal 319
*Monpas 257
Moraes, Dom 329–30; on VE 219
Moraes, Frank 84, 153, 219
Muggeridge, Malcolm 62
*Murias 138–40, 145, 150, 151, 318; VE on 139–41, 216, 221, 298

*Nagas 239, 247, 267, 281, 311; VE on 182, 225–6, 285–8, 348
Naidu, Sarojini 84, 221
Naik, D. J. 279
Narayan, Jayaprakash 280
Narmada dam controversy 320–1
Narmada, Sunderlal (VE's research assistant) 97, 161, 173, 175, 194, 220
Needham, Rodney 280
Nehru, Jawaharlal vi, viii, 35, 42, 45, 63, 68, 133, 144, 153, 236, 259, 270, 271, 279, 295, 304, 313, 324–5; VE's meetings with 108, 224, 249–53, 254–5, 267–9, 272, 285, 290, 297, 301; VE's admiration for 50, 108, 134, 137, 141, 202, 217, 246, 251, 253, 261, 262, 268; praises VE 231, 253, 254, 267–8, 276; views on tribal life 181, 197, 222, 231, 264, 266, 268–9, 275–6, 285, 326
Neill, Bishop Stephen 10, 11–12, 23–4, 316; VE criticizes 91

Newman, Cardinal Henry 18
Nivedita, Sister (alias Margaret Noble) vii
North East Frontier Agency (NEFA): administrative policy in 239, 255, 256–8, 261–7, 270–4, 282–3, 293–4, 294–5, 300, 304, 322–6, 343–8

Orwell, George 1, 131
Oxford University 13–14, 16–17, 25, 134, 258, 299; religious life 18–19, 21, 26; VE's identification with 29, 131, 154, 161, 192–3, 211, 278, 307
Oxford University Press (VE's publishers) 120, 141, 142, 161, 163, 281, 294, 299–300, 305, 307, 326, 331, 332

Padamsee, Alyque 223
Palmer, E. J. (Bishop of Bombay) 27, 39, 50
Panchen Lama 259
Panda Baba (Gond magician) 95–6, 99, 111, 112
Pandit, Vijayalakshmi 275
Panikkar, K. M. 248
Pant, Apa 276
Pant, Govind Ballabh 262; on VE 276–7
*Pardhans 98, 110, 193, 194, 290
Patel, Jehangir 177, 178, 328; funds VE's research 141, 204, 207, 223, 248, 297, 327; VE's relationship with 196, 197–8, 222, 225, 229, 254
Patel, Vallabhbhai 45, 50, 52, 55, 59, 63, 292, 304
Patkar, Medha 320

Patton, William 74, 104; on VE 105–6, 124, 301
Petitpierre, Max 22
Phizo, A. Z. 239, 285
*Phoms 241, 243
Pioneer, The, on VE 324
Pocha, Ala 62, 82–3, 127
Prasad, Rajendra 289
Pusey Hall 26
Pyarelal 231–2

Rada 198–9
Radcliffe-Brown, A. R. 210
Ragini Devi 189
Raisinda 194–5
Rajagopalachari, C. 63, 262, 292
Ramunny, Murkot 257–8, 325
Rathee, K. L. 250, 295, 301
Reynolds, Reginald, on VE 45–6
Richards, Audrey 210
Rivers, W. H. R. 159
Robertson, Algernon 27, 28, 29, 33, 43
Rolland, Romain 72; compares VE to Albert Schweitzer vi
Rolle, Richard 23, 40, 292
Rowse, A. L. 14
Roy, Jamini 189
Roy, Sarat Chandra 109; VE on 119, 146–7
Rustomji, N. K. 301, 327

Sabarmati Ashram 26, 35, 36, 49, 51, 59, 60, 71, 77, 81, 238, 248, 304; VE on 37, 55–6, 79
Sadhu Sundar Singh 28
Sahid 177, 189, 330
Salter, Sir Michael 28
*Santhals 215, 298
*Saoras 175–6, 180, 194–5, 196,

INDEX

198, 317–18; position of women 212–13; VE on 211–13, 216, 220
Sassoon, Victor 196, 197, 198, 203, 222, 226, 236–7, 282
Satyarthi, Devendra 165
Scheduled Areas and Scheduled Tribes Commission 289, 291
Schiff, Leonard 41, 42, 44, 45, 74; on VE 58, 317
Scott, Maeve, on VE 303
Scott, Rev. Michael 285
Servants of India Society 84
Sevagram Ashram 35, 60; VE on 156
Shaw, Gilbert 23
*Sherdupkens 247, 346
Sher-Gil, Amrita 62
Shyam, Jangarh 323
Silbert, Ronnie 226
Singh, Charan, on VE 325
Singh, Har Mander 257–8
Singh, Khushwant 231
Singharo 95, 127
Smith, David Nicol 16, 164
Society for the Propagation of the Gospel 26
Sparrow, Gerald 198–9
Spratt, Philip vii
Squire, J. C. 116
Sri Krishna Prem 278
Sri Madhava Ashish 278
Srinivas, M. N. 121; on VE 158–9; VE on 192
Statesman, The, on VE 309
Stephen, Leslie 310
Stephens, Ian 62
Students Christian Movement 22, 26
Subramaniam, C. 333
Sudarshan, H., on VE 325–6

Swaminathan, J. 323
Sykes, Christopher 17
Symons, Ronald, on VE 278

*Tagins 240, 266
Tagore, Rabindranath 27, 28, 87
Tamara, Sonia, on VE v
*Taraons 257
Tata, J. R. D. 120, 141, 190, 232, 275, 297
Tawang monastery 260, 282; VE on 258–9, 295
Temple, Archbishop William 93
Tennyson, Alfred 8
Thakkar, A. V. 48, 72, 262, 279; VE's relationship with 53–4, 88, 155, 168
Thakkar, Natwar 279
Thakurdas, Purshottamdas 168
Thomas, R. S. 242
Thompson, E. J. vii, 184
Thompson, E. P. vii
Tilak, Bal Gangadhar 34
Todorov, Tzvetan 122–3
Tribal Art and Research Unit (TARU) 204
Tribal Welfare and Research Unit (TWARU) 195, 204, 218, 248, 297, 332
Turner, Victor, on VE 317–18
Tyagi, M. D. 280

*Uraons 118, 220

Vannikar, P. G. 168
Verghese, George 322
Visvanathan, Shiv vi

Waley, Arthur 310; on VE 248
*Wanchos 246, 255, 348
Watts, Alan, on VE 116
Waugh, Evelyn 17

Wavell, Lord 168
Willingdon, Lord 77, 84
Winslow, J. C. 26, 29, 33, 34, 35, 46; personality 27, 30; religious views 26–7, 28, 36, 38, 41, 65; political views 43, 44, 47–8; VE's relationship with 37–8, 39, 45, 48, 51, 58–9, 90
Wood, Alex (Bishop of Nagpur) 60–1, 62, 68, 317; on VE 69–70, 86, 92, 93
Wood, Evelyn, on VE 143

Wooster, Bertie, VE on 55–6, 333–4
Wordsworth, William, VE's love of 10, 11, 16, 219, 235, 299, 381n.47
Wycliffe Hall seminary 2, 26, 29, 182, 316

YMCA 57, 287
Young, Wayland 281
Yusuf Ali, Rashid 250, 257–8, 301